Principles

of

Family Law

by

S. M. CRETNEY, M.A.

Solicitor of the Supreme Court;
Fellow and Tutor of Exeter College, Oxford;
University Lecturer in English Law, University of Oxford

LONDON

SWEET & MAXWELL

1974

First Published 1974
Second Impression 1975

Published by
Sweet & Maxwell Limited of
11 New Fetter Lane London
and printed in Great Britain
by Redwood Burn Limited
Trowbridge & Esher

SBN Hardback 421 191708
     Paperback 421 191805

To A. L. C.

PREFACE

THIS book is intended primarily for the use of degree and other students of Family Law. I have tried not only to explain the law as it is, but also to analyse the reasons for its development and to stimulate discussion of its effectiveness as an instrument of social policy. The book is not intended as a practitioners' manual, in the sense of providing a comprehensive coverage of all the topics within its title; on the contrary I have been deliberately selective, concentrating on extended discussion of what I believe to be the issues central to a student's understanding of the law.

Since this is a students' text it has been produced at a price which it is hoped will be within their means. This has meant the excision of certain chapters which were in the original draft, notably on the courts and the family, the enforcement of financial orders, and tax matters. It may be possible to include chapters on these topics in any future edition. I have excluded all consideration of problems of private international law since I believe these are best treated as part of a separate course.

Family Law is a constantly changing subject; most parts of the text have been extensively revised as developments occurred. Some decisions are, however, so fundamental that mere revision may not be adequate: thus, whilst I have dealt fully with the Court of Appeal decision in *Wachtel* v. *Wachtel*, I suspect that if I were starting the book again I would feel that I could reduce somewhat the discussion of the problems of ascertaining title to matrimonial property. These will often now be (in the pejorative sense) academic.

I hope that the law is accurately stated on the sources available to me on January 1, 1974. I have throughout given references to the Matrimonial Causes Act 1973, which came into force on that date. For convenience a comparative table, showing the derivation of the sections of that Act, will be found after the Table of Statutes. It has not been possible to include references to the new Matrimonial Causes Rules 1973, which come into force on January 11. I have included references to the Guardianship Act 1973, although that has not yet been brought into force.

I have to acknowledge the permission of the Controller of Her Majesty's Stationery Office and Butterworth & Co. (Publishers) Ltd., for permission to reproduce copyright material. I am also grateful to the publishers of the *Modern Law Review*, the *New Law Journal* and the *Solicitors' Journal* who have allowed me to make use of articles which first appeared in their columns. I (in common with all students of the subject) owe a special debt to the Law Commission, whose working

papers and reports are so often the most comprehensive examination of
the problems with which this book is concerned.

Finally, I must thank the publishers who have prepared the Table of
Statutes, and whose skilled help has made my task infinitely easier than
it would otherwise have been.

S. M. CRETNEY.

Exeter College,
Oxford.
February 5, 1974.

CONTENTS

CONTENTS

PART I
INTRODUCTORY

PART II
THE FORMATION OF MARRIAGE

PART III
MATRIMONIAL LITIGATION

PART IV
CHILDREN

TABLE OF CASES

xi

TABLE OF STATUTES

UNITED KINGDOM STATUTES

OTHER STATUTES

MATRIMONIAL CAUSES ACT 1973: COMPARATIVE TABLE

Divorce Reform Act 1969 (c. 55)

1969	1973	1969	1973	1969	1973
s. 1	s. 1 (1)	s. 5	s. 10 (1)	s. 10	Sch. 1,
2 (1)	1 (2)	6	10 (2)–(4)		para. 3
(2)	1 (3)	7 (1)	7	Sch. 1,	
(3)	1 (4)	(2)	Sch. 2,	para. 1 ...	s. 4
(4)	2 (4)		para. 6 (2)	para. 2 ...	49
(5)	2 (6)	8 (1)	s. 17 (1)	para. 3 ...	20
(6)	2 (7)	(2)	17 (1) (2)	para. 8 ...	Sch. 2,
3 (1)–(2) .	6		(3),		para. 5
(3) (a) .	2 (2)		Sch. 1,		(1) (b)
(b) .	2 (1)		para. 8	para. 12 ..	Sch. 1,
(4)	2 (3)	(3)	s. 17 (2)		para. 8
(5)	2 (5)	9 (1)	ss. 4, 20, 49,		
(6)	2 (6)		Sch. 1,		
4	5		para. 8		

Matrimonial Proceedings and Property Act 1970 (c. 45)

1970	1973	1970	1973	1970	1973
s. 1	s. 22	s. 20	— [2]	Sch. 1,	
2 (1)	23 (1)	21	Sch. 1,	para. 1 (b).	Sch. 1,
(2)	23 (3)		para. 15		para. 5
3 (1)	23 (2)	22	s. 38 (1)–(3)	para. 2 ...	Sch. 1,
(a) .	23 (1)		(5)–(7)		para. 4
(2)	23 (1)	22 (1) ...	Sch. 1,	para. 3	
(3)	23 (3)		para. 16	(1)–(4).	Sch. 1,
(4)	23 (3)	23	s. 39		para. 17
(5)	23 (4)	24	26	(5)	Sch. 1,
4	24 (1)–(2)	(1) (b).	ss. 23 (5),		para. 18
5	25		24 (3)	para. 4 ...	Sch. 1,
6	27 (1)–(7)	25	s. 30		para. 22
7	28	26	40	para. 5 ...	Sch. 1,
8	29	27 (1) ...	52 (1)		para. 23
9	31	(2) ...	52 (3)	para. 6 ...	Sch. 1,
10	32	(3) ...	52 (4)		para. 19
11	33 (1)–(4)	28	— [2]	para. 7 ...	Sch. 1,
	(6)	29	Sch. 1,		para. 9
12 (1) ...	Sch. 2,		para. 14	para. 8 ...	Sch. 1,
	paras. 3 (1),	34 (1) ...	ss. 33 (5),		para. 10
	10 (2)		38 (4),	para. 9 ...	Sch. 1,
(2) ...	Sch. 2,		Sch. 1,		para. 24
	para. 3 (2)		para. 23	para. 11 ..	Sch. 1,
13	s. 34	(2) ...	Sch. 2,		para. 20
14	35		para. 4	para. 12 ..	Sch. 1,
15	36	35	s. 3 (2)		para. 21
16 (1) ...	37 (2)–(3)	36	43 (1)–(7)	Sch. 2,	
(2) ...	37 (4)	40 (1) ...	18 (2),	para. 1 (1).	Sch. 2,
(3) ...	37 (5)		Sch. 1,		para. 5
(4) ...	37 (1) (6)		para. 13		(1) (a)
(5) ...	37 (7)	40 (2) ...	18 (3)	(2).	s. 43 (9)
17	41	(3) ...	Sch. 1,	(2)–(3).	44
18 (1) ...	42 (1)		para. 13	para. 2 (1).	Sch. 2,
(2) ...	42 (5)	42 (1) ...	ss. 17 (2),		para. 6 (1)
(3) ...	42 (3)		43 (9), 44,	(2).	s. 50 (1)–(2)
(4) ...	42 (4)		50 (1)–(2)	para. 3 ...	Sch. 2,
(5) ...	42 (6)	43 (2) ...	— [2]		para. 7
(6) ...	42 (7)	Sch. 1,		para. 4 ...	s. 17 (2)
19 (1) ...	42 (2), (6)	para. 1 (a).	Sch. 1,	para. 5 ...	Sch. 2,
(2) ...	42 (5), (7)		para. 2		para. 10 (2)

Nullity of Marriage Act 1971 (c. 44)

1971	1973	1971	1973	1971	1973
s. 1	s. 11 (a)–(c)	s. 5	s. 16	s. 7 (3)	— [2]
2	12	6 (1)	— [2]	(4)	Sch. 1,
3	13	(2)	19 (6)		para. 6
(4)	11 (3)	7 (1)	— [2]	(5)–(6) .	— [2]
4	14	(2)	46, Sch. 2, para. 2		

[1] Previously repealed.
[2] Spent or unnecessary.

ABBREVIATIONS

THE following are the abbreviations most commonly used in the text.

Books

Bedford College Survey: *Separated Spouses*, by O. R. McGregor, Louis Blom-Cooper and Colin Gibson, 1st ed., 1970.

Bevan: *The Law Relating to Children*, by H. K. Bevan, 1st ed., 1973.

Bromley: *Family Law*, by P. M. Bromley, 4th ed., 1971.

Craffe: *La Puissance Paternelle en Droit Anglais*, by Mauricette Craffe, 1st ed., Paris, 1971.

Dicey and Morris: *The Conflict of Laws*, 8th ed. by J. H. C. Morris and others, 1967.

Eekelaar: *Family Security and Family Breakdown*, by John Eekelaar, 1st ed., 1971.

Foote, Levy and Sander: *Cases and Materials on Family Law*, by Caleb Foote, Robert J. Levy and Frank E. A. Sander, Boston and Toronto, 1966.

Graveson and Crane: *A Century of Family Law*, edited by R. H. Graveson and F. R. Crane, 1st ed., 1957.

Hambly and Turner: *Cases and Materials on Australian Family Law*, by David Hambly and J. Neville Turner, 1st ed., Sydney, 1971.

Hay: *William Hay's Lectures on Marriage*, edited by John C. Barry, Edinburgh, 1967.

Jackson: *Matrimonial Finance and Taxation*, by Joseph Jackson, 1st ed., 1972.

Jackson, *Formation, etc.*: *The Formation and Annulment of Marriage*, by Joseph Jackson, 2nd ed., 1969.

Megarry and Wade: *The Law of Real Property*, by R. E. Megarry and H. W. R. Wade, 3rd ed., 1966.

Mortlock: *The Inside of Divorce*, by Bill Mortlock, 1st ed., 1972.

Pettit: *Equity and the Law of Trusts*, by Philip H. Pettit, 2nd ed., 1970.

Ploscowe and Freed: *Family Law Cases and Materials*, by Morris Ploscowe and Doris Jonas Freed, Boston and Toronto, 1963.

Pollock and Maitland: *The History of English Law*, by Sir Frederick Pollock and Frederic William Maitland, Cambridge, 2nd ed., 1898, reissued 1968.

Rayden: *Law and Practice in Divorce and Family Matters*, 11th ed. by Joseph Jackson and others, 1971.

Theobald: *Theobald on Wills*, 13th ed. by Stephen Cretney and Gerald Dworkin, 1971.

Todd and Jones: *Matrimonial Property*, by J. E. Todd and L. M. Jones, Office of Population Censuses and Surveys, 1972. SBN 11 700129 5.

Papers and Reports

Field of Choice: The Law Commission. Reform of the Grounds of Divorce. The Field of Choice. Report on a reference under section 3 (1) (*e*) of the Law Commissions Act 1965, 1966, Cmnd. 3123.

Graham Hall Report: Report of the Committee on Statutory Maintenance Limits, 1968, Cmnd. 3587.

Houghton Committee Report: Report of the Departmental Committee on the Adoption of Children, 1972, Cmnd. 5107.

Houghton Committee Working Paper: Working Paper containing the provisional proposals of the Departmental Committee on the Adoption of Children, 1970, SBN 11 340356 9.

Kilbrandon Report: Report of the Departmental Committee appointed to inquire into the Law of Scotland relating to the Constitution of Marriage. The Marriage Law of Scotland, 1969, Cmnd. 4011.

Latey Report: Report of the Committee on the Age of Majority, 1967, Cmnd. 3342.

Law Commission. Law Commission *Reports* are now numbered, and they are so identified in the text—*e.g.* " Law Commission 52 " refers to the Law Commission's First Report on Family Property. In most instances, the report has been preceded by a *Working Paper*: these are also numbered, and are referred to in the text by the abbreviation " P.W.P."—*e.g.* P.W.P. No. 42 is a reference to the Published Working Paper on Family Property Law. Most of these reports have not been published, in the sense of being made available for public sale; they can, however, be consulted in the leading law libraries.

Morton Commission: Report of the Royal Commission on Marriage and Divorce, 1956, Cmd. 9678.

Payne Committee Report: Report of the Committee on the Enforcement of Judgment Debts, 1969, Cmnd. 3909.

Putting Asunder: Putting Asunder, A Divorce Law for Contemporary Society. The Report of a group appointed by the Archbishop of Canterbury in January 1964, S.P.C.K., 1966.

Statutes

A.E.A.: Administration of Estates Act.

L.P.A.: Law of Property Act.

M.C.A.: Matrimonial Causes Act [and note also M.C.R.: Matrimonial Causes Rules].

PART I

INTRODUCTORY

CHAPTER 1

INTRODUCTION

THE FAMILY AS A LEGAL UNIT

THE meaning of the word "family" can be a matter for elaborate sociological and anthropological discussion.[1] Lawyers have in comparison a deceptively simple approach. Is a mistress a member of a tenant's family so as to be entitled under the Rent Acts [2] to succeed to a controlled tenancy? The answer is said to depend on the answer that an ordinary man would give in the circumstances.[3] This leads to curious results. In one case,[4] a couple had lived in close, but unmarried association, for some twenty years, living in the same house and posing to the outside world as husband and wife. The Court of Appeal held that the man was not a member of the woman's family. Although purporting to follow the "ordinary man" test the court seems to have been influenced by moralistic considerations. Asquith L.J. said [5]:

> "if the relations between them had been platonic I can see no principle on which one could say that they were members of the same family which would not require the court to predicate the same of two old cronies of the same sex innocently sharing a flat. If, on the other hand, the relationship involves sexual relations, it seems to me anomalous that a person can acquire a 'status of irremovability' by having lived in sin, even if the liaison has been, not a mere casual encounter, but one protracted in time and conclusive in character. I would, however, decide the case on a simpler view. To say of two people masquerading, as these two were, as husband and wife—there being no children to complicate the picture—that they were members of the same family, seems to me an abuse of the English language. . . ."

Sir Raymond Evershed M.R. was even more candid [6]:

> "It may not be a bad thing that it is shown by this decision that in the Christian society in which we live one, at any rate, of the privileges which may be derived from marriage is not equally enjoyed by those who are not married."

In contrast, it was held in a later case [7] that the mistress was a member of the tenant's family, even though she had not taken his name

---

[1] See, for an introduction, C. C. Harris, *The Family* (1969) Part I, Chap. 1; Bell and Vogel: *A Modern Introduction to The Family* (1960). A good general account of the sociology of the family is Ronald Fletcher's *The Family and Marriage in Britain* (1966).

[2] 1968 Rent Act, s. 3; Sched. I. 3.

[3] *Brock* v. *Wollams* [1949] 2 K.B. 388.

[4] *Gammans* v. *Ekins* [1950] 2 K.B. 328.

[5] [1950] 2 All E.R. 140 at p. 141 (phrased differently in the Law Reports).

[6] At p. 334.

[7] *Hawes* v. *Evenden* [1953] 2 All E.R. 737.

3

because " all the neighbours knew they were not married." The crucial difference was that this couple had children. The court's reasoning was [8] that there could:

> " be said to be *de facto* an actual family consisting of children and the natural parent or parents of those children. . . . The situation assumed would present *de facto* what might be described as the equivalent of a marriage with the natural consequences of a marriage."

To avoid these judicial semantic exercises Parliament has thought it prudent in other cases to follow Humpty Dumpty's view: "When *I* use a word . . . it means just what I choose it to mean—neither more nor less." [9] Thus, the Family Income Supplements Act 1970 provides [10] that, for the purposes of that Act a family shall consist of " the following members of a household:

> (a) one man or single woman [11] engaged, and normally engaged, in remunerative full time work; and
>
> (b) if the person mentioned in paragraph (a) above is a man [12] and the household includes a woman to whom he is married or who lives with him as his wife, that woman; and
>
> (c) the child or children whose requirements are provided for, in whole or in part, by the person or either of the persons mentioned in the preceding paragraphs."

These problems of legal definition have only become acute in recent years when relationships other than those created by marriage [13] were recognised. It had for long been the principle that *marriage* was an essential pre-requisite to the creation of a *legally recognised* family unit.[14] Only by marriage did a woman obtain the right to be supported by a man; only if his parents were married was their child recognised for the purpose of inheriting property, and so on. This principle is now subject to many exceptions, but it is still one which the courts tend to apply in the absence of any specific rule to the contrary.[15] Hence we first analyse the conditions required by English law [16] if a union is to be recognised as a valid marriage.

---

[8] *Per* Jenkins L.J., *Gammans* v. *Ekins* (*supra*) at p. 332 cited in *Hawes* v. *Evenden* at p. 738.

[9] *Through the Looking Glass.*

[10] s. 1 (1).

[11] A term which also receives a special definition: s. 17 (1), *cf.* the Affiliation Proceedings Act 1957, *infra*, p. 321.

[12] It will be noted that the Act thus recognises the man/mistress relationship, but not the converse. This is one further distinction between *Gammans* v. *Ekins* and *Hawes* v. *Evenden* (*supra*).

[13] Or some other legal act such as adoption.

[14] See Foote, Levy and Sander, pp. 3–7.

[15] See *e.g. Sydall* v. *Castings Ltd.* [1967] 1 Q.B. 302.

[16] This book does not deal with cases involving a foreign element; in many cases English law will recognise a union as a valid marriage because it is so by the law of another country. For details see *e.g.* J. H. C. Morris, *The Conflict of Laws*, Part III.

REQUIREMENTS OF A VALID MARRIAGE

English law, on this subject, although now contained in statutes,[17] has its origins in the Canon Law of the Western church. This imposed rules governing the formation of marriage—for instance, that the parties must not already be married to someone else, and that they must not be too closely related. If these rules were broken, there was no marriage between the parties, whatever the outward appearances. If, for instance, it is proved that at the time of a marriage ceremony between A and B, A was already married to someone else, there can be no marriage between A and B, however solemn and magnificent the ceremony, and however long they may subsequently have cohabited as man and wife. In legal language A has no capacity to marry B.

It was obviously desirable that in such circumstances a formal declaration should be obtainable that (in spite of appearances) the parties had never been married. Provision was therefore made for them to obtain a decree of nullity, which pronounced a union " to have been and to be absolutely null and void to all intents and purposes whatsoever." [18] Before considering the rules about capacity to marry, one important complication must be mentioned.

The concept of the voidable marriage

The Church's doctrine that a valid marriage could never be dissolved [19] meant that a decree of nullity was the only way of escape from a union which had become intolerable. In consequence, the grounds of nullity were considerably extended.[20] This led to great hardship: if a marriage had never existed between A and B, it followed that their children were illegitimate; and not entitled to succeed to their parents' property. Hence, perhaps many years after the parties' deaths,[21] anyone who had an interest might seek to show that the apparent " marriage " had never existed.

Two important developments occurred after the Reformation: first, the grounds on which the validity of a marriage might be attacked were somewhat restricted; secondly, the common law courts prevented the ecclesiastical courts [22] from annulling a marriage on certain grounds [23] after the death of either party.[24] Marriages in the formation of which

---

17 Marriage Acts 1949 to 1970; M.C.A. 1973 (consolidating The Nullity of Marriage Act 1971, as amended by the Matrimonial Proceedings (Polygamous Marriages) Act 1972).

18 *de Reneville* v. *de Reneville* [1948] P. 100.

19 Although in a few very limited circumstances a valid but unconsummated marriage could be: see Hay, p. 59.

20 See, *e.g.* the development of the concept of prohibited degrees, *infra*, p. 9.

21 For the limited Common Law exceptions to this doctrine, see Jackson, *Formation etc.*, pp. 44–53.

22 In whom jurisdiction over marriage was vested.

23 Those subsequently termed " canonical disabilities " (*i.e.* impotence, marriage within the prohibited degrees, lack of age or pre-contract).

24 Two principal reasons are given: (i) to protect the issue of the marriage from being bastardised: *Ray* v. *Sherwood* (1836) 1 Curt. 173, 200; *Fenton* v. *Livingstone* (1859) 5 Jur.(N.S.) 1183, 1189; (ii) the ecclesiastical court was concerned to separate

some basic element was lacking might thus fall into one of two categories: (i) Marriages *void ab initio*. In this case a decree could be made (without interference from the common law courts) by the ecclesiastical court at the suit of any interested person at any time, *i.e.* even after the death of one of the parties. (ii) Voidable Marriages. These could only be attacked during the life-time of both parties to the marriage.

The result has been well summed up as follows [25]:

" the novelty of the post-Reformation law was that it allowed certain of these spineless marriages to acquire posthumous backbones: if these associations could escape being examined in the courts while the parties to them were alive and living together in what, from the premises, were sinful unions, then the common law courts in any case which came before them, would bury the past simultaneously with the interment of one or both of the spouses so-called, and would give to them as a parting gift at the grave the unimpeachable and retrospective reputation valid in England and Wales at any rate, of having lived together in holy wedlock." [26]

---

the offenders, and inflict penance for the wrongdoing consisting in living together when they could not be man and wife; after the death of the parties " such declaration cannot . . . tend to the reformation of the parties." (Blackstone, *Commentaries*, 4th ed. Vol. I, p. 434; see also Poynter, *Ecclesiastical Courts*, 1824, p. 154). The intervention of the temporal court may have been justified partly because marriage ceased to be a sacrament: Article 25 of the 39 Articles; *Fender* v. *Mildmay* [1938] A.C. 1, 27. On the history of this matter see: Pollock and Maitland, pp. 364–399; Jackson, *Formation etc.*, pp. 54–59; F. H. Newark (1945) 8 M.L.R. 203. E. J. Cohn (1948) 64 L.Q.R. 324; D. Tolstoy (1964) 27 M.L.R. 385.

[25] Jackson, *Formation etc.*, p. 54.

[26] See also *de Reneville* v. *de Reneville* [1948] P. 100, 111, *per* Lord Greene M.R.

PART II

FORMATION OF MARRIAGE

The English rules on the formation of marriage can best be discussed under three heads:

(1) Capacity to marry;
(2) Formalities;
(3) Nullity of marriage—*i.e.* the judicial process which declares that a purported marriage has been vitiated by some fundamental defect.

CHAPTER 2

CAPACITY TO MARRY

THE relevant rules can be grouped under the following heads: (i) Monogamy; (ii) Prohibited Degrees; (iii) Minimum Age; (iv) Consents of the Parties; (v) Sex of the Parties and Physical Capacity. If any of these requirements as to capacity was broken, the result in canon law was that there was no marriage. But in some cases the effect of the common law was to make the marriage *voidable* only.[1] Statute subsequently intervened,[2] and the consequences of any defect are now governed by the Matrimonial Causes Act 1973.[3]

I. MONOGAMY

For English law, marriage is "the voluntary union for life of one man and one woman to the exclusion of all others."[4] Hence a purported marriage is void if at the time either party is already lawfully married to a third party.[5] It should be stressed that this is so even if the parties believe the former spouse to be dead,[6] and that the crucial date is that of the ceremony. If the former spouse subsequently dies, the later "marriage" remains void, although the parties could regularise their position by going through a second marriage ceremony—which they would then be free to do. This rule requires no further discussion, but it should be pointed out that the law now attaches *some* of the consequences of a valid marriage even to one which is void.[7]

II. PROHIBITED DEGREES

Rules prohibiting marriage [8] between certain categories of relatives are probably universal [9]:

---

[1] *Supra*, p. 6.
[2] To make marriages within the prohibited degrees, and where either party was under sixteen, void rather than voidable; *infra*, pp. 10 and 16.
[3] ss. 11 and 12; consolidating the Nullity of Marriage Act 1971.
[4] *Hyde* v. *Hyde* (1866) L.R. 1 P. & D. 130, *per* Lord Penzance at 133. There are cases where a *foreign* marriage is recognised as valid even though it is polygamous, but this is outside the scope of this book.
[5] M.C.A. 1973, s. 11 (6); as to what amounts to proof of the existence of a prior marriage, see *infra*, p. 198.
[6] So that there may be a defence to the *criminal offence* of bigamy, *infra*, p. 139.
[7] *Infra*, p. 65.
[8] And sometimes also sexual relations *outside* marriage.
[9] For introductory accounts of anthropological knowledge on the incest taboo, see Lucy Mair, *Marriage* (1971) Chaps. 2 and 3; R. Fox, *Kinship and Marriage* (1967) Chap. 2, and J. Beattie, *Other Cultures* (1964) p. 126 *et seq.*

" It would be difficult—it might even be impossible—to find a community, advanced or primitive, in which some prohibitions against sexual conjunction arising out of relationship have not been laid down. Even the free and easy Kainang of the Brazilian high-lands who recognised monogamous, polyandrous, polygynous and joint marriages and who quite readily married their nieces, step-mothers and mothers-in-law, either alone or in combination, draw the line at marriages between parents and children and between full brothers and sisters." [10]

Yet in spite of the universal existence of *some* rule, its *content* varies considerably.

Most societies prohibit sexual relations between parent and child, and brother and sister. But there are exceptions to this: certain Royal dynasties permitted (or even required) the union of brother and sister. It may be that the exceptional nature of this rule served only to stress the " distinctiveness and uniqueness of the rulers who could perform acts unthinkable for ordinary people." [11]   Once one moves outside the basic family unit of parent and child, even more diversity of attitude is apparent. Some developed Western societies permit marriages be-tween first cousins, yet others proscribe them.

In the United States, for instance, they are allowed in about half the states.[12] Some systems (*e.g.* Judaism [13]) allow a man to marry his niece, whereas others (*e.g.* English law) forbid him to do so. Should a man be allowed to marry his deceased wife's sister or deceased brother's widow? Such marriages are encouraged in some cultures. But only since 1907 and 1921 respectively have they been permitted in England.[14] In order to evaluate the modern English law, we need to consider the purposes which such prohibitions serve.

Prohibitions are normally based either on (a) consanguinity (blood relationship), or (b) affinity (relationship by marriage): my sister is my relation by consanguinity, my wife's sister by affinity.

The evolution of the English law is complex. With rules originally based on the canon law,[15] the result of a breach was merely to make a marriage voidable. But in 1835 Lord Lyndhurst's Act, for reasons which are obscure,[16] declared *void* any marriage within the prohibited degrees celebrated thereafter. This caused great hardship. The rules made no distinction between relationships by affinity and consanguinity; thus marriage to one's wife's sister was as odious as marriage to one's

---

10 Kilbrandon Report, para. 32, quoting from a thesis by E. M. Clive on " Reform of the Scottish Marriage Law."
11 Beattie, *op. cit.* p. 126.
12 Ploscowe, *Sex and the Law*, p. 6.
13 *Cheni* v. *Cheni* [1965] P. 85.
14 Deceased Wife's Sister's Marriage Act 1907; Deceased Brother's Widow's Marriage Act 1921.
15 Itself based on Leviticus, Chap. 18; see Pollock and Maitland, pp. 386–389; Royal Commission into the Law of Marriage relating to the Prohibited Degrees (1848).
16 Possibly a devious manoeuvre to secure the succession to a peerage (since the Act retrospectively *validated* existing marriages); see *per* Sir Brampton Gurdon Hansard (4th Ser.) Vol. 169, col. 1153.

own sister. But this theologically sound view [17] conflicted with social facts: a common problem was that on the death of a wife leaving her husband with a young family to bring up, urgent help would be needed from someone prepared to place herself in *loco parentis*. Amongst the poor the only available help was the widower's sister-in-law. Physical propinquity led to emotional involvement. What could be more natural than marriage?

In the latter part of the nineteenth century annual attempts were made to legalise such unions,[18] but only in 1907 was the law finally changed. The issue aroused great passion, but once this breach of the old religious rules had been made, further piecemeal reforms were introduced over the years.[19]

The prohibited degrees are now [20]:

For a man	For a woman
Mother.	Father.
Daughter.	Son.
Grandmother.	Grandfather.
Granddaughter.	Grandson.
Sister.	Brother.
Aunt.	Uncle.
Niece.	Nephew.
Father's, son's, grandfather's or grandson's wife.	Mother's, daughter's, grandmother's or granddaughter's husband.
Wife's mother, daughter, grandmother or granddaughter.	Husband's father, son, grandfather or grandson.

It will be noted that English law (unlike some systems) permits marriages between first cousins, but not between uncle and niece.

The Rationale of Restriction

The reasons which, over the years, have been given in support of the English rules can be divided into four categories:

(i) those based on religious considerations, asserting that the rules are laid down " by the express words of the divine law, or the consequences plainly deducible from thence " [21];

---

[17] See *e.g.* the evidence given by Dr. Pusey to the 1848 Commission, published in 1849 under the title, " Marriage with a Deceased Wife's Sister Prohibited by Holy Scripture as understood by the Church for 1,500 years."

[18] W. S. Gilbert's " annual blister " (*Iolanthe*).

[19] The Deceased Brother's Widow's Marriage Act 1921; the Marriage (Prohibited Degrees of Relationship) Act 1931. Major controversy was caused by the Marriage (Enabling) Act 1960, which allowed marriages between affines where the previous marriage had been terminated by annulment or divorce, rather than death: see O. M. Stone, 23 M.L.R. 538.

[20] Marriage Act 1949, Sched. 1, as amended. These prohibited degrees include half-blood and illegitimate relationships: *R.* v. *Brighton Inhabitants* (1861) 1 B. & S. 447; Marriage Act 1949, s. 78 (1); Marriage (Enabling) Act 1960, s. 1 (2); *Restall* v. *Restall* (1929) 45 T.L.R. 518.

[21] Blackstone, Book I, Chap. 15, p. 434.

    (ii) those founded on a supposed natural law;
    (iii) those based on eugenic grounds;
    (iv) those based on broader considerations of social policy.

Religion

Prior to the Deceased Wife's Sister's Marriage Act 1907 religious considerations were of overwhelming importance. For many years afterwards, the Anglican church preserved the old rule as a matter of internal discipline, so that a clergyman could be subject to ecclesiastical sanctions if he contracted a marriage between a man and his deceased wife's sister.[22] Today the church seeks to justify its rules by reference to considerations other than those of doctrinal authority [23] so that religious reasons no longer need separate treatment.

Natural law

Early writers justified the rules by the universal horror and repugnance which certain relationships aroused. Aristotle,[24] in a passage much relied on by the Canonists, tells of a blindfolded horse being coupled with its own dam; when the blindfold was removed the horse, struck with horror, flung itself over a cliff. Widespread feelings of outrage remain a factor to be taken into account in assessing the desirability of any change in the prohibitions.[25]

Genetics

Genetic considerations (what a Scottish judge called [26] preventing " the corruption of the stock ") are relevant to the higher chance of mutant genes being present in common in two persons with a close common ancestor.[27] The proportion of genes which different relatives have in common is shown in the following table [28]:

Relationship	Proportion of Genes in Common
Father and daughter Brother and sister	$\frac{1}{2}$
Grandfather and granddaughter Uncle and niece Half-brother and half-sister	$\frac{1}{4}$
First cousins Grand-uncle and grand-niece	$\frac{1}{8}$
Second cousins	$\frac{1}{32}$

22 But he could not treat a lay party to such a marriage as an " open and notorious evil liver " and deny them the sacraments: *R.* v. *Dibdin* [1910] P. 57.
23 See " Kindred and Affinity as Impediments to Marriage " (S.P.C.K.).
24 Historia Animalium 9, 47.
25 This factor was given considerable weight by the Law Commission (Law Commission No. 33), para. 52 (b): " There are some matters of conviction on which men hold strong feelings of right and wrong though they cannot place their fingers on any particular reason for this conviction."
26 Lord Normand: *Philips' Trustees* v. *Beaton*, 1938 S.C. 733, 745–746.
27 Kilbrandon Report, para. 34.
28 *Ibid.*

English law is therefore at least logical in drawing the line above relationships where the proportion of genes in common is $\frac{1}{8}$, but logic does not tell us whether the genetic risk is such as to justify prohibition. There is an increased possibility that recessive genetic characteristics will appear in the offspring of a union between relatives, but these characteristics may be either favourable or unfavourable. Since everything depends on the genetic make-up of the parties there is a case for prohibiting first cousin marriages, save after genetic screening. What is quite clear is that genetic considerations cannot justify a bar on relationships between *affines*. These must be based on social reasons.

Social policy

Two arguments are used. First, most Western societies are based on *exogamy* rather than *endogamy* (that is, marriage outside one's own kinship group rather than within it). But it is difficult to think that in modern Britain the social structure is such that people are likely to marry only within their kinship groups unless they are prevented from so doing by the prohibited degrees rules.

The second social reason is that the rules are designed to exclude disturbing sexual relations from the home circle in order to preserve the purity of the home [29]; " incestuous courtships and marriages are incompatible with the organisation of family life." [30] The reasoned opposition to permitting the marriage of a man with his deceased wife's sister was largely based on this ground: if a man could look on his wife's sister as a potential candidate for his affections, the trusting, intimate, but asexual relation of brother and sister might well be destroyed. Further, such marriages would cause a confusion of roles when the children of the marriage had to be told that their " aunt " had become their mother.[31] It is tempting therefore to lay down a general prohibition of marriage between those whose relationship involves a quasi-parental link. But much depends on the facts of each case. At first sight it seems repugnant that a man should marry his stepdaughter. Yet there is no genetic objection. If the man had stood *in loco parentis* to the woman there would be a social objection. But suppose that a man marries a widow whose daughter is an adult living away from home. Is there any valid objection to his subsequently marrying the daughter after his wife's death? [32]

There will no doubt be few such cases, but the possibility prompted legislation in New Zealand and Australia which permits marriage between persons within the prohibited degrees provided (i) that the relationship is one of *affinity* alone, and (ii) that the consent of the

---

29 Kilbrandon Report, para. 33.

30 See the appendix to the work cited in note 23, *supra*. See also *per* Finlay A.C.J. in *Re Woodcock and Woodcock* [1957] N.Z.L.R. 960 and the evidence of the Church of England to the Morton Commission (cited at para. 1162).

31 Even more so since (after 1960) their (divorced) mother might still be alive.

32 *Re Hoskin and Pearson* [1958] N.Z.L.R. 604.

court is obtained to the marriage. In New Zealand [33] the court has to be satisfied that neither party to the intended marriage has by his or her conduct contributed to the termination of any previous marriage of the other party. In Australia [34] there is no such condition precedent, but the court has to be satisfied before granting an application that the " circumstances of the particular case are so exceptional as to justify granting leave."

The way in which a general discretion might be exercised is illustrated by a New Zealand decision [35] in which a stepfather was given leave to marry his stepdaughter. The court considers the *realities* of the situation. Since the man had never stood *in loco parentis* to the woman, the main factor which might make the union abhorrent was not present. The court also takes into account such factors as the presence or absence of any ulterior motive, *e.g.* a desire for financial gain, and the likely effect on any children of the proposed marriage.

It seems unfortunate that English law should make such marriages impossible in the absence of good reason.

Incest as a crime

Since 1908 it has been an offence for a man knowingly to have intercourse with his daughter, granddaughter, mother or sister. He may, without infringing the criminal law, have intercourse with his aunt or niece although these relationships are within the prohibited degrees for marriage.[36]

Adoption

Special problems arise because of the existence of legal adoption, the principle underlying which is that the adopted child should sever his links with his natural family, and be treated for all purposes as the child of his adopting parents. But the fact of his biological parentage clearly remains relevant in considering *genetic* objections to marriage. The law is: (i) an adopted child remains within the same prohibited degrees to his natural parents and other relatives (including affines) as if he had not been adopted; (ii) an adopter and the person whom he adopts under an adoption order are deemed to be within the prohibited degrees, and they continue to be so notwithstanding that someone else adopts that person by a subsequent adoption order [37]; (iii) there is no other prohibition against marriage arising out of adoption, so that if a couple who have a natural son, S, adopt as their daughter a girl, D, S and D may marry each other.

Three problems arise:

(a) Assuming that there has been a complete severance (as there normally will be) between the natural family and the adopting family,

---

[33] See Inglis, *Family Law*, 2nd ed. p. 43, and Marriage Act, s. 15 (2).
[34] s. 20, Matrimonial Causes Act 1959.
[35] *Re Hoskin and Pearson (supra)*.
[36] Sexual Offences Act 1956, ss. 10, 11.   [37] Adoption Act 1958, s. 13 (3).

there seems no sound reason for preserving the prohibitions on marriage with relations by affinity through the natural parents: they will not have played the part of a relative.

(b) If the adopted child does not know the identity of his natural parents, there is the possibility of a marriage within the prohibited degrees being contracted unknowingly.

(c) It seems, for social reasons, objectionable to allow marriages between adoptive siblings.[38]

There has been some difference of opinion on what should be done.[39] The best solution, it is submitted, would be that adopted in Australia [40]:

> (i) Natural relationships by consanguinity (but not affinity) should remain a bar. It is for consideration whether steps could not be taken to prevent the very small risk of incestuous relationships arising unwittingly; and
> (ii) The child should be treated as the natural child of his adoptive parents. However, the court might permit marriage (other than with an adoptive parent or child, brother or sister) if the relationship only arises because of this rule.[41]

This would have the advantage of giving flexibility so as to avoid hardship, whilst avoiding any possibility of role confusion within the family.

Conclusions

In the light of this discussion, it is suggested:

1. The prohibited degrees of *consanguinity* might be divided into two categories: (a) those of the elementary family (ascendants and descendants, and brother and sister); (b) the other existing prohibited degrees (*i.e.* a man's aunt and niece), together with first cousins. Marriage between persons in class (a) would be barred, on the basis that it can be assumed to be repugnant to public opinion, and is probably objectionable on the social policy and genetic grounds mentioned above. Marriages between persons in class (b) would be prohibited unless the court granted leave after a consideration of the genetic hazards involved in the particular union, as well as any public policy factors.

2. *Either* (a) all prohibitions based on *affinity* should be abolished, or the court should be given a power to dispense couples from the pro-

---

38 But only 29 per cent. of adoptive parents questioned in a survey thought there should be a complete ban on such marriages: Houghton Committee, para. 332.

39 See Houghton Report, paras. 329–333; Law Commission No. 33, para. 50 and the material there cited; Kilbrandon Report, para. 36.

40 Marriage Act 1961, s. 24.

41 This possibility was rejected by the Houghton Committee: " it is difficult to see on what grounds a court, given discretion, could identify cases in which it would be proper to refuse permission to two adults, when there were no biological objections " (para. 332).

hibitions. The Law Commission however concluded [42] that there was
no evidence that public opinion on this point had changed since the
Morton Commission reported in favour of the present rules,[43] and that
" the almost unanimous view " of those who had commented on their
working paper on the subject was that the law should remain as it is.

3. Special consideration should be given to the problems caused by
adoptive relationships.

III. MINIMUM AGE

A marriage is void if either party is under sixteen.[44] This rule should be
distinguished from that [45] requiring parental consent if either party is
under eighteen: this requirement is purely directory, and failure to
comply with it has no effect on the *validity* of the marriage.[46]

The law was changed in two respects in 1929: until then (a) a
boy could marry at fourteen and a girl at twelve; (b) marriages where
one or both parties were under the relevant age were not void. Either
party could avoid the marriage on attaining majority, but it remained
valid unless this was done.[47]

It is instructive to consider the reasons advanced to justify the
change made in 1929. It was not to stamp out a widespread practice of
child marriage: in the twelve years prior to 1929, only three girls of
thirteen, twenty-eight of fourteen, and 318 of fifteen had married in
this country.[48] Yet the debates on the Bill (prompted by the reforming
zeal of Lord Buckmaster) were conducted in an atmosphere of moral
fervour which it is difficult to recapture. Concealed in the melodramatic
oratory three reasons are to be found for raising the age: (i) The " age
of maturity " was *higher* than it had been in the past. (ii) It was inconsistent to have sixteen as the age at which a girl could consent to
sexual intercourse outside marriage if she could marry at twelve.
" Does it not seem to you a remarkable thing that what the girl is incapable of consenting to once she can consent to in perpetuity . . . ? " [49]
It was said that men threatened with prosecution for unlawful intercourse with a girl under sixteen would stifle it by marrying her (so that
she could not be compelled to give evidence). (iii) The League of
Nations was trying to outlaw the institution of child marriage in India
and other oriental countries. Britain could hardly influence opinion

---

[42] Law Commission No. 33, para. 54. The Kilbrandon Report saw no reason to
    change the substance of Scottish law (which prohibits marriage with descendants
    by affinity): para. 38.
[43] See para. 1170.
[44] Marriage Act 1949, s. 2. But foreign marriages between parties one or more of whom
    is under this age may be valid: *Alhaji Mohamad* v. *Knott* [1969] 1 Q.B. 1.
[45] Marriage Act 1949, s. 3, as amended.
[46] s. 48. This requirement is regarded as part of the *formalities* of the marriage
    ceremony: see *infra*, p. 51.
[47] See Jackson, *Formation etc.*, p. 26; Blackstone, Book I, Chap. 15, p. 436.
[48] According to figures given by the Government Spokesman, Lord Salisbury, in the
    debate on the Age of Marriage Bill 1929: Hansard, Lords, Vol. 72, col. 968.
[49] *Per* Lord Buckmaster, *ibid.*, col. 962.

if her own laws were (in the words of the then Bishop of Southwark) on a par with those of Siam and Venezuela.

The reason for making a marriage one or both of the parties to which is under age void rather than voidable followed from the view that sexual relations in such a case should be *illegal*. It was to be a fundamental requirement of social policy that the parties be at least sixteen.

These arguments are by no means all convincing:

The age of maturity

In 1929 it was assumed that the age of puberty had *risen* over the years, yet in 1967 the Latey Committee assumed the opposite. It refused to recommend that the minimum age for marriage be raised to eighteen because scientific evidence showed that the age of puberty had been going *down* by approximately four months in every decade since 1830, and is now 13·2 on average. There seems to have been some confusion in 1929 between physical and emotional maturity.

The criminal law

The argument that it is essential to have the same minimum age for marriage and consent to sexual intercourse has recently found favour with the Kilbrandon [50] and Latey Committees [51] and the Law Commission.[52] Nevertheless, it is open to a number of objections:

(a) The reason why in 1885 it was made a criminal offence to have intercourse with a girl under sixteen (however much she might consent) was to stamp out the child brothel,[53] not to regulate the long-term relationships of young people.[54] The reason why the age of sixteen was chosen for the purposes of this offence [55] was that few marriages took place under that age. It could therefore be assumed that girls under that age were " looked on as immature, and as not having arrived at the age of puberty." [56] The process is circular: the age of sixteen is taken in 1885 as the age of consent to sexual intercourse because few people get married under that age; in 1929, the fact that sixteen is the " age of consent " is seen as a reason for prohibiting legal marriage under that age.

(b) The argument is based on a confusion between the proper function of the civil and criminal law. The fact that behaviour is not so offensive as to call for criminal sanctions does not mean that society should provide an institutional framework for it: the

---

50 Para. 20.   51 Para. 177.
52 Para. 19.
53 For a popular account, see Ann Stafford, *The Age of Consent* (London, 1964).
54 See *per* Salmon L.J., *R.* v. *Commissioner of Police of the Metropolis, ex p. Blackburn* [1968] 2 Q.B. 118, 139, asserting that the object of the law was to protect girls against seduction and thus justifying the police practice of not prosecuting teenage boys for the offence.
55 Note that there is a separate and more serious offence where the girl is under 12: Sexual Offences Act 1956, s. 5.
56 See Hansard, 3rd Ser., Vol. 300, col. 771.

law does not, as we have seen, allow certain relatives to marry, even though intercourse between them does not constitute the crime of incest. The fact that homosexual relations are no longer *per se* criminal does not mean that society will allow homosexuals to " marry," or give a homosexual couple the same tax relief as a married couple. There is equally no necessary correlation between the minimum age for marriage and the age of consent: it might be justifiable to have the age of consent higher than that for marriage (as between 1885 and 1929) if the criminal law is concerned with the commercial exploitation of the young; it might equally be justifiable to have the age of consent lower if it is thought that marriage should only be allowed at an age when emotional stability is likely to have been reached, although there is no sufficient reason to make sexual intercourse between young people a criminal offence.[57] It must, however, be conceded that public opinion might (unreasonably) find it paradoxical that the law should " permit " [*i.e.* not punish] sexual intercourse, whilst not allowing the parties to marry.

The force of example

The old common law rules of fourteen for males and twelve for females remain in some of the United States, whilst in some Islamic states the law is such that scholars can still dispute whether a child still *en ventre* can effectively be given in marriage.[58] The United Nations still tries (with some success)[59] to outlaw the child marriage; but it continues to exist for deep-seated social and religious reasons, and it is difficult to believe that the arguments which are convincing in their application to Streatham are equally cogent in their application to (say) Saudi Arabia.

What is the right age?

Although these reasons for increasing the minimum age may not be convincing, few people today would suggest lowering it.[60] On the contrary, such pressure as there is has been to *raise* the age to eighteen (although perhaps leaving it at sixteen for girls). The argument is based on the fact that the lower the age of marriage the greater the chance of it ending in divorce.

Both the Latey and Kilbrandon Committees (whilst sympathetic to the proposal) rejected it:

[57] The Latey Committee stigmatised this as being tantamount to saying " sex outside marriage was legal, wedlock was not ": para. 103. This is to confuse the two senses of " legal."

[58] The answer is negative because the sex of an embryo would not be known; see C. D. Farran, *Matrimonial Laws of the Sudan* (London, 1963), p. 39. For details of minimum age in other countries, see App. 7 to the Latey Report.

[59] See the Convention on Consent to Marriage, Minimum Age for Marriage and Registration of Marriages (New York, December 10, 1962, London, H.M.S.O., Cmnd. 3616).

[60] See the discussion in the Latey Report, paras. 102–103 and 166–177, and the Kilbrandon Report, paras. 14–21.

(i) As the age of puberty has been going down " this would be a hopeless attempt to swim against the tide "[61] (although this fact was not thought to justify reducing the age to approximate to that of puberty).

(ii) A large number of girls of sixteen and seventeen are pregnant at marriage. There would thus probably be some increase in the number of illegitimate births if eighteen were the minimum. Whether it is right to purchase legitimacy at the cost of sanctioning a relationship which has little chance of success is something which perhaps merits more consideration than it received.

(iii) There are " at least some mature and sensible young couples who are well able to take on the responsibilities of marriage between sixteen and eighteen years of age."[62]

(iv) It is essential to keep the age of consent and the minimum age for marriage the same. This argument has already been considered.

(v) The demand for change is not strong.[63] Thus the law might as well remain as it is, whilst perhaps doing more to prepare young people for the responsibilities of marriage.[64]

Should the court have a power to permit under-age marriages?

There may be cases in which it is felt that the facts justify marriage below the permitted age. Some countries[65] vest a limited dispensing power in the court or a welfare agency. Unfortunately it is difficult to know what circumstances justify the exercise of such a power. In the American case of *Re Barbara Haven*,[66] for instance, a physically mature girl of fourteen years eight months sought leave to marry a " typical fine American youth " of twenty-two for no other reason than that she was in love with him. The court rejected the application. Only the most compelling circumstances could justify giving such consent; being in love was in no sense exceptional, and could not thus justify an exception. A similar attitude has been taken in Australia[67]: in *Re S. G.*[68] permission was refused for an under age Greek girl to marry, notwithstanding that the application was supported by the family and priest, and the marriage was one which seemed eminently in accord with modern Greek cultural traditions. The court held that the " exceptional and unusual circumstances " which the statute required " must relate

61 Latey Report, para. 103.
62 *Ibid.* para. 176.
63 Kilbrandon Report, para. 20.
64 Latey Report, paras. 186–191.
65 *e.g.* Australia, some of the United States, France, Italy, Sweden and Switzerland: see App. 7 to the Latey Report, Law Commission No. 33, p. 22, n. 80.
66 *Re Barbara Haven*, 86 Pa.D. & C. 141 (Foote, Levy and Sander, p. 222). The relevant statute required " special circumstances " to be shown. After the case this was amended so that leave could be given " if in the best interests of the applicant."
67 Under the Marriage Act 1961, s. 11. See Finlay and Bissett-Johnson, *Family Law in Australia*, pp. 53–55.
68 (1968) 11 F.L.R. 326; but *cf. Re W.* [1968] Q.W.N. 45, discussed by Finlay (1970) 1 A.C.L.R. 80; and see Turner (1968) 8 Univ. of W.A.L.R. 319.

to the particular parties concerned and not merely to the class or kind of persons to which those parties belong."

In practice it is in cases where the parties belong to an ethnic group whose social traditions recognise early marriage that the problem is likely to be most acute in contemporary England. English law has recognised a marriage (celebrated abroad) between two Nigerian immigrants where the girl is only thirteen.[69] Should it refuse facilities if they wish to marry here? Certainly membership of such a group might be a better ground for permitting marriage than the fact that the girl is pregnant, which is the basis on which in practice dispensation is most often given.[70]

Consequences of an under-age marriage

It has been suggested that a marriage where one of the parties is under sixteen should not be void but only voidable. The present law may cause hardship—particularly if the parties erroneously believed they were of age.[71] The arguments were well summarised by the Law Commission [72]:

> (a) " If the parties marry genuinely believing that they are both of marriageable age, it is hard on them if subsequently—perhaps many years later—they discover that their marriage is void. The hardship to one party may be still greater if the other has led him or her to think that the other is of marriageable age. It may be possible for the parties, on discovering the true facts, to marry and thereby rectify the position, but this possibility would not be available if they had separated and one or other refused to marry or if one or both were dead; in such event children and other persons might be adversely affected.
>
> (b) If parties have lived together for many years believing their marriage to be valid, it is wrong to let a third party, who has a financial interest in establishing the invalidity of the marriage, challenge it on the ground that, through some error (as where, for instance, the wife was an immigrant with no birth certificate), a party was under sixteen at marriage.
>
> (c) Society should not interfere with a marriage which is valid from the ceremonial aspect unless it is contrary to public policy to regard the particular marriage as valid; it is difficult to see why it should be contrary to public policy to treat as valid a marriage which both parties, now of the age of marriage, want to preserve."

The proposal was however rejected for the following reasons [73]:

> (a) " It may seem hard on innocent persons who after years of marriage discover that the marriage is void because a party was under age at the time of marriage, but this result flows from

---

[69] *Mohammed* v. *Knott* [1969] 1 Q.B. 1; see Karsten (1969) 32 M.L.R. 212.

[70] *Re H.* [1964–65] N.S.W.R. 2004; *Re W.* (*supra*).

[71] This may be a real problem in the case of immigrants from countries without adequate systems of birth certification

[72] Law Commission No. 33, para. 17.

[73] *Ibid.* paras. 18–19. Another suggestion was that such marriages might be ratifiable— *i.e.* void unless ratification took place after attaining the appropriate age. There are more powerful technical objections to this: see para. 19.

the law's requirements as to the observance of fundamental conditions as a foundation for a valid marriage and its refusal to treat cohabitation as equivalent to matrimony. The parties are in a similar predicament where after years of ' married life ' the parties discover that their marriage is void because a former spouse was still alive at the date of marriage."

(b) The essential question is one of social policy. Parliament has decided that sexual intercourse below sixteen should be illegal, and it is wrong to validate it by allowing " marriage." It should not be left to the parties to decide whether the " marriage " is to be valid or void.[74]

(c) The petition might not be presented until many years after the ceremony, so that there would be uncertainty as to the status of marriage.[75]

(d) It is essential that the age of consent and of marriage be the same.[76]

It is submitted that these arguments are not convincing:

(a) The requirement of age is not " fundamental ": the law may recognise such marriage if celebrated abroad between foreigners, even (probably), if they immediately come to live here.[77]

(b) It has already been shown [78] that there is no logical or social necessity to equate the minimum age of marriage and that of consent to sexual intercourse. In any case, the choice of sixteen as the age of consent may need review.

(c) The argument that to allow the parties to decide whether their marriage should continue is open to two objections:

(i) Since the Divorce Reform Act 1969 [79] it is always open to the parties to agree to terminate their marriage. The law thus already recognises " trial " marriages.

(ii) If the argument is that it is objectionable to allow *one* party to avoid the marriage (against the wishes of the other) it might be enacted that the court should only annul the marriage if a case can be made out on social grounds.[80]

(d) To prevent the status of marriage being left in doubt it could be provided that it could only be avoided within (say) three years after the age of sixteen had been reached.[81]

The issue is not, perhaps, of great importance. If the parties discover the defect and still wish to be married, they can go through a marriage ceremony which will almost certainly legitimise their

---

74 *Op. cit.* paras. 18 (b) and (c).
75 *Ibid.* para. 18 (a).
76 *Ibid.* para. 18 (d).
77 *Mohammed* v. *Knott (supra)*, but *cf. Radwan* v. *Radwan (No.* 2) [1973] Fam. 35.
78 *Supra*, p. 17.
79 *Infra*, Chap. 5.
80 This is the law in some parts of the United States, where other interested parties, *e.g.* parents, may apply for such an order. See *Foley* v. *Foley* (1924) 203 N.Y.S. 674 and *cf. Duley* v. *Duley* (1959) 151 A. 2d 255. See generally Ploscowe and Freed, p. 70 *et seq.*
81 See Karsten, *op. cit.* n. 69, *supra*, p. 217.

children.[82]. If the defect is not discovered until after one has died, or
one party wishes to repudiate the marriage, the disastrous consequences
for support and succession rights have been mitigated by attaching many
of the legal incidents of marriage even to a union which is void. This
is dealt with below.[83]

IV. CONSENT OF THE PARTIES

The English law of marriage is based on its being a consensual union.[84]
Problems arise because the outward *expression* of consent may not have
been accompanied by the necessary mental *intention*. A party may have
been insane, and not aware of what he was doing. He may have
believed that his bride was A (whereas in fact she is B); although he
did intend to marry, he did not intend to marry the person who now
claims to be his wife. He may have spoken the words of consent only
because his bride's father was standing behind him with a shotgun;
or he may have spoken them as a joke.

These cases raise an acute juristic dilemma: if the *apparent* consent
was not *real* there should be no marriage; yet it produces uncertainty
if an apparently valid marriage can be avoided by proving the existence
of a state of mind or belief which was in no way evident at the time
of the ceremony. The law therefore refuses to allow private reserva-
tions or motives to vitiate an ostensibly valid marriage,[85] yet there may
be cases in which it holds that there has been no consent at all.

The cases can best be considered under three heads: (1) insanity;
(2) duress and fear; (3) mistake.

1. *Insanity*

Marriage (it has been judicially asserted) [86] is a very simple contract,
which it does not require a high degree of intelligence to understand.
It will only affect the validity of consent if either spouse was, at the
time of the ceremony, incapable by reason of mental illness or defect of
understanding the nature of marriage and the duties and responsibilities
it creates.[87] This is difficult to establish, with the result that in 1937
the legislature introduced an easier way of annulling a marriage where
one party was suffering from mental illness.[88] The reason why petitions
were occasionally still brought on the old ground was that, if established, the marriage was *void*. The only recent English case [89] was

[82] *Infra*, p. 311.
[83] *Infra*, p. 65.
[84] *Infra*, p. 32.
[85] *Per* Sir Jocelyn Simon P., *Szechter* v. *Szechter* [1971] P. 286.
[86] *Per* Hodson L.J., *Re Park* [1954] P. 112, 136.
[87] *Re Park* (*supra*); *Hill* v. *Hill* [1959] 1 All E.R. 281. See also *Fischer* v. *Adams*
(1949) 38 N.W. 2d 337.
[88] See *infra*, p. 60. Insanity might also have constituted grounds for divorce: Matrimonial Causes Act 1965, s. 1 (1) (*a*) (iv).
[89] *Supra*.

brought by the husband's relatives, in an attempt to prevent his property passing to the widow on intestacy. Since the Nullity of Marriage Act 1971 want of consent now makes a marriage *voidable* only: it is therefore unlikely that petitions will be brought on the basis of " common law " insanity. It will be easier (and just as effective) to establish the alternative mental disorder ground.[90]

2. *Duress and Fear* [91]

" Where a formal consent is brought about by force, menace or duress —a yielding of the lips, not of the mind—it is of no legal effect." [92] Public policy requires that marriages should not be lightly set aside [93] so that the principles applied are strict and not to be rashly extended.[94] There are, however, some indications that this has occurred in a number of post-war cases where a marriage ceremony has been used as a means of escape from a totalitarian régime.[95] The conditions seem to be as follows:

(i) There must be *fear*, overriding the party's true intent. Thus, in an American " shotgun " marriage case, the marriage was void because " if there had not been a wedding, there would have been a funeral." [96] It is insufficient if the marriage is, in the absence of fear, deliberately entered into to escape from a disagreeable situation such as penury or social degradation,[97] or out of a sense of obligation to family or religious tradition. Thus the court refused to annul a marriage arranged by the parents of two young Sikhs on this ground: although the bride had never seen her husband before the marriage, and only went through with the ceremony out of a " proper respect " for her parents and the traditions of her people, there was no evidence at all of *fear*.[98]

(ii) It must be sufficiently grave. It has been said that there must be a threat of immediate danger to life, limb or liberty.[99]

(iii) Yet the test is a subjective one. The question is not whether a person of ordinary courage and resolution would yield to the fear, but whether the petitioner did so yield.[1] There is (it is submitted) an in-

---

90 See *infra*, p. 58.
91 See C. Davies (1972) 88 L.Q.R. 549.
92 Bishop, *Marriage and Divorce*, 6th ed., 1881, p. 177, cited in *Szechter* v. *Szechter* (*supra*).
93 *Per* Batt J., *Scott* v. *Sebright* (1886) 12 P.D. 21.
94 *Per* Karminski J., *H.* v. *H.* [1954] P. 258, 267.
95 See *infra*, p. 24, n. 3.
96 *Lee* v. *Lee* (1928) 3 S.W. 2d 672. For other examples, see *Scott* v. *Sebright* (*supra*) (threats to make bankrupt, and ultimately to shoot); *Griffith* v. *Griffith* [1944] I.R. 35 and *Buckland* v. *Buckland* [1968] P. 296 (prosecution for defilement); *Parojcic* v. *Parojcic* [1959] 1 All E.R. 1 (to return to totalitarian country); *Szechter* v. *Szechter* (*supra*) and *H.* v. *H.* (*supra*) (danger of remaining in totalitarian country). See generally Manchester (1966) 29 M.L.R. 622; Brown (1968) 42 Tulane L.R. 837.
97 *Per* Sir J. Simon, *Szechter* v. *Szechter* (*supra*).
98 *Singh* v. *Singh* [1971] 2 All E.R. 828.
99 *Szechter* v. *Szechter*; *Singh* v. *Singh* (*supra*).
1 *Scott* v. *Sebright* (*supra*) at p. 24; *cf. Buckland* v. *Buckland* (*supra*) at p. 301. See, however, C. Davies (1972) 88 L.Q.R. 549, 553.

consistency in accepting a purely subjective test, yet requiring that the threat must be to life, limb or liberty.

(iv) The fear must arise from external circumstances, but not necessarily [2] from acts of the other party. Thus in two cases [3] threats to life and liberty arising from the policies of a totalitarian régime have been held to suffice; the marriages took place to avoid imprisonment by leaving the country.[4]

(v) It is sometimes said that the fear must not be justly imposed. Thus if the threat is of prosecution for defilement, the marriage is valid if the petitioner was guilty.[5] The man is free to elect between scandal and possible punishment on the one hand, and marriage to the girl he has wronged on the other.[6] If the accusation is false the marriage will be void. It will also be void if the petitioner is threatened with a more severe penalty than the courts could impose (as in an American case where the man was told that " statutory rape " [7] was a " hanging matter ").

This is illogical and contrary to authority. It is illogical because the justice of the threat has nothing to do with the subjective question of consent. It is contrary to authority in that canon law held a marriage void even if the petitioner was subjected to a just fear through his own fault.[8]

It has been suggested by the Law Commission [9] that the courts in fact impose their own unarticulated test of social policy in applying this principle:

> " If one reviews the actual decisions reached by the courts rather than some of the reasons which have been advanced in reaching those decisions, the results seem to be about right. What in effect they have done is to distinguish legitimate threats from

---

[2] Although this will be the common case, as in *Hussein* v. *Hussein* [1938] P. 159, where H threatened to kill the petitioner if she did not marry him. The state of mind to which she was reduced can be gauged from the document which H made her sign: " I undersigned Estella agree to marry Mohammed on the following conditions: (i) I know well that he is an old-fashioned Egyptian and I know all about the Egyptian habits and character and I promise to follow all these habits and character without any exceptions: (ii) I promise not to go out anywhere without my husband (iii) I will never have men or boy friends of me nor ask any man or boy to visit me at home nor see any man or boy outside or have any appointments; (iv) I promise not to write to anybody friend of mine in Egypt or anywhere else abroad, man, boy, girl or lady (v) I promise not to dance with any man or boy at home or at another home or at any dancing hall. . . . (vi) I know well that Mohammed is not rich at all and he can't promise anything except just keeping me comfortably; (vii) I confess that I write these conditions with my own wish and without any obligation from any side, and that I am conscious and responsible, and if I break any of these conditions I have to separate and have no right to claim any penny from Mohammed at any court, whether Egyptian or English." Mohammed had evidently been brought up in the Civil Law tradition, and regarded a Marriage Contract as an essential element in a respectable union.

[3] *Szechter* v. *Szechter*; *H.* v. *H.* (*supra*); and see *Parojcic* v. *Parojcic* [1958] 1 W.L.R. 1280.

[4] See also *Buckland* v. *Buckland* (*supra*).

[5] *Buckland* v. *Buckland* (*supra*); *Griffith* v. *Griffith* [1944] I.R. 35.

[6] Per Haugh J., *Griffith* v. *Griffith* (*supra*).

[7] *i.e.* intercourse with a girl below the age of consent.

[8] Hay, pp. 88–90.

[9] Law Commission No. 33, para. 66.

illegitimate ones. They have rightly held that the threat is illegitimate if it is to make a false charge against the person threatened. They have implied that it may be legitimate if the charge is just. But no court has gone so far as to hold that a threat is necessarily legitimate on that ground. We doubt, for example, whether any court would hold that it is a legitimate threat not capable of vitiating consent for an employer to tell the office-boy who has robbed the till that unless he marries the employer's ex-mistress he will be prosecuted. In our view, this is not a matter in which legislative action is required. Any attempt to define duress with the precision appropriate to a statute would, in our view, be likely to do more harm than good. We think that the courts can safely be left to deal with each case on its merits."

Some may question whether it is desirable to allow the courts such a wide discretion. Now that divorce is so much more easily available, it may be that this kind of issue will arise even less frequently than in the past.

3. Mistake and Fraud

Generally neither mistake nor fraud avoids a marriage. " The maxim caveat emptor [let the buyer beware] applies just as much to marriage as it does to the purchase of a horse."

The only cases where mistake is relevant is where it vitiates consent to marriage:

(i) Mistake as to the person (as distinct from his attributes)

If I marry A under the belief that she is B there is no marriage; but if I marry A erroneously believing her to be a chaste virgin of good family and possessed of ample wealth the marriage is valid. In a New Zealand case,[10] H represented to W that he was a well known featherweight pugilist. Her mistake was as to his attributes and not as to his identity, and the marriage was valid.[11] She intended to marry the man physically present, and his name was not an essential condition of the marriage. In an Australian case,[12] where W believed that H was a member of a certain family *with which she was acquainted*, there was held to be a sufficient mistake of identity as distinct from a mere mistake of name. The distinction is a fine one.

(ii) Mistake as to the nature of the ceremony

If one party thinks she is appearing in a police court, or that the ceremony is a betrothal [13] or religious conversion ceremony,[13a] there is no marriage.[14] A mistake as to the *effects of the relationship produced* by the marriage is insufficient: a marriage was valid where H thought

---

10 *C.* v. *C.* [1942] N.Z.L.R. 356.
11 See also *Wakefield* v. *Mackay* (1807) 1 Hag.Con. 394, 398; *Ussher* v. *Ussher* [1912] 2 I.R. 445; *Moss* v. *Moss* [1897] P. 263.
12 *Allardyce* v. *Mitchell* (1869) 6 W.W. & A'B. 45.
13 *Parojcic* v. *Parojcic (supra)*; *Ford* v. *Stier* [1896] P. 1.
13a *Mehta* v. *Mehta* [1945] 2 All E.R. 690.
14 See also *Valier* v. *Valier* (1925) 133 L.T. 830.

the marriage was polygamous entitling him to take further wives,[15] and where H assumed that his Russian wife would be allowed to leave the Soviet Union and live with him.[16]

In addition, if one of the parties is so drunk (or under the influence of drugs) that he does not know what he is doing at the time the marriage should be void.[17] If the marriage ceremony is contracted in jest it should also be invalid,[18] although it would be difficult in practice to show that there had been no real consent.

The same principle has been applied to cases where a " sham " marriage has been contracted in order to acquire a nationality or immigration status. If the intention is to contract a marriage—even although it is only for a limited purpose—it will be valid [19] in the absence of fear or duress.[20]

Other mistakes will not suffice, even if the marriage would never have taken place if the true facts had been known, and even if one party has been fraudulent. Fraud is not a vitiating factor if it induces consent, but only if it procures the appearance without the reality of consent.[21] Hence a marriage into which a woman tricked a man by concealing the fact that she was pregnant by a third party was valid at common law.[22]

There has been some suggestion that the law is too restrictive.[23] One proposal is that a " fundamental mistake as to the obligations of the marriage would suffice, leaving the court to decide each case on its merits and, in due course, to formulate a principle; another solution might be to confine relief to cases where the mistake as to the effect of the ceremony was induced by fraud." This was (rightly it is suggested) rejected by the Law Commission on the grounds that the first proposal would be too vague, and the second would go too far.[24] Given the availability of divorce [25] it is not necessary to extend the grounds for obtaining a decree of nullity.

V. SEX OF THE PARTIES AND PHYSICAL CAPACITY

Sex of the parties

By English law, marriage is a union between a man and a woman. If either party's sex is in doubt, the court will determine the issue.[26]

---

[15] *Kassim* v. *Kassim* [1962] P. 224.
[16] *Way* v. *Way* [1950] P. 71. See also *McDougall* v. *Chitnavis*, 1937 S.C. 390; *cf.* the views of Denning L.J. in *Kenward* v. *Kenward* [1951] P. 124.
[17] *Sullivan* v. *Sullivan* (1812) 2 Hag.Con. 238 (*per* Sir W. Scott).
[18] See *Crouch* v. *Wartenberg* (1912) 112 S.E. 234.
[19] *Silver* v. *Silver* [1958] 1 All E.R. 528.
[20] *H.* v. *H.* (*supra*). See also *Messina* v. *Smith* [1971] P. 322, where a marriage of convenience to obtain a passport was annulled at first instance (although the decree was subsequently set aside), and *Kurma* v. *Kurma*, *The Times*, April 30, 1958.
[21] *Moss* v. *Moss* [1897] P. 263, *per* Sir F. H. Jeune P.
[22] It would now be voidable by statute: see *infra*, p. 60.
[23] American courts granted annulments for fraud very readily; see *Shonfield* v. *Shonfield* (1933) 184 N.E. 60; (1948) 48 Col.L.R. 900.
[24] Law Commission No. 33, para. 67.
[25] *Infra*, Chap. 5.
[26] See *Corbett* v. *Corbett* (*orse. Ashley*) [1971] P. 83.

Physical capacity

Capacity to consummate was in the canon law an implied term in the contract of marriage even though the marriage was formed simply by consent.[27] The theory was that incapacity *existing at the time of the ceremony* prevented a marriage coming into existence at all: physical capacity was as much a basic requirement of marriage as the intellectual capacity to consent. There is a vast theoretical difference between recognising this fact (by granting a decree of nullity) and dissolving a valid marriage because of some supervening cause.[28] There may seem little real difference between the case of a couple who never succeed in consummating the marriage, and that where a husband who " was not interested in women at all " had intercourse on some eight occasions in eighteen years of marriage.[29] In both cases in fact an unhappy union comes to an end because of incompatibility. In the classical theory, however, no marriage ever came into existence in the first case, whereas in the second a valid marriage had to be dissolved by a decree of divorce. The courts still apply not only a code of divorce law which attempts to serve current social needs, but also the law administered in the ecclesiastical courts[30] in granting decrees of nullity before the first Divorce Act of 1857.

The main principles of the doctrine are as follows:
1. The inability to consummate the marriage must exist at the time of the marriage ceremony. It is irrelevant that the parties have had premarital sexual intercourse.[31] It is equally irrelevant that one party may *become* incapable after the ceremony.[32]

2. The inability must be permanent and incurable. It will be deemed to be incurable if any remedial operation is dangerous, or if the respondent refuses to undergo an operation.[33]

The requirement of permanence sometimes leads to unedifying incidents. The ecclesiastical court would adjourn cases to enable further attempts to be made.[34] It might be thought that this practice belongs to a bygone age, but the Court of Appeal adopted a not dissimilar attitude as recently as 1962[35]: there had for sixteen years been frequent but unsuccessful attempts by the parties to have intercourse. The husband ultimately petitioned for nullity on the grounds of the wife's incapacity. Six days before the hearing she underwent an operation. The Court of

---

[27] *Infra*, p. 32.
[28] The legal distinction was blurred when incapacity was classified as a ground on which a marriage was voidable, not void; see *supra*, p. 6.
[29] *P.* v. *P.* [1964] 3 All E.R. 919.
[30] Supreme Court of Judicature (Consolidation) Act 1925, s. 32; Matrimonial Causes Act 1857, s. 22.
[31] *Dredge* v. *Dredge* [1947] 1 All E.R. 29 (wife pregnant at date of marriage; decree granted for non-consummation).
[32] *Brown* v. *Brown* (1828) 1 Hag.Ecc. 523; *cf.* n. 11, p. 57, *infra*.
[33] *S.* v. *S.* [1956] P. 1; *L.* v. *L.* (1882) 7 P.D. 16.
[34] See *D.* v. *A.* (1845) 1 Rob.Ecc. 279.
[35] *S.* v. *S.* [1963] P. 162.

Appeal held that the case should have been adjourned for further evidence of the result of the operation.

3. It is for the petitioner to prove that the inability exists. The court has power to order a medical examination, and may draw adverse inferences against a party who refuses to be examined.[36] It used to be the practice to require the parties to cohabit for three years, but there is now no minimum period.[37]

4. The issue is ability to have sexual relations. Sterility or barrenness is not enough.[38] A great deal of elaborate discussion is to be found in the cases as to precisely what degree of sexual relationship will suffice to seal the marriage bond.[39] What is required is a capacity for *vera copula*, intercourse which is " ordinary and complete, and not incipient, imperfect and unnatural." [40] Little would be gained by discussing the details of the cases: originally they were based on a primitive version of the theory that marriages should be decently buried if they have irretrievably broken down. If the parties do not find sexual satisfaction in marriage, they would be tempted to find solace elsewhere. In the language of an ecclesiastical lawyer:

> " Where the coitus itself is absolutely imperfect, and I must call it unnatural, there is not a natural indulgence of natural desire; almost of necessity disgust is generated, and the probable consequences of other connexions with men of ordinary self control become almost certain . . . no man ought to be reduced to this state of quasi unnatural connexion and consequent temptation. . . ." [41]

But no general doctrine developed in English law under which a union could be legally terminated if the parties were incapable of forming a nórmal sexual relationship and in recent years the courts have adopted a largely mechanical approach to the problem.[42]

5. Most cases of incapacity are not based on physical abnormality, but on psychological impotence. It is no objection that the impotence may only be *quoad hunc* or *hanc*—i.e. that the respondent is capable of having intercourse with other partners.[43]

---

[36] *B.* v. *B.* [1901] P. 39; *W.* v. *W.* [1905] P. 231; M.C.R. 1971, r. 30.

[37] *B.* v. *B.* [1958] 1 W.L.R. 619 (cohabitation for one week).

[38] Even if resulting from the voluntary act of the respondent, and not disclosed to the other: *Baxter* v. *Baxter* [1948] A.C. 274. The Law Commission refused to recommend that non-disclosure of sterility should be a ground for nullity: Law Commission No. 33, para. 33.

[39] *D.* v. *A.* (*supra*); *Snowman* v. *Snowman* [1934] P. 186; *Clarke* v. *Clarke* [1943] 2 All E.R. 540; *White* v. *White* [1948] P. 330; *R.* v. *R.* [1952] 1 All E.R. 1194; *G.* v. *G.* [1952] V.L.R. 402; *B.* v. *B.* [1955] P. 42; *S. Y.* v. *S. Y.* [1963] P. 37; *W.* v. *W.* [1967] 1 W.L.R. 1554.

[40] *Per* Dr. Lushington, *D.* v. *A.* (*supra*).

[41] *Ibid*. at p. 299. For a detailed examination of modern canon law (which in the absence of divorce has tended to extend the availability of nullity), see P. V. Hannington, " The Impediment of Male Impotency," 19 *The Jurist* 29, 187, 309, 465.

[42] See *e.g. S. Y.* v. *S. Y.* [1963] P. 37.

[43] *G.* v. *G.* [1924] A. C. 349.

6. If the parties had the opportunity to consummate the marriage, and failed to do so, the courts might presume the existence of incapacity. Since 1937 wilful *refusal* to consummate has been a separate ground for nullity. The two grounds are often pleaded in the alternative.[44]

7. Either party can petition.[45]

[44] See *infra*, p. 58.
[45] *Harthan* v. *Harthan* [1949] P. 115. In some circumstances, however, knowledge of his own impotence was a bar to a petition: see Bevan, 76 L.Q.R. 267. The only bar is presumably now that contained in s. 13 (1), M.C.A. 1973: *infra*, p. 63.

CHAPTER 3

FORMALITIES FOR MARRIAGE

Two topics fall to be discussed under this heading: (i) The Marriage Ceremony and (ii) Consents of Third Parties.

I. *THE MARRIAGE CEREMONY*

Consent is essential to the *formation* of marriage, but the consequences are laid down by law irrespective of the parties' intentions. In the words of an American judge:

> " When the contracting parties have entered into the married state, they have not so much entered into a contract as into a new relation, the rights and duties and obligations of which rest not upon their agreement, but upon the general law of the state, statutory or common, which defines and prescribes those rights, duties and obligations. They are of law, not of contract. It was a contract that the relation should be established, but, being established, the power of the parties as to its extent or duration is at an end. Their rights under it are determined by the will of the sovereign, as evidenced by law. They can neither be modified nor changed by any agreement of parties. It is a relation for life, and the parties cannot terminate it at any shorter period by virtue of any contract they may make. The reciprocal rights arising from this relation, so long as it continues, are such as the law determines from time to time, and none other." [1]

It is, for example, impossible for a couple to marry on the basis that the husband shall be under no obligation to support his wife. In an ordinary contract, the parties may decide on the terms, but in the marriage relationship this is not so.

A couple may, therefore, be tempted to eschew the all or nothing of legal marriage, securing what they believe to be necessary by private contract. For example, an American couple entered into the following agreement (much more formal, as we shall see, than anything which is done in the Registrar's Office ceremony in England):

> " We, the undersigned, hereby enter into a co-partnership on the basis of the true marriage relation. Recognising love as the only law which should govern the sexual relationship we agree to continue this co-partnership so long as mutual affection shall exist, and to dissolve it when the union becomes disagreeable or undesirable to either party. We also agree that all property that shall be acquired by mutual effort shall be equally divided on the dissolution of said co-partnership. Should any children result from this union, we

---

[1] *Per* Appleton C.J., *Adams* v. *Palmer* (1863) 51 Maine 481, 483.

pledge ourselves to be mutually held and bound to provide them support, whether the union continues or is dissolved." [2]

Such an agreement is substantially devoid of legal effect: it would almost certainly be held illegal and contrary to public policy.[3]

The law insists not only on certain essential conditions if two parties are to marry, but also on compliance with certain forms. The present law is complex and, in many respects, obscure.[4] Before considering the details, it may be helpful to outline the purpose which, it is submitted, a modern system of formalities should serve.

(i) Certainty

There should be no doubt whether or not a marriage has been created, and the precise moment of time at which the parties became man and wife. Otherwise there may be problems about legitimacy and succession rights.

(ii) Proof

It should be easy to *prove* that a valid marriage has been effected—for instance by the provision of an official document.

(iii) Public Records

The existence of a marriage may be of interest to outsiders, perhaps many years in the future. It is important therefore that records should be kept for public inspection.

(iv) Avoidance of deception

It should, as far as practicable, be made impossible for those who are not legally free to marry to go through a marriage ceremony. In particular, since all marriages contracted in England are monogamous, it is desirable to prevent men who are already married from deceiving women into a bigamous marriage.

(v) Consents

The law should ensure that both parties to a marriage consent to it. English law also imposes a requirement of parental consent for the marriage of persons under the age of eighteen. The system should provide checks to ensure that this has been given.

---

2 *Peck* v. *Peck* (1892) 30 N.E. 74.

3 See *Benyon* v. *Nettlefold* (1850) 3 Mac. & G. 94. This point does not seem to be considered in the draft " Cohabitation Contract " at (1973) 123 New L.J. 591.

4 Reforms are under active consideration: see the Kilbrandon Report; the Law Commission's P.W.P. No. 35 prepared by a joint working party of the Law Commission and Registrar-General's Department (" P.W.P. 35 "), and the Report of the Law Commission on Solemnisation of Marriage in England and Wales, Law Commission No. 53.

(vi) Solemnity

A " marriage ceremony is an important family and social occasion." [5]
It should therefore (a) adequately express the significance of the occasion,
and (b) not be surrounded by " unnecessary and irksome restrictions." [6]

In addition to these rather limited aims, some reformers take the
view that the state should use preliminary formalities to discourage
marriages which are unlikely to be successful. A common suggestion is
that the parties be required to submit themselves to a medical examination, but there are also more far-reaching proposals (e.g. for a period of
compulsory betrothal during which detailed counselling can be provided).

It is impossible to understand the modern English law of marriage
formalities without reference to its history. We shall then be in a position
to assess what changes are needed to achieve the above objectives.

A. HISTORICAL ORIGINS

The common law for many years left the regulation of marriage entirely
to the church. Until statute intervened the marriage law was simply
canon law, which allowed marriage to be contracted with great ease and
absence of ceremonial.

For the early church (whilst it was spiritually desirable to have a
religious ceremony) consummation was the essential factor.[7] This caused
problems with regard to the marriage of Joseph and the Virgin Mary [8]
(who according to one interpretation had exchanged vows of life-long
chastity). In the twelfth century, therefore, it was settled that a valid
marriage could be formed by the mere exchange of consents. The vital
requirement was that the words should be in the present tense: *sponsalia
per verba de praesenti*. No other ceremony was needed; the church
might, as a matter of discipline, order the parties to go through a religious
ceremony, but it was the prior consent which created the marriage.

If the consent was in the future tense (not " I do marry you," but
" I promise I will marry you ") an immediately binding marriage was
not created. But if sexual intercourse took place after the promise the
parties immediately became man and wife. The reason was that these
sponsalia per verba de futuro " implied such a present consent at the
time of the sexual intercourse as to complete the marriage in substance,
and give it equal validity with the contract *de praesenti*." [8a] Thus the
church reconciled the two views: that of the early church that consummation was necessary to form a marriage; that, derived from Roman
law, that *consensus non concubitus facit matrimonium*.[9] The result

---

[5] Law Commission No. 53, para. 4.
[6] *Ibid*.
[7] The text relied on was Genesis, 2, 24: " Therefore shall a man leave his father
and his mother, and shall cleave unto his wife: and they shall be one flesh."
[8] See Hay, pp. 306–322.
[8a] Poynter, *Ecclesiastical Courts*, 1824, p. 14.
[9] See generally Pollock and Maitland, pp. 364–385; Jackson, *Formation etc.*, pp. 10–20.

was that " the one contract which . . . should certainly be formal had become the most formless of contracts." [10]

The decrees of the Council of Trent required the presence of a priest and independent witnesses, but they came too late to apply to England, where the old methods of contracting marriage continued until 1735.[11]

In Scotland, they remained in force until 1940,[12] while common law marriages can still be contracted in parts of the United States, enabling couples to avoid the rigour of their own state law by crossing the frontier into a less exigent state.[13] The objections to such informality are considerable:

(i) Hasty marriages are encouraged. In 1856 [14] Lord Brougham recounted that:

" a respectable gentleman in Scotland, whose two daughters went out to ride with a groom, found to his infinite astonishment and no less infinite dismay, that one of them returned to the house an hour after and stated that the groom was her husband, and such a marriage was as perfectly valid by the law of Scotland as if it had been celebrated after proclamation of banns by a regular clergyman."

To put the matter in a more modern setting an American writer has commented that the agreement (which is all that is necessary to form the marriage):

" may be entered into in the privacy of one's own bedroom, in an automobile after a picnic in the country, or after a night's debauch." [15]

In such cases, it seems unlikely that there will be much point in inquiring whether the promises were in the present or future tense. An even more striking illustration of the potential evil of such " quickie " marriages is given by the American case of *State* v. *Ward* [16] in which the defendant, to a charge of statutory rape, asserted that the complainant was his wife. This was found to be the case, on the basis of *sponsalia de praesenti*.

---

10 Pollock and Maitland, p. 369.
11 Save for a period between 1540 and 1548 when legislation of Henry VIII provided that a consummated church marriage could not be invalidated by pre-contract (*i.e.* proof of prior *sponsalia de praesenti* with a third party): see Jackson, *Formation etc.*, pp. 18–19. Note, however, that according to *R.* v. *Millis* (1844) 10 Cl. & F. 534, the presence of an episcopally ordained clergyman was necessary to the validity in this country of a common law marriage.
12 Marriage (Scotland) Act 1939. For history, see Kilbrandon Report, Chap. 1. It is still possible in Scotland to establish retrospectively a marriage " by cohabitation with habit and repute." This arises where couples set up a home together, and live as a married couple. Prior to 1940 this doctrine was justified by the presumption that the parties must have created a marriage by exchange of consents. It is difficult to see what theoretical justification there can be for it now. But the Kilbrandon Report recommends its retention: Chap. 9.
13 See Foote, Levy and Sander, p. 264.
14 Hansard, Vol. 142, col. 206.
15 Ploscowe, *Sex and the Law* (1951), p. 17.
16 (1944) 28 S.E. 2d 785.

(ii) It leads to uncertainty about the validity of marriages. It is not so much that there might be doubts about the validity of A's marriage to B; it is rather that indiscreet and quickly forgotten words breathed under the influence of passion will invalidate a subsequent solemn marriage with C.[17]

English law [18] was reformed by Lord Hardwicke's Act, carried (against strong opposition) in 1753. It did away with the formless common law marriage in England and stipulated a public Church ceremony after the calling of banns on three successive Sundays. (It was possible by licence to dispense with banns, but only if one of the parties had lived in the parish for the previous four weeks.) The consent of parents or guardians of minors had to be obtained, and register entries made. Failure to comply with these requirements made the marriage void. The Act applied to all except members of the Royal Family, Quakers and Jews. Thus, Protestant dissenters and Roman Catholics were compelled to marry according to the Anglican rite, or not at all.[19]

In 1836 the law was changed to permit marriages outside the Church of England. Two parallel systems were thus available: (i) Marriage in the Church of England. This followed the pattern laid down by Lord Hardwicke's Act [20]; (ii) Marriage under the provisions of the new Act.[21] The law is now codified in the Marriage Act 1949,[22] but is still based on the pattern established in 1836.

The process falls into two stages: (i) preliminaries to marriage; (ii) the marriage ceremony.

B. PRELIMINARIES TO MARRIAGE

Civil Preliminaries

The 1836 legislation established the office of Superintendent Registrar. All marriages *other than those to be solemnised in the Church of England* have to be [23] preceded by preliminaries for which he is responsible.

These preliminaries are designed to ensure that notice of the marriage

---

[17] See *Dalrymple* v. *Dalrymple* (1811) 2 Hag.Con. 54.

[18] But note that until 1856 it was possible for English residents to go to Scotland and celebrate a marriage in the traditional form. After that date by the law of Scotland the parties had to reside in Scotland for three weeks, and the number of marriages celebrated at Gretna Green fell sharply. In recent years the only advantage of an elopement to Scotland has been that (once the necessary residence has been established) a valid marriage can be contracted there without any parental consent. See Kilbrandon Report, pp. 25–33.

[19] See O. Chadwick, *The Victorian Church* (1966), Vol. I, p. 143 *et seq.*

[20] The Marriage Act 1823 had preserved the requirements of Lord Hardwicke's Act, but provided that formal defects should only make the marriage *void* if the parties " knowingly and wilfully " contravened the Act.

[21] Marriage Act 1836.

[22] As amended.

[23] But marriages in the Church of England *may* be preceded by one variant of the civil preliminaries—*i.e.* the issue of a Superintendent Registrar's certificate—rather than by the normal ecclesiastical preliminaries: Marriage Act 1949, s. 5 (*d*).

is given (thus providing publicity), but there are three different procedures:

Superintendent Registrar's certificate

This is the counterpart of the ecclesiastical practice of calling banns, and was intended to be the usual procedure. The main requirements are:

(a) *Residence*

Notice has to be given to the Superintendent Registrar of the district or districts where the parties have resided for seven days beforehand.[24] If therefore either party does not live in this country [25] it is impossible to use this procedure.

(b) *Declaration*

The notices must be accompanied by a solemn declaration that there are believed to be no lawful impediments to the marriage, that the residential requirements have been satisfied and that any requisite consents to the marriage of a minor have been given or dispensed with.[26] A wilfully false statement in the declaration is an offence under the Perjury Act 1911. The prescribed form of notice [27] is prominently endorsed with warnings about the criminal consequences of making a false declaration, etc. and with the words "*Marriage according to the law of this country is the union of one man to one woman, voluntarily entered into for life, to the exclusion of all others.*"

(c) *Publicity*

All notices are entered in a marriage notice book which is open to public inspection [28] and is " suspended or affixed " for twenty-one days on a notice-board in " some conspicuous place " in the Superintendent Registrar's office.[29]

(d) *Discovery of impediments*

The object of this procedure is to avoid the celebration of marriages to which there is some legal objection. If there are circumstances which demand inquiry the Registrar will seek to satisfy himself (*e.g.* if one party claims to be a widower or divorcé that this is the case). The Act also contains provisions enabling members of the public to object. Any person may enter a caveat at the office [30] and any person whose consent

---

24 Marriage Act 1949, s. 27 (1).
25 There are special facilities for sailors, residents in Scotland or Northern Ireland (ss. 37–39), and in some other countries: Marriage of British Subjects (Facilities) Acts 1915–16.
26 See *infra*, p. 51.
27 See the Registration of Births, Deaths and Marriages Regulations 1968 (S.I. 2049), Forms 15 and 16.
28 Marriage Act 1949, s. 27 (4).
29 s. 31 (1).
30 s. 29.

is required to the marriage of a minor, may forbid the issue of a certificate by writing " forbidden " by the entry and signing it with a statement of the capacity in which he purports to forbid.[31] In either event the certificate cannot be granted until the objection is withdrawn or found to be invalid.

(e) *Waiting time*

At the end of twenty-one days [32] from the giving of notice, the Registrar must issue a *certificate*. This is the authorisation for the marriage to be solemnised, and has to be produced to whoever celebrates the marriage. This may be done at any time within three months from the day when notice was entered in the marriage notice book.[33]

Superintendent Registrar's certificate and licence

This procedure is commonly (but erroneously) called " Marriage by Special Licence." It is, as we shall see, closely analogous to the Ecclesiastical Common Licence.[34] It is the same in essentials as the ordinary certificate process, but with the following major [35] differences:

(a) *Residence*

Notice need only be given to the Superintendent Registrar of the district in which *one* of the parties has resided for the previous fifteen days.

(b) *Publicity*

Although the notice must be entered into the notice book (which is open to inspection) it is not displayed in the Registrar's office.[36]

(c) *Waiting time*

The marriage may take place at any time after the expiration of *one whole day* from the giving of notice.[37] Thus, if notice is given on Monday, the marriage can take place on Wednesday.

There is thus virtually no publicity, and no time for objection to be raised. The difference is simply one of cost: the fee for giving notice is £1·00 (or £2·00 if notice has to be given to two registrars). If a licence is sought, an additional fee of £5·00 is payable, bringing the total to £6·00.[38] Although intended to be exceptional, this procedure is used in a large proportion of civil marriages—81,782 out of 167,101 in the year 1971.[39]

---

[31] s. 30.
[32] s. 31 (2)—unless, of course, some bar has been discovered.
[33] s. 33.
[34] *Infra*, p. 39.
[35] Certificates for marriage by licence are printed in red (rather than black) and bear a distinctive watermark: s. 40.
[36] s. 32 (1).
[37] s. 32 (2).
[38] Registration of Births, Deaths and Marriages (Fees) Order 1972.
[39] Appendix I, Law Commission No. 53.

Registrar-General's licence

Until 1971 there was no civil procedure which could be used to authorise a marriage outside an Anglican church, register office, or registered building. This caused hardship where the parties wanted to contract a so-called " death-bed marriage." The only way of doing this was to obtain a Special Licence from the Archbishop of Canterbury,[40] which was only given for an Anglican marriage, and then only to those who were free to marry by Anglican canon law. It was thus not available where one of the parties had been divorced if the previous spouse was still alive.

The Marriage (Registrar General's Licence) Act 1970 provides a procedure analogous to the Archbishop's Special Licence, and it is specifically provided that the new procedure shall *not* be used as a preliminary to an Anglican wedding.[41] It can only be used where there is evidence [42] that one of the persons to be married is seriously ill and is not expected to recover and cannot be moved to a place at which marriages can normally be solemnised.[43] Evidence must also be produced that: (a) there is no lawful impediment to the marriage; (b) the requisite consents have been given; (c) there is a sufficient reason why the licence should be granted.[44] The application is forwarded to the Registrar-General, who must issue a licence, provided he is satisfied that there are sufficient grounds, and that no impediment has been shown.[45] The marriage must be celebrated within one month from the date on which notice was entered [46] at the place stated in the notice.[47] There is no prescribed waiting period at all, and any delay will depend on the speed with which the application is handled by the authorities. A fee of £15 is payable, although this may be remitted if it would cause hardship to the parties.[48]

Ecclesiastical Preliminaries

These can be used *only* as a preliminary to marriage according to the Rites of the Church of England. There are three procedures:

Banns

This procedure is used for some 94 per cent. of Anglican weddings.[49] The salient features of the law are as follows:

---

40 *Infra*, p. 40.
41 s. 1.
42 A doctor's certificate is sufficient: s. 3.
43 s. 1 (2).
44 s. 7.
45 s. 7.
46 s. 8.
47 s. 9.
48 s. 17 (1).
49 Law Commission No. 53, Appendix I: 151,540 out of 160,059 in 1971.

(a) *Residence*

If the parties reside in the same parish the banns must be published there[50]; if in different parishes, in each of them.[51] They *may* also be published in any parish church or authorised chapel which is the usual place of worship[52] of one or both of the parties[53] but this will only be *necessary* if the parties are to be married there.[54]

There is no specific requirement as to length of prior residence, or as to what constitutes residence.[55] In practice, seven days' prior residence may be required, since no clergyman is obliged to publish banns unless the parties deliver or cause to be delivered seven days' notice in writing with their full names, places of residence and the period during which each has resided there.[56] In contrast to the civil procedure, there is no requirement of a declaration of capacity or parental consent (nor in theory even of personal attendance to arrange for the calling of banns).

(b) *Publicity*

The banns are entered in an official register, and must be published therefrom[57] " in an audible manner and in accordance with the form of words prescribed by the rubric prefixed to the office of matrimony in the Book of Common Prayer " on three Sundays preceding the solemnisation.[58] There seems to be no right of public inspection of the Register of Banns.

(c) *Discovery of impediments*

The theory is that banns are " primarily addressed to parents and guardians, to excite their vigilance, and afford them fit opportunities of protecting those lawful rights which may be avoided by clandestinity."[59] In the case of civil preliminaries, the Registrar may refuse to issue a licence unless he is " satisfied by the production of written evidence " that the necessary consents have been obtained.[60] But there is no analogous right in the ecclesiastical procedure. The Act simply provides that if a person whose consent is required " openly and publicly declares or causes to be declared in the church . . . at the time of the publication, his dissent from the intended marriage, the publication of

---

[50] There is a great deal of case law on the proper publication of banns: see Jackson, *Formation etc.*, p. 169 *et seq.* Furthermore, the complexities of extra-parochial places, chapelries, etc. is ignored in the discussion in the text.
[51] Marriage Act 1949, s. 6.
[52] In order to qualify for this purpose, the applicant must be enrolled on the Church electoral roll: s. 72.
[53] s. 6 (4).
[54] s. 12 (1).
[55] According to P.W.P. 35, " The residential qualification is often regarded as fulfilled by booking a room in a local hotel and depositing a suitcase in it " (p. 11, n. 52), but *quaere* whether this is legally sufficient: *Fox* v. *Stirk* [1970] 2 Q.B. 463.
[56] s. 8.
[57] " and not from loose papers ": s. 7 (3).
[58] s. 7 (1) (2).
[59] Poynter, p. 27.
[60] This power was only introduced by the Family Law Reform Act 1969, s. 2 (3), although it had prior to this been the practice of Registrars to ask for such written consent: see Latey Report, para. 185.

banns shall be void." [61] In practice no doubt a clergyman would refuse to solemnise a marriage one of the parties to which was under eighteen if he had notice that consent had not been given but in theory he may do so unless public objection has been made.[62]

The best advice to be given to a person under eighteen who wishes to contract a marriage without his parents' consent is therefore to be married after publication of banns in church, preferably in a large town, where the incumbent does not take an officious view of his pastoral responsibilities, and where it is unlikely that members of the congregation will know the parties. Not only will the marriage be valid (in the absence of objection) but no criminal offence will have been committed.[63] He may thus enjoy his married life in defiance of the policy of the law and without fear of penal sanctions.

(d) *Waiting time*

The parties may marry immediately after the third publication. The marriage must be solemnised in one of the churches where the banns have been published.[64] The waiting time will depend on whether or not the clergyman requires seven days' notice before the first publication: it may be less than the corresponding twenty-one days for a Registrar's certificate if it is dispensed with: the absolute minimum would be fifteen days if publication was sought and made without prior notice on Sunday, when the marriage could take place on Monday fortnight. But in practice the waiting time will be rather in excess of twenty-one days.

Common licence

This is the ecclesiastical counterpart of the Superintendent Registrar's certificate and licence. Basic rules are laid down in the Marriage Act,[65] but the details are matters of ecclesiastical law. The main requirements are:

(a) *Residence*

The licence can only permit a marriage in *either* the parish where one of the parties has had his usual place of residence for fifteen days immediately before the grant of the licence *or* the church which is " the usual place of worship " [66] of either or both parties.[67]

(b) *Declaration*

Unlike the procedure by banns, a common licence can only be granted if one of the parties swears on affidavit [68] that he believes that there is

---

61 s. 3 (3). 62 s. 3 (4).
63 Since no declaration will have been made, *cf.* the civil preliminaries where a declaration will have been made that the parties are of age: *supra*, p. 35.
64 Certificates must be provided of the publication of banns in the other relevant churches: s. 11. The marriage must take place within three months of completion of publication: s. 12.
65 ss. 15–16.
66 *i.e.* his name is on the electoral roll: see n. 52, *supra*.
67 s. 15 (1).
68 Thus exposing himself to punishment if its contents are known to be untrue.

no lawful impediment, that the residential qualification is complied with, and, where one of the parties is a minor and not a widow or a widower, that the requisite consents have been obtained or dispensed with.[69] There is no legal power to require written evidence that consent has in fact been obtained,[70] but this is of little practical importance, since the grant of a licence (unlike the analogous civil procedure) seems to be a matter of discretion rather than right.[71]

(c) Publicity, discovery of impediments, and waiting time

A caveat may be entered against the grant of a licence. If it is, no licence can be issued until it is withdrawn or the ecclesiastical judge certifies that it should not obstruct the grant of a licence.[72]

There is no waiting time: once the licence is issued the marriage can take place immediately. In practice it is understood that the formalities of obtaining a licence take some little time.

As with the Superintendent Registrar's Certificate with Licence there is virtually no publicity or opportunity for objection. As with that procedure the cost (£4·50) is a little more than the normal procedure by banns (£1·05 a set, plus £0·70 for a certificate if needed).[73] But, unlike the civil procedure, obtaining a Common Licence is something of a rarity,[74] and may be found considerably more awesome in practice.

Special licence

By an Act of Parliament of 1533 [75] power is reserved [76] to the Archbishop of Canterbury to license marriages at any hour of the day or night in any church or chapel or other meet and convenient place whether consecrated or not. The fee for such licences is £25 [77] and less than 300 are granted annually.[78] Originally, we are told "they were intended exclusively for the use of persons of noble and illustrious quality."

In practice they are today usually granted to permit marriages [79] in churches other than a parish church or authorised Anglican chapel (e.g. college chapels at Oxford and Cambridge or the Queen's Chapel of the Savoy). Until the Marriage (Registrar General's Licence) Act 1970 [80]

---

69 s. 16.
70 The Family Law Reform Act 1969, s. 2 (3), only applies to civil preliminaries.
71 *Middleton* v. *Croft* (1736) 2 Stra. 1056; *Ex p. Brinckman* (1895) 11 T.L.R. 387.
72 s. 16 (2).
73 Law Commission No. 53, paras. 12–13.
74 There were 7,766 licences in 1971; *cf.* 151,540 marriages after banns: Law Commission No. 53, Appendix I.
75 The Ecclesiastical Licences Act.
76 And see also the express savings in Marriage Act 1949, s. 79 (6); Marriage (Registrar General's Licence) Act 1970, s. 19.
77 This is sometimes wholly or partially remitted.
78 Law Commission No. 53, para. 14, n. 66, gives an average of 250, but 450 were issued in 1971: *ibid.*, Appendix I.
79 It is possible and quite common to avoid the expense of a special licence by taking advantage of the procedure authorised by s. 46 of the Act: a marriage takes place after civil preliminaries in a Registrar's office. The couple may then, on production of the Marriage Certificate, have a religious service celebrated. But they are in law married by the civil ceremony: s. 46 (2).
80 *Supra*, p. 37.

it was only by special licence that a deathbed marriage could be celebrated if one of the parties could not be moved; it is still the only way in which such a marriage can be celebrated according to Anglican rites.[81]

C. Solemnisation of the Marriage

There are four main [82] categories of marriage ceremony in English law:

(1) Civil marriage.
(2) Marriage according to a non-Anglican religious ceremony.
(3) Marriage according to the rites of the Church of England.
(4) Quaker and Jewish marriages.

(1) Civil marriage

The parties may state in the notice that they wish to be married in a register office. The ceremony takes place after completion of civil preliminaries in the office with open doors in the presence of the Superintendent Registrar (who acts as celebrant) and a Registrar [83] (whose function is to see to the registration formalities). The ceremony must [84] be purely secular in form, and is simply the exchange of the *sponsalia per verba de praesenti* in a prescribed modern form: " I call upon these persons here present to witness that I, *A.B.*, do take thee, *C.D.*, to be my lawful wedded wife (or husband)." [85] The parties are also required to declare that they know of no lawful impediment to the marriage. It is the practice of Registrars to make the following allocution to the parties: " it is my duty to remind you of the solemn and binding character of the vows you are about to take. Marriage according to the law of this country is the union of one man with one woman, voluntarily entered into, for life, to the exclusion of all others." There is no statutory authority for this.

(2) Marriage according to a non-Anglican religious ceremony

The 1836 Act made provision for the registration of places of worship for the solemnisation of matrimony. This enabled non-conformist chapels and Roman Catholic churches to be used for weddings. Originally, such marriages had to be carried out in the presence of a Registrar of Marriages, but in 1898 [86] it was made possible for an authorised person to be nominated to celebrate marriages without the presence of the Registrar. The authorised person will invariably be a minister of the religious group concerned.

These provisions represent a striking division of function: on the

---

81 Marriage (Registrar General's Licence) Act 1970, s. 1 (1).
82 The Act (Part V) contains special provisions relating to marriages in naval, military or air force chapels.
83 s. 45.
84 s. 45 (2).
85 ss. 45 (3), 46 (1).
86 Marriage Act 1898.

one hand the state is concerned with the preliminary formalities, and licenses both the places where the marriages can take place and those who can solemnise them. On the other hand, the form of the ceremony is left to the parties (and the authorities of the registered building).

(a) *Preliminaries*

The parties must comply with the civil preliminaries. The certificate will state where the ceremony is to be held.[87] This must normally be a registered building in the district where one of the parties resides,[88] but there is power to designate a building elsewhere if this is the nearest place where a particular form of religious ceremony can be conducted, or if it is the usual place of worship [89] of one or both parties.[90]

(b) *Registration of buildings*

The Registrar-General has the responsibility of deciding whether to register a building for the solemnisation of marriages. It is necessary:

(i) That the building should have been previously certified under the Places of Religious Worship Registration Act 1855 as " a place of meeting for religious worship." There is no discretion to refuse certificates under that Act provided the Registrar-General is satisfied that the building falls within this description. But this may involve difficult quasi-theological problems: it has been said that religious worship means reverence or veneration of God or of a supreme being,[91] and that worship means humbling oneself in reverence and recognition of the dominant power and control of an entity or being outside one's own body and life, or that it involves some, at least of the following characteristics: submission to the object worshipped, veneration of that object, praise, thanksgiving, prayer or intercession.[92]

(ii) The building must be a " separate building." [93]

(iii) Application for registration under the Marriage Act must be made by the owner or trustees to the Superintendent Registrar of the registration district where the building is situated,[94] and it must be supported by a certificate signed by at least twenty householders who certify that the building is being used by them as their usual place of public religious worship.[95]

---

[87] ss. 27 (3), 31, 32, 35 (5).
[88] s. 34.
[89] This expression has no technical meaning: *cf. supra*, p. 39.
[90] s. 35, as amended by Marriage Act 1949 (Amendment) Act 1954.
[91] *Per* Lord Denning M.R., *R.* v. *Registrar-General, ex p. Segerdal* [1970] 2 Q.B. 697.
[92] *Per* Winn and Buckley L.JJ., *Ex p. Segerdal (supra)*. In this case the Registrar-General's refusal to register the chapel of the Church of Scientology at East Grinstead under the Act was upheld by the Divisional Court and Court of Appeal.
[93] s. 41 (1), unless it is a Roman Catholic chapel: Marriage Acts Amendment Act 1958, s. 1 (1).
[94] s. 4 (1).
[95] s. 14 (2), as amended.

(c) *The celebrant*

Marriages in registered buildings must be attended *either* by a registrar *or* an " authorised person." The authorisation comes from the trustees or governing body of the building, but must be notified to the authorities.[96] No qualifications are laid down but he will normally be a minister of the religion concerned. The function of the Registrar or authorised person:

> " is not only to ensure that the subsequent process of registering the marriage is duly carried out but also to ensure that the preliminaries have been duly completed and that the formalities are properly observed, for if they are not he will, or should, refuse to allow the marriage to take place. The object of allowing an ' authorised person ' to act instead of a registrar is to minimise the discrimination against religions other than the Church of England, by allowing one of their officials to be present instead of a representative of the State. . . . These provisions relating to authorised persons also have the desirable consequence of relieving the civil authorities of the heavy burden of having to make a registrar available at every marriage in a registered building." [97]

(d) *The ceremony*

The Act provides that the marriage shall be celebrated with open doors in the presence of two or more witnesses, and a registrar or authorised person. The authorised person will often be the celebrant.[98] The marriage may be solemnised " according to such form and ceremony as [the parties] may see fit to adopt." [99] Marriages may thus be celebrated, *e.g.* in Hindu or Islamic form, but:

(i) At some stage the parties have to make the following statements:

> " I do solemnly declare that I know not of any lawful impediment why I, *A.B.*, may not be joined in matrimony to *C.D.*";

and:

> " I call upon these persons here present to witness that I, *A.B.*, do take thee, *C.D.*, to be my lawful wedded wife [or husband]." [1]

When the marriage is in the presence of an authorised person (instead of a registrar) the words " I call upon these persons here present to witness that " [2] may be omitted.

(ii) The consent of the religious authorities is required for a marriage in their building. Hence a traditional form will (presumably) normally be adopted.

96 s. 43.
97 P.W.P. 35, para. 68.
98 P.W.P. 35, para. 87.
99 s. 44 (1).
1 s. 44 (3).
2 *Ibid.*

(3) Marriage according to the rites of the Church of England

(a) Preliminaries

A marriage can take place *either* (a) after completion of any of the ecclesiastical preliminaries, *or* (b) on the authority of a Superintendent Registrar's certificate [3] (but not a certificate with licence).[4] The marriage must take place *either* (i) in one of the churches where banns have been published,[5] *or* (ii) in the church authorised by a common licence,[6] *or* (iii) in the church or other place authorised by a special licence,[7] *or* (iv) if it is by Superintendent Registrar's certificate, in any church or chapel where banns may be called.[8] In this case, the incumbent must agree to the church being used.[9]

It should be noted that a clergyman is entitled to refuse to marry any person whose former marriage has been dissolved (on whatever ground) and whose former spouse is still living, and to refuse to permit such a marriage to be solemnised in his church.[10] Apart from this, a clergyman is bound to celebrate a marriage after due publication of banns or on production of a valid licence, irrespective of the religion (or lack of it) of the parties.[11]

(b) The ceremony

The marriage must be celebrated by a clergyman in the presence of two or more witnesses.[12] The rite is that laid down in the Book of Common Prayer, or any alternative form of service currently authorised.[13]

(4) Quaker and Jewish marriages

These were exempted from the provisions of Lord Hardwicke's Act, and have remained a special category. It is now, however, necessary for one of the forms of civil preliminaries to be completed. In the case of Quaker marriages a special declaration has to be made when giving notice.[14] There is no statutory requirement in the case of Jewish marriages save that it be between " two persons professing the Jewish religion." [15]

The *celebration* of Jewish and Quaker marriages is entirely a matter

---

[3] s. 5 (d). Only 106 such marriages took place in 1971: Law Commission No. 53, Appendix I.
[4] s. 26 (2).
[5] s. 12 (1).
[6] s. 15 (1).
[7] *Supra*, p. 40.
[8] s. 79 (6); *i.e.* parish churches and licensed chapels; a list of the latter is made each year and sent to all registrars and superintendent registrars: s. 73.
[9] s. 17.
[10] Matrimonial Causes Act 1965, s. 8 (2). See generally A. R. Winnett, *Divorce and Remarriage in Anglicanism* (1958); *The Church and Divorce* (1968); and *Marriage, Divorce and the Church* (S.P.C.K., 1971), paras. 6–13 and Appendix 7.
[11] *Argar* v. *Holdsworth* (1758) 2 Lee 515; *Davis* v. *Black* (1841) 1 Q.B. 900.
[12] s. 22.
[13] Under the Prayer Book (Alternative and Other Services) Measure 1965.
[14] s. 47.
[15] s. 26 (1) (d).

for the rules of those religions.[16] They need not be celebrated in a registered building, by an authorised person, or in public. There are special rules for *registration*.[17]

Hours for marriage

Except in the case of Quaker and Jewish marriages, and Marriages by Special [18] or Registrar-General's [19] Licence, it is an offence knowingly and wilfully to celebrate a marriage save between 8 a.m. and 6 p.m.[20] But the marriage will be valid.[21]

Registration of marriages

The objects of a system of registration are to ensure that [22] :

" there is a public record of an event which has important legal consequences both for the parties themselves and for third parties and for the State. The parties need such a record so that their marriage relationship can be established beyond doubt and so that they can present proof of it to others. Third parties need it so that they can determine the status of the parties and the status (*e.g.* legitimacy) of themselves and others in so far as that is dependent on the marriage of the parties. The State needs it because upon it may depend rights and obligations owed by or to the State in relation, for example, to tax, social security, and allegiance. An effective system of registration affords means of proof or disproof and avoids uncertainty where certainty is essential. In addition registration provides statistics regarding marriage which are vital for any serious research into legal, social or demographical problems."

Examination of the details of the system is outside the scope of this book.[23]

Consequence of irregularities

In sharp contrast to the system originally introduced by Lord Hardwicke's Act,[24] the general principle of modern English law is that only contumacious disregard of the marriage formalities will invalidate a marriage. The Act provides that if the parties " knowingly and wilfully " disregard certain requirements the marriage shall be void.[25] Both parties must know of the defect, although it has never been determined whether it is sufficient if they know in fact that the formality has not been observed, or whether they must also know that this will in law invalidate the marriage.[26] The class includes (in the case of Anglican marriages)

---

[16] See for some details Jackson, *Formation etc.*, p. 198 *et seq.*   [17] *Infra.*
[18] ss. 75 (1), 79 (6).
[19] Marriage (Registrar General's Licence) Act 1970, s. 8 (1), although this has been doubted: P.W.P. 45, para. 65 and para. 9, n. 40.
[20] s. 75 (1) (*a*); s. 4.
[21] *Infra*, p. 46.
[22] Report of the Joint Working Party of the Law Commission and the Registrar-General, Law Commission No. 53, para. 104.
[23] See *ibid.* pp. 56–63 for detailed criticisms.
[24] *Supra*, p. 34.
[25] ss. 25 (Anglican Marriages), 49 (Marriage under Certificate).
[26] *Greaves* v. *Greaves* (1872) L.R. 2 P. & M. 423, 424–425 *per* Lord Penzance.

marriages otherwise than in church or chapel where banns may be published, failure to carry out the necessary preliminaries, marriages after duly registered parental objection [27] or after expiry of the banns, etc. and marriages by a person not in Holy Orders.[28] In the case of other marriages the class includes marriages without due notice or without a certificate, marriages after the certificate has expired, marriages in a place other than that specified in the certificate, and marriages in the absence of the registrar, authorised person, etc.[29]

The Act also specifies certain defects evidence of which is not to be given—e.g. lack of parental consent [30]—so that the marriages must be valid.[31]

Unfortunately, the Act is silent as to the consequences of certain irregularities: these include the requirement that the ceremony take place between 8 a.m. and 6 p.m., that it be celebrated with open doors, and that certain prescribed words be used. It seems almost certain that such irregularities will not affect the validity of the marriage. However, it is probably also true that there must be something which can be described as:

> " a ceremony in a form known to and recognised by our law as capable of producing . . . a valid marriage." [32]

Hence a purported " marriage " by African Customary Law in a private house, or an Islamic ceremony outside a registered building, would be wholly ineffective.[33] But this has never been decided, and the law is unclear.

The case for reform

One major difficulty of the marriage laws is their complexity and obscurity. The " proliferation of procedures " outlined above means that " the law is not understood by members of the public or even by all those who have to administer it." [34] Apart from this, the law does not in other respects achieve the objects desirable in a good marriage code [35]:

(i) Certainty

A major objection is that it is not entirely clear what effect certain procedural irregularities will have on the validity of the marriage.[36]

---

27 i.e. a public objection at the calling of banns, or lodging a caveat against the issue of a licence, not simply marrying without obtaining consent, infra, p. 51.
28 s. 25.
29 s. 49.
30 s. 48 (1) (b).
31 s. 48, and see also s. 24.
32 R. v. Bham [1966] 1 Q.B. 159, a criminal prosecution against a celebrant for " knowingly and wilfully " celebrating a Muslim marriage contrary to the provisions of s. 75.
33 But it could be argued that both ceremonies would be capable of producing a valid marriage if celebrated in a Registered Building, with use of the prescribed words.
34 P.W.P. 35, para. 5.
35 Supra, p. 31.
36 Supra, p. 45. The existing law provides a procedure for retrospective validation of marriages where there is doubt as to their validity: Provisional Order (Marriages)

The minimal requirements of a valid marriage (both preliminaries and celebration) should be clearly specified.[37]   It is also unsatisfactory that validity depends on subjective tests of the parties' minds. The law:

> " may come close to leaving it to the option of the parties whether their marriage is to be treated as void or valid, for if they allege that they had knowledge of an irregularity it will be virtually impossible to disprove it, and if they allege that they had not, it will normally be extremely difficult to prove the contrary. As a result the dishonest may be more favoured than the scrupulous. But it is not only the deliberately dishonest who may benefit undeservedly for most people have no difficulty in sincerely convincing themselves that what they would like to have occurred is what in fact occurred, so that the nature of their subsequent testimony about their state of knowledge is likely to vary according to whether they wish to be relieved of the marriage or to remain married." [38]

Obviously flagrant disregard of the marriage laws should be punished, but the sanction should not normally be to invalidate the marriage, unless the defect is quite fundamental.

A more academic problem is that it is not clear in English law at what moment of time the marriage is complete. This may be important in cases of succession disputes. Probably the crucial moment is the formal exchange of consent. In the Australian case of *Quick* v. *Quick* [39] the parties had exchanged the marriage promises but as the man was putting the ring on the woman's finger (and thus before the priest had joined their hands or pronounced them man and wife) she pulled it off, hurled it to the ground, and with the words " I will not marry you " ran out. The court held that they were validly married.

(ii) *Proof and public records*

Although there are defects in the system of marriage registration [40] these are mostly matters of detail, involving at worst delay.[41] Whether the system of demographic registration could be improved to prevent those who lack capacity to contract a marriage (*e.g.* because they are already married) is dealt with below.[42]

(iii) *Avoidance of fraud—consents*

The present system is seriously defective in this respect. The law depends almost entirely on securing publicity for an intended marriage, but the provisions are largely nugatory. The calling of banns may have been effective in rural English parishes a hundred or more years ago,[43] but is no longer so.

Act 1905 as amended. If there is doubt as to the validity of a particular marriage and both parties are still alive it may be resolved by going through a second ceremony.
37 See Law Commission No. 53, Annex, paras. 121–133 for a valuable analysis.
38 *Ibid.*, para. 121.
39 [1953] V.R. 224.
40 Law Commission No. 53, Annex, Part 4.
41 Marriage certificates are prima facie proof of the existence of a marriage: s. 65 (3).
42 p. 48.
43 Although a uniform civil code was proposed in 1836, and only removed to avoid opposition: Law Commission No. 53, Annex, para. 17.

The civil notice requirements are no more satisfactory. The only people who scrutinise marriage notices [44] are press men, seeking news of the impending marriage of some figure of notoriety, and others with a commercial interest in marriage ceremonies. It is easy to avoid publicity by marrying on certificate with licence in a Registrar's Office.

Publicity will not, in modern conditions, ensure that those with legitimate interests in opposing the marriage (*i.e.* (a) the parent or guardian of a child under eighteen who seeks to marry without consent; (b) the wife of a man who is proposing to go through a bigamous marriage ceremony) are discovered. It would seem better to introduce a uniform system under which all persons intending to marry have to give notice in a prescribed form,[45] which would include (a) the production of birth certificates (to ensure that each is over eighteen) (b) evidence of identity and (c) evidence of the termination of a former marriage.[46] If either party is thus shown to be under eighteen, a more searching procedure for checking that parental consent had been given would be introduced. Generally a more *inquisitorial* approach is needed: if the requirement of parental consent is retained,[47] for instance, the law should require service by registered post on those entitled to consent of an official notification of the intended marriage. If a heavier responsibility is placed on Registrars to carry out inquiries, it is clear that reasonable time must be allowed. Although there may be a case for allowing marriage at short notice in special circumstances, the retention of the present licence system (where the ability to pay a small sum of money is the only test) seems difficult to defend.[48] If the present system of dependence on the lodging of objections is retained, it is clearly desirable that provision be made for a central register of objections.[49]

The attempted bigamous marriage causes more intractable problems. One proposal is that the birth certificate of every person married in the United Kingdom be endorsed with a note of any marriage. If that marriage were dissolved another note would be entered on the certificate. Clearly such a system would be expensive, and not wholly effective for many years. Even then the certificate would not show marriages abroad, and people who had not been born in this country would be outside the scheme. What is really needed is a National Register of

---

[44] An unfortunate side effect of the present system arises because the notice has only to be signed by one party. It is by no means unknown for an emotionally disturbed woman to give notice of intended marriage to a public figure with consequent publicity and embarrassment.

[45] *cf.* Kilbrandon Report, paras. 61–64; Law Commission No. 53, Annex, paras. 15–63. The difficult problems of (a) the marriage of " foreigners "—a particularly pressing one in Scotland: Kilbrandon Report, paras. 73–102, and (b) whether a foreign divorce has effectively terminated a marriage, are outside the scope of this book.

[46] *cf.* Law Commission No. 53, Annex, paras. 39–41.

[47] See *infra*, p. 51.

[48] Its abolition has been supported by the Law Commission, who recommend a single formal preliminary to marriage (the Superintendent Registrar's licence) with two very limited exceptions: (1) The Registrar General's Licence (*supra*, p. 37) and (2) The Archbishop's Special Licence: Law Commission No. 53, paras. 11–12.

[49] Law Commission No. 53, Annex, para. 52.

Civil Status, although this idea is " anathema to many." [50] Anything less is an unsatisfactory compromise.[51]

Further possibilities of error or deceit by one party or the other arise because of the laxity of form in the actual solemnisation. Marriage in a registered building [52] by a non-Christian ceremony may give a misleading impression of the effects of the ceremony: the parties may think that Muslim law governs a marriage contracted in a mosque in England. Even if the ceremony takes place in a Register Office there are few effective precautions to ensure that both parties understand that it is a marriage ceremony (as distinct from a betrothal [53]) and that the marriage so created is monogamous.

It would only require minor changes in the law to remedy these problems. But the multiplicity of marriage systems is bound to cause confusion, and the question arises whether the law should not (as in many foreign countries) stipulate a civil ceremony as the only legally effective way of contracting marriage. The parties could then go through any religious ceremony they pleased. The Joint Working Party of the Law Commission and the Registrar-General thought this to be the " simplest and most effective " way of reforming the law, but that it would arouse strong opposition from the churches and general public.[54] Hence, the Commission was content to make suggestions for uniform *preliminaries*, whilst retaining (with added safeguards) the diversity of methods of solemnisation.[55]

Even if the Register Office marriage remains simply one of several alternatives the ceremony could be more solemn, and less bureaucratic, while the material environment of the often rather depressing offices should be improved.[56]

---

[50] P.W.P. 35, para. 115.

[51] See Kilbrandon Report, para. 128, and the cogent criticism in Law Commission No. 53, Annex, paras. 116–117.

[52] See *supra*, p. 41, and generally Law Commission No. 53, Annex, paras. 96–100.

[53] As in *Parojcic* v. *Parojcic* [1959] 1 All E.R. 1 (marriage of Yugoslavs in Oxford Register Office). There are two difficulties: (i) There is a statutory requirement (ss. 44 (3); 45) that the operative words be spoken in English (or Welsh " in any place where the Welsh Language is commonly used ": s. 52), but no *statutory* requirement that this should be intelligible to the parties. " What advantage is to be gained from this parrot-like repetition of what must to the person making them be meaningless noises it is difficult to imagine . . . ," *per* Davies J., *Parojcic* v. *Parojcic* (*supra*). In practice the Registrar General has for some years required superintendent registrars to make sure that where one party is a foreigner who does not fully understand English the prescribed words are translated into a language which he does understand, and to read to the parties a statement which makes it clear that the marriage is monogamous. (P.W.P. 35, para. 94, n. 4); (ii) even if they do understand the words, they may not understand their effect. There is no requirement that the celebrant pronounce the parties to be man and wife: see Law Commission No. 53, Annex, para. 98.

[54] P.W.P. 35, para. 70, *cf.* Law Commission No. 53, Annex, para. 72. See also Kilbrandon Report, para. 108.

[55] The Law Commission was divided on how exigent the rules relating to solemnisation should be: Law Commission No. 53, paras. 21–22.

[56] See the criticisms made in the debate on the Marriage (Registrar General's Licence) Act: Hansard (H.C.) Vol. 795, col. 1602.

(iv) *Preventing unsatisfactory marriages*

Two main proposals have been made:

(a) Compulsory betrothal. A " cooling-off period of compulsory betrothal " [57] is sometimes suggested, particularly in the case of marriages between persons under the age of majority.[58] But the objections are considerable. First, there is no evidence that *precipitancy* is the main cause of such failures. In the racy language of the Latey Commission [59]

> " We should guess that as many marriages fail through too limited experience of people generally as through too limited experience of the particular intended. It is a case of ' What can she know of Henry, who only Henry knows? ' "

Secondly, a formal betrothal might

> " amount to a more definite commitment, harder for either party to break out of, than the personal engagement they might otherwise have. We fear, too, that an arrangement started on the basis of ' Let's register our engagement *in case* we want to get married ' could all too easily harden into ' We've registered our engagement so I suppose we're going to get married. . . .' " [60]

It is sometimes claimed that the waiting period for Church marriages under the existing law serves a purpose similar to that of a compulsory betrothal in that it enables the priest or minister to give the parties advice before the marriage is solemnised.[61]

(b) Medical examination. In some countries, the parties have to undergo medical testing as a preliminary to marriage. If this is done, the question arises whether an unfavourable result will (a) make the marriage illegal; (b) have to be communicated to the other party; or (c) simply be given to the party tested, leaving it to his conscience whether to go ahead or not.[62] The Kilbrandon Report considered that it would be impracticable to make such tests *compulsory*, but supported an extension of voluntary medical counselling.[63]

II. *CONSENTS OF THIRD PARTIES*

Under the Royal Marriage Act 1772 the consent of the Sovereign in Council may be required to the marriage of descendants of George II. A marriage contracted in defiance of the Act is void.[64]

---

[57] Latey Report, para. 178.
[58] Where the risk of divorce is statistically greatest: see Kilbrandon Report, Appendix 3, and (for a graphic representation) Figure 1, p. 136, Latey Report.
[59] Para. 182.   [60] Para. 183.
[61] On the case for provision of counselling and advice before marriage, see the recommendations of the Scottish Marriage Guidance Council: Kilbrandon Report, Appendix 4.
[62] Paras. 42–44.
[63] The Scottish Marriage Guidance Council (*op. cit.* n. 61 *supra*) thought the provision of such facilities would not only detect mental illness, venereal disease and other barriers to marriage, but " make it easier for men and women who intend to marry to raise their own questions or fears about sex."
[64] It may be that, as a result of the exemption from the Act of the issue of princesses who have married into foreign families, there are few if any members of the Royal Family to whom the Act applies: see Farran (1951) 14 M.L.R. 53. But in practice consent is still obtained.

If either party to a marriage is under eighteen (and not a widow or widower[65]) "parental" consent is required.[66] But if a marriage is solemnised without such consent it will be valid.[67] Hence this requirement is usually classified as part of the formalities for marriage, and not a basic question of capacity.

A. *Whose Consent is Required?*

The basic policy of the law is that the consent of both parents is required if both are alive; if they are not, consent is required from the survivor and any guardian.[68]

The detailed statutory provisions are, however, "complicated and incomplete."[69] The rules are[70]:

1. Where the Infant is Legitimate

Circumstances	*Person or Persons whose consent is required*
Where both parents are living	
(a) if parents are living together;	Both parents.
(b) if parents are divorced or separated by order of any court or by agreement;	The parent to whom the custody of the infant is committed by order of the court or by the agreement, or, if the custody of the infant is so committed to one parent during part of the year and to the other parent during the rest of the year, both parents.
(c) if one parent has been deserted by the other;	The parent who has been deserted.
(d) if both parents have been deprived of custody of infant by order of any court.	The person to whose custody the infant is committed by order of the court.
Where one parent is dead	
(a) if there is no other guardian;	The surviving parent.
(b) if a guardian has been appointed by the deceased parent.	The surviving parent and the guardian if acting jointly, or surviving parent or the guardian if the parent or guardian is the sole guardian of the infant.
Where both parents are dead	The guardians or guardian appointed by the deceased parents or by the court under section 3 or 5 of the Guardianship of Minors Act 1971.

[65] Consent is required if the first marriage has been ended by divorce.
[66] See Marriage Act 1949, s. 3; Family Law Reform Act 1969, s. 2. Consent is only a statutory pre-requisite to a marriage after civil preliminaries or by common licence; if it is after banns, consent is not required, but the parent or other third party may object: s. 3 (3) *supra*, p. 38.
[67] *Supra*, p. 46.
[68] Law Commission No. 53, Annex, para. 54.
[69] *Ibid*. para. 47.
[70] Marriage Act 1949, s. 3 (1), 2nd Sched.

2. Where the Infant is Illegitimate

Circumstances	Person whose consent is required
1. If the mother of the infant is alive.	The mother, or if she has by order of any court been deprived of the custody of the infant, the person to whom the custody of the infant has been committed by order of the court.
2. If the mother of the infant is dead.	The guardian appointed by the mother.

If the infant is a ward of court, the consent of the court must be given as well.[71]

The Act makes no provision for the case where the parents are divorced, but there is no custody order or agreement[72]: presumably both must then consent. It is manifestly unsatisfactory that the question of entitlement to consent may depend on the difficult legal question of whether one parent has deserted the other, and that the consent of the father of an illegitimate child is never (apparently) required.[73]

Consent may be dispensed with in two groups of case:

(a) Where consent of a prescribed person " cannot be obtained by reason of absence or inaccessibility or by reason of his being under any disability." In such circumstances either the consent may be dispensed with by the superintendent registrar, or the court may consent.[74]

(b) If a person whose consent is required refuses to give it, application can be made to the court.[75]

The High Court and County Court have jurisdiction to give consent in such cases, but the vast majority of applications are made to Magistrates' Courts. Since cases are not reported it is impossible to say what principles[76] are applied. Cases on the analogous Australian legislation[77] lay down that refusal is unreasonable if based on grounds personal to the parent (e.g. that he needs the services of the child), because the applicant did not seek consent in a normal and proper manner, if the facts upon which he relies as a ground for refusing consent are not true, or if they could not reasonably support the refusal. But the test is whether the parent has been unreasonable, not whether the court agrees with his refusal.[78] It seems probable that English magistrates simply do what they think is in the best interests of the

---

[71] s. 3 (6).
[72] If the child was 16 at the time of his parents' divorce there is not likely to be either: see *Hall* v. *Hall* (1946) 175 L.T. 355, *infra*, Chap. 8.
[73] But the Law Commission decided that any change in this rule would cause embarrassment and further complication: Law Commission No. 53, Annex, para. 55.
[74] s. 3 (1) proviso (*a*).
[75] s. 3 (1) proviso (*b*).
[76] There are no published statistics for the exercise of this jurisdiction since the age of majority was reduced from 21 to 18. In the years before that change there were some 600 applications a year, of which something over half were granted: see Latey Report, para. 570.
[77] Finlay and Bissett-Johnson, pp. 58–60; Hambly and Turner, pp. 40–56.
[78] See *Re an Infant* (1963) 6 F.L.R. 12; *Re V.* (1964) 6 F.L.R. 266.

parties. It is no doubt desirable that issues of this kind should be solved without too much formality, but a great deal must depend on the idiosyncrasies of the magistrates involved.

B. *Justification for the Rules*

The case for requiring parental consent has been examined in recent years by the Latey Committee, the Kilbrandon Committee, and the Law Commission.[79] As a result of the Latey Committee's majority recommendation, consent is no longer required when both parties are eighteen.[80]

There has been a difference of opinion as to whether the requirement of parental consent should not be scrapped altogether. The arguments in favour of this course have been summarised as follows[81]:

" (a) The requirement is easily evaded and short of making marriages void in the absence of consents no steps can be taken which will be wholly effective in preventing evasion.

(b) Consents are not required in Scotland and there is no pressure for their introduction there.[82]

(c) There is no available evidence to show that parents are better judges of the suitability of a match than the child who proposes to marry.

(d) It may well be that parental opposition (armed with a legal sanction) merely strengthens the child's determination.

(e) It is notorious that if the girl becomes pregnant parental opposition is likely to be withdrawn (though arguably this should be regarded as a further reason for objecting). Hence, the requirement may encourage an unwanted or premature pregnancy which places an additional strain on the marriage.

(f) Where children are living with and dependent on their parents, it may be reasonable to defer to the parents' judgment; that, however, would generally happen in practice (*cf.* Scotland) whether or not the law required it; and persuasion, without the teeth of legal sanctions, may well be more effective than threats. Today, however, many children are self-supporting and some are living on their own by the age of 16 or 17. In such circumstances to allow the absent parents to retain a veto on marriage is unjustified."

The Latey Committee, however, had unanimously recommended that the requirement be retained where either party was under eighteen (although a majority favoured abolition of the requirement for eighteen year olds). They thought that there was a valid distinction between sixteen and seventeen year olds and the eighteen to twenty-one age group. Eighteen to twenty-one year olds were more mature, while the younger group might wish to marry simply as part of a rebellion against parental

---

79 P.W.P. 35, paras. 35–36.
80 Family Law Reform Act 1969, s. 2.
81 P.W.P. 35, para. 35.
82 The Kilbrandon Report rejects proposals that parental consent should be required under Scots law, largely because there was no evidence that public opinion was in favour of this change: see paras. 22–23.

authority. Young people of sixteen and seventeen were factually more dependent on parents than the over eighteens; hence the sanction of the law was "much less a piece of irrelevant outside ammunition in the parents' locker and much more a genuine part of a situation that actually exists." [83] What of the argument that a couple who cannot get parental consent may "start a baby" to force their parents' hands? The Committee thought that in the case of sixteen and seventeen year olds "there were signs that parents are less likely to be bulldozed into giving permission for this reason than they used to be" [84] and that sixteen year olds who know that they can marry at eighteen without consent will be readier to wait for two years. Finally, the Committee was impressed by the fact that "very few people viewed with any enthusiasm the marriage of young people—especially boys—under eighteen; the young themselves (once safely past eighteen) thought of the idea with a shudder. . . ." [85] (The fact that a specially commissioned survey found that the majority (60 per cent.) of young people favoured the retention of twenty-one as the age for free marriage did not deter the Committee from recommending a reduction to eighteen.) Finally, the Committee thought that since comparatively few marriages do take place under eighteen "it must be assumed that parents saying 'No' is at least one factor in the situation." [86] It is difficult to support the Committee's assumptions. In effect they are based simply on a feeling that the young are mature at eighteen, but not at sixteen or seventeen. This may well be true, but it is insufficient to justify a *legal* bar. As the Committee said [87] in recommending the reduction of the age from twenty-one to eighteen:

"... this is not because we think that parents should never discourage their children's marriages but because this is not the way to do it; not because we think well of marriages made in defiance of parents but because we think that the law now contributes to the defiance; not because the family is too weak to use this weapon but because it is strong enough to do without it. It is because good parents know that the way to help their sons and daughters of any age is to hold tight with loose hands that we recommend removing the knuckle-duster of the law."

In short the effective factor is the state of the parent-child relationship, not the legal prohibition. This is as true where the child is sixteen as where he is eighteen; in the words of the Committee again: "law is useless as a strengthener of family ties, and indeed by the friction it causes between the generations may well help to wear them through." [88]

[83] Para. 161.
[84] Para. 162.
[85] Para. 159.
[86] Para. 159.
[87] Para. 165.
[88] Para. 106.

It is submitted that the case for retaining the requirement of parental consent is weak. In practice it is unlikely to be removed: the law has so recently been reformed, and there would be little pressure for this further change.[89]

[89] See Law Commission No. 53, para. 48. The Law Commission considered that steps should be taken to make it more difficult for the consent requirement to be evaded: *ibid.* paras. 49–50.

CHAPTER 4

NULLITY OF MARRIAGE

IF a marriage is, in its inception, affected by lack of capacity, or grave formal irregularity, it may be avoided. A decree of nullity is the normal way of doing this.

The position is complicated because of the existence for historical reasons of two categories of defective marriage—the void and voidable.[1] The main differences[2] between the two categories can be summarised as follows:

Void	*Voidable*
No valid marriage ever existed.	The marriage is valid unless annulled.
Any interested party[3] may take proceedings.	Only the parties can take proceedings.
The question can be raised at *any* time, even after the death of both parties.	It can only be litigated while both parties are alive.
A decree is not necessary; the marriage does not exist and a court decree merely records the fact.	Unless a decree is obtained the marriage remains in force.

It should, however, be noted at the outset that many of the incidents of a valid marriage have been attached even to a void " marriage," *provided* that a *decree* of nullity is obtained. Although it is never necessary to obtain a decree annulling a void marriage, it may be very much in the " wife's " interests to do so in order to claim financial provision.

The law of nullity is now codified in the Matrimonial Causes Act 1973,[4] and it is convenient to consider the substance of the modern law as laid down in that Act under three heads: (i) Grounds on which a petition may be presented; (ii) Bars to the making of a decree; (iii) Effects of a decree. It should however be noted that the Act's provisions (generally) only apply to marriages taking place after July 31, 1971.[5] References to the old law are only made for comparison. For full

---

1 " A very unnatural distinction," *Ray* v. *Sherwood* (1836) 1 Curt. 173, 188; *supra*, p. 5.
2 See also the distinction suggested by Lord Guest, in *Ross Smith* v. *Ross Smith* [1963] A.C. 280: " In a void marriage the decision depends upon the ascertainment of a state of facts instantly verifiable at the date of the marriage. . . . Where a marriage is voidable the decision depends on supervening circumstances, such as . . . impotence which may be *quoad hanc* and therefore not ascertainable until after the parties have cohabited."
3 As to what constitutes a sufficient interest, see Jackson, *Formation etc.*, pp. 100–102.
4 Which consolidates the codifying Nullity of Marriage Act 1971, which was based on the Law Commission's Report on Nullity of Marriage, Law Commission No. 33.
5 M.C.A. 1973, ss. 11 and 12. This was the date when the Nullity of Marriage Act 1971 came into force.

accounts of the old law reference should be made to the standard textbooks.[6]

I. GROUNDS

A. *Void Marriages*

It is provided [7] that a marriage celebrated after July 31, 1971, shall be void on the following grounds, only, that is to say:

> (*a*) that it is not a valid marriage under the provisions of the Marriages Act 1949 to 1970 (that is to say where:
>> (i) the parties are within the prohibited degrees of relationship;
>> (ii) either party is under the age of sixteen; or
>> (iii) the parties have intermarried in disregard of certain requirements as to the formation of marriage);
>
> (*b*) that at the time of the marriage either party was already lawfully married;
>
> (*c*) that the parties are not respectively male and female.

These are cases in which society has " an interest in seeing that the legal estate of marriage does not come into existence." [8] The details have been discussed in the preceding chapters, to which reference should be made.

The Act makes it clear that there are no other grounds on which a marriage is void (*i.e.* in respect of which a *decree of nullity* can be obtained). But there may be other cases in which the court will make a *declaration as to matrimonial status* (*i.e.* that A is or is not married, rather than that " a marriage " between A and B is void) is unaffected.[9]

B. *Voidable Marriages*

There are six grounds [10] on which a marriage may be avoided:

(a) Non-Consummation owing to incapacity [11]

This is the classical " canonical disability," the details of which have been discussed. It is possible for either party to petition—*i.e.* an im-

---

[6] Rayden, Chap. 6; Jackson, *Formation etc.*, and (for less exhaustive treatments) Bromley, *Family Law* (4th ed.) Chap. 3; *Tolstoy on Divorce* (7th ed.) Chap. 3.

[7] M.C.A. 1973, s. 11 (*a*)–(*c*). The Matrimonial Proceedings (Polygamous Marriages) Act 1972 adds an additional ground (now s. 11 (*d*), M.C.A. 1973) " in the case of a polygamous marriage entered into outside England and Wales, that either party was at the time of the marriage domiciled in England and Wales." " Polygamous marriage " includes a potentially polygamous union. Consideration of the scope of this provision is outside the scope of this work: for details see (1972) 116 S.J. 654 (Cretney), and *Radwan* v. *Radwan* (*No.* 2) [1973] Fam. 35.

[8] *Per* A. W. Lyons M.P. introducing the Bill into the Commons. Hansard (H.C.) Vol. 810, col. 1165, January 29, 1971.

[9] The use most likely to be made of it is in cases where the recognition of a foreign decree of divorce or nullity is in issue. It should also be noted that sometimes a foreign law is applied by the English courts to determine the validity of the marriage. This complex subject is outside the scope of this book, but the jurisdiction is expressly preserved (s. 14, M.C.A. 1973). As to the possibility that a declaration might be used as an alternative to a decree of nullity, see *infra*, p. 67.

[10] And no more.

[11] s. 12 (*a*); note that this does not in terms stipulate that the incapacity *exist* at the date of the marriage, *cf.* p. 27, *supra*.

potent spouse may petition on the grounds of his own impotence, unless he is debarred from so doing.[12]

(b) Non-Consummation owing to wilful refusal [13]

For a decree to be granted " a settled and definite decision come to without just excuse " by the respondent must be found.[14] This is a question of fact involving an examination of the whole history of the marriage.

If the parties have agreed that a civil marriage ceremony shall be followed by a religious ceremony, it is a " just excuse " for refusing to consummate the marriage that such a ceremony has not taken place. The courts have gone even further, and held that one party's refusal to go through the religious ceremony is a failure to implement it, and itself amounts to wilful refusal to consummate the marriage.[15] In *Kaur* v. *Singh*,[16] for instance a marriage was arranged between two Sikhs. A civil ceremony took place, but (as the parties well knew) in order fully to marry by Sikh religion and practice, a religious ceremony (which it was the husband's role to arrange) was necessary. He refused to do so, and it was held that the wife was entitled to a decree on the grounds of his wilful refusal to consummate. The result would apparently be the same if he had tried to have intercourse, but the wife refused.[17]

It has been held that refusal to have intercourse unless contraceptives are used is not a refusal to consummate the marriage.[18]

(c) Lack of valid consent

The Canon Law doctrine was that *consent* was basic to the formation of marriage; if there were no true consent (whether because of insanity, duress, or for some other reason) the " marriage " was void.[19] Such " marriages " could, however be ratified [20] : if the vitiating factor were removed, and the parties continued to live together voluntarily as man and wife, the existence of the marriage could not be put in issue.

The Nullity of Marriage Act 1971 implemented the recommendation of the Law Commission [21] that lack of consent should be a ground on which a marriage is *voidable*.[22] The Commission's reasons were:

---

[12] Under s. 13 (1) (a) of the Act. See *infra*, p. 63.   [13] s. 12 (b).

[14] *Horton* v. *Horton* [1947] 2 All E.R. 871.

[15] *Jodla* v. *Jodla* [1960] 1 All E.R. 625; *Kaur* v. *Singh* [1972] 1 All E.R. 292.

[16] *Supra.*

[17] *Jodla* v. *Jodla* (*supra*).

[18] *Baxter* v. *Baxter* [1948] A.C. 274. On historical grounds, the decision is open to criticism: see 11 M.L.R. 176 (Gower) and *G.* v. *G.* [1952] V.L.R. 402. As to insistence on the practice of *coitus interruptus* see *Cackett* v. *Cackett* [1950] P. 253; *White* v. *White* [1948] P. 330, *cf. Grimes* v. *Grimes* [1948] P. 323.

[19] *Supra*, p. 22. There is some judicial support for the view that marriages effected by force, fear, fraud or drunkenness were voidable only, but this view is convincingly refuted by Tolstoy, 27 M.L.R. 385, although it is arguable that fraud can be distinguished from the other cases: see Jackson, *Formation etc.*, p. 285 et seq.

[20] Jackson, *Formation etc.*, p. 357 et seq.

[21] Law Commission No. 33, p. 4 et seq.

[22] See now M.C.A. 1973, s. 12 (c).

" Whereas a bigamous marriage or one within the prohibited degrees is, both in theory and in practice, void without the necessity of a decree of nullity and can never be ratified, a marriage alleged to be void on the ground of lack of consent—whether due to duress, mistake or insanity—cannot in practice be treated as a void marriage without the court first investigating the circumstances and making a decree, so that the transfer of such a marriage from the void into the voidable category of marriages would not create hardship to the parties. The case for such transfer is strengthened by the doctrine of ratification which enables a party to decide for himself whether he wishes the marriage to take effect; why, if the parties wish their marriage to be valid, should they run the risk of having the marriage impeached by third parties? " [23]

To some extent, the doctrine of ratification [24] has been given statutory force, since no decree can be granted on this ground unless proceedings are started within three years of the marriage.[25]

Originally, the Commission had thought that if the reason for the lack of consent were *insanity* the " marriage " should remain *void*, because [26]

" first, . . . a marriage, where one of the parties is in this mental state and does not understand what he is doing, is meaningless and, secondly, . . . the insane party is, in general, unable to consult a solicitor or take intelligent advice as to what action he should pursue with regard to the marriage, *i.e.* he cannot make a rational decision whether to accept the marriage or to take steps to have it set aside."

This was finally rejected because :

(a) Since 1937, there had been a statutory ground under which the existence of a mental disorder in the respondent at the time of the marriage had been a ground on which the marriage could be annulled as voidable,[27] and " the distinction between a mental disorder which makes a marriage voidable and unsoundness of mind which makes a marriage void is a source of confusion, and artificial.[28]

(b) " It also seems artificial that the marriage of a person subject to recurrent attacks of insanity should be absolutely void if the celebration of the marriage coincides with a period of aggravation of the illness depriving a person of the requisite degree of understanding, but is valid, though voidable, if such aggravation takes place the day before or the day after the celebration."

This argument is difficult to reconcile with the basic doctrine of nullity that there is a fundamental difference between cases where a vitiating factor exists at the moment of the ceremony, and those where a super-vening factor causes the marriage to break down (the former being retained as grounds for annulment, the latter being only a basis for divorce). What is really artificial is the whole concept that a " voidable "

---

23 Law Commision No. 33, para. 12.
24 As to the analogous bar of *approbation* see *infra*, p. 63. For a full comparative consideration of these doctrines, see (1963) 26 M.L.R. 249 (D. Lasok).
25 s. 13 (2), M.C.A. 1973. See *infra*, p. 61.   26 P.W.P. No. 20, para. 46.
27 s. 9, Matrimonial Causes Act 1965; see now *infra*, p. 60.
28 Law Commission No. 33, para. 14 (*a*).

marriage has never come into existence, rather than that an unsatisfactory union is being dissolved.[29]

(c) Since a court hearing will, in practice, be necessary before the plea could be relied on, the marriage is " for practical purposes, valid unless successfully challenged." [30]

(d) " There are marriages of insane persons which benefit such persons. If, for instance, a woman marries a man of unsound mind and is willing to look after him and her care and presence are beneficial to the man, we can find no good reason why the marriage should be null and void or why third parties should be allowed to interfere with it by having it declared to be a nullity." [31]

It may be objected (i) that this argument is inconsistent with the Commission's insistence that a " marriage " where one of the parties (perhaps unknown to either) happens to be a few days below the age of sixteen must, as a matter of policy, be void notwithstanding the parties' wish to keep it in existence [32]; (ii) the argument that third parties should not be able to interfere (perhaps after the husband's death) if the woman's care and presence are " beneficial to the man " sounds less attractive if (say) the wife's motive in marrying him is mercenary. A woman who married a person of unsound mind would no longer be treated unfairly even if the marriage were void, since the " widow " may ask the court for reasonable provision out of the deceased's estate if she entered into the marriage *bona fide*.[33] This might be a more satisfactory solution.

(e) " Under existing law a third party can, with leave of the court, institute nullity (and divorce) proceedings on behalf of the insane person as his next friend [34]; there is, therefore, a safeguard in the event of its being in the interest of the insane person to obtain a decree of nullity, the insane person being himself unable to take this step because of his mental condition."

(d) Grounds originating in the Matrimonial Causes Act 1937

The remaining three grounds on which a marriage may be voidable originate in the Matrimonial Causes Act 1937:

> (i) *that at the time of the marriage the respondent was suffering from venereal disease in a communicable form;*
> (ii) *that at the time of the marriage the respondent was pregnant by some person other than the petitioner* [35]*; and*
> (iii) *that at the time of the marriage either party, though capable of giving a valid consent, was suffering (whether con-*

29 See *infra*, p. 69.
30 Law Commission No. 33, para. 14 (*c*).
31 *Ibid.* para. 14 (*d*).
32 *Supra*, p. 16. Consent is at least as fundamental to the concept of marriage as age.
33 Law Reform (Miscellaneous Provisions) Act 1970, s. 6, *infra*, p. 67.
34 Law Commission No. 33, p. 5, n. 12.
35 s. 12 (*e*) and (*f*) M.C.A. 1973. These are identical to the provisions in earlier legislation: the Law Commission rejected a proposal that a wife should be able to have the marriage annulled if some other woman was at the time of the marriage pregnant by the husband: see Law Commission No. 33, para. 75.

tinuously or intermittently) from mental disorder within the meaning of the Mental Health Act 1959 of such a kind or to such an extent as to be unfitted for marriage.[36]

It should be noted that this last subsection is intended to cover the case where, although the respondent is capable of giving a valid consent to the marriage, his mental disorder [37] made him incapable of carrying on a normal married life.[38]

These three grounds were introduced because of the lack of matrimonial relief for fraudulent or wilful concealment of material facts.[39] A man who discovered that his wife was carrying another man's child had, at common law [40] no ground of matrimonial relief: deceit was not a ground for annulment, and the pregnancy did not establish that she had committed adultery since the marriage.

II. BARS

The Matrimonial Causes Act 1973 [41] contains an exhaustive [42] codification of the grounds on which a decree may be refused, replacing the complex and ill-defined bars inherited from the ecclesiastical courts. The Act applies only to marriages contracted after July 31, 1971,[43] so that the old bars remain of importance for some time to come. Consideration of them is outside the scope of this book.

There are three bars, two of which originate in the Matrimonial Causes Act 1937, whilst the third (approbation) is based on a bar applied in the ecclesiastical court.

Time

In the case of proceedings on the ground of (a) lack of consent, (b) mental illness, (c) venereal disease, (d) pregnancy *per alium*, it is an absolute bar that proceedings were not instituted within three years of the marriage.[44] The old law has been changed in two respects: (a) the time bar now applies to petitions based on lack of consent [45] as well as the three new grounds introduced in 1937; (b) the period has been extended from one year to three years.

---

[36] s. 12 (*d*). Some minor changes have been made from the earlier legislation: the most significant is that it is no longer a ground for annulment that the respondent was subject to recurrent attacks of epilepsy. See generally Law Commission No. 33, paras. 69–74.

[37] As defined: Mental Health Act 1959, s. 4.

[38] *Bennett* v. *Bennett* [1969] 1 W.L.R. 430, 434.

[39] Morton Commission, para. 267.

[40] *Moss* v. *Moss* [1897] P. 263.   [41] s. 13.

[42] Nullity of Marriage Act 1971, s. 3 (4).

[43] Save (*semble*) that the bar of collusion (which remained as an anomaly) no longer operates in any case: Nullity of Marriage Act 1971, s. 6 (1); Law Commission No. 33 p. 18, paras. 37–38, n. 65.

[44] s. 13 (2).

[45] The reason for introducing this was because a " party to such a marriage should decide as soon as possible whether to avoid it or to accept it as a valid marriage, and three years is more than sufficient in which to make such a decision." For the reasons for not extending the bars to other grounds see Law Commission No. 33, paras. 83–86.

The reasons for this latter change were [46] that the rigid [47] time limit of one year led to hardship if, for example, the petitioner went abroad immediately after the marriage, or did not [48] discover the defect in time.

Knowledge of defect

A petition founded on (a) venereal disease or (b) pregnancy *per alium* will fail unless the petitioner can satisfy the court that, at the date of the marriage, he was ignorant of the facts alleged: the fact that the husband knows that the wife is pregnant is not in itself a bar, he must also know that she was pregnant *by another man*.[49]

Knowledge is no longer a bar to a petition based on the existence of a mental disorder. The Law Commission thought [50]

> "First, it is not just mental disorder which is a ground for relief, but mental disorder 'of such a kind or to such an extent' as to cause the respondent to be 'unfitted for marriage,' so that even if the disorder is known to the petitioner at the time of marriage, its gravity or its future development or its impact on the marriage may not be then apparent to him. Secondly, the petitioner may know that the respondent had previously suffered from mental disorder to a more or less severe degree, but such disorder may be quiescent at the time of marriage and medical prognosis as to its future course may be inconclusive. It would be hard on the petitioner if, contrary to his hopes and expectations, there were a recurrence of the disorder, so that it became clear that the respondent had all along been "unfitted for marriage" and the petitioner then found himself barred from relief, although his only fault may have been an over-optimistic evaluation of the medical advice he had been given."

This is true, but it seems inconsistent with the doctrine that nullity is relief in respect of a defect existing at the date of the marriage; the argument is really that a petitioner should be able to escape from a marriage if things turn out a lot worse than he had expected.

Until the 1971 Act there was a third statutory bar: no marital intercourse must have taken place after the petitioner discovered the existence of the grounds for a decree. This bar was removed since:

(a) the courts had made the test an objective one, and it was thought unjust to deprive a petitioner of relief " merely because, not realising that he has grounds for terminating the marriage, he tries

---

[46] Law Commision 33, paras. 79–80.

[47] ". . . the requirements of the Act are strict and must be strictly observed." *Per* Karminski L.J., *Sullivan* v. *Sullivan* [1970] 1 W.L.R. 1008 and see *Chaplin* v. *Chaplin* [1949] P. 72 (wife fraudulently concealed from husband serving overseas fact of child's parentage; *held*: no jurisdiction to extend time limit).

[48] If only because of a failure, resulting from lack of intelligence or initiative, to obtain advice: *Sullivan* v. *Sullivan* (*supra*), where the husband petitioner was said (*per* Winn L.J. at p. 1010) to be " virtually illiterate and virtually unable to express himself with any clarity, almost wholly lacking in any memory of the relevant matters."

[49] *Stocker* v. *Stocker* [1966] 1 W.L.R. 190.

[50] Law Commission No. 33, para. 78.

to make the best of it and does not immediately break off marital relations." [51]

(b) " the law should encourage reconciliation, a factor strongly stressed in recent legislation providing for matrimonial relief, and if a petitioner discovers the existence of a defect, for example, mental disorder or pregnancy by another, he should not be placed in the position that if he attempts a reconciliation and it fails he thereby loses all right to relief." [52]

The abolition of this bar is consistent with the policy of the law which abolished condonation as a bar to divorce: one of the reasons underlying that bar [53] was that it would be grossly unfair to a wife (who might become pregnant as a result of the intercourse) to allow the husband to " approbate and reprobate." This is no longer seen as such a serious objection. The fact that the petitioner has had intercourse with the respondent with knowledge of his right to have the marriage annulled *may* however form the basis of a defence on the new statutory bar of approbation.

Approbation [54]

Approbation was, in the practice of the ecclesiastical courts, conduct on the part of the petitioner [55] which so plainly implied on his part a recognition of the existence and validity of the marriage as to render it inequitable and contrary to public policy that the validity of the marriage should be questioned by him.[56]

The Nullity of Marriage Act introduced [57] a statutory codification of the law, which was intended to remove the uncertainty and obscurity of the old law, it applies to *all* voidable marriages celebrated after July 31, 1971 [58]:

" The court shall not grant a decree of nullity on the ground that a marriage is voidable if the respondent satisfies the court:

(a) that the petitioner, with knowledge that is was open to him to have the marriage avoided, so conducted himself in relation to the respondent as to lead the respondent reasonably to believe that he would not seek to do so; and
(b) that it would be unjust to the respondent to grant the decree."

The following points should be noted:

(a) the bar is *absolute*. This was because [59]

---

[51] *Ibid.*, para. 81.
[52] *Ibid.*
[53] See *infra*, p. 103.
[54] For full discussions of the pre-1971 law see Lasok: " Approbation of Marriage in English Law and the Doctrine of Validation " 26 M.L.R. 249; Jackson, *Formation etc.*, Chap. 8.
[55] *G.* v. *M.* (1885) 10 App.Cas. 171, 199, *per* Lord Watson.
[56] *Ibid.* at p. 186, *per* Lord Selborne L.C.
[57] s. 3 (1), now s. 13 (1), M.C.A. 1973.
[58] The day on which the Act came into force: s. 7 (5).
[59] Law Commission No. 33, para. 43.

" it is of general advantage to know as soon as possible and with as much certainty as possible whether a marriage is valid or not and undesirable uncertainty may arise if, notwithstanding approbation, the parties are free to challenge the marriage at any time, in the hope that the court will exercise its discretion to declare the marriage invalid. The validity or invalidity of the marriage should not depend on the court's discretion, but should be determined by the relevant facts."

It is submitted that this argument loses much of its validity given (i) that the effect of annulling a marriage no longer differs very much from the effect of dissolving it; and (ii) that a party who wishes to terminate a valid marriage can almost invariably do so.[60]

(b) There is no reference to public policy. Under the old law there was authority for the view that the court might hold that a marriage had been approbated in spite of the absence of injustice to the parties if public policy so required.[61] Now the only relevant factors are (i) the conduct of one party *towards the other* (*i.e.* not towards outsiders) and (ii) the absence of injustice *to the respondent*. The reason for dispensing with the public policy consideration was [62] that the bar

" should be so defined as to encourage parties to do their best to overcome their difficulties. If the bar can be too readily invoked they may be discouraged (or their lawyers may discourage them) because of the risk that they will thereby lose any chance of having the marriage annulled should their efforts fail. . . . If there is a defect rendering the marriage voidable either party should be entitled (subject, in certain cases, to the three-year time-limit) to have it annulled unless his conduct after he knew his position has been such as to lead the other party reasonably to believe that he would not seek to have the marriage annulled and it would be unjust to the other for him to do so. Lawyers cannot advise their clients with any certainty if there is a risk of individual notions of public policy being invoked."

The abolition of this requirement could make a difference in cases where a couple adopt a child in the hope that it will normalise their relationship, whilst making clear to each other that this is not to take away their right to seek annulment. It could no longer be a relevant consideration [63] that the adoption application " involves a representation to the court that the joint adopters are husband and wife." Although this may seem a striking change it is submitted that the Law Commission were clearly right in their proposal: if it is desired to protect the *child* in such cases adequate measures now exist for this purpose.[64]

60 See Chap. 5, *infra.*
61 *Tindall* v. *Tindall* [1953] P. 63, 72; *Slater* v. *Slater* [1953] P. 235, 244.
62 Law Commission No. 33, para. 44.
63 *Cf. W.* v. *W.* [1952] P. 152. This case might be decided in the same way, however, on the basis that the adoption was a representation by the one spouse to the other that he would not petition.
64 s. 41, M.C.A. 1973, requiring the court to declare by order that satisfactory arrangements for any children have been made: *infra,* p. 272.

III. EFFECTS OF A DECREE

If a marriage was void (a) any children of the union were illegitimate, for their parents had never been married; (b) no legal consequences could flow from the relationship which (*ex hypothesi*) did not exist: thus, a man could not logically be required to maintain the woman with whom he had been living in reliance on the void ceremony; for they were not, and never had been, more than man and paramour.

In the case of a voidable marriage the same consequences followed: although the marriage was valid until avoided the decree, if and when made, operated *retrospectively* and declared the marriage " to have been and to be absolutely null and void to all intents and purposes whatsoever." [65] Once the decree was pronounced the marriage became void *ab initio*.

Over the years, the harshness stemming from this principle was mitigated:

Legitimacy of children of voidable marriage

When new grounds on which a marriage could be annulled were introduced in 1937 the legislature provided that any child born of a marriage which was avoided under the provisions of the Act [66] should be a legitimate child of the parties notwithstanding the annulment. There was thus legislative acceptance of the fact that the traditional rule could cause hardship, and the newly accepted principle was applied to all *voidable* marriages in 1949.[67] It was [68] provided:

> Where a decree of nullity is granted in respect of a voidable marriage, any child who would have been the legitimate child of the parties to the marriage if at the date of the decree it had been dissolved instead of being annulled shall be deemed to be their legitimate child.

Legitimacy of children of void marriages

The harsh consequences of declaring a marriage void were mitigated by the canon law doctrine of the putative marriage [69]; this doctrine produced the legal consequences of a valid marriage (such as the legitimacy of offspring) *provided* (a) that the marriage in question was not clandestine, and (b) one of the parties had acted in good faith.[70] English ecclesiastical law began by accepting this doctrine [71] but the

---

[65] *de Reneville* v. *de Reneville* [1948] P. 100, 111.
[66] Save where the ground was wilful refusal to consummate. The reason for this exception was that it appears to have been overlooked that children may be born of an unconsummated union by *fecundatio ab extra*. (*Clarke* v. *Clarke* [1943] 2 All E.R. 540), by artificial insemination (*R. E. L.* v. *E. L.* [1949] P. 211), or as a result of pre-marital intercourse (*Dredge* v. *Dredge* [1947] 1 All E.R. 29, where the child of the " non-existent marriage " was 17 at the date of the suit.)
[67] s. 4 (1), Law Reform (Miscellaneous Provisions) Act 1949.
[68] s. 11, Matrimonial Causes Act 1965; now Sched. I, para. 12, M.C.A. 1973.
[69] See generally E. J. Cohn, 64 L.Q.R. 324, 331.
[70] See Hay, p. 235 and for a full discussion of the difficulties Cohn, *op. cit.*, pp. 331–333.
[71] Jackson, *Formation etc.*, p. 52; Cohn, *op. cit.*, p. 334.

acceptance did not survive the reign of Edward III.[72] Thenceforth the more strictly logical view was taken: if there was no marriage any issue must be bastards.[73] It was not until 1959 that English law finally accepted that the offspring of a void marriage could be " treated as " the legitimate child of his parents if at the time of the act of intercourse resulting in his birth (or at the time of the celebration of the marriage if later) both or either of the parties reasonably believed that the marriage was valid.[74]

Other legal consequences of a " void " marriage

If a " marriage " does not exist, it logically follows that none of the rights and duties of marriage subsist between the parties. But, provided that a *decree* of nullity is obtained, the court now [75] has exactly the same powers to order one party to make financial provision for the other as if a valid marriage had been dissolved. Similarly, a " wife " or " husband " who has obtained such a decree can apply to the court for reasonable provision out of the other's estate after his death.[76] These powers depend on the existence of a *decree*. If a man fails to maintain his " wife," it would have been an answer to her claim for maintenance at Common Law that the " marriage " was void; it is still an answer if she seeks to enforce her right by proceedings under the Matrimonial Proceedings (Magistrates' Courts) Act 1960,[77] or by proceedings in the High Court [78] for wilful neglect to maintain. But *if* she gets a *decree*

[72] *Ibid.* For a discussion of the reasons for this attitude see F. H. Newark, " The Operation of Nullity Decrees," 8 M.L.R. 203, 208, Cohn, *op. cit.*, p. 335 *et seq.*; Jackson, *Formation etc.*, p. 52 *et seq.*

[73] This was however mitigated by (a) rules whereby a child who had, during his father's lifetime been held out as legitimate, could not be bastardised after his death, nor could the legitimacy of a bastard be put in issue after his death if he had entered on land as his father's heir, and remained in unquestioned seisin all his life. See Jackson, *Formation etc.*, pp. 44–50; (b) the post-Reformation distinction of void and merely voidable marriages.

[74] Legitimacy Act 1959, s. 2 (1). This is subject to the conditions in s. 2 (2)–(3) of the Act: see *infra*, pp. 313–315 for a full consideration.

[75] Powers to make financial provision in nullity cases were first introduced by Matrimonial Causes Act 1859, s. 5, which enabled the court to vary ante- or post-nuptial settlements. This in itself was a remarkable power since, if the marriage were avoided, at Common Law the consideration for the settlement wholly failed, and the funds would result to the settlor: *Re Wombwell's Settlement* [1922] 2 Ch. 298. Under this power, the court could direct that the funds should not so result (although *quaere* whether this would apply to funds settled by a third party—*e.g.* the parents of the couple: see also *Clifton* v. *Clifton* [1936] P. 182). The power to award periodical payments was first conferred by Matrimonial Causes Act 1907, s. 1. The powers are now identical with those on divorce or judicial separation: M.C.A. 1973, ss. 23, 24, *infra*, p. 185.

[76] Matrimonial Causes Act 1965, s. 26. This presupposes that a person whose *void* marriage has been annulled is within the definition of " former spouse " in s. 26 (6)—*i.e.* " a person whose marriage with the deceased was annulled. . . ." It can be argued that where the marriage is *void ab initio* there has been no " marriage " which could be annulled. Perhaps this is the basis on which it is stated in Rayden, p. 540, note (b) that the jurisdiction " extends to the former spouse of a voidable marriage, but not a void marriage." The contrary assumption was however made by the Law Commission (Report on Breach of Promise of Marriage, Law Commission No. 26, p. 17, para. 49).

[77] *Ivett* v. *Ivett* (1930) 94 J.P. 237, 143 L.T. 680. That Act gives relief to " a married woman " etc., and a party to a void union is not such.

[78] Because it is based on the common law duty.

of nullity the court will have power to order provision (although, of course, there may be cases in which, in the exercise of its discretion, it will decline to do so).[79]

A further break with principle was made in the Law Reform (Miscellaneous Provisions) Act 1970.[80] This enables a person who has in good faith entered into a void marriage with a person now deceased to apply to the court for reasonable provision out of his estate, exactly as if the applicant were his widow, or had obtained a decree of nullity carrying with it the right to be considered for financial provision. The legal consequences of a marriage which is null and void thus seem to resemble those of a valid marriage, which has been ended by divorce.

It is not possible to avoid these consequences by simply asking the court to make bare declarations as to status,[81] which do not give the court any power to make ancillary orders [82] (whether for financial provision, custody of the children or otherwise). It has been twice held [83] that if the relief sought is a declaration that the marriage is *void ab initio*, the form in which the relief must be given is a decree of nullity, and not a bare declaration under the Rules of the Supreme Court. The bare declaration is appropriate if, for instance, the point which is really in issue is the validity of a foreign decree of divorce, as a result of which (so it has to be decided) H and W are no longer man and wife,[84] or (alternatively) that the decree was ineffective so that they remain man and wife.[85]

It does not follow from this that any woman can involve a man in potential financial liability to her by the simple expedient of petitioning for nullity on the grounds that there is no subsisting marriage between them: she must be able to establish one of the grounds exhaustively set out in the Matrimonial Causes Act 1973.[86] All those grounds refer to " a marriage " [87] and presuppose some kind of ceremony between the parties. It would not be possible for a woman who had lived with a man as his mistress for many years to get a decree of nullity: she could not point to the necessary " existence of an act allegedly creative of a marriage status." [88]

But granted that there must be *something* which purports to be a

---

[79] See *infra*, p. 190; *Corbett* v. *Corbett* (*No. 2*) [1971] P. 110, and the authorities cited in *Rayden*, p. 713, n. (*b*).

[80] *Infra*, p. 177.

[81] R.S.C. Ord. 15, r. 16; *Har-Shefi* v. *Har-Shefi* [1953] P. 161.

[82] This was assumed to be the case in *Kassim* v. *Kassim* [1962] P. 224 and (*sub silentio*) in *Corbett* v. *Corbett* [1971] P. 83; it also seems to follow from the wording of ss. 21, 23, 24, and 42, M.C.A. 1973, which refer either to a " decree " of nullity (ss. 23, 24), a " petition for nullity " (s. 22) or " proceedings for nullity " (s. 42). A petition for a bare declaration would seem to be within none of these definitions.

[83] By the same judge of first instance: *Kassim* v. *Kassim* (*supra*); *Corbett* v. *Corbett* (*supra*). See the Law Commission P.W.P. No. 48, particularly at p. 8 *et seq.*

[84] *Har-Shefi* v. *Har-Shefi* (*supra*); *Garthwaite* v. *Garthwaite* [1964] P. 356.

[85] *Garthwaite* v. *Garthwaite* (*supra*).

[86] *Supra*, p. 57.

[87] M.C.A. 1973, s. 11.

[88] Jackson, *Formation etc.*, p. 86.

marriage, it is uncertain where the dividing line is to be drawn. It is by no means clear whether two immigrants who *bona fide* believed that they could contract a marriage in Islamic form in England without complying with the forms of English law could subsequently be able to obtain a decree of nullity.[89] It has been held [90] that a man who went through a ceremony of marriage with a person who was psychologically a transexual, but sexually a male is entitled to a decree of nullity. In that case there was some doubt as to the respondent's sex.[91] But suppose that two homosexuals, knowing that each is biologically the same sex as the other, go through a ceremony of marriage,[92] is it to be supposed that the court could grant a decree? There is no real authority on the point, but it is suggested that it would not: notwithstanding the rule that a decree of nullity can be obtained if it is shown that the parties are not respectively of the male and female sex, it remains true that " marriage " still, in English Law, means the " union of one man and one woman." [93] If the parties are clearly, demonstrably, and known by each not to be male and female it is difficult to see how a court could hold that there was a marriage, even a void one.

Retrospective effect of decrees of nullity

A decree of nullity pronounces a marriage " to have been and to be absolutely null and void to all interests and purposes whatsoever." [94] Until the Nullity of Marriage Act 1971 the courts gave effect to the retrospective wording of the decree. A striking illustration is seen in *Re Rodwell*,[95] where the question was whether the deceased's daughter was a " dependant " within the meaning of the Inheritance (Family Provision) Act 1938; she would only be such if she had " not been married." The daughter had in fact contracted a marriage, but it had been annulled. Pennycuick J. held that because of the retrospective effect of the decree she qualified. The rule was clearly both " anomalous and inconvenient " [96] and the precise scope of its application was uncertain.[97]

---

[89] See Law Commission No. 53, Annex, para. 120 and *R. v. Bham* [1966] 1 Q.B. 159; see also *Manson* v. *Heaslip* [1949] 1 W.W.R. 717 (British Columbia) where it was held that a private and secret declaration of consent was so totally ineffective, that the court would not make a decree of nullity.

[90] *Corbett* v. *Corbett* [1971] P. 83.

[91] The true sex of the respondent (April Ashley) was in issue at the trial.

[92] One correspondent suggested to the Law Commission that such unions should be legalised: see Law Commission No. 33, para. 32, and see also the speech of Mr. Leo Abse M.P. on the Report Stage of the Nullity of Marriage Bill, Hansard (H.C.) Vol. 814, col. 1827 (April 2, 1971).

[93] *Hyde* v. *Hyde* (1866) L.R. 1 P. & D. 130.

[94] *Per* Pilcher J., *Hutter* v. *Hutter* [1944] P. 95, 101.   [95] [1970] Ch. 726.

[96] *Per* Pennycuick J., *Re Rodwell* at p. 731; see also the trenchant criticism by Tiley in (1969) 32 M.L.R. 210 (on *Re d'Altroy's Will Trusts* [1968] 1 W.L.R. 120), and *Theobald on Wills*, 13th ed., para. 342.

[97] As for instance in the case where H (who has grounds for the annulment of his marriage to W) goes through a form of marriage to B, without obtaining any decree. The marriage with B is clearly void for bigamy, since until a decree the marriage to W remained valid. But suppose W now obtains a decree of nullity. Can it be said that the marriage to B is valid, because (as a result of the decree of nullity) no subsisting marriage existed when it was celebrated? The authorities were confused: *Newbould* v. *Att.-Gen.* [1931] P. 75; *Mason* v. *Mason* [1944] N.I. 134 (retro-

It is now [98] provided that:

A decree of nullity granted after July 31, 1971 in respect of a voidable marriage shall operate to annul the marriage only as respects any time after the decree has been made absolute,[99] and the marriage shall, notwithstanding the decree, be treated as if it had existed up to that time.[1]

IV. CRITICISM AND REFORM

The law of nullity has lost much of its practical importance, because:

   (a) many of the legal consequences of marriage have now been attached to even a void marriage, and

   (b) all marriages can now be dissolved by divorce at the instance of one party. It is no longer necessary for one party to an unhappy marriage either to convict his spouse of a matrimonial offence, or, if he could not, assert that the marriage was a nullity.

The Nullity of Marriage Act 1971 introduced a number of largely technical reforms into the law, but there are two issues, on which the Law Commission recommended no change in the law, which merit further consideration:

Should the Concept of Voidable Marriages be Retained?

There is a school of thought that all the present grounds on which a marriage is voidable should be abolished as grounds of nullity, and included instead among the factual situations from which irretrievable breakdown of marriage can be inferred, and thus a divorce obtained. It is clear that the rigid distinction between divorce for *supervening* cause and nullity for a defect existing at the date of the marriage has come under strain: increasingly the law of nullity does consider developments since the marriage.[2]

The Law Commission summarised the argument in favour of abolishing the concept of the voidable marriage as follows:

   " the two remedies are in substance similar and the difference between them is really only a matter of form [3]; in each case there is a marriage valid until the decree is made and that decree terminates the marriage, but, in the case of nullity, the decree misleadingly declares the marriage to have never existed; that being so, it is

spective effect validates second marriage), but *cf. Wiggins* v. *Wiggins* [1959] 1 W.L.R. 1013 (second marriage remains bigamous), and see *R.* v. *Algar* [1954] 1 Q.B. 279; *Re Eaves* [1940] Ch. 109. For a full discussion, see Jackson, *Formation etc.*, pp. 92–96.

[98] M.C.A. 1973, s. 16.

[99] See p. 108, *infra*.

[1] It is submitted that this equates the effect of a nullity decree with a decree of divorce. Although the marriage is " annulled " it *has* existed: *cf.* Bromley's, *Family Law*, 4th ed., p. 531.

[2] Apart from the obvious case of wilful refusal as a ground (see *infra*, p. 71), consider (i) the Law Commission's arguments in favour of treating lack of consent arising from insanity as a ground on which a marriage should be voidable only (p. 59, *supra*), and (ii) the justification for no longer treating knowledge of the respondent's mental illness as a bar (p. 62, *supra*).

[3] *Turner* v. *Turner* (1888) 13 P.D. 37, 40; *Inverclyde* v. *Inverclyde* [1931] P. 29, 42.

more logical to terminate the marriage by a divorce [4] which records the realities of the situation." [5]

These arguments were rejected by the Law Commission [6] on grounds which, in view of their importance, are set out *verbatim*:

"(a) It is not true to say that the difference between a nullity decree of a voidable marriage and a decree of divorce is a mere matter of form. It may be that the consequences of the two decrees are substantially similar, but the concepts giving rise to the two decrees are quite different: the decree of nullity recognises the existence of an impediment which prevents the marriage from initially becoming effective, while the decree of divorce records that some cause for terminating the marriage has arisen since the marriage. This distinction may be of little weight to the lawyer, but is a matter of essence in the jurisprudence of the Christian Church.

"(b) The Church attaches considerable importance to consent as a prerequisite to marriage. Consent to marriage includes consent to sexual relations and, hence, impotence can be regarded as having the effect of vitiating consent. Likewise, the grounds under section 9 (1) (*b*), (*c*) and (*d*) of the Act of 1965 (mental disorder, epilepsy, pregnancy by another or venereal disease) can be considered to fall under the head of conditional consent and are acceptable to the Church. Except with regard to wilful refusal to consummate, which the Church of England considers should cease to be a ground for nullity and be a ground for divorce, the Church is satisfied with the existing law of nullity. Therefore, so radical a change as is involved in the substitution of a decree of divorce for a decree of nullity in respect of matters which the Church regards as relevant to the formation of marriage and irrelevant to divorce, is likely to be unwelcome to the Church. It is also likely to be resented by people not necessarily belonging to the Church who associate a stigma with divorce and who would therefore prefer to see such matters as impotence and mental disorder, which are illnesses, remain grounds for annulling the marriage rather than causes for dissolving it.

"(c) It may be that many people do not appreciate the distinction between divorce and nullity. They, presumably, would not oppose turning a nullity of a voidable marriage into a divorce. If, however, such a change is likely to cause offence to a substantial minority, then the proposal cannot be recommended unless some worthwhile advantage is to be gained from the change. The only advantage to be gained would be one of the present voidable marriages (*i.e.* one voidable for wilful refusal to consummate) might be thought by some to fit in more " neatly " among divorces than among nullities.

"(d) The assimilation of voidable marriages and dissolvable marriages could not be complete so long as we retained the bar on divorce within three years of marriage. Such a bar would be wholly inappropriate to nullity cases."

---

[4] " It may be that it would be more logical to treat impotence as a ground of divorce, as it is in America, where the jurisdiction is not hampered by the rules of the Canon Law ": *Re Eaves* [1940] Ch. 109, 122.

[5] Law Commission No. 33, para. 23.

[6] *Ibid.*, para. 24.

It is submitted that the only one of these arguments which is of any substance is that in para. (c)—*i.e.* that there is no point in causing offence to a minority unless some clear benefit is to be obtained as a result. The other arguments are wholly unconvincing: firstly, it is not possible for modern secular family law to follow the doctrines of the Church. Those who attach importance to these doctrines can always seek approval from the Church authorities as well as a secular termination, in precisely the same way that Roman Catholics have done for many years.[7] Secondly, the argument from the " three year bar " in divorce cases is totally specious: it would be a simple matter of drafting to provide that if a petition were presented on " nullity " grounds, the bar should not apply. In any case, the continued existence of this bar in relation to divorce should not be taken as sacrosanct.[8] Furthermore, it is submitted that there is a compensating advantage to be gained as the price of offending those members of the Church of England who would be distressed at the prospect of obtaining a decree of divorce rather than nullity. Nullity petitions involve great humiliation and distress to those who appear in them by reason of the nature of the allegations which are made, and the methods by which evidence is obtained.[9] If decrees of divorce could be obtained without parading these essentially personal problems the sum total of misery would be alleviated. It may be said that this would not be the case, given that it would still be necessary to prove *e.g.* wilful refusal as the fact on the basis of which the petition is brought. It is suggested (a) that most of the grounds could in any case be subsumed under s. 1 (2) (*b*) Matrimonial Causes Act 1973 [10] (*i.e.* unreasonable behaviour); (b) if it were clear to both parties that the union would be terminated under some head or other of the Act, they might well prefer an agreed divorce (*e.g.* based on two years' separation) rather than exposing their personal problems in a court of law.

Should Wilful Refusal Remain as a Ground for Nullity, rather than Divorce?

Wilful refusal was not a ground for annulment, under the practice of the ecclesiastical courts inherited by the Divorce Court in 1857,[11] although refusal (or failure) to consummate might have been used as *evidence* of incapacity.[12] It became a ground for annulment in 1937.[13] This offends against the principle that nullity is " granted for some defect or incapacity existing at the date of the marriage. Wilful refusal is something

---

[7] See F. J. Sheed, *Nullity of Marriage.*
[8] See *infra*, p. 108.
[9] See *supra*, p. 28 and for a detailed account of the procedure, Jackson, *Formation etc.*, p. 319 *et seq.*
[10] *Infra*, p. 115.
[11] s. 6, Matrimonial Causes Act 1857.
[12] *Supra*, p. 27. It will be recalled that " incapacity " extends to psychological as well as physiological incapacity, and that it may be simply *quoad hunc* or *quoad hanc.*
[13] See p. 72.

that happens after the marriage. . . ." [14] Strong pressure has been exercised over the years by the Church of England to remove wilful refusal from the grounds of nullity: if it were not for this exception, the law of nullity applied in the secular courts could be recognised by the Church as being not inconsistent with its own doctrine.[15]

The case put forward in favour of removing wilful refusal as a ground for nullity was:

(a) On grounds of *logic*, it cannot be said that a marriage "valid at the time it was made, can be declared void *ab initio* as a result of a subsequent event.[16]

(b) Wilful refusal would justify a finding that the petitioner could not reasonably be expected to live with the respondent,[17] and thus lead to a finding that the marriage had broken down irretrievably, and to a divorce. It may have been understandable to make wilful refusal a ground for nullity at a time when it might not have been sufficient grounds for divorce; there can be no such justification for retaining it now.

(c) It would make little real difference to the availability of nullity in cases of non-consummation; in many cases [18] wilful refusal and incapacity are pleaded in the alternative, and much depends on the individual judge's preference as to whether the decree was based on incapacity or wilful refusal.[19] If only incapacity were a ground, many decrees now pronounced for refusal would be successful on the ground of incapacity.

(d) Wilful refusal involved a finding that one party was at fault, where in nullity the principle is that "nobody is at fault." [20]

---

13 Matrimonial Causes Act 1937, s. 7 (1) (*a*) following the recommendations of the Gorell Barnes Commission (1912, Cd. 6478). The Commission did not consider the conceptual problem, but apparently considered that refusal indicated a failure to disclose unfitness to marry to the other party. There was again little discussion of the matter during the passage through Parliament of the 1937 Act.

14 Morton Commission, para. 89.

15 See *The Church and the Law of Nullity of Marriage* (1955), pp. 38, 48, and also Morton Commission, paras. 88, 89, 283; "Putting Asunder" pp. 67, 124–125.

16 *The Church and the Law of Nullity of Marriage* (1955) p. 34.

17 s. 1 (2) (*b*), M.C.A. 1973, *infra*, p. 115.

18 In a five year average for the years 1964–69 the figures are:

Incapacity and Wilful Refusal	498
Incapacity alone	148
Wilful refusal alone	193
	839

If there were doubt, presumably the alternatives would be pleaded.

19 See A. W. Lyon, Standing Committee C Report on Nullity of Marriage Bill, February 17, 1971, col. 12 and Edward Lyons, *ibid.* col. 16.

20 Lord Hodson, Hansard (H.L.) Vol. 318, col. 943, May 11, 1971. This statement can only be accepted if it is limited to petitions based on incapacity. Clearly in some nullity cases (*e.g.* a petition on the grounds of duress, see *supra*, p. 23) one of the parties may be at fault. Again, it might be objected that "fault" is no longer required as a basis for divorce.

The case for retaining wilful refusal as a ground for nullity is:

(a) Objections on the ground of illogicality are unsound for three reasons:

(i) Wilful refusal almost invariably results from a state of mind which dates back to the time of the marriage celebration.[21] The impediment *exists* at the time of celebration; its *manifestation* is deferred until afterwards.[22]

(ii) An unconsummated marriage has never become a true marriage.[23] This was recognised by the Canon Law which, contrary to the general rule, was prepared to allow divorce *a vinculo matrimonii* in such cases.[24] Furthermore

" [f]ailure to consummate, whether it be because the respondent is unable or because he is unwilling to have sexual intercourse, deprives the marriage of what is normally regarded as one of its essential purposes. Parties would think it strange that the nature of the relief should depend on the court's decision whether non-consummation was due to the respondent's inability or whether it was due to his unwillingness. From the parties' point of view the relevant fact would be that the marriage had never become a complete one.[25] To tell them that, in the eyes of the law, failure to complete it due to one cause results in their marriage being dissolved, would seem to them to be a strange result." [26]

(iii) Even if it is illogical, that is unimportant: wilful refusal had worked satisfactorily for thirty-four years.

(b) As to the argument that it was inconsistent to have behaviour which could be a ground for divorce as a ground for a nullity petition, it was said:

(i) A petition for divorce may not be presented until three years have elapsed from the date of marriage.[27] To make petitioners complaining of wilful refusal wait three years would cause hardship.[28]

(ii) It did not necessarily follow that a divorce would be obtainable because of wilful refusal. The parties might be old, the

---

21 *Per* Lord Hailsham, Hansard (H.L.) Vol. 318, col. 9, May 11, 1971.
22 But if innate tendencies existing at the date of the marriage are to form the basis of nullity petitions, nullity should presumably have been available in most divorces on the ground of cruelty.
23 See n. 19 *supra.*
24 Albeit not as a general rule, but only for special reasons: *e.g.* if one party became a nun: Hay, p. 59.
25 But this seems unconvincing: there can perfectly well be cases in which nullity is not available to terminate an unconsummated union. Suppose that H and W are involved in a car accident as they drive to their honeymoon, with the result that H becomes impotent. His wife cannot petition for nullity on the ground of incapacity, because the incapacity did not exist at the time of the ceremony. Nor can she petition on the basis of wilful refusal, because the non-consummation results from incapacity. (It should be pointed out that the Act does not specifically state that the inability should exist at the time of the marriage; if so, the law has been changed: *cf. Briggs* v. *Morgan* (1820) 2 Hag.Con. 324, 331; *Brown* v. *Brown* (1828) 1 Hag.Ecc. 523; *B.* v. *M.* (1852) 2 Rob.Ecc. 580; *Napier* v. *Napier* [1915] P. 184, 189–190; *S.* v. *S.* [1963] P. 162.)
26 Law Commission No. 33, para. 27 (b).
27 s. 3, M.C.A. 1973. See *infra*, p. 108.
28 Law Commission No. 33, para. 27 (d). See also Lord Hailsham in Hansard (H.L.) Vol. 317, col. 819.

case might be regarded as one of desertion for an insufficient period,[29] or there might be other special circumstances which would lead a court to say that it was not unreasonable to expect the petitioner to continue to live with the respondent.

(c) The argument that it would make little real difference to nullity cases was countered by a statistical argument: since a five year average of petitions alleging wilful refusal *alone* (*i.e.* not in the alternative to incapacity) gave a figure of 193 petitions, and since the average number of decrees granted for wilful refusal was 333, it followed that an average of at least 140 were granted in cases where the petitioner had not been sure whether the failure to consummate resulted from incapacity or refusal. This was thought to support the Law Commission's argument [30] that

" [w]ilful refusal to consummate is in most cases the alternative allegation to impotence as it is often uncertain whether the respondent's failure to consummate is due to one cause or the other; the petitioner may not know whether the respondent refuses to consummate the marriage because he is unable to have sexual intercourse or because, though able to have sexual intercourse, he does not want to have it; in such cases the court must draw an inference from the evidence before it and it seems unreal that the relief granted to the petitioner—nullity or divorce—should depend in any given case on the court's view as to which of the two reasons prevented the consummation of the marriage." [31]

In the end, the Law Commission's view that wilful refusal be retained was accepted simply because in the debates on the Nullity of Marriage Act 1971 the Lord Chancellor refused to accept a change; if the amendment was insisted on, there was every possibility that the Bill would be lost *in toto*.[32] Faced with this threat the advocates of change withdrew,[33] but it is difficult to avoid the conclusion that they had the better of the argument: arguments in favour of preserving wilful refusal as a ground for nullity on the basis of the artificiality of any other course ignore the fact that the whole doctrine of nullity seems artificial. It is equally

---

[29] See *per* A. W. Lyon M.P., Hansard (H.C.) Vol. 810, col. 1174. Desertion must have existed for two years if it is to be a basis for a divorce: s. 1 (2) (*c*), M.C.A. 1973, *infra*, p. 119.

[30] Law Commission No. 33, para. 27 (a).

[31] The Law Commission (para. 27 (c)) also put forward a highly technical justification for the present rule. In cases where the petitioner is not domiciled here English courts may be prepared to assume jurisdiction to hear the petition if it is for a decree of nullity, but not if it is for divorce. Hence, it was said, if " wilful refusal to consummate were to become a ground for divorce while impotence remained a ground for nullity, a petitioner might find himself unable to allege the two grounds in the alternative, although he himself might not know which of these was the effective cause preventing consummation of his marriage." It is difficult to believe that there is a statistically significant number of cases in which this would be a factor.

[32] *Per* Lord Hailsham, Hansard (H.L.) Vol. 318, col. 944, May 11, 1971.

[33] Not without a feeling of some resentment at the unfairness of the tactics employed: see Lord Simon of Glaisdale, *ibid*.

difficult to believe that their defeat matters very much. To some extent concentration on this narrow issue enabled Parliament to avoid discussing a far more important problem—whether the concept of the voidable marriage should be retained at all.[34]

---

[34] *Supra*, p. 69.

PART III

MATRIMONIAL LITIGATION

FAMILY law is primarily concerned with pathological situations—

> " The normal behaviour of directors of a company towards their shareholders . . . is regulated by law, and must be. The normal behaviour of husband and wife or parents and children towards each other, is beyond the law—as long as the family is ' healthy.' The law comes in when things go wrong." [1]

Hence it is primarily concerned with *litigation*. This can be classified under two main heads:

(i) Litigation concerned with the status of marriage between two parties.

(ii) Litigation concerned with financial matters.

We therefore consider:

(a) The law of divorce (including, for convenience, judicial separation and the analogous magistrate's jurisdiction [2]).

(b) The law of matrimonial property and support obligations.

---

[1] O. Kahn-Freund and K. W. Wedderburn, Editorial Foreword to *Eekelaar*, p. 7.
[2] Nullity has been dealt with above; see Chap. 4.

CHAPTER 5

DIVORCE

THIS Chapter is divided as follows:
  (i) The Social Policy of Divorce Legislation.
  (ii) The Matrimonial Offence and Bars.
  (iii) The Modern Law of Divorce.
  (iv) Other Kindred Matrimonial Litigation.

THE SOCIAL POLICY OF DIVORCE LEGISLATION [3]

DIVORCE RATES AND THEIR SIGNIFICANCE [4]

IN 1858 [5] there were 244 divorce petitions. In 1914 for the first time the number exceeded 1,000; in 1942 it rose above 10,000.[6] In the first year of the operation of the Divorce Reform Act 1969 there were 110,017 petitions, and in 1972, 111,077.[7] This is only a crude indication of divorce rates, but whatever statistical test is adopted [8] there is an upward trend [9] over the years.

It should not be assumed that this necessarily represents an increase in the number of marital breakdowns:

  (i) All divorces evidence breakdown of a marriage, but not all breakdowns are evidenced by divorce. A man who leaves his wife and establishes a " stable illicit union " [10] with another partner has done much the same as a man who divorces one wife and remarries, but it is only in the latter case that the breakdown is reflected in the Divorce Statistics.

  (ii) The rise in the rate may simply " reflect the fact that a growing

---

[3] See Max Rheinstein, *Marriage, Stability, Divorce and the Law* (1972).
[4] See generally: " Field of Choice " paras. 5–12; McGregor, *Divorce in England* (1957); *Eekelaar*, pp. 32–47; W. J. Goode, *World Revolution and Family Patterns* (1963).
[5] The first year in which divorce by judicial process was available.
[6] See Royal Commission Report, App. II, Table 1.
[7] Civil Judicial Statistics, 1971, Cmnd. 4982, and 1972, Cmnd. 5333, Table 10.
[8] The number of decrees absolute of divorce per 1,000 of the married population is the most meaningful of the readily available figures: this was 0·4 in 1931, 2·6 in 1951, 3·1 in 1966, 3·6 in 1968, 4·1 in 1969, and 4·6 in 1970: see Table 14 and the graph at p. 57, Social Trends (No. 1, 1970), and Table 7, Social Trends (No. 3, 1972) (H.M.S.O.), " Field of Choice " para. 10 and App. C. Other tests sometimes used are (i) the divorce rate per 1,000 marriages; (ii) the rate per 1,000 population; (iii) the rate per 1,000 married women (at specified ages). All statistical information is given in the Registrar-General's Annual Statistical Reviews—most recently for 1971, Part II. Commentaries on the statistical tables are published periodically.
[9] With, however, considerable short-term fluctuations, influenced by (*e.g.*) the availability of legal aid: this is graphically illustrated in *Eekelaar*, p. 34, and see " Field of Choice " para. 5 and App. B; the *Bedford College Survey*, p. 147.
[10] " Field of Choice " paras. 33 *et seq.* This may appear to outsiders to be a valid marriage: there is nothing to stop a woman adopting the surname of the man with whom she is living; " Mrs." is a courtesy title without legal significance.

segment of society is coming to regard divorce as more respectable
than other outcomes of a broken home." [11] With increasing acceptance of divorce as a socially tolerable solution,[12] fewer marriages
may be kept alive, in name only, for the sake of appearances.

(iii) Divorce was for many years in practice only open to the
comparatively rich. To get a realistic idea of the number of marriage
breakdowns involving recourse to the courts, applications in
magistrates' courts must be brought into account.[13]

Even if the number of irretrievable marriage breakdowns has
increased, this does not necessarily indicate (as is often assumed) any
decline in respect for the institution of marriage, or of the quality of
family life:

(i) A high (and increasing [14]) proportion of those who are divorced
remarry, and there are indications that the subsequent marriages are
not unstable. The fact that couples who have been prevented for
many years from legalising a " stable illicit union " should now seek
divorce to enable them to do so scarcely suggests that marriage as
an institution is in jeopardy. Nor do attitude surveys support the
view: although an increasing number of engaged couples discuss
the possibility of divorce, only a very small number enter marriage
with the idea of getting divorced if it turns out badly.[15]

(ii) Changes in social, economic and demographic circumstances
reinforce this concentration on marriage as a personal relationship,
which becomes meaningless if the relationship is in fact destroyed.[16]
Marriage no longer has a social function if the spouses' relationship
is destroyed. It is no longer necessary to preserve the bond for
economic reasons. The expectation that marriage should be a
source of happiness, and the belief that if this does not materialise
fulfilment may legitimately be sought in a second union is much more
widespread than before the Second World War when the view that

---

11 " Field of Choice " para. 11.
12 Until the Second World War, " [d]ivorce remained a serious barrier in public life
and, in Court circles an insuperable one."—A. J. P. Taylor, *English History 1914–45*
(1965), p. 170.
13 " In the early years of the century, divorce petitions made up less than one tenth of
all matrimonial proceedings; by the end of Hitler's War they amounted to less than
half; today they have risen to nearly two-thirds." *Bedford College Survey*, p. 31,
graphically illustrated at Fig. 1, p. 32 (*ibid.*). Those now obtaining magistrates'
orders may be doing so as an interim measure pending divorce proceedings: see
infra, p. 210, and *ibid.*, Chap. 9, *passim*.
14 See Table 14, Social Trends No. 1; Registrar-General's Statistical Review of England
and Wales, 1971, Part II, Table H2, p. 58; *Rowntree, op cit.*, n. 11, *infra*; T. P.
Monahan, " The Changing Nature and Instability of Remarriages," in *Selected Studies
in Marriage and the Family*, N.Y. (1962).
15 See generally on this topic: M. G. Marwill, *The Comparative Sociology of Divorce
in Divorce, Law and Society* (ed. H. A. Finlay, 1965); and on statistical aspects:
Rowntree, " Some Aspects of Marriage Breakdown in Britain during the last 30 years "
(1964) 18 *Population Studies* 147; Rowntree and Carrier, " The Resort to Divorce in
England and Wales 1858–1957 " (1958) 11 *Population Studies* 188; R. Chester, " The
Duration of Marriage to Divorce " (1971) 22 *British Journal of Sociology* 172.
16 See generally R. Fletcher, *The Family and Marriage in Britain* (1966); J. Dominian,
Marital Breakdown (1968); Bill Mortlock, *The Inside of Divorce* (1972).

there was a duty to preserve even an unhappy marriage was common. Lord Hugh Cecil's beliefs were no doubt untypical even in 1937 but they were not uncommon:

" The only argument for more divorce really is the hardship of indissoluble marriage, but this is no argument for it assumes a right of happiness. There is no such right. The path of virtue may often lead to unspeakable misery. It was hard in the War to stay in the front line places, it was hard to be wounded, mutilated and maimed for life, it was hard to be scourged and crucified. Is any unhappy marriage worse? If not, the Christian must endure as his Lord endured." [17]

It is sometimes said that an increase in the divorce rate is disturbing because of the effect of divorce on children:

" . . . the future of the country depends on the way in which children are brought up. They are best brought up in the happiness and security of a sound family life. This in turn rests on the maintenance of the institution of marriage." [18]

But the truism that children should be brought up in the happiness and security of a sound family life is not helpful in determining the question whether, given marital disharmony, it is in the interests of the children to terminate the marriage.[19] It is one thing to say that, given the possibility of divorce, every precaution will be taken to ensure the minimum harm to any children; it is quite another to say that the availability of divorce should itself be restricted in an attempt to increase the proportion of stable and happy marriages.

The most serious consequence said to follow from the ready availability of divorce is that this by itself creates " a habit of mind in the people " [20] and thus does weaken the security of marriage. The argu-

---

[17] Hansard (H.L.), Vol. 105, col. 21. The history of the Anglican Church's attitudes to divorce is traced in A. R. Winnett, *Divorce and Remarriage in Anglicanism* (1958). The influential Report of the Archbishop of Canterbury's group (" Putting Asunder " 1966) (discussed *infra*, p. 87) adopted the premise that the Church could recognise fully the validity of a secular divorce law within the secular sphere, without compromising its own doctrine (see particularly Chap. 2). The Report of the Archbishop's group on the Christian Doctrine of Marriage (" Marriage, Divorce and the Church ") (1971) rejects the concept of indissolubility. The Roman Catholic Church still adheres to this, although this is mitigated by an extended application of the concept of nullity, and is the subject of much discussion: see G. Vass S.J., " Divorce and Remarriage in the Light of Recent Publications," 11 *Heythrop Journal* 251; V. J. Pospishill, *Divorce and Remarriage: Towards a New Catholic Teaching* (1967).

[18] Lord Denning M.R., foreword to W. Latey, *The Tide of Divorce* (1970).

[19] This is a matter on which both the Archbishop's group (see " Putting Asunder " para. 57 and App. D) and the Law Commission (see " Field of Choice " paras. 49–50) rightly thought it impossible to generalise: " Sometimes the children will suffer more if their quarrelling parents stay together than they would if they parted; sometimes they will not. Sometimes they will suffer more if the parting is followed by a divorce; sometimes they will not. Sometimes they will suffer further if there is a remarriage; sometimes they will gain thereby. All one can be sure of is that it is in the best interests of the children that their parents' marriage should be a happy one and not break up. The truism is recognised by all parents, but, unhappily, not all of them are able, however hard they try (and we believe that most of them try desperately hard), to preserve a happy home and marriage. Inevitably some marriages will break up notwithstanding that there are children." (" Field of Choice " para. 50.)

[20] See the dissenting report by the Archbishop of York, Sir William Anson, and Sir Lewis Dibdin to the Gorell Barnes Commission Report (1912) Cd. 6478, p. 185.

ments of Hume [21] and Paley [22] have been cogently summarised by Lord Stowell [23] in a much quoted passage:

> " the general happiness of the married life is secured by its indissolubility. When people understand that they *must* live together, except for a very few reasons known to the law, they learn to soften by mutual accommodation that yoke which they know they cannot shake off. . . . If it were once understood that upon mutual disgust married persons might be legally separated, many couples who now pass through the world with mutual comfort, with attention to their common offspring, and to the moral order of civil society, might at this moment have been living in a state of mutual unkindness, in a state of estrangement from their common offspring, and in a state of the most licentious and unreserved immorality. In this case, as in many others, the happiness of some individuals must be sacrificed to the greater and more general good."

The view that easier divorce means less security and happiness appealed to the Morton Commission in 1956 [24]: the " root of the problem " was

> " a tendency to take the duties and responsibilities of marriage less seriously than formerly . . . there is less disposition to overcome difficulties and to put up with the rubs of daily life, and in consequence, there is an increasing disposition to regard divorce, not as the last resort, but as the obvious way out when things begin to go wrong." [25]

Critics have pointed out that there is no evidence establishing such a causal connection.[26] It is impossible to establish by evidence whether increased demand for divorce is the cause or result of easier divorce laws. Even if it is thought likely that facilitating divorce is an influence on the breakdown of marriage, it is clear that it is only one among many.[27]

THE POLICY OF THE LAW

The underlying policy which has found expression in the development of divorce law since 1857 has, in many ways, been remarkably consistent:

(i) No law should be so lax as to lessen the regard for the sanctity of marriage. Hence, there should be a restriction on the availability of divorce.

(ii) No law should be so harsh as to lead to its disregard, encouraging

---

[21] Essay XVIII: " Of Polygamy and Divorce."

[22] *Moral and Political Philosophy* (8th ed., 1791) Chap. 7.

[23] *Evans* v. *Evans* (1790) 1 Hag.Con. 35.

[24] And to some witnesses, including J. E. S. Simon Q.C.: Evidence, May 7–8, 200–201.

[25] Para. 47.

[26] See O. Kahn-Freund (1956) 29 M.L.R. 573, particularly at pp. 577–578; O. R. McGregor, *Divorce in England* (1957) and in (1956) 7 *British Journal of Sociology*.

[27] This was accepted even by the Morton Commission, which (para. 46) drew attention to the " rapid and far-reaching social changes " of the past 30 or 40 years, and asserted that it " is perhaps inevitable that at such a time there should be a tendency to regard the assertion of one's own individuality as a right, and to pursue one's personal satisfaction, reckless of the consequences to others. The teaching of modern psychology has been widely interpreted as laying emphasis on self-expression and the harmfulness of repression, with the consequent assumption that much that had previously held sexual licence   check could be jettisoned."

the formation of illicit, if permanent, extra-marital relationships.[28] Subsidiary aims, given greater or lesser emphasis from time to time, have included:

(a) The law should protect those likely to be adversely affected by divorce, particularly the wife [29] and the children.

(b) No law should outrage the popular sense of justice. The law should not " assist anyone to gain advantage from his own wrong doing, particularly if it causes injury to an innocent party." [30]

(c) The law should be based on understandable and respected principles, and not be thought hypocritical.[31]

(d) It should facilitate reconciliation between estranged spouses.

(e) It should be fair to others affected by the marriage, such as the husband's mistress and their children.

(f) So far as possible, the law should encourage harmonious relationships between the parties and their children after the divorce by " taking the heat " out of the divorce proceedings.[32]

For many years divorce policy in England was influenced by theological arguments, but by 1966 the Church of England had come to accept that " [h]ow the doctrine of Christ concerning marriage should be interpreted and applied within the Christian Church is one question: what the Church ought to say and do about secular laws of marriage and divorce is another question altogether." [33] The withdrawal of doctrinal [34] Anglican opposition to reform was a powerful influence in the ultimate acceptance of the Divorce Reform Act 1969.

The changes in legislative attitudes to divorce can most easily be considered under three heads:

(i) the Doctrine of the Matrimonial Offence; (ii) the decline of the Matrimonial Offence Doctrine; (iii) divorce for irretrievable breakdown.

The Doctrine of the Matrimonial Offence

Until 1857 the only way of obtaining freedom to remarry was by obtaining a private Act of Parliament. Although in form legislative, the procedure

---

28 Based on the Gorell Barnes Commission's Statement of Principle (1912) Cd. 6478, para. 135.
29 Bentham (*Theory of Legislation*, ed. C. M. Atkinson (1914), pp. 292 *et seq.*) was amongst the first to stress that (a) child-bearing; and (b) diminishing physical attractiveness over the years made it necessary to encourage life-long unions, whilst nevertheless permitting divorce subject to safeguards. Opposition to the Divorce Reform Act 1969 largely centred on the fact that it would allow an " innocent " wife to be divorced, and would thus be a " Casanova's Charter."
30 Sir J. Simon, " The Seven Pillars of Divorce Reform " (1965) 62 L.S.Gaz. 344: see also the eloquent appeal to the House of Lords by the [nonagenarian] former Lord Chancellor, Lord Simonds, that they should follow " the pattern of justice, decency and honour, and refuse to the man who comes before you the benefit of his own wrong." (Hansard (H.L.), Vol. 303, col. 1300.)
31 See " Field of Choice," para. 17.   32 *Ibid.*
33 " Putting Asunder," para. 6. See also *ibid.*, pp. 6–15, 80–95. For the Church's attitude to divorce as a matter of internal discipline, see *Marriage, Divorce and the Church* (1971).
34 Although Church spokesmen opposed the Bill as finally presented, on the ground that it did not include adequate protection for the weak.

was in substance judicial,[35] based on proof of adultery. The Matrimonial Causes Act 1857 created a new and somewhat more accessible tribunal, but did not change the principles on which divorce was granted, *i.e.*:

(a) The grounds upon which divorce could be obtained were limited to " a few extreme and specific provocations "—*i.e.* the matrimonial offences—which were considered such that the parties could no longer " discharge their mutual difficulties by continuing . . . to cohabit with each other."

(b) The petitioner had to show that he was free from guilt.

(c) There must be no connivance or collusion between the parties to escape from the solemn obligation of matrimony.

Hence, the only ground for divorce was adultery,[36] and connivance, condonation and collusion [37] were absolute bars to a petition.[38]   The petitioner's own adultery, delay, cruelty, desertion, or conduct conducing to adultery were discretionary bars.[39]

Adultery remained a prerequisite to divorce until 1937.   The reasons for this stress on physical infidelity were:

(a) The historical precedent of the private Divorce Acts, the justification for which was originally to prevent illegitimate children being foisted on " the unhappy husband whose bed had been violated." [40]

(b) Scriptural justifications for divorce were usually based on adultery.[41]

(c) A wife's adultery was totally inconsistent with the continuance of the marriage, and (unlike other matrimonial offences) could not be forgiven.[42]   The same argument justified treating a wife (who could not get a divorce solely on the grounds of adultery) differently from

---

[35] For a full historical account, see First Report of the Commissioners into the Law of Divorce (1853).   See also Jackson, *Formation and Annulment of Marriage*, Chap. 2, Bishop, *Divorce Bills in the Imperial Parliament* and D. Morris, *The End of Marriage*, Chap. 2.

[36] A *wife* petitioner had to show either incestuous adultery; adultery and bigamy; rape, sodomy or bestiality; adultery with cruelty; adultery and desertion for at least 2 years. The parliamentary debates in 1857 were largely concerned with the question whether a wife should be treated differently from her husband: see *e.g.* Hansard, Vol. 145, col. 496.   Equality was not obtained until the Matrimonial Causes Act 1923 allowed a wife to petition on the ground of adultery alone.   (Since 1884, failure to comply with a decree of Restitution of Conjugal Rights was treated as statutory desertion, so that a wife who could establish adultery could obtain a divorce immediately by obtaining a decree of Restitution which her husband ignored: s. 5, Matrimonial Causes Act 1884.)

[37] See *infra*, p. 103.

[38] s. 30, Matrimonial Causes Act 1857.   [39] s. 31, *ibid.*

[40] *Mr. Lewkenor's Case*, 13 State Trials 1308—although in this case the Act did not permit remarriage.

[41] For a full examination of the Biblical Texts, see the report of the Gorell Barnes Committee, and the evidence at Vol. III, p. 544.   For a modern interpretation, see Hugh Montefiore, " Jesus on Divorce and Remarriage," in *Marriage, Divorce and the Church* (1971), pp. 79–95.

[42] See First Report of the 1853 Royal Commission, who regarded adultery as " an offence which destroys altogether the primary objects of the married state, by introducing, in some instances, a confusion of offspring; by cutting off, in others, all hope of succession; and by diverting, in all, the affection and feelings into strange channels, which reason and religion forbid them to flow in " (p. 39).

the husband: "it was possible for a wife to pardon a husband who had committed adultery; but it was hardly possible for a husband ever really to pardon the adultery of a wife. . . .[43]

The exclusive reliance on adultery was never universally accepted[44] and came under increasing attack over the years.[45] It was alleged that the " adultery " was often simulated, and divorce in reality consensual.[46]

Adultery remained a prerequisite for divorce until the Matrimonial Causes Act 1937 allowed either spouse to petition because of the other's cruelty, desertion for three years, or supervening incurable insanity.

The Decline of the Matrimonial Offence Doctrine

The retention of the matrimonial offence as the basis of divorce law came under increasing attack after 1937:

> (i) Over 90 per cent. of divorce petitions were undefended. The procedure was " based on the assumption that the litigation is contentious "[47] but in many cases the parties had in fact agreed on divorce.

> (ii) The 1937 Act allowed divorce because of the respondent's incurable insanity. Divorce was thus allowed for misfortune, and a serious inroad into the offence principle had been made.[48]

---

[43] Hansard (H.C.) Vol. 145 (3rd ser.) col. 490. Other justifications for the discrimination were (a) the possibility of a wife foisting spurious children on the husband; (b) if a wife could sue solely because of her husband's adultery, it might tend to collusive divorces (see 1853 Commission, para. 40); (c) the wife might infect her husband with contagious disease. (It did not seem to be regarded as significant that a husband might infect his wife.) The Matrimonial Causes Act 1923 gave the wife the right to petition on the grounds of adultery alone.

[44] See Milton, *The Doctrine and Discipline of Divorce*, who thought that the Canon Law should have regarded spiritual and civil companionship rather than carnal coupling as the true basis of marriage: " . . . he who affirms adultery to be the highest breach, affirms the bed to be the highest of marriage, which is in truth a gross and boorish opinion, how common so ever; so far from the countenance of scripture, as from the light of all clear philosophy or civil nature."

[45] Notably by the Gorell Barnes Commission whose report was ultimately the basis of the Matrimonial Causes Act 1937, and in many ways foreshadowed the modern concept of breakdown.

[46] Notably in the so-called Hotel Cases, in which husband and wife agreed on a divorce, and the husband would then arrange to provide evidence of adultery (in fact never committed) perhaps with the assistance of a professional companion—a process satirised by A. P. Herbert in *Holy Deadlock* (1934) where the process was summed up: " The husband ' behaved like a gentleman '; good lawyers were engaged, a good many pennies had to be put in the slot, but the divorce emerged from the machine at last as easily as a motor licence, and rather more easily than a passport." Even after new grounds were introduced in 1937, adultery remained the commonest ground for divorce (rather more than 50 per cent. of cases) and it was often suggested that many of the cases were in fact consensual: it provided divorce without the delay inherent in desertion (which had to have continued for 3 years) and without the stigma of findings of cruelty. There is no agreement on the extent of the continued use of the " hotel divorce ": see on the one hand the evidence of L. C. B. Gower to the Morton Commission (Minutes of Evidence 16–17), and C. P. Harvey Q.C. (1953) 16 M.L.R. 129, particularly at pp. 131–132, but *cf.* the conclusions of the Morton Commission (at para. 69 (ix) to (xii)) and the Law Commission (" Field of Choice " para. 26) who thought that in " recent years the bogus *hotel case* . . . has become far less common." For the courts' increasing suspicion of petitions based on such evidence, see *Rayden*, para. 14, p. 152 and the authorities there referred to.

[47] " Field of Choice " para. 20.

[48] " Field of Choice " para. 21.

(iii) After decisions of the House of Lords [49] in 1964 a decree might be made for cruelty against a respondent who was not morally blameworthy. Increasingly the question became simply whether the petitioner could be expected to endure the marital situation.

(iv) Although generally proof of an offence by the respondent was still necessary, it was no longer so important to establish that the respondent was an aggrieved and innocent victim. By statute,[50] collusion was made into a discretionary [51] rather than an absolute bar, and the scope of the bar of condonation was restricted.[52] In those cases where the court had a discretion to refuse a divorce because the respondent had himself committed a matrimonial offence, the courts increasingly adopted the principle that if a marriage had broken down no public interest was served by keeping it legally in existence.[53] If full and frank disclosure were made,[54] discretion would normally be exercised.[55] Increasingly both parties were granted a decree, so that " the guilty/innocent dichotomy " was blurred.[56]

In 1951 a Royal Commission was appointed [57] to inquire into the law. All except one member [58] favoured the retention of the matrimonial offence principle, and nine were opposed to the introduction of breakdown

---

[49] *Gollins* v. *Gollins* [1964] A.C. 644; *Williams* v. *Williams* [1964] A.C. 698.

[50] Matrimonial Causes Act 1963, s. 4.

[51] The fact that both parties were agreed in wanting a divorce was no longer a sufficient reason for preventing their obtaining one: see *Nash* v. *Nash* [1965] P. 266; *M.* v. *M.* [1967] P. 313; *Gosling* v. *Gosling* [1968] P. 1; *Main* v. *Main* [1965] 1 W.L.R. 819, and N. Michaels (1966) 29 M.L.R. 241; Bevan (1966) 82 L.Q.R. 371.

[52] Matrimonial Causes Act 1963, ss. 1 and 2, containing (*inter alia*) the so-called " kiss and make-up " provisions designed to facilitate reconciliation. Those were given a restrictive operation by the courts: see (1966) 82 L.Q.R. 525 (Irvine); Mortlock, *The Inside of Divorce*, pp. 44–46.

[53] *Blunt* v. *Blunt* [1943] A.C. 517; *Masarati* v. *Masarati* [1969] 1 W.L.R. 393; *cf. Bull* v. *Bull* [1968] P. 618.

[54] A respondent seeking the exercise of discretion had to file a " discretion statement "; it was the duty of the petitioner's solicitor to make clear to his client his duty of full disclosure: see *Pearson* v. *Pearson* [1971] P. 16—a rule which sometimes led to absurd and embarrassing results: *Barnacle* v. *Barnacle* [1948] P. 257 (where the petitioner had not understood the meaning of adultery, and the trial judge gave examples of misunderstanding on other occasions: " ' it is not adultery if she is over 50.' . . . ' I did not think it was adultery during the daytime '; ' I thought it meant getting a girl into trouble '; ' I thought it meant drinking with men in public houses ' " (p. 261)).

[55] *Per* Sachs L.J., *Masarati* v. *Masarati* (*supra*) at p. 396. The court's attitude had changed very much since " [j]ust after the first world war men were refused discretion on account of a single weekend at an hotel after the wife had long deserted them " (*per* Sachs L.J., *ibid.* at p. 396). Latterly discretion was asked for and obtained in some 30 per cent. of all cases; in 1965 out of a total of 11,221 divorces and judicial separations granted in cases dealt with in the [London] Principal Probate Registry, discretion was exercised in 3,850 cases and refused in only 3. Even where the adultery was not disclosed, but only came to light as the result of an intervention by the Queen's Proctor after decree nisi the court frequently exercised its discretion: in 1965, 54 interventions by the Queen's Proctor were heard and allowed, but discretion was exercised in 34 of these: see " Field of Choice " p. 12, notes 30, 32, 33.

[56] " Field of Choice " para. 21.

[57] The Morton Commission—appointed after a Bill to allow divorce after 7 years' separation (introduced by Mrs. Eirene White) had received a second reading in the House of Commons.

[58] Lord Walker.

as even an alternative ground for divorce.[59] This group asserted that the proper function of the law was to give relief where a wrong had been done, not to provide a dignified and honourable means of release from a broken marriage.[60]

Divorce for Irretrievable Breakdown

The fact that the Commission was so divided on its principal recommendation did nothing to inhibit Divorce Reformers. In 1963 Mr. Leo Abse presented a bill which (inter alia) [61] would have allowed divorce after seven years' separation. This was unsuccessful, but in the House of Lords debate the Archbishop of Canterbury [62] announced the appointment of a Committee to investigate the formulation of a principle of breakdown of marriage, free from any trace of the idea of consent, which conserved the point that offences and not only wishes are the basis of breakdown, and which would be protected by a far more thorough insistence on reconciliation procedure.

Putting Asunder

The report of this group, " Putting Asunder," was published in 1966. It favoured, as the lesser of two evils,[63] the substitution of the doctrine of breakdown for that of the matrimonial offence. The primary and fundamental question should be [64]:

> " Does the evidence before the court reveal such failure in the matrimonial relationship, or such circumstances adverse to that relationship, that no reasonable probability remains of the spouses again living together as husband and wife for mutual comfort and support? "

If so, the legal tie should be dissolved. A divorce decree should be seen simply as a judicial recognition of a state of affairs with a consequent redefinition of status.[65] The Committee considered that the court should carry out a detailed inquest into

> " the alleged fact and causes of the ' death ' of the marriage relationship. It would have to be made possible for the court . . . to inquire effectively into what attempts at reconciliation had been made, into the feasibility of further attempts, into the acts, events, and circumstances alleged to have destroyed the marriage, into the truth of statements made (especially in uncontested cases), and into all matters bearing upon the determination of public interest." [66]

59 Nine members of the Commission were prepared to adopt the principle of breakdown to a limited extent—i.e. either party could obtain a divorce if there had been 7 years' separation and the other did not object. Four were prepared to dispense with the respondent's consent, if he had been to blame for the separation.

60 Para. 69 (xiii). The Commission has been very fiercely attacked (e.g. by Professor O. R. McGregor, Divorce in England (1957)). But the Commission's thorough examination of divorce law and practice led to many changes, particularly in relation to the protection of children and other ancillary matters.

61 The Bill amended the law of collusion, and provided the " kiss-and-make-up " procedure. These sections became law as the Matrimonial Causes Act 1963.

62 Hansard (H.L.), col. 1547.

63 " Putting Asunder," para. 68.   64 Ibid., para. 55.

65 Ibid., para. 66.   66 Ibid., para. 84.

But to prevent the law from being brought into disrepute,[67] the court would be obliged to refuse a decree (notwithstanding proof of breakdown) if:

(i) to grant it would be contrary to the public interest in justice and in protecting the institution of marriage.[68] This bar would apply where " to put it crudely—it just would not do to let the petitioner get away with it," [69] and also in cases where both parties had combined to deceive the court [70]; or,

(ii) the petitioner failed to satisfy the court in the matter of maintenance for the respondent and her children, and failure was against the public interest.[71]

Detailed proposals were made for securing (a) the welfare of children,[72] and (b) any prospects of reconciliation.[73]

The Law Commission—The Field of Choice

The report was immediately referred by the Lord Chancellor to the Law Commission. The Commission took as its basic assumption that [74]

" a good divorce law should seek to (i) buttress, rather than to undermine, the stability of marriage; and (ii) when, regrettably, a marriage has irretrievably broken down, to enable the empty legal shell to be destroyed with the maximum fairness, and the minimum bitterness, distress and humiliation."

They rejected the view that a divorce law, which is directed essentially towards dissolving the marriage bond, can do nothing towards upholding the status of marriage:

" It can and should ensure that divorce is not so easy that the parties are under no inducement to make a success of their marriage and, in particular, to overcome temporary difficulties. It can also ensure that every encouragement is afforded to a reconciliation and that the procedure is not such as to inhibit or discourage approaches to that end." [75]

The second objective was amplified under two heads:

" First, the law should make it possible to dissolve the legal tie once that has become irretrievably broken in fact. If the marriage is dead, the object of the law should be to afford it a decent burial. Secondly, it should achieve this in a way that is just to all concerned, including the children as well as the spouses, and which causes them the minimum of embarrassment and humiliation. Above all, it should seek to take the heat out of the disputes between husband and wife and certainly not further embitter the relationships between them or between them and their children. It should not merely bury the marriage, but do so with decency and

---

67 *Ibid.*, para. 98.
68 *Ibid.*, para. 66.
69 *Ibid.*
70 *Ibid.*, para. 97.
71 *Ibid.*, para. 65.
72 *Ibid.*, para. 92.
73 *Ibid.*, paras. 88, 90.
74 " Field of Choice " para. 15.
75 *Ibid.*

dignity and in a way which will encourage harmonious relationships between the parties and their children in the future." [76]

The existing divorce law, although not without merit was found wanting [77]:

" It does not do all it might to aid the stability of marriage, but tends rather to discourage attempts at reconciliation. It does not enable all dead marriages to be buried, and those that it buries are not always interred with the minimum of distress and humiliation. It does not achieve the maximum possible fairness to all concerned, for a spouse may be branded as guilty in law though not the more blameworthy in fact. The insistence on guilt and innocence tends to embitter relationships, with particularly damaging results to the children, rather than to promote future harmony. Its principles are widely regarded as hypocritical. In particular, it has failed to solve four major problems with which a reformed divorce law must grapple." [78]

The four problems were:

(1) The failure to provide adequate help in exploring all possibilities of reconciliation.

(2) The problems of stable illicit unions, where substantial numbers of children were illegitimate because one or both parents, although living as man and wife, could not obtain the legal freedom to remarry.

(3) The problem of securing justice to wives.

This was seen under three heads: (a) Financial justice; (b) deprivation of status; (c) a petitioner taking advantage of his own wrong.

(a) The Commission considered [79] that radical reform was needed in the law relating to family property (including pension rights) and financial provision (and its enforcement) to this end. Such reform " could go some way both to mitigate the inevitable hardship caused by a break-up of the home and to eradicate the additional hardship which may result from a subsequent dissolution of the marriage." [80] There should certainly be a bar to divorce if the husband had not made the most equitable provision for the wife that was possible in the circumstances. It might even be necessary to go further [81]:

" by providing an additional safeguard whereby a divorce cannot be forced on the wife if it is impossible for the husband to make provisions which protect her from disproportionate hardship." But—" If such a safeguard cannot be dispensed with it is much to be hoped that resort to it could be infrequent: it is offensive to decency and derogatory to respect for family ties to preserve the legal shell of a dead marriage for purely monetary considerations. Moreover, a rich husband can easily make satisfactory financial provision for his wife and get his divorce; a poor man cannot, and it will be argued that it would be discriminatory for the law

[76] Ibid., para. 17.
[77] Ibid., paras. 23–28.
[78] Ibid., para. 28.
[79] Ibid., para. 39.
[80] Ibid. See infra, Chap. 6.
[81] Ibid., para. 40.

to refuse him a divorce on that account. Fortunately, the orders which the court makes can be varied subsequently if the circumstances of the parties alter, and this may enable an initial injustice to be corrected. In most cases, as we have said, the hardship will already have resulted from the break-up of the home and a refusal of a divorce cannot mend this."

(b) The problem of deprivation of status was regarded as less serious. Any such loss had to be balanced against the advantage to society of allowing stable illicit unions to be regularised.

(c) It might be desirable to have a discretionary bar to divorce if to grant it would be offensive to the principle that no man should take advantage of his own wrong. But any such bar should be narrowly drawn [82]:

" The expedient of preserving the sanctity of marriage by insisting that one who has shown a wanton contempt for it should be punished by remaining married seems illogical and unattractive, especially if, as is usually the case, it involves punishing others as well."

There should be a discretion to refuse a decree if the petitioner wilfully failed to provide the required information, or had attempted to deceive the court.[83]

(4) The problem of protection for children. The Commission rejected suggestions that no divorce at all should be possible if there were infant children.[84] There is no evidence that divorce necessarily involves damage to children; and it is the fact of marital disharmony, rather than the severance of the legal tie, which often causes most harm.

The Commission rejected the Archbishop's group's proposal for a full inquest into the marriage because:

(i) An inquiry into causes might be necessarily humiliating and distressing to the parties, so that one of the criteria for reform would be broken.

(ii) It would be impracticable without a vast increase in expenditure of money and human resources.[85]

It was concluded that the " field of choice " was between three alternatives, summarised as follows [86]:

" (a) *Breakdown without inquest*—a modification of the breakdown principle advocated in *Putting Asunder*, but dispensing in most cases with the elaborate inquest there suggested. The court would, on proof of a period of separation and in the absence of evidence to the contrary, assume that the marriage had broken down. If, however, this were to be the sole comprehensive ground of divorce, it would not be feasible to make the period of separation

---

[82] *Ibid.*, para. 44, and see the further discussion at paras. 114–119.
[83] *Ibid.*, para. 109.
[84] As proposed by Sir J. Simon: (1965) 62 L.S.Gaz. 344.
[85] " Field of Choice " para. 2.
[86] " Field of Choice " pp. 54–55. For a fuller elaboration, see *ibid.* paras. 71–105. For a critique of " Breakdown " and " Consent " principles see (1967) 30 M.L.R. 121 (MacKenna); see also (1967) 30 M.L.R. 180 (Kahn-Freund).

much more than six months.[87] If, as seems likely, so short a period is not acceptable, breakdown cannot become the sole ground, but might still be introduced as an additional ground on the lines of proposal (c) below.

(b) *Divorce by consent*—This would be practicable only as an additional, and not a sole comprehensive, ground. It would not be more than a palliative and would probably be unacceptable except in the case of marriages in which there are no dependent children. Even in the case of childless marriages, if consent were the sole criterion, it might lead to the dissolution of marriages that had not broken down irretrievably.

(c) *The separation ground*—This would involve introducing as a ground for divorce a period of separation irrespective of which party was at fault, thereby affording a place in the law for the application of the breakdown principle. But since the period would be substantially longer than six months, it would be practicable only as an addition to the existing grounds based on matrimonial offence. The most comprehensive form of this proposal would provide for two different periods of separation. After the expiration of the shorter period (two years is suggested) either party, subject to safeguards, could obtain a divorce if the other consented, or, perhaps, did not object. After the expiration of the longer period (five or seven years) either party, subject to further safeguards, could obtain a divorce even if the other party objected."

The Divorce Reform Act was made possible [88] by a compromise between the Law Commission and the Archbishop's group: (a) the basic principle is that of the Archbishop's group—*i.e.* that breakdown should be the sole ground for divorce; *but* (b) breakdown is to be inferred from the commission of certain facts akin to the old matrimonial offences *or* (i) two years' separation if the respondent consents, or (ii) five years' separation if he does not.

Its major practical innovations (discussed in detail below) are:

(i) It accepts the principle of divorce by consent, albeit only after a period of separation.

(ii) It permits divorce by repudiation after five years' separation. It does not contain any express provision preventing a petitioner from relying on his own wrong.[89]

THE MATRIMONIAL OFFENCE AND BARS

THE MATRIMONIAL OFFENCE

Divorce law is no longer based on the concept of the matrimonial offence, but it is still necessary to have some understanding of the topic: proof of adultery or desertion may be the basis for decrees of divorce or judicial separation, while these offences together with persistent cruelty are still

[87] Because there might be cases where speedy dissolution was imperative.
[88] See Appendix to the Law Commission's Third Annual Report.
[89] For criticisms of the basis of the Act, see O. M. Stone, " Moral Judgments and Material Provision in Divorce " (1969) 3 *Family Law Quarterly* 371.

the basis of much of the jurisdiction of the magistrates' courts.[90] Detailed consideration of the complex case law on these topics is outside the scope of this work, and reference should be made to the standard textbooks.[91]

ADULTERY

Although one learned judge has said " [n]obody has yet attempted to define adultery, and I do not propose to rush in where wiser men have not," [92] the elements of the offence are clear [93] : there must be voluntary or consensual sexual intercourse between a married person and a person (whether married or unmarried) of the opposite sex not being the other's spouse. The following points should be noted:

(i) Voluntary or Consensual: it is a defence to a charge of adultery against a wife if she can establish that she was raped.[94] Similarly a person may be able to establish that he lacked the necessary mental capacity to consent to intercourse.[95]

(ii) Sexual Intercourse: adultery presupposes a " carnal union between a man and a woman." [96] Mere indecent familiarities are not enough.[97]

(iii) The Parties: it is not necessary for *both* parties to be married: for example, a single woman who has intercourse with a married man commits adultery.[98]

The standard of proof of adultery is high.[99] In many cases, the evidence is a confession made to an inquiry agent; in other cases, it is often circumstantial (*e.g.* the birth of a child of whom the husband cannot be the father).

CRUELTY

The concept of legal cruelty has caused great difficulty: judges have " always carefully refrained from attempting a comprehensive definition of cruelty for the purposes of matrimonial relief. . . ." [1] The Court of Appeal (in a case [2] decided in the light of two decisions [3] of the House

---

[90] *Infra*, p. 211.
[91] *e.g., Rayden*, pp. 174–203 (Adultery), 219–271 (Desertion), 1101–1124 (Cruelty).
[92] *Per* Karminski J., *Sapsford* v. *Sapsford* [1954] P. 394.
[93] Based on the definition in *Rayden*, accepted by the courts in *e.g. Barnett* v. *Barnett* [1957] 1 All E.R. 388; *Dennis* v. *Dennis* [1955] P. 153.
[94] *Redpath* v. *Redpath* [1950] 1 All E.R. 600.
[95] *Long* v. *Long* (1890) 15 P.D. 24; *S.* v. *S.* [1962] P. 133.
[96] *Per* Karminski J., *Sapsford* v. *Sapsford* (*supra*).
[97] *Ibid. Dennis* v. *Dennis* [1955] P. 153. Artificial insemination by a donor is not adultery: *Maclennan* v. *Maclennan*, 1958 S.L.T. 12, although the point has never been decided in England, *cf. Orford* v. *Orford* (1921) 58 D.L.R. 251, and see G. W. Bartholomew (1956) 21 M.L.R. 236; Tallin, 34 Can.Bar Rev. 1; Smith (1968) 67 *Michigan Law Review* 127; Departmental Committee on Human Artificial Insemination. Cmnd. 1105.
[98] *Abson* v. *Abson* [1952] P. 55 (where the woman was divorced); *Chorlton* v. *Chorlton* [1952] P. 169.
[99] *Blyth* v. *Blyth* [1966] A.C. 643; *cf. Preston-Jones* v. *Preston-Jones* [1951] A.C. 391.
[1] *Per* Lord Tucker, *Jamieson* v. *Jamieson* [1952] A.C. 525. The quotation continues " and experience has shown the wisdom of this course," a proposition which may be thought doubtful.   [2] *Le Brocq* v. *Le Brocq* [1964] 1 W.L.R. 1085.
[3] *Gollins* v. *Gollins* [1964] A.C. 644; *Williams* v. *Williams* [1964] A.C. 698.

of Lords) has emphasised a " plain-words " approach: " ' Cruel ' means
' cruel ' . . . ' cruel ' is not used in any esoteric or ' divorce court ' sense
of that word, the conduct complained of must be something which an
ordinary man or jury . . . would describe as ' cruel ' if the story were fully
told." [4] But although everything which constitutes legal cruelty must be
" cruel " in the ordinary sense of the word not everything which
is " cruel " in the ordinary sense of the word constitutes legal cruelty:
the petitioner must show (a) conduct of the requisite gravity, and
(b) injury to health or reasonable apprehension thereof:

Conduct

(i) The conduct complained of must be of a grave and weighty nature,[5]
such as to constitute cruelty in the ordinary sense of that word,[6] such
that the other spouse should not be called on to endure it,[7] and to make
continued cohabitation virtually impossible.[8] This must be distinguished
sharply from " the ordinary wear and tear of married life." [9]

(ii) It is not necessary to establish a desire or intention to injure.[10]
If there is conduct dangerous in itself (*e.g.* gross physical violence) a
decree will be granted whatever the respondent's state of mind. But in
borderline cases, the existence of an intention is highly relevant: a man
who (knowing that his wife is severely allergic to dogs) deliberately leaves
her with no means of escape from a kennels would be guilty of cruelty;
if he did not know of his wife's condition, his behaviour (however thought-
less) could not be said to be so.

(iii) The question is, not what are standards of a reasonable man or
woman, but whether " *this* conduct by *this* man to *this* woman, or *vice
versa*, is cruelty." [11] The personal characteristics of each spouse may be
taken into account in deciding whether (a) there is anything about the
respondent to excuse conduct which would otherwise be cruel, and (b)
whether a hypersensitive petitioner can establish cruelty where a more
robust petitioner would have been left unmoved. These questions only
become relevant in borderline cases: in clear cases of physical violence
there is no room for argument about the expectations of the parties.

Injury to health

There must, as a general rule, be hurt or injury to health,[12] or a
reasonable apprehension thereof. If a complaint of *physical* violence is

---

4 *Per* Harman L.J., *Le Brocq* v. *Le Brocq* (*supra*) at p. 1089.
5 *Mulhouse* v. *Mulhouse* [1966] P. 39; *Saunders* v. *Saunders* [1965] P. 499. This
requirement has " never been challenged," *per* Lord Morris (dissenting), *Gollins* v.
Gollins.
6 *Gollins* v. *Gollins* (*supra*) *per* Lord Evershed, *cf. per* Diplock L.J., *Hall* v. *Hall* [1962]
1 W.L.R. 1246: " I await with some philological excitement an example of conduct
which is ' grave ' without being ' weighty,' " *Le Brocq* v. *Le Brocq* [1964] 3 All
E.R. 464; *Saunders* v. *Saunders* (*supra*).
7 *Gollins* v. *Gollins* per Lord Pearce.   8 *Saunders* v. *Saunders* (*supra*).
9 *Per* Asquith L.J., *Buchler* v. *Buchler* [1947] P. 25; *Gollins* v. *Gollins* (*supra*), *per*
Pearce L.J. at p. 694.   10 *Gollins* v. *Gollins*; *Williams* v. *Williams* (*supra*).
11 *Per* Pearce J., *Lauder* v. *Lauder* [1949] P. 277, and see *per* Lord Reid, *Gollins* v.
Gollins at p. 664.   12 Including mental health.

proved, the court will not require any further evidence of general injury to health.[13]

Examples of cruelty

It may be helpful to summarise some common examples of cruelty:

(i) Conviction of criminal offences which involve directly or indirectly the other party, or are particularly relevant to their relationship: *e.g.* a persistent course of dishonesty and fraud involving the husband in embarrassment with his bank, tradesmen and employers,[14] (b) sexual offences, such as indecent exposure,[15] or sexual assaults on the wife's children.[16]

(ii) Sexual Matters: *e.g.* the practice of perversions,[17] excessive sexual demands,[18] infecting the petitioner with Venereal Disease,[19] submitting to a sterilisation operation against the wishes of the other party.[20]

(iii) Nagging,[21] neglect and insults,[22] violent and obscene language.[23]

(iv) Physical violence.

DESERTION

Desertion is based on the rejection by one party of all the obligations of marriage.[24] The courts have consistently refused to define it,[25] and for many years adopted a restrictive attitude to the concept for fear that too wide a definition would lead to divorce by consent after a period of separation.[26] The effect of the courts' struggles with changing policy considerations over the years has been to introduce many " metaphysical niceties " [27] into the law, and it is difficult to make clear statements of principle without considerable risk of over-simplification.

The main characteristics of the offence are: (i) the fact of separation; (ii) the intention to desert; (iii) the lack of any justification for the separation; (iv) the lack of consent by the respondent.

Two important complications should be mentioned at the outset:

(i) until an action is brought, desertion remains an *inchoate* offence.[28] It can be terminated by the party in desertion demonstrating that he no

---

13 *Mulhouse* v. *Mulhouse* [1966] P. 39, 57.
14 *Stanwick* v. *Stanwick* [1970] 3 All E.R. 983.
15 *Crawford* v. *Crawford* [1956] P. 195.
16 *Ivens* v. *Ivens* [1955] P. 129, *Cooper* v. *Cooper* [1955] P. 99.
17 *Gardner* v. *Gardner* [1947] 1 All E.R. 630; *Statham* v. *Statham* [1929] P. 131.
18 In practice, a very common complaint: see *e.g. Holborn* v. *Holborn* [1947] 1 All E.R. 32; *Walsham* v. *Walsham* [1949] P. 359.
19 *Browning* v. *Browning* [1911] P. 161. An infected husband is guilty of cruelty if he knowingly has intercourse with his wife against her will, or if she is unaware of his infection: *Foster* v. *Foster* [1921] P. 438.
20 *Bravery* v. *Bravery* [1955] P. 129.
21 *King* v. *King* [1953] A.C. 124; *J.* v. *J.* (1967) 111 S.J. 792.
22 *Lauder* v. *Lauder* [1949] P. 277.
23 *Hand* v. *Hand* (1967) 111 S.J. 604.
24 *Per* Evershed M.R., *Perry* v. *Perry* [1952] P. 203.
25 See *e.g. Weatherley* v. *Weatherley* [1947] A.C. 628, 671, *per* Lord Jowitt L.C.
26 Desertion only became by itself a ground for divorce in 1937.
27 *Per* Diplock L.J., *Hall* v. *Hall* [1962] 1 W.L.R. 1246.
28 *Perry* v. *Perry* [1952] P. 203.

longer has the necessary intention to desert (often by making an offer to return).

(ii) Although it is based on *factual* separation, it does not follow that the guilty party is necessarily he who leaves: the party who stays behind may by reason of conduct on his part have made it intolerable for the other spouse to stay, in which case, he (by effectively expelling or driving out the other) is in " constructive desertion." A simplified illustration of the complex way in which these factors may interlock may be helpful: H leaves W, who takes proceedings in the magistrates' court for maintenance. She cannot allege cruelty since there is no evidence that her health has suffered as a result of any conduct on H's part, so she alleges desertion. H may claim (i) that he left only because W's conduct drove him out; it is she, therefore, who is in desertion; (ii) that even if that is not so, her behaviour or other circumstances *justified* his leaving. Even if he *is* in desertion he may, at any time,[29] make an offer to resume cohabitation. If W refuses that offer she may be held to have thereby put herself in desertion, even if H had been in desertion up to that moment. All, therefore, depends very much on the court's assessment of H's reasons for leaving. Even more depends on the extent to which H or his advisers manipulate the device of the " offer to return."

Separation De Facto

Factual separation is an absolute pre-requisite to desertion,[30] but " desertion is not the withdrawal from a place, but from a state of things." [31]

There must be a separation of *households*, not a separation of houses. If the parties, although physically present under the same roof, live completely separate lives, the *factum* of desertion is present: the crucial factor is generally whether one spouse continues to provide any marital or household duties in common with the other.[32]

It follows that refusal to perform marital obligations does not by itself suffice: in particular, a respondent's refusal to have sexual relations with the other does not constitute the *factum* of desertion.[33]

The typical instance of desertion is where one spouse leaves the matrimonial home, but it is not necessary that there should be a matrimonial home, and a husband's failure without good cause, to establish a matrimonial home may by itself lead to the inference of desertion.[34]

---

29 *i.e.* even after a matrimonial order has been made (see *infra*, p. 141) unless it contains an effective non-cohabitation order.
30 See *e.g. Price* v. *Price* [1970] 1 W.L.R. 993.
31 *Per* Lord Merrivale, *Pulford* v. *Pulford* [1923] P. 18, 21.
32 *Smith* v. *Smith* [1940] P. 49; *Naylor* v. *Naylor* [1962] P. 253; *cf. Hopes* v. *Hopes* [1949] P. 253; *Le Brocq* v. *Le Brocq* (*supra*).
33 *Weatherley* v. *Weatherley* [1947] A.C. 628. Conversely, participation in one or two acts of intercourse after desertion has started will not necessarily terminate it: the question is whether there has been a resumption of cohabitation: *Perry* v. *Perry* [1952] P. 203. The bar of condonation (see *infra*, p. 103) does not generally apply to simple desertion.
34 *Milligan* v. *Milligan* [1941] P. 78, 83; see also *Dunn* v. *Dunn* [1949] P. 98.

Animus Deserendi

The mental element required is an intention to bring the matrimonial union permanently to an end,[35] inferred from the words and conduct of the spouse alleged to be in desertion.[36] It follows that not every separation will be desertion, since (a) there may be good cause for the separation; (b) the absconding spouse may be incapable of forming the necessary intention; or (c) the separation may have been by agreement.

Good cause

The respondent may be justified in leaving the petitioner against the latter's will either (i) by necessity; or (ii) because of the respondent behaviour.

(i) *Necessity*

In these cases, the defence is really one of " reasonable excuse "[37]:

" [f]or example, a husband may be deported or a wife may be sent to prison for life; each such circumstance affords good cause for separation, and in the absence of any further circumstance neither husband nor wife could be termed a deserter. Similarly, it seems to me that if the health of one spouse demands a state of isolation or separation, the law would be flying in the face of good sense if it were not to recognise that as affording justification for the spouses living separately. . . ."[38]

Nevertheless, the excuse which is advanced must be the real reason for the separation: it follows that if that is (for instance) the need to avoid injury to health, the husband will be guilty of desertion if he makes it clear that he intends to live apart from the petitioner even if and when she recovers.

It is justifiable to say: " I cannot return to you at present," but not: " I will never return to you."[39] (Unless, presumably, it is clear that the condition justifying separation is permanent.)[40] The logic of this distinction is irrefutable, but it gives rise to results reminiscent of the worst kinds of scholasticism: everything is made to depend on the precise words used by a spouse who is probably labouring under the stress of deep emotion. It seems absurd that a wife's rights may depend on her paying lip service at least to a willingness to return whenever it may be safe to do so.

(ii) *The petitioner's behaviour*

One spouse may be justified in leaving the other because of his

---

[35] *Lang* v. *Lang* [1955] A.C. 402.
[36] *Per* Sir W. Greene M.R., *Pardy* v. *Pardy* [1939] P. 288, 302.
[37] See Irvine " Reasonable Cause " and " Reasonable Excuse " as justification for separation (1967) 30 M.L.R. 659.
[38] *Per* Sir J. Simon P., *G.* v. *G.* [1964] P. 133 (husband's behaviour terrified children; separation justified).
[39] *Keeley* v. *Keeley* [1952] 2 T.L.R. 756; *Lilley* v. *Lilley* [1960] P. 158; *Tickle* v. *Tickle* [1968] 2 All E.R. 154.
[40] *G.* v. *G.* (*supra*).

behaviour. This is an area of the law in which there is much confusion. The primary duty of husband and wife is to cohabit; a husband should not be obliged to support his wife, against his will, in a separate establishment.[41] If conduct is not of sufficient gravity to justify a charge of cruelty, it is not of sufficient gravity to excuse withdrawal from cohabitation.[42] Injury to health is not required. If a matrimonial offence [43] has been committed,[44] it gives just cause to live apart from the offender.[45]

Incapacity

Mental illness may prevent the formation of the intention to desert. It is a question of fact whether this is so, and the onus is on the petitioner.

If by reason of insanity one spouse has deluded beliefs about the conduct of the other, the rights of the parties in relation to the charge of desertion are to be adjudicated on as if that belief were true.[46]

The necessary intention to desert must be present throughout the relevant period. If insanity of such a kind as to prevent the continuance of the *animus deserendi* supervened, desertion was, at common law, terminated. This rule has now been altered by statute [47]:

" . . . the court may treat a period of desertion as having continued at a time when the deserting party was incapable of continuing the necessary intention if the evidence before the court is such that, had that party not been so incapable, the court would have inferred that that intention continued at that time."

Consensual separation

If and so long as [48] both parties consent to a separation, there can be

---

41 See *infra*, p. 220.
42 *Per* Sir J. Simon P., *Young* v. *Young* [1964] P. 152, 158; see also *Pike* v. *Pike* [1954] P. 81; *Timmins* v. *Timmins* [1953] 1 W.L.R. 757; *Thoday* v. *Thoday* [1964] P. 181. Examples of such behaviour are *e.g.* wife's persistent charges of unnatural offences: *Russell* v. *Russell* [1895] P. 315 (C.A.) affd. (H.L.) [1897] A.C. 395; *Pike* v. *Pike* (*supra*); failure to provide suitable home for wife on leaving mental hospital: *Clark* v. *Clark* [1956] 1 W.L.R. 345; wilful and unjustifiable refusal of sexual intercourse: *Synge* v. *Synge* [1900] P. 180; *Hutchinson* v. *Hutchinson* [1963] 1 W.L.R. 280, *cf. Beevor* v. *Beevor* [1945] 2 All E.R. 200, and p. 100 *infra*.
43 Provided it has not been condoned, conduced to or connived at: *Wells* v. *Wells* [1954] 3 All E.R. 491. Belief that a " grave sin " has been committed is insufficient: *Kacmarz* v. *Kacmarz* [1967] 1 All E.R. 416.
44 Or is reasonably believed by the petitioner to have been committed.
45 *Glenister* v. *Glenister* [1945] P. 30.
46 *Perry* v. *Perry* [1963] 3 All E.R. 766. See also *Lilley* v. *Lilley* [1960] P. 169; see also *Kacmarz* v. *Kacmarz* (*supra*).
47 s. 2 (4), M.C.A. 1973, also applicable to judicial separation (s. 17 (1) *ibid.*). The provision does not affect the necessity for the existence of *animus deserendi* at the *start* of the period. The Act appears to give the court a discretion, but it is not clear how this is to be exercised: *Kacmarz* v. *Kacmarz* (*supra*) at pp. 421–422, *per* Cairns J.
48 *Nutley* v. *Nutley* [1970] 1 All E.R. 410. Even if the parties are separated by virtue of a formal separation deed this may not be effective: if one party is in fundamental breach of his duties under it (*e.g.* to maintain his wife) and the other elects to treat this as a repudiation (rather than treating it as still in force, *e.g.* by trying to enforce it) the separation is no longer consensual: *Pardy* v. *Pardy* [1939] P. 288; *Hall* v. *Hall* [1960] 1 All E.R. 91.

no desertion. But the fact that one spouse is glad that the other has gone does not mean that he has consented to the separation.[49] The court makes allowance for the emotional realities of the situation, and the consent must have been freely given.[50]

Supervening Desertion

Desertion, as we have seen, requires the coexistence of the fact of separation with an intention to desert. If there is a factual separation it will become desertion if the necessary *animus* supervenes,[51] even if (at the time of the intention coming into existence) the parties were physically unable to live together (for instance because one of them is then in prison). If, however, the separation is *consensual* in origin, it must be clear that the separation is no longer in reliance on it. If the parties agree to separate, the fact that one or both of them subsequently forms the intention not to return will not by itself convert the separation into desertion: it must be shown that the consent is no longer in force, either because it was given for a limited time or purpose which has expired or been accomplished, or because the consent has been withdrawn or because one party no longer relies on the consent and *has communicated this fact to the other party*. It is necessary for the consensual element to be lost on both sides.[52] This gives rise to absurd results. A husband leaves his wife for a business voyage; that separation is regarded (apparently) [53] as justified (rather than consensual); if it can be shown that he subsequently formed an *animus deserendi* desertion begins, without the necessity for any communication to the other. But if the wife leaves, with the husband's *agreement*, to look after her ailing parents, the fact that she then forms an *animus deserendi* is irrelevant because the agreement will still be in force unless and until something happens to terminate it.[54] This distinction, although perhaps logically justifiable, is difficult to apply in those cases where the separation is both justifiable *and* consensual. Suppose that a husband as a matter of politeness asks his wife if she minds his going off on a business trip. It seems absurd that, if he subsequently decides to abandon her, she may be worse off because she has consented to something which she probably could not in any case object to.

Constructive Desertion

The doctrine of constructive desertion has been explained by the Judicial Committee as follows [55]:

[49] *Harriman* v. *Harriman* [1909] P. 123; *Pizey* v. *Pizey* [1961] P. 101.
[50] " Go if you like, and when you are sick of her, come back to me." Not a valid consent: *Haviland* v. *Haviland* (1863) 32 L.J.P.M. & A. 65.
[51] *Pardy* v. *Pardy* [1939] P. 288.
[52] *Pardy* v. *Pardy* (supra); *Nutley* v. *Nutley* (supra).
[53] See *Pardy* v. *Pardy* (supra) at p. 302.
[54] *Nutley* v. *Nutley* (supra).
[55] *Lang* v. *Lang* [1955] A.C. 402.

" Since 1860 [56] in England . . . , it has been recognised that the party truly guilty of disrupting the home is not necessarily or in all cases the party who first leaves it. The party who stays behind (their Lordships will assume this to be the husband) may be by reason of conduct on his part making it unbearable for a wife with reasonable self-respect, or powers of endurance, to stay with him, so that he is the party really responsible for the breakdown of the marriage. He has deserted her by expelling her: by driving her out."

Examples of such behaviour are:

(a) One party physically expels the other.

(b) One party orders the other to leave. Not every such order entitles the spouse to whom the order is directed to leave: it must be clear that the expulsive words were meant [57] and that they were used in a context which justified the spouse who leaves in accepting them as an order to leave.[58] The words must be an *order*, and not a mere *permission*.[59] These are questions of fact.[60]

(c) One party has been guilty of conduct which is *equivalent to* driving the other away.[61] Since this means that a spouse who leaves the matrimonial home may brand the other as a deserter, the courts therefore construed the doctrine restrictively,[62] stressing the need for both *factum* (the outward conduct) and *animus* (the intention) to be present on the part of the alleged deserter.

Factum

The factum of constructive desertion is the course of conduct which is pursued by the husband.[63]

A bewildering variety of language has been used in describing the requisite degree of gravity. The conduct must be:

" such that a reasonable spouse in the circumstances and environment of these spouses could not be expected to continue to endure. This, I apprehend, is what is meant by such expressions as ' serious,' ' convincing,' ' grave and weighty.' " [64]

but need not be such as can be described as cruel in the accepted and

---

[56] *Semble* a reference to *Graves* v. *Graves* (1864) 3 Sw. & Tr. 350; but note that the House of Lords might have to consider whether there was sufficient warrant for the doctrine. In *Gollins* v. *Gollins* [1964] A.C. 644 the existence of the doctrine seems to have been assumed.

[57] *Dunn* v. *Dunn* [1965] 1 All E.R. 1043.

[58] *Charter* v. *Charter* (1901) 84 L.T. 272 (where the complaining spouse was held to have in fact left of her own free will).

[59] *Buchler* v. *Buchler* [1947] P. 25.

[60] *Dunn* v. *Dunn* (supra).

[61] *Per* Bucknill J., *Boyd* v. *Boyd* (1938) 55 T.L.R. 3.

[62] See *e.g. per* Lord Greene M.R., *Buchler* v. *Buchler* [1947] P. 25; see also *per* Denning L.J., *Pike* v. *Pike* [1954] P. 81: " This is yet another case in which the doctrine of constructive desertion has been allowed to run wild. A wife leaves the home, refuses to return to it, and then promptly charges her husband with constructive desertion."

[63] *Buchler* v. *Buchler*; *Lang* v. *Lang* (supra).

[64] *Per* Diplock L.J., *Hall* v. *Hall* [1962] 1 W.L.R. 1246.

decided meaning of that term.[65] It has been said [66] that the distinction is: cruel conduct is unforgivable; on the other hand, conduct may still be sufficiently grave and weighty to justify a finding of constructive desertion even although it is forgivable. The practical difference is that the aggrieved party is bound to forgive conduct which amounts to constructive desertion, subject to certain conditions, so that is open to the deserting spouse to terminate the desertion by making a bona fide offer to resume matrimonial relations.[67]

Animus

In the simplest sense, the *animus* is the intention to bring the married life to an end by driving the other spouse from the home.

The main difficulty arises if the husband (a) did not, in fact, appreciate that his conduct if persisted in, would, in all human probability, result in the wife's departure, or (b) that, whilst he did appreciate that, he nevertheless *desired* that she should stay (" since people often desire a thing but deliberately act in a way that makes that desire unrealisable " [68]).

There is an acute judicial [69] conflict on this issue, between those who hold that such an intention must exist and those who say that the husband is conclusively presumed to intend the natural and probable consequences of his acts, so that if his conduct is so bad or so unreasonable that his wife is forced to leave him, he must be presumed to have intended her to leave and he is guilty of constructive desertion.[70] Those who saw divorce as being concerned to protect an ill-used spouse, rather than to punish a guilty one, tended to favour this latter view.

This controversy is now unlikely to be resolved: a wife who leaves her husband will be able to divorce him in any case at the end of five years,[71] while desertion is no longer so important in relation to financial matters.[72]

---

[65] *Ogden* v. *Ogden* [1969] 2 All E.R. 135, 140 *per* Sir J. Simon P. (Div.Ct.); *reversed* C.A. [1969] 3 All E.R. 1055, see *Le Brocq* v. *Le Brocq* [1964] 3 All E.R. 464, *Marsden* v. *Marsden* [1968] P. 544. But the relationship is very close: see *Young* v. *Young* [1964] P. 152; *Slon* v. *Slon* [1969] P. 122; *Pike* v. *Pike* (*supra*) and *Thoday* v. *Thoday* [1964] P. 181; *Ogden* v. *Ogden* [1969] 3 All E.R. 1055. If the case is brought under the Matrimonial Proceedings (Magistrates' Courts) Act 1960 (see *infra*), a charge of cruelty may also fail because (a) it lacks the necessary element of persistence, (b) there has been no act of cruelty within 6 months prior to the summons. These factors would not prevent the same facts supporting a charge of constructive desertion.

[66] By the Divisional Court in *Ogden* v. *Ogden* [1969] 2 All E.R. 135, particularly *per* Baker J. at pp. 143–144; *cf.* however *Gollins* v. *Gollins*, *per* Lord Pearce.

[67] *Infra*, p. 101.   [68] *Lang* v. *Lang* [1955] A.C. 402 at p. 427.

[69] And academic: Allen (1955) 73 L.Q.R. 512; Goodhart (1961) 79 L.Q.R. 98 (all written before *Gollins* v. *Gollins* [1964] A.C. 644); Bates (1970) 33 M.L.R. 144. See *Gollins* v. *Gollins* (*supra*); *Hall* v. *Hall* [1962] 3 All E.R. 581; *Saunders* v. *Saunders* [1965] P. 499.

[70] See *per* Denning L.J., *Hosegood* v. *Hosegood* [1950] W.N. 218.

[71] s. 1 (2) (*e*), M.C.A. 1973, *infra*, p. 121.

[72] See *infra*, p. 194. The only court in which the question is likely to be litigated is a magistrates' court: even there, in the kind of case under consideration where a wife has good cause for leaving her husband, she could probably obtain maintenance on the ground of his neglect to maintain her, even if she could not establish desertion: see *infra*, p. 219; *Brannan* v. *Brannan* [1973] Fam. 120.

Termination of Desertion

A spouse who has been deserted must take his partner back—

" and thereafter her desertion is at an end. If he will not receive her, he becomes himself a deserter. He cannot say: 'You have deserted me; I will not forgive you for running away and therefore, you cannot return.' During the whole of the current period he must affirm the marriage." [73]

This principle is simply a corollary of the requisite of an *animus deserendi*: not only must there be a physical separation, one spouse must intend to destroy the marriage. However coherent in theory it gives rise to much manipulation in practice: where there has been a separation, a well-advised spouse will send a letter to the other seeking to put him in desertion; at any time a spouse who is accused of desertion may try to rebut the charge simply by making a so-called bona fide offer to return— something he can normally do with impunity because neither spouse is in the least anxious to resume married life. The area of law provides great scope for the more astute tacticians amongst divorce practitioners.[74]

The requirements of an effective offer to resume cohabitation are as follows [75]:

(i) The offer must be genuine in the sense that it must be to return permanently and the offerer must have both the intention and the means to implement it if it is accepted.[76]

(ii) The offer must not be subject to unreasonable (or, at any rate, unnegotiable) conditions.[77] But even if the offer is subject to conditions, the offeree must not ignore it altogether, or refuse to entertain it.[78]

The law is not concerned with affection, but with obligation: in *Price* v. *Price* [79] it was not in dispute that the wife hated the husband, and had hated him for some time before she left. Hating him as she did, she was prepared to go back to him in order to be maintained, and her offer to return was therefore genuine.

This doctrine only applies with modifications if the offer is made by a person who is in *constructive* desertion. For if, say, the wife has left because of her husband's adultery, she cannot be required to condone that adultery [80] by returning to him. Hence she could refuse any offer to resume cohabitation, however genuine and sincere it might have been, without putting herself in desertion. The same result followed if she had

73 Per Hodson L.J., *Perry* v. *Perry* [1952] P. 203, 231–232.
74 As to whether there can be *mutual* desertion see *Hosegood* v. *Hosegood* (1950) 66 T.L.R. 735, 740; *Price* v. *Price* [1970] 2 All E.R. 497, C.A., [1968] 3 All E.R. 543; Irvine (1967) 30 M.L.R. 46.   75 *Fraser* v. *Fraser* [1969] 3 All E.R. 654.
76 *Parkinson* v. *Parkinson* (1959) The Times, April 14; *Storey* v. *Storey* (1962) 106 S.J. 429; [1965] 1 All E.R. 1052n.; *Barnard* v. *Barnard* (1952) [1965] 1 All E.R. 1050n.; *Turpin* v. *Turpin* (1960) [1965] 1 All E.R. 1051n.
77 See *Dunn* v. *Dunn* [1967] P. 217; *Pratt* v. *Pratt* [1939] A.C. 417; *Fletcher* v. *Fletcher* [1945] 1 All E.R. 582; *Slawson* v. *Slawson* (1942) 167 L.T. 260.
78 *Gallaher* v. *Gallaher* [1965] 2 All E.R. 967.
79 [1951] 1 All E.R. 877 (Pilcher J.); affd. [1951] P. 413 (C.A.); see also *per* Brandon J. *Fraser* v. *Fraser* [1969] 3 All E.R. 654, 663.
80 Or, logically, cruelty: *cf. Bowron* v. *Bowron* [1925] P. 187, 195; *Edwards* v. *Edwards* [1948] P. 268.

reasonable ground to believe [81] that the husband had been guilty of adultery, even if in fact he was not.[82]

More generally, if the deserting party has given the other just cause for living apart from him, the deserted spouse may be entitled to refuse an offer to return, either outright, or unless the deserter is prepared to abide by conditions and assurances of better behaviour for the future.[83] Unless the deserting spouse has committed another matrimonial offence, or been guilty of conduct so gross and outrageous that no spouse could be expected to take him back [84] a spouse who rejects an offer to resume cohabitation because it does not contain adequate promises or assurances for the future should, it would appear, specify the promises or assurances she is seeking.[85] Otherwise it may be held that she has rejected a bona fide offer without cause.

Other ways in which desertion may be terminated

These can be dealt with summarily:

(i) A resumption of cohabitation destroys the *factum* of desertion, and is thus the counterpart of the bona fide offer to return (which destroys the *animus*).[86]

(ii) If one party *subsequently* consents to the other living apart (*e.g.* enters into a separation agreement) the desertion ends.[87]

(iii) Other supervening events may remove the duty to cohabit, *e.g.* a court order (such as a decree of judicial separation [88] or a magistrates' matrimonial order containing a non-cohabitation clause [89]) which releases the parties from the duty to live together will terminate desertion.

BARS

In the old law of divorce, it was essential not only that the respondent should be guilty, but that the petitioner should be innocent and justly aggrieved by the other's wickedness. This premiss led to the development of bars to relief in two main cases: (a) where the petitioner himself was a wrongdoer, so that he could not generally complain of the other's offence; (b) if his conduct suggested that he was not in reality labouring under a proper sense of grievance.

---

81 See *supra*, p. 97.
82 *Everitt* v. *Everitt* [1949] P. 374; see generally Tiley, " Desertion and the Bona Fide Offer to Return " (1967) 83 L.Q.R. 89 arguing that in such a case the offer *does* terminate the *desertion*.
83 *Thomas* v. *Thomas* [1924] P. 194; *Bowron* v. *Bowron* [1925] P. 187; *Edwards* v. *Edwards* (*supra*); *W.* v. *W.* (*No.* 2) [1954] P. 486; *Lewis* v. *Lewis* [1956] P. 205.
84 *Edwards* v. *Edwards* (*supra*).
85 *Ogden* v. *Ogden* [1969] 3 All E.R. 1055.
86 *Cf.* s. 2 (5), M.C.A. 1973.
87 But it is presumed to continue in the absence of evidence to the contrary: *Sifton* v. *Sifton* [1939] P. 221.
88 See *infra*, p. 140.
89 See *infra*, p. 141.

Although the bars were abolished for divorce and judicial separation by the Divorce Reform Act 1969,[90] their importance is not solely historical: the complainant's adultery or desertion, connivance, condonation and wilful neglect or misconduct conducing to adultery still remained relevant in magistrates' courts. Adultery and desertion have already been discussed; the remaining bars are discussed in bare outline here, in view of their diminishing importance. Reference must be made to the standard practitioners' works [91] for full treatment.

CONNIVANCE

Connivance means [92] consent to or acquiesence in adultery committed by the other spouse: it is a bar based on the principle [93] " volenti non fit injuria," *i.e.* that one cannot complain of an act to which one has freely consented. It is normally of the essence of connivance that it *precedes* the event [94]: it must be distinguished from mere toleration of adultery which has already started.[95] But connivance at the continuance of an adulterous association *may* show that there must have been connivance from the outset.[96]

Once connivance is established, the complainant will be barred from complaining of adultery with *any* third party,[97] unless he can establish that there is no causal connection between the connivance and the adultery now complained of.[98] This is a question of fact.

There is no connivance if the petitioner merely seeks proof of adultery.[99] It will be different if, by lulling the parties into a false sense of security and failing to take steps to prevent an intimate friendship developing, he effectively promotes or encourages the inception of the adultery.[1]

CONDONATION

" Condonation is the reinstatement of a spouse who has committed a matrimonial offence in his or her former matrimonial position in knowledge of all the material facts of that offence with the intention of remitting it, that is to say, with the intention of not enforcing the rights which accrue to the wronged spouse in

---

[90] Sched. 2. Collusion as a bar to nullity and presumption of death suits was abolished by the Nullity of Marriage Act 1971, s. 6.
[91] See *Rayden*, pp. 1136–1155.
[92] Literally meaning " to wink at " (" connivere ").
[93] *Per* Denning L.J., *Douglas* v. *Douglas* [1951] P. 85, 96, referring to *Forster* v. *Forster* (1790) 1 Hag.Con. 144, 146, *per* Sir William Scott and *Rogers* v. *Rogers* (1830) 3 Hag.Ecc. 57, 58, *per* Sir John Nicholl.
[94] *Per* Lord Merriman P., *Churchman* v. *Churchman* [1945] P. 44, 50, and see generally Tiley (1965) 28 M.L.R. 712.
[95] *Stevenson* v. *Stevenson* [1947] W.N. 83.
[96] See n. 94.
[97] " Can a man, consenting to adultery with A, but not . . . with B . . . say . . . ' Non omnibus dormio.' This is language not to be endured ": *Lovering* v. *Lovering* (1792) 3 Hag.Ecc. 85, *per* Sir William Scott at p. 87.
[98] *Godfrey* v. *Godfrey* [1965] A.C. 444; see (1960) 80 L.Q.R. 466 (A. L. Goodhart).
[99] *Douglas* v. *Douglas* [1950] 2 All E.R. 748; *Mudge* v. *Mudge* [1950] P. 173.
[1] *Manning* v. *Manning* [1950] 1 All E.R. 602.

consequence of that offence. The reason for the rule that condonation bars relief is that it would generally be inequitable to
permit a spouse who has forgiven an offence to go back on the
decision. Matrimony involves mutual obligations and rights; a
reinstatement in the matrimonial position therefore involves the
enjoyment, or the possibility of enjoyment, of those rights through
approbation of the marriage, and the spouse who does that cannot
in fairness subsequently be allowed to reprobate it." [2]

Condonation is thus an application to the matrimonial offence of a
general concept of justice [3]: if A acts in a way inconsistent with his legal
duties to B, B may either accept the repudiation, and treat himself as
discharged from any further performance of his own duties to A, or he
may (notwithstanding the breach) elect to affirm the relationship, insisting
on A's performance of his own further obligations.[4] But he must do one
or the other: the doctrine is an application of the fundamental principle
that " one may not at the same time approbate and reprobate or in the
more homely expression blow hot and cold." [5]

The elements of condonation are:
  (i) the *fact* of reinstatement;
  (ii) the *intention* to forgive;
  (iii) *knowledge* of the offence.

Reinstatement in fact

Mere words of forgiveness, written or oral, are not by themselves
sufficient to operate as condonation: the innocent party must not only
have intended to waive the offence, but must have manifested that
intention by restoring the guilty party to his or her former position.[6]
The analogy with the general doctrine of estoppel is clear: it is necessary
not only that a representation should be made, but that it should be
intended to be acted on, and in fact be acted on by the other party to his
detriment.[7]

What is a sufficient resumption of cohabitation is a question of fact.
Sexual intercourse is now neither conclusive nor necessary.[8]

Intention to forgive

" Forgiveness " must be understood, not in a psychological or theological sense, but in a legal sense as implying merely that the legal
remedy for the wrong committed by the other spouse is to be waived.[9]

---

[2] *Per* Sir J. Simon P., *Inglis* v. *Inglis* [1968] P. 639, 651.
[3] *Hearn* v. *Hearn* [1969] 3 All E.R. 417, 425.
[4] *Ibid.*
[5] *Howard* v. *Howard* [1965] P. 65, 73.
[6] *Fearn* v. *Fearn* [1948] P. 241, *per* Bucknill L.J.
[7] See *per* Phillimore L.J., *Quinn* v. *Quinn* [1969] 3 All E.R. 1212, 1223.
[8] See *Henderson* v. *Henderson* [1944] A.C. 49; *Tynan* v. *Tynan* [1969] 3 All E.R. 1472; *Cook* v. *Cook* [1949] 1 All E.R. 384.
[9] *Per* Wrangham J., *Tynan* v. *Tynan* (*supra*) at p. 1474, referring to *Rayden on Divorce*, 10th ed., p. 284, n. (*a*) [see now 11th ed., p. 1140, n. (*a*)], also approved in *Hearn* v. *Hearn* (*supra*) at p. 422.

Hence there is no necessity for affection [10] in determining whether there has been forgiveness (or reinstatement).

It is not generally helpful to regard forgiveness as a separate requirement of condonation,[11] since the courts will infer it from the resumption of cohabitation: it is no good a husband whose wife has been reinstated showing that he had never forgiven his wife, that he had showed no affection to her,[12] that he still deeply resented her adultery,[13] that the motive for the resumption of cohabitation was economic, or for the sake of the children, or to conceal from the world that the marriage has run into trouble,[14] or that their life together was uneasy and painful, full of animosity and unhappiness.[15]

Until 1963, resumption by a husband [16] of sexual intercourse with his wife was *conclusive* proof of condonation of adultery [17] of which he knew. This rule was abolished by statute [18]; if the parties have sexual intercourse, it is evidence of condonation, which may be rebutted.[19]

The same Act also tried to deal with one of the social problems arising from the concept of condonation: if a wife resumed cohabitation with her adulterous husband to see if they could affect a reconciliation, the result might be (a) that she had condoned his adultery, and (b) by subsequently leaving him (when it became clear that reconciliation was not possible) she had put herself in desertion.[20] A so-called " kiss-and-make-up " provision was therefore introduced [21]; this still applies in Magistrates' Courts proceedings

" adultery or cruelty shall not be deemed to have been condoned by reason only of a continuation or resumption of cohabitation between the parties for one period not exceeding three months, or of anything done during such cohabitation, if it is proved that cohabitation was continued or resumed, as the case may be, with a view to effecting a reconciliation."

This is unfortunately drafted [22]:

---

10 *Hearn* v. *Hearn* (*supra*) at p. 424; *Inglis* v. *Inglis* [1968] P. 639.
11 " . . . The true definition of condonation is that it is a conditional waiver of the right of the injured spouse to take matrimonial proceedings, and it is not forgiveness at all in the ordinary sense," *per* McCardie J., *Cramp* v. *Cramp* [1920] P. 158, 163, approved in *Hearn* v. *Hearn* (*supra*). See also *Quinn* v. *Quinn* [1969] 3 All E.R. 1212.
12 *Hearn* v. *Hearn* (*supra*).
13 *Tynan* v. *Tynan* (*supra*).
14 *Hearn* v. *Hearn* (*supra*).
15 *Inglis* v. *Inglis* [1968] P. 639.
16 The rule did not apply to a wife: *Henderson* v. *Henderson* [1944] A.C. 49, 53, either because (i) she might lack the means to separate herself from the husband: *Keats* v. *Keats* (1859) 1 Sw. & Tr. 334, or (ii) since a wife might become pregnant, she was far more likely to be prejudiced by a resumption of sexual relations: *Tilley* v. *Tilley* [1949] P. 240, 260; *Fearn* v. *Fearn* [1948] P. 241, 254.
17 Or cruelty.
18 Matrimonial Causes Act 1965, s. 42 (1).
19 *Cf. Morley* v. *Morley* [1961] 1 All E.R. 428.
20 Thus, perhaps, affecting her right to financial provision.
21 See s. 42 (2), Matrimonial Causes Act 1965; see generally Hall [1965] C.L.J. 51; Michaels (1965) 28 M.L.R. 101; Irvine, " The Concept of ' Reconciliation ' and the Matrimonial Causes Act 1963 " (1966) 82 L.Q.R. 525.
22 See [1965] C.L.J. 51 (J. C. Hall).

(i) there may be only *one* period of cohabitation (however short) [23];

(ii) it must not last for more than three months. If the parties stay together for longer than that, they must show that there was not a condonation at common law, either for want of reinstatement or forgiveness [24];

(iii) the exception only applies where the resumption of cohabitation is *with a view to reconciliation*, not in cases where a reconciliation has already been achieved [25];

(iv) a resumption of cohabitation may still be very strong evidence of condonation [26];

(v) the onus of proof that the resumption was conditional on reconciliation is on the petitioner, and the respondent must know that he is to some extent " on probation," [27] in the sense that the resumption of cohabitation is a trial attempt only.

Knowledge of the offence

There can be no condonation unless the petitioner has knowledge of the offences in question; if H tells W that he has committed adultery with X, her condonation of that adultery will not condone adultery (of which she does not know) with Y,[28] unless there is an avowed forgiveness of *any* adultery, known or unknown.[29] Essentially, the spouse seeking forgiveness must disclose all material facts which might reasonably weigh with the other in deciding to forgive; if he does not, there is no condonation.[30]

Conditional forgiveness

Condonation is forgiveness, but forgiveness conditional upon proper conduct [31]; the law implies a condition that the guilty spouse shall henceforth be true to his marriage vows [32] and treat the other with conjugal kindness.[33] The bar of condonation " continues only so long as the matrimonial conduct of the repentant spouse continues to be such as the divorce court can accept as consistent with matrimonial duty. . . ." [34]

23 *Cf.* the analogous provisions of s. 3, Divorce Reform Act 1969, *infra*, p. 120.
24 See *e.g. Tynan* v. *Tynan* (*supra*): parties cohabited for 4½ months.
25 *Brown* v. *Brown* [1967] P. 105; *Herridge* v. *Herridge* [1965] 1 W.L.R. 1506; *Quinn* v. *Quinn* [1969] 1 W.L.R. 1394. See (1965) 81 L.Q.R. 172.
26 *Quinn* v. *Quinn* [1969] 3 All E.R. 1212.
27 *Quinn* v. *Quinn* (*supra*).
28 *Bernstein* v. *Bernstein* [1893] P. 292; see also *Inglis* v. *Inglis* [1968] P. 639; *Tilley* v. *Tilley* [1949] P. 240, 262–263; *cf. Wells* v. *Wells* [1954] 1 W.L.R. 1390.
29 *Keats* v. *Keats* (1859) 28 L.J.P. 57, 62; *Lowther* v. *Lowther* (1944) *The Times,* November 11, (1945) *The Times,* February 6.
30 *Inglis* v. *Inglis* (*supra*); see also *Burch* v. *Burch* [1958] 1 All E.R. 848. The cases in which condonation is procured by a fraudulent misstatement of fact are presumably best explained as illustration of this principle: *e.g.* a wife who procures forgiveness by a false statement that she is not pregnant by the co-respondent: *Roberts* v. *Roberts* (1917) 117 L.T. 157. Distinguish a representation as to *future* conduct: *Henderson* v. *Henderson* [1944] A.C. 49, wife promised to break off adulterous association; subsequent repudiation by her did not affect condonation.
31 Gorell Barnes Report, Cd. 1912, para. 375.
32 *Newsome* v. *Newsome* (1871) L.R. 2 P. & D. 306, 312, *per* Lord Penzance.
33 *Durant* v. *Durant* (1825) 1 Hag.Ecc. 733, 762, *per* Sir John Nicholl.
34 *Beard* v. *Beard* [1946] P. 8, 22, *per* Scott L.J.

If the condition was broken, the condoned matrimonial offence would be *revived*. It was not necessary that the conduct relied on to revive a condoned matrimonial offence should by itself be such as would constitute a matrimonial offence. Hence desertion by the forgiven spouse for however short a period revives the condoned offence.[35] But conduct falling short of a matrimonial offence will only revive a condoned offence if it is a substantial breach of duty,[36] such as if persisted in would make married life together impossible,[37] and break up the marriage.[38] In essence the question is one of fact: Is the present conduct of sufficient gravity to exonerate the one spouse from his previous express or implied promise to forgive the other? [39]

The condition is implied by law: it is, however, possible to condone an offence by express agreement in terms excluding any possibility of revival.[40]

The fact that a single act of adultery could be revived perhaps many years later gave rise to a considerable amount of criticism [41]; legislation now provides that [42] adultery which has been condoned shall not be capable of being revived.

The doctrine of revival is less important given the new basis for divorce; it may still have some importance in Magistrates' Courts where conduct falling short of cruelty may revive condoned persistent cruelty.

" CONDUCT CONDUCING " [43]

Conduct conducing was a *discretionary* bar to a suit for divorce or judicial separation based on adultery, desertion or unsoundness of mind. It has been abolished as such, but remains an *absolute* bar to the making of a magistrates' court order on the grounds of adultery.[44] In effect, the conduct must be the *cause* of the adultery [45]: the conduct must be after the marriage,[46] and it must be neglect of, or towards the respondent. If the husband is sent to prison for theft that is not misconduct conducing to his wife's adultery [47] but if he leaves his wife destitute it may be.[48] The defence is not often found today, although it may arise if a man consents to the grant of a foreign divorce decree which he knows to be

35 *Beard* v. *Beard* [1946] P. 8; *Kafton* v. *Kafton* [1948] 1 All E.R. 435.
36 *Beard* v. *Beard* (*supra*) at p. 22, *per* Scott L.J.
37 *Richardson* v. *Richardson* [1950] P. 16; *Ives* v. *Ives* [1968] P. 375, 400.
38 *Jelley* v. *Jelley* [1964] 2 All E.R. 866; see also *Cundy* v. *Cundy* [1956] 1 All E.R. 245.
39 *Cundy* v. *Cundy* (*supra*).
40 *Rose* v. *Rose* (1883) 8 P.D. 98.
41 See *e.g. per* Vaisey J. (dissenting) *Beard* v. *Beard* (*supra*).
42 Matrimonial Causes Act 1965, s. 42 (3) re-enacting s. 3, Matrimonial Causes Act 1963.
43 The usual abbreviated form of " wilful neglect or misconduct conducing."
44 s. 2 (3) (*a*), Matrimonial Proceedings (Magistrates' Courts) Act 1960, *infra*, p. 212.
45 *Brown* v. *Brown* [1956] P. 438 where the authorities are reviewed.
46 *Allen* v. *Allen* (1859) 28 L.J.P. & M. 81, although it has been said that a man who lived with his wife before marriage is bound to take greater care of her, in view of his knowledge of her propensities: *Hawkins* v. *Hawkins* (1885) 10 P.D. 177.
47 *Cunnington* v. *Cunnington* (1859) 1 Sw. & Tr. 475.
48 *Haynes* v. *Haynes* [1960] 2 All E.R. 401.

invalid.[49] There is a close relationship between connivance and conduct conducing: in the latter, the petitioner foresees that adultery is likely without wishing it to be so; in the former his motive is to bring it about.[50]

THE MODERN LAW OF DIVORCE

Divorce is granted on the petition of one or both spouses. The petition is issued in a county court, but the case may be transferred to the High Court if it is contested, or in certain other cases.[51] For historical reasons,[52] the court first grants a decree nisi. The marriage is only ended when that decree is made *absolute*.[53]

THREE YEARS' DELAY

No petition for divorce can be presented before the expiration of the period of three years from the date of the marriage, unless it is shown that the case is one of exceptional hardship suffered by the petitioner or one of exceptional depravity on the part of the respondent.[54]

Although the courts have refused to lay down general rules to fetter the exercise of their discretion,[55] the section has been restrictively interpreted.[56] Adultery may constitute " exceptional depravity " if, but only if, on the facts a sensible, right-thinking, contemporary Englishman would so regard it.[57] If the petition is based on the respondent's unreasonable behaviour, there must be aggravating circumstances.[58] The main consideration is whether the conduct is such as to make reconciliation quite impossible.[59]

If it is to qualify as exceptional, hardship to the proposed petitioner

---

49 *Clayton* v. *Clayton* [1932] P. 45.   50 *Haynes* v. *Haynes* (*supra*).

51 See M.C.A. 1967, s. 1, and the rules made thereunder.

52 See Morton Commission, paras. 947 *et seq.*

53 See *Re Seaford* [1968] P. 53. A decree nisi can now be made absolute 6 weeks after it has been pronounced, unless the court gives special leave for a shorter period (which it will rarely do): M.C.A. 1973, s. 1 (5); Matrimonial Causes (Decree Absolute) General Order 1972; Practice Note (Divorce: Decree Absolute) [1972] 1 W.L.R. 1261; *Dryden* v. *Dryden* [1973] Fam. 217.

54 M.C.A. 1973, s. 3.

55 *Fisher* v. *Fisher* [1948] P. 263. *Cf. V.* v. *V.* [1966] 3 All E.R. 493, where the trial judge refused an application based on allegations (i) that the husband had struck his wife with a bottle some weeks after the marriage; (ii) he refused to go out to work; (iii) he assaulted the wife while she was pregnant; (iv) she had discovered him, after an attempted reconciliation, committing adultery on the couch in the matrimonial home. The Court of Appeal held that the judge's view, that this was " no worse than many spouses have to put up with " was plainly wrong: there was more than one offence, the charges were unusually serious, and the adultery was in scandalous circumstances. *Cf. W.* v. *W.* [1967] P. 291.

56 Applications are heard in private: the paucity of reports makes it difficult to determine on what basis the discretion is exercised: see Morton Commission, para. 217.

57 *Bowman* v. *Bowman* [1949] P. 345; *cf. Blackwell* v. *Blackwell* (1973) 117 S.J. 939.

58 *E.g.* throwing the wife downstairs, breaking bones: *Brewer* v. *Brewer* [1964] 1 W.L.R. 403.

59 *Bowman* v. *Bowman* [1949] P. 345; *Brewer* v. *Brewer* [1964] 1 W.L.R. 403; *C.* v. *C.* [1967] P. 298 (*supra*).

must transcend the inevitable hardship caused by divorce. The test is subjective: the fact that further delay will have a serious effect on a highly-strung petitioner may thus justify a finding of exceptional hardship.[60]

If leave is granted, and it subsequently appears that it was obtained by any misrepresentation or concealment of the nature of the case, the court may either dismiss [61] the petition, or grant a decree but direct that it be not made absolute for three years from the date of the marriage.

The bar does not prevent a petition being presented solely on the basis of matters arising within three years of the marriage[62]: a petition can still be based on a single act of adultery committed within the first three years of marriage.[63]

Nullity and judicial separation petitions are not subject to the bar: a spouse may petition for judicial separation on the basis of (say) a single act of adultery, and subsequently petition for divorce on the same [64] facts.

If a prima facie case of exceptional hardship or depravity is made out, the court has a discretion whether to grant leave or not. In exercising this it must have regard to the interests of any child of the family [65] and to the question whether there is reasonable probability of a reconciliation between the parties if the petition is not presented until the end of the three year period.[66]

Criticism

The conventional view is that this provision constitutes

> " a useful safeguard against irresponsible or trial marriages and a valuable external buttress to the stability of marriages during the difficult early years. It therefore helps to achieve one of the main objectives of a good divorce law." [67]

This seems questionable:

(i) No such bar exists in Scotland. Statistical comparisons suggest that its absence has no effect on the divorce rate.[68]

(ii) It is difficult to reconcile the need to establish " exceptional depravity " with the view that marriages should be dissolved with the minimum of bitterness, distress and humiliation.

---

60 *Hillier* v. *Hillier and Latham* [1958] P. 186; *Brewer* v. *Brewer* (*supra*).
61 Another petition on the same, or substantially the same facts may then be presented after the three-year period: s. 3 (4); *Stroud* v. *Stroud* (*No.* 2) [1963] 1 W.L.R. 1083.
62 M.C.A. 1973, s. 3 (4).
63 Provided that the petitioner finds it intolerable to live with the respondent: see *infra*, p. 112.
64 M.C.A. 1973, s. 4.
65 s. 3 (2), M.C.A. 1973. The expression is defined by s. 52 (1), as to which see *infra*, p. 280.
66 s. 3 (2). As to the relevance of prospects of reconciliation to making out hardship or depravity *cf. Bowman* v. *Bowman* (*supra*), and *Szagmeister* v. *Szagmeister* (1969) 15 F.L.R. 240, and the other Australian authorities referred to therein. See also H. A. Finlay (1970) 1 A.C.L.R. 81.
67 " Field of Choice " para. 19. See also Morton Commission, para. 215, " Putting Asunder," pp. 116–117, and para. 78.
68 See Divorce: The Grounds Considered, Cmnd. 3256, 1967, para. 30; *Mortlock*, pp. 11–12.

(iii) It is inconsistent to impose a three-year bar in divorce, whilst permitting immediate judicial separation (which will almost certainly destroy any prospect of reconciliation) and nullity (granted for certain kinds of sexual incompatibility but not others).

The provision was introduced in 1937 as a manoeuvre to facilitate the passing of the Matrimonial Causes Act of that year.[69] It is doubtful whether its repeal would increase the divorce rate. Abolition would enable the parties to unsuccessful marriages to make a fresh start.[70]

DIVORCE REFORM ACT 1969

The Breakdown Principle

The Divorce Reform Act 1969 [71] introduced the principle that " the sole ground on which a petition for divorce may be presented to the court by either party to a marriage shall be that the marriage has broken down irretrievably."

This provision is however of only limited effect [72]:

(i) The court may not dissolve a marriage, even if it has broken down, unless the petitioner satisfies the court of one or more of five " facts," [73] three of which are based on the old matrimonial offences.[74]

(ii) Although the facts are not " grounds " for divorce but merely *evidence* of breakdown, proof of one of them will raise a presumption (in practice a strong presumption [75]) that there has been a breakdown which is irretrievable:

> " If the court is satisfied on the evidence of any such fact . . . then, unless it is satisfied on all the evidence that the marriage has not [76] broken down irretrievably, it shall [77] . . . grant a decree nisi of divorce." [78]

In legal theory, a simple assertion by the petitioner cannot suffice: the court must consider all the evidence and form its own conclusion.[79]

---

69 See A. P. Herbert, *The Ayes Have It*, p. 65, and the Parliamentary Debates (particularly H.C. Vol. 326, col. 2609).

70 See *Mortlock*, pp. 11–15.

71 s. 1; *cf.* now M.C.A. 1973, s. 1 (1).

72 " Of no real legal significance " (*per* Lord Simon of Glaisdale, The Riddell Lecture (1970), see *Rayden*, p. 3232); " virtually deprived of all effect " by what follows (*per* Lord Reid, Hansard (H.L.) Vol. 303, col. 1271) but *cf.* E. J. Griew [1972 A] C.L.J. 294, 304.

73 s. 1 (2), M.C.A. 1973. *Richards* v. *Richards* [1972] 1 W.L.R. 1073 is a case where the court found that the marriage had irretrievably broken down, but refused a decree because no relevant " fact " had been proved.

74 See *supra*, p. 91.

75 *Santos* v. *Santos* [1972] Fam. 247. And see *per* Ormrod J., *Pheasant* v. *Pheasant* [1972] 1 All E.R. 587, 589J (" a very strong inference ").

76 The relevant time is the date of the hearing: a petition will be granted even if the marriage had *not* broken down irretrievably when the petition was filed: *Pheasant* v. *Pheasant* (*supra*) at p. 588.

77 This general rule is subject to exceptions if (a) leave has been obtained to present a petition within 3 years of the marriage by misrepresentation or concealment (see *supra*, p. 109), (b) in certain cases, if the grant of a decree would cause grave financial or other hardship to the respondent: see s. 5, M.C.A. 1973, *infra*, p. 127.

78 s. 1 (4).

79 *Ash* v. *Ash* [1972] Fam. 135, 141.

In practice, it will be very difficult for a respondent to discharge the onus placed on him of proving [80] that there has *not* been an irretrievable breakdown [81]:

> " If even one of the parties adamantly refuses to consider living with the other again, the court is in no position to gainsay him or her. The court cannot say, ' I have seen your wife in the witness-box. She wants your marriage to continue. She seems a most charming and blameless person. I cannot believe that the marriage has really broken down.' The husband has only to reply, ' I'm very sorry; it's not what *you* think about her that matters, it's what *I* think. I am not prepared to live with her any more.' He may add for good measure, ' What is more, there is another person with whom I prefer to live.' The court may think that the husband is behaving wrongly and unreasonably; but how is it to hold that the marriage has not irretrievably broken down? " [82]

The most that can be hoped for is that the evidence may lead the court to think that there is a reasonable possibility of a reconciliation (in which case it has power to adjourn the proceedings for such period as it thinks fit to enable attempts to be made to effect a reconciliation).[83]

The Divorce Reform Act also abolished the old bars to divorce [84]: divorce is no longer dependent on proof of one spouse's guilt; hence the innocence or otherwise of the petitioner is no longer decisive. It should particularly be noted that the Act contains no provision enabling the court to withhold a decree merely because to grant it would be inconsistent with generally accepted principles of justice and equity.

We shall consider the details of the new law under the following heads: (i) " Facts " upon which a petition may be based; (ii) Circumstances in which a decree may be refused.

Facts evidencing breakdown

It is provided [85] that " On a petition for divorce it shall be the duty of the court to inquire, so far as it reasonably can, into the facts alleged by the petitioner and into any facts alleged by the respondent."

The function of the court is thus inquisitorial: it has a duty not merely to weigh up the evidence the parties choose to place before it, but also, if it thinks fit, to go further in order to get at the truth: the procedure is intended to involve judicial care as opposed to rubber-stamping.[86] In practice it is doubted whether this is of any importance: neither the

---

80 The court must be " satisfied." It is not clear what *degree* of proof is required, probably that there must be a clear finding by the court that the marriage has not broken down irretrievably: see *Blyth* v. *Blyth and Pugh* [1966] A.C. 643.

81 But note that in *Pheasant* v. *Pheasant* (*supra*), Ormrod J. would have hesitated to find that the marriage had broken down irretrievably (see at p. 592). *Quaere* whether this expression of doubt accurately reflects the onus of proof.

82 *Per* Lord Simon of Glaisdale, Riddell Lecture, n. 72 *supra*.

83 s. 6 (2), see p. 135, *infra*.

84 s. 9, D.R.A. 1969.   85 s. 1 (3), M.C.A. 1973.

86 *Santos* v. *Santos* (*supra*) at p. 264. But note that a special procedure has now been introduced for certain consensual divorces which it is difficult to distinguish from " rubber-stamping ": *Practice Direction* [1973] 1 W.L.R. 1442.

machinery of the courts,[87] nor the nature of the relevant questions,[88] leave the court with much choice save to accept what evidence the parties choose to give.

The facts alleged by the petitioner will be those which entitle him to a divorce; those alleged by the respondent may be matters casting doubt on the validity of the petitioner's case, and particularly facts on the basis of which the respondent hopes to establish that the marriage has not irretrievably broken down.

The " facts " are [89]:

Adultery

> " That the respondent has committed adultery and the petitioner finds it intolerable to live with the respondent." [90]

It is necessary to prove (i) the fact of the respondent's adultery, *and* (ii) that the petitioner finds it intolerable to live with the respondent. This dual requirement seems at first sight intended to give effect to the view that an act of adultery should no longer " be regarded as an independent and self-sufficient reason for dissolving a marriage; its import would be determined by the part it had actually played in the relationship between the husband and wife concerned." [91] But it is unlikely that it effectively does so :

(i) The test is subjective, not objective.[92] That is to say: it is sufficient if the petitioner does in fact find it intolerable to live with the respondent; it is immaterial that a reasonable person might not find it so.[93]

However, the court must be satisfied that the petitioner does (however unreasonably) find living with the adulterous spouse intolerable. Mere assertion may not be sufficient,[94] and some reason, explanation or justification for it will normally be given, since in the discharge of its inquisitorial function the court might otherwise be unconvinced.

" Intolerable " is a strong word : a petitioner may be held not to find living with his spouse intolerable, even although he would prefer not to do so. It is not sufficient that he " is merely attracted to another mode of life," [95] or simply prefers to live with someone else.[96] Again, a wealthy couple who decide on divorce so as to get the valuable tax advantages

---

[87] See *Mortlock*, particularly at p. 32 and pp. 52–54.
[88] This provision was originally designed to prevent the court being deceived by collusion between the parties. Collusion is, however, no longer a bar. The provision could still be relevant if the parties put a wholly false case forward, *e.g.* a petition based on two years' separation when they were in fact still living together.
[89] s. 1 (2), M.C.A. 1973.
[90] s. 1 (2) (*a*).
[91] " Putting Asunder " para. 80.
[92] *Goodrich* v. *Goodrich* [1971] 1 W.L.R. 1142; *Pheasant* v. *Pheasant* (*supra*) at p. 590B.
[93] *Cf.* this requirement (*i.e.* " the petitioner finds . . .") and the next " fact " (*i.e.* the respondent has behaved in such a way that the petitioner *cannot reasonably be expected* to live with the respondent ").
[94] *Roper* v. *Roper and Porter* [1972] 1 W.L.R. 1314; *cf. Pheasant* v. *Pheasant* (*supra*) at 590A: " the criterion is adultery coupled with the assertion [*sic*] that the petitioner finds it intolerable to live with the respondent."
[95] J. Levin (1970) 33 M.L.R. 632, 635.
[96] *Roper* v. *Roper and Porter* (*supra*).

conferred by that status[97] may find their attempts to obtain a legal divorce without resorting to a factual separation frustrated by a judicial inquiry: it is the fiscal consequence of marriage, not the fact of living with each other, which is intolerable.

It is also provided [98] that if the parties to a marriage have lived with each other for six months or more after it became known to the petitioner that the respondent had committed adultery, the petitioner cannot rely on that act of adultery. If, however, they have lived together for six months or less, the fact " shall be disregarded in determining . . . whether the petitioner finds it intolerable to live with the respondent." This seems to envisage an inquiry into whether the petitioner does genuinely find it intolerable to live with his spouse or not.

(ii) There need be no causal link between the respondent's adultery and the fact that the petitioner finds it intolerable to continue to live with him [99]: if so, the petitioner is entitled to a divorce provided that *for whatever reason*,[1] he finds it intolerable to live with the respondent, even if the adultery has not played any significant part in the breakdown of the marriage.

This view of the independent operation of the two requirements leads [2] to striking results:

> H and W are free-thinkers who have throughout their marriage licensed each other to commit adultery. As a result of a change of political views on W's part, H finds her company intolerable. He is entitled to a divorce.

> H has frequently committed adultery. W has always put up with this, although she finds it deeply distressing. On one occasion in a mood of despair induced by H's behaviour she commits adultery herself. H does not object, and they continue to live together. They are involved in a car accident, caused by H's drunken driving some four months after W's adultery. H is uninjured, but W is paralysed and now requires constant attendance. H finds this situation intolerable. He is entitled to a divorce.

> " . . . A finds married life intolerable because the expenses of maintaining a household have compelled him to adopt a more frugal style of living than he was accustomed to as a bachelor. He therefore takes Mrs. A to a wife-swopping party, and presents his petition on the following day." [3]

---

[97] *E.g.* their investment income will not be aggregated.

[98] s. 2 (1)–(2), M.C.A. 1973.

[99] *Anderson* v. *Anderson* (1973) 117 S.J. 33; *Goodrich* v. *Goodrich* (*supra*); *Cleary* v. *Cleary* (1973) 117 S.J. 834, C.A., overruling *Roper* v. *Roper* (*supra*).

[1] *E.g.* because the husband blows his nose more than his wife likes: *per* Faulks J., *Roper* v. *Roper* (*supra*) at p. 1317.

[2] When taken in conjunction with the abolition of the old bars of collusion, connivance etc. and the absence of any general bar on grounds of injustice.

[3] J. L. Barton, " Questions on the Divorce Reform Act 1969 " (1970) 86 L.Q.R. 348, 349. A will probably *increase* his expenses, since his wife will be entitled to maintenance at a level commensurate with A's position. See *infra*.

These strange results could be avoided if the section were construed [4] as if it read " that the respondent has committed adultery *by reason of which* the petitioner finds it intolerable to live with the respondent." This construction may be supported [5] by reference to the provisions directing the court to disregard up to six months' living together after discovery of the adultery in determining whether or not the petitioner finds it intolerable to live with the respondent [6]:

> " If it be thought necessary to enact that co-habitation for not more than six months after the discovery of the adultery relied upon shall not be taken into account in determining whether the petitioner finds it intolerable to live with the respondent, it is a fair inference that such co-habitation would otherwise be material. It can be material, however, only on the assumption that it must be the respondent's adultery which makes it intolerable to live with the respondent. If it were sufficient that the petitioner found life with the respondent intolerable for some other reason, the date at which the petitioner discovered the respondent's adultery would not even be relevant. It would be the petitioner's conduct after the events which were alleged to have made it intolerable to live with the respondent which would have to be looked to." [7]

The arguments in favour of the independent construction of the two phrases are:

(i) it gives effect to the plain words of the section. If Parliament had intended to give the section the meaning imported by adding " by reason of which " it would have been simple to do so.[8]

(ii) the result is consistent with the aim set out in the Divorce Reform Act, namely that breakdown of marriage should be the sole ground for divorce. Breakdown is not,[9] but adultery is, a justiciable issue. Once it has been established, the court draws the inference of irretrievable breakdown unless there is evidence to the contrary.

(iii) The reason why literal construction of the Act seems strange is that it produces results unjust [10] to a party who wishes to preserve the existence of the marital status. But the Act is not concerned with such

---

[4] As was done in *Roper* v. *Roper* (*supra*): wife formed liaison with R. Subsequently agreed that H would live with Mrs. R, and W with R. After 18 months H left Mrs. R. W (who continued to live with R) refused decree under s. 1 (2) (*a*): she did not find it intolerable to live with H by reason of his sporadic adultery, which would never have started but for W's conduct.

[5] In addition to reliance on " common sense " (as in *Roper* v. *Roper* (*supra*) at p. 1317).

[6] s. 2 (1)–(2), M.C.A. 1973.

[7] *Barton, op. cit.*, p. 350.

[8] The parliamentary history shows quite clearly that the construction was positively rejected: see Hansard (H.L.) Vol. 304, cols. 1222–1249. The court will not refer to Hansard, but have found this self-denial taxing in construing the Divorce Reform Act: see *Roper* v. *Roper* (*supra*) at p. 1317F, and *McGill* v. *Robson* [1972] 1 W.L.R. 237 at p. 238, and *Wachtel* v. *Wachtel* [1973] Fam. 72, 93, *per* Lord Denning M.R.

[9] *Pheasant* v. *Pheasant* (*supra*) at p. 589G,

[10] As to whether divorce on this basis involves a " stigma " see *Wachtel* v. *Wachtel* [1973] 2 W.L.R. 366, 372, *per* Lord Denning M.R.; *cf. Huxford* v. *Huxford* [1972] 1 All E.R. 330; *Collins* v. *Collins* [1972] 2 All E.R. 658 and *Spill* v. *Spill* [1972] 1 W.L.R. 793.

considerations. It is immaterial that the divorced spouse is [11] " wholly innocent " and the petitioner " wholly responsible " for the breakdown. This is not a reason for keeping in existence the empty legal shell [12] of a marriage which has in fact broken down.

Two further strange consequences stem from the new provision:

(i) It apparently permits immediate divorce by consent (provided that one of the spouses is prepared to commit adultery).

The old law required injury to the petitioner (which he could not establish if he had agreed to the act of which complaint was made) but there is no such requirement [13] under the new law; there is no jurisdiction to refuse a divorce because it is collusive. Adultery is merely the outward and provable sign of a broken marriage. Unlike some of the problems on the interpretation of the Act, this is not academic. A significant proportion of divorces are granted to spouses, one or both of whom wish to remarry quickly. In such cases, two years may seem too long to wait.[13a] If however the law is to allow immediate divorce by consent [14] it is not clear why an act of adultery should be required as part of the price.

(ii) The Act does not stipulate that the adultery should have been committed *since the marriage*. If W (a spinster), having had intercourse with X (a married man),[15] marries H, he may divorce her at any time; if H and W have intercourse with each other whilst both are married to third parties either can divorce the other.[16] The possibility is no doubt entirely academic.

Unreasonable behaviour

" that the respondent has behaved in such a way that the petitioner cannot reasonably be expected to live with the respondent." [17]

Petitions brought under this head are, if defended, unlikely to avoid the

---

[11] It is doubtful whether there are many cases in which these clear judgments can justly be made: see *Mortlock, op. cit.,* particularly at pp. 17, 22–25.

[12] " Field of Choice " para. 15.

[13] If it be held that the adultery must be what makes it intolerable for the petitioner to live with the respondent a petition based on adultery at which the petitioner had connived would fail. [13a] See p. 137 *infra.*

[14] Lord Simon has said " [i]t will obviously require vigilance to ascertain whether it will involve a substantial re-introduction of the ' rigged adultery ' divorce which was found so objectionable." (Riddell Lecture, *supra*.) But it is not clear on what grounds a decree could be refused, unless it is shown that the adultery pleaded has not taken place—as was often said to happen under the old law: see C. P. Harvey, " On the State of the Divorce Market " (1953) 16 M.L.R. 129, 131–132; A. P. Herbert, *Holy Deadlock*, 1934.

[15] Which is adultery: see the definition at p. 92 *supra.*

[16] Subject to proof that he finds it intolerable to live with her. S. 3 (3) of the Divorce Reform Act, which prevented a petitioner basing his suit on adultery if the parties had cohabited for 6 months or more after it became known to him that the respondent had committed adultery, only applied where the adultery had been committed *since the celebration of the marriage.* Hence if either party had committed adultery before the marriage there was a *permanent* vested right in the other to determine the marriage at will. But M.C.A. 1973, s. 2, removed the additional words.

[17] M.C.A. 1973, s. 1 (2) (*b*).

" embarrassment and distress " [18] of defended cruelty cases under the old law. The standard practitioners' manual gives a precedent [19]:

> " The respondent is a man of ungoverned temper and drunken habits, and has habitually used violent and obscene language to the practitioner. [Set out in chronological order the various specific allegations relied on in separately numbered paragraphs, giving particulars as to date and place.] "

Examples of the sort of defence which may be filed are also given:

> " The respondent admits that he struck the petitioner a blow on the jaw as alleged in paragraph 18 of the petition; the same was in self-defence, to prevent the petitioner from wounding him with a knife with which she was attacking him. . . ."

Provision is made for the preparation of a schedule of allegations and counter allegations, in which each counter allegation is to be set out against the allegation to which it relates.[20] The present provision thus enables the parties to act out their grievances and resentments in the institutionalised framework of a court of law [21]: it will involve precisely that hostile litigation which under the old doctrine of the matrimonial offence led " to unnecessary bitterness and frequently has harmful effects on the children who may well love both parents. . . ." [22] It does away with the technicalities of the matrimonial offence, but preserves the concept of breach of marital obligation,[23] with its corollary of guilt and innocence.

The test is objective [24]: can the petitioner " reasonably be expected " to live with the respondent? [25]—not " has the respondent behaved reasonably? "

The decision is one for the court,[26] and normally involves a value judgment about the behaviour of the respondent and its effect on the petitioner.[27] The character, personality, disposition and behaviour of *this* petitioner and *this* respondent [28] must be considered [29]:

> " . . . can this petitioner, with his or her character and personality, with his or her faults and other attributes, good and bad, and having regard to his or her behaviour during the marriage, reasonably be expected to live with this respondent? " [30]

---

18 " Field of Choice " para. 25. As to whether a " stigma " is necessarily involved, see *Spill* v. *Spill* [1972] 1 W.L.R. 793, 795H, but *cf.* per Lord Denning M.R. in *Wachtel* v. *Wachtel* (a case where cross-decrees were granted to both parties under the present provision after a hearing on the merits lasting five days)—" It [*i.e.* a divorce] carries no stigma, but only sympathy. It is a misfortune which befalls both. No longer are there long contested divorce suits. Nearly every case goes uncontested " (at p. 89G).   19 See *Rayden*, Form 21, p. 3046, paras. 9, 10, 11.
20 M.C.R. 1971, r. 35.
21 But it may be a legitimate function of the legal system to supply such a facility.
22 " Field of Choice " para. 25 (c).
23 See *Pheasant* v. *Pheasant* [1972] 2 W.L.R. 353, 357.
24 *Ash* v. *Ash* [1972] Fam. 135; *Pheasant* v. *Pheasant* [1972] 2 W.L.R. 353; *Katz* v. *Katz* [1972] 1 W.L.R. 955; *Richards* v. *Richards* [1972] 1 W.L.R. 1073.
25 Not simply is she tired of him or fed up with him: *Katz* v. *Katz* (*supra*) at p. 960C.
26 *Katz* v. *Katz* (*supra*) at p. 960B.
27 *Richards* v. *Richards* (*supra*) at p. 1079 per Rees J.
28 *Pheasant* v. *Pheasant* [1972] 2 W.L.R. 353, 357.
29 *Ash* v. *Ash* (*supra*) at p. 140.
30 *Ash* v. *Ash* (*supra*) per Bagnall J. at p. 140C.

Since a breach of obligation by one spouse towards the other is involved,[31] it follows that—

> " a violent petitioner may reasonably be expected to live with a violent respondent; a petitioner who is addicted to drink can reasonably be expected to live with a respondent similarly addicted; a taciturn and morose spouse can reasonably be expected to live with a taciturn and morose partner; a flirtatious husband can reasonably be expected to live with a wife who is equally susceptible to the attractions of the other sex; and if each is equally bad, at any rate in similar respects, each can reasonably be expected to live with the other." [32]

But it is not always necessary to establish a " breach of obligation " where the respondent's behaviour is attributable to mental illness: the test is not whether the respondent is morally culpable, but simply whether the facts are such that, after making all allowances for his disabilities and for the temperaments of both parties, the character and gravity of his acts are such that the petitioner cannot reasonably be expected to live with the respondent.[33] Hence, if the respondent has used gross physical violence to the petitioner, it is immaterial that he is not responsible for his actions.[34] Nevertheless, difficult problems will be found in determining the " reasonableness " of expecting one spouse to put up with the consequences of misfortune, such as physical or mental illness.[35] If suffering to the petitioner caused by the *mental* illness of the respondent is sufficient, is it different if his partner is struck down by *physical* disease such as disseminated sclerosis, or cerebral thrombosis, " illnesses that for years encumber all communication or active co-operation in the home "? [36] How far is one spouse required, by reason of the matrimonial obligation, to endure the consequences of the incapacity of the other? [37]

The Act requires that the respondent should have " behaved " in such a way that the petitioner cannot reasonably be expected to live with him: " behaviour is something more than a mere state of affairs or a state of mind . . . [it] is action or conduct by the one which affects the other." [38] Hence if an accident or illness renders a spouse comatose, the petitioner will not be able to rely on this " fact." Similarly, it cannot be sufficient that the respondent suffers from some contagious or other disease such as leprosy. Although it may no longer be reasonable to expect the petitioner to live with his spouse, this is not attributable to behaviour.

It is not clear whether behaviour not directly connected with the

---

[31] *Pheasant* v. *Pheasant* (*supra*) at p. 357.
[32] *Ash* v. *Ash* (*supra*) *per* Bagnall J. at p. 140E.
[33] *Katz* v. *Katz* (*supra*) at p. 961, *per* Sir George Baker P. (adapting Lord Reid's *dictum* in *Williams* v. *Williams* [1964] A.C. 698, 723); see also *Richards* v. *Richards* (*supra*) at pp. 1078–1079.
[34] *Cf. Williams* v. *Williams* [1964] A.C. 698.
[35] See *e.g. Priday* v. *Priday* [1970] 3 All E.R. 554 (cruelty petition under the old law).
[36] *Ibid. per* Cumming-Bruce J. at p. 561H.
[37] The basis of the refusal of a decree in *Priday* v. *Priday* was that it was impossible to characterise the sufferings of a schizophrenic spouse as " cruelty." But that is no longer necessary.
[38] *Per* Sir George Baker P., *Katz* v. *Katz* (*supra*) at p. 960A.

relationship of husband and wife [39] will suffice: if a man is convicted of a criminal offence (such as falsifying accounts or dangerous driving) can it be unreasonable to expect the wife to continue to live with him? The answer probably depends on the gravity of the offence, whether it is repeated, and any peculiar susceptibilities of the wife: an isolated conviction for dangerous driving could scarcely be sufficient, but if often repeated might be so. A single conviction for fraudulent conversion would not normally make it unreasonable to expect the wife to continue to live with the husband, but might do so if it were accompanied by aggravating circumstances (such as a mean course of fraud on old people) or if the wife were particularly susceptible to the disgrace following such a conviction (for instance, if husband and wife were solicitors). Repeated convictions for serious offences will certainly suffice.

The requirement that the behaviour should be " since the celebration of the marriage " was removed from the Divorce Reform Bill during its passage through Parliament; the object was to ensure that it would not be a defence that the conduct had only began some time after the marriage. The result may be that pre-marriage behaviour discovered after the marriage could ground a petition: if a wife conceals the fact that at the time of the marriage she is pregnant by another man a decree might be made: the wife has behaved (*i.e.* by marrying the husband without disclosing that she is bearing another man's child) in such a way as to justify his refusal to go on living with her.[40] It is an open question whether other pre-marital misconduct (*e.g.* that the husband had lived with another woman) could found a successful petition.

Two other possibilities may be mentioned: firstly, if the respondent has deserted the petitioner, two years must normally elapse before a petition can be brought,[41] but desertion accompanied by aggravating circumstances [42] may constitute unreasonable behaviour, and found an immediate petition. Secondly adultery may constitute behaviour which makes it unreasonable to expect cohabitation to continue.[43] In practice this will only arise where adultery cannot be relied on under section 1 (1) (*a*) (*e.g.* because after it was committed the parties cohabited for six months or more [44]). It is true that section 2 (3) of the Act provides:

[39] If it is so connected, it could be cruelty under the old law; see *e.g. Ingram* v. *Ingram* [1956] P. 390 (wife's fascist activities and treasonable conduct cruelty to husband serving in Royal Air Force, as striking at roots of matrimonial relationship) so also convictions for indecent conduct: *Boyd* v. *Boyd* [1938] 4 All E.R. 181; *Cooper* v. *Cooper* [1955] P. 99; *Ivens* v. *Ivens* [1955] P. 129.

[40] A view supported by the fact that, subject to conditions (as to which see p. 61 *supra*) he could have the marriage annulled. In *Sullivan* v. *Sullivan* [1970] 2 All E.R. 168 similar facts were held not to amount to constructive desertion under the old law because misconduct *during the marriage* was a pre-requisite. Note that behaviour *after* proceedings have started may suffice: *Shears* v. *Shears* (1972) 117 S.J. 33.

[41] s. 1 (1) (*c*), M.C.A. 1973.

[42] *Cf. Cade* v. *Cade* [1957] 1 All E.R. 609, 617, 619.

[43] Lord Simon P. has argued that this provision could " cover in itself all cases of adultery which might be thought in justice to give entitlement to a divorce ": Riddell Lecture, p. 3233.

[44] s. 2 (1) (2), *supra*, p. 113. *Cf. Chalcroft* v. *Chalcroft* [1969] 1 W.L.R. 1612.

" Where . . . the petitioner alleges that the respondent has behaved in such a way that the petitioner cannot reasonably be expected to live with him, but the parties to the marriage have lived with each other for a period or periods after the date of the occurrence of the final incident relied on by the petitioner and held by the court to support his allegation, that fact shall be disregarded in determining for the purposes of section 1 (2) (*b*) above whether the petitioner cannot reasonably be expected to live with the respondent if the length of that period or of those periods together was six months or less."

This, however (unlike the bar to a petition based on adultery), does not provide that acts taking place prior to the six months' cohabitation shall be *disregarded*. It merely *permits* the court to take into account the period of cohabitation " *after the date of the occurrence of the final incident* " in deciding whether the petitioner cannot reasonably be expected to live with the respondent. If the total period is *less* than six months, it *must* be disregarded; if it is longer it is relevant, and the longer the period the more difficult it will be to show that the petitioner cannot reasonably be expected to live with the respondent. But the petitioner is entitled to rebut this inference—for instance by proving her inability to get alternative accommodation.[45]

Apart from this statutory bar it would seem that if the petitioner is proved to have forgiven the respondent's acts, he cannot normally rely on those acts as showing that he cannot reasonably be expected to live with the respondent.[46] To this extent, the old bar of condonation [47] is revived under another name.

Desertion

" That the respondent has deserted the petitioner for a continuous period of at least two years immediately preceding the presentation of the petition." [47a]

It will be noted:

(i) A period of two years' desertion [48] is required.

(ii) It must immediately precede [49] the presentation of the petition.[50]

(iii) The period must be " continuous." However, as one of the

---

45 *Bradley* v. *Bradley* [1973] 1 W.L.R. 1291.

46 See *Katz* v. *Katz* (*supra*) at p. 961C, *per* Sir George Baker P.

47 *Supra*, p. 103.   47a M.C.A. 1973, s. 1 (2) (*c*).

48 *Cf.* the three years which was a ground for divorce under the old law: Matrimonial Causes Act 1965, s. 1 (1) (*a*) (ii). The new law reproduces—M.C.A. 1973, s. 2 (4)— the rule that the court may treat a period of desertion as continuing notwithstanding the respondent's supervening insanity: see *supra*, p. 97.

49 But a period of desertion immediately preceding a decree of judicial separation (or a magistrate's *separation* order: see *infra*, p. 141) is deemed immediately to precede the filing of a subsequent divorce petition if the parties have not resumed cohabitation, and the order has been continuously in force since it was granted: M.C.A. 1973, s. 4 (3).

50 Hence it is an *inchoate* offence until then: *Perry* v. *Perry* [1952] P. 203.

measures " designed to encourage reconciliation " [51] it is provided [52] that:

" In considering for the purposes of section 1 (2) above whether the period for which the respondent has deserted the petitioner . . . has been continuous, no account shall be taken of any one period (not exceeding six months) or of any two or more periods (not exceeding six months in all) during which the parties resumed living with each other, but no period during which the parties lived with each other shall count as part of the period of desertion . . ."

Hence resumptions of cohabitation alone cannot prevent desertion being continuous for the purposes of this provision, provided that the total does not exceed six months: if H deserted W in January 1970, W can petition in July 1972 even if they have resumed cohabitation for six months. This is true even if there were not one period of six months' cohabitation, but twenty-six periods of one week or even ninety weekends spread through the thirty months since desertion began. But this rule only applies to determine whether desertion has been *continuous*: the court may draw the inference from frequent cohabitation that desertion never started,[53] or that (having started) it had been *determined* by a complete resumption of cohabitation.[54] Similarly, if a bona fide offer to return [55] is accepted (even if subsequent cohabitation lasts for less than six months) the desertion is still terminated. The offer terminates desertion because it destroys the offeror's *animus deserendi*, not because cohabitation is resumed. There may still, therefore, be tactical advantages in making such an offer.

The expression " has deserted the petitioner " includes not only simple, but also *constructive* desertion, *i.e.* where the respondent behaves in such a way as to drive the petitioner away.[56] In most such cases, the petitioner will be able to rely on section 1 (2) (*b*) without waiting for two years to go by.[57] Constructive desertion may, however, be relevant:

(i) Where the petitioner has been expelled from the matrimonial home without violence. The respondent will be in constructive desertion, yet the expulsion by itself does not necessarily make it unreasonable for the petitioner to live with the respondent. Thus a petition under section 1 (2) (*b*) will fail, but a petition under section 1 (2) (*c*) may succeed after two years.

(ii) A respondent charged with desertion under this provision may reply that, on the contrary (although he admits that he left), the petitioner drove him out and is therefore guilty of constructive desertion.

51 The heading of Divorce Reform Act 1969, s. 3, replaced in M.C.A. 1973 by the less tendentious " Supplemental provisions as to facts raising presumption of breakdown."
52 M.C.A. 1973, s. 2 (5).
53 *Mummery* v. *Mummery* [1942] P. 107; *Ives* v. *Ives* [1968] P. 275; *France* v. *France* [1969] P. 46.
54 *Mummery* v. *Mummery* (*supra*).
55 *Supra*, p. 101.   56 *Supra*, p. 98.
57 There seems little merit in the view that because the Act makes specific provision for " desertion," proceedings based on facts which also justify other charges must be brought under the " desertion " head. *Cf.* Barton (1970) 86 L.Q.R. 348, 350.

The two year period of factual separation is no shorter than that required under section 1 (2) (d) for a divorce based on separation and consent. In many cases, there will be no overlap: a couple may be separated without either being in desertion,[58] in which case the " desertion " " fact " is not available. Where a spouse has been deserted, but is prepared to agree to a divorce, it *may* be advantageous to consent to divorce under the separation head on the basis that more advantageous financial provision can be agreed than the court would order.[59]

Separation

The Act contains two provisions:

(i) that the parties to the marriage have lived apart for a continuous period of at least two years immediately preceding the presentation of the petition and the respondent consents to a decree being granted [60];

(ii) that the parties to the marriage have lived apart for a continuous period of at least five years immediately preceding the presentation of the petition.[61]

These provisions constitute the real novelty of the Act: they permit divorce by consent, and divorce of a blameless spouse by repudiation.

The differences between the two are:

(a) The respondent must *consent* to a decree based on two years' separation. It should be noted:

(i) A positive consent is required.[62] As originally drafted [63] the Bill simply required that the respondent should not object. The change was made to provide greater safeguards for the respondent. It may however mean that respondents with conscientious scruples about divorce will refuse to take the positive step although they would not have *objected* (particularly given the inevitability of divorce after a further three years' separation).

(ii) The capacity required to give a valid consent to dissolution is exactly the same as that for the formation of marriage: does the respondent know and understand what he is doing, and its consequences? [64] This will only cause problems where the respondent is under a mental disability (or is very young); the onus of establishing consent is on the petitioner.

(iii) Rules of Court [65] seek to ensure that the respondent is given such information as will enable him to understand the consequences to him of his consenting to a decree being granted [65a]:

58 *E.g.* because the *separation* is consensual.
59 Since the decision in *Wachtel* v. *Wachtel* (*infra*, p. 194) there would seem little prospect of a petitioner *increasing* her right to financial provision by proving that the other is in desertion.   60 M.C.A. 1973, s. 1 (2) (d).
61 M.C.A. 1973, s. 1 (2) (e).
62 *McGill* v. *Robson* [1972] 1 W.L.R. 237.
63 " What I cannot help knowing is originally in the Bill," *per* Sir George Baker P., *ibid.* at p. 238.   64 *Mason* v. *Mason* [1972] Fam. 302.
65 s. 2 (7), M.C.A. 1973; App. 2, M.C.R. 1971, Forms 5 and 6.
65a See p. 122.

(a) that his rights of intestate succession [66] will cease on decree absolute; (b) that rights to a pension which depend on the marriage continuing or upon the respondent being left a widow, the right to a State widow's pension,[67] and rights of occupation under the Matrimonial Homes Act 1967 [68] (unless the court otherwise orders) will all cease; (c) that there may be other consequences applicable in the respondent's particular circumstances on which the advice of a solicitor should be sought. The rules also provide forms to be used to signify consent; it has not yet been decided whether the court can grant a decree if these forms are not used, but other proof of consent is available.[69]

(iv) Consent will normally be given prior to the hearing of the petition but since the relevant point of time is that of the pronouncement of decree nisi the respondent has until then an absolute right, for any or no reason, to withdraw consent.[70] The proceedings will then be stayed.[71] This may be an effective way of exercising pressure on a petitioner to make advantageous financial arrangements for the respondent.

(v) Consent may be given conditionally—*e.g.* on terms that the respondent will not be asked to pay costs.[72]

(vi) Even after decree nisi, the court may [73]—

" on an application made by the respondent at any time before the decree is made absolute, rescind the decree if it is satisfied that the petitioner misled the respondent (whether intentionally or unintentionally) about any matter which the respondent took into account in deciding to consent to the grant of a decree."

The question is entirely subjective: *did* this particular respondent in fact take the matter into account? (not: would a reasonable respondent have done so?). Thus, if H leads his wife to believe that he wants a divorce so that he can marry X (when in fact he does not intend to do so), or even that if he is divorced he will *not* marry X, but Y (when in fact he intends to marry X), or that his mistress is pregnant (when she is not), or that she is not pregnant (when she is) application may be made to have the decree rescinded.[74] The court's power is, however, *discretionary.* It might not be exercised if the change of mind were for altogether trivial reasons.

(b) There are differences in the application of the special provisions [75]

[65a] Rules also provide a special " rubber-stamp " procedure in 2 year cases, by which a decree can (subject to certain restrictions) be granted entirely on the papers: see *Practice Direction* (*Matrimonial Causes: Special Procedure*) [1973] 1 W.L.R. 1442.

[66] *Infra*, p. 165.   [67] *Infra*, p. 201.
[68] *Infra*, p. 168.   [69] *McGill* v. *Robson* (*supra*).
[70] *Beales* v. *Beales* [1972] 2 All E.R. at 674.
[71] M.C.R. 1971, r. 16.   [72] See *Beales* v. *Beales* (*supra*).
[73] M.C.A. 1973, s. 10 (1).
[74] See *Beales* v. *Beales* [1972] 2 All E.R. 667, 672B: If husband consented to divorce on basis that costs will not be sought against him, he could apply for recission if such an order were made.
[75] ss. 5 and 10, M.C.A. 1973.

designed to protect the respondent depending on whether the two or five year period is relied on. This is dealt with in detail below.[76]

In the case of both " facts " :

    (i) the separation must be " continuous," but by continuous the Act does not necessarily mean continuous. This is because of the " provision designed to encourage reconciliation " [77] whereby up to six months cohabitation must be left out of account. The effect is:

> " during the over-all period of at most five years and six months [78] immediately preceding the presentation of the petition, the parties must have lived apart for at least five years, but . . . these five years may be broken up into any number of shorter periods provided that the total time spent living apart amounts to five years in the over-all period of five years and six months." [79]

Apart altogether from this provision isolated visits will not necessarily interrupt a period of living apart.[80]

    (ii) the separation must have been for a period immediately preceding the presentation of the petition.

    (iii) the parties must have " lived apart " for the relevant period. It is provided [81] that " For the purposes of this Act a husband and wife shall be treated as living apart unless they are living with each other in the same household."

This means that husband and wife can be treated as living apart, even if they are living under the same roof, unless that living is in the same household.[82] The fact is thus similar to the test of factual separation under the old law of desertion.[83] If both parties live under the same roof, the question whether they are living in the same household depends largely on whether one party continues to provide matrimonial services (such as cooking). But the crucial question is whether the parties are living together as husband and wife.[84] In the absence of such sharing of services, two "households" may be formed in the same house.[85] Further, the expression " living with each other " means " living with each other as husband and wife." [86] Even if the wife is providing services for her husband, they will be treated as living apart if the evidence clearly establishes that he is there as a paying guest, and not as a husband.[87]

Does every occasion of the husband and wife not living with each other in the same household constitute living apart for the purposes of the Act or is a mental element required? [88] There are two crucial

---

[76] *Infra*, p. 126.
[77] s. 3 (5), D.R.A., now s. 2 (5), M.C.A. 1973; see n. 51, p. 120 *supra*.
[78] *Mutatis mutandis* for the two-year period.
[79] See *Rayden*, p. 272, para. 114; but *cf. Santos* v. *Santos*, p. 124 *infra*.
[80] s. 2 (6), *infra*, p. 124.
[81] s. 2 (6).
[82] *Mouncer* v. *Mouncer* [1972] 1 W.L.R. 321.
[83] *Mouncer* v. *Mouncer* (*supra*); *Hopes* v. *Hopes* [1949] P. 227.
[84] Barton (1970) 86 L.Q.R. 348, 350.
[85] See *e.g. Hollens* v. *Hollens* (1971) 115 S.J. 327.
[86] *Per* Lord Denning M.R., *Fuller* v. *Fuller* [1973] 2 All E.R. 650, 652.
[87] *Fuller* v. *Fuller* (*supra*).
[88] See *Rayden*, p. 273, para. 115.

questions: (i) does the period of separation only start to run when at least one spouse decides that he is unwilling to continue the matrimonial relationship? (ii) If so, need he *communicate* his decision to the other spouse before the period starts? The difficulties which may arise can be illustrated by examples:

> H is sentenced to ten years' imprisonment. After he has been confined for five years, W (who until then has stood by him) falls in love with X and wishes immediately to marry him. H does not want a divorce. Can W petition under section 1 (2) (*e*)?
>
> H was afflicted with a mental illness in 1967 since which date he has been confined in a mental hospital. He has never behaved in an unreasonable way to W. She decided more than five years ago that she would not resume married life with H, but has never told him (a) because it would upset him, and (b) because at that time she did not wish to remarry. She has now met someone she wishes to marry. There is no hope of H ever recovering sufficiently to leave hospital. Can W obtain a divorce under section 1 (2) (*e*)? [89]
>
> H, with W's agreement, took up employment abroad in 1971. He has now met another woman (who refuses to permit extra-marital relations) whom he wishes to marry. W recognises that the marriage has irretrievably broken down, and is prepared to consent to a divorce. Can H rely on section 1 (2) (*d*)?

The Court of Appeal [90] has held that living apart only commences when one party recognises that the marriage is at an end—he and his spouse are, in common parlance, " separated," rather than simply living apart by force of circumstances. Until that date the spouses are not " living apart," although they may " be apart." [91] However, it is not necessary for the one spouse's decision to be communicated to the other.

The reasons for this decision were:

(a) There is a stream of authority on analogous Australian,[92] New Zealand,[93] United States [94] and Canadian [95] living-apart provisions, running " uniformly and clearly in favour of mere physical separation *not* constituting ' living apart.' " [96] What is required is " both a physical

---

[89] Note that, prior to the passing of the Divorce Reform Act, W would have been able to petition for divorce on the grounds of H's incurable insanity: Matrimonial Causes Act 1965, s. 1 (1) (*a*) (ii).

[90] *Santos* v. *Santos* [1972] Fam. 247.

[91] *Per* Henry J., *Sullivan* v. *Sullivan* [1958] N.Z.L.R. 912.

[92] See H. A. Finlay and A. Bissett-Johnson, *Family Law in Australia*, pp. 330–339; see also J. Neville Turner, " Australian and German ' Breakdown ' Provisions Compared " 18 I.C.L.Q. 896; McCall (1960) 5 U.West A.L.R. 51; Nygh (1966) 6 *Journal of Family Law* 219, *cf. Macrae* v. *Macrae* (1967) 9 F.L.R. 441, *per* Walsh J.A. (at pp. 463–464)—not cited to the Court of Appeal.

[93] See Inglis, *Family Law*, 2nd ed., p. 150; Sims, *Divorce Law and Practice in New Zealand*, 8th ed., p. 118.

[94] See W. Wadlington (1966) 52 Virginia L.Rev. 32.

[95] Under the Canadian Divorce Act 1967–68 (noted by B. M. Bodenheimer, 2 *Family Law Quarterly* 213): see for an examination of the cases (1972) 35 M.L.R. 113, 116–120 (R. L. Deech), *Rowland* v. *Rowland* (1969) O.R. 615.

[96] *Per* Sachs J. at p. 257.

separation and a mental attitude on the part of one or both of the spouses. . . .[97] The relationship does not end so long as both spouses bona fide recognise it as subsisting [98]:

> " living apart does not begin until that date at which, if the spouse in question were compellingly asked to define his or her attitude to cohabitation, he (or she) would express an attitude averse to it. Until this state is reached, cohabitation is not . . . broken. When it is reached, living apart begins." [99]

Parliament and the draftsman (it was said) must have been aware of these decisions. It makes no difference that some of the statutes use the expressions " have separated," or " living separate and apart."

(b) In a number of English cases on other statutory provisions, it has been held that, in determining whether a husband and wife are " living together "—

> " the law has regard to what is called the consortium of husband and wife, which is a kind of association only possible between husband and wife. A husband and wife are living together, not only when they are residing together in the same house, but also when they are living in different places, even if they are separated by the high seas, provided the consortium has not been determined." [1]

(c) There is nothing in the scheme of the Act as a whole to negative this ordinary meaning of the words used. In particular, if mere physical separation were required, absurdity would arise under section 1 (2) (d) when read in conjunction with section 2 (5) [2]:

> " . . . the spouses can spend up to 20 per cent. of their time together without interrupting the continuity of the separation (i.e. six months in two years and six months). Thus . . . a man who came home on leave for less than 20 per cent. of the two to two-and-a-half years immediately preceding the filing of the petition would be in a position to satisfy the court under head (d), even though he and his wife had been on excellent terms until they had a row on the last day of his last leave. . . . Unless—contrary to our view—the Act intended to permit divorce by consent simpliciter, such a result would be absurd. . . ." [3]

(d) The Act provides that " [f]or the purposes of this Act a husband and wife shall [sic] be treated as living apart unless they are " living with each other in the same household." The Court of Appeal rejected an argument that this dual requirement contemplates an association under the same roof if the spouses are not to be treated as " living apart." The provision was probably intended simply to establish that even if two

---

[97] Per Hutchinson J., Sullivan v. Sullivan [1958] N.Z.L.R. 912, 922.
[98] Per Cussen J., Tulk v. Tulk [1907] V.L.R. 64, 65, approved in Main v. Main (1949) 78 C.L.R. 636, 642, and held to be " very persuasive " in Santos v. Santos, at p. 257.
[99] Per Turner J., Sullivan v. Sullivan (supra) at p. 924; see also per Crisp J., Collins v. Collins [1961] 3 F.L.R. 17.
[1] Per Darling J., R. v. Creamer [1919] 1 K.B. 564, 569. See also Bradshaw v. Bradshaw [1897] P. 24; Eadie v. I.R.C. [1924] 2 K.B. 178; Nugent and Head v. Jacob [1948] A.C. 321.
[2] i.e. up to 6 months' cohabitation to be excluded in calculating the period, and whether it has been continuous: supra, p. 123.   [3] Per Sachs L.J. at p. 261.

spouses were living in the same house, they could be held to be living apart if not living in the same household.[4] The section does not use the expression " house," but " household," which has an abstract meaning; the phrase " living together " has a well settled meaning in family law, and if it had been intended to refer to a purely physical fact Parliament could easily have used some clearer expression.

It is submitted that this conclusion is unfortunate:

(i) An Act which is based on simple clear-cut evidential guides should not be complicated by unnecessary investigation into mental states. A factual separation gives an easily justiciable *indication* of breakdown. If the petitioner has only recently formed the intention to repudiate the marriage, this *may* justify the court in rejecting the prima facie inference of breakdown, by holding that it is not satisfied that the marriage has irretrievably broken down.

(ii) Any injustice, caused by requiring no more than a physical separation, is inherent in the scheme of the Act. It is not mitigated by the Court of Appeal's decision that an *uncommunicated* intention to terminate the marriage suffices. If the intention had to be communicated in order to start the period of separation, at least the respondent could then try to persuade the petitioner to change his mind.

(iii) The Court of Appeal's interpretation encourages the formation of a secret but recorded intent to terminate the marriage at an early stage, and this runs counter to the Act's professed object of facilitating reconciliation in matrimonial causes. The wife whose husband is confined in a mental hospital will be well advised to place on record her intention to abandon the marriage: if she puts such thoughts out of her mind, loyally holding on to the marriage, she will have to wait another five years from the date when she finally gives up hope. This is particularly harsh when it is recalled that the English Act (unlike some of the Commonwealth provisions to which reference has been made) does not allow divorce on the specific grounds of insanity or imprisonment.[5]

Circumstances in which a decree may be refused

Even if one or more of the above " facts " are proved, the court may nevertheless refuse to dissolve the marriage:

(1) If it is satisfied that the marriage has not broken down irretrievably.[6]

(2) If a decree nisi has been made on the basis of two years' separation, it may be rescinded if the petitioner misled the respondent about any matter which the respondent took into account in deciding to consent to the decree.[7]

---

4 See *supra*, p. 95 and *cf. Smith* v. *Smith* [1940] P. 49; *Hopes* v. *Hopes* [1949] P. 227, and *Evans* v. *Evans* [1948] 1 K.B. 175.
5 Parliament rejected amendments of the Divorce Reform Bill designed to implement the interpretation of the Act adopted by the court in *Santos* v. *Santos*: see Hansard (H.L.) Vol. 304, cols. 1082–1130.
6 M.C.A. 1973, s. 1 (4), *supra*, p. 110.   7 *Supra*, p. 122. M.C.A. 1973, s. 10 (1).

(3) If there are children of the family a decree must not normally be made absolute unless the court has satisfied itself about the arrangements for their welfare.[8]

(4) The Act contains two provisions designed primarily to protect the " innocent " wife which apply only to petitions based on separation:

Refusal of decree in five year separation cases on grounds of grave hardship to respondent

" (1) The respondent to a petition for divorce in which the petitioner alleges five years' separation may oppose the grant of a decree on the ground that the dissolution of the marriage will result in grave financial or other hardship to him and that it would in all the circumstances be wrong to dissolve the marriage.

(2) Where the grant of a decree is opposed by virtue of this section, then,

(a) if the court finds that the petitioner is entitled to rely in support of his petition on the fact of five years' separation, and makes no such finding as to any other fact mentioned in section 1 (2) above, and

(b) if apart from this section the court would grant a decree on the petition,

the court shall consider all the circumstances, including the conduct of the parties to the marriage and the interests of those parties and of any children or other persons concerned, and if of opinion that the dissolution of the marriage will result in grave financial or other hardship to the respondent and that it would in all the circumstances be wrong to dissolve the marriage it shall dismiss the petition.

(3) For the purposes of this section hardship shall include the loss of the chance of acquiring any benefit which the respondent might acquire if the marriage were not dissolved." [9]

It should be noted:

(i) The section is not available unless the only fact pleaded and proved is five years' separation, *i.e.* where the decree is being sought against an " innocent " spouse who does not consent to it being made.

(ii) It provides a defence to the petition, but a defence of last resort. It is only to be used if " apart from this section [the court] would grant a decree nisi " [10]; the five year separation fact and irretrievable breakdown must first be established. The defence if successful will thus, contrary to the general policy of the Act, keep in existence an " empty legal shell." [11]

(iii) The petition must be dismissed if *two* matters are established:

---

[8] p. 272 *infra*.
[9] M.C.A. 1973, s. 5, based on D.R.A. 1969, s. 4, slightly amended to take account of drafting defects: see Law Commission No. 51, Appendix, para. 1.
[10] s. 5 (2) (*b*).
[11] " Field of Choice " para. 15.

(a) that dissolution will result in " grave financial or other hardship to the respondent " [12] and (b) " that it would in all the circumstances be wrong to dissolve the marriage." [13]

A number of difficulties arise:

(a) The hardship must be " grave ": this must mean something more than the hardship [14] almost inevitably arising when a wife is " put away " under this provision, and the onus of proof is on the respondent.[15] The words have to be considered subjectively in relation to the particular marriage and the circumstances of the parties [16]: the loss of a very small sum may be grave hardship to a woman with a small income.[17]

(b) The hardship must result from the *dissolution* of the marriage, not from its *breakdown* (which, *ex hypothesi*, has already occurred).[18]

What is in point is the contrast between the respondent's position as a *separated* wife and her position as a *divorced* woman.

The financial differences resulting from *dissolution* are [19]

(i) the husband will be able to contract a further marriage, thus involving himself in legal obligations to his second wife. Without a divorce he could not confer any legal entitlement to financial provision on any other woman. It is doubtful whether this will make any substantial difference. In assessing the husband's capacity to pay maintenance to a separated wife the mistress's moral claim on his resources is not disregarded [20] and if that moral claim is converted to a legal one, the *quantum* of any maintenance claim by the second wife will probably be reduced to give effect to the first wife's rights.[21]

(ii) The Act defines [22] " hardship " as " including " the loss of the chance of acquiring any benefit which the respondent might acquire if the marriage were not dissolved. These benefits will normally [23] be:

[12] In order to give the respondent an opportunity to decide whether to defend on its ground the Rules provide that the petition must contain details of the petitioner's financial proposals, and that he must swear an affidavit of means and commitments.
[13] *Mathias* v. *Mathias* [1972] Fam. 287.
[14] *Ibid. per* Davies L.J. at p. 301.
[15] *Ibid. per* Davies L.J.
[16] *Talbot* v. *Talbot* (1971) 115 S.J. 870, approved in *Mathias* v. *Mathias* (*supra*), *Parker* v. *Parker* [1972] Fam. 116.
[17] *Dorrell* v. *Dorrell* [1972] 3 All E.R. 343.
[18] *Talbot* v. *Talbot* (*supra*).
[19] There may be special circumstances in relation to the special facts of a particular marriage: see *Mathias* v. *Mathias* (*supra*) where the wife (unsuccessfully) argued that grave hardship would be caused by (a) the loss of her right to have a maintenance award deducted from her husband's army pay, and (b) the loss of her financial security as the wife of a serving soldier.
[20] " It is the practice of the judges and registrars of [the Family] Division to refuse to draw a rigid line between legally enforceable obligations and ' moral ' obligations or to insist on shutting their eyes to the latter . . . ": *per* Rees J., *Roberts* v. *Roberts* [1970] P. 1; see also *Attwood* v. *Attwood* [1968] P. 591, *infra*, p. 198.
[21] It is " . . . quite impossible for the courts to ignore the just claims of the first wife because the man has taken on himself other obligations, although the courts have to take into account those obligations as involving a reduction in the capacity of the man to pay for the upkeep of his first wife." *Per* Hobson L.J. *Cockburn* v. *Cockburn* [1957] 3 All E.R. 260, 263.   [22] s. 5 (3).
[23] There may be special circumstances: see *Trippas* v. *Trippas* [1973] 2 W.L.R. 585.

(a) loss of the right to succeed as a surviving spouse on the husband's intestacy.[24] In practice, the chance of a man who is separated from his wife (and living with someone else) failing to make a will excluding his wife from benefit is remote.

(b) the loss of a widow's entitlement [25] to National Insurance benefits or payments from a private pension scheme.[26]

Most of the cases in which the court has found " grave financial hardship " have been based on loss of such rights.[27] In *Parker* v. *Parker*,[28] for instance, a wife aged forty-seven was entitled, contingently on surviving her husband, to a pension under the police pension scheme. It was held that this loss of possible future security after the death of her husband, at a time when she would most need it, was a grave hardship when considered in the light of her probable financial stringency on attaining the age of sixty.[29]

It has been held that grave financial hardship may be made out even if a reduction in pension would be fully compensated for by payment of increased supplementary benefit [30]:

" the fact that social security is available to a wife is not a reason for a man refusing to carry out, or being excused from carrying out, his obligation to maintain his wife." [31]

But that consideration is relevant only in determining what financial provision the husband can reasonably be expected to make. It is only when the courts' powers in this regard are exhausted [32] that the question arises whether grave financial hardship will result from the dissolution. That question, it is submitted, should be answered solely by reference to the respondent's overall financial position, and not by reference to its source. Social Security payments may be far more dependable than a husband's maintenance payments.

(c) There has been little extended judicial discussion [33] of what grave [34] hardship " other " than financial will suffice.

It might perhaps be shown if a woman had a job for which marriage was a condition. If her husband were able to provide adequate funds she would not suffer financial hardship but the deprivation might nevertheless constitute grave hardship.[35] On the other hand it seems difficult to accept

---

[24] See *infra*, p. 165.
[25] *i.e.* not a surviving divorced former wife's.
[26] See the explanation *infra*, pp. 201 to 204.
[27] *Parker* v. *Parker* [1972] Fam. 116. *Dorrell* v. *Dorrell* (*supra*); *Julian* v. *Julian* (1972) 116 S.J. 763; *cf. Lee* v. *Lee* (1973) 117 S.J. 616.
[28] *Supra*.
[29] *Per* Cumming-Bruce J. at p. 123.
[30] *Dorrell* v. *Dorrell* (*supra*).
[31] *Per* Sir G. Baker P. at p. 348.
[32] And note the petitioner's rights under M.C.A. 1973, s. 10. See *infra*, p. 131.
[33] See however *Banik* v. *Banik* [1973] 1 W.L.R. 860, *cf. Parghi* v. *Parghi* (1973) 117 S.J. 582.
[34] This word qualified both financial *and* other hardship: *Parker* v. *Parker*; *Dorrell* v. *Dorrell* (*supra*).
[35] See *Lee* v. *Lee* (1973) 117 S.J. 616 (decree refused; wife would be unable to look after disabled son).

that a respondent's religious objections to divorce, sense of social stigma, or deprivation of marital status can by themselves constitute " grave hardship." A Roman Catholic (for instance) will still be able to regard the marriage as indissoluble, even although the secular courts have purported to dissolve it.[36] So far as social stigma is concerned, the court has to be satisfied that grave hardship is in fact caused to the respondent [37] while loss of status is inherent in the scheme of the Act.[38] This provision seems unlikely to be of much practical importance.[39]

(i) If, *but only if,* the court is satisfied that such hardship will result, it will proceed to the next stage, and consider whether it would " in all the circumstances " be wrong to dissolve the marriage.[40] Attention is specifically directed to:

(a) The conduct of the parties to the marriage.[41] Under this head the court might, for example, take into account that the " innocent " respondent had contributed to the breakdown of the marriage,[41a] so that it would not be wrong to dissolve the marriage. Conversely, the petitioner's own misconduct might be a factor to take into account in deciding whether it would be wrong to dissolve the marriage. Conduct includes for this purpose lack of candour in disclosing the petitioner's financial position.[42]

(b) The interests of those parties. It will obviously be a material factor that the petitioner may wish to re-marry [43]; it may also be thought to be in the interest of the respondent that the empty legal shell be destroyed, in the hope that she will find a happy future with another man as husband.[44]

(c) The interests of any children. It is clearly material to consider the interests of the children of the parties (although given that the spouses

---

36 *Cf. Painter* v. *Painter* (1963) 4 F.L.R. 216. In *Banik* v. *Banik (supra)* the Court of Appeal held that social ostracism attaching to divorced women was capable of constituting grave hardship; *cf. Banik* v. *Banik (No. 2)* (1973) 117 S.J. 874.

37 *Ibid.*

38 *Cf. Macrae* v. *Macrae* (1967) 9 F.L.R. 441.

39 *Cf.* the Australian legislation, permitting the court to withhold a decree if it would be " harsh and oppressive " to the respondent: see Finlay and Bissett-Johnson, *Family Law in Australia,* pp. 385–393; *Painter* v. *Painter* (1963) 4 F.L.R. 216; *Raggett* v. *Raggett* (1968) 13 F.L.R. 316; *McDonald* v. *McDonald* (1967) 9 F.L.R. 441; *Taylor* v. *Taylor (No. 2)* (1961) 2 F.L.R. 371; *Judd* v. *Judd* [1961] 3 F.L.R. 207, and generally, D. M. Selby, " The Development of Divorce Law in Australia " (1966) 29 M.L.R. 473.

40 *Parker* v. *Parker (supra)* at p. 118E. It follows that there is no discretion to refuse a decree merely because it is " wrong in all the circumstances to do so." Lord Reid's attempt to give the court such power was described by Lord Denning M.R. " a niggling little amendment which should not take up the time of your Lordships " [Hansard (H.L.) Vol. 304, col. 182] but the result is that the court has no discretion to refuse a decree in cases " where the petitioner had not only been patently responsible for ending the common life, but had blatantly flouted the obligations of marriage and treated the other party abominably " [" Putting Asunder " para. 66, p. 52–53].

41 Adequate notice of such allegations must be given: *Parker* v. *Parker (supra)* at p. 119. Voluminous pleadings may result: see the example given in *Rule* v. *Rule* [1971] 3 All E.R. at 1373B.

41a *Brickell* v. *Brickell* [1973] 3 All E.R. 508.

42 *Dorrell* v. *Dorrell (supra)*.

43 In *Parker* v. *Parker (supra)*, the husband would increase his prospects of promotion in the police force if he were able to regularise his adulterous relationship.

44 *Mathias* v. *Mathias (supra)* where the wife was 32, the husband 35.

have already been separated for five years, it is unlikely that their interests will be adversely affected by divorce [45]). The interests of the petitioner's illegitimate children (who will be legitimated by his marrying their mother) will often be in point. The interests of children of neither party may occasionally be relevant: for example the welfare of his mistress's children (by a previous union) might be promoted by giving her the stability and respectability of marriage with the petitioner.

(d) The interest of any other persons concerned. The obvious example is the petitioner's mistress, whom he will marry if he is made free to do so. But there might be other persons concerned: if the respondent's wife had a relative dependent on her, it might be relevant to consider the impact on him or her of the wife's loss of succession and pension rights.

The court then weighs up these factors and the desirability in the public interest of ending " empty ties " against the " grave financial or other hardship " which it has found will be caused to the respondent.[46] It is only if, having done so, it is of opinion that it would be wrong [47] in all the circumstances to do so, that it must dismiss the petition; it may well not be " wrong " to destroy the empty legal shell, even at the expense of grave hardship to the wife. There have been few cases in which a decree has been refused. In *Julian* v. *Julian*,[48] for instance:

The husband was 61, and the wife 58. Neither was in good health. The wife was getting maintenance, which could be increased to £946 per annum. But this would cease if the husband pre-deceased her, and she would lose her right to a police widow's pension of £790 per annum. The only financial provision the husband could make for her after his death was an annuity of £215. Grave financial hardship was thus clearly established. The court also held that it would be wrong in all the circumstances to dissolve the marriage: it could not be said to be hard on the husband to deprive him of the chance to remarry, given his age, health and circumstances.

The section seems thus likely to be used primarily to protect middle-aged and elderly wives [49] against the loss of pension rights, and then only very sparingly.

Special protection for respondent in separation cases: proceedings after decree nisi [50]

" (2) The following provisions of this section apply where—

---

[45] *Cf. Mathias* v. *Mathias* (*supra*) where the wife claimed that the birth of further legitimate children would diminish the existing child's expectations under a settlement. In the case of settlements made since 1970, illegitimate children may well be beneficiaries: s. 15, F.L.R.A. 1969.

[46] *Talbot* v. *Talbot*; *Mathias* v. *Mathias* (*supra*).

[47] *i.e.* " unjust " or " not right ": *Brickell* v. *Brickell* (*supra*), *cf.* p. 511.

[48] *Julian* v. *Julian*; *Lee* v. *Lee* (*supra*). In *Dorrell* v. *Dorrell* the hearing was adjourned so that the husband could make proposals.

[49] *Cf. Mathias* v. *Mathias* (*supra*).

[50] M.C.A. 1973, s. 10 (2), reproducing (with some drafting amendments) s. 5, D.R.A. 1969.

   (a) the respondent to a petition for divorce in which the petitioner alleged two years' or five years' separation coupled, in the former case, with the respondent's consent to a decree being granted, has applied to the court for consideration under subsection 3 below of his financial position after the divorce; and

   (b) the court has granted a decree on the petition on the basis of a finding that the petitioner was entitled to rely in support of his petition on the fact of two years' or five years' separation (as the case may be) and has made no such finding as to any other fact mentioned in section 1 (2) above.

  (3) The court hearing an application by the respondent under subsection (2) above shall consider all the circumstances, including the age, health, conduct, earning capacity, financial resources and financial obligations of each of the parties, and the financial position of the respondent as, having regard to the divorce, it is likely to be after the death of the petitioner should the petitioner die first; and subject to subsection 4 below, the court shall not make the decree absolute unless it is satisfied—

   (a) that the petitioner should not be required to make any financial provision for the respondent, or

   (b) that the financial provision made by the petitioner for the respondent is reasonable and fair or the best that can be made in the circumstances.

  (4) The court may if it thinks fit proceed without observing the requirements of subsection 3 above if—

   (a) it appears that there are circumstances making it desirable that the decree should be made absolute without delay, and

   (b) the court has obtained a satisfactory undertaking from the petitioner that he will make such financial provision for the respondent as the court may approve." [51]

This section is intended to give financial protection to a respondent. Its scope is more limited than that given by section 5.[52] It should be noted:

  (i) The application will be heard *after* a decree nisi has been granted.[53] If successful the decree nisi will not be made absolute, thus leaving the parties in an unsatisfactory twilight zone between marriage and divorce.

  (ii) An application can be made under this section, both (a) by a respondent who does not want to be divorced [54] *and* (b) by a respondent who consents to divorce.[54]

  (iii) Unlike section 5, this section is concerned solely with financial matters. The object of the inquiry is to satisfy the court (a) that the petitioner should not be required to make any financial provision for the respondent, or (b) that the financial provision made by the petitioner for the respondent is reasonable and fair or the best that can be made in the

[51] See *Grigson* v. *Grigson* (1973) *The Times,* November 6.
[52] *Mathias* v. *Mathias* [1972] Fam. 287.　　　　　[53] M.C.R. 1971, r. 57, Form 11.
[54] So that the petition is based on 5 years' separation.

circumstances. It enables the court to carry out a detailed investigation into financial arrangements,[55] and is in some way comparable to provisions requiring the court to approve arrangements for children [56]: although in principle it has been found right to dissolve the marriage, this should not finally be done until arrangements have been made to cope with consequential problems. Often the section will be used in conjunction with an application under section 5. That may have failed, either (a) because the court is not satisfied that " grave financial hardship " will result from the dissolution, or (b) because it is thought right to dissolve the marriage even though such hardship will result. In either case section 10 enables the respondent to probe thoroughly the financial consequences [57] and seek a fair solution. It nevertheless recognises that the financial provision made by the petitioner is only " the best that can be made in the circumstances." This will often be the case when the court accepts that the divorce will inevitably result in grave financial hardship.

It is at first sight difficult to see why a respondent who has consented to a divorce should nevertheless be able to apply under section 10 to prevent the decree being made absolute [58]: if a consenting respondent has been *misled* the decree can be rescinded under section 10 (1) of the Matrimonial Causes Act 1973.[59] There are, it is suggested, two possible uses for the section: (i) it ensures that an investigation is made. The wife may suspect that she has been misled, and yet not have sufficient evidence to justify rescission. In any case she may herself want a divorce so that rescission would be inappropriate. (ii) A wife who recognises that divorce is inevitable may be able to secure favourable financial treatment by using the section to put pressure on her husband. This may be particularly helpful if she wants to persuade him to offer financial provision of a kind that the court cannot order. The court has virtually unfettered power to deal with her husband's income as it arises and to order transfers of his property. But there is no way (save by ordering a lump sum—which the husband may not possess) by which the court can *order* the husband to satisfy the wife's reasonable expectations after the husband's normal retiring age.[60] She is at risk in two ways: (a) if the husband survives until retirement age and then draws a pension, it is true that he could be ordered to pay maintenance to his wife out of it. But even in this case, given (i) that his pension is likely to be less than his normal earnings and

---

[55] *Grigson* v. *Grigson* (*supra*).

[56] s. 41, M.C.A. 1973, see pp. 271–274 *infra*.

[57] Hence, it is highly relevant whether the petitioner has not been frank in disclosing his financial affairs: *Dorrell* v. *Dorrell* (*supra*). Note that the decree will not be made absolute unless and until the proposals have actually been carried out: *Wilson* v. *Wilson* [1973] 1 W.L.R. 555.

[58] See Passingham, *The Divorce Reform Act 1969*, pp. 27–28.

[59] *Supra*, p. 122. S. 10 (1) only applies where the petition has been based on s. 1 (2) (*d*), not where a respondent has, under a misapprehension, withdrawn her objection and allowed a section 1 (2) (*e*) petition to go undefended. In this use, s. 10 may be used to prevent the decree being made absolute, and the court may rescind the decree under its inherent jurisdiction: *Parkes* v. *Parkes* [1971] 1 W.L.R. 1481.

[60] See Law Commission No. 25, pp. 145 *et seq.*

(ii) that he may by then have acquired other financial responsibilities, the court might order a smaller payment to the first wife than she had previously been receiving. (b) The husband might die before attaining pension age. In this case, a pension could, under a private pension scheme, only be paid if a former wife were a beneficiary under the terms of the trust deed. If she were not, she could receive nothing.[61] In this kind of case the court could use its powers under section 10 to encourage the husband to make proper arrangements.[62]

Provisions Designed to encourage Reconciliation [63]

The divorce law was often criticised because, far from encouraging reconciliation between estranged couples, it made it less likely: the risk of such an attempt constituting the bar of condonation led lawyers to advise their clients to have no dealings with the other spouse.[64]

The Divorce Reform Act introduced for the first time the notion of reconciliation as a positive feature of matrimonial litigation. There are three provisions, all of which are welcome. But it is doubtful if they have had any significant effect.[65]

Discussion with a solicitor

A petitioner's solicitor must file a certificate as to whether he has discussed with the petitioner the possibility of a reconciliation [66] and given him the names and addresses of persons qualified to help in this regard.[67] This does not *require* a solicitor to discuss reconciliation with his client: there may be cases in which that would be wholly inappropriate. The object of the procedure has been officially stated as being [68]:

> " . . . to ensure that parties know where to seek guidance when there is sincere desire for reconciliation; it is important that reference to a marriage guidance counsellor or a probation officer should not be regarded as a formal step [69] which must be taken in all cases irrespective of whether or not there is any prospect of a reconciliation."

Even if counselling fails to bring the parties together it may serve a valuable function in identifying the issues (*e.g.* as to children or financial

---

[61] As in *Parker* v. *Parker* (*supra*), where the husband made proposals to avoid the hardship before the decision on the wife's s. 5 application had been concluded.

[62] But it may not be right to place too heavy a burden on the husband as the price of decree absolute: *Talbot* v. *Talbot* (*supra*).

[63] See generally E. J. Griew, " Marital Reconciliation—Contexts and Meanings " [1972A] C.L.J. 294. *Mortlock*, Chap. 12; Hambly and Turner, pp. 10–14, 298–299, and the material there referred to.

[64] See " Field of Choice " paras. 29 *et seq.*

[65] " The fact is that the reconciliation provisions are a dead letter " *per* J. Jackson Q.C. (1973) 89 L.Q.R. at p. 424; *cf.* E. J. Griew, *op. cit.*, *supra*, at p. 307.

[66] M.C.A. 1973, s. 6 (1); M.C.R. 1971, r. 12 (3) and Form 3. The provision was influenced by Australian legislation (" Field of Choice " para. 31).

[67] For details see *Practice Direction (Divorce: Reconciliation) (No.* 2) [1972] 1 W.L.R. 1309.

[68] *Ibid.*

[69] *Cf.* the compulsory reconciliation procedure provisions of some foreign laws.

matters [70]) which can be settled by agreement, and in reconciling individuals to the inevitability of divorce.[71]

Adjournment of proceedings

If at any stage of proceedings for divorce it appears to the court that there is a reasonable possibility of a reconciliation between the parties to a marriage, the court may adjourn the proceedings for such period as it thinks fit to enable attempts to be made to effect such a reconciliation.[72] A procedure now exists [73] whereby the services of the court welfare officer can be used if the court considers that there is a reasonable possibility of reconciliation, or that there are ancillary proceedings [74] in which conciliation might serve a useful purpose.

Resumption of cohabitation

The Act contains provisions designed to enable the parties to resume cohabitation for a period or periods up to six months without prejudicing their right to divorce.[75] These are dealt with under the facts of adultery,[76] unreasonable behaviour [77] and separation.[78]

AGREEMENTS

Financial matters are even more important under the new divorce law, since there will be few cases in which a divorce will not ultimately be granted, if even one party wants it. The indissoluble marriage has disappeared from English law. The result should be a strong incentive to the parties to agree on financial matters: the respondent may be able to use the petitioner's desire to get a divorce quickly (*i.e.* after two years' separation rather than five) to persuade him to offer her better terms than she could rely on getting if the case were contested. The petitioner will know that sooner or later he can get a divorce, but may prefer to avoid the possibility of the court interfering under section 5 or 10 by agreeing financial terms with the respondent. The Act facilitates this process: rules have been made [79]

" enabling the parties to a marriage, or either of them, on application made either before or after the presentation of a petition for divorce, to refer to the court any agreement or arrangement made or proposed to be made between them being an agreement or arrangement which relates to, arises out of, or is connected with, the proceedings

---

70 See *Practice Note* (*Divorce: Conciliation*) [1971] 1 W.L.R. 223.
71 See N. Tyndall, *Reconciliation and The Divorce Reform Act 1969* [1971] L.S.Gaz. 37–39.
72 s. 6 (2), M.C.A. 1973, again based on Australian provisions: " Field of Choice " para. 32.
73 See n. 70 (*supra*).
74 *E.g.* relating to children or financial matters.
75 s. 2, M.C.A. 1973.
76 *Supra*, p. 112.
77 *Supra*, p. 115.
78 *Supra*, p. 121.
79 M.C.R. 1971, r. 6.

for divorce which are contemplated or, as the case may be, have begun, and for enabling the court to express an opinion, should it think it desirable to do so, as to the reasonableness of the agreement or arrangement and to give such directions, if any, in the matter as it thinks fit." [80]

It should be noted that there is no *obligation* to refer an agreement to the court, and this provision is only likely to be used in exceptional cases.[81] Nor has the court any wider powers than to express an opinion on the reasonableness of the agreement and to give directions. But the section may be resorted to if the agreement is that, in exchange for some advantage, a defence is dropped, or the parties agree to rely on section 1 (2) (*d*): the fact that the agreement has been referred to the court may avoid the risk of the court at a later stage feeling it necessary to make inquiries; more important, if the court does express the view that a financial arrangement is " reasonable " it would be difficult for the respondent to invoke section 10 of the Act in an attempt to extort a more ample settlement.

THE EFFECTS OF THE ACT [82]

The principal result of the Act will be to release from the bonds of marriage a substantial number of persons whose spouses refused to divorce them under the old law. Further, a substantial number of children under sixteen may be legitimated (about 180,000 according to the Law Commission's calculations [83]) by the marriage of their parents. It should not be assumed that all or even most of the persons now enabled to obtain a divorce will bother to do so; they may not wish to take the risk of provoking their spouses to seek maintenance, or the risk that publicity will be given to the legal irregularity of an existing union,[84] while not all of them will wish to marry for a second time. Finally, the Act's recognition of consensual divorce may mean that a significant number of divorces (93 per cent. of which are undefended under the old law) will be founded on two years' separation.

The effect of the Act in removing " bitterness, distress and humiliation " from divorce proceedings should not be exaggerated [85]:

(a) There may be advantages in proceeding on one of the " offence " facts:

(i) If an " offence " fact can be established, the court's powers under sections 5 and 10 of the Act do not come into play;

---

[80] M.C.A. 1973, s. 7.

[81] Practice Direction (*Decrees and Orders: Agreed Terms*) [1972] 1 W.L.R. 1313; *Thomas* v. *Thomas* (1972) 117 S.J. 88. The court cannot generally interfere with agreements made by the parties, unless undesirable pressure is applied, or the interests of a child are affected: *Beales* v. *Beales* [1972] Fam. 210.

[82] See M. D. A. Freeman, " The Search for a Rational Divorce Law " [1971] C.L.P. 178.

[83] " Field of Choice " paras. 33–37.   [84] See *Mortlock*, p. 156.

[85] See *e.g.* *Ackerman* v. *Ackerman* [1972] Fam. 1. The number of *defended* divorce cases has not fallen significantly since the Act: see Hansard Vol. 861, col. 347.

(ii) Proof of an " offence " will avoid the necessity to wait for five years from the time of separation to obtain a divorce from a spouse who is unwilling to consent;

(iii) At the moment, many divorce petitions follow proceedings for maintenance brought in Magistrates' Courts under the Matrimonial Proceedings (Magistrates' Court) Act 1960. That jurisdiction still depends exclusively on the matrimonial offence.

(b) It is too early to estimate the long term effect of the Act on divorce rates. In 1972, 106,560 were granted on petitions filed under the Divorce Reform Act. Of these, 20,669 were founded on separation and consent, while 22,030 were founded on five years' separation. But the most popular single ground remained adultery (32,960 decrees) and there were still many (21,710) based on unreasonable behaviour.[86]

(c) Misconduct by one of the parties may, if " gross and obvious," still be relevant in fixing the financial provision to be made after divorce. Even if they will not often be relied on by the court, allegations of such behaviour will probably continue to be made in an attempt to influence financial settlements.

PRESUMPTION OF DEATH AND DIVORCE

Since 1937 the court has had power to make decrees of presumption of death and dissolution of marriage.[87] Such a decree effectively dissolves the marriage, even if it turns out that the other spouse was, in fact, still alive.[88]

The Act provides that [89]:

> " Any married person who alleges that reasonable grounds exist for supposing that the other party to the marriage is dead may, . . . present a petition to the court to have it presumed that the other party is dead and to have the marriage dissolved, and the court may, if satisfied that such reasonable grounds exist, grant a decree of presumption of death and dissolution of the marriage."

The task of a petitioner in satisfying the court that reasonable grounds exist for supposing that the other party to the marriage is dead is facilitated by the provision that [90]:

> ". . . the fact that for a period of seven years or more the other party to the marriage has been continually absent from the petitioner and the petitioner has no reason to believe that the other party has

---

86 See Civil Judicial Statistics 1972, Cmnd. 5333, Table 10. In the text, the figures include cases where decrees have been based on more than one fact (e.g. adultery and unreasonable behaviour). Surprisingly, almost as many decrees (10,420) were granted to wife petitioners as to husbands (11,577) under the so-called " Casanova's charter " of five years' separation.

87 Matrimonial Causes Act 1937, s. 8 (1) (now s. 19 (1)–(5), M.C.A. 1973).

88 Since the decree is one of divorce, applications for financial provision can then be made.

89 s. 19 (1), M.C.A. 1973. There are no absolute or discretionary bars to a decree on this ground: M.C.A. 1973, s. 19 (6); see Law Commission No. 33, p. 55.

90 s. 19 (3), M.C.A. 1973.

been living within that time shall be evidence that the other party is dead until the contrary is proved."

The onus of proof is on the petitioner.[91]

It has been held [92] that the words " the petitioner has no reason to believe that the other party has been living within " the seven year period should be read as : " if nothing has happened within that time to give the petitioner reason to believe that the other party was then living." The object of the statute is to provide its own clear-cut test as to when the death can be presumed for the specific purpose of allowing the other to remarry.[93] Hence, matters occurring before the seven year period should be excluded except so far as those matters are related to others super- vening during that time : the fact that one spouse was known to be alive a few days before the start of the period does not give the other " reason to believe " that he was alive within the period, even although it may be very likely that he was. The test of whether there is " reason to believe " relates to the standards of belief of a reasonable man : " pure speculation " is excluded.[94]

Seven years' absence (subject to the above) by itself establishes a presumption. If seven years' absence cannot be shown, the petitioner may still obtain a decree if he can show reasonable grounds : if a man were known to have been a passenger on a plane which disappeared without trace, a decree could be granted. It is a matter to be decided on the facts of the particular case.[95]

The court, as in other divorce cases, pronounces first a decree nisi. If, before it has been made absolute, affirmative proof is given that the respondent is still alive, the decree must be rescinded.[96] After decree absolute, the matter cannot be reopened.

If no such decree is obtained to dissolve a marriage, any subsequent marriage will be void for bigamy [97] if it is *proved* that at the time of the second marriage the first marriage was still in existence.[98] Difficulties arise as to what is sufficient proof for this purpose in the common case

---

[91] *Parkinson* v. *Parkinson* [1939] P. 346; *Thompson* v. *Thompson* [1956] P. 414. Has he to make inquiries? See *Rayden*, p. 288, n. (*c*), for a submission that " purely supine and negative absence of belief would not be sufficient on which to found a decree; but . . . all inquiries must be made which the circumstances suggest, including, in ordinary circumstances, advertisements." The matter was left open in *Thompson* v. *Thompson* (*supra*), *per* Sachs J. at p. 421. If the court were uneasy it could exercise its discretion not to grant a decree: *Thompson* v. *Thompson* (*supra*). The words of the section (" the court *may* . . . make a decree ") should be contrasted with those of s. 1 (4), M.C.A. 1973 (" . . . the court . . . *shall* . . . grant a decree of divorce ").
[92] *Thompson* v. *Thompson* (*supra*).
[93] *Ibid.*
[94] *Parkinson* v. *Parkinson* [1939] P. 346.
[95] *MacDiarmaid* v. *Att.-Gen.* [1950] P. 218.
[96] *Manser* v. *Manser* [1940] P. 224 (where the respondent was in court at the hearing of the application to rescind).
[97] M.C.A. 1973, s. 11 (*b*). It does not follow that the criminal offence of bigamy has been committed: see *infra*, p. 139.
[98] If there is *doubt* as to the validity of the *first* marriage, however the court may apply a presumption of validity to the second: *Taylor* v. *Taylor* [1967] P. 25.

where a man who has been married to W1 subsequently goes through a ceremony of marriage with W2, without the first marriage being dissolved, and without affirmative evidence that W1 has died. Can a decree of nullity for bigamy then be obtained in respect of the marriage to W2? Once the first marriage is shown to have existed, the court is put on inquiry as to the validity of the second.[99] Apart from positive evidence, the court may apply a presumption of law [1] that if there is no acceptable affirmative evidence that a person was alive at some time during a continuous period of seven years or more, his death at some time during that period will be presumed, *provided*:

(i) that there are persons who would be likely to have heard from him during that period;

(ii) that those persons have not heard from him; and

(iii) that all due inquiries have been made appropriate to the period.

There is no " magic " for this purpose in seven years' absence [2]; the three additional requirements must also be satisfied. If, for instance, there exist reasons why the missing spouse might have wished not to be heard of, or if he were a solitary person, the court might well refuse to presume death; if, on the other hand, he had been a gregarious man leading a public life, who had been in poor health or following a dangerous occupation, his death might more easily be presumed.

These matters are of less importance than was once the case because of (i) the availability of divorce after five years' separation; (ii) the fact that even when a marriage is void, the court may, on granting a decree of nullity, order one party to make financial provision for the other.[3] Furthermore, the children of a void marriage are not necessarily to be treated as illegitimate.[4]

For the sake of completeness it should be said that it is a statutory defence [5] to a prosecution for bigamy that the accused's husband or wife has been, at the time of the ceremony, continually absent for seven years, and not known by the accused to be living during that time.

SEPARATION ORDERS

The Superior Courts have power to make decrees of judicial separation; the Magistrates' Courts have power to make orders with similar consequences.

---

[99] *Tweeney* v. *Tweeney* [1946] P. 180; *Re Peete* [1952] 2 All E.R. 599; *Re Watkins* [1953] 2 All E.R. 1113; *Chard* v. *Chard* [1956] P. 259.

[1] *Chard* v. *Chard* [1956] P. 259 where the (unsatisfactory) case law is analysed; see also *Jackson*, pp. 150–155.

[2] *Per* Harman J., *Re Watkins* [1953] 2 All E.R. 1113, 1115.

[3] *Supra*, p. 66.

[4] *Supra*, p. 65.

[5] Offences against the Person Act 1861, s. 57.

Judicial Separation

Originally the purpose of a judicial separation decree [6] was to protect the wife but it became increasingly the means whereby she could invoke the court's ancillary powers to order her errant husband to make financial provision for her whilst denying him the right to remarry. It was thus capable of causing very considerable hardship.[7]

The introduction of divorce on the basis of five years' separation means that after a period a respondent spouse can convert a decree of judicial separation obtained against him into a decree of divorce. The only circumstances in which the empty legal shell of a marriage can now be preserved at the instance of one party is if one of the bars provided by the Divorce Reform Act 1969, exists.[8] Judicial separation is now primarily a short-term remedy which may be of use in the following cases: (a) where a decree of divorce cannot yet be obtained because three years have not elapsed since the celebration of the marriage; (b) where neither party wishes to remarry, although the petitioner wishes to take advantage of the court's ancillary powers.[9]

The Divorce Reform Act 1969 amended the law so as to be consistent with the new code of divorce [10]; a petition for judicial separation may be presented to the court by either party to a marriage on the ground that any of the facts now set out in section 1 (2) of the Matrimonial Causes Act 1973 exists.[11] It is specifically provided [12] that in the case of petitions for judicial separation, the court is not to be concerned with the question of whether or not the marriage has broken down irretrievably.[13] Provided one of the relevant facts is proved [14] the court is bound to grant a decree. All the old absolute and discretionary bars to a decree have been abolished; the defence to a petition for divorce based on the grave financial or other hardship to the respondent does not apply to judicial separation.[15] The only exceptions to the rule that proof of a specified fact gives a right to a decree is that the court must not make a decree unless it has by order expressed its satisfaction as to the arrangement for any children; if it purports to do so, the decree is a nullity.[16]

---

[6] The direct lineal descendant of the divorce " *a mensa et thoro* " of the ecclesiastical courts.

[7] See, for example, *Sansom* v. *Sansom* [1966] P. 52. Although strongly attacked as other than a temporary remedy by the Gorell Barnes Committee the Morton Commission favoured its retention on (*inter alia*) the surprising ground that the door was left open for reconciliation: para. 303.

[8] *Supra*, p. 112.

[9] Hence, presumably, the fact that two decrees were pronounced in 1972 on the basis of two years' separation with consent: Civil Judicial Statistics 1972, Cmnd. 5333, Table 10.

[10] See now M.C.A. 1973, s. 17.

[11] *Supra*, p. 111.

[12] s. 17 (2).

[13] The Act paradoxically (in view of the fact that the court is not concerned with irretrievable breakdown) applies to Judicial Separation suits the power to adjourn proceedings to enable attempts at reconciliation to be made: s. 17 (3).

[14] s. 17 (2).

[15] ss. 5 and 10, M.C.A. 1973, *supra*. Note also s. 18 (2), *infra*, p. 141.

[16] s. 41, M.C.A. 1973, *infra*, p. 272.

Effects of a decree of judicial separation

There are three main consequences of a decree of judicial separation:

(1) The court's ancillary financial and custody powers may be invoked.

(2) It is no longer obligatory for the petitioner to cohabit with the respondent.[17] That obligation has not, in modern times, been enforceable,[18] but since a decree terminates the duty to cohabit, neither party can thereafter be in desertion.

It should be noted that the decree is an order that the petitioner be no longer bound to cohabit with the respondent; it is not an order that the respondent shall cease to live with the petitioner.[19] It follows that the court will not necessarily exclude a husband against whom a decree of judicial separation has been granted from the matrimonial home; it will only do so if the wife needs protection from molestation or for some other cogent reason.[20]

(3) For the purposes of intestate succession, a decree operates as a divorce[21]: neither spouse has any right to succeed to the property of the other on intestacy.[22]

Magistrates' Separation Orders

The jurisdiction of Magistrates' Courts to make " matrimonial orders " is considered in detail in Chapter 6 in so far as it is concerned with the making of maintenance orders. Since 1878, however, these courts have also had power to include a so-called "non-cohabitation clause" in matrimonial orders.[23] Until 1971 such a provision had effect in all respects as a decree of judicial separation.[24] But the Matrimonial Proceedings and Property Act 1970[25] introduced a distinction. Whereas judicial separation affects the devolution of the spouses' property on death, a Magistrates' Court order has no such effect.[26] The reason given for this distinction[27] is that a Magistrates' Order is " essentially a summary remedy provided for the immediate protection of the applicant and, even in the rare[28] case where there is a non-cohabitation clause, is not any clear evidence of the breakdown of the marriage." This assertion rests on a doubtful assumption of fact[29] but seems unlikely to be of much practical significance.

---

[17] s. 18 (1), M.C.A. 1973.
[18] As to the effect of a decree for Restitution of Conjugal Rights (abolished by s. 20, Matrimonial Proceedings and Property Act 1970) see Law Commission No. 23.
[19] Per Ormrod J., Montgomery v. Montgomery [1965] P. 46.
[20] Infra, p. 172, n. 1.
[21] s. 18 (2), M.C.A. 1973.
[22] This rule does not prevent a spouse applying to the court for reasonable provision to be made for her as a spouse under the Inheritance (Family Provision) Act 1938.
[23] s. 2 (1) (a), Matrimonial Proceedings (Magistrates' Courts) Act 1960.
[24] Ibid.   [25] s. 40 (now s. 18 (2), M.C.A. 1973).
[26] s. 18 (3), M.C.A. 1973.
[27] Law Commission No. 25, para. 79, n. 74.
[28] But see infra, p. 142.
[29] Infra, p. 142 as to the use made of non-cohabitation orders. The assertion that the order is not clear evidence of the breakdown of the marriage also seems questionable.

The use made of the powers to include a non-cohabitation clause is an apt illustration of the distinction between textbook law and court practice.[30] The court has a complete discretion whether to include a non-cohabitation clause in a matrimonial order.[31] In theory, therefore, it is possible for such a clause to be inserted even if the only ground of complaint is wilful neglect to maintain or simple desertion.[32] Yet, ever since 1906,[33] the courts have consistently [34] stated that the discretion to make a separation order should only be exercised when this is *necessary for the protection of the wife or children.* It has therefore been assumed that separation orders are rarely made.[35] But the practice of the courts was otherwise: in the Bedford College sample,[36] they were inserted in 30 per cent. of live orders, and in 40 per cent. of all live orders originally made in the last two years of the survey (*i.e.* 1964–65).[37] In 38 per cent. of the cases, persistent cruelty (which might have justified " protecting " the wife) was not alleged.[38] There was evidence of local variations in practice.[39]

There is evidence that on occasions the non-cohabitation clause has by inadvertence not been struck out of the printed form used for the court's order.[40] But the reason seems often to be that local authorities require a wife to get an order continuing a non-cohabitation clause as a condition of transferring to her the tenancy of a local authority house or flat,[41] while in one case [42] it was revealed that the Canadian Immigration authorities were not prepared to allow deserting husbands to be given an immigrant's visa unless an order containing a non-cohabitation clause had been obtained. The fact that a non-cohabitation clause terminates desertion is less important as a result of the passing of the Divorce

---

30 For full accounts, see C. Gibson " The Separation Order: A Study in Textbook Law and Court Practice " (1970) 33 M.L.R. 63; the Bedford College Survey, pp. 59–66. These sources are extensively drawn upon in the following paragraphs.
31 *Corton* v. *Corton* [1965] P. 1, 3, *per* Sir J. Simon P.
32 *Per* Lord Hodson, *Gollins* v. *Gollins* [1964] A.C. 644, 681.
33 Prior to that date a non-cohabitation clause was inserted as a matter of routine into most matrimonial orders (92 per cent. in 1903). But in *Dodd* v. *Dodd* [1906] P. 189 this practice was condemned by Sir Gorell Barnes P. on the basis that the intention of the legislature was that such orders should only be made in cases of cruelty and drunkenness, where protection was necessary.
34 *Taylor* v. *Taylor* (1907) 23 T.L.R. 566; *Gollins* v. *Gollins* [1964] A.C. 644; *Corton* v. *Corton* [1965] P. 1; *Jolliffe* v. *Jolliffe* [1965] P. 6; *Vaughan* v. *Vaughan* [1965] P. 15; *Halden* v. *Halden* [1966] 1 W.L.R. 1481, 1483; *Wall* v. *Wall* [1968] 1 W.L.R. 306.
35 See n. 27, *supra* (Law Commission: " very rare "); Graham Hall Committee Report, para. 28 (" only rarely "). In *Tarr* v. *Tarr* [1971] 1 All E.R. 817 C.A. Lord Denning M.R. concluded from the insertion of a non-cohabitation clause in an order that " it must have been a bad case of cruelty " (at p. 818C).
36 See Bedford College Survey, pp. 59–66.
37 Bedford College Survey, Table 15, p. 65. It should be noted that the most recent and widely publicised decisions condemning indiscriminate use of non-cohabitation orders would probably not have made an impact by this time: *Corton* v. *Corton* [1965] P. 1; *Jolliffe* v. *Jolliffe* [1965] P. 6.
38 *Ibid.*, Table 16.
39 *Ibid.*, p. 65.
40 See *e.g. Cohen* v. *Cohen* [1947] P. 147; *Jolliffe* v. *Jolliffe* [1965] P. 6.
41 See *Montgomery* v. *Montgomery* [1965] P. 46.
42 *Wall* v. *Wall* [1968] 1 W.L.R. 306.

Reform Act 1969.[43] But it is still not devoid of significance: it is no doubt possible for a wife who has been deserted to obtain a divorce in due course on the basis of five years' separation, but there are disadvantages in taking this course.[44]

The questions which a court *should* ask before making such an order are briefly as follows [45]:

(i) Is a separation order [46] really necessary for the protection of the complainant?

(ii) Is the case " a more than ordinarily serious case "? [47]

(iii) Is there any reasonable prospect of reconciliation? [48]

This has been said to be perhaps the most important consideration: a non-cohabitation clause would entitle a complainant to reject offers of reconciliation; if there is no such clause genuine offers must be accepted if the risk that the complainant will by rejecting put herself into desertion is to be avoided.[49]

In practice (apart from the fact that it may indirectly [50] enable a wife to obtain local authority housing) the " protection " afforded by a separation order is very limited; if it is needed the aggrieved spouse will obtain an injunction against molestation (enforceable by the sanction of imprisonment) whether or not he has a separation order.[51] The conclusion seems irresistible that the time has come for the separation order to be consigned to the "museum of legal history," [52] leaving Magistrates' Courts to their proper function of providing for financial needs.[53]

---

43 *Supra*, p. 110.
44 Apart from the length of time which must elapse, the possibility that a petitioner on this ground will be treated less generously than one who can establish one of the " offence " facts, *supra*, p. 112.
45 *Corton* v. *Corton* [1965] P. 1.
46 *i.e.* a non-cohabitation clause.
47 See *Tarr* v. *Tarr* [1971] 1 All E.R. 817, n. 35, *supra*.
48 *Cf.* the Law Commission's view that the making of a separation order did not necessarily mean that the marriage had irretrievably broken down, n. 7, *supra*.
49 This is perhaps a less important consideration in the light of the Divorce Reform Act, *supra*.
50 *Supra*, p. 142.
51 See *infra*, p. 172, n. 1; see also [1973] Legal Action Group Bulletin pp. 175, 277.
52 Bedford College Survey, p. 60.
53 It may often be advantageous for a wife petitioner who is primarily concerned with financial matters to seek judicial separation rather than a magistrate's order; see B. Passingham (1971) 68 L.S.Gaz. 173.

CHAPTER 6

MATRIMONIAL PROPERTY AND FINANCIAL OBLIGATIONS

" DIVORCE," it has been said by an eminent lawyer [1] " has become less about divorce and more about money." The parties to an unhappy marriage now have to accept that, sooner or later, it can be dissolved. The main scope for dispute is therefore about the financial arrangements which should be made.

Until 1970 although the courts had wide power to order income payments on divorce they had very limited powers over the parties' capital assets.[2] In order to achieve fairness in this respect the courts developed the law of property rights, so as to give both spouses some interest in " family assets." [3] This undoubtedly led to some distortion of orthodox concepts of property law.

The Matrimonial Proceedings and Property Act [4] gave the courts wide discretionary powers over the whole family finances, but for some time there was doubt as to how liberally these powers would be exercised.[5] These doubts have now been resolved,[6] so that the ascertainment of the parties' strict property rights will often be unnecessary [7] in disputes consequent on divorce. But the problem may still be relevant in some such cases,[8] and will be relevant if the dispute is between one spouse and strangers—e.g. a creditor, seeking to enforce his debt against one spouse's property,[9] or as to rights of inheritance.[10]

We therefore consider in turn :

    (i) Matrimonial Property;

    (ii) Financial Obligations on Breakdown;

    (iii) The Case for Reform.

---

[1] Jackson, p. v.

[2] See Law Commission 25, and P.W.P. No. 9, Part I; *Wachtel* v. *Wachtel* [1973] Fam. 72, 90.

[3] See *Pettit* v. *Pettit* [1970] A.C. 777 *per* Lord Diplock at p. 819.

[4] The greater part of which is now consolidated in M.C.A. 1973.

[5] *Infra*, p. 206.

[6] *Wachtel* v. *Wachtel* (*supra*).

[7] *Kowalczuk* v. *Kowalczuk* [1973] 2 All E.R. 1042, *per* Lord Denning M.R. at p 1045; *Gordon* v. *Gordon* (1973) *The Times*, October 13.

[8] *Glenn* v. *Glenn* [1973] 1 W.L.R. 1016; p. 207 *infra*.

[9] *Ex p. Solomon* [1967] Ch. 573; *Re Cole* [1964] Ch. 175.

[10] *Re Cummins* [1972] Ch. 62.

MATRIMONIAL PROPERTY [11]

" PROPERTY " RIGHTS AND " PERSONAL " RIGHTS

A fertile source of confusion in this complex and controversial field is the use of the word " property " in different senses by lawyers and laymen. In legal language, a property right is:

> " definable, identifiable by third parties, capable in its nature of assumption by third parties, and having some degree of permanence or stability." [12]

Apparently similar rights may be either proprietary or purely personal. The difference is crucial: if my right is proprietary I can, in principle, assert it against third parties, even innocent purchasers. If it is personal, then I cannot enforce it against a third party at all. I may be able to sue the grantor of the right for damages, but that will not always be an adequate remedy particularly if he is insolvent and cannot pay damages.

In *National Provincial Bank Ltd.* v. *Ainsworth*,[13] for instance, H had deserted W. It was conceded that she had a right to be provided with housing by her husband, and that she could have obtained an injunction from the courts to stop him interfering with it. Unfortunately W only found out that H had mortgaged the house to the bank *after* the transaction had been completed. H became insolvent. The House of Lords held W's right was incapable of binding the Bank: " the rights of husband and wife must be regarded as purely personal . . . these rights as a matter of law do not bind third parties." [14]

The difference between this very limited lawyers' concept and the sociologists' is exemplified in this quotation [15]:

> " Since, in our societies, marriage is the basis of the normal family, it follows that marriage must have a profound effect upon the property of the spouses."

This is undoubtedly correct if " property " is used in the wide sense of " wealth." But if " property " is given the restricted lawyers' sense the conclusion is demonstrably untrue: the fact that I allow my wife to use my car, and even that I may consult her before trading it in for a new model, in no way means that she has rights in it that will bind a purchaser. If such rights follow from common use, presumably our children would have similar rights over the television set.

This confusion has had a number of unfortunate consequences. For

---

[11] The most comprehensive analysis, with detailed suggestions for reform, is the Law Commission's Published Working Paper on Family Property Law (1971) P.W.P. No. 42; see also M. D. A. Freeman, " Towards a Rational Reconstruction of Family Property Law " [1972] C.L.P. 84.

[12] *Per* Lord Wilberforce, *National Provincial Bank Ltd.* v. *Ainsworth* [1965] A.C. 1175, at p. 1248.

[13] *Supra.*

[14] *Per* Lord Upjohn at p. 1233; *cf. Caunce* v. *Caunce* [1969] 1 W.L.R. 286 where it was conceded that the wife had a proprietary interest.

[15] O. Kahn-Freund, *Matrimonial Property Law in England* (ed. Friedmann, 1955).

the policy of the law is to *restrict* the number of proprietary interests which can be created:

(i) The more interests there are which are capable of binding innocent purchasers, the less trust will be placed in the system of property rights. If a man lends money on mortgage, or buys a house, he wants to be quite sure that his right is not going to be defeated by the existence of a third party's right. The more complex the web of proprietary rights, the more difficult it becomes to ensure that a purchaser will get what he paid for.

(ii) The time spent, and thus the *cost* of investigating titles is bound to be increased. Cheaper conveyancing necessitates a reduction in the number of rights to be examined.

Conversely the confusion of terminology has led lawyers astray: policy considerations which would have been appropriate to recognition of a proprietary right have been used to defeat claims to a *personal* adjustment against the other spouse.[16] Such considerations (*e.g.* that the right claimed should be easily identifiable by potential purchasers) are largely irrelevant if all that is involved is the adjustment of rights between the two spouses on breakdown without affecting third party rights.

Separate Property—The Historical Paradox

Since 1870 the basic principle of English law is that marriage has no effect on the spouse's property rights:

> " There is not one law of property applicable where a dispute as to property is between spouses or former spouses and another law of property where the dispute is between others." [17]

This principle was accepted after long agitation representing " separation of property " as the only way in which justice could be achieved for married women. The apparent paradox that this very system, then the panacea for all a married woman's disabilities, has recently been attacked on grounds of its injustice is comprehensible if the law is viewed historically in its response to changing social and economic pressures.

The common law [18]

At common law husband and wife become one: " the very being or legal existence of the woman is suspended during the marriage, or at least is incorporated into that of the husband." [19] It followed from

---

16 See *e.g. Jansen* v. *Jansen* [1965] P. 478, where the claimant's counsel specifically denied that he was making a proprietary claim (p. 483) but asserted a personal claim for the value of work done to the property. This concession was ignored; the courts dealt with the cases as if property law was dominant.

17 *Per* Viscount Dilhorne, *Gissing* v. *Gissing* [1971] A.C. 886, at p. 899.

18 For full accounts see Blackstone, *Commentaries*, 4th ed. Book I, Chap. 15, and Dicey, *Law and Opinion in England*, 2nd ed., 371–395.

19 See *Blackstone*, p. 442.

this for instance that all the wife's personal property [20] vested in her husband on marriage. Such a system seems to modern eyes to rest " on the doctrine that what is mine is yours, but what is yours is not mine. . . ." [21] Yet in reality the system was not so unfair: it was developed in a society when land was the major form of substantial wealth, and there were special rules for the ownership of land. A husband's interest in his wife's freehold land only continued during the subsistence of the marriage (" coverture ").[22] The husband could alienate these rights, but not any greater rights than he himself possessed. It followed, therefore, that the land would revert to the wife's own kinship group not later than the husband's death. Conversely, if the wife survived the husband, she took an interest for her life in *his* freehold land by way of dower. Reduced to its simplest essential, this was a right to one-third of the land to which the husband had been absolutely entitled during the marriage.

The role of equity

These rules, therefore, gave the wife some kind of protection if the family fortune were in land. It was left to Equity to develop this protection and extend it to *all* forms of capital. Equity used two main techniques:

(a) *Separate property*

If, prior to her marriage, the wife's property were given to third parties she had no interest which the law could transfer to her husband. This remained the case even if the property were held by third parties on terms that they would apply it for the wife's benefit. This system developed so that a transfer at any time to trustees to hold to the wife's " separate use " would prevent any interest vesting in the husband. A prudent parent would thus ensure that a proper settlement was made on marriage, securing (*inter alia*) (*a*) that his daughter's existing property was held for her separate use, and (*b*) that any after-acquired property was so held.[23]

(b) *Restraint on anticipation*

The wife ultimately acquired the right to deal with her separate property; her instructions to the trustees to transfer the property to a third party had to be obeyed. This was so even if the wife was acting at her husband's direction. An unscrupulous husband could, by the skilful use of " kicks and kisses " (either the one or the other, or sometimes a judicious combination) persuade his wife to hand over property

---

20 Except for her so-called " paraphernalia."

21 J. S. Mill, *The Subjection of Women*, (1869) Everyman's Library ed., p. 263.

22 If a child capable of inheriting the land were born alive, the husband's interest was enlarged from one for the parties' joint lives to an interest for his life.

23 This was done by the machinery of a covenant to settle after-acquired property: see Hanbury's *Modern Equity* (9th ed.), pp. 140–142.

to him or his creditors.   The restraint on anticipation was a conveyancing device, inserted in marriage settlements, which prevented the wife getting control of anything beyond the *current income* of the property.   The capital would thus be preserved intact.

The demand for separate property

So far we have dealt with capital owned by the wife.   Under the Common Law theory that husband and wife were one, the right to her earnings (and any savings made out of them) vested in her husband. Equity was powerless to intervene, because this income did not arise from " property " which could be settled.   This became a major social problem with the expansion of the wage economy after the Industrial Revolution.   There was nothing to stop a man leaving his wife destitute, and then returning to seize the small savings built up by her own labour and thrift.[24]   Public opinion was influenced by the following factors:

(i) The fact that it was a woman's *earnings* alone which could not be protected in any way against her husband seemed particularly offensive to women authors whose writings [25] had a powerful influence.

(ii) This was connected with the feelings of frustration which led middle-class women to campaign for the opportunity to engage in socially productive work.   The law can be changed more easily than social and economic conventions and it was thought that a change might influence social conventions.

(iii) Suffrage reformers [26] used the legal disabilities of married women as a notable illustration of the practical grievances which could be remedied by enfranchisement.

(iv) The complexity of the law (particularly as to whether the husband was liable for goods ordered on credit by a wife) [27] caused difficulty to tradesmen.   Much of the nineteenth-century case law on the property rights of husband and wife was financed by hapless tradesmen who did not mind who paid them so long as someone did.   All too often, they would end up unpaid, and with a large additional bill for legal costs.

The solution which commended itself to most informed opinion was that of separation of property.   The reasons can be summarised as follows:

---

[24] See Report of the Married Women's Property Bill Committee, B.P.P. 1867–68, vii. 399. An unsuccessful attempt to deal with this particular problem was made by s. 21, Matrimonial Causes Act 1857.

[25] There is an extensive periodical literature: a characteristic title was Francis Power Cobbe's " Criminals, Idiots, Women and Minors. Is the Classification sound? " (1869). A full bibliography, by O. R. McGregor, is " The Social Position of Women in England, 1850–1914 " (1955) *British Journal of Sociology*, Vol. 6, p. 48.   The best monograph on the legal position of women is " Rights and Duties of Englishwomen. A Study in Law and Public Opinion " by Erna Reiss (1934).   A broader account of the feminist movement is to be found in " The Cause " by Ray Strachey (1928).

[26] See *e.g.* " The Legal Disabilities of Women " by C. Pankhurst (in *The Case For Women's Suffrage* 1907, ed. Villiers) dealing with the comparatively few disabilities which existed after the Married Women's Property Act 1882.

[27] See Morison, *A Century of Family Law* (ed. Graveson and Crane) Chap. 6.

(a) It was simple. The complexities of the law stemmed from the special régime applicable to married persons, and would disappear if the spouses' marital status no longer affected their property rights.

(b) The concept was familiar to the middle classes. A fundamental change in property law might have appeared revolutionary to a Victorian legislature, but to universalise separate property:

> " did no more than give to every married woman nearly the same rights as every English gentlemen had for generations past secured under a Marriage Settlement for his daughter on her marriage." [28]

(c) It lacked the alien connotations of European community systems.[29] Separation systems had been successful in other parts of the English-speaking world.

(d) It accorded with the currently fashionable notions of philosophical individualism: the legal subordination of one sex to the other should (it was said) be replaced by " a principle of perfect equality, admitting no power or privilege on the one side, nor disability on the other." [30] For John Stuart Mill and his followers [31] equality of property rights was a positive good in that it would help to achieve social and moral equality.

Reforms were introduced over the years.[32] The question of who owns property acquired during the currency of the marriage has prima facie to be decided by applying principles of law applicable to the settlement of claims between strangers.

The reason for the extraordinary paradox that a system which was created to further married women's rights should now be seen as a crying injustice is that, in the same way as the Common Law failed to provide adequate rights when capital began to be invested in wealth other than land, and just as the rules of Equity failed to provide for wage-earners, so the system of separation has failed to deal adequately with the economic realities of married life in the twentieth century. The main factor has been the inflation of property values, and in particular the growth of owner occupation of housing (financed by instalment mortgage) coupled with the fact that inflation has led to a substantial increase in property values over the years. If a house had been bought for £250 in 1939 (the deposit of, say £25, being provided by the husband) it might well be now worth over £10,000. There is nothing in the principle of

---

[28] Dicey, *Law and Opinion in England*, Lecture XI, p. 389. See also C. S. Kenny, " History of the Law of England as to the effects of Marriage on Property," 1879: the reform merely afforded to " the mangle, the teapot and the sewing machine the same protection which diamonds and consols had always purchased for themselves in the teeth of the law."

[29] *Ibid*.

[30] J. S. Mill, *The Subjection of Women*, p. 263.

[31] Even his opponents were often prepared to concede that " separate property " was a desirable reform.

[32] Married Women's Property Acts 1870, 1874, 1882, 1884, 1893, 1907, 1908, and finally the Law Reform (Married Women and Tortfeasors) Act 1935. The 1870 and 1882 Acts were the most important, and introduced the general principle of separate property.

separate property to confer any rights to this valuable asset on the wife—
even although the wife might have spent all her adult life working in the
house and she might have given up paid work so as to look after domestic
matters.   The law failed to recognise that a wife's contribution to the
marriage partnership, by her services in the home, is comparable to that
of her husband as breadwinner.[33]   In the words of Lord Simon of
Glaisdale:

> " The wife spends her youth and early middle age in bearing
> and rearing children and in tending the home; the husband is thus
> freed for his economic activities.   Unless the wife plays her part,
> the husband cannot play his.   The cock bird can feather his nest
> precisely because he is not required to spend most of his time sitting
> on it." [34]

We now examine the modern law under the following heads:

(i) The relevant basic rules of the Common Law and Equity.   Under
this head we shall note the various judicial attempts to redress particular
injustices by bold interpretations of the law.

(ii) The piecemeal reforms which have been made by statute:

(a) The Married Women's Property Act 1964 has given certain
rights to a wife over savings from a housekeeping allowance.

(b) The Matrimonial Homes Act 1967 protects the wife's *right
of occupation* of the matrimonial home against persons dealing with
the property.

(c) The Matrimonial Proceedings (Property and Maintenance)
Act 1970 enables a wife in certain circumstances to assert a proprietary interest in the matrimonial home if she has made substantial
improvements to it.

(d) The Inheritance (Family Provision) Act 1938 gave a widow
the right to apply to the court for reasonable provision out of her
husband's estate if his will and/or the laws of intestacy fail to do so.

(e) The Law Reform (Miscellaneous Provisions) Act 1970
introduced a special property régime for engaged couples.

THE RULES OF LAW AND EQUITY

In this section we are concerned with two separate issues: (1) the rules
governing the ownership of property in a family context; (2) the rules
governing the devolution of property on the death of a family member.
These are now largely statutory, but it is easier to deal with them in this
section since they are part of the basic structure of family property law.

The Ownership of Property

It is in connection with land that most matrimonial property law has
developed; this analysis concentrates on the special rules relating to

---

[33] Morton Report, para. 626.
[34] " With all my Worldly Goods," Sir J. Simon, Holdsworth Lecture, Birmingham,
1964.

land with references where appropriate to any distinctive rules relating to other property.

In the absence of any relevant statutory provision,

> " the rights of the parties [to a marriage] must be judged on the general principles applicable in any court of law when considering questions of title to property, and *though the parties are husband and wife these questions of title must be decided by the principles of law applicable to the settlement of claims between those not so related, while making full allowances in view of that relationship.*" [35]

Those principles are of two kinds: formal and substantive.

Formalities

The *formal* rules prescribe that certain transactions must be effected by deed or be in, or evidenced in, writing. These rules are not relaxed simply because the parties are husband and wife [36]:

(a) Section 52 of the Law of Property Act 1925 provides:

> " All conveyances of land or of any interest therein are void for the purpose of conveying or creating a legal estate unless made by deed."

Hence it will always [37] be clear from documentary evidence who owns the legal estate in land.

However, proprietary interests can also exist *in equity*: although the legal title to the matrimonial home is in the husband, he may hold it as trustee on trust,[38] for example for himself and his wife jointly.

(b) Section 53 of the Law of Property Act 1925 contains three rules:

> " (i) No interest in land can be created or disposed of except by writing signed by the person creating or conveying the same. . . .[39]
> (ii) A declaration of trust respecting any land or any interest therein must be manifested and proved by some writing signed by some person who is able to declare such trust. . . .[40]
> (iii) A disposition of an equitable interest or trust subsisting at the time of the disposition, must be in writing signed by the person disposing of the same. . . ." [41]

(c) Finally, section 40 of the Law of Property Act 1925 requires *contracts* for the sale or other disposition of land or interests therein to be evidenced in writing.

Hence, the general policy is that all interests in land (equitable as

---

35 *Pettit* v. *Pettit* [1970] A.C. 777, 813, *per* Lord Upjohn.
36 *Spellman* v. *Spellman* [1961] 2 All E.R. 498; *Re Cole* [1964] Ch. 175.
37 There are exceptions in the case of short leases: s. 54 (2) Law of Property Act 1925.
38 If there is concurrent ownership in equity a trust for sale will be imposed: see *infra*, p. 160.
39 Law of Property Act 1925, s. 53 (1) (*a*).
40 *Ibid.*, s. 53 (1) (*b*).
41 *Ibid.*, s. 53 (1) (*c*). This (alone) applies to interests in all types of property.

well as legal), must be effected by, or evidenced in writing.[41a]   But this
is subject to a major qualification: section 53 of the Law of Property Act
does *not* "affect the creation or operation of resulting, implied, or
constructive trusts." [42]   Hence it is only by showing the existence of
such a trust that a wife can be held to have a proprietary interest in a
matrimonial home, the legal estate of which is vested in her husband.

Substance

There are two principal fact-situations: first, cases where the legal estate
is in one spouse alone, and the other claims nevertheless to be entitled
to a (necessarily equitable) interest; secondly, cases where the legal estate
is vested in both spouses, the dispute being as to the extent of the
beneficial interests of each or the exercise of their rights.

Legal estate in one spouse alone

1. If there is a document in writing, it may be effective either as a
contract for the disposition of an interest in land or as a declaration of
trust, provided: (a) It is intended to be legally binding.[43]   If the parties
are *not* living in amity or are separated, or about to separate, it can be
presumed that they intend to create legal relations [44]—or at least there
is no presumption against creating such a relationship.[45]

(b) It is sufficiently certain. This is related to the last rule: lack of
precision may indicate that a legally binding agreement is not envisaged.[46]

(c) It makes out either (i) a *contract* (in which case, however, it must
be supported by consideration, or be under seal), or (ii) a declaration
of trust (in which case there must be sufficient evidence of intention).[47]
A voluntary agreement to make a gift will not do.[48]

(d) It is *signed* (if a declaration of trust " by some person able to
declare such trust "; if a *contract* by the defendant " or by some other
person thereunto by him lawfully authorised ").[49]   In either case the
document need only be *evidenced* in writing, as distinct from being *in*
writing.

(e) If it is a " contract by an estate owner . . . to convey or create
a legal estate " it must be registered as a Class C (iv) Land Charge,
otherwise it will be void against a purchaser of a legal estate for money

---

[41a] But an agreement between the parties as to the extent of their respective contributions
to the purchase price (as distinct from an agreement as to the *quantum* of their
beneficial interests in the property) does not require to be evidenced in writing:
Cowcher v. *Cowcher* [1972] 1 W.L.R. 425.
[42] *Ibid.*, s. 53 (2).
[43] *Balfour* v. *Balfour* [1919] 2 K.B. 571; *Jones* v. *Padavatton* [1969] 1 W.L.R. 328.
[44] *Merritt* v. *Merritt* [1970] 2 All E.R. 760, *per* Lord Denning M.R. at 762A.
[45] *Per* Widgery L.J., *ibid.* at 763C. See also *Davis* v. *Vale* [1971] 2 All E.R. 1021, *per*
Edmund Davies L.J.
[46] *Gould* v. *Gould* [1970] 1 Q.B. 275.
[47] See Pettit, *Equity and the Law of Trusts* (2nd ed.), p. 63.
[48] *Jones* v. *Lock* (1865) L.R. 1 Ch.App. 25.
[49] s. 53 (1) (*b*); s. 40, L.P.A. 1925. Alternatively, the doctrine of part performance may
apply: *Steadman* v. *Steadman* [1973] 3 W.L.R. 698.

or money's worth.[50]   This will rarely be in point because the agreement will only be to transfer an *equitable* interest. Even if the agreement were to transfer the legal estate, it would remain enforceable between the parties, but not against a purchaser.

2. If there is no written agreement or evidence, the other spouse will not be entitled to a proprietary interest unless he or she can establish the existence of a resulting, implied, or constructive trust. In *Gissing* v. *Gissing* [51] the husband said to his wife: " Don't worry about the house—it's yours. I will pay the mortgage payments and all other outgoings." This promise was ineffective at law: there was no *written* [52] document and thus section 52 of the Law of Property Act 1925 was not complied with. The wife failed to discharge the onus of establishing an implied, resulting or constructive trust.

The legal estate prima facie carries with it the whole beneficial interest.[53]   Cases in which the legal estate has been displaced can be considered under three heads:

(a) cases where the courts presume an original intention on the basis of the application of the presumptions of advancement and resulting trust, to hold the property jointly;

(b) cases where the courts presume an original common intention on the basis of other evidence as to the parties' intention;

(c) cases when the courts impose a trust in the absence of evidence of agreement.

The presumption of advancement and resulting trust [54]

If property is conveyed into the name of someone other than the person who has provided the purchase money, there is a resulting trust in the absence of admissible evidence to the contrary.[55]   In its application to the acquisition of the matrimonial home, this means that prima facie the beneficial interest will be held for the benefit of the person who provided all or part of the purchase money,[56] even if he is not the legal estate owner: if a wife provides all or part of the purchase price of property conveyed into her husband's name, this presumption may be applied to give her an interest—in the proportions in which the purchase money was provided. If for example the cost was £6,000, and A provides £2,000 while B (who owns the legal estate) provides £4,000, there is a resulting trust to A of one third.[57]   The parties will hold as tenants

---

50 Land Charges Act 1972, s. 4 (6). Analogous provisions exist if the title is registered.
51 [1971] A.C. 886.
52 *Cf. Merritt* v. *Merritt (supra).*
53 See *per* Lord Dilhorne at p. 900; *per* Lord Pearson at p. 902; *per* Lord Diplock at p. 910.   54 See *Scott on Trusts*, 3rd ed., p. 339 *et seq.*
55 *Anon.* (1683) 2 Ventr. 361; *Dyer* v. *Dyer* (1788) 2 Cox Eq. 92.
56 Or is treated as providing some part of the purchase money, possibly by agreement: *Cowcher* v. *Cowcher* [1972] 1 W.L.R. 425.
57 *Re Roger's Question* [1948] 1 All E.R. 328; *Diwell* v. *Farnes* [1959] 2 All E.R. 379; *Bull* v. *Bull* [1955] 1 Q.B. 234; *Cowcher* v. *Cowcher (supra).*

in common unless they put up the purchase price *equally*, when it would seem that a *joint tenancy* arises.[58]

If certain special relationship (including that of husband and wife) exist this presumption may be displaced by the (stronger, but still rebuttable) presumption of *advancement—i.e.* that a *gift* is intended:

> " there is a rule of equity which still subsists, even though in this day and age one may feel that the presumption is more easily capable of rebuttal—a rule that if the husband makes a payment for or puts property into the name of a wife, he intends to make an advancement to her." [59]

In *Pettit* v. *Pettit* these presumptions came under some attack. " The strength of the presumptions must have been much diminished " it was said,[60] because the presumption of advancement depended on the wife's economic subservience: it would

> " be an abuse of the legal technique for ascertaining or imputing intention to apply to transactions between the post-war generation of married couples ' presumptions ' which are based on inferences of fact which an earlier generation of judges drew as to the most likely intentions of earlier generations of spouses belonging to the propertied classes of a different social era." [61]

Although the presumptions were not entirely without adherents in *Pettit*,[62] subsequent cases suggest that they will be applied rarely, perhaps only as a last resort in the absence of any other evidence (including evidence of conduct from which an intention can be inferred).[63]

Evidence is not normally admissible if it involves the disclosure of an improper or fraudulent motive. Thus, if a husband fraudulently puts property into his wife's name to protect it from his creditors [64] these facts cannot be relied on to rebut the normal principle that it was intended to belong to her beneficially. Even if a husband, without fraudulent intent, puts property into his wife's name to avoid it being taken by his creditors if his business fails, he will not be able to rebut the presumption. This is evidence that he in fact *did* intend her to benefit; if this were not so, the transaction would be fraudulent, and thus again the presumption would apply.[65] In its application to matrimonial property, however, this

---

[58] *Lake* v. *Gibson* (1729) 1 Eq.Cas.Abr. 290; *Aveling* v. *Knipe* (1815) 19 Ves. 441; *Robinson* v. *Preston* (1858) 4 K. & J. 505.

[59] *Per* Lord Evershed M.R., *Silver* v. *Silver* [1958] 1 All E.R. 523, 525.

[60] *Per* Lord Reid at [1970] A.C. p. 793.   [61] *Per* Lord Diplock at p. 824.

[62] Lord Upjohn, for instance, thought (at p. 813) that " when properly understood and properly applied to the circumstances of today I remain of the opinion that they remain as useful as ever in solving questions of title."

[63] See particularly *Falconer* v. *Falconer* [1970] 3 All E.R. 449. If the property is put into the wife's name the cases suggest that the presumption of advancement operates, but this presumption is rebutted if *both* have contributed to the purchase price. A wife who pays nothing may therefore be better off than one who contributes: see T. K. Earnshaw, (1971) 121 New L.J. 96 and 120.

[64] *Gascoigne* v. *Gascoigne* [1918] 1 K.B. 223; see also *Re Emery's Investment Trust* [1959] 1 All E.R. 471.

[65] *Tinker* v. *Tinker* [1970] P. 136: on these topics generally see *Pettit*, Chap. 4; *Snell*, Chap. 4.

exclusionary rule has been held only to apply where moral guilt is involved. In *Heseltine* v. *Heseltine* [66] the wife had transferred property to the husband so that (i) death duty might be avoided if she survived seven years and (ii) the husband could show he was a man of sufficient wealth to become an underwriting member of Lloyd's. The husband claimed that the wife should not be allowed to deny the making of an absolute gift, since this would involve revealing that the transactions had been shams designed to deceive Lloyd's and the Revenue. It was held that she could give evidence of her true intention. The exclusionary rule is based on the principle that a man canot take advantage of his own wrong. In the present case it did not apply because:

> "The wife here has done no wrong. She only did what her husband asked her. That should not be taken against her." [67]

Evidence of intention

If there is admissible evidence of the parties' intention, at the date of acquisition, the court will give effect to it by imposing a trust of the proceeds of sale in the shares agreed on. The intention to be found is that the spouse who does not have the legal estate vested in him shall nevertheless be entitled to an interest in the proceeds of sale by virtue of the contributions he or she makes or is deemed to have made. [68] The courts will not be deterred by the difficulty of finding clear evidence: "The court cannot refuse to decide a case on the ground that the path to conclusion is not floodlit by clear evidence." [69]

The court may draw inferences which a reasonable man would draw from the parties' conduct [70]: they may have formed an intention "without having used express words to communicate this intention to one another; or their recollections of the words used may be imperfect or conflicting by the time any dispute arises." [71]

It is impossible to give clear rules as to when [72] such an inference can properly be drawn, but the following guidelines can be extracted from *Gissing* v. *Gissing* and subsequent decisions which are founded on the same juristic basis—*i.e.* that the court determines what the parties did in fact decide; it does not, and cannot ascribe intentions which the parties demonstrably never had [73]:

[66] [1971] 1 All E.R. 952.
[67] *Per* Lord Denning M.R. at p. 955.
[68] But *cf. Cowcher* v. *Cowcher* [1972] 1 All E.R. 943, 950 (for the view that what is in question is an inferred agreement as to the proportions in which the purchase money is to be treated as being provided rather than the shares in which the property is to be held, see also J. Levin (1972) 35 M.L.R. 547).
[69] *Per* Lord Morris, *Pettit* v. *Pettit* at p. 803.
[70] *Per* Lord Diplock, *Gissing* v. *Gissing* at p. 906.
[71] *Ibid.*
[72] "My Lords, I do not think that any useful purpose will be served by my expressing any views on what will suffice to justify the drawing of such an inference" *per* Lord Dilhorne, *ibid.*, 901.
[73] *Per* Lord Morris, *Gissing* v. *Gissing* at p. 898. For a close and valuable analysis of the cases see Dymond's *Death Duties* (15th ed.), pp. 448–459. See also L. Neville Brown (1971) 4 Ottawa L.R. 331.

(a) The underlying principle is that if both spouses contribute to the acquisition, they intend to be joint beneficial owners.

(b) In the simplest case, each party will pay part of the purchase price. The normal principle of the proportionate resulting trust will then apply.

(c) The same principle applies if the house is bought with the aid of a mortgage, but its application to the facts causes more problems:

(i) A payment towards the deposit is a contribution which leads to the inference that joint ownership was intended.

(ii) The same follows even in the absence of a contribution to the initial payment if the wife makes subsequent "*regular, substantial and direct* " contributions to the periodical mortgage payments.

(iii) It was not entirely clear after the House of Lords cases whether, in the absence of a contribution to the deposit, *indirect* contributions to the periodical payments sufficed to raise the necessary inference of original intention.[74]

This problem arises if, for instance, the husband pays all the mortgage payments, but is relieved of *other* household expenditure by his wife's earnings. On one view, such indirect contributions suffice if, but only if, *either* (a) husband and wife have consistently applied a system of meeting all expenses (including those of the house purchase) out of a common fund formed by the pooling of their resources,[75] or (b) if those contributions are *directly referable* to the acquisition costs.[76] Hence, they will qualify if the family budget has been re-arranged by virtue of the wife's earnings to enable the husband to pay the mortgage instalments. The clearest evidence of such connection would be if the Estate Owner could not have paid the instalments and discharged his other obligations had it not been for the wife's earnings. In the absence of such a causal connection indirect contributions will not suffice.

Another view is that no such causal relationship needs to be traced; the only question is whether there has been a substantial contribution in money or money's worth to family expenses.[77]

> "It is sufficient if the contributions made by the wife are such as to relieve the husband from expenditure which he would otherwise have had to bear. By so doing the wife helps him indirectly with the mortgage instalments because he has more money in his pocket with which to pay them. It may be that he does not strictly need her help—he may have enough money of his own without it— but if he accepts it (and thus is enabled to save more of his own money), she becomes entitled to a share." [78]

[74] The view that it does can be supported by reference to the speeches of Lords Reid and Pearson in *Gissing* at pp. 896, 903. Lord Diplock thought indirect contributions were only relevant *if* the wife had made an initial contribution to the deposit: see at p. 909.   [75] *Cowcher* v. *Cowcher* [1972] 1 All E.R. 943, 955, *per* Bagnali J.

[76] As in *Falconer* v. *Falconer* [1970] 3 All E.R. 449 where the indirect contributions consisted of joining in a guarantee of the Estate Owner's mortgage, and paying certain bills for " extras " connected with the house.

[77] *Per* Lord Denning M.R., *Falconer* v. *Falconer* (*supra*) at p. 452; *Wachtel* v. *Wachtel*, *supra* at p. 92.

[78] *Per* Lord Denning M.R., *Hazell* v. *Hazell* [1972] 1 All E.R. 923, 926.

This view is difficult to support on orthodox trust principles. If it is correct, it is difficult to understand why *Gissing* v. *Gissing* was not decided differently:

> The parties were married in 1935. The wife worked throughout the marriage, and was instrumental in getting the husband work with the same employer. The house in dispute was bought in 1951. The wife made no direct contribution to the acquisition costs, but paid for certain fittings and the cost of laying the lawn. She also paid for her own clothes and clothes for their son.

The House of Lords unanimously held that the wife had acquired no interest in the house. Yet the wife's contributions throughout the marriage must have " relieved the husband from expenditure which he would otherwise have had to bear." Nevertheless, the principle stated above appears to have formed the *ratio decidendi* of at least one case in the Court of Appeal,[79] so that it must be accepted as law for the time being unless and until considered again by the House of Lords.

Indirect contributions often result from the wife going out to work and earning a wage, and it suffices if her contribution is in the provision of services for which the husband would otherwise have had to pay, as in *Nixon* v. *Nixon*[80] where the wife's regular unpaid assistance in a market stall and shop sufficed. But contributions which cannot be regarded as in money's worth will not suffice.[81]

It should constantly be borne in mind that under the principle developed in the two House of Lords cases the question is *not*: does an indirect contribution suffice to give the wife an interest? It is: does the whole of the evidence (including the actions of the parties) justify the inference that they intended from the beginning to be treated as joint owners?[82] But the courts have not generally accepted that it must be possible to infer that the spouses' common answer to an officious bystander's question " Ought you not to record that you are intending to pay for this house in equal (or some other) shares? " would be " No; that goes without saying."[83]

Quantification of the spouses' interests is dealt with below.

Trusts imposed in the absence of agreement

A constructive trust may be imposed even in the absence of agreement, " in order to satisfy the demands of justice and good conscience."

---

79 *Hargrave* v. *Newton* [1971] 3 All E.R. 866. Other cases in which the " indirect contribution " view has been asserted by the Court of Appeal might have been decided in the same way on narrower grounds: *Davis* v. *Vale* [1971] 2 All E.R. 1021; *Falconer* v. *Falconer* (*supra*); *Hazell* v. *Hazell* [1972] 1 All E.R. 923. For a more orthodox view *cf. Cowcher* v. *Cowcher* (*supra*), and *Macfarlane* v. *Macfarlane* [1972] N.I. 59.
80 [1969] 3 All E.R. 1133, *cf. Simon* v. *Simon* (1971) 115 S.J. 673. See also *Muetzel* v. *Muetzel* [1970] 1 All E.R. 443; *Smith* v. *Baker* [1970] 2 All E.R. 826; *Re Cummins (dec'd.)* [1972] Ch. 62.
81 *Wachtel* v. *Wachtel* [1973] Fam. 72, 92, *per* Lord Denning M.R.
82 *Kowalczuk* v. *Kowalczuk* [1973] 2 All E.R. 1042.
83 *Cf. per* Bagnall J., *Cowcher* v. *Cowcher* (*supra*) at p. 955 where this is seen to be the proper test.

1. THE TRADITIONAL RULES OF EQUITY.[84] The general principle of English law is that if A expends money on B's property, this does not give A any interest in such property.[84a] The doctrine of equitable estoppel[85] may apply, however, if a wife has incurred expenditure on the property, in the belief (encouraged by her husband) that she already owned, or would be given, some proprietary interest in it.[86] Often cases when this doctrine might have been applied will now be solved by reference to section 37 of the Matrimonial Proceedings and Property Act 1970,[87] but the doctrine may still be relevant if for any reason that Act does not apply.[88]

There are other limited fields in which traditional doctrines of equity such as mistake[88] may be invoked, but these have only a limited application.

2. IMPOSING THE JUST SOLUTION. It is often difficult in matrimonial cases to reconcile the demands of doing justice on the facts with the rigid demands of orthodox property law. Two techniques have been used in an attempt to do what is just, rather than simply what is the law:

(a) *Section 17 of the Married Women's Property Act 1882.* This gave power to a judge to " make such order . . . as he thinks fit " where any question arose between husband and wife as to the title to or possession of property. It was claimed that this gave the court " a free hand to do what is just " in all the circumstances, ignoring the strict legal rules governing the title to property.[89] The House of Lords denounced this view as heretical[90]: " no Parliament of that era could have intended to put the husband's property at the hazard of the unfettered discretion of a judge (including a county court judge)." [91] This provision simply gives the parties the advantage of a summary procedure,[91a] and gives the court a discretion as to the *enforcement* of the parties' proprietary or possessory rights.

(b) *Lord Denning's view of the Trust.* In a number[92] of recent

---

[84] " The more-than-handy husband " by J. Tiley [1969] C.L.J. 92.
[84a] *Campion* v. *Cotton* (1810) 17 Ves. 263; *Ramsden* v. *Dyson* (1866) L.R. 1 H.L. 129; *Re Vandervell's Trusts (No. 2)* [1973] 3 W.L.R. 744, 772.
[85] *Ramsden* v. *Dyson* (1866) L.R. 1 H.L. 129 as interpreted by Lord Upjohn in *Pettit* (p. 818). See also *Unity Joint Stock, etc.* v. *King* (1858) 25 Beav. 72; *Chalmers* v. *Pardoe* [1963] 3 All E.R. 552. For a wider view of the constructive trust doctrine see *per* Lord Denning M.R., *Hussey* v. *Palmer* [1972] 1 W.L.R. 1286 at 1290.
[86] *Snell*, p. 565.
[87] *Infra*, p. 175.
[88] For possible applications of other traditional equitable doctrines, see Tiley, *op. cit.*
[89] See *per* Denning J., *H.* v. *H.* (1947) 63 T.L.R. 645, 646; *Hine* v. *Hine* [1962] 3 All E.R. 345, 347. *Appleton* v. *Appleton* [1965] 1 All E.R. 44, 46.
[90] *Pettit* v. *Pettit* [1970] A.C. 777.
[91] But note that 23 years previously Parliament had by s. 5 of the Matrimonial Causes Act 1859 given the courts (although not county courts) an entirely unfettered discretion to vary that most sacrosanct of Victorian institutions, the marriage settlement.
[91a] It also gives the court power to order a sale, which it does not have under the discretionary powers of breakdown; see *Glenn* v. *Glenn* [1973] 1 W.L.R. 1016.
[92] See *Heseltine* v. *Heseltine* [1971] 1 All E.R. 952; *Davis* v. *Vale* [1971] 2 All E.R. 1021; *Farquharson* v. *Farquharson* (1971) 115 S.J. 444; *Hazell* v. *Hazell* [1972] 1 All E.R. 923. See also *Cooke* v. *Head* [1972] 1 W.L.R. 518; *Hussey* v. *Palmer* [1972] 1 W.L.R. 1286; *cf. Richards* v. *Dove* (1973) The Times, November 17.

cases Lord Denning has suggested that the court may impose a trust wherever it would be " inequitable " for the estate owner to claim the property as his own.[93] " Inequitable " is not used in any technical sense: according to this view a trust may be imposed wherever the circumstances made it just to do so. This may be because of the wife's contributions to the family budget,[94] because of the husband's conduct,[95] or because the property was acquired by joint efforts for joint *use*.[96] Lord Denning has in terms stated that it is not necessary to establish even an implied agreement or common intention.[97] It is also implicit in his judgments that the court may look at the circumstances as they exist at the time of the marriage breakdown, and do what seems just in the circumstances as they then exist [98] (including the wife's right to maintenance [99]).

It is difficult to reconcile these views with the House of Lords insistence on the application of orthodox property law concepts.[1] It is true that this insistence leads to artificiality and injustice.[2] But in the absence of legislation inferior courts are obliged to follow decisions of the House of Lords.[3] It is submitted that this doctrine does not do so. It is not in any case necessary to have recourse to doctrines of this kind to do justice between the parties when a marriage breaks down: the court has ample *discretionary* powers to deal with this situation on the basis of an adjustment of the parties' *personal* rights.[4]

Quantifying the beneficial interests

(i) If each party's contribution has been a *cash* contribution to the purchase price, the beneficial interests will normally be proportionate to the cash sums provided.[5]

(ii) Greater difficulty is found if the house has been bought with the aid of a mortgage. Proportionate distribution by reference solely to the (often small) initial deposit might cause grave injustice. Hence—

(a) If it is clear that one spouse has *limited* his contribution to a

---

93 *Heseltine* v. *Heseltine* (*supra*) at p. 955F.
94 As in *Hazell* v. *Hazell* (*supra*) but not (apparently) to contributions not in money's worth: *Wachtel* v. *Wachtel* (*supra*) at p. 92.
95 As in *Heseltine* v. *Heseltine* (*supra*).
96 As in *Cook* v. *Head* [1972] 2 All E.R. at p. 41F. For some time, the courts sought to develop a special code for " family assets," but this had apparently been checked by the decision of the House of Lords in *Pettit* v. *Pettit* (*supra*). See Miller (1970) 86 L.Q.R. 98 and O. Kahn-Freund, " Matrimonial Property: where do we go from here? " (J. Unger Memorial Lecture, 1971.)
97 See *Hazell* v. *Hazell* (*supra*) at p. 925G; *Cooke* v. *Head* (*supra*) at p. 41F.
98 *Heseltine* v. *Heseltine*; *Davis* v. *Vale*; *Farquharson* v. *Farquharson* (*supra*).
99 But this may be intended only to apply to *quantum*: see *Farquharson* v. *Farquharson* (*supra*).
1 See *Pettit* v. *Pettit*; *Gissing* v. *Gissing* (*supra*).
2 *Cf. per* Lord Denning M.R., *Davis* v. *Vale* (*supra*) at pp. 1024–1025.
3 See *Broome* v. *Cassell & Co. Ltd.* [1972] A.C. 1027.
4 See *infra*, p. 190, and *Wachtel* v. *Wachtel* [1973] Fam. 72; *cf. Cowcher* v. *Cowcher* (*supra*) *per* Bagnall J. at p. 955E.
5 See *supra*, p. 153.

finite sum, his interest will be calculated in the proportion that bears to the total purchase price.[6]

(b) If one spouse puts up the whole deposit while the other assumes liability for the mortgage repayments it is impossible to separate and quantify the contributions.[7]

While excessive use of the maxim " Equality is Equity " has been criticised, it is (perhaps) the usual inference that the proceeds are divisible equally,[8] but this is far from inflexible [9]: there may be a case for quantifying the share in the light of all the circumstances at the time of division, since the parties can be taken to have agreed that the extent of their share should be quantified in this way.[10]

Legal estate in both spouses

In this case two main problems arise: (a) quantifying each party's *beneficial* interests; (b) resolving disputes between them as to how their property rights should be exercised.

(a) The beneficial interest

The rules can be summarised [11] as follows:

1. If there is an express declaration of the beneficial trusts, that is conclusive, or (at least) requires a high degree of proof of fraud or mistake if it is to be rebutted.[12] If the conveyance states that the parties hold the property upon trust for themselves as joint tenants beneficially (which presupposes an *equal* division) it will be very difficult for one of them subsequently to assert that he is entitled to more than 50 per cent. of the sale proceeds.

2. It is not entirely clear what suffices to rebut this presumption.[13] It may be necessary to prove that at the *date of the conveyance* there existed a common intention which was not carried out. It is not sufficient that the parties are at cross-purposes (*e.g.* that the wife believes they are taking equally, the husband that she is to have only a share proportionate to her financial contribution).

This is likely to cause injustice. No doubt the parties will have agreed that the property should in some way belong to them both. But

---

6 *Re Rogers' Question* [1948] 1 All E.R. 328.
7 *Rimmer* v. *Rimmer* [1959] 1 Q.B. 63; *Ulrich* v. *Ulrich* [1968] 1 W.L.R. 188.
8 *Per* Lord Denning M.R., *Heseltine* v. *Heseltine* [1971] 1 All E.R. 952, 954.
9 See *e.g. Smith* v. *Baker* [1970] 2 All E.R. 826; *Nixon* v. *Nixon* [1969] 3 All E.R. 1133; *Muetzel* v. *Muetzel* [1970] 1 All E.R. 443; *Falconer* v. *Falconer* [1970] 3 All E.R. 449; *Heseltine* v. *Heseltine* [1971] 1 All E.R. 952; *Cooke* v. *Head* [1972] 2 All E.R. 38.
10 See *per* Lord Diplock, *Gissing* v. *Gissing* [1971] A.C. 886, 909; and *per* Lord Denning M.R., *Davis* v. *Vale* [1971] 2 All E.R. 1021, 1027. As to the difficulties of adjustment of accounts between spouses when one has been left in sole occupation of a mortgaged house see: *Falconer* v. *Falconer* (*supra*); *Cracknell* v. *Cracknell* [1971] P. 356; *Cooke* v. *Head* (*supra*).   11 See (1970) 34 Conv.(N.S.) 156 (G. Miller).
12 *Per* Lord Upjohn in *Pettit* v. *Pettit* at p. 813 followed in *Re John's Assignment Trusts* [1970] 2 All E.R. 210; see also *Wilson* v. *Wilson* [1963] 1 W.L.R. 601; and *cf. Bedson* v. *Bedson* [1965] 2 Q.B. 666.
13 *Brown and Staniek* v. *Brown* (1969) 211 E.G. 283; see also *Wilson* v. *Wilson* [1969] 1 W.L.R. 1470; *Boydell* v. *Gillespie* (1970) 216 E.G. 1505 and *Re John's Assignment Trusts* (*supra*); *cf. Mayes* v. *Mayes* (1969) 210 E.G. 935.

the everyday use of words differs somewhat from the lawyer's: the expression " in equal shares " means that the property is to be held on a tenancy in common, so that the interests will devolve under the owner's intestacy or will (*i.e.* not necessarily to the other spouse). It is unlikely that husband and wife will appreciate these conveyancer's subtleties.

3. In the absence of any indication on the face of the title documents, or other evidence, the same principles set out above [14] apply, but:

(a) If the husband provides the purchase money, there will be a beneficial *joint* tenancy as distinct from tenancy in common.[15]

(b) If the wife provides it all, there will probably be a joint beneficial interest, not a resulting trust to her (as would be the case on a strict application of the presumptions). This is because no other reason can today be for this course of action.[16]

4. In addition to the other possibilities set out above (*i.e.* inferences of intention derived from conduct),[17] a joint owner who spends money on the trust property may have a *lien* on it in respect of the cost or additional value thus accruing. This may be based on an implied agreement, or on the equitable doctrine that a beneficiary cannot take anything out of a fund without making good what he owes to it. If expenses are incurred by one spouse in the management or improvement of the property, he is entitled [18] to be indemnified.

5. The beneficial interests may be varied by subsequent agreement.[19]

6. If the interest of the spouses is a *joint* tenancy either may *sever* it, thus converting it into a tenancy in common.[20] This may be important if either party is concerned to regulate the devolution of the property after death. For instance, if one spouse has children by another union he may want his share of the house to go to them rather than to the other spouse.

Severance can take place either—

(a) by giving notice in writing to the other spouse under section 36 (2) Law of Property Act 1925;

(b) by " an act of any one of the persons interested operating upon his own share." [21] Examples of such acts are a sale, mortgage

14 *Supra*, p. 153.
15 *Re Eyken's Trusts* (1877) 6 Ch.D. 115.
16 Per Lord Upjohn, *Pettit* v. *Pettit* (*supra*) at p. 815, *cf. Grzeczkowski* v. *Jedynska* (1971) 115 S.J. 126.
17 And to the provisions of s. 37, Matrimonial Proceedings and Property Act 1970, see *infra*, p. 175.
18 See also *Rowley* v. *Ginnever* [1897] 2 Ch. 503; *Re Rhodesia Goldfields Ltd.* [1910] 1 Ch. 239, *per* Swinfen Eady J. at p. 247 and see *Mayes* v. *Mayes* (1969) 210 E.G. 935; *Re Sims' Question* [1946] 2 All E.R. 138.
19 See Bevan and Taylor (1966) 30 Conv.(N.S.) 354, 436, Scammell [1967] C.L.P. 120, and Gareth Miller (1970) 34 Conv.(N.S.) 156 but unless the appropriate formalities are observed it will be necessary to have further recourse to the doctine of constructive trusts.
20 *Re Draper's Conveyance* [1969] 1 Ch. 486, where Lord Denning's view in *Bedson* v. *Bedson* [1965] 2 Q.B. 666, that there could be no severance (described in the same case by Russell L.J. as " being without the slighest foundation in law or equity ") was not accepted.
21 *Williams* v. *Hensman* (1861) 1 J. & H. 546, 557.

or settlement of the share.[22]   It is clear that it is impossible to sever a joint tenancy by will; by the time the will has taken effect the deceased's share will have accrued to the other.   This is an important practical problem.   A spouse whose marriage is on the verge of break-up may want to sever, to protect the interest of her own children.   Giving notice to the other may be seen as a hostile step and precipitate a crisis.   The simplest solution would be to allow severance by will.

(b) *Exercise of the parties' rights*

Property owned jointly or in common is subject to a trust (*i.e.* an imperative obligation) to *sell*; there is only a *power* to postpone sale.[23] The consequence of this distinction is that the trustees (*i.e.* the spouses if they both hold the legal estate) must be unanimous if they are to exercise the power to postpone sale; if one wants to sell, there should be a sale.   This rule is not however absolute.   If there is a dispute, application can be made to the court under section 30 of the Law of Property Act 1925, " for an order directing the trustees for sale to give effect thereto."   The decision is then within the court's discretion,[24] and a sale will not be ordered if, either (a) it would be inequitable so to do, or (b) some purpose of the trust remains to be discharged.

The application of these principles can be seen by contrasting two decided cases.   In *Jones* v. *Challenger*[25] the house had been bought as a home in which the spouses could live; that purpose had been brought to an end by divorce; a sale was ordered.   There were no young children; if there had been, it might well have been held that the original trust's purposes were still in existence.[26]   Nor was it inequitable that the wife should want to realise her investment.   In *Bedson* v. *Bedson*[27] on the other hand, the husband was carrying on a business in the house and a sale would ruin him.   Since it would have been inequitable, the court refused to order a sale; the husband was ordered to pay the wife £1 a week in respect of her interest in the house.[28]

---

[22] *Megarry and Wade*, 3rd ed. pp. 417–419.   In *Re Draper* (*supra*) it was held that the wife's act in issuing a summons under s. 17, Married Women's Property Act 1882 seeking a sale of the house was sufficient.   This has been criticised (see (1968) 84 L.Q.R. 462) on the grounds that it was a mere unilateral declaration, and thus insufficient.   In *Re John's Assignment Trusts* (*supra*), Goff J. assumed that proceedings brought by a wife for an order for sale had severed a tenancy.   It seems clear that if an *order* for sale is made, this effectively severs the tenancy.

[23] This is generally assumed to be the case, but it is not always clear how the result follows from the language of the statute: see *Megarry and Wade*, 3rd ed. p. 423 *et seq.*; Rudden, (1963) 27 Conv.(N.S.) 51.

[24] *Re Buchanan-Wollaston's Conveyance* [1939] Ch. 738; see also *Re Solomon* [1967] Ch. 573.

[25] [1961] 1 Q.B. 177.

[26] See *Rawlings* v. *Rawlings* [1964] 2 All E.R. 804, *per* Salmon L.J.

[27] [1965] 2 Q.B. 666.

[28] It is not entirely clear under what jurisdiction this order was made; it appears that the court has no power to order the grant of a tenancy to one of the trustees: *Re John's Assignment Trusts* (*supra*) at p. 214.   *Bedson* v. *Bedson* was distinguished on the ground that only an interim order was made in that case.

In deciding how to exercise its discretion the court takes the parties' conduct into account. A wife who has been deserted by the husband will normally be allowed to stay in possession, but there may be circumstances when this will not be so.[29] The question in each case is: what would be reasonable and just in all the circumstances? [30]

Conveyancing Problems

The imposition of a trust for sale causes difficulties in conveyancing. These are outside the scope of this book [31] but the general principles are:

(a) If the legal estate is vested in one spouse on trust for himself and a spouse, a second trustee should be appointed to convey the legal estate, and enable the equitable interest to be over-reached;

(b) if this is not done, the purchaser will probably nevertheless get a good title if he takes without notice, actual or constructive, of the equitable interest. If the title is registered, however, it is possible that the purchaser will take subject to the equitable interest if the spouse entitled thereto is in actual occupation.[32]

Joint Bank Accounts

In the case of land the claim which the courts often have to decide is whether the beneficial interest belongs to both husband and wife, even though the legal title is only in one. In the case of bank accounts, the claim is often the converse—*i.e.* that although husband and wife have had a joint account, the balance in it and any investments made out of it belong only to one of them. The practice of opening joint accounts is now common, but often gives rise to serious problems on the death of one party in agreeing with the Estate Duty Office what (if any) share of the account forms part of his estate.[32a]

The problem has to be decided by reference to general principles, but the courts have established a number of guidelines specially applicable to this kind of property:

1. If the parties pool their resources in a common fund, then they will each have an interest as beneficial joint tenants in the whole of the

---

29 See *Jackson* v. *Jackson* [1971] 3 All E.R. 774. As to the principle on which Plowman J. decided that case at first instance (*i.e.* that a wife's right to be housed is commensurate with her right to maintenance) *cf. Jones* v. *Jones* [1971] 1 W.L.R. 396, and *Re Hardy's Trust* (1970) 114 S.J. 864.

30 *Jackson* v. *Jackson* (*supra*).

31 Rudden, " The Wife, the Husband and the Conveyancer " (1963) 27 Conv.(N.S.) 51, Megarry and Wade 3rd ed. 423 *et seq. Waller* v. *Waller* [1967] 1 W.L.R. 451; *Caunce* v. *Caunce* [1969] 1 W.L.R. 286; *Re Rogers' Question* [1948] 1 All E.R. 328; *Bull* v. *Bull* [1955] 1 Q.B. 234; *Cook* v. *Cook* [1962] P. 181; [1962] P. 235; J. F. Garner, " A Single Trustee for Sale " (1969) 33 Conv.(N.S.) 246; Farrand, *Contract and Conveyance*, p. 178; *Marks* v. *Attallah* (1966) 110 S.J. 709; D. J. Hayton, " Overriding Rights of Occupiers of Matrimonial Homes." (1969) 33 Conv.(N.S.) 254; T. B. F. Ruoff, " Protection of the Purchaser in English Law." (1969) 32 M.L.R. 121, 131; *Hodgson* v. *Marks* [1971] Ch. 892, Leeming, (1971) 35 Conv.(N.S.) 255.

32 *Cf. Hodgson* v. *Marks* (*supra*), and see Leeming, (1971) 35 Conv.(N.S.) 255; R. H. Maudsley (1973) 36 M.L.R. 25; J. L. Barton (1972) 88 L.Q.R. 14.

32a Dymond's *Death Duties* (15th ed.), p. 484 *et seq.*

fund.[33]   Thus if both husband and wife pay their incomes into a joint bank account, on the death of one the survivor will normally be entitled to the whole balance by the *jus accrescendi,* and one half of it will be an asset in the deceased's estate.

2. If funds are withdrawn from a common pool account, property bought with the proceeds will prima facie belong to the spouse who acquires the title: if a wife buys shares in her own name by drawing on a joint bank account, they will prima facie belong to her absolutely.[34] This will not be so if there is evidence that the assets so acquired were intended to be held in the same way as the fund, but this would be unusual.[35]

3. The common fund will only apply if there is a *pooling* of resources. Otherwise (in the absence of other evidence of intention) the presumptions of advancement and resulting trust must be applied to determine the ownership. Hence if the husband has his salary paid into a joint bank account, prima facie the account will belong to the spouses as joint tenants.[36]

It is sufficient to rebut any presumption if it can be shown that the account was in joint names for reasons of convenience only.[37]   One very common (and sensible) reason for having a joint bank account is to enable the wife to continue to draw cash after the husband's death before probate has been granted. It has been held [38] that such an account (on which the husband continued to draw) has for the purposes of this rule been opened for convenience only.

Although an account may originally have been put into joint names for convenience only, the intention may change so that a joint interest will arise.[39]   It is a matter for inference in the light of all the available evidence.

Relevance of the Rules for Determining Title

It has been pointed out that many of the developments of matrimonial property law were prompted by a desire to achieve an equitable division of " family assets " on marriage breakdown. Since the court now has extensive powers to divide up such assets on a discretionary basis, and is prepared to use them,[40] it will rarely be necessary to determine property

33 *Jones* v. *Maynard* [1951] Ch. 572; *cf. Gage* v. *King* [1961] 1 Q.B. 188.
34 *Re Bishop, deceased* [1965] Ch. 450.
35 See *Jones* v. *Maynard (supra).*
36 *Re Figgis* [1969] 1 Ch. 123, *cf. Heseltine* v. *Heseltine* [1971] 1 All E.R. 952, where the whole balance on a joint account fed largely with the wife's capital belonged to her.
37 *Re Figgis, deceased* [1969] 1 Ch. 123, *Marshall* v. *Crutwell* (1875), L.R. 20 Eq. 328; *Hoddinott* v. *Hoddinott* [1949] 2 K.B. 406; *Harrods Ltd.* v. *Tester* [1937] 2 All E.R. 236; *Heseltine* v. *Heseltine (supra),* (account only in joint names " for convenience of administration for the family purposes.")
38 *Thompson* v. *Thompson* (1970) 114 S.J. 455.
39 *Re Figgis (supra).* Semble such a new intention will only affect monies subsequently paid into the account: *cf.* s. 53 (1) (*c*), L.P.A. 1925.
40 *Infra,* p. 206.

rights if divorce or other matrimonial proceedings are to take place.[41] It may, however, still be necessary to resort to these rules if:

(a) The question does not arise in consequence of the breakdown of the parties' marriage, but as a result of the death or insolvency of either of them.

(b) Neither party wishes to take other matrimonial proceedings (although judicial separation may be sought by a spouse who does not want a divorce in order to invoke the wide discretionary powers). Furthermore, the procedure of section 17 of the Married Women's Property Act 1882 may still be invoked if an order for the *sale* of part of the property is required.[42]

Succession on Death
Wills

Any adult person of sound mind [43] may dispose of all his property on death by making a will complying with the formalities prescribed by the Wills Act 1837.[44] Until 1938 the power thus conferred on a man to disinherit his wife and children was absolute [45]; the Inheritance (Family Provision) Act 1938 gave the court a limited power to override the deceased's testamentary provisions by ordering provision to be made out of his estate for the maintenance of his widow and a limited category of other dependants. This is dealt with elsewhere.[46]

The privilege is exercised comparatively rarely: only 24 per cent. of a representative sample of husbands and 10 per cent. of wives had made wills [47] (although more than two-thirds of those who had not did have some vague intention to do so in the future).[48]

Intestacy

Under the system of intestate succession introduced by the Administration of Estates Act 1925 the whole of the deceased's property is held (after payment of debts etc.) for the following:

If the intestate leaves a spouse and issue [49]

The surviving spouse takes:

(i) The personal chattels [50] absolutely.

---

41 *Hunter* v. *Hunter* [1973] 1 W.L.R. 958, 961; *Wachtel* v. *Wachtel* [1973] Fam. 72, 92; *Gordon* v. *Gordon* (1973) The Times, October 13; *cf. Glenn* v. *Glenn* [1973] 1 W.L.R. 1016.
42 *Glenn* v. *Glenn* (*supra*); this power was exercised in *Harnett* v. *Harnett* [1973] 2 All E.R. 593.
43 See *Theobald*, Chap. 5.
44 s. 9. See *Theobald*, Chap. 6.
45 Although fixed rights of inheritance were known to early English Law: *Pollock and Maitland*, Vol. II, p. 348. The final vestiges of these rights (dower and curtesy) were abolished in 1925: Administration of Estates Act 1925, s. 45.
46 See *infra*, p. 177.
47 *Todd and Jones*, para. 5.1.
48 *Ibid.*, para. 5.2.
49 However remote. The expression also includes any illegitimate child of the intestate and the issue of such child: Family Law Reform Act 1969, s. 14.
50 Defined in s. 55 (1) (*x*), A.E.A. 1925. See *Theobald*, para. 602.

(ii) A "statutory legacy," currently amounting to £15,000.[51]

(iii) A life interest in one-half of the balance of the estate.

Subject to the spouse's rights, the estate is held " on the statutory trusts " for the issue of the intestate. These trusts are defined in the Act.[52] For present purposes it suffices to note that in the common case the intestate's children will be entitled to the capital when they attain eighteen; if any child of the intestate predeceases him leaving children, they take the child's presumptive share.

If the intestate leaves a spouse but no issue

(a) *If he also leaves a parent, a brother or sister* [53] *the surviving spouse takes*

(i) the personal chattels absolutely

(ii) a statutory legacy of £40,000

(iii) one half of any balance absolutely.

The other half is held for the intestate's surviving parent or parents (in equal shares) absolutely, but if he leaves no parent, on the statutory trusts for the brothers and sisters.

(b) *If he leaves no such close relatives* the whole estate goes to the surviving spouse.

If the intestate leaves no surviving spouse

(a) If he leaves issue, the whole estate is held on the statutory trusts for their benefit.

(b) If he leaves no issue but is survived by one or both parents, then they take (in equal shares if both survive) absolutely.

(c) If he leaves neither issue nor parent the following relatives (if surviving) take in order:

(i) Brothers and Sisters

(ii) Grandparents

(iii) Uncles and Aunts

(d) In default the estate passes as *bona vacantia* to the Crown. In this event provision may as a matter of grace be made for " dependants " (whether kindred or not), of the intestate, and other persons for whom the intestate might reasonably have been expected to make provision.[54] This power may be used to provide some part of the estate for the deceased's " Common Law wife " (*i.e.* mistress) who has no rights on his intestacy.

The salient feature of this code of distribution is the generosity with which it treats the surviving spouse: it is only in the case of comparatively large estates that he or she will not inherit the whole of the intestate's property. There may be cases where his generosity causes

---

[51] See Family Provision (Intestate Succession) Order 1972, operative in the case of deaths on or after July 1, 1972. Interest is payable on the legacy from the date of death until payment.

[52] A.E.A. 1925, s. 47, as amended.

[53] Or issue of such.

[54] A.E.A. 1925, s. 46 (1) (vi). See generally Ing, *Bona Vacantia.*

injustice, particularly where a parent with dependent children marries a second time: the spouse will take to the prejudice of the dependants.[55]

The surviving spouse also has the right to require the intestate's interest in the matrimonial home in which the surviving spouse was resident at the time of the intestate's death to be appropriated in or towards satisfaction of his or her share.[56]

STATUTORY REFORMS

The Married Women's Property Act 1964

If a husband provided his wife with an allowance out of his income for housekeeping, any sums not spent on this purpose remained his, and he was entitled to any property bought with such savings.[57]

This rule seemed symptomatic of the injustices done to married women (particularly those who devoted their lives to looking after the home). The Morton Commission therefore recommended that savings made out of a housekeeping allowance should belong half to the husband and half to the wife.[58] The Married Women's Property Act 1964 [59] implements this:

> " If any question arises as to the right of a husband or wife to money derived from any allowance made by the husband for the expenses of the matrimonial home or for similar purposes, or to any property acquired out of such money, the money or property shall, in the absence of any agreement between them to the contrary, be treated as belonging to the husband and wife in equal shares."

This gives a genuine proprietary interest in such savings: it applies not only if a marriage breaks down, but if one of the spouses becomes insolvent or (for succession and estate duty purposes) on the death of either.

Unfortunately, the Act raises a number of problems:

(i) What is an " allowance " for this purpose? Does it cover the case where the wife has a power to draw on the husband's bank account?

(ii) What does " for the expenses of the matrimonial home or for similar purposes " mean? It is not clear whether payment of mortgage instalments is " an expense of the matrimonial home " or an expense of acquiring it.[59a]

(iii) It is not clear whether the Act operates retrospectively [60]—i.e. whether it applies to savings made out of an allowance before the Act came into force or not. The general principle is that Acts of Parliament

---

55 See *Sivyer* v. *Sivyer* [1967] 3 All E.R. 429.
56 Intestates' Estates Act 1952, Sched. 2.
57 *Blackwell* v. *Blackwell* [1943] 2 All E.R. 579; *Hoddinott* v. *Hoddinott* [1949] 2 K.B. 406.   58 Para. 701.
59 See O. M. Stone (1964) 27 M.L.R. 576.
59a *Tymosczuk* v. *Tymosczuk* (1964) 108 S.J. 656.
60 So held in *Tymosczuk* v. *Tymosczuk* (*supra*), but doubted in *Re John's Assignment Trusts* (*supra*).

do not effect changes of substance in the law (particularly when the change would affect vested property rights) but the resulting accountancy problems may be almost insoluble.

(iv) If the savings are invested the Act applies. But if part is " invested " in an entry on the Football Pools, are any winnings " derived from " the allowance? [61]

Even when it is clear what the legal effect of the Act is, these consequences sometimes seem bizarre:

(i) the Act creates a *tenancy in common* so that the fund will be held jointly by the spouses during their lives, but on death the share passes under the deceased's will or intestacy.

(ii) If a wife buys something obviously intended for her own personal use (*e.g.* a fur coat) the Act apparently entitles the husband to a half share in it (unless the courts find there is an implied agreement to the contrary).

(iii) The Act does not confer any rights on a husband whose wife makes an allowance to him.

The Matrimonial Homes Act 1967

In *National Provincial Bank Ltd.* v. *Ainsworth* [62] the House of Lords made a sharp distinction between personal obligations and property rights. A husband is under an obligation to provide his wife with housing. She can protect herself by getting an injunction against his selling the house over her head.[63] But if a disposition takes place her rights could not bind a purchaser.

In practice, the real threat to the wife was that her husband might mortgage the house as security for a loan, and then get into financial difficulties (no doubt exacerbated by the expense of keeping two households going). The mortgagee would be entitled to possession of the house, and could sell it free of the wife's personal rights. These are not worth very much against an insolvent husband.

The Matrimonial Homes Act 1967 [64] was passed to remedy this situation. Its primary object was to give a wife [65] a shield against eviction or exclusion by her husband [66]; that protection is made to bind third parties [67] by constituting those rights into a *charge*—

" having the like priority as if it were an equitable interest created

---

[61] *Cf. Hoddinott* v. *Hoddinott* (*supra*).

[62] [1965] A.C. 1175. For a full discussion of the problems caused by this case, see Crane: After the Deserted Wife's Licence (1965) 29 Conv.(N.S.) 254.

[63] *Lee* v. *Lee* [1952] 2 Q.B. 451.

[64] See Crane (1968) 32 Conv.(N.S.) 85; (1969) 33 Conv.(N.S.) 148; Stone (1968) 31 M.L.R. 305; Kahn-Freund (1970) 33 M.L.R. 601, 610.

[65] The Act applies irrespective of sex, and accords protection to husbands as well as wives. To avoid circumlocution the text assumes (unless otherwise indicated) that the estate owner is the husband, and that the wife has no proprietary interest.

[66] *Per* Megarry J., *Wroth* v. *Tyler* [1973] 1 All E.R. 897, 907.

[67] The Morton Commission (paras. 662 *et seq.*) had recommended that this be done but a court order was needed for full protection against a third party.

at whichever is the latest of the following dates, that is to say—
(a) the date when [the husband] . . . acquires the estate or interest;
(b) the date of the marriage; and (c) the commencement of this
Act " (*i.e.* January 1, 1968).[68]

Thus if H buys a house on July 1, 1970, and gets married on November 1,
the wife's charge will attach as from that latter date.

The charge is registrable as a Class F land charge.[69] Unless and
until so registered the charge will be void against a purchaser [70] of the
land or of any interest therein.[71] The Act thus reconciles the conflicting
policies of giving protection to a wife and yet enabling transactions in
land to take place without the purchaser having to make difficult and
embarrassing enquiries about the vendor's matrimonial status. An
intending purchaser searches for Land Charges as a matter of routine.
If his search reveals no charge he can be confident that he will take
free of a claim under the Act. At the same time, it is easy for the wife
to register.

An illustration may be helpful: suppose that H (who is married to W)
buys Blackacre as a matrimonial home. At that moment a charge
attaches to it in W's favour. But if—as is commonly done—H immediately
(on the same day, and indeed in fact—as distinct from legal theory [72]—
as part of the same transaction) mortgages the property to a Building
Society, the wife's charge is not registered at the date of that mortgage
and the Building Society will not be bound by it. H defaults on the
mortgage payments, the Building Society will be entitled to enforce the
mortgage, by possession, sale etc.[73] If W registers at any time after
completion her right will bind subsequent purchasers. Thus if H contracts a second mortgage the second mortgagee will be subject to W's
rights. In practice no mortgagee would lend money on a property
subject to a Class F charge.[74]

A charge may only be registered over one property at any one time.[75]
A wife may choose against which of several houses (*e.g.* a country cottage
or a town flat) she registers; and she may register successive charges.
If she registers more than one charge at a time the Chief Land Registrar
is bound to cancel the first charge.[76] A charge may not be registered
over property which has never been a matrimonial home.[77]

---

[68] s. 2 (1) 1967. Although the Law Reform (Miscellaneous Provisions) Act 1970 generally
applies the matrimonial property rules to engaged couples, the Matrimonial Homes Act
seems not to be so extended.
[69] s. 2 (7) Land Charges Act 1972. Analogous provisions exist in the case of properties
the title to which is registered under the Land Registration Act 1925: s. 2 (7).
[70] *i.e.* including a mortgagee.
[71] s. 4 (8) Land Charges Act 1972. It is expressly provided that the wife's rights do not
constitute an overriding interest: s. 2 (7), Matrimonial Homes Act.
[72] *Church of England Building Society* v. *Piskor* [1954] Ch. 553.
[73] *Hastings and Thanet Building Society* v. *Goddard* [1970] 3 All E.R. 954.
[74] There is provision to enable W to *postpone* her charge to another person's, or to
release it altogether; there is also provision protecting the position of a contracting
purchaser: see ss. 4, 6, Matrimonial Homes Act 1967.
[75] s. 3, Matrimonial Homes Act.
[76] *Ibid.*   [77] See s. 1 (7) (8), M.H.A. and *cf. Nanda* v. *Nanda* [1968] P. 351.

What and Who is Protected

The rights which are protected are those which subsist from time to time between husband and wife. Those are called " rights of occupation," and are defined in the Act as [78] :

> " if in occupation, a right not to be evicted or excluded from the dwelling house or any part thereof by the other spouse except with the leave of the court given by an order under this section; if not in occupation, a right with the leave of the court so given to enter into and occupy the dwelling house."

The rights being *personal* in nature [79] (although protected by registration as if they were proprietary) come to an end on termination of the marriage by death or legal process : " a spouse's rights of occupation shall continue only so long as the marriage subsists and the other spouse is entitled." [80]

The act of registering the wife's charge does nothing to extend her rights against her husband. If on being informed that his wife has registered a Class F Land Charge, the husband suffers a fatal heart attack, the wife's rights die with him. In practice a more important threat arises from the fact that the wife's rights end on divorce. If an *English* court grants a divorce this fact will be taken into account in fixing the financial provision which the husband is ordered to make for the wife [81]; but if a *foreign court* grants a decree it may not do so. This is a real problem, since the decrees of foreign courts are increasingly regarded as effective to dissolve marriages.[82] The only way in which the charge can be crystallised or perfected [83] is by application to the court. The Act provides—

> " So long as one spouse has rights of occupation either of the spouses may apply to the court for an order declaring, enforcing, restricting or terminating those rights or regulating the exercise by either spouse of the right to occupy the dwelling house." [84]

The Act also [85] gives the court power to make an order which will extend the rights of occupation beyond the marriage, but this power is only exercisable " in the event of a matrimonial dispute or estrangement." It follows therefore that a spouse will be well advised to apply to the court for such an order. Merely registering a Class F charge gives a protection which may be illusory.

---

[78] s. 1 (1).
[79] They do not avail against an insolvent husband's creditors: s. 2 (5); *Wroth* v. *Tyler* (*supra*).
[80] s. 2 (2).
[81] *Infra*, p. 190.
[82] See the Recognition of Divorces and Legal Separation Act 1971, 115 S.J. 778 (Samuels). See also *Turczak* v. *Turczak* [1970] P. 198; Karsten (1970) 33 M.L.R. 205; Cretney (1969) 119 New L.J. 1121.
[83] See *per* Lord Denning M.R., *Baynham* v. *Baynham* [1968] 1 W.L.R. 1890. The court may make an interim order.
[84] s. 1 (2).
[85] s. 2 (2) (*b*) proviso.

The Act gives no rights over the household *furnishings*: a spiteful husband may make life unbearable for his wife by removing essential furniture. Nor does it protect anyone except the wife against eviction: if she takes in lodgers or guests, the husband may exclude them.[86]

Rights to contribute

The Act provides [87] that where a spouse is entitled to occupy a dwelling house, any payment or tender by him of mortgage instalments or other outgoings shall be as good as if made by the other spouse. Even if a mortgagee has priority over the wife's charge, she will be able to stay in possession provided she can keep up the mortgage instalments. Supplementary Benefit is available for the interest (but not capital) portion of the instalments. If a wife does so contribute she will almost certainly acquire a proprietary interest in the house.[88]

Special Problems on the Act

(a) *Joint owners and the Act*

The Act was passed to protect the wife who had no proprietary interest in the house. It only applied—

"where one spouse is entitled to occupy a dwelling house by virtue of an estate or interest or contract or by virtue of any enactment ... and the other spouse is not so entitled. ..."[89]

It did not therefore apply where the *legal estate is vested in both spouses.*[90] No effective disposition can take place without both spouses' concurrence, and there is no need for protection.

If the legal estate was vested in the husband on trust for himself and his wife as joint owners the wife would have an equitable interest in the property. Was such a wife "not so entitled"—*i.e.* to occupy? The answer was not clear.[91] The Act was therefore amended to enable such a wife to register a Class F land charge,[92] without prejudicing her proprietary interests.[93]

(b) *Can a spouse who is not in occupation register?*

The Act was primarily intended to protect the wife who had been deserted by her husband [94] against the risk that he would sell the house

---

[86] *Per* Megarry J., *Wroth* v. *Tyler* (*supra*) at p. 908.
[87] s. 1 (5).
[88] *Supra*, p. 153.
[89] s. 1 (1).
[90] See *Gurasz* v. *Gurasz* [1970] P. 11.
[91] Law Commission 25, paras. 59–60.
[92] Matrimonial Proceedings and Property Act 1970, s. 38.
[93] The wife's rights as an equitable owner would be defeated by a bona fide purchaser for value: *Caunce* v. *Caunce* (*supra*) at least in the case of unregistered land, see *supra*, p. 163. Registration does not affect a purchase with notice of the wife's equitable interest but in practice it would put off any bona fide purchaser.
[94] Although it " is in no way confined to desertion or any other matrimonial offence but confers all the rights that it gives forthwith on marriage." *Per* Megarry J., *Wroth* v. *Tyler* (*supra*) at p. 906.

over her head: hence there is something to be said on policy grounds for limiting the protection to the case where the wife is still in occupation. But it seems strange to deprive a wife who has been (perhaps temporarily) driven out by her husband of the protection of the Act.

This has caused difficulty. The rights of a spouse not in occupation are " with the leave of the court " to enter into and occupy the dwelling house; these are defined as " rights of occupation," [95] and constitute a charge.[96] It could be argued that *until the leave of the court was obtained* the wife has no charge; if she has no charges, she has nothing to register. This reasoning has been rejected [97]: the non-occupying wife had a right of entry which was conditional on the court's leave being obtained [98]; which is sufficient to give her a registrable charge under the definition in the Act.

(c) *Can the court, under the Act, order a spouse-owner out of his house?*

The Act is primarily concerned with protecting the wife against a purported disposition to a third party, but it does contain power for the court to regulate the exercise by either spouse of the right to occupy the house. Does that include power to make an order wholly prohibiting exercise by the husband of the right to occupy normally incidental to his proprietary right? The difficulty arises from a distinction drawn in the Act: (a) on the one hand the court may " *declare, enforce, restrict or terminate* " rights of occupation; (b) on the other, it may only *regulate* the exercise by either spouse of the right to occupy the house. The Act contains no definition of " right to occupy," but it defines " rights of occupation " in a way which suggests that it refers only to the rights of the non-owner. Hence it has been held [99] that the court cannot " terminate " the right of a husband-owner to occupy the house, it can only " regulate " it, *e.g.* by ordering that he should not use the kitchen save at certain times. Power to regulate does not include a power to prohibit. In practical terms, the effect of this restriction may not be great:

(i) It applies only to the court's jurisdiction under the Matrimonial Homes Act. It in no way affects the court's inherent power to protect a wife from molestation, or to preserve her rights pending divorce proceedings. It is immaterial that the power stems from the inherent jurisdiction rather than from the Matrimonial Homes Act.[1]

---

95 s. 1 (1) (*b*).   96 s. 2 (1).

97 *Watts* v. *Waller* [1972] 3 W.L.R. 365, *cf. Rutherford* v. *Rutherford* [1970] 3 All E.R. 422.

98 This suggestion was first made by Lord Denning M.R. in *Baynham* v. *Baynham* [1968] 1 W.L.R. 1890.

99 By the House of Lords: *Tarr* v. *Tarr* [1972] 2 W.L.R. 1078. See also *Maynard* v. *Maynard* [1969] P. 88.

1 See *e.g. Gurasz* v. *Gurasz* [1970] P. 11, and *Maynard* v. *Maynard* (*supra*) in both of which injunctions were made under the inherent jurisdiction, although the application had been made under the Act. But the power is sparingly exercised: see Prichard [1973] C.L.J. 227; *Phillips* v. *Phillips* [1973] 1 W.L.R. 615.

(ii) In many cases, the dispute about the home will be simply part of the background to a divorce hearing. When the divorce is dealt with, the court has the widest powers to give the wife such proprietary interest in the matrimonial home as may seem appropriate.

(d) *Application to rented property*

During the currency of the marriage, the tenant's wife will have rights of occupation under section 1 (1) of the Act. She is thus entitled not to be evicted by her husband, and she can apply to the court to declare and fix her rights.[2]

The Act also confers special protection:

(a) any payment by way of rent or rates by the wife is " as good as if made or done " by the other spouse. So long as she pays the rent therefore,[3] the landlord cannot evict her.

(b) The wife's occupation is treated for the purposes of the Rent Act 1968 as possession by the other spouse. The effect of this provision is to preserve for the wife the complex rights of security of tenure and succession [4] conferred by the Rent Acts.

There is a limited power to protect the wife of a protected tenant after divorce or nullity. The court, on pronouncing a decree of divorce or nullity, can transfer such a tenancy to the wife, with effect from the date when the decree is made absolute. The transferee becomes liable to perform the obligations of the tenancy (*e.g.* to pay the rent); the husband ceases to be liable in respect of future performance of the obligations.[5] This provision gives a divorced wife security in occupation of property at a fair rent but there are some curious anomalies: the transfer can only take effect on decree absolute of divorce and is not available in judicial separation or neglect to maintain.[6] Furthermore it only applies to tenancies within the Rent Acts and not for instance, to council house tenancies.

(e) *Apart from the Act, can the Common Law protect unregistered rights of occupation?*

A wife who fails to register will lose her rights against a bona fide purchaser. But she may not do so if the sale is a " sham "[7] as distinct from a genuine sale (even at a low price and with the ulterior motive of defeating the wife's claim).[8]

Apart from this limited exception, neither common law nor equity will protect a wife who could have, but has not, registered under the Act. It introduced a clear statutory code for this purpose which replaced any

---

[2] s. 1 (2).
[3] But see *Penn* v. *Dunn* [1970] 2 All E.R. 858 for one flaw in this protection.
[4] For details see *Megarry on the Rent Acts*, p. 188.
[5] s. 7 as amended.
[6] Nor is it available to a deserted widow.
    Rent Act 1968, Sched. I para. 2.
[7] *Ferris* v. *Weaven* [1952] 2 All E.R. 233, approved in *National Provincial Bank Ltd.* v. *Ainsworth*, see [1965] A.C. 1175, 1257, 1258.
[8] *Miles* v. *Bull* (*No.* 1) [1969] 1 Q.B. 258.

old equitable doctrines, which might possibly have protected her apart from the Act.

Criticism

Apart from the points already mentioned, the Act can be criticised on a number of grounds:

(i) The wife is in practice likely to be at a severe disadvantage in knowing what to do; the Act contains nothing to require prior notice of any transaction to be given to her.[9] By the time she consults a solicitor the husband may have carried out transactions to her disadvantage.

The Act's protection would be more generally effective if it were a matter of routine to register a charge in favour of the wife whenever a matrimonial home is bought. If relations remain good no one would suffer. If there were discord the wife would be adequately protected without the necessity of taking a step which may be practically difficult, and will be seen as a hostile act. This is not the present practice.[10] The authorities were concerned that the Land Charges Registry would be swamped by a flood of applications,[11] and Solicitors were concerned as to the professional propriety of taking a step which could be adverse to the interests of the husband if he alone was their client.

(ii) It may be difficult for solicitors to ensure that an application is effective:

(a) The wife may not know [12] whether title is registered or not, with the result that an inappropriate registration is made.

(b) Registration of a land charge, to be fully effective, has to be against the correct full name of the owner. For present purposes that is the name into which he has had the property conveyed. It is by no means impossible that the wife will register her charge against a variant of that name (e.g. Jack instead of John or vice versa); if she does she is not protected against a purchaser who searches against the correct names (which he, unlike the wife, will know from seeing a copy or abstract of the conveyance).[13]

(iii) There is no provision whereby the estate owner is notified of the registration of a charge. This may cause difficulties if he subsequently bona fide enters into a contract to sell the property.[14]

(iv) A malicious or spiteful wife is given a very powerful weapon: she can register a Class F charge, even after the husband has contracted

---

9 Per Megarry J., Miles v. Bull (supra) at p. 261.

10 See Wroth v. Tyler (supra) at p. 909D.

11 There are some 40 applications a week under the current practice: Chief Land Registrar's Report, 1969–70, p. 7.

12 The solicitors could find out by searching the Index Map, but this takes time.

13 Oak Co-operative Building Society v. Blackburn [1968] Ch. 730, see Cretney, 112 S.J. 450; Diligent Finance Ltd. v. Alleyne (1972) 23 P. & C.R. 346.

14 See Watts v. Waller (supra); Wroth v. Tyler (supra).

to sell, and thus make it impossible for him to perform his contract—
perhaps at the cost of heavy damages.[15]

Generally speaking, however, the Act does meet the problem reasonably well. Many criticisms of it, *e.g.* that it gives the wife no protection
if her husband is adjudicated bankrupt,[16] or against the building society
which has advanced the purchase price [17]—imply a policy of throwing
the social cost of housing deserted wives onto individual creditors (rather
than society as a whole) whose implications would be very far-reaching.

The Matrimonial Proceedings and Property Act 1970, Section 37
One of the ways in which the courts tried to give effect to the idea that
marriage was a partnership was to hold that if a spouse carried out
improvements in the matrimonial home he should " be given credit for a
just proportion on any realisation of the house. A percentage of the
proceeds ought to go to him commensurate to the enhancement due to
his work in improving the property." [18]

It was always unclear on precisely what juristic basis such a claim
was based. Even after the decision of the House of Lords in *Pettit* v.
Pettit [19] the principles were not wholly clear, " since their Lordships
did not speak with one voice." [20] The Law Commission took the opportunity to recommend [21] that the uncertainty of this aspect of the law
should be immediately resolved. This was implemented by section 37,
Matrimonial Proceedings and Property Act 1970.[22]

> " It is hereby declared that where a husband or wife contributes
> in money or money's worth to the improvement of real or personal
> property in which or in the proceeds of sale of which either or both
> of them has or have a beneficial interest, the husband or wife so
> contributing shall, if the contribution is of a substantial nature and
> subject to any agreement between them to the contrary express or
> implied, be treated as having then acquired by virtue of his or her
> contribution a share or an enlarged share, as the case may be, in
> that beneficial interest of such an extent as may have been then
> agreed, or, in default of such agreement, as may seem in all the
> circumstances just to any court before which the question of the
> existence or extent of the beneficial interest of the husband or wife
> arises (whether in proceedings between them or in any other
> proceedings)."

It should be noted:

---

15 The husband could always apply to have the charge vacated under s. 1 (2) (*supra*,
  p. 170), " but problems of time and costs will often make it prudent to bow to
  even the most unreasonable demands." *Per* Megarry J., *Wroth* v. *Tyler* (*supra*) at
  p. 909. It is clear, however, that such an application was not made in that case.
16 See s. 2 (5). On this general problem see C. Palley, 20 N.I.L.Q. 132.
17 *Supra*, p. 169.
18 See *Appleton* v. *Appleton* [1965] 1 W.L.R. 25; *Jansen* v. *Jansen* [1965] P. 478.
19 [1970] A.C. 777; Cretney (1969) 32 M.L.R. 570.
20 Law Commission 25, para. 55, p. 28.
21 Law Commission 25, para. 56.
22 See Oerton (1970) 120 New L.J. 1008, and the correspondence at *ibid.* 1072.

(i) The Act only deals with the limited problem of contributions to the improvement (as distinct from the *acquisition*) of property.[23]

(ii) The contribution must be in *money or money's worth*. A wife who uses a legacy to pay for an extension to the house will be entitled, as will a wife who carries out such an improvement herself. The test seems to be: is it the sort of work for which one would normally expect to have to pay?

(iii) It must be " of a *substantial* nature." This is intended to prevent a claim arising in the case of the " do-it-yourself job which husbands often do." [24] The Act has been held to apply to the installation of a water heater, sink unit, three fireplaces, and a wall and iron gates.[25]

(iv) It must effect an " improvement." This would seem to be used in contra-distinction to " maintenance." The distinction may result in some curious anomalies: if a husband who is a jobbing builder takes time off from work to carry out extensive repairs to the roof or structure of the house, or being an electrician, to rewire [26] the house, neither of these expensive services seems to give him any claim under the Act. But he does have a claim if he instals a pre-fabricated garage, although the value of this work is much less.

(v) The contribution must be identifiable with the relevant contribution; mere general contributions to looking after the home will not suffice.[27]

(vi) The provisions of the Act yield to agreement between the spouses, either express or implied from their conduct. The agreement may be negative—*i.e.* that, notwithstanding the work, *no* interest shall be acquired, or positive—*e.g.* that the shares shall be a certain percentage of the proceeds of sale. On the strict wording of the Act, the agreement must be contemporaneous with the improvement.

(vii) The Act confers a genuine proprietary right which will be recognised in bankruptcy or for Estate Duty purposes, but it is a right of a rather special kind:

(a) Quantification of the shares is left to the court's discretion. The Law Commission said [28] that this discretion was—

" a very limited one exerciseable only in circumstances where a discretion is inevitable because of the informality of family arrangements. It differs fundamentally from the wider discretion which the courts need after the marriage breaks down."

In the only reported case,[29] the court regarded the effect that the

---

23 For the rules applicable in such cases see p. 152, *supra*. In *Davis* v. *Vale* [1971] 2 All E.R. 1021, 1024–1025, Lord Denning M.R. seems to treat this provision as having a wider significance.
24 *Per* Lord Denning M.R., *Button* v. *Button* [1968] 1 W.L.R. 457, 461.
25 *Davis* v. *Vale (supra)*, and see Lord Denning M.R. in *Kowalczuk* v. *Kowalczuk* [1973] 2 All E.R. 1043, 1045.
26 *Ibid.*, where " connecting " the house to the supply was sufficient.
27 *Harnett* v. *Harnett* [1973] 3 W.L.R. 1; *Kowalczuk* v. *Kowalczuk (supra)*.
28 Law Commission 25, para. 58, and explanatory note to draft clause 27 (p. 103).
29 *Griffiths* v. *Griffiths* [1973] 1 W.L.R. 1454.

improvements had on the *value* of the house as crucial in achieving a just solution.

(b) Legal proceedings seem necessary, in the absence of agreement, to quantify the shares. Perhaps the courts will escape from this dilemma by saying the reference to " proceedings " implies that the spouses have such shares as a court *would have* considered to be just. But that is not what it says. The point may be academic, since either (i) the spouses will be alive and litigious, or (ii) the spouses will be alive and ready to agree, or (iii) one spouse will have died in which case it is unlikely that recourse will be had to the Act.

(c) If the spouses are joint tenants the acquisition of an enlarged share under the Act should in theory sever the joint tenancy. It destroys the unity of interest.[30]

The Inheritance (Family Provision) Act 1938 [31]

The English family provision Acts [32] leave a testator free to dispose of his property as he wishes, but give the court discretion to award reasonable provision out of his estate for the maintenance of certain dependants if this is not achieved by the will (or intestacy). The main features of the law are:

Only certain relatives may apply

Only the following relatives of the deceased (called " dependants ") [33] can apply:

(a) A wife or husband. This expression does not include a mistress. But it has been extended [34] to include persons who have in good faith entered into a void marriage, which had not been annulled. A former spouse whose marriage has been dissolved or annulled may apply under the analogous provisions of section 26, Matrimonial Causes Act 1965.

(b) A daughter who has not been married or who is by reason of some mental or physical disability incapable of maintaining herself.

It would seem that a daughter whose marriage has been annulled has " been married " for the purposes of the Acts.[35] The fact that a daughter is, or has been, cohabiting with a man as his wife does not disentitle her from applying for provision from her parent's estate.[36]

---

30 See *Megarry and Wade*, p. 406, 416.

31 See Tyler, *Family Provision* (1971); F. R. Crane, " Family Provision on Death in English Law " (1960) 35 N.Y.U.L.R. 984; J. Gold (1938) 1 M.L.R. 296; O. M. Stone, " The Economic Aspects of Death in the Family," 8 J.S.P.T.L.(N.S.) 188; Hopkins (1971) 35 Conv.(N.S.) 72; Law Commission P.W.P. No. 42, p. 155 *et seq.*

32 The 1938 Act as amended by (i) the Intestates' Estates Act 1952; (ii) the Family Provision Act 1966; (iii) Family Law Reform Act 1969; (iv) the Law Reform (Miscellaneous Provisions) Act 1970. These enactments are together referred to as " the Family Provision Acts."

33 Inheritance (Family Provision) Act 1938, s. 1 (1).

34 Law Reform (Miscellaneous Provisions) Act 1970, s. 6; see Law Commission No. 26; Cretney (1970) 33 M.L.R. 534.

35 s. 16, M.C.A. 1973 (*supra*, p. 68) *cf. Re Rodwell* [1970] 1 Ch. 726.

36 But it may affect her prospects of success: see *Re Andrews* [1955] 1 W.L.R. 1105.

(c) A son [37] who is not over twenty-one.

(d) A son who is, by reason of some mental or physical disability, incapable of maintaining himself.

Time limit on applications

Applications must be made within six months from the date on which representation to the deceased's estate was first taken out.[38] However, in the case of deaths since July 1, 1966,[39] the court has an unfettered discretion [40] to extend the period.

Courts having jurisdiction

Since 1967 the county court has had jurisdiction if the net estate of the deceased does not exceed £5,000.[41] Applications under the Act to the High Court are made to the Chancery Division, but applications from a former wife [42] to the Family Division. This may lead to a situation where the deceased's former wife applies to one court, and the children to another.

What has to be established

The Family Provision Acts provide that if, on the application of a dependant, the court is of the opinion that the disposition of the deceased's estate effected by his will, or by the law of intestacy or by a combination of both, is not such as to make reasonable provision for the maintenance of that dependant, the court may order reasonable provision to be made out of the deceased's estate for the maintenance of that dependant subject to such conditions as it may impose.[43]

After some judicial difference of opinion,[44] it seems that this test is objective:

> " The question is simply whether the will or other disposition has made reasonable provision, and not whether it was unreasonable on the part of the deceased to have made no provision or no larger provision for the dependants." [45]

Thus in *Re Franks* [46] a mother who died in child-birth had not been unreasonable in failing to make a new will providing for the baby. Nevertheless, since the provision was not reasonable, the court awarded main-

---

[37] The expressions " son " and " daughter " include adopted, legitimated, or (in the case of deaths occurring on or after January 1, 1970) illegitimate children: Inheritance (Family Provision) Act 1938, s. 5 (1); Adoption Act 1958, s. 16; see Legitimacy Act 1926, s. 3 (1); Family Law Reform Act 1969, s. 18 (1), 18 (3).

[38] s. 2 (1).

[39] s. 5 (2) Family Provision Act 1966.

[40] *Re Ruttie* [1970] 1 W.L.R. 89; *Re Stone* [1969] C.L.Y. 3676.

[41] Or such larger sum as may from time to time be fixed by order of the Lord Chancellor: Family Provision Act 1966, s. 7 (1), (5).

[42] Under s. 26, Matrimonial Causes Act 1965.

[43] s. 1 (1).

[44] *Re Goodwin* [1969] 1 Ch. 283. See 85 L.Q.R. 331 (Cretney); *Re Gregory* [1970] 1 W.L.R. 1455; *Miillward* v. *Shenton* [1972] 1 W.L.R. 711.

[45] *Per* Megarry J., *Re Goodwin* (*supra*).

[46] [1948] Ch. 62.

tenance. The objective test also allows circumstances (*e.g.* a fall in the value of the residuary estate) occurring after the death to be considered.[47] However, in applications by a *former* spouse under section 26 of the Matrimonial Causes Act 1965, the court has to be satisfied before making an order that *it would have been reasonable* for the deceased to make provision for the dependant. There may therefore be a stronger case for applying a subjective test on such applications,[48] but the trend of authority seems to be moving towards an objective solution in this case as well.[49]

Factors to be taken into account

The Act [50] contains three specific provisions:

(i) The court must have regard to the nature of the property representing the deceased's net estate and must not order any such provision as would necessitate an improvident realisation.

(ii) The court must have regard to any past, present or future capital or income from any source of the applicant, to his conduct in relation to the deceased and otherwise, and any other matter or thing which in the circumstances it may consider relevant or material.

(iii) The court must have regard to the deceased's reasons, so far as they are ascertainable, for making or not making provisions for a dependant, and may accept such evidence of those reasons as it considers sufficient. The court will test the reasonableness or otherwise of such reasons objectively.[51]

Apart from this, decided cases establish a number of general principles.[52]—as for instance that if the deceased's estate is small he may be entitled to discharge his moral obligations in preference to purely legal ones,[53] particularly if state aid is available to the claimant.[54] It is no longer true that an application by a surviving husband will succeed [55] only in exceptional circumstances.

The Act specifically provides that the court shall not be bound to assume that the law relating to intestacy makes reasonable provision in all cases.[56] This is particularly important now that a surviving spouse

---

47 See *Re Clarke* [1968] 1 W.L.R. 415; *Re Goodwin* (*supra*); *Lusternik* v. *Lusternik* [1972] Fam. 125.
48 See *Re Bellman* [1963] P. 239; *Re Eyre* [1968] 1 All E.R. 968; *Re Harker-Thomas* [1969] P. 28.
49 *Re Shanahan* (*dec'd.*) [1972] 2 W.L.R. 63.
50 s. 1 (5), (6) and (7); s. 26 (4) and s. 26 (5), Matrimonial Causes Act 1965 contain similar provisions.
51 *Re Blanch* [1967] 1 W.L.R. 987; *Re Milliken* [1966] N.I.L.R. 68 (N.I.); *Re Gregory* (*supra*).
52 See *Theobald*, paras. 336–340; *Tyler* (*op. cit.*) Chaps. 6, 7, 11.
53 *Re Joslin* [1941] Ch. 200; *Re Charman* [1951] 2 T.L.R. 1095; *Re E.* [1966] 1 W.L.R. 709.
54 *Re E.* [1966] 1 W.L.R. 709; *Re Clayton* [1966] 1 W.L.R. 969; *Re Goodwin* [1969] 1 Ch. 283; *Millward* v. *Shenton* (*supra*), *Re Canderton* (1970) 114 S.J. 208.
55 See *Theobald* (12th ed.), para. 331; *Re Sylvester* [1941] Ch. 87; and *Re Clayton* [1966] 1 W.L.R. 969.
56 s. 1 (8).

will take the whole of all save large estates on intestacy.[57] In *Re Sivyer*[58] the intestate left a net estate of some £4,000. In addition to his widow who on his intestacy would be entitled to the whole of an estate of this size, he left a thirteen-year-old daughter by a previous marriage. It was held that the daughter was entitled to provision out of the estate.

Orders that can be made

The court is only empowered to award *maintenance*.[59] It has no jurisdiction to consider whether the capital provision made for dependants is reasonable. Thus the provision made by the court is normally by way of periodical payments of income. These may stipulate payments of specified amounts (*e.g.* £100 per annum) or a proportion of the income (*e.g.* half the annual income).[60] The order must provide for the termination of the payments not later than:

(a) In the case of a wife or husband, her or his remarriage.

(b) In the case of a daughter who has not been married or who is under disability, her marriage or the cesser of her disability, whichever is the later.[61]

(c) In the case of a minor son, his attaining the age of twenty-one years.

(d) In the case of a son under disability, the cesser of the disability.[62]

Since 1966 the court has had power to make an order providing for a lump sum payment.[63] But the power is still one to make provision for *maintenance*.[64] It may be that lump sum orders will generally only be made in the case of comparatively small estates, unless special need can be shown. The object of this provision is fundamentally different from that of the court's powers to order capital provision on divorce or other breakdown proceedings.[65]

Variation of orders

The court has a power to vary orders made under the Act, but this is very restricted[66] and will rarely be practicable.[67] There is a wider power to vary under the Matrimonial Causes Act.[68]

Defects of the law

Although the Act enables rough justice to be done in many cases, it suffers from a number of defects.[69] Perhaps the most important are:

---

[57] *Supra*, p. 165.   [58] [1967] 3 All E.R. 429.
[59] Inheritance (Family Provision) Act 1938, s. 1 (1).
[60] Family Provision Act 1966, s. 3 (2), removing the difficulty exposed by *Re Gale* [1966] Ch. 236.   [61] *Re Pointer* [1941] Ch. 60; 57 L.Q.R. 20.
[62] Inheritance (Family Provision) Act 1938, s. 1 (2).
[63] Family Provision Act 1966, s. 4.
[64] *Sivyer* v. *Sivyer* (*supra*).
[65] See *infra*, p. 190.
[66] s. 4 (1).
[67] See (1973) 117 S.J. 517 (A. Samuels).   [68] s. 27 (4).
[69] See P.W.P. 42, Part III, for a full consideration.

(a) *It can easily be evaded*

The Act only operates on the deceased's "net estate." [70] This means property of which the deceased had power to dispose by his will (otherwise than by virtue of a special power of appointment), less the amount of his funeral, testamentary expenses, debts and liabilities and estate duty payable out of his estate on his death. [71]

If the deceased gives property away during his lifetime, it will not be subject to the Act—although the court may take such dispositions into account in assessing the reasonableness of the testamentary provisions. [72]

The deceased may also have taken property out of the court's jurisdiction, whilst reserving some control over it during his lifetime, *e.g.*:

(a) By settling property on trust for himself for life, with remainder as the settlor by deed or will appoints to his mistress, illegitimate children, or others. Further protection could be given by reserving to the settlor power to revoke the settlement, wholly or partially, or to add beneficiaries. [73]

(b) By means of Life Assurance policies written in trust. Many pension schemes are of this type. Provided any interest of the deceased's estate is discretionary, the policy monies will not fall under the definition of net estate.

(c) By making *donationes mortis causa*. If the donor recovers, he can revoke the gift.

(b) *The definition of "dependants" is too narrow*

The Act only applies to a spouse and "children" of the deceased. It does not, for example, extend to a child of the deceased's widow's former marriage, even though the deceased may have accepted full responsibility for it. The limitations on the age of child applicants may exclude deserving cases—*e.g.* a son of twenty-two who has been encouraged to embark on a long course of professional training.

The Law Reform (Miscellaneous Provisions) Act 1970 [74]

This Act abolished the action for breach of promise of marriage. It introduced a special code to deal with some of the proprietary problems which may arise from the termination of an engagement.

Gifts

Under the old law a gift made in contemplation of marriage by one party to the other was *conditional* on the marriage taking place, and

---

70 s. 1 (1). See also s. 26 (2), Matrimonial Causes Act 1965.
71 s. 5 (1).
72 *Re Carter* (1968) 112 S.J. 136.
73 *Re Manisty's S.T.* [1973] 2 All E.R. 1203.
74 See Cretney (1970) 33 M.L.R. 534, from which the text is largely derived.

was in the nature of a *pledge*, so that it could not be recovered by the party in default.[75] The Act makes a distinction between engagement rings [76] and other conditional gifts. The Law Commission [77] thought that it was of " overriding importance " to do away with inquiries into fault, and recommended that a donor " should not be precluded from recovering the gift on termination of the agreement by reason of the fact that he was responsible for the termination." [78] The Act accepts that general principle. At the same time, it introduces a new presumption [79] that the gift of an engagement ring is an *absolute* gift. This rule is intended to preserve the right of a jilted woman to throw the ring away rather than return it to her former fiancé.[80] The Act reconciles the recognition of this desire with the need to avoid judicial investigation of culpability by changing the law of property, and at the price of allowing the donee of a ring who has wrongly terminated an engagement to keep the ring. In the case of engagement rings, the presumption of an absolute gift may be rebutted (*e.g.* if the ring is a family heirloom); in the case of other gifts the old law must still be referred to in order to decide whether the gift was conditional or absolute.[81] If it is construed as a conditional gift, it may be doubted whether the Act [82] fully implements the proposal that the right to recover should no longer depend on absence of fault: it provides [83] that a donor " shall not be prevented from recovering the property *by reason only of his having terminated the agreement.*" But under the old law it was not termination *alone*, but termination *without good cause* which prevented recovery. A donor may therefore still be debarred from recovery if he has not himself terminated the agreement, but behaved in such a way as to justify his fiancée in repudiating it.

Some examples may make the working of the rules clearer:

M gives F an engagement ring and a gold eternity ring. After a violent quarrel, he forcibly ejects her from his flat, saying that everything is over between them. F can keep the engagement ring: it is presumed to have been an absolute gift [84]; he can, however, recover the eternity ring, since this would be a conditional gift. It is immaterial that M was entirely to blame for the rupture.

M gives F a valuable engagement ring. Shortly afterwards he discovers that F has three illegitimate children, and is cohabiting

---

75 *Cohen* v. *Sellar* [1926] 1 K.B. 536; *Jacobs* v. *Davis* [1917] 2 K.B. 532.

76 Which are not defined; *cf. Elkington* v. *Amery* [1936] 2 All E.R. 86. *Quaere* whether a ring given to a man by a woman on the occasion of their engagement can be within this description.

77 Law Commission 26.

78 Law Commission 26, para. 45; s. 3 (1) Law Reform (Miscellaneous Provisions) Act 1970.   79 s. 3 (2).

80 See Standing Committee C Report, February 11, 1970.

81 *Cf. Moate* v. *Moate* [1948] 2 All E.R. 486.

82 Although it follows the Law Commission's draft.

83 s. 3 (1), italics supplied.

84 *Ibid.*

with another man. He breaks off the engagement. F can keep the ring.

M and F become engaged. M gives F an engagement ring, and F in return gives him a gold signet ring. F breaks off the engagement so that she can marry X. She is entitled to keep the engagement ring, and (*semble*) can sue him for the return of the signet ring, since it was (probably) a conditional gift and (perhaps) not within the meaning of " engagement ring " in the Act.

M gives F a large quantity of furniture to furnish the home which they plan to establish after their marriage. She subsequently discovers that he is suffering from a venereal disease for which he refuses treatment. She breaks off the engagement. Although the gift was no doubt conditional, M (contrary to the policy of the Act) may not be able to recover. He has not terminated the agreement, and therefore the provision in the Act that he is " not prevented from recovering the property by reason only of his having terminated the agreement " *semble* is ineffective. Hence the Common Law still applies, and since M is the party in default, F could successfully resist a claim by him.

Property adjustment

First, as a matter of procedure, the Act applies section 17 of the Married Women's Property Act 1882 [85] " to any dispute between, or claim by, one [*sic*] of them in relation to property in which either or both had a beneficial interest while the agreement was in force " [86] provided that proceedings are instituted within three years of the termination of the agreement. The aim of this reform is simply to give the advantages of a summary procedure [87] to disputes between the formerly betrothed.

A far more fundamental change is that the Act applies the proprietary rules relating to husband and wife to the determination of beneficial interests in property acquired during the currency of the engagement.[88] These include, not only the common law rules whereby a beneficial interest in property may be obtained by financial contribution to its acquisition or improvement,[89] but also the new statutory principles [90] whereby a contribution in money or money's worth to the improvement of property (provided it is of a " substantial " nature) confers a proprietary interest.

Certain special problems may arise in the case of property acquired during an engagement:

---

85 As extended by s. 7 of the Matrimonial Proceedings (Property and Maintenance) Act 1958.   86 s. 2 (2).
87 For a description, see J. H. Hames, " Applications under section 17 of the Married Women's Property Act 1882 (Oyez Practice Notes, No. 42, 3rd 1971). There is no power to vary property rights under this procedure: see *supra*, p. 158, and *Kowalczuk* v. *Kowalczuk* [1973] 2 All E.R. 1042, 1046.
88 s. 2 (1).   89 *Supra*, p. 156.
90 s. 37 of the Matrimonial Proceedings and Property Act 1970; *supra*, p. 175.

(i) The rules only apply *if* the agreement is terminated: if a fiancé gives up his job as a bricklayer to carry out improvements on his fiancée's house, and is then adjudicated bankrupt, the trustee in bankruptcy will not (so long as the parties remain engaged) be able to rely on the Act to claim a beneficial interest in the house for the benefit of creditors. He would have been able to do so had the parties been married.

(ii) The rule applies *however* an engagement is terminated, so that if the bricklayer-fiancé dies (rather than become bankrupt) his share in the property will pass under his will or intestacy,[91] and thus to his fiancée only if he has made a will in her favour.

(iii) Although the Act applies the same rules as are applicable to husband/wife disputes, it does not confer any power to vary those strict rights in the interest of the parties or their children.[92] If our bricklayer married his fiancée, had children and then deserted her, the court [93] could order his share in the matrimonial home to be settled.[94] If, however, he failed to marry her, he could call for his share of the proceeds of sale of the house, and could not be compelled to make any capital provision for his children.

(iv) The rules only apply to interests acquired during the currency of the engagement: it may, therefore, still be important to know at what moment of time the agreement came into being.[95] Difficulties may be found in deciding whether a so-called "unofficial engagement" is "an agreement between two persons to marry one another."

FINANCIAL OBLIGATION ON BREAKDOWN [96]

The law on the enforcement of spouses' obligations to provide financial support for one another is complex and confusing:

(i) When financial support from the other party is sought in legal proceedings, fundamentally different codes apply in (a) the Superior Courts (High Court and county court), and (b) Magistrates' Courts. Different rules also apply where the sole ground of complaint is neglect to provide maintenance on the one hand and cases where other matrimonial relief (*e.g.* divorce or separation) is sought, or complaint is made of misconduct (*e.g.* cruelty or desertion) other than financial neglect on the other.

(ii) Second, the state now recognises [97] that every person whose income falls below a certain level is *entitled* to a supplementary cash allowance. Yet it is also recognised that members of a family have an

---

[91] *Supra*, p. 165.
[92] *Cf.* the wider powers of property adjustment on breakdown of marriage; *supra*, p. 165.
[93] In proceedings for divorce, nullity or judicial separation.
[94] *Ulrich* v. *Ulrich and Fenton* [1968] 1 W.L.R. 180; *Smith* v. *Smith* [1970] 1 W.L.R. 155; M.C.A. 1973, s. 24.
[95] It may also be important for the application of the presumption of advancement: *Moate* v. *Moate* (*supra*), and possibly the doctrine of undue influence: *cf. Zamet* v. *Hyman* [1961] 1 W.L.R. 1442; *Re Lloyds Bank* [1931] 1 Ch. 289.
[96] For special rules relating to children see Chap. 7.
[97] Ministry of Social Security Act 1966, s. 4 (1).

obligation to support one another, which they should not be able to cast upon the State. Wives who are in urgent need of support will in practice obtain it from the Supplementary Benefits Commission, who will then seek to compel the husband to meet his obligation. In effect, therefore, the State underwrites the performance of family support obligations.

(iii) Traditionally, the courts were concerned with *maintenance* out of income.[98] But since 1970 the courts have had " the widest possible powers " [99] in readjusting the overall financial position (capital as well as income) of the parties to a marriage which has broken down. The full implications of this revolutionary change have yet to be worked out.

For analytical purposes it is necessary to treat the various procedures separately, but in practice they interlock. Furthermore the role of the Supplementary Benefits Commission is often at least as important as that of the courts, and the role of the Magistrates' Courts is as important as that of the Superior Courts.

We shall consider in turn:

(i) Financial remedies in the Superior Courts ancillary to other relief.

(ii) Financial remedies in Magistrates' Courts on grounds other than neglect.

(iii) Financial remedies obtainable in both the Superior Court and Magistrates' Court on the ground of wilful neglect to maintain.

(iv) The effect of the social security system.

(v) Other methods of obtaining financial aid without direct recourse to the courts, including maintenance by agreement.

ANCILLARY [1] FINANCIAL PROVISION IN THE SUPERIOR COURTS

We shall first of all consider the orders that can be made, then the principles applied by the court in exercising its discretion.

Orders that can be made Ancillary to Divorce, Nullity or Judicial Separation

All orders can be made in favour of either party [2]: the court has power to order a wife to maintain her husband,[2a] and *vice versa*. In practice there will be few cases in which an order against a wife would be appropriate.

Maintenance pending suit [3]

This is in effect an interim [4] maintenance award:

98 *Per* Bagnall J., *Harnett* v. *Harnett* [1973] 3 W.L.R. 1.
99 *Per* Lord Denning M.R., *Wachtel* v. *Wachtel* [1973] Fam. 72, 91.
1 *i.e.* in theory the financial relief is ancillary to the principal relief (*e.g.* divorce).
2 To avoid circumlocution, the text assumes that the order is made in favour of the wife against the husband.   2a *Griffiths* v. *Griffiths* [1973] 1 W.L.R. 1454 (lump sum).
3 See *Jackson*, Chap. 2.
4 Although, confusingly, an *interim* order for maintenance pending suit may be made: M.C.R. 1971, r. 78 (3), *Jackson*, p. 17.

" On a petition for divorce, nullity of marriage or judicial separation, the court may order . . . either party to the marriage to make to the other such periodical payments for his or her maintenance and for such term, being a term beginning not earlier than the date of the presentation of the petition and ending with the date of the determination of the suit, as the court thinks reasonable." [5]

The order cannot continue beyond the determination of the suit (*i.e.* the granting of a decree absolute, or the dismissal of the petition), nor can it begin earlier than the date of presentation of the petition. In practice there may be considerable delay before an order is actually made because of the procedural requirements [6]   The order when made, may be backdated, but:

" the fact of the matter is that time goes by in . . . a way which is appallingly difficult for clients to bear. It can't be helped; people have to get instructions, draft affidavits, swear affidavits, answer affidavits and so on and so on. . . .[7]   Although the order may be backdated a wife " can't live on backdated orders. . . ." [8]

In practice, it is often the wife of independent means who can wait for an order for maintenance pending suit. In other cases the husband will either pay maintenance voluntarily,[9] or the wife will (a) have applied to the Magistrates' Court for an order or (b), obtained supplementary benefit.

Periodical payments, secured or unsecured [10]

The court may order the husband to make regular income payments to the wife.

It is provided [11]:

" On granting a decree of divorce, a decree of nullity of marriage or a decree of judicial separation or at any time thereafter (whether, in the case of a decree of divorce or of nullity of marriage, before or after the decree is made absolute), the court may make any one or more of the following orders, that is to say:

(a) an order that either party to the marriage shall make to the other such periodical payments, for such term, as may be specified in the order;

(b) an order that either party to the marriage shall secure to the other to the satisfaction of the court such periodical payments, for such term as may be so specified. . . ."

Secured or unsecured?

If the order is *secured*, the husband is required to set aside a fund

---

[5] M.C.A. 1973, s. 22.
[6] M.C.R. 1971, Rules 68–73.
[7] *Per* Ormrod J., *Lanitis* v. *Lanitis* [1970] 1 All E.R. 466, 472.
[8] *Cf. Jackson*, pp. 15–16.
[9] In which case credit for the payments will be given against any back-dated order.
[10] See *Jackson*, Chaps. 4 and 3.
[11] s. 23 (1), M.C.A. 1973.

of capital (often a fund of stocks and shares) which will usually be vested in trustees, and can be resorted to if the maintenance payments are not made as they fall due. The order normally directs [12] that an annual sum be secured on certain property. Carrying this into effect may require special conveyancing skills, so there is power to refer the settling of the necessary documents to one of the conveyancing counsel of the court.[13] The fund remains the property of the husband: it is *only* if he defaults in making payments that the income from the security can be used, or if need be part or all of it be sold, to make good the default.

The advantages of having secured provision are:

(a) It provides a tangible fund for enforcement. If an order is *unsecured*, enforcement will depend both on the husband's having sufficient means to pay, and being present within the jurisdiction of the court.[14] A secured order remains enforceable even if the husband disappears, loses all his other assets, ceases to earn, or becomes bankrupt.[15]

(b) A secured order may continue for the lifetime of the wife: the husband may die, but the fund remains.[16] There is no power to order unsecured payments to continue beyond the parties' *joint* lives.[17] The reason is that to require payments to be made out of his estate would cause hardship and difficulty: it would probably be impossible to distribute any of his assets (*e.g.* to a second wife) until the death of the payee. This objection does not apply to secured payments: the security fund will be retained separately after the husband's death, and the rest of his property distributed.

The court has an unfettered discretion as to whether to order security, and if so what proportion of the total maintenance should be secured: traditionally it was regarded as a form of relief only suitable if the husband had substantial assets; normally no more than one-third of a man's free investments would be tied up in this way.[18] In recent years, however, the courts have been readier to order security if there seemed a special need for it.[19] The Law Commission recommended the courts

---

[12] *Cf. Powys* v. *Powys* [1971] P. 340.   [13] s. 30, M.C.A. 1973.

[14] Emigration is an effective way of avoiding payment of maintenance; however, the provisions of the Maintenance Orders (Reciprocal Enforcement) Act 1972 when brought fully into effect may provide more effective remedies: see Bromley (1972) 35 M.L.R. 625.

[15] *Shearn* v. *Shearn* [1931] P. 15, *per* Hill J.

[16] *Ibid.*

[17] All that a wife with an unsecured order who survives her husband can do is to apply for provision out of his estate: see *supra*, p. 177. This is unsatisfactory since (a) there may be little or no property left, (b) the wife's claim will be assessed in competition with others, on the basis of the facts existing at the husband's death.

[18] *Shorthouse* v. *Shorthouse* (1898) 78 L.T. 687; *Barker* v. *Barker* [1952] P. 184, 194-195; *cf. Hulton* v. *Hulton* [1916] P. 57.

[19] See *Aggett* v. *Aggett* [1962] 1 W.L.R. 183 where maintenance was secured on the husband's only valuable asset (a house) in view of the fact that the wife had set up a guest house in it which was her only means of earning a living, and that the husband (who had shown himself irresponsible and unconcerned for her welfare) might well go abroad leaving her without any other means of support. See also *Foard* v. *Foard* [1967] 2 All E.R. 660.

to be more ready to award secured provision, and saw no reason why, in suitable cases, the matrimonial home should not be used as security.[20]

Duration of the order

Orders (whether secured or unsecured) automatically determine on the remarriage of the payee.[21]   Before 1970 this was not the case: if a wife remarried, the husband would apply for the order to be varied. The court would then consider all the circumstances, particularly the effect remarriage had on the wife's *financial* position.   The change in the law was made because the Law Commission's tentative proposal [22] that all periodical maintenance payments should cease on remarriage received " almost unanimous support, which includes that of the various women's organisations that favoured us with their comments."

It is submitted that the change was unfortunate. Application of the new rule may mean that a divorced woman loses substantially by marrying (as distinct from living in a *de facto* illicit relationship) with a man poorer than her first husband. Particular difficulty may arise if the mother has custody of a child. The child's *own* maintenance will not be affected, but it may have unfortunate consequences if the *mother's* standard of living suddenly drops. Even if such situations infrequently arise it is desirable to have the powers when needed.[23]

Lump sums and other capital provision orders [24]

The Act contains four separate provisions enabling capital provision to be made in all cases of divorce, judicial separation and nullity:

(a) The court may order payment of a lump sum (*i.e. cash*).[25] It is provided:

> (i) that a lump sum order may be made for the purpose of enabling the wife to meet liabilities reasonably incurred in maintaining herself or the children before making an application to the court.[26]

> (ii) that a lump sum order may provide for payment by instalments, in which case payment may be secured.[27] This provision is designed to deal, for example, with the kind of case where the husband owns a valuable holding in a private company [28] but little

---

20 Law Commission 25, para. 11. For a recent case where payments were to be secured by means of a second mortgage on the husband's house, see *Parker* v. *Parker* [1972] Fam. 116.
21 s. 28 (1) M.C.A. 1973.
22 See Working Paper No. 9, paras. 40, 69; Law Commission 25, para. 14.
23 See *e.g. O'Regan (formerly Douglass)* v. *Douglass* (1969) 13 F.L.R. 417.
24 See *Jackson*, Chaps. 5, 7, 8.
25 s. 23 (1) (*c*).
26 s. 23 (3) (*a*). This provision was included in the 1970 Act because it abolished the wife's agency of necessity. This may have been used to enable the wife to purchase necessaries (or contract loans for their purchase) at the husband's expense: see Law Commission 25, paras. 10, 108.
27 s. 23 (3) (*c*).
28 Or is a partner in a business.

else. It may be fair to order him to pay his wife a lump sum, but unreasonable to expect him either to sell part of the share capital in disadvantageous circumstances, or to transfer shares to the wife. A lump sum order payable by instalments would enable him to raise cash over a period of time, while the obligation could be secured on his holding of shares.

(b) It may [29] order specified property to be transferred to the other spouse. This will normally be done as an *alternative* [30] to a lump sum order. But since it enables the court to direct the transfer of shares, land (*e.g.* the matrimonial home) or an interest under a settlement to the other spouse, it may be used in those cases where there is a particular case for the transfer of a specific asset (*e.g.* the matrimonial home, or one spouse's share in it).

The power extends to reversionary property: if, for instance, the husband's father died leaving his estate to his widow for life, remainder to the husband, the court may (even during the widow's lifetime) order his interest to be transferred to the wife: she would receive the fund on the termination of the widow's life interest (and could sell it or use it as security for a loan before then).

(c) The court may [31] also direct property to be settled for the benefit of the wife and children of the family. For instance, the court might order a settlement of shares belonging to the husband on trust for the wife for life or until remarriage, with remainder to the children on attaining twenty-one.[32]

(d) The court may *vary* existing settlements. It is provided [33] that an order may vary [34]

> " for the benefit of the parties to the marriage and of the children of the family or either or any of them any ante-nuptial or post-nuptial settlement (including such a settlement made by will or codicil) made on the parties to the marriage."

The relationship of this provision to the capital transfer provisions set out above requires explanation. An order for the transfer of property can only be made if the husband is " entitled " to it even although that entitlement may be to an interest under a settlement [35] (as explained above); an order for variation can only be made so as to alter the terms of a settlement, but it is not necessary that either party should have any present entitlement thereunder.[36] This power was originally intended to enable marriage settlements of the traditional Victorian pattern to be

---

[29] s. 24 (1) (*a*) M.C.A. 1973.
[30] Law Commission 25, para. 68.
[31] s. 24 (1) (*b*) M.C.A. 1973.
[32] See for example the order made in *Harnett* v. *Harnett* (*supra*).
[33] s. 24 (1) (*c*), (*d*) M.C.A. 1973.
[34] There is an express power to extinguish or reduce either party's interest: s. 24 (1) (*d*) M.C.A. 1973.
[35] But *cf. per* Bagnall J., *Harnett* v. *Harnett* (*supra*) at p. 598A.
[36] *e.g.* the settlement may be a discretionary settlement under which no beneficiary has any " interest."

varied. It may still be used for that purpose, although settlements (and variation) are now often influenced by considerations of tax advantages. Detailed treatment of such variations and of the details of the statutory provisions are outside the scope of this work.[37]

Under the old law the power to vary settlements was important since it was one of the very few methods of altering the distribution of *capital* on the breakdown of marriage. The court gave a wide interpretation to the word " settlement " (so that a purchase of a dwelling-house in joint names fell within the definition).[38] It may no longer be necessary to postulate the existence of a " settlement " in these cases since the court has express power to transfer one spouse's interest to the other.[39] These provisions are so all-embracing that using non-technical language " . . . when all appropriate orders have been made the result, though not the method, has been to distribute the property owned by either of the parties among them and their children." [40]

Principles Applied by the Court in Exercising its Discretion

The Matrimonial Proceedings and Property Act 1970 [41] set out detailed rules governing the manner in which its powers to order financial provision are to be exercised. After some initial hesitation [42] it has been held [43] that the statute does not codify the old law, but introduces revolutionary [44] reforms. Hence, the statutory provisions are not to be construed in the light of cases decided under the old law.[45]

Maintenance pending suit

These specific guidelines do not, however, apply to maintenance pending suit; the only statutory provision being that the court may make such order as it " thinks reasonable."

The old practice of the courts was to give the wife a sum which would bring her income up to one-fifth of the joint incomes: if the husband had an income of £2,000, and the wife nothing she would get £400 per annum; if he had an income of £10,000 and she an income of £1,500 she would get £800 per annum to bring her income up to £2,300. This was a smaller proportion than could be expected under a final order. Various explanations were given for the distinction between interim orders and

---

37 See further *Rayden*, pp. 650–671; Law Commission 25, paras. 64–77; Passingham, *Matrimonial Proceedings and Property Act 1970*, pp. 18–21; *Jackson*, Chap. 9.
38 *Brown* v. *Brown* [1959] P. 86; see also *Cook* v. *Cook* [1962] P. 235.
39 Although the same result could be achieved by extinguishing one spouse's interest under s. 24 (1) (*d*); see the application in *D'Este* v. *D'Este* [1973] Fam. 55.
40 Per Bagnall J., *Harnett* v. *Harnett* (*supra*) at p. 598.
41 s. 5 (now s. 25, M.C.A. 1973).
42 *E.g.* " obviously intended to codify the existing law and practice." *Ackerman* v. *Ackerman* [1972] 2 All E.R. 424F, *per* Phillimore L.J. (who was, however, subsequently a party to the decision in *Wachtel* v. *Wachtel* (*infra*) where the contrary was asserted).
43 *Wachtel* v. *Wachtel* [1973] Fam. 72; *Trippas* v. *Trippas* [1973] 2 All E.R. 1.
44 Per Lord Denning M.R., *Trippas* v. *Trippas* (*supra*) at p. 4.
45 *Wachtel* v. *Wachtel* (*supra*) at p. 91; *Trippas* v. *Trippas* (*supra*) at p. 7, *per* Scarman L.J., but see p. 195 *infra*, on the principles referred to in s. 25 (1), M.C.A. 1973.

orders made at the conclusion of the suit.[46] The Law Commission thought [47] that:

"the criteria determining whether an order should be made are different. Payments ordered at the conclusion of the principal suit will depend to some extent on the court's findings regarding the respective conduct of the parties; payments ordered pending the outcome of the suit will be made prior to the court's adjudication on conduct, and indeed, before there has been a full investigation of the parties' means."

But it is doubtful whether this is any longer so since the parties' conduct will rarely affect financial orders.[48] It remains true that the court may not be in possession of all the relevant facts (e.g. about the wife's earning capacity), so perhaps the award should attempt to enable the wife to live approximately in the fashion to which she has been accustomed, without hardship, pending the outcome of the case.

Other orders

It is the duty of the court in deciding whether to exercise its powers of ordering financial provision (other than maintenance pending suit) for a party to the marriage and, if so, in what manner—e.g. whether to order periodical payments alone, or to secure some part of them, or to order capital adjustments—" to have regard to all the circumstances of the case" including the following seven specified matters [49]:

"(a) the income, earning capacity, property and other financial resources which each of the parties to the marriage has or is likely to have in the foreseeable future;
(b) the financial needs, obligations and responsibilities which each of the parties to the marriage has or is likely to have in the foreseeable future;
(c) the standard of living enjoyed by the family before the breakdown of the marriage;
(d) the age of each party to the marriage and the duration of the marriage;
(e) any physical or mental disability of either of the parties to the marriage;
(f) the contributions made by each of the parties to the welfare of the family, including any contribution made by looking after the home or caring for the family;
(g) in the case of proceedings for divorce or nullity of marriage, the value to either of the parties to the marriage of any benefit (for example, a pension) which, by reason of the dissolution or annulment of the marriage, that party will lose the chance of acquiring."

The court is then—

"so to exercise those powers as to place the parties, so far as it is practicable and, having regard to their conduct, just to do so, in the

---

46 *Poynter*, 2nd ed. at p. 250; *Sherwood* v. *Sherwood* [1929] P. 120; *Waller* v. *Waller* [1956] P. 300; *Slater* v. *Slater* [1962] P. 94.
47 Law Commission 25, para. 6
48 See *infra*, p. 194.
49 M.C.A. 1973, s. 25 (1).

financial position in which they would have been if the marriage had not broken down and each had properly discharged his or her financial obligations and responsibilities towards the other."

The court is thus given a specific target, involving three questions which have to be answered in relation to each party [50]: (a) What would that party's financial position have been if the marriage had not broken down? (b) How far is it practicable to place that party in that financial position? (c) How far is it just to do so?

(a) *What would that party's financial position have been had it not been for the breakdown?*

This must be based on a close consideration of the existing facts,[51] but also involves an assessment of future probabilities [52]: had the marriage continued what would the wife have enjoyed by way of housing, pension and succession rights, and even gifts [53] from the other spouse? The Act in effect establishes a presumption that a wife is potentially entitled to benefit at some time from all her husband's capital assets, in addition to her right to be maintained out of her husband's income, supplemented by her own if she has any.[54]

(b) *How far is it practicable to place that party in that financial position?*

In almost every case it will not be practicable to place both parties in the hypothetical financial position.[55] Attempts to do so may involve somewhat complex property settlements.[56] It is abundantly clear that capital provision orders (particularly related to the former matrimonial home [56a]) will be appropriate, even in the case of parties of modest means.

In practice, the courts will often adopt the one-third principle [57] as

[50] *Per* Bagnall J., *Harnett* v. *Harnett* (*supra*) at p. 598.
[51] Closer consideration may have to be given to this than had been the court's practice in the past: see *per* Scarman L.J., *Trippas* v. *Trippas* (*supra*) at pp. 9–10. A suggested form of affidavit of means, including a questionnaire designed to provide the information most likely to be required, has been prepared by the Divorce Registry (in consultation with the Law Society). It is set out in *Practice Note* (*Affidavit of Means*) [1973] 1 W.L.R. 72. For a detailed account of the problems which may be encountered, see *Jackson*, particularly at pp. 31–45.
[52] In *Trippas* v. *Trippas* (*supra*); *Hunter* v. *Hunter* [1973] 1 W.L.R. 958, 968.
[53] *Trippas* v. *Trippas* (*supra*), where a lump sum order was made on the basis that if the marriage had continued the husband would probably have transferred capital to the wife.
[54] *Harnett* v. *Harnett* (*supra*) at p. 601.   [55] *Ibid.* at p. 598.
[56] *Hunter* v. *Hunter* (*supra*).   [56a] *Hector* v. *Hector* [1973] 3 All E.R. 1070.
[57] The " one-third rule " originated in the practice of the ecclesiastical courts in making alimony (*i.e.* periodical maintenance) orders. It had a chequered career in the twentieth century: long accepted as " a guide, a sound working rule . . . , yet not an absolute rule " (*per* Lord Hanworth M.R., *Stibbe* v. *Stibbe* [1931] P. 105, 110) subsequently described as " discredited " by Sir Jocelyn Simon P. (*Kershaw* v. *Kershaw* [1966] P. 13, 17). But only a week before the Court of Appeal (*Williams* v. *Williams* [1965] P. 125), had described it as a " convenient proportion." The rule served a useful purpose since " it meant that in thousands and thousands of cases . . . maintenance orders would be agreed by negotiation between solicitors and so the expense involved in a fight over maintenance at court would be avoided " (D. Morris, *The End of Marriage*, 1971, p. 110) and was often applied in practice: see *e.g. Brister* v. *Brister* [1970] 1 W.L.R. 644 and (after the Divorce Reform Act 1969) *Ackerman* v. *Ackerman* [1972] Fam. 225, 234, *per* Phillimore L.J.

a starting point [58]; this means (i) that the wife will receive periodical payments so as to make her income (if any) up to one-third of the joint incomes of herself and her husband [59]; (ii) she will receive one-third of the " family assets "—*i.e.* " gross earnings which are acquired by one or other or both of the parties, with the intention that there should be continuing provision for them and their children during their joint lives," [60] such as the matrimonial home. Maintenance payments for children will be in addition to those orders for the wife. This guide is " not a rule and must not be so regarded." [61] The Act gives the court complete flexibility,[62] and there will be many cases (particularly where the parties' means are modest [63]) in which one-half of the family assets [64] will be the appropriate fraction for the wife.[65] Conversely if the marriage has *de facto* existed for a short time,[66] or if the husband's capital is substantial,[67] a smaller fraction will be given. These considerations are amongst the " circumstances " the court is statutorily required to consider, and may justify a lower starting point than would otherwise be appropriate.

[58] *Wachtel* v. *Wachtel* (*supra*) at pp. 94–95.

[59] *E.g.* husband's income £5,000 per annum, wife's income £1,000 per annum. Wife will receive periodical payments of £1,000 per annum to bring her income up to £2,000 per annum, one-third of the joint income (£6,000), *supra* at p. 92.

[60] *Per* Lord Denning M.R., *Wachtel* v. *Wachtel*. It may not be limited to assets within this definition (see *e.g. Trippas* v. *Trippas*) but in the case of a wealthy man with substantial means a smaller fraction would no doubt be used: *Harnett* v. *Harnett* (*supra*) at p. 601E.

[61] *Per* Lord Denning M.R., *Wachtel* v. *Wachtel* (*supra*) at p. 94; *cf.* " the non-existent one-third rule," *Krystman* v. *Krystman* [1973] 1 W.L.R. 927, *per* Davies L.J.; " the so-called one-third rule," *Trippas* v. *Trippas* (*supra*) at p. 9.

[62] *Trippas* v. *Trippas* (*supra*) at p. 7, *per* Scarman L.J.; *Wachtel* v. *Wachtel* (*supra*) at p. 94, *per* Lord Denning M.R.; *Chamberlain* v. *Chamberlain* [1973] 1 W.L.R. 1557.

[63] Nothing " precludes this court from doing rough justice on the basis of approximate equality, provided it is, on the whole, just to both parties. . . ." *Per* Scarman L.J., *Trippas* v. *Trippas* (*supra*) at p. 9; *Harnett* v. *Harnett* (*supra*) at p. 601, *per* Bagnall L.J.

[64] As to why one-half is not the usual fraction, see Lord Denning M.R., *Wachtel* v. *Wachtel* (*supra*) at p. 95:
    " If we were only concerned with the capital assets of the family, and particularly with the matrimonial home, it would be tempting to divide them half and half, as the judge did. That would be fair enough if the wife afterwards went her own way, making no further demands on the husband. It would be simply a division of the assets of the partnership. That may come in the future. But at present few wives are content with a share of the capital assets. Most wives want their former husbands to make periodical payments as well to support them; because, after the divorce he will be earning far more than she; and she can only keep up her standard of living with his help. He also has to make payments for the children out of his earnings, even if they are with her. In view of those calls on his future earnings, we do not think she can have both—half the capital assets, and half the earnings."
    Cf. the justification advanced (in relation to permanent alimony after judicial separation) under the old law, *per* Sir Jocelyn Simon P., *Sansom* v. *Sansom* [1966] P. 52: it " often worked out soundly and fairly . . . because in a typical case the court was concerned with three groups of needs—those of the wife, those of the husband and those of the children for whose support the husband was liable. . . ."

[65] But the same principle may not apply if the wife is wealthier than the husband, see *per* Bagnall J., *Harnett* v. *Harnett* (*supra*) at p. 601: " Where the wife has some capital, that must be taken into account in determining what she should be given by the husband. It would be unlikely that she would be required to transfer capital to the husband unless her assets were substantially greater than his ": *cf. Griffiths* v. *Griffiths* (*supra*).

[66] *Krystman* v. *Krystman* (*supra*), *cf. Brett* v. *Brett* [1969] 1 W.L.R. 487.

[67] *Harnett* v. *Harnett* (*supra*).

(c) *How far is it just to do so?*

In the early days of the divorce jurisdiction, a wife who had committed adultery (or deserted her husband) would normally [68] receive no maintenance, or at most a " compassionate allowance to save her from utter destitution." [69] But " the law is a living thing moving with the times and not a creature of deed or moribund ways of thought " [70]; even under the matrimonial offence doctrine of divorce it finally became accepted, (at least in theory [71]), that the court should hesitate to reduce a wife's maintenance because of her misconduct. This should only affect her rights if it were of a really serious nature and in the category of the disruptive, the intolerable, the unforgivable.[72]

Under the new law, the court is specifically required to have regard to the parties' conduct in determining how far it is just to place them in the position they would have been in apart from the marriage breakdown. This must mean—

> " that if a wife's conduct was found to a given extent to be worse than her husband's she would be placed in a financial position, compared with the hypothetical position, to that extent lower than his position, similarly compared." [73]

It therefore seemed probable [74] that the assessment of financial provision would almost inevitably involve a detailed investigation by the court into the parties' conduct,[75] hearing their mutual recriminations and petty squabbles [76] for days on end, thus frustrating the declared aim of enabling the " empty legal shell " of a broken marriage to be destroyed with " the minimum bitterness, distress and humiliation." [77] The courts have, however, avoided this danger. First, it was held that there would be few cases in which the parties' finances were such that findings as to conduct could properly affect the order made.[78] Finally, the Court of Appeal [79] has asserted the principle that regard will *only* be had to misconduct where it is:

> " ' both obvious and gross,' so much so that to order one party

---

[68] The court had a discretion to award maintenance, but in practice it was " used sparingly and in cases where the wife would have suffered great hardship if the order had not been made ": Morton Commission, para. 502.

[69] *Per* Willmer J., *Dailey* v. *Dailey* [1947] 1 All E.R. 847, 850 (a nullity case) *cf.* the principle applied in the ecclesiastical courts: " such bad wives as have violated their vows shall have such provision . . . as clerks convict . . . and shall be fed with the bread of affliction and with the water of adversity ": *Manby* v. *Scott* (1660) Smith's *Leading Cases* at p. 441.

[70] *Porter* v. *Porter* [1969] 1 W.L.R. 1155, *per* Sachs L.J.

[71] The old phrases and concepts survived in conventional advocacy: *Wachtel* v. *Wachtel* (*supra*) at p. 77, *per* Ormrod J.

[72] *Ackerman* v. *Ackerman* [1972] Fam. 1, *per* Sir George Baker P. (reversed by C.A. [1972] Fam. 225, but not so as to affect the point); *Porter* v. *Porter* [1971] P. 285.

[73] *Per* Bagnall J., *Harnett* v. *Harnett* (*supra*) at p. 599.

[74] See Cretney (1970) 33 M.L.R. 667.

[75] See *e.g. Ackerman* v. *Ackerman* (*supra*) at first instance.

[76] *Per* Lord Denning M.R., *Wachtel* v. *Wachtel* (*supra*) at pp. 89–90.

[77] " Field of Choice," para. 15.

[78] *Ackerman* v. *Ackerman* (*supra*); *O'Brien* v. *O'Brien and Smith* [1972] Fam. 20.

[79] *Wachtel* v. *Wachtel*; *Trippas* v. *Trippas* (*supra*).

to support another whose conduct falls into this category is repugnant to anyone's sense of justice." [80]

It has also been said that:

" the conduct of both parties must be considered. If the conduct of one is substantially as bad as that of the other then it matters not how gross that conduct is; they will weigh equally in the balance. . . . [T]o satisfy the test the conduct must be obvious and gross in the sense that the party concerned must be plainly seen to have wilfully persisted in conduct, or a course of conduct, calculated to destroy the marriage in circumstances in which the other party is substantially blameless." [81]

It follows that conduct will hardly ever come into consideration,[82] notwithstanding the plain words of the Act.[83]

The specified " Circumstances "

Many of these embody common-sense principles, originating in long-standing judicial decisions, which will thus continue to be applied where relevant under the new law.

Income and financial resources

Ability to pay

The courts look at the *realities* of the parties' financial position. Thus, in *J.* v. *J.* [84] the husband was a property developer, living at the rate of more than £1,100 per annum. His taxable income was only £70 per annum,[85] but the court took £1,200 as his income for assessment purposes. Similarly, if he is provided with free board and lodging by his mistress,[86] that will be taken into account, as will other voluntary allowances,[87] tips and regular overtime pay.[88] The court is concerned not only with what money a man has, but with what he *could* have if he liked.[89] Hence earning capacity will be taken into account if the husband voluntarily gives up his job.[90]

---

[80] *Per* Lord Denning M.R., *Wachtel* v. *Wachtel* (*supra*) at p. 90; J. C. Hall [1973] C.L.J. 230.

[81] *Per* Bagnall J., *Harnett* v. *Harnett* (*supra*) at p. 601.

[82] *Trippas* v. *Trippas* (*supra*); *Harnett* v. *Harnett* (*supra*) at p. 601; *Brickell* v. *Brickell* [1973] 3 All E.R. 508. For a case where the wife was refused an order on the grounds of her gross and obvious misconduct which was wholly responsible for the breakdown, see *Cuzner* v. *Underwood* (1973) 117 S.J. 465.

[83] *Ackerman* v. *Ackerman* (*supra*); *Pheasant* v. *Pheasant* [1972] Fam. 202, *per* Ormrod J.: " ' conduct ' is still a factor, and a factor which is likely to continue to influence decisions until the attitudes of the public and their advisers and of those who administer the law change." Note also that both the Law Commission and Archbishop's Group thought it must remain a factor: *Field of Choice*, para. 25, " Putting asunder," para. 39 *et seq.*

[84] [1955] P. 215; on appeal [1955] P. 236.

[85] The gap was bridged by his ability to borrow money.

[86] *Ette* v. *Ette* [1965] 1 All E.R. 341; *Donaldson* v. *Donaldson* [1958] 1 W.L.R. 827.

[87] *Martin* v. *Martin* [1919] P. 283.

[88] *Klucinski* v. *Klucinski* [1953] 1 All E.R. 683.

[89] *N.* v. *N.* (1928) 44 T.L.R. 324, 327, *per* Lord Merivale P.; *McEwen* v. *McEwen* [1972] 2 All E.R. 708.

[90] *Cf. Jacobson* v. *Jacobson* (1961) 105 S.J. 991; *McEwen* v. *McEwen* (1971) 115 S.J. 739; and *Luton* v. *Luton* (1962) *The Times*, February 27.

Supplementary benefit

In many cases there will not be sufficient money available to give two households even a subsistence living standard, so that Supplementary Benefit will be needed. This is not regarded as one of the financial resources available to the husband within the meaning of the Act.[91] The court will first of all consider what would be a fair figure without regard to social security payments. An order will not normally be made which would depress the husband below subsistence level.[92] The courts will take account of the fact that the wife will be eligible for benefit, but this does not mean that the husband will be allowed to throw onto the community the obligation which he ought himself to bear: he will be made to pay such an amount as will keep him at (but not significantly above) subsistence level even if the effect is that his payments will not increase the wife's total income, but simply reduce what she receives in benefit.[93] A simplified example may make this clearer. A husband, living with another woman and one child, has a weekly income [94] of £20. If he were without income the Supplementary Benefits Commission would pay weekly benefit for him and his household [95] of £15·35. The wife who has two children aged between five and nine has no income or capital, and no relevant earning capacity. The allowance she would get from the Commission would be £12·05. Suppose that the court would regard £11 per week as the appropriate maintenance for the husband to pay his wife and family. If that were ordered, it would leave him with only £9, and thus £6 below the Supplementary Benefit (*i.e.* "subsistence") level. So the court will probably make an award of £4. That means the husband's household has £16; the wife's has £4, which will be supplemented to £12·05 by a weekly payment from the Supplementary Benefits Commission. The cost to the taxpayer will be £8·05 alone. Had the court adopted the attitude: "it is no use making this man pay anything; his wife will not get any benefit from it since her Supplementary Benefit will simply be reduced by the amoun. of the husband's payments," it would have cost the community £12.

Wife's earning capacity

If a wife is in receipt of earnings they will be taken into account,[96] (unless it would be unreasonable to expect her to carry on [97]). What is

---

91 *Barnes* v. *Barnes* [1972] 3 All E.R. 872, 874, *per* Edmund Davies L.J.

92 *Ashley* v. *Ashley* [1968] P. 582; *Roberts* v. *Roberts* [1970] P. 1; *Attwood* v. *Attwood.*

93 *Ashley* v. *Ashley* (*supra*); *Roberts* v. *Roberts* (*supra*); *Barnes* v. *Barnes* (*supra*). See *infra*, p. 227 as to the ways in which the S.B.C. in effect guarantee the husband's payments up to the level of the appropriate allowance.

94 Taxation and Rent Allowances are ignored.

95 As to the rights of second wives, mistresses etc., see *infra*, p. 198.

96 As in *Wachtel* v. *Wachtel* (*supra*). See *Rose* v. *Rose* [1951] P. 29; *Higgs* v. *Higgs* [1941] P. 27.

97 *Levett-Yeats* v. *Levett-Yeats* (1967) 111 S.J. 475; *Attwood* v. *Attwood* [1968] P. 591.

the position if she is not working, but could do so? [98]   Generally it does not " lie in the mouth of a wrongdoing husband to say that the wife ought to go out to work simply in order to relieve him from paying maintenance." [99]   But if she is in fact able to go out to work, some deduction from maintenance will normally be made to take account of that.[1]   Even if she does not wish to work, the recent decisions suggest that the court will often think it in her own interest to do so, particularly if she were young and childless, had worked before marriage, and was quite able to do so.[2]   Such a wife should not necessarily [3] expect to get as much as a woman who " is deserted after years of married life looking after the husband and building up the husband in his profession or work, and rearing the family."

The court will in most cases only " take into account " earning capacity,[4] *i.e. some* reduction will be made, as distinct from automatically reducing the award by the total of the wife's potential earnings.   A computation is made, then " weight is given to other relevant considerations." [5]

Financial needs and obligations [6]

Need is presumably to be interpreted by the standards the parties have come to expect.   Maintenance includes " much more than food, lodging, clothes, travelling and so on.   It includes, for instance, charity and making arrangements for the future. . . ." [7]   Hence it is immaterial that the wife is able to make savings from her allowance.[8]

Obligations—competing dependants

It is in considering " obligations " that the most acute problems are met: there may be competing claims between two or more former wives,

98 The Morton Commission (para. 493) found a feeling that the court does not take into consideration sufficiently, or at all, the fact that a wife may well be able to obtain employment but chooses not to do so while she can receive money from her husband. " We are agreed that in principle it is undesirable nowadays that a woman should receive maintenance if she is well able to support herself, and would in fact have had to do so if she had been left a widow." Although there has been no formal implementation of this recommendation, the court seems readier to take earning capacity into account (at least in the case of the lower income groups).

99 Denning L.J., *Rose* v. *Rose* [1951] P. 29; see also *Le-Roy Lewis* v. *Le-Roy Lewis* [1955] P. 1.   1 *J.* v. *J.* [1955] P. 215; *Rose* v. *Rose* (*supra*).

2 *Rose* v. *Rose* (*supra*); see also *Mathias* v. *Mathias* [1972] Fam. 287.

3 *Per* Baker J., *P.* (*J. R.*) v. *P.* (*G. L.*) [1966] 1 W.L.R. 788; and *Coleman* v. *Coleman* [1972] 3 All E.R. 886, 888A, where the court showed little sympathy for a mother who refused to work. It may be different if the wife's earnings could, in the context of the husband's means, more appropriately be thought of as " pin-money "; see *Brett* v. *Brett* [1969] 1 W.L.R. 487. The most recent statement of principle is in *Attwood* v. *Attwood* [1968] P. 591. See also *P.* (*J. R.*) v. *P.* (*G. L.*) [1966] 1 W.L.R. 788: 43-year-old wife who had not contemplated work since she had been a model as a young woman not expected to work.

4 Sir J. Simon P., *Attwood* v. *Attwood* (*supra*) at p. 596.

5 *Per* Sir J. Simon P., *Roberts* v. *Roberts* [1970] P 1. This ensures that the wife still has an incentive to work.

6 Age and ill-health are separately referred to: see M.C.A. 1973, s. 25 (1) (*d*) and (*e*), neither of which clauses were in the original Law Commission draft.

7 *Per* Scott L.J., *Acworth* v. *Acworth* [1943] P. 21, 22–23.

8 *Acworth* v. *Acworth* (*supra*); *Sansom* v. *Sansom* [1966] P. 52.

between a wife or former wife and a mistress, and between the children (legitimate or illegitimate) of several unions. The courts tried to formulate principles under the old law to balance these competing claims:

(a) A spouse is presumed, on marriage, to take the other " subject to all existing incumbrances, whether known or not—for example, a charge on property, or an ailment which impairs earning capacity, or an obligation to support the wife or child of a prior dissolved marriage." [9]   Thus, a wife who marries a man whose child has been receiving an education at fee-paying schools may have her claim in subsequent divorce proceedings deferred to that obligation,[10] at least if there will be sufficient for her subsistence. In the case of people of small means this general principle is applied somewhat pragmatically [11]: the first wife has a just claim, but the second marriage results in a reduction of capacity to pay for the first wife's upkeep.[12]   Her claim would not " be dealt with as a matter of strict calculation on one side or other of the account " [13] but would be " taken into account " in arriving at a just solution. If, therefore, the first wife had a maintenance order of £8 per week, and the husband now has an income of £25 per week, the court would not necessarily simply deduct the £8 from his income, and treat the husband's income (on the second wife's application) as only £17. It would try to decide what an appropriate figure for the second wife would be, taking into account the obligation to pay £8 to the first wife.

(b) The courts refuse to draw a rigid line between legally enforceable obligations, and those which " a little quaintly though conveniently " [14] are called " moral " obligations (e.g. to a mistress [15]).   Such claims are " taken into account " in assessing competing claims.[16]

Other financial obligations

If a financial obligation was contracted during the marriage, and

---

9 Per Rees J., Roberts v. Roberts [1970] P. 1, 8.

10 Wiliams v. Williams [1965] P. 125.

11 Cf. the more rigid application of the principle in Davis v. Davis [1964] V.L.R. 278; Burton v. Burton [1928] N.Z.L.R. 496; Richards v. Richards [1942] N.Z.L.R. 313; Lyne v. Lyne [1951] N.Z.L.R. 287.

12 Cockburn v. Cockburn [1957] 1 W.L.R. 1020.

13 Collins v. Collins [1943] P. 106, 108, per Lord Merriman P., approved in Powell v. Powell [1951] P. 257, and Roberts v. Roberts [1970] P. 1. Cf. Williams v. Williams [1965] P. 125 where the Court of Appeal held that the cost of educating a child of the first marriage should be deducted from the income for assessment purposes.

14 Per Rees J., Roberts v. Roberts (supra) at p. 3.

15 Roberts v. Roberts (supra).

16 Before the Divorce Reform Act 1969 it was possible to draw some distinction between the claims of a second wife and those of a mistress. It was up to the innocent first wife to decide whether to release her husband from his marriage; there could thus (it was said) be no injustice in giving weight to legal obligations arising from the second marriage, although not to the extent of ignoring the first wife's claim. Conversely, if the first wife refused to allow the husband to contract a further marriage it could correspondingly rarely be right to postpone her claim to that of a mistress, " even though this must be taken into account for whatever weight it is held to bear." (per Rees J., Roberts v. Roberts (supra)). Now that an " innocent " wife can be divorced against her will it may be: (a) that the courts will be less ready to give weight to the claims of a mistress; and (b) may be readier to enforce the first wife's claim in priority to all others.

still enures to the wife's benefit, it may be brought into account as a deduction from the wife's entitlement [17]: the most obvious example is where a wife continues to occupy a house which the husband is buying with the aid of a mortgage.[18] The *interest* element (as distinct from the capital repayment) may be equated to rent; since the wife is receiving the whole benefit, it will be a deduction from the amount she would otherwise receive.   It is different if the wife is no longer living in the house, so that the benefit enures to the husband.[19] The same principle will apply if household goods are being paid for by deferred payments.[20] If the husband is contributing to a pension scheme which will enure for the wife's benefit,[21] the wife may have to give credit for the payments, although difficult problems of assessment may arise.[22]

Standard of living

The wife's standard of living should not suffer more than is inherent in the circumstances.[23] In the case of the wealthy, standards can be approximately preserved by income provisions coupled with suitable capital transfers from one to the other. If the parties are of moderate or small means, the inevitable reduction should (other things being equal) be evenly distributed so that each has the same standard of living.[24]

Age and duration of marriage

The duration of the marriage has always been relevant, particularly as a credit factor where, for other reasons (such as her misconduct [25]) the wife's provision might have been reduced. On the other hand, if the marriage has only lasted a very short time, the wife may not get any provision at all [26] unless that would produce an unjust result.[27] Age will normally be relevant in relation to financial needs, but under this head it may be possible for the court to give special weight in the case of the wife who has been cast on one side by a husband who finds her charms diminishing with age, even though she may only have been married for a comparatively short period.

[17] *Roberts* v. *Roberts* (*supra*).
[18] The statement to the contrary in *Rayden*, p. 718 is inconsistent with *Sansom* v. *Sansom* and does not appear to be supported by the authorities relied on. It is only correct if the wife is no longer living in the house in question.
[19] *P.(J.R.)* v. *P.(G.L.)* [1966] 1 W.L.R. 788; see also *Porter* v. *Porter* (1973) 117 S.J. 34.
[20] The analogy is inexact, since in hire purchase transactions the charges cannot be regarded as equivalent to a rent for use.
[21] See *infra*, p. 202.
[22] *Sansom* v. *Sansom* [1966] P. 52. See also *Parry* v. *Parry* (1966) 111 S.J. 247.
[23] *Kershaw* v. *Kershaw* [1966] P. 13.
[24] *Kershaw* v. *Kershaw* [1966] P. 13; *Attwood* v. *Attwood* [1968] P. 591.
[25] *Porter* v. *Porter* [1969] 1 W.L.R. 1155.
[26] *Lombardi* v. *Lombardi* [1973] 1 W.L.R. 1276; *Krystman* v. *Krystman* [1973] 1 W.L.R. 927 (fortnight's cohabitation after shot-gun marriage; separation for 26 years; no children; no order).
[27] *Brett* v. *Brett* [1969] 1 W.L.R. 487 (5½ months from marriage to breakdown: no reduction); *P.(J.R.)* v. *P.(G.L.)* [1966] 1 W.L.R. 788 (12 months: no reduction). These cases were, however, decided on the matrimonial offence principle and might now be decided differently.

Physical or mental disability

Special need arising from physical disability needs no comment. In the case of persons suffering from mental disability, special provisions apply, the details of which are outside the scope of this book.[28]

Contributions to the welfare of the home, etc.

This provision clearly recognises that the wife who looks after the home and family contributes as much to the family assets as the wife who goes out to work. If a wife has looked after home and family for a long period she will normally be given a share in it under this provision.[29]

Loss of prospective benefit

A wife who is divorced, or whose marriage is annulled, ceases to be a wife. If her former husband predeceases her, she will not be his widow. She will, therefore, no longer be entitled to succeed on his intestacy; she may no longer be eligible to benefit under the terms of a superannuation fund, and her position under the National Insurance legislation may also suffer. These consequences do not generally follow if the wife is judicially separated: she remains her husband's wife, and, after his death, his widow. For that reason, the court is not required to consider this matter in judicial separation proceedings.[30]

The present provision is largely (but not exclusively [31]) concerned with the loss of pension rights.[32] The rights in question are those conferred directly on a widow by the scheme. Such rights do not vest in the husband's estate, and cannot therefore be reached by application under the Family Provision Acts.[33] The basic problem is:

> " She may have been married for 20 years or more during which the husband has been a member of a superannuation scheme under which the wife, if she survives him, would be entitled to a pension or lump sum, or, if not entitled, would be the likely recipient of benefits either at the discretion of the trustees or as a result of a nomination by the husband. On the dissolution of the marriage her prospective rights or expectations are normally destroyed, since she can no longer become his widow. . . . It should be borne in mind, however, that if the wife is divorced while young (and most divorces affect women under 35) the probability is that unless she is handicapped by the care of young children she will be able to find pensionable employment and may well remarry in due course and

28 See *Rayden*, p. 275.
29 *Wachtel* v. *Wachtel* (*supra*).
30 It seems to have been overlooked that a judicially separated wife no longer has any right to succeed on the intestacy of her husband: s. 18 (2) M.C.A. 1973. In that respect she is as badly off as a divorced woman, and logically the court should have been enabled to consider that loss in her case as well as that of the divorced wife. This is, however, a point of little practical importance: the right to succeed on intestacy is of little real value.
31 *Trippas* v. *Trippas* (*supra*).
32 For a full treatment see the Law Commission's Published Working Paper No. 9, paras. 182–210, reprinted in Law Commission 25, p. 145 *et seq*.
33 *Supra*, p. 177.

thereby acquire a pension expectancy in right of her new husband.
When that occurs there is little hardship if she forfeits her expectancy
in right of her former husband. The real hardship arises in respect
of women left with children to bring up and, more especially, in
respect of the older women—those who are 45 or older when
divorced. Statistics show that these have a poor expectation of
remarriage so that if they lose their hope of an occupational pension
in right of the first husband they are likely to lose all hope of an
occupational pension; even if they can find pensionable employment,
which may not be easy at their age, the pension is likely to be small."

Pensions are derived from two main sources:

The State scheme

The main characteristics of the present state scheme [34] are:

(i) it is *contributory* (*i.e.* benefit depends on the insured person's
contributions over the years);

(ii) it is *obligatory* (*i.e.* adults are normally required to pay
contributions);

(iii) it confers rights [35] not only on the insured contributor, but
on his wife, and his widow. [36]

The effect of divorce on a woman is:

(i) a married woman is not (unless she is employed [37]) obliged to
pay contributions. An unmarried woman (including a divorcée) is. On
divorce, therefore, a woman who is not employed is faced with a substantial financial obligation (currently £1·057 per week [38]). A divorced
woman who obtains employment is also liable, but her contributions [39]
can at least be met out of earnings.

(ii) The Act confers rights on wives and *widows* after retirement
age. The cost of these benefits is actuarially calculated, [40] and taken
into account in assessing the contributions and benefits. This calculation
is based on the fact that a man can only have one widow, and no more
than one wife at the same time. [41] If former wives were also entitled
the extra cost would fall on the general body of contributors. This has
been thought inconsistent with the contributory nature of the scheme. [42]

---

[34] It is to be reformed: see *infra*, p. 204.

[35] These benefits are not confined to retirement or widows' benefits but they alone are
considered here.

[36] The scheme is complicated by the addition of a graduated element in both contributions and pensions; that is ignored in the present discussion.

[37] And then she has a right to contract out: see National Insurance Act 1965 (subsequently called " the 1965 Act ") s. 102.

[38] National Insurance and Supplementary Benefit Act 1973, Sched. 2, Part IV. But if
her total income is below a low subsistence level she may be exempted from liability
to pay: see 1965 Act, s. 10.

[39] Which will in any case be lower.

[40] See the 1965 Act, s. 86, as amended by National Insurance Act 1969, s. 10.

[41] But it is no longer a bar that the marriage may have been, at some time, actually
polygamous: see National Insurance Act 1971, s. 12, and regulations made thereunder
(S.I. 1150 of 1972).

[42] See P.W.P. No. 9, para. 187. But note that (a) it would be theoretically possible to
provide for a single widow's or retirement pension to be divided amongst all the
former wives of a deceased contributor. This would not be worthwhile, since on

However, the divorced woman is treated favourably in one respect.[43] For the purpose of *retirement pension* [44] (*i.e.* the pension which becomes payable at age sixty or later on the husband's retirement) a divorced woman:

1. If she is over sixty *when divorced*,[45] becomes entitled to the same rate of retirement pension she would have had if her husband had died at the time, *i.e.* the single person's pension, currently £7·75 per week.[46]

2. If she is divorced before reaching the age of sixty, she can get such a retirement pension as would have been earned by her husband's contributions *during the marriage*. The longer the marriage the larger the pension, but it will never be the full amount, and may be very much less.[47]

Occupational pension schemes

Private pension schemes represent a considerable source of accumulated savings. In 1969, there were over twelve million employees covered by such schemes; in 1967, some two million persons were receiving benefits, and schemes had an income from contributions of some £1,265 million. The total value of occupational pension funds is probably now in excess of £15,000 million.[48] The proportion of male non-manual workers covered by such schemes is as high as 75 per cent.[49] A husband may have had 15 per cent. of his annual salary paid into a Pension Fund over the period of the marriage. This represents a considerable accumulation of wealth; and also probably (apart from the matrimonial home) the spouses' only substantial asset. It is thus vital to ensure that it is available to the divorced wife.

current levels, it would reduce all the payments to below-subsistence level; (b) if a pension were so reduced *and the former-wife and widow had no other means*, each would be entitled to have it supplemented by Supplementary Benefit. On current levels, her income would not be substantially below the pension level: see *infra*, p. 225. The taxpayer bears the whole cost of Supplementary Benefit. It is not known what the additional cost to the taxpayer of providing (as of right and irrespective of means) the widow's and retirement pension would be; (c) it would theoretically be possible to require a man's contributions during marriage to be earmarked for the benefit of his then wife, and if he divorces her, to require him to pay an increased contribution to cover her pension rights. This has been rejected because it would produce administrative complications, and would involve employers in making inquiries into marital status: P.W.P. No. 9, para. 190.

[43] Following the Morton Commission, paras. 712–716. See the National Insurance (Married Women) Regulations 1948; Regulation 8C (inserted by the National Insurance (Married Women) Amendment Regulations 1957).

[44] As distinct from widow's pension (*i.e.* the pension payable on the husband's death if she has children or is over 50).

[45] Or if the marriage is voidable (but not void) and annulled

[46] National Insurance and Supplementary Benefit Act 1973, Sched. I.

[47] Under the Labour Government's pension proposals (Cmnd. 3883, para. 83) a divorced woman would also have been entitled to take over the husband's record for the period *before* as well as during marriage. This proposed change, coupled with the larger pensions to be expected under the earnings-related scheme, led the Law Commission to conclude (Law Commission 25, para. 112) that the main difficulty in relation to pension provision was not in relation to the state scheme, but occupational schemes.

[48] *Per* Lord Aberdare, Hansard (H.L.) Vol. 342, col. 1111.

[49] Cmnd. 3883, paras. 112–113. See also Occupational Pension Schemes (H.M.S.O.) (1966).

Each scheme must be considered separately. There are wide variations, and many are complicated by tax avoidance considerations.
The main variants are as follows:

(i) No provision at all is made for widows or other dependants.
The contributor alone is entitled to a pension. Such schemes are
uncommon.[50]

(ii) The fund is held on trust to apply it at discretion for the benefit
of a wide class of beneficiary. In practice, the trustees will usually follow
the known wishes of the employee in exercising their discretion. A widow
would normally be a member of the class. A former wife is less likely to
be so, and the trustees are less likely to exercise their discretion in her
favour even if she is.

(iii) The employee is given a right to a pension and may give up
part of this entitlement in exchange for a smaller pension for a surviving
widow. A divorced wife would rarely benefit.

(iv) The scheme may confer an entitlement to a widow's pension.
A former wife would not be entitled.

It follows that there are two main ways in which the divorced wife's
position can be protected:

(i) It may be possible for the husband to enter into an agreement
with the pension fund trustees whereby his former wife is to benefit.
But the husband has no present entitlement such as would enable an
immediate order to be made against him. The only possibility is
that the court will exercise its powers under sections 5 and 10, of
the Matrimonial Causes Act 1973 to persuade the husband to deal
with the matter.[51]

(ii) The court may, in view of " the loss of the expectation that
she will be maintained in her old age out of the husband's own
earnings or pension " [52] order the husband as from the date of
divorce to make additional financial provision for the wife, to
compensate her for this loss, so far as possible by making her own
arrangements. This will be particularly appropriate if the husband
has some capital which can be transferred; otherwise the only practicable alternative will be to increase the periodical payments to
enable pension provision for the wife to be made out of them.[53]

The court's attention is specifically directed to this matter by the
clause under discussion. At most this will " alleviate indirectly " the
problem.[54] As the Law Commission accepted, the problem of utilising
savings in private pension funds for the divorced wife " remains
unsolved and, after full consultation, we believe it to be incapable of
direct and complete solution." [55]

[50] And will not be entitled to approval under the new pension legislation, see *infra*,
    p. 204.
[51] *Supra*, p. 127.
[52] P.W.P. No. 9, para. 204. See *e.g. Parker* v. *Parker* [1972] Fam. 116.
[53] P.W.P. No. 9, paras. 190–207.
[54] Law Commission 25, para. 112.
                                                          [55] *Ibid.*

Effect of the Social Security Act 1973

This Act (which does not come into force until 1975) makes radical changes in the State Pensions scheme. Instead of the present flat rate scheme,[53] every person will be entitled to two pensions: (1) A standard flat-rate pension from the state basic pension scheme. This is intended to be the basic minimum pension. The idea that this is funded by past contributions is scrapped; this scheme will be financed out of current revenue. (2) An earnings related pension. This may be derived either from a recognised private occupational scheme, or in default from the state reserve scheme. It is government policy to encourage private schemes: these will only be recognised if they meet certain requirements, designed primarily to ensure that a decent personal pension with adequate provision for widows[57] is provided. The state reserve scheme will be available for those who have no qualifying occupational scheme: it will be funded (*i.e.* based on invested contributions) and the scale of pensions will include an element of bonus to give the benefit of appreciation in the fund's investments.

This scheme may greatly improve the pension expectations of the average worker. Paradoxically the greater its success, the greater the potential hardship to a wife on divorce. The new legislation does nothing to remedy the disadvantages pointed out above: a wife may still not pay contributions in her own right[58]; if so, she will be entirely dependent on her husband's contributions, and stands to forfeit increased benefits if the marriage is terminated.

Loss of other benefits

Although the Act specifically refers to loss of a pension, it is not limited to such practical benefits. In *Trippas* v. *Trippas*[59] the wife was given a lump sum on the basis that, had the marriage continued it was likely that the husband would have settled on her part of the proceeds of a takeover of his family business.

Exercise of the discretion to make lump sum and other capital provision orders[60]

The only exceptions to the general principle that the whole of the parties' property can be dealt with by the court on breakdown are that there is no power over:

(i) The *capital* of a settlement which is not a nuptial or post nuptial settlement.[61] If a testator settles property on his bachelor son for life, the settlement is outside the definition, and the court

---

[56] With small graduated supplements.
[57] Normally a pension equal to one-half of the husband's pension.
[58] Except that a married woman *cannot* contract out of the earnings-related pensions provisions.
[59] *Supra.*
[60] See generally G. Miller (1971) 87 L.Q.R. 66; *Jackson*, Chaps. 5, 7–9.
[61] *Supra*, p. 190, and M.C.A., s. 24 (1) (*c*).

cannot vary the settlement. It could order the son to settle his life interest, but that cannot affect the settled *capital*.

(ii) Assets which, by their nature, are not " owned " by either spouse (*e.g.* interests under a discretionary pension scheme).[62] There are five advantages to capital provision[63]:

(i) Difficulties of enforcement are avoided. If the husband fails to comply with a lump sum order the wife may enforce it by bankruptcy proceedings.[64] Once the property has been transferred the husband has no further means of defaulting.[65]

(ii) Provision of capital assets will often be the only effective way in which a wife can be compensated for loss of expectations, pension rights,[66] and given security against bad times or illness.[67]

(iii) The only effective way of giving much recognition to the wife's contributions to the welfare of the family by looking after the home and caring for the family will usually be by transferring to her a share of the matrimonial home and other family assets.

(iv) It " enables the parties to start afresh without relics of the past hanging like millstones round their necks." [68]

(v) It is virtually impossible (as a result of the taxation system and other economic factors) to maintain the customary life style of the affluent out of income alone. For example, a house which costs £40,000 to buy may cost £4,000 per annum to rent. The rent has to be paid out of taxed income, which will mean that a very large sum of pre-tax income has to be set aside simply to cover the rent. Even at the (comparatively) modest income level of £10,000 per annum each pound of taxable income will only be worth £0·30 in the wife's pocket.[69]

The court had no power to order any capital provision until 1963, when they were given power to avoid lump sums. But these were seen as appropriate only to deal with the financial problems of the

---

[62] *Supra*, p. 202. In this case, however, the court may be able, under s. 10, M.C.A. 1973 (if the petition is based on one of the separation " facts "), to exercise pressure so that such interests can be brought into account.

[63] See Law Commission 25, para. 9 (Lump Sums), 64–77 (other capital provision).

[64] *Curtis* v. *Curtis* [1969] 1 W.L.R. 422.

[65] See *Jones* v. *Jones* [1971] 3 All E.R. 1201, 1206. Hence a capital order may be made for a larger sum than would otherwise be appropriate: *Bryant* v. *Bryant* (1973) *The Times*, November 7.

[66] See *Trippas* v. *Trippas* (*supra*).

[67] *Jones* v. *Jones* (*supra*).   [68] Law Commission 25, para. 9.

[69] On the assumption that the income is unearned (which includes any periodical payments the wife receives from the husband): see generally on the problem, and the principles applied, *Davis* v. *Davis* [1967] P. 185. *Schlesinger* v. *Schlesinger* [1960] P. 191 (a case in which the court had no power to order a lump sum) sharply demonstrates the difficulties of providing out of income for the wife of a wealthy man: the husband had a notional income of some £110,000 per annum; in order to give his wife £5,000 or £6,000 per annum after tax, the court had to order £20,000 per annum. Even that would not provide accommodation of the sort enjoyed by the parties as husband and wife.

wealthy [70] and in a limited number of other exceptional circumstances,[71] as where it would coerce an unwilling husband by fear of bankruptcy,[72] where settlement of a capital asset enabled the wife to earn her own living,[73] or where capital was needed for special non-recurrent purposes such as major structural repairs to the house in which the wife has made her home.[74]

For some time after the introduction of extended powers in 1970 [75] the indications were that the courts did not accept the Law Commission's " considered opinion " [76] that lump sum awards (or in the alternative,[77] capital provision orders) should be made more readily.[78] But the Act specifically requires husband and wife to be put in the same position as they would have been had the marriage not broken down, and it is now recognised that this can only be done by using capital provision orders. It follows that the court will consider whether to make a capital provision order in all cases.[79] This will often be an order related to the matrimonial home [80] and the court would not make an order for transfer of other assets unless the husband has available sufficient capital for the purpose.[81]

Difficulty might arise because a lump sum award, once made, cannot normally be varied, nor can it be recovered if the wife remarries. Periodical payments, on the other hand, *must* cease on remarriage.[82] If a lump sum were regarded as the capitalised value of future income payments,[83] it could be said to be unfair to a husband to make an order

---

[70] " As a practical matter, it is clear than an order for a lump sum payment can only properly be made against a husband possessed of sufficient capital uses to justify it. It is not to be expected, therefore, that the question is likely to arise except in relatively rare cases." *Per* Willmer L.J., *Davis* v. *Davis* (*supra*) at p. 192. As to the factors to be taken into account, see *Jackson* at p. 123. It is not necessary for the wife to point to any specific *need* for capital, although housing is highly relevant: *Jones* v. *Jones* (*supra*).

[71] *Ibid.* See also *Hackluytt* v. *Hackluytt* [1968] 1 W.L.R. 1145, 1149.

[72] *Curtis* v. *Curtis* (*supra*); *Brett* v. *Brett* (*supra*).

[73] *Von Mehren* v. *Von Mehren* [1970] 1 W.L.R. 56 (house used by wife as guest house). Note also (a) the provision enabled a stable home to be provided for the wife and children, and (b) the property involved was to be settled so that there was no risk of the wife dissipating it.

[74] *Hackluytt* v. *Hackluytt* (*supra*).

[75] Matrimonial Proceedings and Property Act 1970, s. 4.

[76] Law Commission 25, para. 9.

[77] *Ibid.* para. 68.

[78] *Millward* v. *Millward* [1971] 3 All E.R. 526, by inference from Russell L.J.'s remarks at p. 529J; see also *Jones* v. *Jones* [1971] 3 All E.R. 1201, and *per* Karminski L.J., *Von Mehren* v. *Von Mehren* (*supra*) at p. 61: " . . . the cases in which lump sums can be ordered are of necessity relatively rare. I rely only on my own experience in these matters, but I would hazard a guess that it is in only a small minority of cases, in possibly not as much as 5 per cent. of the total of maintenance orders, when an order of this kind could possibly be made."

[79] *Wachtel* v. *Wachtel* (*supra*) at p. 95.

[80] *Hunter* v. *Hunter* (*supra*); *Williams* v. *Williams* [1971] P. 271.

[81] *Wachtel* v. *Wachtel* (*supra*) at p. 96.

[82] But see *Jankov* v. *Jankov* (1970) 14 D.L.R. (3d) 88 (Nova Scotia) and *Coleman* v. *Coleman* [1972] 3 All E.R. 886, 891E, *per* Sir G. Barker P.

[83] This was the accepted view under the old legislation: see *Brett* v. *Brett* [1969] 1 W.L.R. 487; but it has now been rejected: *Trippas* v. *Trippas* (*supra*) at p. 4, *per* Lord Denning M.R.

without considering the likelihood of the wife remarrying (thus determining her periodical maintenance, but not her lump sum award). The courts have however refused to reduce the wife's provision to take account of this possibility because the wife has earned it by her contribution in looking after the home and family.[84] Normally a lump sum award should be *outright*; it may, however, be put into settlement if there are young children to ensure that they are protected.[85]

The increased readiness of the courts to make discretionary capital awards should reduce the need to distort the traditional rules of property law in order to achieve justice between them.[86] It has been said that it will often be desirable to determine existing property rights as a preliminary to the exercise of this jurisdiction,[87] but the better view seems to be that this would only be academic: even if one spouse does establish a claim as a matter of property law, this would simply go to reduce or extinguish his discretionary award.[88]

Variation of Orders

Since one of the objects of a *capital provision order* is to achieve finality, the general principle is that no variation should subsequently be possible.[89]   To this there are two exceptions:

(a) if orders for settlement of property or variation of an existing nuptial settlement [90] are made *on judicial separation*, the court may vary them if (i) the separation decree is rescinded, or (ii) the marriage is subsequently dissolved.[91]

(b) although the *total amount* of a lump sum order is never variable, the court may vary any provisions relating to *instalments* or *security* for such an order [92]—*e.g.* if a husband is ordered to pay the wife £10,000 by ten annual instalments of £1,000 secured on his shareholding in Abracadabra Ltd., the court could vary it by providing that it be paid in fifteen instalments, and that the security be changed. It cannot, however, change the total of the award.

[84] *Wachtel* v. *Wachtel* (*supra*) at p. 96.
[85] *Wachtel* v. *Wachtel* (*supra*); *Harnett* v. *Harnett* (*supra*) at p. 601E; *Mesher* v. *Mesher* (1973) *The Times*, October 13; *cf. Chamberlain* v. *Chamberlain* [1974] 1 All E.R. 33.   [86] *Supra*, p. 206.
[87] *Glenn* v. *Glenn* [1973] 1 W.L.R. 1016.
[88] See *Hunter* v. *Hunter* (*supra*) at p. 962; *Wachtel* v. *Wachtel* (*supra*) at p. 922. But note that there is no express power to order a sale of property under the M.C.A. jurisdiction: *Glenn* v. *Glenn* (*supra*).
[89] Law Commission 25, paras. 87–88.
[90] Lump Sum Orders and Transfer of Property orders are not included: s. 31 (2), M.C.A. 1973. If the decree is subsequently rescinded, the reasoning is no doubt that the parties can make their own arrangements (which they may not be able to do if there is a settlement with other interests). If the separation is converted into a divorce, the court will presumably be able to make *further* capital provision orders (under the general wording of s. 23 and s. 24 which s. 31 does not cut down in this regard), and it was presumably thought undesirable that it should be able to order *repayment* (although a new order could be made effectively achieving this—*i.e.* by ordering the payee to pay a sum to the payer: Law Commission 25, para. 89).
[91] s. 31 (4).
[92] s. 31 (2) (*d*); see Law Commission 25, para. 89, and notes to draft clause 9 (para. 3, p. 79).

The Act also provides that lump sum or capital provision orders shall not be made on applications to vary periodical awards[93]: to do otherwise was thought inconsistent with the principle that decisions on capital provision should be finalised on making the decree.[94] But the Act permits the making of capital provision orders " on granting a decree . . . or at any time thereafter." It is thus in theory possible for a wife who did not get such an order to apply, perhaps many years later, for the court to make an *original* capital provision order in her favour, even though such an order could not be made on an application to vary. But, in the exercise of its discretion, the court will not allow the declared policy of the Act to be outflanked in this way unless there are special circumstances.[95] Nor, although it is given power to order payment of a " lump sum *or sums* "[96] will the court in effect vary a lump sum order by subsequently making a further award: this provision is intended to enable the court to make more than one lump sum award in a single order—*e.g.* one sum to cover past expenses, a further sum payable immediately, and a further sum payable by instalments.[97]

Periodical payment orders[98] are, in contrast, primarily designed to provide maintenance, and can be reviewed[99] on any change of circumstances. In exercising its wide power to " vary or discharge the order or to suspend any provision thereof temporarily and to revive the operation of any provision so suspended "[1] the court is directed[2] to—

> " have regard to all the circumstances of the case, including any change in any of the matters to which the court was required to have regard when making the order to which the application relates. . . ."

Hence, the court will consider not only any change in the parties' means or responsibilities, but will also take account of the statutory direction to place them in the financial position in which they would have been had the marriage not broken down. It is not the case that periodical payment orders must be " crystallised " at the time of divorce: a wife is prima facie entitled to share in any increase in her husband's means.[3]

An application to vary an order for secured periodical payments may

---

[93] s. 31 (5).
[94] Law Commission 25, para. 90; see also *Marsden* v. *Marsden* [1973] 1 W.L.R. 641.
[95] *Williams* v. *Williams* [1971] 3 W.L.R. 92; *Powys* v. *Powys* [1971] P. 340; *Jones* v. *Jones* [1971] 3 All E.R. 1201; *Coleman* v. *Coleman* [1972] 3 All E.R. 886.
[96] s. 23 (1) (c).
[97] *Coleman* v. *Coleman* (*supra*).
[98] *i.e.* maintenance pending suit and periodical payments (secured or unsecured): s. 31 (2).
[99] s. 31 (1).
[1] *Ibid.*
[2] s. 31 (7).
[3] *Jones* v. *Jones* (*supra*); *Sansom* v. *Sansom* [1966] P. 52; *cf. Lombardi* v. *Lombardi* [1973] 1 W.L.R. 1276. This seems inconsistent with the desire that the book should be closed once and for all: see *Wachtel* v. *Wachtel* (*supra*) at p. 96.

be made [4] after the death of the husband; in this case the court must consider the changed circumstances resulting from his death.[5]

Avoidance of Dispositions

The court has power to restrain one party from disposing of or transferring property out of the jurisdiction if it is satisfied that this is intended to defeat a claim for financial relief. If a disposition has already been made to anyone except a bona fide purchaser, it may be set aside.[6] Details of these rules are outside the scope of this book.[7]

MAGISTRATES' COURTS [8]

Historical Background

The extensive jurisdiction of Magistrates' Courts originated in the need to protect women of the poorer classes from physical assaults by husbands. The Matrimonial Causes Act 1878 [9] provided that a husband convicted of an aggravated assault on his wife could be ordered [10] to pay to her a weekly sum by way of maintenance; the court could also give the wife custody of any children, and make an order that she was no longer bound to cohabit with the husband. There was little parliamentary debate,[11] and it cannot have been foreseen how revolutionary the measure was. The remedies thus given were, and are still, the basis of the matrimonial jurisdiction of magistrates, although their scope has been much extended—in particular—

(a) the right to relief no longer depends on the husband's conviction for a criminal offence, and

(b) there is no longer any limit on the amount of maintenance that can be ordered.

Originally the Magistrates' Courts' jurisdiction was used by women

---

[4] Within a time limit: s. 31 (6), (8) and (9).

[5] s. 31 (7).

[6] s. 37, M.C.A. 1973.

[7] See Law Commission No. 25, paras. 97–98.

[8] For a comprehensive examination of the operation of this jurisdiction, see the Bedford College Survey and the Graham Hall Report (the most comprehensive official examination of the subject). The Report of the Departmental Committee on Matrimonial Proceedings in Magistrates' Courts (" The Arthian Davies Committee ") (1959, Cmnd. 638) was the basis of the codification of the law now embodied in the Matrimonial Proceedings (Magistrates' Courts) Act 1960, but contains little of interest save on points of detail. A more comprehensive examination of the jurisdiction was made by the Royal Commission on Marriage and Divorce, (1956 Cmnd. 9678, Part XIV). The Report of the Committee on the Enforcement of Judgment Debts (" the Payne Committee ") (1969, Cmnd. 3909) is a useful source of information on the problems of enforcing orders and also relies heavily on the (then unpublished) results of the Bedford College Survey. D. Marsden, *Mothers Alone* (Revised Ed. 1973) contains a valuable, if impressionistic, sociologist's account of the working of the law (see particularly Chap. 10, " Family Law for the Poor "). A joint Home Office/Law Commission Working Party is examining this jurisdiction. Its Working Paper (No. 53) was published too late for consideration in the text.

[9] s. 4.

[10] By the court which had convicted him, whether assizes, quarter sessions, or justices.

[11] *Hansard*, 3rd Ser., Vol. 239, col. 191, March 29, 1878.

who could not afford proceedings in the Superior Courts. The introduction of legal aid has reduced the proportion of cases.[12] Whereas at the beginning of the century some 93 per cent. of matrimonial suits were heard in Magistrates' Courts, today the figure is less than 25 per cent. In 1972 there were 25,472 applications to Magistrates' Courts for Matrimonial Orders [13]; in the same year 111,077 divorce petitions were filed.[14] Even if the use made of Magistrates' Courts is declining, the case load is still considerable.[14a] One view is that, from being simply the poor woman's substitute for the Divorce Court, the Magistrates' Court has " become for many complainants simply a staging post on their way to the High Court as petitioners." [15] Women get maintenance orders in the Magistrates' Court, and subsequently go to the Divorce Court to destroy the marriage tie. But in a large number of cases no divorce proceedings follow. In either case it is the magistrate's order (remaining in force even after a subsequent divorce), which continues to regulate the wife's financial position.

There remains something of a class distinction between the Divorce Court and the Magistrates' Court: whereas the former is now open to all, the latter still deals " only with the lower income groups. People of means still go to the High Court . . . " [16] (or perhaps come to some voluntary arrangement) in order to avoid the " stigma attaching to proceedings in Magistrates' Courts among the middle class, and possibly the lower middle class. . . ." [17] The Bedford College Survey concluded that " the matrimonial jurisdiction of magistrates is used almost entirely by the working class and very largely by the lowest paid among them." [18] Whereas 21 per cent. of all married men fall into the Registrar General's social classes I and II,[19] no more than $5\frac{1}{2}$ per cent.[20] of defendant husbands in magistrates' matrimonial cases do so. Again, 70 per cent. of the sample of defendants against whom magistrates' orders were made in 1965 had incomes of less than £16 per week (at a time when the average earnings of men in manufacturing industry were £18 per week); only 8 per cent. had incomes of £20 or more.[21] Most women complainants

---

12 For a diagrammatic representation of the two jurisdictions, see Fig. 1 in Bedford College Survey.

13 In addition to 6,647 applications for affiliation orders, and 7,051 applications for orders under the Guardianship of Infants Acts: see Civil Judicial Statistics 1972 (Cmnd. 5333), Table M.   14 Civil Judicial Statistics 1972, Table 10.

14a There were 27,905 applications in 1970, and 26,009 in 1971.

15 Graham Hall Committee Report, para. 35.

16 G. G. Raphael, of the Magistrates' Association, Evidence to the Morton Commission (1951–55), Minutes, p. 320, Q. 2441.

17 A. J. (later Sir Arthur) Driver, subsequently President of the Law Society, ibid. p. 755, Q. 7179.   18 p. 70.

19 Class I: " Professional "; Class II: " Intermediate "; Class III: " Skilled "; Class IV: " Partly Skilled "; Class V: " Unskilled."

20 The inadequacy of court records may lead to an upgrading of many occupations: see Bedford College Survey, p. 68.

21 Bedford College Survey, pp. 69–70. Research done by the Oxford Centre for Socio-Legal Studies on orders made in 1971 produced similar results: 89 per cent. of defendant husbands in a sample had incomes under £30 (at a time when the average wage of male manual workers was £28·20). But these figures should be treated with caution since it is obviously in the interest of defendants to understate their income.

in the courts will be to some extent dependent on Supplementary Benefit, and the substantive law must be viewed in the context of its inter-relation with the Social Security system.

The Substantive Law

There are two characteristics of the Magistrates' jurisdiction which sharply differentiate it from that of the Superior Courts: it is based on the matrimonial offence,[22] and " misconduct " is generally an absolute bar to the making or continuance of an order.

Grounds

The Act [23] provides that *either* husband or wife may apply to the court for an order on any of the following grounds:

(a) *Desertion* (however short the period).

(b) *Persistent cruelty* to the complainant, her child, or the defendant's child if he had become a " child of the family." [24] Unlike the old divorce ground of cruelty, the conduct must be *persistent*: one assault in the course of a row cannot constitute persistent cruelty,[25] although a single assault coupled with a history of mental cruelty would suffice,[26] and it may be that a series of acts on the same day could have the necessary quality of persistence.[27]

(c) *Conviction* [28] of any of a number of *offences involving assault* [29] against the complainant or a child, or indecency on such a child.[30]

(d) *Adultery.*

(e) Having intercourse with the complainant while knowingly suffering from a *venereal disease*, unless she knows of the infection and does not object.[31]

(f) Habitual *drunkenness* or *drug addiction.*[32]

In addition the wife may complain if the husband has compelled her to submit herself to prostitution or has been guilty of conduct likely to result, and in fact resulting in *submission to prostitution*.

Wilful neglect to provide maintenance is also a ground: this is dealt with separately below [33] as is the Magistrates' jurisdiction over children.[34]

---

22 For the offences see *supra*, p. 91.
23 Matrimonial Proceedings (Magistrates' Courts) Act 1960, s. 1. For a general comment see Stone, (1961) 24 M.L.R. 144.   24 As defined, s. 16.(1). See *infra*, p. 274.
25 *Goodman* v. *Goodman* (1931) 95 J.P. 95.
26 *Crawford* v. *Crawford* [1956] P. 195; see also *Buxton* v. *Buxton* [1967] P. 48.
27 *Broad* v. *Broad* (1898) 78 L.T. 687.
28 It is the conviction which enables the court to make the order: *Bryant* v. *Bryant* [1914] P. 277; since a probation order or conditional or absolute discharge is not a conviction (Criminal Justice Act 1948, s. 12 (1)) no order can be made under this head in such a case: *Cassidy* v. *Cassidy* [1959] 1 W.L.R. 1024.
29 See s. 1 (1) (*c*).   30 As defined.
31 If the complainant did not know of the infection the defendant must have " insisted," a term which means something short of compulsion: *Rigby* v. *Rigby* [1944] P. 36.
32 As defined: s. 16 (1).
33 *Infra*, p. 217.   34 *Infra*, p. 258.

Desertion is the most common of the grounds, being alleged by 70 per cent. of complainants in the Bedford College Survey's sample [35] (47 per cent. of the total number of complaints). It is followed by wilful neglect to maintain (47 per cent. and 31 per cent.), and the only other offence with any significant showing is adultery (11 per cent. and 7 per cent.). "Other grounds" were only alleged by four out of a sample of 1,271.

Bars

(i) If the cause of complaint is the respondent's adultery, no order shall be made unless the court is satisfied that the complainant has not *condoned* or *connived at*, or by wilful neglect or misconduct, *conduced to* that act of adultery.[36]

(ii) If the complainant is proved to have committed an act of *adultery* during the subsistence of the marriage, no order can be made unless the court is satisfied that the defendant has condoned, connived at, or by wilful neglect or misconduct conduced to that adultery.[37]

Orders that can be made

(a) *Periodical payments to the wife*

The court may order the husband to pay to the wife such weekly sum as the court considers reasonable in all the circumstances of the case.[38]

(b) *Periodical payments to the husband*

The court may order the wife to pay to the husband such weekly sum as it considers reasonable in all the circumstances of the case if, but only if, it appears reasonable to make such an order by reason of the impairment of the husband's earning capacity through age, illness or disability of mind or body.[39]

These orders can be made whatever ground of complaint is established—*e.g.* a husband can be ordered to pay periodical sums to the wife even if the complaint is only of neglect to maintain children.[40] This is of little importance now that orders, unlimited in amount, may be made to the child.[41]

There is no financial limit on the amount of such orders, although in fact most orders are of small amounts.[42] The differences between the powers of Magistrates' and the Superior Courts are:

---

[35] p. 59.   [36] s. 2 (3) (a); for the meaning of these terms see *supra*, p. 102.
[37] s. 2 (3) (b).
[38] s. 2 (1) (b). Save in the case of orders on the grounds of drug addiction or drunkenness, only the *complainant* is entitled to an order: s. 2 (2).
[39] s. 2 (1) (c). There are also provisions for periodical payments to children, custody and related matters: *infra*, p. 260.
[40] *Northrop* v. *Northrop* [1968] P. 74; Brown (1968) 31 M.L.R. 121; Donaldson [1967] C.L.J. 177.   [41] *Infra*, p. 258.
[42] Maintenance Orders Act 1968. See the Graham Hall Report, paras. 121–135, Bedford College Survey, pp. 79–83. Less than one in five of orders made in a sample were of an amount sufficient to keep the recipient's family at subsistence level (assessed by the Supplementary Benefit yardstick). The Committee thought that the removal of the limit of £7·50 for orders in favour of a wife would affect less than 1 per cent. of such orders.

(i) Magistrates have no power to order capital provision, of however small an amount.[43]

(ii) Magistrates have no power to order secured provision.

In addition to these formal differences, Magistrates' Courts may still be reluctant to make orders (even in the rare cases where these would be appropriate) at more than a subsistence level. Although originating in a need to protect women from physical assault, " [t]oday the main concern of the magistrates' domestic court is to determine issues which will affect the wife's financial position. . . ." [44]

(c) Separation Orders

This power is dealt with elsewhere.[45]

Duration of Orders

(i) If an order has been made it *must* be discharged [46] if it is shown that the complainant has at any time during the subsistence of the marriage [47] committed an act of adultery, unless it is shown that the defendant has condoned it, connived at it, or by wilful neglect or misconduct conduced to it.[48] It should be noted that an application is needed: the order is not *automatically* discharged. If on the application the husband proves adultery, the court has no discretion and must discharge the order.

(ii) An order now automatically determines on the *remarriage* [49] of the payee.

(iii) Orders do *not* automatically determine on divorce [50]; indeed, as has been said, they commonly continue in force. The position is the same if a *voidable* marriage is annulled,[51] if the marriage is *void* it may well be that the order is automatically determined, in so far as it is based on the premiss that the parties are married.

These rules give rise to the possibility that orders of two different courts could be in force at the same time. The courts try to avoid this happening. If, therefore, proceedings in the Divorce Court have been

---

[43] *Cf.* the Graham Hall Committee's recommendation (para. 226): power to make small lump sum awards would be particularly valuable where the wife has incurred expenses, and in dealing with disputes over furniture, etc.

[44] Graham Hall Committee, para. 28.

[45] *Supra*, p. 141.

[46] Save as to provisions relating to children: s. 8 (2) (*b*), *infra*, p. 259.

[47] If, therefore, the wife relies on a Magistrates' Order for maintenance after divorce it will not automatically terminate if she has intercourse with a married man.

[48] s. 8 (2).

[49] Matrimonial Proceedings and Property Act 1970, s. 30 (1). This was the only change of principle introduced by that Act into magisterial law. It was necessary to make it since otherwise a well advised woman would always have preferred to get a Magistrates' (rather than a High Court) Order. Provision is made for enforcing repayment of money paid in ignorance of the remarriage: *ibid.*, s. 31.

[50] *Wood* v. *Wood* [1957] P. 254. It has been estimated that about 50 per cent. of wives receiving maintenance under Magistrates' Orders subsequently found themselves in the Divorce Court. Bedford College Survey, p. 140.

[51] M.C.A. 1973, s. 16.

instituted, the justices will normally as a matter of practice refuse to adjudicate on the issue and leave it to the High Court.[52]

The converse situation may also arise—if, for instance, a wife who has relied on a Magistrates' Order now wishes to take proceedings in the Divorce Court because of the wider range of financial relief now available there. It is provided that the Divorce Court may direct that a Magistrates' order shall cease to have effect, so that the matter can be dealt with *de novo* by the Superior Court.[53]

Variation

The court has a general power to vary orders, by adding, deleting or altering provisions.[54] It may also revoke an order, or revive one previously revoked.[55] These *discretionary* powers should be contrasted with the *mandatory* revocation of orders on proof of the payee's adultery.[56] Under this head the court will normally be concerned with a change of circumstances of either party, or simply to take account of the effects of inflation. Surprisingly, the Bedford College Survey suggests that most (*i.e.* about 75 per cent.) variation applications result in a *reduction* in maintenance.[57]

Time Limits

A complaint must be made within six months of the date when the cause of complaint arose.[58] However, desertion and wilful neglect to maintain are continuing offences, so that proceedings need not be started within six months of their commencement. In cruelty cases, there must have been an act of cruelty within six months, but provided this is so, evidence may be (and normally is) also given of conduct before the start of this period.[59] In adultery, the six months period begins when the adultery first became known to the complainant.[60]

It should also be noted that adultery and cruelty are not to be deemed to have been condoned by reason only of a continuation or resumption of cohabitation between the parties for *one* period not exceeding *three* months, or of anything done during such cohabitation, if it is proved that cohabitation was continued or resumed, as the case

---

52 The Act contains a general provision enabling the justices to refuse to adjudicate if they form the opinion that any matter in question between the parties would be more conveniently dealt with by the High Court: s. 5. See *R.* v. *Middlesex Justices, ex p. Bond* [1933] P. 158; *Kaye* v. *Kaye* [1965] P. 100. The court may make an *interim order* particularly if it suspects that the husband has filed a divorce petition simply to block the magistrates' hearing: see *Lanitis* v. *Lanitis* [1970] 1 W.L.R. 503.
53 s. 7 (3) Matrimonial Proceedings (Magistrates' Courts) Act 1960; s. 33, Matrimonial Proceedings and Property Act 1970.
54 Magistrates' Courts Act 1952, s. 53; Matrimonial Proceedings (Magistrates' Courts) Act 1960, s. 8.
55 *Ibid.* See generally *Rayden*, 11th ed., p. 1180.
56 s. 8 (2), *supra*, p. 213.
57 pp. 83–87.
58 Magistrates' Courts Act 1952, s. 104.
59 *Donkin* v. *Donkin* [1933] P. 17; *Bond* v. *Bond* [1967] P. 39.
60 Matrimonial Proceedings (Magistrates' Courts) Act 1960, s. 12 (1).

may be, with a view to effecting a reconciliation.[61] This is still the law in Magistrates' Courts, notwithstanding the fact that the analogous provision in divorce law is now considerably more flexible.[62]

Registration of Orders

An order obtained in the Superior Courts can be enforced in the Magistrates' Court (and vice versa).[63] This is because the methods of enforcement differ. In most cases there are advantages in enforcing an order in the Magistrates' Court. If, however, the husband has property or means, the methods of securing that they are applied in fulfilment of the wife's maintenance order may be better in the High Court. In practice the vast majority of applications are for the registration in the Magistrates' Court of a High Court order.

Administrative Machinery

The most important factor in the collection of maintenance obligations in Magistrates' Courts is the power to order periodic payments to be made to the justice's clerk, rather than direct to the wife: this power *must* be exercised unless, upon express representations by the applicant, the court is satisfied that it is undesirable so to do. There are a number of advantages to this:

(i) The Collecting Officer keeps proper accounts. Proof of arrears is therefore simplified. If it were not for this it would be easy for a husband to claim that he had made payments direct to the wife; investigation of such claims would cause considerable delay.

(ii) The parties are kept at arm's length, but the clerk's office is in touch with both.

(iii) All matters relating to the making, variation, and collection of orders, as well as decisions on arrears, are centralised in a single building, under the supervision of responsible officials. This centralisation of the enforcement process in the official person of the clerk is reinforced by the rule that the clerk is required, if requested in writing and unless it appears to him unreasonable so to do, to proceed *in his own name* for enforcement of arrears.[64]

In practice, formal enforcement procedures are perhaps often less important than their supplementation by

"a good deal of informal threat, exhortation and encouragement from the clerk's office, much of the routine business of which involves correspondence with maintenance defaulters threatening enforcement proceedings if orders are not paid regularly or arrears reduced." [65]

---

61 Matrimonial Causes Act 1965, s. 42 (2). It has been held that resumption of cohabitation in consequence of a reconciliation is not the same as resumption with a view to reconciliation: see *Brown* v. *Brown* [1964] 2 All E.R. 828; *Herridge* v. *Herridge* [1966] 1 All E.R. 93, and generally Irvine (1966) 82 L.Q.R. 525; Hall [1965] C.L.J. 51; Michaels (1965) 28 M.L.R. 101; Griew [1972A] C.L.J. 294; *Mortlock*, pp. 45–46.
62 *Supra*, p. 123.
63 Maintenance Orders Act 1968.   64 Magistrates' Courts Act 1952.
65 Graham Hall Report, para. 56.

Defects of the Law

There are two main problems facing the reformer. The first is whether the procedural complexity of so many interlocking jurisdictions should be retained, and if not, what should replace it. The other is whether, assuming that the present system is retained, the law should still be based on the matrimonial offence. In support of this principle, it is argued [66] that if " guilt " ceased to be the test the issues would not be clear enough for a lay tribunal to assess. Even if this justified the retention of the matrimonial offence as the *cause of action* it does not follow that there should be rigid bars if the wife herself committed an offence. But it is submitted that the argument is in any case fundamentally unsound:

(i) It assumes that laymen (even guided by their clerk) are more likely to comprehend the refinements of the law of desertion or condonation than the simple test of need (even if in determining this they are given a discretion to take culpability into account).

(ii) It assumes that the technicalities of matrimonial offences such as desertion necessarily give a reliable indication of guilt. This is not so. For example, because of the housing shortage, an offer of accommodation elsewhere may tempt a wife to leave, even although technically without just cause, thus putting herself in desertion. Again, much may depend on the form of words which is used: a mentally ill spouse who says: " I am *never* coming back," will be held to be in desertion, and thus disentitled to maintenance.[67] One who had been educated in the law could certainly phrase his refusals to cohabit in such a way that he would, whilst conveying exactly the same message, not have put himself in desertion: " I will not come back to you until I am cured." [68] Furthermore, under the present law, proof of one of the grounds entitles the complainant to an order, even though she may be wholly to blame for the breakdown of the marriage. It is the practice of courts to take the complainant's own conduct into account when fixing the amount of maintenance, but (as the Graham Hall Committee put it [69])

> " there is no way of assessing the weight attached to this factor by different courts in different circumstances. Nor have we been able to discover whether particularly reprehensible conduct on the part of a defendant ever leads the court to fix a sum of maintenance larger than the complainant's needs would otherwise have required."

(iii) The bar of adultery operates unfairly: a woman who has substantially fulfilled all her matrimonial obligations and yet been deserted by a cruel husband loses all right to maintenance from him under *this*

---

[66] P.W.P. No. 9, para. 9; *cf.* Milner: " The Place of ' Fault ' in Economic Litigation between Husband and Wife " (1959) 109 L.J. 215.
[67] See *e.g. Nutley* v. *Nutley* [1970] 1 W.L.R. 217; *Fraser* v. *Fraser* [1969] 1 W.L.R. 1797.
[68] *Tickle* v. *Tickle* [1968] 1 W.L.R. 937; *Lilley* v. *Lilley* [1960] P. 158.
[69] Para. 94.

code if she commits a single act of adultery. The wife's right to maintenance in Superior Court ancillary proceedings would not be affected.

WILFUL NEGLECT TO MAINTAIN

Since 1886 it has been possible for a wife to obtain a financial order on no other ground than that the husband has wilfully neglected to maintain her.[70] The interpretation of the statutory provisions has been strongly influenced by the view that they are simply a statutory method of enforcing the husband's duty to maintain his wife at common law, of which an explanation is therefore necessary.

The Common Law Right to Maintenance

It is necessary to distinguish the position while the parties continue to live together from that after a separation. A husband was obliged to maintain his wife [71] to the extent of providing her with necessaries,[72] but so long as they lived together, it was entirely for him [73] to fix the standard of living. As recently as 1953 an American court refused to interfere where a husband (aged eighty) had not given the wife any money for her own use for thirty-three years, and had not even taken her to the cinema for twelve years. The matrimonial home was a run-down shack with no bathroom. The sole touch of luxury was provided by the husband's two cars, although the more modern of these was manufactured in 1929. The reason for this frugal way of life was not poverty since the husband had assets worth some $200,000. It was held that—

> " The living standards of a family are a matter of concern to the household and not for the courts to determine, even though the husband's attitude towards the wife, according to his wealth and circumstances, leaves little to be said in his behalf. As long as the home is maintained and the parties are living as husband and wife it may be said that the husband is legally supporting his wife, and the purpose of the marriage obligation is being carried out." [74]

This rule was originally justified by the undesirability of having domestic differences unravelled before a jury, perhaps consisting largely of merchants. Hence the Common Law right to maintenance is " not a right to an allowance but to be supported by being given bed and board." [75]

---

70 Or dependent children: see *infra*, p. 258. The Superior Courts have only had power to make orders on this ground since 1949: Law Reform (Miscellaneous Provisions) Act 1949, s. 5. The powers are now contained in Matrimonial Proceedings (Magistrates' Courts) Act 1960, s. 1 (1) (*h*) and M.C.A. 1973, s. 27.

71 *Manby* v. *Scott* (1660), most conveniently to be read in *Smith's Leading Cases* (13th ed.), p. 418.

72 *Blackstone's Commentaries on the Laws of England* (4th ed.), p. 442.

73 At least in the absence of totally unreasonable behaviour on his part: *Gollins* v. *Gollins* [1964] A.C. 644 (neglect may amount to cruelty).

74 *McGuire* v. *McGuire* (1953) 59 N.W. 2d 336 (Nebraska Supreme Court) at p. 342; see also *Commonwealth* v. *George* (1948) 56 A. 2d 228.

75 *Per* Hodson L.J., *Lilley* v. *Lilley* [1960] P. 169.

If the husband deserted the wife, or if his misconduct [76] drove her away from the matrimonial home, the rule was modified to the extent that he was no longer sole judge of what was fit. He had to provide reasonable expenses for " necessaries " " according to her husband's degree." [77] Hence articles of food and dress which would be luxuries for a workman's wife might be " necessaries " for a duchess.[78]

The wife did not even have these limited rights if she were separated for some reason other than his misconduct. If she committed adultery,[79] for instance, she forfeited all rights to maintenance, whatever the extenuating circumstances.[80]

The methods of *enforcing* the right were limited in the extreme. Disputes between husband and wife were exclusively within the jurisdiction of the ecclesiastical court [81]; the Common Law courts never ordered a husband to maintain his wife,[82] but gave her an *indirect* remedy: so long as she was entitled to be maintained, the wife could bind her husband by her contract for the supply of " necessaries " such as food, clothing, housing, and legal services. The agency was *irrevocable*: it did not matter that the husband forbade his wife to incur the liabilities, or tradesmen to supply the goods.[83] A newspaper advertisement of the type " I John Smith hereby give notice that I will not be liable for debts incurred by my wife Mary Smith " was ineffective to avoid liability, although in practice it may have tempered the enthusiasm of shopkeepers

---

[76] As distinct from a reasonable exercise of his marital right: see *Jackson* v. *Jackson* [1932] All E.R. Rep. 553 where the husband's insistence on occupying a house next door to his mother's, and taking the house-keeping out of the wife's hands, did not justify her leaving him.

[77] *Per* Blackburn J., *Bazeley* v. *Forder* (1868) L.R. 3 Q.B. 559, 562.

[78] *Phillipson* v. *Hayter* (1870) L.R. 6 C.P. 38.

[79] Unless he has condoned it or connived at it: *Wilson* v. *Glossop* (1888) 20 Q.B.D. 354; *Harris* v. *Morris* (1801) 4 Esp. 41.

[80] For instance, the fact that the husband had treated her with great cruelty, driving her from the matrimonial home, and had himself frequently committed adultery: *Govier* v. *Hancock* (1796) 6 Term. 603; see also *Stimpson* v. *Wood* (1888) 57 L.J.Q.B. 484. As to the position if the separation is consensual see *infra*, p. 220.

[81] *Manby* v. *Scott, Smith's Leading Cases*, 13th ed., 481.

[82] The wife's remedy for desertion was a decree of Restitution of Conjugal Rights from the ecclesiastical court. If the husband disobeyed, he would be excommunicated (or after the Ecclesiastical Courts Act 1813, imprisoned). If he were guilty of other matrimonial offences the wife could seek a divorce *a mensa et thoro* (*i.e.* judicial separation) on making which the ecclesiastical court could order payment of alimony.

[83] Although referred to as an " agency " this is part of matrimonial law, rather than agency. Distinguish agency arising by the application of normal contractual principles: (i) the wife, *if cohabiting with her husband*, was *presumed* to have his authority to pledge his credit for necessary goods and services within the domestic department normally in her management. This presumption could be rebutted if, *e.g.* the husband had prohibited her from pledging his credit; (ii) the husband might be estopped from denying that his wife had authority to pledge his credit to a particular tradesman for goods and services (not only necessaries). This would arise if, by his conduct (*e.g.* by paying without objection for similar goods ordered by her in the past) he had held her out as authorised to incur liabilities on his behalf. In order to terminate this liability the husband must inform the individual tradesmen that the wife no longer possesses his authority, *e.g.* by a circular letter, or by press advertisement if it can be proved that the particular shopkeeper saw the advertisement. For full accounts of agency principles, see *Bowstead on Agency* (13th ed.), p. 93; *Sutton and Shannon on Contract*, (7th ed., 1970), p. 575.

in advancing credit. The agency was terminated by anything which terminated the Common Law duty to maintain [84]: a shopkeeper could only rely on it if he were confident that the wife had not committed adultery, and was not in desertion.

The agency of necessity was abolished [85] by the Matrimonial Proceedings and Property Act 1970,[86] because it was an anachronism: the courts now have adequate powers to enforce the duty to maintain directly, by proceedings (either in the Superior Courts or Magistrates' Court) alleging wilful neglect to maintain. But although the *procedure* has been improved, the substance of the law still reflects the Common Law duty.

Wilful Neglect—the Basis of Liability

The expression " has wilfully neglected to provide reasonable maintenance " is the basis of liability in both High Court and Magistrates' Court. It has been the subject of considerable judicial exegesis [87]:

There must be neglect

If a husband has complied fully with an existing court order he can be guilty of neglect only if he knows that there has been a change in the wife's financial circumstances.[88] Further, the offence is neglect to provide *reasonable* [89] *maintenance*: this has to be considered by reference to the husband's Common Law liability to maintain, and (it has been said [90]) " has to be interpreted against the background of the standard of life which he previously has maintained." But the wife is entitled to benefit from an increase in the husband's means and standard of life after the separation.[91] This reflects the position at Common Law: prior to separation the standard of living is entirely a matter for the husband; after separation it is a question of what is reasonable in all the circumstances.[92]

The neglect must be wilful

This means that the husband knows what he is doing, and intends to do what he is doing; it does not connote any malice or wickedness.[93] Hence:

---

84 Hence an isolated act of adultery was sufficient, even if unknown to the creditor and husband: *Wright (H. S.) and Webb* v. *Annandale* [1930] 2 K.B. 8.

85 For reasons set out in detail in P.W.P. No. 9, para. 52.

86 s. 41. The Act also gave the court power to make interim maintenance awards and to order lump sum payments in respect of maintenance which the other spouse should have provided in the past; see p. 188, *supra*.

87 See L. Neville Brown (1960) 23 M.L.R. 1.

88 *Smith* v. *Smith* (1962) 106 S.J. 111, applied in *Baynham* v. *Baynham* [1968] 1 W.L.R. 890.

89 Reasonableness is assessed at the date of the application: *Tulip* v. *Tulip* [1951] P. 378.

90 *Per* Hodson J., *Scott* v. *Scott* [1951] P. 245, 248; and see *Ridley* v. *Ridley* [1953] P. 150.

91 *LeRoy-Lewis* v. *LeRoy-Lewis* [1955] P. 1; *Sansom* v. *Sansom* [1966] P. 52.

92 *Supra*, p. 217. See also *Bradley* v. *Bradley* [1956] P. 326.

93 *Brannan* v. *Brannan* [1973] 2 W.L.R. 7, 15.

(a) the husband must be shown to have sufficient means, *i.e.* either a sufficient income,[94] or a sufficient capacity to earn money.[95]

(b) he must know that the wife is in need,[96] at least if the spouses had parted on terms which did not impose an immediate obligation on the husband to pay maintenance.[97]

(c) there must be a subsisting Common Law obligation to support the wife. Hence an order will not be made against a husband if:

(i) the wife has committed adultery.[98] Reasonable belief that she has done so also justifies refusal to maintain,[99] but if the belief is shown to be unfounded the liability revives.[1] In the case of proceedings before magistrates there is also a *statutory* bar against the making of an order if the wife has committed adultery, unless the husband has condoned, connived at, or by wilful neglect or misconduct conduced to it.[2]

(ii) the wife has been guilty of cruelty, or other conduct justifying the husband in leaving her.[3]

(iii) the wife is in desertion.[4] In this case, however, the obligation is suspended [5] and will revive if desertion is terminated (*e.g.* by the wife making a bona fide offer to return [6]).

If the parties are separated in circumstances not amounting to desertion, the husband is not *necessarily* obliged to maintain the wife: a man is under no liability to maintain his wife in a separate establishment. If she remains and insists on remaining in a separate establishment without good cause and without his consent, she forfeits her right to maintenance, even though she has no intention to remain permanently

---

94 Taking into account his liabilities: *Williams* v. *Williams* [1965] P. 125.

95 *Earnshaw* v. *Earnshaw* [1896] P. 160.

96 *Stringer* v. *Stringer* [1952] P. 171; *Pinnick* v. *Pinnick* [1957] 1 All E.R. 873; *Jones* v. *Jones* [1959] P. 38.

97 *E.g.* if there were a consensual separation, with no term express or implied that the husband should maintain the wife: *Lilley* v. *Lilley* [1960] P. 158; *Northrop* v. *Northrop* [1968] P. 74.

98 *Jones* v. *Newtown and Llanidloes Guardians* [1920] 3 K.B. 381. *Weatherley* v. *Weatherley* (1929) 94 J.P. 38; *Roast* v. *Roast* [1938] P. 8; *West* v. *West* [1954] P. 444; *National Assistance Board* v. *Parkes* [1955] 2 Q.B. 506. It is true that in the unsatisfactory decision of *Spence* v. *Spence* [1965] P. 140 Lloyd-Jones J. treated the " difficult and important " point as open to question, but this is inconsistent with the other authorities cited above.

99 *Chilton* v. *Chilton* [1952] P. 196; *West* v. *West* [1954] P. 444; *Cooke* v. *Cooke* [1961] P. 16.

1 But the husband will be under no obligation in respect of the period when the belief *was* reasonable: *West* v. *West* [1954] P. 444.

2 Matrimonial Proceedings (Magistrates' Courts) Act 1960, s. 2 (3); *supra*, p. 102. It has been suggested that, in the High Court, even adultery which has been condoned, connived at, or conduced to, may be a bar, but this seems difficult to accept as a general position either on principle or authority: P.W.P. 9, para. 30. (Conduct conducing may, however, be a purely *statutory* concept: *ibid.*)

3 *Young* v. *Young* [1964] P. 152; *Ratcliff* v. *Ratcliff* [1964] 1 W.L.R. 1098.

4 *Lilley* v. *Lilley* [1960] P. 158. So also if the wife is in constructive desertion (*i.e.* has by her conduct driven the husband away, as to which see *supra*, p. 198): *Winnan* v. *Winnan* [1949] P. 74.

5 *Jones* v. *Newtown and Llanidloes Guardians* [1920] 3 K.B. 381.

6 *Price* v. *Price* [1951] P. 413; *Young* v. *Young* [1964] P. 152; generally p. 101, *supra*.

apart (so that she is not guilty of desertion).[7] If the parties are separated *by agreement* the husband is only liable if it is a term of the agreement, express or implied, that she should receive maintenance.[8] If he does not maintain her, the wife's duty is to return to him, and she cannot complain that he is wilfully neglecting to maintain her.[9] But the fact that the husband has a good defence to a charge of desertion does not necessarily exculpate him from liability to support his wife: the matrimonial misconduct inherent in the phrase " wilful neglect " may be no more than the failure to maintain.[10] A husband whose delusions furnished him with a defence to a charge of desertion was still guilty of wilful neglect.[11]

If the separation agreement provides for the payment of maintenance, payment of the stipulated sums is very strong (but not conclusive) evidence against neglect.[12] In such cases the wife may now be better advised to seek a variation of the order.[13]

If separation is justified *by force of circumstances or necessity* (*e.g.* if the husband is away on military or naval service, or because of the illness of one party [14]) the husband remains under an obligation to support the wife.

Orders that can be made

The Superior Courts [14a]

The Matrimonial Proceedings and Property Act 1970 [15] removed many limitations and procedural defects [16] in the High Court procedure. The court can now:

(i) Order periodical payments, unlimited in amount,[17] secured or unsecured.[18] If secured, they may continue during the applicant's life.[19]

(ii) Order a lump sum payment.[20] This may be payable by instalments; in which case it may be secured.[21] The Act specifically provides that the order may be made to enable the wife to discharge liabilities or expenses reasonably incurred in maintaining her (or the children) before the making of the application.[22] This power may be used to overcome

---

7 *Price* v. *Price* [1951] P. 413; *Pinnick* v. *Pinnick* [1957] 1 All E.R. 873; *Lindwall* v. *Lindwall* [1967] 1 All E.R. 470.
8 *Baker* v. *Baker* (1949) 66 T.L.R. 81; *Lilley* v. *Lilley* [1960] P. 158; *Young* v. *Young* [1964] P. 152; *Northrop* v. *Northrop* [1968] P. 74.
9 *Northrop* v. *Northrop*, per Diplock L.J. at p. 116 (" I am constrained by the authorities . . . so to hold "). If the husband unjustifiably refuses to take the wife back he is then guilty of desertion.
10 *Brannan* v. *Brannan* [1973] 2 W.L.R. 7, 14.
11 *Brannan* v. *Brannan* (*supra*).
12 *Morton* v. *Morton* [1954] 2 All E.R. 248; *Tulip* v. *Tulip* [1951] P. 378.
13 *Supra*, p. 207.
14 *Lindwall* v. *Lindwall* [1967] 1 All E.R. 470; *Lilley* v. *Lilley* [1960] P. 158; *Tulip* v. *Tulip* [1951] P. 378.
14a High Court and County Court. " High Court " is used in the text.
15 s. 6 (and see now s. 27, M.C.A. 1973).
16 See Law Commission 25, paras. 18–22.
17 s. 27 (6) (*a*) M.C.A. 1973.
18 s. 27 (6) (*b*).
19 s. 27 (6) (*b*); s. 28 (1) (*b*).
20 s. 27 (6) (*c*).
21 s. 27 (7) (*b*), *supra*, p. 186.
22 s. 27 (7) (*a*). As to the liability to maintain *children*, see *infra*, p. 274.

any possible hardship resulting from the abolition of the wife's agency of necessity.[23]

There is *no* power to make any other capital provision order [24] (*e.g.* to transfer a house or shares [25]).

(iii) Make interim awards prior to the determination of liability,[26] if it appears that the applicant (or a child) is in immediate need of financial assistance.[27]

Magistrates' Courts

The courts' principal [28] remedy is the award of weekly periodical payments of any amount.[29] These cannot be secured, nor is there power to award a lump sum.[30]

Orders in favour of a husband

Both the High Court and Magistrates' Courts now [31] have power to make an order against the wife on the grounds that she has wilfully neglected to provide reasonable maintenance for her husband. But orders can only be made if

" by reason of the impairment of the applicant's earning capacity through age, illness or disability of mind or body, and having regard to any resources of the applicant and the respondent respectively which are, or should properly be made, available for the purpose, it is reasonable in all the circumstances to expect the wife so to provide or contribute." [32]

Duration of Orders

Effect of wife's subsequent [33] adultery

(a) *Magistrates' Courts*

There is a *statutory obligation* to discharge the order if it is subsequently proved that the wife has, during the subsistence of the marriage,

---

[23] *Supra*, p. 219. P.W.P. No. 9, para. 48.
[24] *Cf.* ancillary orders in divorce, judicial separation and nullity, *supra*, p. 188.
[25] This is because an order on the grounds of wilful neglect does not necessarily indicate that the marriage has broken down; a property adjustment would thus be inappropriate. But this reasoning is unconvincing. A decree of judicial separation does not (in theory) pre-suppose that the marriage has broken down (see s. 17 (2)), yet the full range of powers is there available. Further, the distinction between ordering a lump sum payment of £10,000 and the transfer of a house worth £10,000 seems slender (as is the distinction between ordering a lump sum of £50 to reimburse a wife for hire-purchase instalments she has paid, and ordering a transfer to her of a 3-piece suite of the same value).
[26] s. 27 (5).
[27] This is not a requirement for maintenance pending suit in other cases; *supra*, p. 185.
[28] But once the complaint is made out, any order permitted by the Act can be made: *Northrop* v. *Northrop* (*supra*).
[29] Maintenance Orders Act 1968.
[30] *Cf. supra*, p. 188.
[31] The power was introduced in Magistrates' Courts in 1960 (Matrimonial Proceedings (Magistrates' Courts) Act 1960, s. 1 (1) (i)) and in the High Court in 1970 (M.P.P.A. s. 6 (1) (*b*) (i), now s. 27 (1) (*b*) (i), M.C.A. 1973).
[32] *Cf.* the unrestricted power to make ancillary orders in favour of a husband: *supra*, p. 185. For an explanation of the inconsistency, see Law Commission 25, para. 65.
[33] As to the effect of adultery on *making* an order see p. 220, *supra*.

committed adultery, unless the husband has condoned, connived at, or by wilful neglect or conduct conduced to the adultery.[34]

(b) High Court

It has been held [35] that there is no question of importing the Common Law doctrine of discharge by adultery into the statutory provisions for variation and discharge. The " highly anomalous result " [36] is that a wife will not obtain an order in the High Court if she has or is reasonably thought to have committed adultery [37] but if " she refrains from adultery until she has obtained an order . . . she retains her order unless and until the court in its discretion varies or discharges it; she may, apparently, get it increased notwithstanding her adultery." [38]

Effect of cohabitation, remarriage, etc.

(a) Magistrates' Courts

Although a wife can get an order even if she is still cohabiting [39] with her husband, it is *unenforceable* until they cease to cohabit, and no liability accrues under it while the parties are cohabiting. If cohabitation *continues* for three months after an order has been made, it ceases to have effect. If the parties, having once separated *resume* cohabitation, the order ceases.[40] This results from a conflict between the principle that a husband should not be obliged to pay an allowance to his wife [41] and the need to secure for the wife who would otherwise be destitute sufficient money to enable her to flee from her husband's tyranny.[42] It may be questioned whether this is still valid given the availability of help from the Supplementary Benefits Commission.[43]

(b) High Court

There are no provisions as to the effect of a resumption of cohabitation. Application would have to be made to vary or discharge the order.[44]

Divorce does not automatically affect orders made under either jurisdiction. In practice it will often be desirable to reconsider the order.

Remarriage terminates any order, whether in the High Court or Magistrates' Court.[45]

---

[34] s. 8 (2) Matrimonial Proceedings (Magistrates' Courts) Act 1960. Orders for children are not necessarily affected: s. 8 (3), and *infra*, p. 258.
[35] *Spence* v. *Spence* [1965] P. 140.
[36] P.W.P. No. 9, para. 30.
[37] *Supra*, p. 220.
[38] P.W.P. No. 9, para. 40.
[39] As distinct from *residing*: *Evans* v. *Evans* [1948] 1 K.B. 175; *Wheatley* v. *Wheatley* [1950] K.B. 39; *Hopes* v. *Hopes* [1949] P. 227; *Naylor* v. *Naylor* [1962] P. 253.
[40] However short the resumption: s. 7, Matrimonial Proceedings (Magistrates' Courts) Act 1960.
[41] *Supra*, p. 217.
[42] Morton Commission, para. 1014.
[43] *Infra*, p. 224. The Morton Commission recommended that orders be fully enforceable during cohabitation: 1042–1049.
[44] *Caras* v. *Caras* [1955] 1 W.L.R. 254.
[45] s. 28, s. 52 (3), M.C.A. 1973; s. 30 Matrimonial Proceedings and Property Act 1970.

Defects of the Law

(1) It is unsatisfactory that the law differs between Magistrates' Courts and the Superior Courts on such topics as the effect of subsequent adultery and resumption of cohabitation.

(2) The influence of the old Common Law rules is anomalous. In particular it no longer seems appropriate that commission of a matrimonial offence should be a bar.

The law on support obligations during a consensual separation [46] is also unsatisfactory: the reliance on implied terms is unjust, since (i) it is not clear when such a term will be implied; (ii) an astute husband may too easily show that any such term has been excluded.[47] Liability should depend simply on whether the one had failed to make a proper contribution in all the circumstances towards the other's reasonable maintenance. It seems preferable to lay down general guidelines [48] for the exercise of the court's discretion (as in the case of ancillary relief) than to depend on the relics of the Common Law.

THE EFFECT OF THE SOCIAL SECURITY SYSTEM [49]

The Supplementary Benefits Scheme [50]

Since 1948 [51] every person in Great Britain of or over the age of sixteen [52] whose resources are insufficient to meet his requirements has been entitled to receive a " supplementary allowance " [53] from the National Assistance Board (now the Supplementary Benefits Commission). The first source of finance to the deserted wife is thus usually the Supplementary Benefits Commission: 87 per cent. of wife respondents who completed a questionnaire publicised in the *News of the World* had applied for assistance at some time since separation [54]; since 1963, an average of more than 100,000 wives each year have been in receipt of assistance.[55] The gross cost [56] of providing benefit to separated wives and divorced women with legitimate children in 1965 was in excess of £32,000,000.[57] But although benefit is a right, it is a right of a very special kind; entitlement to benefit

---

[46] See L. N. Brown (1968) 31 M.L.R. 121.

[47] *Northrop* v. *Northrop* [1968] P. 74.

[48] *Cf.* s. 25, M.C.A. 1973.

[49] See generally Aikin, 8 J.S.P.T.L. 167.

[50] T. Lynes, *The Penguin Guide to Supplementary Benefit* (1972) is an excellent general account. The Supplementary Benefits Commission publishes a valuable *Supplementary Benefits Handbook*, while the legislation and regulations are collected in an H.M.S.O. publication: E. O. F. Stocker and P. G. Nilsson (ed.): *The Law Relating to Supplementary Benefits and Family Income Supplements.*

[51] National Assistance Act 1948. For the influence of the old poor law see L. N. Brown (1955) 18 M.L.R. 113.

[52] With certain exceptions: *infra*, p. 225.

[53] Ministry of Social Security Act 1966, s. 4 (1). This Act repealed and replaced the National Assistance Act 1948. Persons over retirement age receive a " Supplementary Pension."

[54] Bedford College Survey, p. 154.

[55] *Ibid.*, pp. 158–161, Table 106; App. D, Graham Hall Report; see the annual Reports of the Supplementary Benefits Commission (now Department of Health and Social Security).

[56] Certain amounts (less than £3m.) were recovered from husbands. See *infra*, p. 226.

[57] Graham Hall Report, App. D, Table 17 (a), col. 7.

is determined [58] by the Commission which has a very wide discretion,[59] either to meet exceptional needs [60] or exceptional circumstances [61] or on the other hand to withhold benefit (e.g. if it is thought that the applicant is work-shy [62]). Although the discretionary powers may be more valuable for an individual claimant than a " precisely prescribed right because they give the scheme a flexibility of response to varying situations of human need," [63] their existence may put an applicant in a position of dependence on apparently all-powerful officials of the Commission which can easily cause resentment.

Certain general points should be noted:

(i) Benefit is only available to those in need: a person's requirements and resources are calculated on a basis laid down in the Act.[64] If his requirements exceed his resources, benefit will normally be payable. The modest scale [65] of " requirements " is laid down annually by Parliament, and an allowance may also be paid in respect of rent.

(ii) The resources and requirements of a married couple living together are aggregated.[66] A wife living with her husband cannot claim benefit in her own right.[67] If a couple are " cohabiting as man and wife " [68] the same principle is applied, unless there are " exceptional circumstances." The application of this rule has caused much controversy.[69] It may make a deserted wife fearful that if she has men visitors (or men lodgers) she will be deprived of her supplementary allowance.[70]

(iii) A person who is in full-time work cannot normally receive benefit. A separated wife who is in full-time, but low-paid, work may be entitled to Family Income Supplement if she has at least one dependent child.[71] If she only works part-time (less than thirty hours a week [72]) she will retain her right to Supplementary Benefit.[73] She has a choice therefore between part-time earnings plus Supplementary Benefit, or full-time earnings plus Family Income Supplement.[74]

[58] Subject to a right of appeal to a local Supplementary Benefit Appeal Tribunal: see s. 18, Ministry of Social Security Act 1966.
[59] For different views on this see The Penguin Guide at pp. 23–26, R. M. Titmuss (1971) Political Quarterly 113–132, Supplementary Benefits Handbook (1971), p. 1.
[60] E.g. special diets.   [61] E.g. to visit sick relatives.
[62] See generally The Penguin Guide, Chap. 5 (" Below the Minimum ").
[63] Supplementary Benefits Handbook, p. 1.
[64] Sched. II, as amended.
[65] Currently £7·15 weekly for a single householder, £2·05 for a child less than 5.
[66] Sched. II, para. 3.
[67] Cf. the Common Law rules: the wife living with her husband has no right to an " allowance "; after separation an objective assessment is made.
[68] Sched. II, para. 3 (1).
[69] See, for an explanation of the Commission's practice, " Cohabitation: the administration of the relevant provisions of the Ministry of Social Security Act 1966 (1971) "; see also the Report of the Committee on Abuse of Social Security Benefits, Cmnd. 5228.
[70] See Marsden, passim.
[71] Family Income Supplements Act 1970.
[72] Supplementary Benefits Handbook, para. 2.
[73] A woman with a dependent child under 16 living with her is not required to register for work as a condition of receiving benefit—see Handbook, paras. 7–8. But officials apparently sometimes suggest that they " ought " to do so: The Penguin Guide, p. 29.
[74] The Penguin Guide, pp. 186–187.

The Commission will meet a claim by a wife whose husband has left her unsupported, but may try to recover the cost of so doing from him, since the law imposes a *duty* on a man or woman to maintain his or her spouse and children (legitimate or illegitimate).[75] In practice, therefore, the Commission will try (having paid the wife) to contact the husband to find out why he is failing to maintain his dependants. If he offers to do so, his offer will be accepted if it is reasonable in relation to his circumstances. But often it is necessary to enforce the duty. This is done in two ways:

(i) The Commission may apply to a Magistrates' Court for an order directing him to reimburse the Commission.[76] This procedure is used only infrequently: there were 302 applications by the Board in 1971.[77] It is the policy of the Commission to persuade a woman to take proceedings herself, rather than for the Board to do so.[78] This is justified by the Commission on three grounds: (a) the possibility of reconciliation will receive proper consideration when she is brought into direct contact with the court officials; (b) the court order may be for a greater sum than the current rate of supplementary benefit; (c) such an order will not lapse if she becomes ineligible for benefit (*e.g.* by going out to work). It is also said that husbands would be even more reluctant to pay to the Board than to the wife,[79] while on occasion a moralistic attitude is displayed—getting her own order is " a step towards her independence." [80] Some women feel that the Supplementary Benefits Commission put pressure on them to take legal proceedings,[81] but this is always denied by the Board. In any case, the procedure is not, in economic terms, very effective: although some 41 per cent. of wives in receipt of assistance in 1965 had a court order against their husbands (and a further 11 per cent. had out-of-court arrangements with the husband), the net contributions received by the Board was only £2,065,000 towards expenditure of £27,444,000 (*i.e.* £7·50 for each £100), while the wives themselves received direct from the husband a further £2,754,000.[82] Of those husbands who were subject to a court order or voluntary arrangement, only 28 per cent. complied with its terms regularly; in 64 per cent. of the cases no payments at all were made. In approximately half the cases of complete default, the reason was that the husband could not be traced, or had insufficient means.[83]

---

75 Ministry of Social Security Act 1966, s. 22 (1). For the history of this duty and its enforcement, see Bedford College Survey, pp. 149–153; " National Assistance and the Liability to Maintain One's Family ": L. Neville Brown (1955) 18 M.L.R. 113; *National Assistance Board* v. *Wilkinson* [1952] 2 Q.B. 648. See also L. Neville Brown, " Separation Agreements and National Assistance " (1956) 19 M.L.R. 623.

76 Ministry of Social Security Act 1966, s. 23.

77 Department of Health and Social Security Annual Report 1971, Cmnd. 5019, para. 12.17.

78 *Supplementary Benefits Handbook* (1971), para. 150.

79 Payne Committee Report, para. 1301.

80 Marsden, p. 150.

81 Marsden, p. 152; Morris, *Prisoners and their Families*, p. 269.

82 Bedford College Survey, p. 159, Table 105.

83 *Ibid.*, p. 161, Table 106.

(ii) It is a criminal offence persistently to refuse or neglect to maintain oneself or any person whom one is obliged to maintain under the Act.[84] The power is infrequently used in cases of genuine separation.[85]

The truth is that many of the problems are not problems of enforcement but of economics; improvements in procedure will not put more money into the pockets of husbands or enable them to meet commitments beyond their capacity to pay.[86] It follows again that much of the burden will in fact be passed on to the state. It is therefore often suggested that the Social Security authorities should pay to the separated wife an adequate maintenance allowance (not pitched at the subsistence level of Supplementary Benefit, but at a " moderate but adequate " level [87]). It would then be for the Commission to recover what it could from the husband, but the responsibility could be taken away for the wife altogether.[88]

A problem of legal theory arises if the Board does decide to proceed on its own initiative. It used to be thought that the husband was not bound under the Act to support his wife unless he would be so at Common Law.[89] This is no longer a rigid rule. In deciding whether to make an order the court is directed to " have regard to all the circumstances." [90] Factors which would relieve the husband at common law (e.g. that the wife has committed adultery) are " highly relevant " to the decision whether to make an order in favour of the Board, but may not be conclusive.[91] There may thus be a rule of practice, but there is no rule of law: a husband may be obliged to maintain a wife for Supplementary Benefit purposes although the obligation could not be directly enforced by her.[92]

Underwriting support obligations

If the wife has an order against the husband, it is quite probable that it will not be complied with regularly.[93] A practice has therefore developed whereby, if a woman qualifies for supplementary benefit, and

---

[84] s. 30.
[85] In 1971 there were 614 prosecutions, but not all would be separation cases.
[86] Payne Committee Report, para. 1306.
[87] See this concept developed by M. Wynn, *Family Policy* (1970).
[88] Payne Committee Report, para. 1305; Graham Hall Committee Report, para. 219 and paras. 231–240; Bedford College Survey, pp. 162–163. The argument normally advanced against this is the cost. It is often forgotten that the state already contributes extensively through tax relief to the more affluent separated spouse. This should clearly be taken into account.
[89] *N.A.B.* v. *Wilkinson* [1952] 2 Q.B. 648; *N.A.B.* v. *Prisk* [1954] 1 All E.R. 400.
[90] s. 23 (2) Ministry of Social Security Act 1966.
[91] *N.A.B.* v. *Parkes* [1955] 2 Q.B. 506. The point seems to have been left open in *Brannan* v. *Brannan* [1973] 2 W.L.R. 7, 17.
[92] *Imam Din* v. *N.A.B.* [1967] 2 Q.B. 213.
[93] *Supra*, p. 226; Graham Hall Report, Table 42; Bedford College Survey, Chap. 6.

has a maintenace order within the scale rate, the Commission will, in
return for her authorising the court to pay over any receipts to the
Commission, give her an order book for the full Supplementary Benefit,[94]
which she can cash at the local post office.   The result is that the wife
" receives regularly her full entitlement regardless of whether the order
is paid regularly, intermittently, or never.   This reform has relieved many
women of the harassing anxiety of irregular payments and of the humiliating inconvenience of fruitless visits to the court collecting office." [95] But
if the wife's order is for a larger amount than her Supplementary Allowance the Commission is reluctant to adopt this procedure if it might
involve it in the work of repaying the wife.   In such cases the practice
will only be followed if it seems likely from experience that the husband
will not pay regularly.[96]

Other Social Security Benefits

Apart from Supplementary Benefit, Family Income Supplement and
Retirement Pensions,[97] which have already been referred to, there is a
substantial number of other benefits [98] which may be paid for the benefit
of a divided family—e.g. Family Allowances, which are payable in respect
of children (other than the eldest) who are under the upper limit of the
compulsory school age.[99] A full examination is outside the scope of this
work.

MAINTENANCE AGREEMENTS, ETC.

The law permits husband and wife to make enforceable private agreements about financial matters, and it was the policy of the Divorce
Reform Act 1969 to encourage such agreements.[1] A number of special
problems arise:

Legality of separation agreements

Agreements fall into two main classes: separation agreements and
maintenance agreements.   Many separation agreements also include
financial terms; not all maintenance agreements include an agreement
to separate since (i) this might prejudice the parties' right to allege
desertion,[2] (ii) the agreement may be made as a part of a divorce settlement when reference to separation would clearly be otiose.
    After some conflict, it was settled in the nineteenth century [3] that a

---

[94] i.e. as if no payment were received from the husband.
[95] Bedford College Survey, p. 157.   See also Report of the Ministry of Social Security
    for 1967 (Cmnd. 3639, 1968), para. 38.
[96] Handbook, para. 151, The Penguin Guide, pp. 150–151.
[97] See supra, p. 201.
[98] A convenient summary is in The Penguin Guide, pp. 14–16.
[99] Family Allowances Act 1965; see Eekelaar, pp. 133–135.
[1] Supra, p. 135.
[2] Supra, p. 97.
[3] Wilson v. Wilson (1848) 1 H.L.C. 538; (1854) 5 H.L.C. 40; Hunt v. Hunt (1862)
    4 De G.F. & J. 221.

separation agreement was not void as conflicting with public policy[4] *provided* the separation has actually occurred or is inevitable. But the law is still influenced by the old notions[5]:

(i) Agreements or dispositions which *tend to encourage the violation of the marriage tie* are void (*e.g.* a provision increasing a legacy to a husband in the event of a separation from his wife).[6]

(ii) Hence, an agreement between husband and wife, whereby they make arrangements in the event of a future separation, is altogether void. If, however, the husband and wife, while living apart, agree to *resume* cohabitation, enforceable financial arrangements in the event of a *future* separation may be made in the same agreement. This rule promotes, rather than hinders, reconciliation.

The sanctity of contract

Prima facie an agreement is binding and can only be varied by consent. The husband wants to buy off the wife once and for all; the wife wants to know that, come what may, she is entitled to certain provision. But over the years provision which seemed fair and reasonable in a period of stable prices can become hopelessly inadequate for the wife. The courts dealt with this in two ways:

(i) A covenant by the wife to accept stipulated payments in lieu of any other right to apply to the court for maintenance is ineffective on public policy grounds.[7] The wife's right to future maintenance is a matter of public concern which she cannot barter away.[8] Hence a wife who had expressly covenanted to accept certain financial provision and not to apply to the court was held entitled to seek further maintenance in divorce proceedings.[9]

(ii) Even if the husband makes the stipulated payments, the wife can allege wilful neglect to provide reasonable maintenance.[10] Payment of

---

4 *Cf.* the attitude of the ecclesiastical courts: *Mortimer* v. *Mortimer* (1820) 2 Hag.Con. 310.

5 See generally *Fender* v. *St. John-Mildmay* [1938] A.C. 1; and see *per* Lord Atkin, *Hyman* v. *Hyman* [1929] A.C. 601, 625; such agreements " still looked at askance and enforced grudgingly " but the true position is " Agreements for separation are formed, construed and dissolved and to be enforced on precisely the same principles as any respectable commercial agreement, of whose nature indeed they sometimes partake."

6 See *e.g. Re Johnson's Will Trusts* [1967] Ch. 387: annuity to testator's daughter to be increased if she were divorced or separated; evidence that testator concerned to protect his daughter against her husband. Held void. The condition might well influence the wife's mind if she were contemplating separation or divorce: see generally *Theobald*, Chap. 43 and para. 1568.

7 If the covenant by the wife was the sole consideration for the agreement to pay, the wife would not be able to enforce those provisions against the husband (unless they could be severed from the rest of the agreement: *Goodinson* v. *Goodinson* [1954] 2 Q.B. 118), since there would be no consideration for them: *Coombe* v. *Coombe* [1951] 2 K.B. 215; *Bennett* v. *Bennett* [1952] 1 K.B. 249.

8 *Cf. Re M.* [1968] P. 174 (wife not barred by prior agreement from claim under s. 26, M.C.A. 1965).

9 *Hyman* v. *Hyman* [1929] A.C. 601.

10 *Supra*, p. 221; *Morton* v. *Morton* [1942] 1 All E.R. 273; *Tulip* v. *Tulip* [1951] P. 378; *Dowell* v. *Dowell* [1952] 2 All E.R. 141; *Morton* v. *Morton* [1954] 2 All E.R. 248; *N.A.B.* v. *Parkes* [1955] 2 Q.B. 507; *Pinnick* v. *Pinnick* [1957] 1 All E.R. 837.

the agreed amounts is of strong evidential value; the courts will not lightly upset, or go behind, the terms of an agreement freely entered into.[11] Nevertheless if new circumstances have arisen since the agreement (*e.g.* illness or merely a change in the value of money) which the wife brought to the husband's attention then, provided that he is under a duty to maintain her,[12] a further order can be made.[13] The wife thus had the best of both worlds.   A husband might well ask:

> "Why should I enter into an agreement?   If I do, and I fall out of work, or if my means become less, I am bound by the terms of the agreement, but why should I, or any other husband, enter into an agreement if the other party is not going to be bound by it? "[14]

The Morton Commission recommended that the law should be rationalised[15]:

> (a) as a general rule maintenance agreements should be binding and enforceable on the parties;
>
> (b) *either* party should be able to apply to the court for an order varying the terms of the agreement if fresh circumstances have arisen.[16]

These proposals were implemented in 1957,[17] and the law was further amended by the Matrimonial Proceedings and Property Act 1970[18]:

(a) *Void provisions*

Any provision purporting to restrict the right to apply to the court for financial provision is void; but any other financial arrangements contained in the agreement are valid (unless they are void or unenforceable for any other reason).[19] The agreement need not be made for the purpose of the parties living separately[20]: hence, if a man and wife enter into a formal agreement regulating their financial affairs it is subjected to the provisions of the Act.[21]

---

11 *Morton* v. *Morton* [1954] 2 All E.R. 248, 254, *per* Singleton L.J.; but *cf. Gorman* v. *Gorman* [1964] 1 W.L.R. 1440, 1445, *per* Willmer L.J.

12 *Supra*, p. 220.

13 *Tulip* v. *Tulip*; *N.A.B.* v. *Parkes* (*supra*).   *Cf.* the position at Common Law where a wife's agreement to accept an allowance was a bar to her pledging the husband's credit: *Sandilands* v. *Carus* [1945] K.B. 270.

14 *Morton* v. *Morton* [1954] 2 All E.R. 248, 253, *per* Singleton L.J.

15 And uncertainty removed about the wife's right to sue if the deed contained a clause purporting to oust the jurisdiction of the court: see note 7, *supra*.

16 Paras. 727 *et seq.*

17 Maintenance Agreements Act 1957.

18 ss. 13–15 (now ss. 34–36, M.C.A. 1973), implementing Law Commission 25, paras. 94–96, which should be referred to for an explanation of the minor changes.

19 s. 34 (1), M.C.A. 1973.   The Act (s. 34 (2)) defines " maintenance agreement " so that it only applies to an agreement *in writing*: if the agreement is oral (see *e.g. Peters* v. *I.R.C.* [1941] 2 All E.R. 620) the Common Law rules still apply: the ouster of jurisdiction is ineffective; the wife can sue *unless* the sole consideration for the agreement was the agreement not to sue; n. 7, *supra*.

20 s. 34 (2).

21 *i.e* including the provisions for variation, *infra, cf. Ewart* v. *Ewart* [1959] P. 23.

(b) *Power to vary agreements*

The Act provides [22] that if a maintenance agreement [23] is in existence either party may apply to the court [24] for a variation order. The court's powers are sweeping [25] : it may—

" by order make such alterations in the agreement—

    (i) by varying or revoking any financial arrangements contained in it, or

    (ii) by inserting in it financial arrangements for the benefit of one of the parties to the agreement or of a child of the family

as may appear to that court to be just having regard to all the circumstances, . . . and the agreement shall have effect thereafter as if any alteration made by the order had been made by agreement between the parties and for valuable consideration."

The very broad definition of " financial arrangements " should be noted. This expression means [26]

" provisions governing the rights and liabilities towards one another when living separately of the parties to a marriage (including a marriage which has been dissolved or annulled) in respect of the making or securing of payments or the disposition or use of any property, including such rights and liabilities with respect to the maintenance or education of any child, whether or not a child of the family."

Apart from the normal case of a variation of periodical payments, this means that the court could vary agreements about the occupation of the matrimonial home (or furniture) [27]; more surprisingly, it would seem clear that the court [28] has power to *insert* a provision for a lump sum or other capital provision into an agreement, in sharp contrast to the *prohibition* on varying *court orders* for periodical payments in this way.[29] The fact that such powers exist does not, however, mean that they will be exercised.

As a condition precedent to the exercise of these powers, the court must be satisfied *either*:

" (a) that by reason of a change in the circumstances in the light of which any financial arrangements contained in the agreement were made or, as the case may be, financial arrangements were omitted from it (*including a change foreseen by the parties when making the agreement*), the agreement should be altered so as to make different, or, as the case may be, so as to contain, financial arrangements, *or*

    (b) that the agreement does not contain proper financial arrangements with respect to any child of the family. . . ." [30]

The italicised words were added in the 1970 Act to reverse decisions of

---

22 s. 35.
23 *i.e.* a written agreement which *either* (a) contains " financial arrangements " (as defined, see *infra*) *or* (b) is a separation agreement which does not itself contain financial arrangements and where no other written agreement does so.
24 A Magistrates' Court can only vary periodical maintenance payments: s. 35 (3).
25 s. 35 (2).
26 s. 34 (2).
27 s. 34 (2).
28 But not a Magistrates' Court: s. 35 (3).
29 s. 31 (5), M.C.A. 1973, *supra*, p. 207.   30 s. 35 (2).

the courts to the effect that only a change of circumstances " quite outside the realisation of expectations of the parties " [31] took place, with the result that a party who chose a lower but consistent income in preference to a higher speculative and problematical income would be unable to obtain a variation simply because he had made the wrong choice. The law has now been given an even greater power of intervention: in inflationary times one inevitably thinks of a wife who can apply for an agreed amount to be increased in the light of her husband's business success. But the provision could work the other way: under the old law a husband could not apply for a reduction of the amounts payable however drastic the change in his circumstances unless these were completely outside the range of the parties' expectations.

Even if there has been a change in circumstances the Act simply confers a *discretion* on the court, for it has to be satisfied that " by reason " of the change " the agreement *should be* altered." [32] Under the same wording in the previous legislation the Court of Appeal [33] held that it must follow from the change of circumstances that the agreement had become *unjust*. Hence, a voluntary reduction in earning capacity (by a husband who gave up work in insurance to take a teacher's training course) was not a ground on which a variation could be made. Harman L.J. asserted that " [t]he more we stick to the sanctity of a contract of this sort the safer we shall be," and it seems probable that the court will exercise its jurisdiction sparingly.

If the agreement is varied, the increase must, in accordance with the Act's general policy,[34] be for a period terminating not later than the payee's remarriage.[35] If the agreement provides for the continuation of payments after the death of either party, the surviving party (or the personal representatives of the deceased) may, subject to restrictions,[36] also apply for a variation.

The function of agreements

The advantage of a *separation agreement* in its traditional form [37] was that it provided maintenance for the wife without the scandal and publicity of divorce or other proceedings: the agreement would terminate desertion, and it would often contain a clause whereby the spouses agreed not to petition in respect of any other existing cause of complaint.[38] Now these advantages have gone. Either party can obtain a divorce without

---

[31] *K.* v. *K.* [1961] 2 All E.R. 266; *Ratcliffe* v. *Ratcliffe* [1962] 3 All E.R. 993.
[32] *Per* Holroyd Pearce L.J., *K.* v. *K.* (*supra*) at p. 269.
[33] *Ratcliffe* v. *Ratcliffe* (*supra*); and see *Gorman* v. *Gorman* [1964] 1 W.L.R. 1440.
[34] *Supra*, p. 188.
[35] s. 35 (4). Increased provision for children must also comply with the Act's general rules: *infra*, p. 269.
[36] s. 36.
[37] For precedents (with helpful explanatory comments) see *Encyclopaedia of Forms and Precedents* (4th ed.), Vol. 10, p. 905.
[38] The so-called " *Rose* v. *Rose* clause ": (1882) 7 P.D. 225; (1883) 8 P.D. 98; *L.* v. *L.* [1931] P. 63; *H.* v. *H.* [1938] 3 All E.R. 415; *Keeble* v. *Keeble* [1956] 1 W.L.R. 94.

proving anything apart from the separation, and the stigma of divorce has been much reduced.[39]

A separation agreement may still have certain advantages:

(a) It can record the facts as to the separation, and thus be used as evidence in subsequent divorce proceedings.[40]

(b) It may give the husband some limited financial protection:

    (i) It will usually prohibit the wife from pledging the husband's credit. The only case then in which he could be liable on contracts made by her would be if he were estopped from denying that she had his authority.[41]

    (ii) Compliance with its terms provides some evidence that the husband is not guilty of wilful neglect to maintain the wife.[42]

(c) It may help the wife since:

    (i) If the husband falls into arrears she can sue on the contract: there is no discretion (as there is with maintenance orders [43]) to remit arrears. Furthermore (again unlike maintenance order payments) the arrears could be the foundation of bankruptcy proceedings.[44]

    (ii) It may give her a certain amount of security since the agreement may contain terms (*e.g.* as to pensions or the use of specific assets [45]) which the court could not, or would not, order.

But as against this, there are strong reasons why a husband's advisers may hesitate to recommend a long-term separation agreement.[46] The wife can go back on any agreement not to take further proceedings, and if there is a sufficient change in circumstances the court has an unlimited discretion to vary the agreement. And if there is to be the expense and publicity of a divorce it might as well be dealt with as soon as possible.

Agreements as to financial provision in connection with *divorce proceedings* are, on the other hand, likely to become increasingly common. Such agreements can be varied under the provisions presently under

---

39 It must be regarded as an open question (perhaps one of construction of the relevant clause) as to whether a *Rose* v. *Rose* clause could operate to deprive a party of the right to sue for divorce under the Divorce Reform Act. But the essence of the clause was its forgiveness of matrimonial offences. Now that such are irrelevant, and it is the policy of the law to bury the empty legal shell of dead marriages, there seems little to be said on policy grounds for permitting an agreement, perhaps many years old, to prevent this being done.

40 It may also be useful to show that the parties are " separated " for tax purposes: *Peters* v. *I.R.C.* [1941] 2 All E.R. 620.

41 *Supra*, p. 218, n. 83.

42 *Hyman* v. *Hyman* [1929] A.C. 601, *per* Lord Atkin at p. 629.

43 See *Rayden*, p. 800.

44 Conversely no action will lie for sums payable after the bankruptcy: *Victor* v. *Victor* [1912] 1 K.B. 247. But it is the *threat* of bankruptcy (particularly against a trader) which is the most effective part of the process.

45 See *e.g. Ewart* v. *Ewart* [1959] P. 23.

46 In 1972 there were only 111 applications in the High Court and county court *inter vivos* to vary maintenance agreements: Civil Judicial Statistics, 1972, Cmnd. 5333, Table 10 (ii).

consideration,[47] but this is no hardship since a court *order* would be at least as readily variable.[48] Provision exists for the parties to refer such agreements to the court,[49] although they need not do so.[50]

The only way in which a once-for-all settlement, not subject to review, can be achieved is for the court to dismiss all claims by the wife for financial relief.[51] This is a power which will only be exercised after careful consideration.[52]

REFORM OF MATRIMONIAL PROPERTY LAW [53]

Although the courts now have wide powers to achieve an equitable distribution of assets acquired by the spouses' joint efforts, this does not satisfy the claims of many spokesmen for women's rights, because:

(i) The wife is given no fixed right, but only the chance that a (usually male) judicial discretion (or " whim ") will be exercised in her favour.

(ii) This defect is aggravated by the fact that the exercise of the discretion may still to some extent involve an assessment of the parties' conduct.[53a]

(iii) There is uncertainty as to the interest which each spouse has, or is to be given, in important family assets (such as the matrimonial home).[53b]

Similar objections apply to succession on death. The court has power to intervene if " reasonable provision " is not made for a spouse or divorced spouse; but this power is discretionary.

Demands were increasingly made [53c] for a system of *community of property* or some other fundamental reform, so as to ensure (a) that the wife has fixed rights; (b) that those rights guarantee her equality of

---

[47] Agreements made more than six months after the dissolution or annulment of the marriage were outside the scope of the comparable provisions in Matrimonial Causes Act 1965, ss. 23–25, but they are so no longer: s. 35 (1).

[48] *Supra*, p. 207.

[49] *Supra*, p. 135. A condition in an agreement making it " subject to the approval of the court " means that it will become binding and operative once the court has approved it. Neither party can resile from it unilaterally before the court has considered the matter: *Smallman* v. *Smallman* [1972] Fam. 25.

[50] *Supra*, p. 135.

[51] See *L.* v. *L.* [1962] P. 101, 118 (*per* Willmer L.J.); *Coleman* v. *Coleman* [1972] 3 All E.R. 886, 893.

[52] See *Jackson*, p. 217.

[53] See *Comparative Law of Matrimonial Property* (ed. A. Kiralfy) (1972) and P.W.P. No. 42, Part 5 (which is the most comprehensive treatment of the field of choice affecting property régimes, and is an indispensable starting point for any serious consideration of the issues involved).

[53a] But this is less likely to be so after the decision in *Wachtel* v. *Wachtel* (*supra*). But it remains the case that the courts' powers are discretionary, and that a husband may allege " gross and obvious " misconduct against his wife in an attempt to reduce the provision to be made.

[53b] Since *Wachtel* v. *Wachtel* (*supra*) the court is more likely to recognise non-financial contributions by the wife to the welfare of the home.

[53c] See the debates on the Matrimonial Property Bill (Hansard, January 24, 1969, Vol. 776, cols. 801–896).

treatment with her husband. We consider in turn, first community systems; then two alternatives which have been suggested: —

(1) Special Rules for the Matrimonial House; and

(2) Legal Rights of Inheritance.

(1) *Community System*

The essence of a community system is that, by virtue of the marriage, the spouses' property is at some stage subjected to joint ownership. Such systems take different forms,[53d] however, and the following policy questions must be answered before any sensible choice can be made:

1. Is the wife's right to depend on (a) the *status* of marriage, or (b) the extent of her *contributions* to the acquisition of property? If the former, it is immaterial how long or short a period the marriage has lasted.

Traditionally, in the exercise of discretionary jurisdiction, it has been the *status* of marriage which gives a wife a right to be kept in the position in which she would have been if the husband had discharged his marital obligation to maintain her on a scale appropriate to his station in life.[54]

2. What property is to be bound? In its crudest form, community of property means that all property owned by either spouse *at the time of the marriage* passes into the community, as does all property acquired during the currency of the marriage (whether by the spouses' efforts or by a gift to one or other of them). Such a system gives effect in its simplest form to the " status " concept of marriage. An alternative system is that of *Community of Acquisition*, whereby only property acquired *after* the marriage is brought into the system. This gives effect to the " contribution " theory: the spouses share what they acquire by their efforts during marriage, but keep what they had before. In many systems, even property acquired during the marriage which is in no way related to the existence of the marriage or the efforts of the parties (such as gifts or legacies from third parties) is excluded.

As an alternative it is sometimes suggested that English law should recognise a special régime relating only to one class of property, *i.e.* the matrimonial home. The basis for this is that the home is the only substantial asset in most cases, is often intimately linked with the efforts of the parties, and that to introduce such a limited system would not cause the major conceptual upheaval necessarily involved in other systems of community. These suggestions are dealt with separately below.

3. Who is to manage the community property? Since third parties may be affected by the existence of either of the two forms of community régime so far mentioned, it has to be decided whether one party is to be given special powers to deal with the property (*e.g.* by signing cheques),

---

[53d] See for a brief analysis Hambly and Turner, pp. 400–404.

[54] See *Brett* v. *Brett* [1969] 1 W.L.R. 487, *supra*, p. 191; but *cf. Wachtel* v. *Wachtel* (*supra*).

the other relying on personal remedies against him in case of abuse. If this is not done, a third party could not safely deal with community property unless he satisfied himself that *both* spouses consent to the transaction. The former system, under which one party (generally the husband) becomes administrator of the community lends itself to abuse, and is scarcely consistent with modern ideas of equality of the sexes; the latter is complex and cumbrous.

4. Is it to be possible to contract out of the system? This is, in some ways, the most important question of all. Not to allow contracting out is a severe limitation on personal freedom; furthermore some wealthy men and women would evade the system by making settlements of their property, so that it would not be caught by the community.[55] The man who owns a majority shareholding in a private company is unlikely to wish to put this property into the community, with its inevitable corollary that if the marriage goes wrong he will cease to have voting control; if it is the wife who has a substantial inherited shareholding it is equally unlikely that her family will view with much enthusiasm the prospect of half of it going to her husband, if the marriage goes wrong or on the wife's death. The case against permitting contracting out is that it may leave the system only operative in practice between couples who have no property. If it is to be permitted care has to be taken to protect women against contracting out without full consideration of the implications, perhaps under pressure. Is it allowed *after* marriage? If so it might well be done in most cases when the husband acquired some substantial property rights, thus defeating the objects of the system.

5. What part of the property is to be liable for the debts of each party? Under the existing system of separation of property a creditor can seize the property (with certain unimportant exceptions) of the debtor. If, however, the debtor has *no* property of his own but only an interest in a community pool, it has to be decided what part (if any) of the pool he should be able to seize; even if the system is one of community of acquisitions (so that the debtor may have *some* separate property of his own) it would be inequitable to confine the creditor to that property, particularly if the debt has been incurred for the benefit of the community (*i.e.* post-marital acquisitions) fund.

Another related problem arises if several sorts of régime co-exist— *e.g.* community on the one hand, and separation for those who have contracted out. Since third party rights may be affected by the choice of régime, it is desirable to have a simple but certain way of enabling those who may be affected to find out what the régime is. In countries with a long-established tradition of notarised contracts and public documentation of civil status this causes fewer problems than would be the case in England, where a novel system would have to be devised for the purpose.

---

55 This argument is less valid if the community is confined to acquisitions.

6. Is the court to have power to vary the fixed rights if it seems fair in all the circumstances to do so?

7. Is the court to have power to impose additional maintenance obligations?

Unless the answer to both these questions is in the affirmative, a wife may be worse off than under the existing law, unless there is sufficient capital in the community pool. Yet the demands of feminists are largely based on the need to do away with " discretionary " maintenance. In most cases there would be insufficient property to allow this to be done.[56]

8. When is the community to come into operation? As originally understood, community is brought into operation by the fact of marriage, and operates from the moment the marriage takes place. A variant (commonly called " *deferred community*," " community of surplus " or " participation ") has been evolved to avoid some of the difficulties inherent in traditional community schemes.

The basic feature of this kind of deferred community system is that the parties' proprietary rights are unaffected *until* something occurs requiring a dissolution of " the community." When this event does occur (and it will commonly, but not necessarily, be the dissolution of the marriage) the parties' property is divided between them on the basis of equality. In strict legal analysis this is not a system of community (because marriage as such has no effect on the property, and property is never held in common) but one of separation of property coupled with a claim for equalisation of property rights. Unlike the existing English system of separation this gives fixed rights; unlike the existing English system, it can be brought into operation other than on dissolution of the marriage. Generally the community only extends to assets acquired during the currency of the marriage.

The great advantage of a system of deferred community is that it allows each spouse " to acquire, deal with and dispose of his or her own property independently during the marriage, and to defer the sharing of property until the end of the marriage." [57]

Deferred community

Of all community systems this alone preserves the principle of independent management during marriage. For this reason it alone has been thought a possible practical reform in England. For a full consideration of the problems involved, reference should be made to the Law Commission's Published Working Paper [58] and the sources there referred to.

In outline, it is basically a system of *separation* of property until the occurrence of an event which causes the community to crystallise. At

---

56 See this justification for a one-third (rather than one-half) rule, *per* Lord Denning M.R., *Wachtel* v. *Wachtel* (*supra*) at p. 95.
57 P.W.P. 42, para. 5.10.
58 *Supra*.

that time the parties' property (although generally only such property as has been acquired since the marriage otherwise than by gift or legacy from third parties) is divided so as to give them each an equal share. Thus, if a husband and wife who had no property at the date of marriage, and have acquired none since by gift or legacy, are now divorced, and it is found that the husband has assets worth £25,000 and the wife £5,000, this aggregate of £30,000 will be divided so that each is left with £15,000. It follows that the husband must transfer assets valued at £10,000 to his wife.

Some obvious problems occur:

(i) *When* does a dissolution occur? It invariably does so on the dissolution of the marriage, by death or judicial process. Most systems allow dissolution by mutual consent or by one party unilaterally (perhaps only with leave of the court) at other times—for instance, if one spouse feels it necessary to protect herself against the other's prodigality. To allow such a dissolution may be, in effect, to prefer the spouse to the ordinary commercial creditors.

(ii) What is to stop a husband quietly disposing of his assets, so that by the time the other spouse realises what is happening, there is little left to divide? The answer can only be found in an extended power to disallow transactions [59] save in favour of purchasers, with an additional power (perhaps) to make a prodigal spouse give corresponding credit for his excessive dissipation of the family fund. In the example given above, if the husband had only £15,000 (instead of £25,000) because he had given £5,000 to his mistress and spent £5,000 gambling, these amounts would be brought into account by him, and he would still have to transfer £10,000 to his wife.

(iii) Since normally only acquisitions during marriage are brought in, there may be the problem of identifying and valuing the relevant assets. Ideally on marriage each party would have an inventory of his property drawn up. If this is not done, the law may adapt the crude presumption that the spouse had *no* property at the time. This scheme secures a community of family [60] assets in the case of property acquired *during* the marriage. It is sometimes suggested that only property acquired for use (and not assets acquired for investment purposes) should be brought into the pool, but to translate this distinction into the clarity of a legislative code would be difficult if not impossible. An even more limited scheme restricts the community to the matrimonial home. This is considered below.

Although deferred community systems have the advantage of comparative simplicity and fairness, they involve a number of problems.

---

[59] S. 37, M.C.A. 1973 contains a limited power to set aside dispositions intended to defeat a wife's claim for financial provision under the existing law.
[60] See O. Kahn-Freund, *Matrimonial Property: where do we go from here?* (1971); M. P. A. Freeman, " Towards a Rational Reconstruction of Family Property Law " [1972] C.L.P. 84.

The only real protection given to a spouse is his right to call for a dissolution of the community: this is inevitably a hostile step, which may not be taken in a wish to avoid the final rupture of relations. Principally, however, it is clear that discretionary powers will be needed to secure the wife's position in addition to the fixed rights to share property. In the case of a marriage terminating in divorce, most wives will need support out of the husband's future earnings, as well as a half share in any capital. The exercise of a discretion is not avoided.

In the case of marriage ending on death, given that a surviving spouse takes a minimum of £15,000 on the other's intestacy, the proposed system would make little difference save where the estate is significantly more than £15,000 or the husband has made a will disinheriting his wife.

It seems, therefore, that although the introduction of a system of deferred community may be a desirable reform, it is unlikely to have the major beneficial consequences sometimes claimed for it.

The Law Commission concluded that there is no need to introduce a system of deferred community into English law, having regard to the broad interpretation by the court of its power to order financial provision on divorce, and to the Commission's two proposed reforms:

(a) that co-ownership of the matrimonial home be introduced; and

(b) that the Family Provision legislation be extended to give the court further powers on death.

Special rules for the matrimonial home

Fifty-two per cent. of married couples are now owner occupiers.[61] In most cases, the home is their only substantial asset.[62] Those who do now own a house rarely have any substantial assets.[63] It has therefore been suggested that, if special rules were introduced for this asset it would not be necessary to undertake the more fundamental changes involved in a general reform of matrimonial property law.[64]

Apart from conferring protected rights of occupation for a wife[65] four main proposals have been made:

(a) restrictions on the husband's power to dispose of or deal with the matrimonial home without his wife's consent;

(b) so-called homestead laws, usually combining restriction on disposition with some measure of exemption for the matrimonial home from creditors' claims;

(c) a *presumption* that the home is jointly owned (which may be rebutted by evidence);

(d) compulsory joint ownership limited to the matrimonial home.

61 *Todd and Jones*, pp. 9, 20–21.   62 *Ibid.*, and P.W.P. 42, para. 1 (1).
63 *Todd and Jones*, p. 20.
64 Law Commission No. 52: First Report on Family Property: A New Approach.
65 Already effected by the Matrimonial Homes Act 1967, *supra*, p. 168. Reform of that Act is a matter of detail although the extension of the same principle to household goods is a desirable policy: P.W.P. 42, Part 2.

(a) *Restraint on dealings*

This system could prevent a husband mortgaging (or even selling) the house over his wife's head. There are certain difficulties:

(i) How is a purchaser to be put on notice of the fact that he is dealing with a matrimonial home? Registration by the wife is one obvious solution, but (as under the Matrimonial Homes Act) unless registration is effected as a matter of routine, the wife might in practice not register until too late. It might be possible to overcome this difficulty by making it mandatory to state in the conveyance or transfer on acquisition whether the property was to be used for a matrimonial home, but (first) this would not provide any protection against the husband who simply lied to his solicitors; (secondly) it would provide no protection in the case of houses bought before marriage.

(ii) There would be difficulties in borderline cases in deciding what is to count as a matrimonial home: for instance, is a house used partly for business purposes to be within the definition?

(b) *Homestead legislation*

In so far as this goes beyond a restraint on disposition by one spouse without the other's consent, it also provides protection against execution by a man's creditors. There might be a case for allowing a debtor as against his creditors to keep sufficient property to provide a minimal standard of living. But this could only be done as part of a major re-appraisal of the legal principles relating to enforcement of debts. It would be absurd to exempt the home, but not its contents. Clearly it would be necessary to impose a financial limit on the protection accorded if the scandal of a debtor living with the sanction of the law in considerably greater style than his defeated creditors, is to be avoided.

(c) *Presumption of ownership*

In effect, this would reverse the existing law, which presupposes that the beneficial title is the same as the legal title. It would however be difficult to decide how far and in what circumstances the wife's rights were to bind third parties.

(d) *Joint ownership*

Under this system a matrimonial home would, in the absence of agreement to the contrary, be owned jointly by husband and wife. It has been supported by the Law Commission [65a] on the grounds that:

> " It would reflect the realities of family life in which husband and wife regard the home as ' theirs ' [65b] without considering the legal title or the principles of trust law. It would apply during the subsistence of the marriage and would give security of ownership to the spouse who is now considered by the law as having no proprietary interest in the home. It would recognise that each spouse contributes to the marriage and to the family and that the

---

[65a] Law Commission No. 52, para. 25.
[65b] In practice an increasing proportion of married couples (74 per cent. in 1970–71) acquire the matrimonial home jointly: *Todd and Jones*, pp. 76–83.

joint efforts of both made possible the purchase and maintenance of the home. It would eliminate the uncertainties of litigation in which ownership rights are established by proof of financial contribution."

A Working Party has been set up to advise the Law Commission on the formidable conveyancing problems which will be involved in the change.[65c]

Legal Rights of Inheritance [66]

It is sometimes suggested that the demand for " fixed rights " could be met by introducing a system of fixed succession rights on death. Under such a system, a spouse and other dependants would be entitled, irrespective of the provisions of the deceased's will, to a certain share in his estate—probably a proportion of the estate, with a certain minimum. Since the existing law of intestacy secures that, in most cases, a spouse inherits the whole of the other spouse's property if he dies intestate, the proposal would only be advantageous in cases where the deceased has made a will reducing the dependants' rights.[67] It is not clear whether this is a widespread problem. Unless it is, the proposal would seem to have few advantages over a deferred community system, save that of simplicity.

The Law Commission concluded [68] that a surviving spouse should expect to have a claim on the family assets at least equal to that of a divorced spouse. This would involve a change in family provision law, giving the court extended powers and removing the concept of " maintenance " as the proper consideration. If this were done, there would be no need to add a system of fixed legal rights of inheritance, which would lead to " uncertainty and confusion." [69]

[65c] Law Commission No. 52, App. I, para. 62.
[66] Proposals are considered in detail in P.W.P. 42, Part 4. See *Todd and Jones*, pp. 45–49, for attempts to assess public opinion on family inheritance rights.
[67] It would set a fixed minimum standard of provision for a surviving spouse: P.W.P. 42, para. 4.70.
[68] Law Commission No. 52, paras. 31–45.
[69] Para. 44.

PART IV

CHILDREN

Chapter 7

PARENT AND CHILD

At one time, the law of parent and child lent itself to the traditional exposition of a legal textbook.[1] It could be clearly laid down that a father was entitled to certain rights (subsumed under the description of custody) over his children until they reached the age of twenty-one, and that his right was absolute even against the mother of a child at the breast.[2] These rights could be described, and shown to be extensive: for instance, a right to the child's services, the right to punish it, the right to determine its religion, and so on. It is true that correlative duties were placed on the father to maintain and educate his children, but these were only duties of imperfect obligation, which the courts would not enforce directly (although they might to some limited extent be able to do so indirectly).[3] The law is now not only vastly more complex; it is also far less certain in its application, so that it is difficult to formulate " rules " with the clarity of the old textbook writers.[4] The reason for the complexity is not only the " cascade of legislation "[5] which now governs the rights and duties of parents to their children, but also the fact that the welfare of children has become a major preoccupation of public law agencies. This latter trend has involved not only the creation of children's social services on a large scale, but also the " steadily widening powers of removal of offspring from their parents at the behest of public officials."[6]

It is outside the scope of this work to give a comprehensive account of the law relating to children.[7] We shall consider (i) the basic concepts of custody and guardianship; (ii) the legal machinery for determining issues of custody and guardianship; (iii) the relevance of the social services. Separate chapters are devoted to illegitimacy and adoption.

---

[1] See e.g. W. Macpherson, A Treatise of the Law relating to Infants (1842); A. H. Simpson, A Treatise on the Law and Practice relating to Infants (1st ed. 1875, 4th ed. 1926); J. D. Chambers, A Practical Treatise on the Jurisdiction of the High Court of Chancery over Infants (1842).

[2] R. v. de Manneville (1804) 5 East 221.

[3] See per Cockburn C.J., Bazeley v. Forder (1868) L.R. 3 Q.B. 559, 565, and per Lord Eldon L.C., Wellesley v. Beaufort (1825) 2 Russ. 1, 22.

[4] For historical surveys, see T. E. James, Child Law (1962) and P. H. Pettit in A Century of Family Law (1957) Chap. 4. The best and most comprehensive survey is Mauricette Craffe's La Puissance Paternelle en Droit Anglais (1971).

[5] Per Sachs L.J., Hewer v. Bryant [1970] 1 Q.B. 357, 371.

[6] J. C. Hall, " The Waning of Parental Rights " [1972B] C.L.J. 248.

[7] Reference should be made to Clarke Hall and Morrison's Law Relating to Children and Young Persons (8th ed. 1972), and H. K. Bevan, The Law Relating to Children (1973).

CUSTODY AND GUARDIANSHIP

These are the two key concepts in any discussion of parent–child law [8]:
basically custody describes the " bundle of powers " [9] exercisable over a
child; guardianship is a formula used to attribute those powers [10] to a
particular individual or individuals.[11]   Hence a parent may properly be
described as the " guardian " of his child.[12]

GUARDIANSHIP

The Common Law of guardianship was deeply rooted in medieval concepts of land-holding.[13]   No part of our law was more disjointed and
incomplete.[14]   Nineteenth-century commentators distinguished as many
as thirteen different kinds of guardianship,[15] all with different incidents,
but all involving the attribution of some rights to the guardian.   For
present purposes it is sufficient to note that the father of a legitimate
child was his guardian for all purposes.[16]

Over the years the father's primacy was reduced in three ways:
first, the Court of Chancery, on behalf of the Crown as *parens patriae*,
might interfere to deprive the father of some or all of his rights.[17]
Secondly, statute gave the mother of a child certain rights,[18] culminating
in the Guardianship Act 1973 which will make the mother's rights equal
with those of the father.[19]   Thirdly, statutes attached increasing
importance to the welfare of the child, rather than the rights of parents,
until finally this was made the first and paramount consideration in case
of disputes.[20]

---

[8] For a full analysis, see J. M. Eekelaar, " What are Parental Rights? " 89 L.Q.R. 210.

[9] *Per* Sachs L.J., *Hewer* v. *Bryant* (*supra*) at p. 373.

[10] Or some of them: in theory, a child may have several guardians (*e.g.* a guardian of
the person, and a guardian of the estate) but in practice the word now normally means
guardian of the person: see *Rimington* v. *Hartley* (1880) 14 Ch.D. 630, 632. s. 7,
Guardianship Act 1973 provides that a guardian appointed under the Guardianship of
Minors Act 1971 (see *infra*, p. 252) shall " besides being guardian of the person of the
minor . . . have all the rights, powers and duties of a guardian of the minor's
estate. . . ." s. 7 (2) preserves the right of the High Court to appoint a guardian of a
minor's estate.

[11] The word may have a special meaning conferred on it in a statute. See *e.g. R.* v.
Croydon Juvenile Court Justices, ex p. Croydon London Borough Council [1973]
2 W.L.R. 61.

[12] But *cf.* O. M. Stone, in " Parental Custody and Matrimonial Maintenance," 1966
B.I.I.C.L., p. 10: " It would be more accurate to say that a guardian is a person
empowered to exercise the rights vested in the father at Common Law."

[13] See *Pollock and Maitland*, Vol. I, pp. 318–329; Vol. II, pp. 436–447.

[14] *Op. cit.* Vol. II, p. 443.   [15] Simpson, *op. cit.* 3rd ed. Part III, Chap. XI.

[16] *R.* v. *de Manneville* (1804) 5 East 221; *R.* v. *Greenhill* (1836) 4 Ad. & E. 624;
Thomasset v. *Thomasset* [1894] P. 295; *Re Agar-Ellis* (1883) 24 Ch.D. 317.

[17] See *Re Agar-Ellis* (*supra*), particularly at pp. 317, 326, 334–339, and generally Craffe,
op. cit. pp. 68–83.

[18] See Craffe, *op. cit.* pp. 105–143. The first legislative intervention was the Custody of
Infants Act 1839 (" Talfourd's Act ") which gave the court power (provided she had
not committed adultery) to commit the custody of children to their mother up to the
age of 7, and access up to majority. This was prompted by a number of exceptionally
harsh cases, exposed by the victim of one, Caroline Norton: see " Observations on
the Natural Claim of a Mother to the Custody of her Children as Affected by
Common Law Right of the Father, Illustrated by Cases of Particular Hardship."

[19] s. 1 (1). But the Act has not yet been brought into force.

[20] Craffe, *ibid.*, and pp. 143–184.

Modern English Law has never had a coherent doctrine of *patria potestas*, in the way that Roman Law and the systems derived from it have.[21] It tends " to think not in terms of general rights, but of particular remedies available in particular courts, and sometimes under particular statutes." [22] The concept of guardianship is, however, important, because in the absence of an express court order or valid administrative act, it is the " guardian " of a child who has rights and duties over him.

CUSTODY

In its broadest sense, custody means the sum total of the rights which a parent may exercise over his child. These rights continue [23] until a male child attains the age of eighteen [24] (or, at least in the case of a girl, marries at an earlier age [25]). If a divorce court makes an unqualified order giving " custody " to one parent, it will be assumed that these rights thereby vest in that parent.[26] However, " custody " is often used in a narrower sense [27]—sometimes as simply referring to the power of physical control over the child's movements, and sometimes to refer to residual rights not more specifically dealt with. An example may make this last point clearer: it is quite common for divorce courts [28] to make so-called " split orders " giving " custody " to parent A, and " care and control " [29] to parent B. This means that parent B has the right to have the child under his physical control, but that other parental rights are vested in parent A.[30] It is therefore not sufficient in such cases to ask: " who has custody of a child? " It will usually be necessary to specify which rights are in question.[31]

---

[21] *Pollock and Maitland*, Vol. II, p. 438; Craffe, *op. cit.* (preface by René David), and *cf.* pp. 30–34. [22] Stone, *op. cit.* n. 12 at p. 31.

[23] In the absence of court or other lawful interference.

[24] Twenty-one until the coming into force of the Family Law Reform Act 1969, s. 1: see *Todd* v. *Davison* [1972] A.C. 392 at p. 404, *per* Viscount Dilhorne.

[25] See the discussion of this difficult point in Hall, *op. cit.* n. 6, *supra* at pp. 264–265.

[26] But *cf.* n. 30, *infra*.

[27] See, for instance, the dispute as to the meaning of the expression " in the custody of a parent " in the Law Reform (Limitation of Actions, etc.) Act 1954, s. 2 (2): *Todd* v. *Davison* [1972] A.C. 392; *Hewer* v. *Bryant* (*supra*).

[28] See further *infra*, p. 263. Orders are also sometimes made giving custody to both parents with care and control to one: see *Jussa* v. *Jussa* [1972] 1 W.L.R. 881. Split orders can be made by magistrates under the Guardianship of Minors Act 1971, but *not* under the Matrimonial Proceedings (Magistrates' Courts) Act 1960: *Re W.* [1964] Ch. 202; *Wild* v. *Wild* [1969] P. 33. [29] As to " access " see *infra*, p. 263.

[30] Not necessarily all: in *Re T.* (*orse. H.*) [1963] Ch. 238 it was held that a mother to whom custody of a child had been given had no power to change the infant's name by deed poll. In so far as such a power existed, it remained vested in the child's father as the " natural guardian." See *per* Buckley J. at pp. 241–242: " An order for custody is as its name implies, an order which gives the person in whose favour it is made the right to the custody of the child, and to bring the child up, subject of course to any direction which the court may think right to make from time to time under its jurisdiction in relation to the matter. It does not deprive the father, who is not given the custody of the child, of all his rights and obligations in respect of his child. He remains, subject to the rights conferred on the person to whom custody is given by the court, the natural guardian of the person of the child, and among the residual rights which remain to him are any rights he may have at law with regard to the name of the child." See also *Y.* v. *Y.* [1973] 2 All E.R. 574, 578.

[31] If the expression appears in a statute, it must be interpreted so as to give effect to the intention of Parliament as deduced from the scope and purpose of the legislation. *Todd* v. *Davison* (*supra*).

A detailed examination of the rights incidental to custody in the broadest sense would serve little useful purposes, since if there is no dispute the question whether there is a " right " will not normally arise, and if there is a dispute the court will nowadays resolve the matter by reference to the child's welfare rather than the guardian's right.[32] Nevertheless, the residual rights are of some importance, and a brief account is therefore given of them.

The right to physical possession

The guardian's Common Law right to legal possession of the child [33] is of little practical importance. First, once the child had reached the " age of discretion " [34] the Common Law courts refused to enforce it by means of the writ of *habeas corpus*. Secondly, if the Wardship jurisdiction is invoked,[35] the court will decide the case by reference to the best interests of the child, not necessarily ordering the return of a child (even of tender years) to his parents.[36] Thirdly, if the child is beyond the control of his parent or guardian, or for a wide range of reasons is otherwise in need of care and control, a supervision or care order may be made placing the child [37] under supervision or in the care of a Local Authority.[38]

Power to control education

The old books contain amazing examples of cases where this right was enforced. In *Tremain's* case [39] the child

> " being an infant, . . . went to Oxford, contrary to the orders of his guardian, who would have him go to Cambridge. And the Court [40] sent a messenger to carry him from Oxford to Cambridge. And upon his returning to Oxford, there went another *tam* to carry him to Cambridge, *quam* to help him there."

---

[32] Even if a parent has " the right " to take some important step affecting a child, he should not seek to exercise it (in cases where legal proceedings have been taken affecting the child) without leave of the court or the agreement of the other spouse: *Y.* v. *Y.* (*supra*).

[33] See *e.g. Fleming* v. *Pratt* (1823) 1 L.J.(o.s.)K.B. 195.

[34] Probably 16 in the case of a girl, but 14 in the case of a boy: see the discussion in Craffe, *op. cit.* pp. 220–224 and *R.* v. *Howes* (1860) El. & El. 332; *Re Agar-Ellis* (1883) 24 Ch.D. 317, 326, *per* Brett M.R.; *Thomasset* v. *Thomasset* [1894] P. 295, 298, *per* Lindley L.J., and *per* Lord Denning M.R. in *Hewer* v. *Bryant* (*supra*) at p. 369, the right " is a dwindling right which the court will hesitate to enforce against the wishes of a child, and the more so the older he is. It starts with a right of control and ends with little more than advice." And see also *Krishnan* v. *Sutton London Borough Council* [1970] Ch. 181, *infra*, p. 307.

[35] Which can be invoked throughout minority: see *infra*, p. 281.

[36] See *e.g. J.* v. *C.* [1970] A.C. 668, *infra*, p. 289. *Cf. Eekelaar*, *op. cit.* n. 8 *supra*, at pp. 216–217.

[37] If he is under 17 (or 16 and married): Children and Young Persons Act 1969, ss. 1, 70 (1).

[38] *Infra*, p. 296.

[39] (1719) 1 Strange 167. See also *Hall* v. *Hall* (1749) 3 Att. 721 where the court, having ascertained that a young gentleman of 16 had no reasonable complaint against the master at Eton, told him that the guardian was the best judge of his education, and that he would if necessary be compelled to return.

[40] Of Chancery, exercising the Wardship jurisdiction.

Cases of refusal to go to school would now be dealt with under the care order procedure referred to above,[41] but the right remains of some importance in that, other things equal, the guardian (*i.e.* he with custody in the full sense) may make decisions as to the schooling appropriate for his child.[42] If dispute arises, the matter would be decided on " welfare " principles.[43]

Choice of religion

At common law, a father had an absolute right to determine the religion of his child, and his wishes had to be respected after his death.[44] This principle again now yields to the welfare of the child.[45]

Right to services

At common law the father had a right to the domestic services of his infant and unmarried children. It is not possible to enforce this action directly, but it remains of importance: it is an actionable tort to do an act [46] wrongfully depriving the parent of his child's services. Hence, a parent may have an independent cause of action against (say) a motorist who negligently injures his child. This subject is full of anomalies, and it has been suggested that the right should be replaced by an action to recover expenses reasonably incurred as the result of a tortious injury inflicted on a dependent child.[47]

Administration of property

Section 7 (1) of the Guardianship Act 1973 provides that a guardian under the Guardianship of Minors Act shall have all the rights, powers and duties of a guardian of the minor's estate, including in particular the right to receive and recover in his own name for the benefit of the minor, property of whatever descriptions and wherever situated which the minor is entitled to receive or recover. When brought into force [48]

[41] And see *infra*, p. 296.

[42] There is a statutory duty to provide education: Education Act 1944, s. 114.

[43] *J.* v. *C.* (*supra*); see further *infra*, p. 289.

[44] *Andrews* v. *Salt* (1873) 8 Ch.App. 622.

[45] See the discussion in *Bromley*, pp. 300–304; *Bevan*, pp. 426–432; and note that theory and practice often conflicted: see *e.g. Re Agar-Ellis* (1878) 10 Ch.D. 49. *Cf. per* Lord Upjohn, *J.* v. *C.* [1970] A.C. 668 (a case itself prompted by an application by foster parents to change the child's religion: see particularly the judgment of Ungoed-Thomas J. [1969] 1 All E.R. 801H). It should be noted that agreements that a child should be brought up in a particular religious faith are not binding for the right is given for the benefit of the child. Such an agreement may be evidence that the parent has abdicated his right to choose: *Andrews* v. *Salt* (1873) 8 Ch.App. 622, 636–637; *Re Agar-Ellis* (1878) 10 Ch.D. 49, 60, 71.

[46] Provided the act is not rape, seduction or enticement: see s. 5, Law Reform (Miscellaneous Provisions) Act 1970 (implementing the recommendations in Law Commission No. 25, paras. 101, 102). The Act also abolished the action for harbouring a child.

[47] 11th Report of the Law Reform Committee, 1963, Cmnd. 2017; *cf.* now the Law Commission: Report on Personal Injury Litigation—Assessment of Damages (Law Commission No. 56, para. 157).

[48] The Act (Sched. 3) repeals the Tenures Abolition Act 1660 which gave the guardian certain powers of management; but its extent was confused and unsatisfactory.

this will resolve the confusion of the law, and reverse decisions that were such that a personal representative who paid over a child's legacy to a guardian did not normally get a good discharge.[49] In practice problems connected with the management of property rarely arose since the property was normally vested in trustees or personal representatives, and not in the guardian as such.

Right to consent to marriage

This right is now governed by statute.[50] The consent of both parents is required if they are living together. If, however, custody has been given by court order to one parent or a third party, he or she must consent, and if either or both parents are dead any guardian has a similar right. In effect, therefore, the right is still an incident of guardianship, in the wide sense used here.

Miscellaneous rights

The residual powers of a guardian are often in practice the most important. They include the power to consent to the carrying out of medical treatment on a child under the age of sixteen,[51] and the right to veto the issue of a passport.[52] The fact that such rights vested at common law in the father to the exclusion of the mother of a child, led to demand for reform [53] which has now been met by the Guardianship Act 1973.[54]

LEGAL MACHINERY

We now consider how to determine in whom the rights of guardianship are vested. The relationship may arise: (a) by birth; (b) by appointment by deed or will, or (c) by Court Order.[55] Since Court Orders can always override guardianship of the first two types, we shall then consider the procedures and principles applied by the courts in determining issues affecting the custody of children.

HOW GUARDIANSHIP ARISES [56]

By birth

(i) *At common law*

The custody of infant legitimate children is vested in the father until they attain the age of majority.[57] It is, therefore, the father (to the

---

49 *Philips* v. *Paget* (1740) 3 Atk. 80; and see *Re Somech* [1957] Ch. 165.
50 *Supra*, p. 51; Marriage Act 1949, Sched. 2.
51 See s. 8, Family Law Reform Act 1969.
52 *Hewer* v. *Bryant* (*supra*) at p. 373. For the present practice see Hansard (H.L.), Vol. 340, col. 669; (H.C.), Vol. 856, col. 451.
53 See the debates on Dame Joan Vickers' Guardianship of Infants Bills in 1962 and 1965: H.C. Deb. 655, col. 417; Vol. 671, col. 881.
54 s. 1, *infra*, p. 251.
55 Parental rights cannot be acquired in any other way—*e.g.* a stepfather has (in the absence of a court order or other appointment) no "rights": *Re N. (Minors) (Parental Rights)* [1973] 3 W.L.R. 866.
56 Special considerations apply to illegitimate children: see *infra*, p. 335.
57 See n. 16, *supra*. As to adoption, see p. 340.

exclusion of the mother) who has the right to consent to medical treatment or exercise any other parental right.

On the father's death, the mother (if surviving) becomes the guardian (although she may have to act jointly with a guardian appointed by the father or by the court [58]).

(ii) *Under the Guardianship Act 1973*

This Act effects a radical change in the law by providing that the mother should have the same rights and authority as the law allows to a father. It further provides that the rights and authority of the mother and the father shall be equal, and exercisable by either without the other. Hence, once the Act is brought into force, a mother may on her down initiative, exercise any parental right.

If the parents disagree on any question affecting the child's welfare, either of them may apply to the court for directions. The court may then make such orders as it thinks proper. This power is restricted to the resolution of particular problems; the court cannot on such an application make any order affecting custody or the right of access of either parent. If one parent wishes to achieve such a result he must apply for custody under the Guardianship of Minors Acts 1971–73.

By appointment by deed or will

Either parent of a legitimate [59] child may by deed or will appoint any person [60] to be guardian of the child after his death.[61]

Any guardian so appointed will (in the absence of any objection by the survivor) act jointly with the surviving parent.[62] If guardians are appointed by both parents, they will, after the death of the surviving parent, act jointly.[63] If a surviving parent objects to the testamentary guardian acting, or if he dies or refuses to act, there is special provision for resolving the matter by application to the court. This is dealt with below.[64]

Appointment by the court

A guardian may be appointed by the court in the following ways:

(i) *Under the inherent jurisdiction*

The High Court has inherent jurisdiction to appoint a guardian for a child.[65] In practice, however, the power is now of little importance: any appointment will be made under statutory powers.

---

[58] s. 3, Guardianship of Minors Act 1971.
[59] For the position of an illegitimate child see *infra*, p. 336.
[60] s. 3 (1) (*b*) and s. 3 (2) (*b*) imply that any number of guardians may be appointed.
[61] Hence, even if an appointment is made by deed, it will not be effective until death, and may be revoked, either by a subsequent deed, or by will: *Ex p. Ilchester* (1803) 7 Ves. 348, 367; *Shaftesbury* v. *Hannam* (1677) Cas. *temp.* Finch 323.
[62] s. 4 (3); s. 3 (1), 3 (2).
[63] s. 4 (5).
[64] p. 252.
[65] *Johnstone* v. *Beattie* (1843) 10 Cl. & Fin. 42; *Re McGrath* [1893] 1 Ch. 143. The power arises from the court's delegated exercise of the Crown's rights as *parens patriae*, but is probably exercisable even if the child is not made a ward: see *Re McGrath*

(ii) *Under the Guardianship of Minors Acts 1971–1973* [66]

The court may appoint a guardian in the following circumstances:

(a) On the application of the intended guardian, if the child has no parent, guardian of the person [67] and no other person having parental rights [68] with respect to him.[69] This section may be used where, for instance, both parents have been killed in an accident (without themselves having appointed a guardian) to enable a relative to be given the legal rights of guardianship.

(b) To replace a guardian removed under the Act.[70]

(c) If *either* parent dies without having appointed a guardian. A guardian so appointed will act jointly with the surviving parent.[71]

(d) If *either* parent dies, and the guardian whom he or she has appointed dies, or refuses to act. Again, the guardian appointed will act jointly with the surviving parent.[72]

If the surviving parent objects to the testamentary guardian appointed by the other, the appointment is ineffective. However, application can be made to the court which may either:

(i) refuse to make any order (in which case the surviving parent remains sole guardian); or

(ii) order that the testamentary guardian shall act jointly with the surviving parent (notwithstanding the latter's objection); or

(iii) order that the testamentary guardian shall be the sole guardian of the child.[73] If such an order is made, the court may [74]

" (a) make such order regarding—
  (i) the custody of the minor; and
  (ii) the right of access to the minor of his mother or father, as the court thinks fit having regard to the welfare of the minor; and
(b) make a further order requiring the mother or father to pay to the guardian such weekly or other periodical sum towards the maintenance of the minor as the court thinks reasonable having regard to the means of the mother or father."

(*supra*) and *cf. Re E.* [1956] Ch. 23; *Re N.* [1967] Ch. 512 and *L.* v. *L.* [1969] P. 25. In practice the point is academic: if it is desired to invoke the machinery of the High Court the child will be made a ward, in which case the court may appoint a guardian (who will, however, always act subject to the court's discretion), or if no appointment is made, the court itself becomes in effect the child's guardian: *Re E.* (*supra*), and see p. 283, *infra*.

[66] The Guardianship of Minors Act 1971 was a consolidation measure, making no change to the substantive law.

[67] As distinct from a guardian of the estate: see *supra*, p. 249.

[68] If, however, a local authority has assumed parental rights over a child under s. 2, Children Act 1948 (see *infra*, p. 300) the court may nevertheless entertain an application for the appointment of a guardian under this section. If it makes an appointment the Local Authority's resolution ceases to have effect: Guardianship of Minors Act 1971, s. 5 (2). As to the meaning of " parental rights," see *Re N.* (*supra*, n. 55).

[69] Guardianship of Minors Act 1971, s. 5 (1).

[70] *Ibid.* s. 6, see *infra*, p. 253.

[71] *Ibid.* s. 3.

[72] *Ibid.* If a guardian is appointed under either head (c) or (d) he will continue to act after the death of the surviving parent, jointly with any guardian appointed by that parent: s. 4 (6).

[73] *Ibid.* s. 4 (4).   [74] *Ibid.* s. 10.

These powers may be exercised at any time, and include power to vary or discharge any previous order.

The power to order a joint appointment is obviously one which must be exercised with great care; it should only be done if the appointees are likely to co-operate.[75]

If joint guardians are appointed,[76] the Act confers two special powers:

(i) A power to apply to the court for directions if they are unable to agree on any question affecting the child's welfare [77];

(ii) If either parent is one of the joint guardians, power [77a]

> " (a) to make such order regarding—
>> (i) the custody of the minor; and
>> (ii) the right of access to the minor of his mother or father, as the court thinks fit having regard to the welfare of the minor;
> (b) to make an order requiring the mother or father to pay such weekly or other periodical sum [78] towards the maintenance of the minor as the court thinks reasonable having regard to the means of the mother or father;
> (c) to vary or discharge any order previously made."

Removal of guardians [79]

The High Court (but not the other courts exercising guardianship jurisdiction [80])—

> " may, in its discretion, on being satisfied that it is for the welfare of the minor, remove from his office any testamentary guardian or any guardian appointed or acting by virtue of this Act, and may also, if it deems it to be for the welfare of the minor, appoint another guardian in place of the guardian so removed." [81]

It will be noted that there is no power to remove a parent (who derives his authority otherwise than from the Act) under this section.[82] If, however, a parent has died having appointed a testamentary guardian, that guardian may, if he considers the surviving parent unfit to have the custody of the minor, apply to the court,[83] which may either—

> " (a) refuse to make any order (in which case the mother or father shall remain sole guardian); or
> (b) make an order that the guardian so appointed—
>> (i) shall act jointly with the mother or father; or
>> (ii) shall be the sole guardian of the minor."

[75] Re H. (an infant) [1959] 3 All E.R. 746.
[76] Either by the court, or by operation of an appointment
[77] s. 7.   [77a] s. 11.
[78] Such orders may continue until the child is 21: s. 12.
[79] There is also an inherent power: Duke of Beaufort v. Berty (1721) 1 P.Wms. 703, 705.
[80] Infra, p. 254.
[81] s. 6. Most of the cases have a period flavour, but see Re Savini (1870) 22 L.T. 61 (breach of undertaking). See also Re Read (1889) 5 T.L.R. 615; Ex p. Nickells (1891) 7 T.L.R. 498; F. v. F. [1902] 1 Ch. 688.
[82] In practice, cases where removal of the parent were thought necessary would be dealt with either under the wardship jurisdiction (see infra, p. 281) or under the social service legislation (see infra, p. 295).
[83] i.e. any court with jurisdiction (not only the High Court).

In practice, the choice will presumably be between making no order, and excluding the parent.

The courts with jurisdiction

One of the great advantages [84] of the statutory procedure under the Guardianship of Minors Act is that it can be exercised by the county court and magistrates' court, as well as by the High Court. But

" A magistrates' court shall not be competent to entertain—
(*a*) any application (other than an application for the variation or discharge of an existing order under this Act) relating to a minor who has attained the age of sixteen unless the minor is physically or mentally incapable of self-support; or
(*b*) any application involving the administration or application of any property belonging to or held in trust for a minor, or the income thereof." [85]

PROCEDURES FOR RESOLVING CUSTODY ISSUES

We have now seen how guardianship arises. But there are many ways of dealing with the incidents of custody short of the appointment of a guardian (and indeed a guardian may need to invoke the courts' ancillary powers). The exercise of some of these powers may effectively deprive a parent or guardian of most of the right normally allocated to that status. We consider these under the following heads:

(1) Statutory powers under the Guardianship of Minors Acts 1971 and 1973.
(2) Statutory power exercisable in matrimonial proceedings.
(3) The inherent jurisdiction of the court.

We shall then deal with the principles applied by the courts in exercising these powers. Questions of financial obligations to children (maintenance) are intimately linked with other questions of custody so that they are dealt with here, but the public law aspects of child care are, for the sake of clarity, dealt with separately.[86] In practice there is often a close interrelationship between these matters.[87]

Statutory Powers under the Guardianship of Minors Acts 1971–73

Disputes Between Parents

The preamble to the Guardianship of Infants Act 1925 [88] recited that

". . . Parliament by the Sex Disqualification (Removal) Act 1919, and various other enactments, has sought to establish equality in law between the sexes, and it is expedient that this principle should obtain with respect to the guardianship of infants and the rights and responsibilities conferred thereby. . . ."

[84] Unlike the inherent wardship jurisdiction, see *infra*, pp. 306 *et seq*.
[85] s. 15 (2).
[86] See p. 295, *infra*.
[87] See further p. 305.
[88] Repealed by the consolidating Guardianship of Minors Act 1971.

The principle was not, however, achieved by directly interfering with the common law rights of guardianship. Instead, it gave the mother of a minor the like powers to apply to the court in respect of any matter affecting the minor as are possessed by the father,[89] and directing the court on such an application to give effect to the minor's welfare rather than parental rights.[90]

The Act therefore provided machinery whereby a parent who does not wish to (or cannot [91]) take matrimonial proceedings,[92] can nevertheless have issues affecting the children [93] resolved by the court.[94]

The Guardianship Act 1973 has a different emphasis: both parents have equal rights [95]; the mother need not apply to the court to assert her wishes. But if the parents do disagree there is a right of application to the court.[96]

If either of the parents do apply to the court for the resolution of *a particular problem*, the court is specifically debarred from making an order regarding the custody of a minor, or the right of access to him of either parent.[97]

If one parent seeks *custody* for himself to the exclusion of the other, or for a third party, he must apply under section 9 of the Guardianship of Minors Act 1971. If such an application is made by either parent [98] the court may make such order regarding the custody of the minor, and the right of access to the minor of his mother or father as it thinks fit " having regard to the welfare of the minor and to the conduct and wishes of the mother and father." The principles on which such orders are made are considered below,[99] but it should at this stage be recalled that in a proper case, a " split " order may be made giving care and control to one spouse, and custody to the other.[1] That means that the physical custody of the child will be in the parent with care and control, but the other will have (subject to application to the court) all the residual powers of guardianship. It is doubtful whether such orders will continue

---

89 s. 2, Guardianship of Minors Act 1971.
90 s. 1. See *infra*, p. 289.
91 *E.g.* because he cannot establish any grounds, or is subject to a bar: see *supra*, p. 211.
92 Whether in the High Court or Magistrates' Court (under the Matrimonial Proceedings (Magistrates' Courts) Act 1960, *supra*, p. 211). There have been times when there were procedural advantages in taking proceedings under the guardianship legislation in respect of the children, in parallel with an application for matrimonial relief under other legislation, and it is open to an applicant to do this: see the Graham Hall Report, para. 79, and *Re Kinseth* [1967] Ch. 223 (when the justices could award larger sums for maintenance under the guardianship legislation than in the exercise of their matrimonial legislation).
93 Including adopted children: Adoption Act 1958, s. 13, and illegitimate children, notes 98 and 7, *infra*.
94 High Court, County Court or Magistrates' Court: see *supra*, p. 254.
95 s. 1, Guardianship Act 1973.
96 s. 1 (3) *ibid*.
97 s. 1 (4) *ibid*.
98 Including the father of an illegitimate child: s. 14 (1), *infra*, p. 337.
99 p. 289.
1 *Re W. (J. C.)* [1964] Ch. 202; *Jussa* v. *Jussa* [1972] 2 All E.R. 600, 604. This is not possible under the Matrimonial Proceedings (Magistrates' Courts) Act 1960: *W. (C.)* v. *W. (R.)* [1969] P. 33. See *infra*, pp. 260, 262.

to be made once the provision [2] giving each parent equal rights of custody has been brought into force.

Again, even if custody and care and control are not separated, but vested in one parent to the exclusion of the other, he or she will almost invariably [3] be granted *access, i.e.* the right to see the child, normally at specified times. The court may occasionally not make an order for custody at all, but simply allocate care and control. In that event, the rights of both parents to have a say (subject to further application to the court) will remain.[4]

It is now [5] provided that the court may, if " exceptional circumstances " exist, make a supervision order, or commit the care of the minor to a local authority.

If the court makes an order giving *custody* [6] of a legitimate child [7] to either parent or a third party it

" may make a further order requiring payment to that person by the parent or either of the parents excluded from having that custody of such weekly or other periodical sum towards the maintenance of the minor as the court thinks reasonable having regard to the means of that parent." [8]

It is specifically provided that " maintenance " includes " education." [9] There is now [10] no financial limit on the amounts which any court may order under the Act (but only in exceptional cases can *magistrates'* courts entertain applications if the child is sixteen or over [11]). Orders may require maintenance to be paid until the child attains twenty-one; sums payable for the benefit of a person over eighteen may be paid to him direct.[12] Orders may be varied.[13]

It is in practice unlikely that custody proceedings will be taken unless the marriage is in a state of collapse, but the Act [14] specifically provides that orders for custody or access may be obtained—

" notwithstanding that the parents of the minor are then residing together, but—

[2] Guardianship Act 1973, s. 1. For some difficulties in the making of split orders, see B. Harris (1972) 122 New L.J. 300.
[3] But see *infra*, p. 294.
[4] *Re M.* [1967] 3 All E.R. 1071; *cf. Laxton* v. *Laxton* [1966] 2 All E.R. 977.
[5] Guardianship Act 1973, s. 2, modelled on the provisions of the Matrimonial Proceedings (Magistrates' Courts) Act 1960, considered *infra*, p. 260. Either parent may be ordered to pay maintenance.
[6] Not only care and control, at p. 980, *per* Davies L.J.
[7] If the child is illegitimate there is no such right: s. 14 (2). The mother must obtain an affiliation order: *infra*, p. 321.
[8] s. 9 (2), as amended by the Guardianship Act 1973, Sched. 2, Pt. II. Until that amendment is brought into force, financial orders could only be made against the *father* if custody were awarded to the mother. *Semble*: there is no power to order maintenance if a joint custody order is made.
[9] s. 20 (2).
[10] As a result of the Maintenance Orders Act 1968.
[11] s. 15 (2), *infra*, p. 261.
[12] s. 12 (1).
[13] s. 9 (4).
[14] s. 9 (3).

(a) no such order shall be enforceable, and no liability thereunder shall accrue, while they are residing together [15]; and

(b) any such order shall cease to have effect if for a period of
three months after it is made they continue to reside
together."

In effect, therefore, an order can be obtained without disturbing the *status
quo*. But the provision for its ceasing to have effect clearly indicates
that such orders are regarded as preliminaries to separation.

If the court on such an application gives custody to someone other
than either parent these restrictions do not apply unless the court so
directs.[16]

Disputes Involving Third Parties

There is no power under the Guardianship of Minors Acts 1971–73
for anyone to apply to the court save (a) the mother or father of the child,
or (b) a guardian appointed under the provisions set out above [17] to act
jointly with the parent, or to the exclusion of the parent.[18] Anyone else
who wishes to intervene in the child's affairs must either (a) make him
a ward of court,[19] or (b) direct the attention of one of the social work
agencies to his case.[20]

To this principle there is one very limited exception. A person aged
between eighteen and twenty-one in respect of whom a guardianship
order has been in force at any time in his minority may apply [21] to the
court *in his own right* for a maintenance order against either of his
parents until he attains twenty-one.[22] The order may be unlimited in
amount, but it is provided that no liability under the order shall accrue
at a time when the parents are residing together, and that the order shall
cease if they reside together for three months after the making of the
order.[23] This restriction, however, no longer applies if custody is given
to someone other than a parent.[24] The result is absurd: whatever the
case for or against giving a young person an independent right to be
maintained, there seems no merit in making the duration of the right
depend on the question of the intimate relationship between his parents.[25]

---

15 As to the interpretation of this expression, see *Evans* v. *Evans* [1948] 1 K.B. 175;
Thomas v. *Thomas* [1948] 2 K.B. 294; *Wheatley* v. *Wheatley* [1950] 1 K.B. 39; *cf.*
Naylor v. *Naylor* [1962] P. 253.
16 s. 9, as amended by Guardianship Act 1973, Sched. 2.
17 *Supra*, p. 252; see ss. 10, 11.
18 If there is no person with parental rights, however, application may be made to the
court for the applicant to be appointed guardian: s. 5, *supra*, p. 252.
19 *Infra*, p. 281.   20 *Infra*, p. 295.
21 Or either parent may on his behalf.
22 But generally only to the county court or High Court: s. 15 (2), *supra*, p. 254.
23 s. 12 (2).
24 Guardianship Act 1973, Sched. 2, Pt. II.
25 The reason for this restriction is that similar restrictions apply to applications by the
parent under s. 9, Guardianship of Minors Act 1971, and when the provision was
introduced by the Family Law Reform Act 1969, s. 4 (consequent on lowering the age
of majority to 18), it was desired to change the law no more than was absolutely
necessary, pending publication of the Law Commission's then awaited report on
Financial Provision. Unfortunately, neither that report (Law Commission 25) nor
the legislation implementing its recommendations did anything to rationalise the
situation.

Statutory Powers Exercisable in Matrimonial Proceedings

Magistrates' Courts

The early legislation giving magistrates jurisdiction in matrimonial disputes [26] enabled provision to be made for the custody and maintenance [27] of the children. But this was very much dependent on, and subsidiary to, what was seen as the main issue—the rights and duties of husband and wife the one to the other. Orders for custody and maintenance were prizes for a successful wife.[28] Such orders depended on her proving her case, while adultery was an absolute bar.[29] The modern code, contained in the Matrimonial Proceedings (Magistrates' Courts) Act 1960,[30] to a large exent recognises: (i) that the court's power to make orders affecting children should not necessarily depend on success in the litigation between husband and wife; (ii) that it may be desirable to invoke the assistance of outside agencies to provide satisfactory arrangements for the children; and (iii) that the spouses may have obligations to children other than those of their own marriage.

When an order may be made

The court only has power to make orders if, either: (a) a complaint has been made alleging one of the " grounds " set out in the Act [31]: these include persistent cruelty to the children,[32] or wilful neglect to provide reasonable maintenance for the children,[33] or (b) a complaint is made for the *variation* of an existing matrimonial order—

" (i) by the revocation, addition or alteration of provision for the legal custody of a child; or
(ii) by the revocation of a provision committing a child to the care of a local authority or a provision that a child be under the supervision of a probation officer or local authority,"

[26] *Supra*, p. 209.
[27] The power to award maintenance was only conferred in 1920: s. 1 (1), Married Women (Maintenance) Act 1920.
[28] " An order for the custody of the children is an order in favour of the wife "; *per* Lord Merriman P., *Kinnane* v. *Kinnane* [1954] P. 41.
[29] Until the Summary Jurisdiction (Separation and Maintenance) Act 1925, s. 2 (2) (*b*), gave the court power to make a fresh order in such circumstances.
[30] Following the Report of the Morton Commission (paras. 408–412) and the Report of the Departmental Committee on Matrimonial Proceedings in Magistrates' Courts (1959) Cmnd. 638.
[31] s. 1, see *supra*, p. 211.
[32] s. 1 (1) (*b*) (ii) and (iii).
[33] s. 1 (1) (*h*) and (*i*). The obligation only extends to children who are, or would but for the neglect have been, dependants, *ibid*. That expression means a person: " (a) who is under the age of sixteen years; or (b) who, having attained the age of sixteen but not of twenty-one years, is either receiving full-time instruction at an educational establishment or undergoing training for a trade, profession or vocation in such circumstances that he is required to devote the whole of his time to that training for a period of not less than two years; or (c) whose earning capacity is impaired through illness or disability of mind or body and who has not attained the age of twenty-one years." (s. 16 (1)). Under the code applicable to divorce proceedings a child of 16 or over who is receiving training qualifies for consideration whether or not he is also in gainful employment: see *infra*, p. 269. Such anomalies result from the patchwork nature of the legislation.

or (c) for the revocation of a matrimonial order consisting of or including any of the provisions set out at (b) above.[34] But the court's powers do not now depend on grounds of complaint being made out. On the contrary, it is provided [35]:

(a) that whether or not the court makes the order sought, it may make such orders [36] concerned with the children as " after giving each party to the proceedings an opportunity of making representations, the court thinks proper in all the circumstances "; and

(b) " the court shall not dismiss or make its final order on any complaint in a case where the powers conferred on the court by this subsection are or may be exercisable until it has decided whether or not, and if so how, those powers should be exercised."

The effect of these provisions (it has been well said [37]) is that " once a party to a marriage brings a domestic dispute to the justices, the question of their children's welfare *must* be investigated, whether the complainant likes it or not." There is [38] also power to get a report from a probation officer or local authority children's officer if the court feels it has insufficient information to make a decision on custody, access or maintenance. The Act thus seems to make the children's position independent of the relationship between their parents, but this is not entirely so:

First, as with applications under the Guardianship of Minors Act,[39] although an order may be made while the husband and wife are cohabiting,

> " (*a*) the order shall not be enforceable and no liability shall accrue thereunder until they have ceased to cohabit "; and
> (*b*) if they continue to cohabit for the period of three months beginning with the date of the making of the order, the order shall cease to have effect at the expiration of that period.[40]

It is true that, unless the court in making the order directs otherwise, this provision does not apply to provisions in effect committing the child to the custody or care of third parties, or for the making of payments to third parties.[41]

Second, although it is true that orders for children's maintenance and custody may be made even if the complainant is shown to have committed adultery,[42] it is (rather weakly) provided [43] that the court " shall not be bound " to grant an application for revocation of such provisions based on the complainant's adultery.

---

[34] Matrimonial Proceedings (Magistrates' Courts) Act 1960, s. 4 (1).
[35] *Ibid.*
[36] *Infra*, p. 260.
[37] M. Puxon, *Family Law* (2nd ed. 1971), p. 100.
[38] s. 4 (2).
[39] *Supra*, p. 256.
[40] s. 7 (1). The order will also cease to have effect if the parties *resume* cohabitation after separation: s. 7 (2), and see s. 8 (2) (*a*).
[41] s. 7 (1) proviso.
[42] s. 2 (4).
[43] s. 8 (2) (*b*).

Orders that can be made

The court's order may contain any of the following provisions:

(a) *Provision for the legal custody of any child of the family* [44] *who is under the age of sixteen years.*

It should be noted:

(i) the court may, under this provision, commit the child to the custody of any individual (*e.g.* another relative). The principle on which the court will exercise these powers is dealt with below [45]: at this stage it should be noted that there is no bar to the unsuccessful or guilty party getting custody.

(ii) Split orders giving custody to one parent and care and control to the other cannot be made under this jurisdiction. [46]

(iii) No provision can be made under this Act for the custody of a child over sixteen (although the High Court and county court could make such orders under the Guardianship of Minors Act, [47] and *maintenance* may be ordered under the present Act for children over sixteen in certain cases). [48]

(iv) It is not necessary for the court to make *any* order for custody. If it does not do so, custody will remain in the mother and father. [49]

(b) *If there are "exceptional circumstances making it impracticable or undesirable" for the child to be entrusted to either of the parties or to any other individual, the care of the child may be committed to the local authority.* [50] This power is not often exercised, although it has been held that the inability of a parent to provide a home (coupled with the absence of any other suitable individual) is a sufficiently " exceptional " circumstance. [51]

(c) *If there are " exceptional circumstances making it desirable that the child should be under the supervision of an independent person "* [52] an order may be made providing for his supervision by a probation officer or local authority.

(d) *Access* may be given [53] to either husband or wife (or to the child's parent, if he is a third party [54]).

---

[44] See *infra*, p. 275.
[45] See *infra*, p. 289.
[46] But they can be made under the Guardianship of Minors Acts 1971–73, see p. 255, *supra*.
[47] *Supra*, p. 247.
[48] *Infra*, p. 261.
[49] Guardianship Act 1973, s. 1; *Hayes* v. *Hayes* [1948] W.N. 361.
[50] s. 2 (1) (*d*). In the year ended March 31, 1970 only 89 children came into care under this provision (out of a total of 51,542): Cmnd. 4559, Table I.
[51] *F.* v. *F.* [1959] 3 All E.R. 180, see also *G.* v. *G.* (1962) 106 S.J. 858, and note the detailed provisions of s. 3.
[52] s. 2 (1) (*f*).
[53] But not if he is in care: s. 2 (4). Access cannot be given to a person to whom custody has been given: *Wild* v. *Wild* (*supra*). This was one of the reasons why the court held there was no jurisdiction to make " split orders giving care and control to one, and custody to the other."
[54] See *infra* on the definition of " child of the family."

(e) *Maintenance, etc.* The Act provides [55] that the defendant or complainant (or both) may be ordered to make weekly payments (which can now [56] be of any amount) for the child's maintenance. It should be noted:

(i) That although an order can be made *against* either party, it can only be made *in favour* of (i) a person to whom custody has been given by the order (or by some other English court order), or (ii) a local authority to whose care the order has committed the child. It is, therefore, only in the case where custody has been given to some third party that maintenance orders against both spouses will be possible. There is no power to order maintenance to be paid to any individual who has not been given the legal custody of the child.[57]

(ii) If, however, the child is over sixteen but under twenty-one, the court may order payments to be made for such period as may be specified in the order (with a top limit of twenty-one). This power can only be exercised if the child is, or will be, or if such payments were made would be, a dependant.[58] In this case the payments can be to the child, to a local authority to whose care he has been committed, or, it would seem, to any other person specified in the order.

(iii) There are special rules for assessing the *quantum* of awards made against a person who is not the parent of a child.[59]

It seems that in practice the Magistrates' Courts in the exercise of their maintenance jurisdiction allocate more of the total sum which they consider the husband has available to the children than to the wife. This is said to be because husbands are more prepared to make payments for their children than for their wife.[60] Since 1968 the court has not been limited in the amount it can award either a wife or a child.

Divorce Courts [61]

It has long been part of the conventional wisdom that those who suffer most from divorce are the children of the parties. It is not clear how far this is true: the evidence suggests that harm is done to children by the breakdown of normal family life. As has already been pointed out [62] divorce is a *consequence* of breakdown; it is far from clear that it is a *cause* of breakdown. It is necessary—it has been said [63]—

" to distinguish between a number of important factors which can make up a divorce situation. One is the breakdown in the relation-

---

55 s. 2 (1) (*h*).
56 Maintenance Orders Act 1968.
57 *Wild* v. *Wild* (*supra*).
58 See s. 16 (1) (*b*) and (*c*), *supra*, n. 33.
59 s. 2 (5); see *infra*, p. 278.
60 Graham Hall Report, para. 131. It seems, however, that the figures show no better standard of compliance overall with orders in respect of children than with any other orders. It may, therefore, be that husbands " so express themselves at the time of the hearing and comply better with the order initially." *Ibid.*, para. 139.
61 *i.e.* courts exercising jurisdiction in Divorce, Judicial Separation and Nullity.
62 *Supra*, p. 72.
63 See *Eekelaar*, p. 261.

ship between the parties manifested by hostility between them in the household. Another is the departure of one of the spouses accompanied, perhaps, by the intruding presence of a third party. Then there is the divorce process itself which, depending on the form it takes, may or may not aggravate the tensions inherent in the situation. Any or all of these factors may harm the children. It is not necessarily the legal fact of divorce which is the major cause of the harm, if it is, indeed, a factor at all. If harm does result from the legal process this may even be attributable to the tensions created by the traditional legal requirement of the establishment of matrimonial guilt against one party."

For many years, the expressed aim of those concerned with divorce policy has been to do everything possible to mitigate any adverse effects divorce may have on the child.[64] This has resulted in:

(i) Exceptionally wide powers being given to the court to make orders for custody and financial matters.

(ii) Attempts to secure that satisfactory arrangements are made for children before the marriage is finally dissolved. We deal with these in turn.

Custody, etc.

The legislation follows the pattern set out above in making the court's powers independent of the outcome of the suit. Orders for the custody and education of any child of the family[65] who is under the age of eighteen may be made, either[66]

> (a) in any proceedings for divorce, nullity of marriage or judicial separation, before, by or after the final decree; *or*

> (b) where such proceedings are dismissed after the beginning of the trial, either forthwith or within a reasonable period after the dismissal.

There is also power to make such orders when proceedings are brought on the ground of wilful neglect.[67]

In practice, controversial matters relating to custody are adjourned into chambers, and are tried after the decree *nisi* has been granted.[68] But the issue must be settled before the decree is made absolute. Orders for *custody* are in practice not normally made in relation to children over sixteen.[69]

The court has a wide range of auxiliary powers:

(i) It is common to make " split orders " giving custody to one parent, and care and control to the other. The practice grew up in the days when

---

[64] Morton Commission, para. 362.
[65] Defined below, p. 280.
[66] s. 42 (1), M.C.A. 1973. But the court will not normally exercise its statutory jurisdiction to interfere with the decision of a local authority acting within its powers: *H.* v. *H.* [1973] 1 All E.R. 801.
[67] Under s. 27, M.C.A. 1973, but such orders have effect only when an order under the section is in force: s. 42 (2).
[68] *Rayden*, pp. 881–882. As to the practice followed, see *ibid.*, pp. 884–885.
[69] *Hall* v. *Hall* (1946) 175 L.T. 355.

it was thought that custody issues should be decided in the context of each spouse's guilt or innocence [70]:

> "Cases often arise in the Divorce Court where a guilty wife deserts her husband and takes the children with her, but the father has no means of bringing them up himself. In such a situation the usual order is that the father, the innocent party, is given the custody of the child or children, but the care and control is left to the mother. That order is entirely realistic. By giving the father the custody, it recognises that he, the innocent party, is at least entitled to a voice in the bringing up of the child or children, and is entitled to the consideration of the court when any question arises as to what is to be done for the child. . . ." [71]

However, although the general concept is clear, the precise rights allocated to custody and care and control are not.[72] In practice, difficulty would be resolved by further application to the court.

The court may decide not to make any order as to legal custody, but simply to give care and control to one parent. This may become a more common practice once the provision giving each parent equal rights of custody has been brought into force.[73] Access [74] will normally [75] be given to a parent who does not have custody or care and control.

(ii) The court may instead of making a custody order, if it thinks fit, direct that proper proceedings be taken for making the child a *ward of court*. This power seems very little used,[76] and it is not clear what useful purpose would be served by it. If independent supervision is required the court now has the means of procuring it: the Act [76a] provides that where—

> "the court has jurisdiction . . . to make an order for the custody of a child and it appears to the court that there are exceptional circumstances [77] making it desirable that the child should be under the supervision of an independent person, the court may, as respects any period during which the child is, in exercise of that jurisdiction, committed to the custody of any person, order that the child be under the supervision of an officer appointed under this section as a welfare officer or under the supervision of a local authority."

It will be noted that this power can only be exercised if (a) there are exceptional circumstances,[78] and (b) the court has made a custody order. Not surprisingly the power is very infrequently exercised.[79] The reason for these restrictions seems to have been (a) that it was considered that

---

70 For the contemporary attitude, see *infra*, p. 291.
71 *Per* Denning L.J., *Wakeham* v. *Wakeham* [1954] 1 W.L.R. 366, 369. Such orders are also used where young children are left in the care and control of the mother, on account of their years.
72 See A. Samuels, (1973) 117 S.J. 460.
73 *Clissold* v. *Clissold* (1964) 108 S.J. 220; Guardianship Act 1973, s. 1, *supra*, p. 251.
74 *i.e.* the right to visit the child.
75 But see *infra*, p. 294.
76 See Report of the Denning Committee, Cmd. 7024 (1947), para. 32 (i).
76a s. 43.   77 See *infra*, p. 264.
78 *Ibid.*
79 See Law Commission P.W.P. 15, p. 8, para. 10 (c) and p. 15, para. 9.

the law ensured that arrangements for children were fully considered at the time of the divorce. Hence, only in exceptional circumstances would further supervision be needed[80]; (b) that the object of supervision was to see that arrangements for custody were reviewed, particularly if there were a change of circumstances.[81] When orders are made, it is thought that they are usually beneficial.[82] In practice, the supervision may be of a very informal kind, involving perhaps annual or twice yearly visits to the child.[83] If they were to be made frequently, not only would the strain placed on the supervisors be considerable, but the children supervised might feel insecure about their future.[84]

(iii) If it appears to the court that there are exceptional circumstances making it impracticable or undesirable for the child to be entrusted to either of the parties to the marriage or to any other individual, the court may make an order committing the care of the child to the *care of a local authority*.[85] This power was conferred as a result of the recommendation of the Morton Commission[86] because there might be occasions in which neither spouse could provide adequate arrangements for the child's upbringing, in which case it might be possible to place the child in the care of a relative, or even an outsider ("although conditions would have to be really bad before that course would be contemplated ").[87] If none of these solutions were possible, the only alternative would be to give the court power to require a local authority to take the child into care.[88] The procedure is therefore very much a last resort[89]: 127 children were placed into care under it in the twelve months ended March 31, 1970.[90]

Since such orders are only made when the parents' home conditions are unsatisfactory it is provided that while an order is in force, the child shall continue in the care of the local authority notwithstanding any claim by a parent or other person.[91]

(iv) The court also has a number of miscellaneous auxiliary powers in dealing with custody cases:

(a) The court may direct that the child be separately represented by a *guardian ad litem*, either the Official Solicitor or some other proper person. This power is used to ensure that the child's interests are properly presented, by evidence and argument, particularly in cases

[80] Morton Commission, para. 396.
[81] *Ibid.*, P.W.P. 15, para. 5, p. 26.
[82] P.W.P. 15, p. 21, para. 16.
[83] P.W.P. 15, p. 21, para. 17. However, although the Morton Commission (para. 396) did not contemplate that the supervision would be of a formal kind, it seems that there is a regional difference in approach: P.W.P. 15, p. 21, para. 17, and see p. 24, para. 8, p. 21, para. 13.
[84] Morton Commission, para. 396.
[85] M.C.A. 1973, s. 43.
[86] Para. 395.
[87] *Ibid.*
[88] *Infra*, p. 296.
[89] *N.B.* the *requirement* of " exceptional circumstances."
[90] Cmnd. 4559, Table I.
[91] s. 43 (3).

where otherwise they might not be.[92] In practice, such orders are rarely made.[93]

(b) It may seek a report from a welfare officer—who will in London be one of the full-time welfare officers available in the Royal Courts of Justice, or in the provinces be the Principal Probation Officer who combines the task of Divorce Court Welfare Officer with his other duties.[94] Fairly extensive use is made of this power.[95] The procedure was described as follows by the Morton Commission [96]:

> " The court welfare officer interviews both parents and visits their homes. He sees the children against the background of the home they are living in; if it seems desirable he may talk privately with the children. It is also often necessary to visit head teachers, doctors and clergymen in order to obtain information which may assist the court."

The result of his inquiries is embodied in a report to the court.[97]

Inevitably, such orders are more often thought appropriate where there is a dispute as to custody,[98] but the power may be invoked in any case where the judge considers it desirable. The sort of case which is thought to merit an inquiry has been said [99] to include the following: if either party asks for a report, if the children are to be split, given to a person intending to remarry, if the petitioner is of low IQ, to a parent alleged to have treated his spouse with cruelty, to a parent cohabiting with a non-spouse, or to a wife respondent. Others were if a girl, or very young child, were to be placed with her father, if difficulties were likely regarding access, or where there was a contest as to custody, insufficient information, or the slightest doubt.

There is a great divergence of judicial practice in the readiness with which a welfare officer's report is called for,[1] and also some regional variation.[2] It is almost universally thought that reports do provide useful assistance in reaching a decision [3]: the only dispute is as to whether more extensive use should be made of them.

Apart from this power to obtain a welfare officer's report, it should be borne in mind that the court may refer auxiliary issues (including those affecting children) to the court welfare officer if it is considered that conciliation by him might serve a useful purpose in resolving the issues between the parents, or at least identifying the issues on which they remain at variance.[4]

---

[92] As for instance where his status as a child of the family (see *infra*, p. 280) is in question. On the duties of such a guardian, see *per* Ormrod J., *Re L.* [1968] P. 119, 136; *Re Taylor's Application* [1972] 2 Q.B. 369.   [93] P.W.P. 15, p. 14, para. 3.

[94] P.W.P. 15, p. 18.

[95] 2,493 cases in 1966: *op. cit.* p. 18, para. B.1.   [96] Para. 387.

[97] As to the problems which disclosure of the report to the parties may cause, see *Official Solicitor* v. *K.* [1965] A.C. 201.

[98] See P.W.P. 15, pp. 6–7.

[99] By welfare officers, see: *op. cit.* pp. 6, 19.

[1] *Op. cit.* pp. 6–7.

[2] *Op. cit.* p. 18.   [3] *Op. cit.* p. 7.

[4] See *Practice Direction* [1971] 1 All E.R. 894; *S.* v. *S.* [1968] P. 185.

But although the court may be helped by a welfare report, or the agreement of the parties, the final decision is for the court itself. It has been held that if courts do differ from the welfare officer's report, it is essential for them to explain why they have done so.[5]

(v) There is a wide power to *vary or discharge* orders, and to make fresh orders from time to time while the child is under the age of eighteen.[6]

(vi) Although the essence of what has been said above is that the court should preserve the maximum flexibility in dealing with issues affecting children from time to time, there is one (it is thought very rarely used) power which is intended to govern the future. It is provided[7] that—

> " Where the court makes or makes absolute a decree of divorce or makes a decree of judicial separation, it may include in the decree a declaration that either party to the marriage in question is unfit to have the custody of the children of the family."

The effect of such a declaration is twofold :

(a) A parent ceases to be entitled as of right on the death of the other parent to the custody or guardianship of the child.[8]

(b) The parent against whom such a declaration is made will have the onus of establishing that he is now a fit and proper person to be entrusted with custody.[9]

Maintenance and property
Provision by cash payments

In proceedings for *divorce, judicial separation or nullity* the court may order *either* party to make :

(a) periodical payments,

(b) secured periodical payments,

(c) a lump sum payment.[10]

Such orders may direct payments to the other spouse, to a third party for his benefit, or to the child himself. They can be made either[11] :

(a) before or on granting the decree or at any time thereafter;
or

(b) where the proceedings are dismissed after the beginning of the

---

5 *Clark* v. *Clark* (1970) 114 S.J. 318 (Div.Ct.).
6 s. 42 (6), (7), M.C.A. 1973.
7 s. 42 (3), M.C.A. 1973.
8 s. 42 (4), M.C.A. 1973 (derived from s. 7, Guardianship of Infants Act 1886); *cf.* s. 3, Guardianship of Minors Act 1971, *supra*, p. 251.
9 See *Skinner* v. *Skinner* (1888) 13 P.D. 90; *Webley* v. *Webley* (1891) 64 L.T. 83; *Woolnoth* v. *Woolnoth* (1902) 18 T.L.R. 453; *S.* v. *S.* [1949] P. 269.
10 s. 23 (1) and (2), M.C.A. 1973. As to the meaning of these terms, see *supra*, p. 185. It is provided that lump sum awards may be payable by instalments (secured if so ordered) and that a lump sum award may be made for the purpose of enabling any liabilities or expenses reasonably incurred by or for the benefit of that child before the making of an application for an order under this section to be met.
11 s. 23 (1) and (2), M.C.A. 1973.

trial, either forthwith or within a reasonable period after the dismissal.

In the case where a decree is granted, the powers referred to can be exercised from time to time; if the proceedings are dismissed, but an order made under (b) above, a further order may be made from time to time.[12]

Apart from these proceedings, *either* party can apply for an order on the grounds that the other has wilfully neglected to provide, or to make a proper contribution towards, reasonable maintenance for any child of the family for whose maintenance it is reasonable in all the circumstances to expect the respondent to provide or towards whose maintenance it is reasonable in all the circumstances to expect the respondent to make a proper contribution.[13] If the ground of complaint is made out, the court may order payments as above.

Provision by property adjustment

The powers classified by the Law Commission under this head are intended to enable the court to adjust the family's property rights if, but only if, the marriage has finally broken down.[14] They are thus available only in divorce, judicial separation and nullity (*i.e.* not in wilful neglect proceedings) and then only if a final [15] decree is made (unlike the provisions discussed above, which can be ordered even if a decree is not made). The powers in question are [16]

(a) Transfer of property.

(b) Settlement of property.

(c) Variation of ante-nuptial or post-nuptial settlement. It should be noted that the Law Commission's view was that in general, if children are to benefit from property adjustments, that should be by means of a settlement, not an out-and-out transfer.[17] The power to order an outright transfer of property to a child (or to someone else for his benefit) was seen " as one to be exercised only as an alternative to a lump sum payment in cash where needed for the advancement or education of a child." The Commission did

"not favour a rule which would enable the spouses' assets to be given immediately to the children; this would put them in a better financial position than if the marriage had not broken down whereas the object is simply to preserve their former position and to protect their reasonable expectations." [18]

Quantum of awards

The court has a wide discretion in determining the quantum of

---

[12] s. 23 (4).
[13] s. 27 (1), (3). As to the meaning of wilful neglect, see *supra*, p. 219.
[14] Law Commission 25, para. 49.
[15] s. 24 (3), M.C.A. 1973.   [16] See *supra*, p. 188.
[17] Law Commission 25, para. 70; see also *Wachtel* v. *Wachtel* [1973] Fam. 72, 90.
[18] Law Commission 25, para. 73. See also *Chamberlain* v. *Chamberlain* [1973] 1 W.L.R. 1557.

awards. It is provided [19] that in deciding whether to exercise its powers in judicial separation, nullity or divorce proceedings, and if so in what manner, the court shall:

> "have regard to all the circumstances of the case including the following matters, that is to say—
>
> > (a) the financial needs of the child;
> > (b) the income, earning capacity (if any), property and other financial resources of the child;
> > (c) any physical or mental disability of the child;
> > (d) the standard of living enjoyed by the family before the breakdown of the marriage;
> > (e) the manner in which he was being and in which the parties to the marriage expected him to be educated or trained;
>
> and so to exercise those powers as to place the child, so far as it is practicable and, having regard to—
>
> > (a) the income, earning capacity, property and other financial resources which each of the parties to the marriage has or is likely to have in the foreseeable future; and
> > (b) the financial needs, obligations and responsibilities which each of the parties to the marriage has or is likely to have in the foreseeable future [20]
>
> just to do so, in the financial position in which the child would have been if the marriage had not broken down and each of those parties had properly discharged his or her financial obligations and responsibilities towards him."

These guidelines were designed [21] to produce the result of:

> "preserving as far as possible, the pecuniary position of the child as it would have been had the marriage not broken down. However, the expectation of the child can be preserved only so far as that is consistent with justice to the parents. . . . If the marriage is dissolved the probability is that both parents will remarry and possibly one or both will have more children than was likely if they had remained married to one another. It would clearly be unjust to insist on a settlement that would leave nothing for the new dependants."

It has been said that in the vast majority of cases the financial position of a child is simply to be afforded shelter, food and education according to the means of the parents [22] so that capital provision orders will be infrequently appropriate. But if the family assets are substantial the courts may preserve a share for the children.[23] In many cases, of course, the determining factor will be the inability of the parties to provide sufficient funds to keep two families at the same level as one. There are no guidelines where the suit is on the grounds of wilful neglect: the court is

---

[19] s. 25 (2), M.C.A. 1973.
[20] s. 25 (1) (a) and (b) incorporated by reference.
[21] Explanatory Note 3 to Draft Clause 5, Law Commission 25, p. 71.
[22] *Harnett* v. *Harnett* [1973] 2 All E.R. 593, 598. The order in that case gives effect to this view by directing a settlement of property on terms giving children *use* thereof until the age of 25 or earlier marriage, but no share of the capital.
[23] *Wachtel* v. *Wachtel* (*supra*).

simply directed to do " as it thinks just." [24]   In practice, no doubt, considerations (a) to (c) above would be taken into consideration in deciding on what was a just maintenance award to make.

If the child is not the child (either biologically or by adoption) of the spouse against whom the order is made, special criteria apply.   This is considered below.[25]

Age limits

Before the Matrimonial Proceedings and Property Act 1970 there was a remarkable lack of consistency in the various statutory provisions regarding the maximum age to which orders in favour of children could extend.   That Act [26] introduced clear principles.[27]

(1) Periodical financial provision (whether secured or unsecured, and whether in nullity, divorce, judicial separation or wilful neglect proceedings) will not be ordered beyond the child's sixteenth [28] birthday. However, the court has an *unfettered* discretion to extend payments up to the child's eighteenth birthday.[29]   The reasoning behind this was that, if a child had left school but was not fully self-supporting at sixteen it was right, to enable periodical payments to be made to him, even in the absence of special circumstances.[30]

(2) Most financial provision orders cannot normally be made in respect of a child over seventeen, and periodical orders *must* determine when the child attains eighteen [31] *unless* either

> (a) the " child is, or will be, or [if provision extending beyond 18 were made] would be, receiving instruction at an educational establishment or undergoing training for a trade, profession or vocation, whether or not he is also, or will also be in gainful employment; or
> (b) there are special circumstances which justify the making of an order [which is not so restricted]." [32]

These restrictions do not apply to the powers, to *vary* nuptial settlements or to order a *settlement* of property.   Capital provision may thus be ordered for a child which may continue to take effect after he has attained majority—*e.g.* a husband could be ordered to make a settlement of capital on his children at age twenty-five; until they attained that age the income would be payable to them (unless accumulated).

The underlying philosophy of the Act is that " special justification " must be shown if an order is to be made or continued in respect of an adult child.[33]   This justification will often be education (which is there-

---

[24] s. 27 (6), M.C.A. 1973.   [25] p. 280.
[26] Now consolidated in M.C.A. 1973.
[27] See the discussion in Law Commission 25, paras. 33–41.
[28] The formula used in the Act (s. 29 (2)) is " the date of the birthday of the child next following his attaining the upper limit of the compulsory school age " so that when the school leaving age is raised to 16, orders will be continued to the 17th birthday.
[29] s. 29 (2) (a).
[30] Within the meaning discussed below—see Law Commission 25, para. 38.
[31] s. 29 (1), (2) (b).
[32] s. 29 (3).   [33] Law Commission 25, para. 39.

fore specifically included) but there may be sufficient other "special circumstances." These will often be ill-health, but there may be other cases where an order would be made, *e.g.* if a father had promised to maintain his son until he was called to the Bar.[34]

These new rules received no consideration in Parliament,[35] and are, it is submitted, unfortunate. No doubt there would be widespread agreement with the Law Commission's premiss that "maintenance obligations of parents should normally end at the age of majority at the latest." [36] But it might be better to leave the application of this social norm to the courts' discretion rather than to impose a rigid bar, the only exception to which is a statutory "special circumstances" which may well receive elaborate judicial exegesis. It is unfortunate that Parliament should not have discussed the conflict between the Law Commission's view and that previously expressed by the Latey Commission [37] (accepting the views of the President and judges of the Divorce division) that the courts should have power to make maintenance awards without limit of age. It is not encouraging to find that the Law Commission apparently did not regard it as a "special circumstance" that a young person was not fully self-supporting,[38] and that as a matter of policy the courts should not order the parents of a permanently disabled child to maintain him for life.[39]

The new principles introduced in 1970 increased the chaos of enactments dealing on different principles with child support obligations. A young person may have (fundamentally different) rights under the Divorce code, the Affiliation Proceedings Act 1957, the Guardianship of Minors Acts 1971–73, and the Matrimonial Proceedings (Magistrates' Courts) Act 1960.[40]

It should be noted that guardians and certain other third parties may apply for financial provision on behalf of a child.[41] But the position of a young person who had no third party to look after his interests (*i.e.* because he is eighteen or more), is unsatisfactory: he has no right to bring his claims before the court.[42] It was regarded as undesirable " to give a child (particularly an adult child) a power to take his parents to court to obtain finance because, for example, he wanted to embark on a scheme of training which they were not prepared to support." This applies principles which are, no doubt, valid in the normal united family but are less so in a state of family breakdown: a child who could reasonably expect financial support should not be prevented from apply-

---

[34] Law Commission 25, para. 39.
[35] The debates on the Bill were truncated to enable it to be passed before Parliament was dissolved for the 1970 Election.
[36] Law Commission 25, para. 40.
[37] Para. 249.
[38] Law Commission 25, para. 38.
[39] *Ibid.*, para. 40.
[40] See for examples Cretney (1970) 33 M.L.R. at p. 676.
[41] M.C.R. 1971, r. 69.
[42] See Law Commission 25, para. 42.

ing for it merely because on this one issue his parents agree (possibly because the mother thinks her own maintenance will be reduced if the father has to support a child). In any case, as has already been pointed out, a child of eighteen or more *has* an independent right to apply to the court under the Guardianship of Minors Act provided that he has at some earlier time been the subject of an order under that Act.

Ensuring proper arrangements

Divorce cases were traditionally contests between adults: there was, therefore, a significant risk that the interests of the children would not be adequately safeguarded. Particular concern was expressed by the Morton Commission on the following points [43]:

> " (i) The court does not deal with the position of the children where no application is made for custody. It cannot be assumed that parents, influenced by strong feelings arising from divorce, are always likely to make the best arrangements for the children. There is at present no guarantee in such cases that the arrangements for the children have been maturely considered.
>
> (ii) Where an application for custody is unopposed it may be assumed that the court will grant the application. In the absence of any evidence to the contrary, it is indeed difficult to see on what grounds refusal could be justified. Yet the parent making the application may not always be the more suitable to have custody. There may, for instance, have been an understanding between husband and wife that if one of them will release the other by getting a divorce, the latter will allow the successful party to have the children.
>
> (iii) Where custody is contested between the parties, other difficulties arise. Each of them is anxious to have custody, but it is open to question whether the contest always indicates that the parties are moved solely or even primarily by the desire to safeguard the children's interests. Passions are aroused in divorce and judgments distorted. One party may contest the other's claim to custody from spiteful or selfish motives. The children are then in danger of becoming pawns in the struggle of wills. In circumstances of that kind, the judge in deciding custody may in the end be forced back to the test of which of the parents was the innocent party in the divorce suit.
>
> (iv) In a contested application for custody the procedure is unsatisfactory in that too much reliance is placed on affidavit evidence, the parties are not usually present and the application may be heard by a different judge from the judge who has tried the main issue."

The Commission concluded [44] that a procedure was needed to ensure that the parents themselves had given full consideration to the question of their children's future welfare, and to make the control of the court over the welfare of the children more effective. This was to be done by

---

43 Para. 366.
44 Para. 372.

a rule that the decree nisi should not normally be made absolute unless and until the court had satisfied itself that the arrangements proposed for the care and upbringing of the children were the best that could be devised in the circumstances.[45] Legislation to give effect to this proposal was enacted in 1958 [46]; some changes of detail were made in 1970 on the recommendation of the Law Commission.[47] The law is now contained in section 41 of the Matrimonial Causes Act 1973:

(1) The court shall not make absolute a decree of divorce or of nullity of marriage, or grant a decree of judicial separation, unless the court, by order, has declared that it is satisfied—

(a) that for the purposes of this section there are no children of the family [48] to whom this section applies; or

(b) that the only children who are or may be [49] children of the family to whom this section applies are the children named in the order and that—

(i) arrangements [50] for the welfare of every child so named have been made and are satisfactory or are the best that can be devised in the circumstances; or

(ii) it is impracticable for the party or parties appearing before the court to make any such arrangements; or

(c) that there are circumstances [51] making it desirable that the decree should be made absolute or should be made, as the case may be, without delay notwithstanding that there are or may be children of the family to whom this section applies and that the court is unable to make a declaration in accordance with paragraph (b) above.[52]

It is provided [53] that " welfare " includes the custody and education of the child and financial provision for him.

The following points should be noted:

(i) If the court fails to make the declaration, any final decree will be void.[54] It follows that a subsequent marriage relying on that decree will itself be void. But if the declaration is erroneous (if, e.g. it declares that

---

[45] Para. 373.

[46] s. 2, Matrimonial Proceedings (Children) Act 1958.

[47] Law Commission 25, paras. 45–46.

[48] For the meaning of this expression see p. 280, infra.

[49] If there is a dispute as to whether a child is or is not within the definition, the court may (without prejudice to his status) make the declaration.

[50] The court should not approve arrangements unless they are of a reasonably permanent character: McKernan v. McKernan (1970) 114 S.J. 284.

[51] The Morton Commission thought that this power would be used in cases where the making of a decree absolute would normally be expedited: see Report, para. 375.

[52] If the court does make a decree absolute under s. 17 (1) (c), it must obtain a satisfactory undertaking from either or both of the parties to bring the question of arrangement for the children before the court within a specified time: s. 17 (2).

[53] s. 41 (6).

[54] s. 41 (3).

there are no children to whom the section applies, when in fact there are [55]) the decree will be valid.

(ii) The section applies to any minor child of the family who is either (a) under the age of sixteen, or (b) under eighteen and receiving educational instruction or training for a trade, profession or vocation (whether or not he is also in gainful employment).[56] There may, however, also be adult " children " for whom arrangements should be made: the court may therefore direct that the section shall apply to such a child if there are special circumstances which make it desirable in the interest of the child that the section should apply.[57]

(iii) It will be noted that even if the arrangements proposed are not satisfactory, the court may still make a declaration if they are " the best that can be devised in the circumstances." [58]

(iv) There are procedural rules designed to ensure that the court has adequate information for its decision.[59]

The Morton Commission attached great importance to these proposals. Not only would they ensure that the court would investigate the children's interests, thus making their welfare just as important as the question of divorce. There would be a further " positive and beneficial result " :

> " If the interests of the children were thus placed in the forefront the parents themselves would, we believe, be led increasingly to recognise their responsibility towards their children, and to appreciate that the fact of divorce, far from diminishing that responsibility, makes it all the more important that they should strive to make the best arrangements which they can devise for the children in the new situation created by the dissolution of the marriage. . . . [T]he main merit of the scheme we put forward is that it would encourage . . . a sense of parental responsibility. And if parents were thus made to realise at the outset their obligations to their children we would hope that they would sometimes decide to abandon the idea of divorce for the sake of their children." [60]

Although the Act no doubt ensures that the parties give some thought to the arrangements to be made for children, it seems doubtful whether the rule has anything like such a decisive influence as the Morton Commission intended. In 1966, Mr. John Hall (at the request of the Law Commission) undertook a survey into the functioning of the law.[61]

---

[55] *Cf. P.* v. *P.* [1970] P. 161 (child born after decree nisi); and *B.* v. *B.* [1961] 2 All E.R. 396 (declaration inadvertently not made). Since 19 judges (out of 97) asked whether they had ever suspected that there might be another child of the family in existence apart from those disclosed answered " yes," it is as well that the decree is unimpeachable if an order is made, however incorrect the assumptions on which it is based: P.W.P. 15, p. 4.

[56] s. 41 (5) (*a*).

[57] s. 41 (5) (*b*).

[58] *Cf.* s. 10 (3) (*b*), M.C.A. 1973, adopting a similar formulation in providing protection for divorces based on separation.

[59] A statement as to the present and proposed arrangements must be filed with the petition: M.C.R. 1971, r. 8 (2), and Form 4.

[60] Paras. 376–377.   [61] Published (1968) as Published Working Paper 15.

This revealed a considerable divergence of judicial practice. If there is no dispute between the parents, some judges " obviously feel that it is generally better to adopt the parents' own wishes; whereas others ' do not really think the agreement of the parents has much bearing on the matter '. . . ." [62] Inevitably the court will often appear to be merely " rubber-stamping " the proposals [63]: " judges are hampered by insufficient time and facilities (and perhaps also by the fact that their experience before appointment was in quite different fields) to enable them at the hearing of the petition to conduct a wholly satisfactory enquiry into the arrangements which are proposed. . . ." [64] Also there is no machinery (apart from the rarely invoked supervision order) [65] to ensure that the arrangements proposed are in fact carried out.[66]

It seems probable that few decrees are ever refused, but the procedure does ensure (a) that parties have to give some thought to the arrangements, and (b) the possibility that a decree may be refused sometimes has a salutary effect.[67]

CHILDREN IN RESPECT OF WHOM THE STATUTORY POWERS MAY BE EXERCISED

Powers under the *Guardianship of Minors Acts 1971–73* can only be invoked by a *parent* [68] or legally appointed guardian of the child,[69] and financial orders can only be made against a parent.

In the case of the powers under the *Matrimonial Proceedings (Magistrates' Courts) Act 1960*, and under the *Matrimonial Proceedings and Property Act 1970*,[69a] however, the position is more complex. The National Assistance Act 1948,[70] adopted the principle that a man or woman should be under an obligation to support his spouse, and his or her *own* children. This therefore made the blood tie the exclusive test of responsibility. But a family group may include children, such as the children of one spouse by a previous marriage, or the wife's illegitimate children, who have *in fact* been taken into the group, and come to rely on it for support. If there is a family dispute it is equally *their* home which may be broken up in consequence. Hence it seemed to many that the spouses should not be allowed to disclaim the responsibilities assumed when the children were taken into the family.[71] After some hesitation,[72]

---

[62] P.W.P. 15, p. 9.
[63] *Ibid.*, p. 34.
[64] *Ibid.*, p. 13.
[65] *Supra*, p. 263.
[66] See P.W.P. 15, pp. 27–32.
[67] *Ibid.*, p. 10.
[68] Including a natural and adoptive parent.
[69] *Supra*, p. 250.
[69a] Now M.C.A. 1973.
[70] s. 42.
[71] Morton Report, para. 393.
[72] See the Parliamentary debates on the 2nd Reading of the *Matrimonial Proceedings (Children) Bill*, February 7, 1968, Hansard (H.C.) Vol. 581, and on the Matrimonial Proceedings (Magistrates' Courts) Bill 1960, Hansard (H.L.) Vol. 220.

Parliament broadened the area of legal family responsibility in divorce court and magistrates' court proceedings by recognising that *acceptance* of a child of the other spouse into the family might impose a legal duty to maintain it [73]; but it was still necessary for the child to be the offspring of *one* of the spouses. This compromise between a test based on the blood tie and a test based on acceptance into the family was somewhat illogical and could produce anomalies.[74] Furthermore, the courts gave a restrictive interpretation to the formula about " acceptance " of a child. The Matrimonial Proceedings and Property Act 1970 substantially amended the law in its application to proceedings in divorce courts, but the old test still applies under the Matrimonial Proceedings (Magistrates' Courts) Act 1960. It is therefore necessary to consider the two separately.

Magistrates' Courts

Children of the family

The courts' powers (*e.g.* to order custody, access or maintenance) can only be exercised in relation to a " child of the family." This is defined [75] to mean:

(a) *Any child of both parties*

This includes any biological child of both parties, whether legitimate or illegitimate, and any child adopted by them both jointly [76]; and

(b) *Any other child of either party who has been accepted as one of the family by the other party*

This provision requires explanation:

(i) The child must be a child of *one* party to the marriage. This will, however, include a child *adopted* by one party,[77] as well as his or her illegitimate child by another partner, or the child of a previous marriage. But the orphan child of a relative cannot be within this definition however dependent he is on the spouses.

(ii) He must have been " accepted as one of the family by the other party." This seemingly simple formula has received elaborate judicial exegesis:

(1) There cannot be an acceptance without some mutual arrangement between the natural parent and his spouse to treat the child as if he were the child of both.[78] If, therefore, the natural parent refuses from the outset to allow the other to have any control or exercise any of the rights of a parent over the child, there cannot be an acceptance.[79] Undue possessiveness by the natural parent is relevant in determining whether

---

73 And corresponding rights to seek custody, access, etc.
74 Law Commission 25, para. 24.
75 s. 16 (1) M.P.(M.C.)A. 1960.
76 *Ibid.*
77 *Ibid.*
78 *Bowlas* v. *Bowlas* [1965] P. 450; *Dixon* v. *Dixon* [1967] 3 All E.R. 659.
79 *P. (R.)* v. *P. (P.)* [1969] 3 All E.R. 777; *G.* v. *G.* (1965) 109 S.J. 831; conversely, there cannot be an acceptance under duress: *S.* v. *S.* (1969) 113 S.J. 426.

there has been a sufficient mutuality, but only as one fact amongst many to be taken into account.[80]

(2) Whether there has been an acceptance or not is a question of fact [81] which must be ascertained by reference to an objective, not a subjective test.[82] In normal circumstances, the fact that a man marries a woman with children and establishes a joint home is evidence of the fact of acceptance.[83] Payment by the non-parent of the expenses of a family unit which includes the child will in the absence of a clear contrary intention lead to a conclusion that there has been an assumption of responsibility, notwithstanding that other resources may be available to contribute to the child's maintenance.[84]

(3) The acceptance must be into a *family*, not a mere collection of bricks and mortar.[85] Simply allowing a child to live in the matrimonial home does not constitute acceptance; conversely, there can be acceptance even if there is no matrimonial home.[86]

(4) The relevant time for determining whether there has been an acceptance is normally the date of the marriage. A consent to accept a child into the family given before marriage, however strongly it is expressed, may be withdrawn if there is an intervening change of mind.[87] But if there is an acceptance still in force at the date of the marriage it cannot subsequently be withdrawn because of the subsequent behaviour either of the natural parent or of the child.[88] It is, however, possible, provided the intention is made clear at the time of the marriage, for the non-parent to stipulate for a period of probation, reserving his decision whether to accept the child until a later date.[89]

There may be an acceptance *after* the marriage,[90] provided there remains a family into which the child can be accepted.[91]

(5) It has been held in a number of cases [92] that there can be no acceptance unless the acceptor had full knowledge of all the relevant

---

[80] *Dixon* v. *Dixon* (*supra*), *cf.* p. 662.

[81] *Bowlas* v. *Bowlas* (*supra*).

[82] *Snow* v. *Snow* [1972] Fam. 74.

[83] *Bowlas* v. *Bowlas* (*supra*), at p. 459 (*per* Davies L.J.).

[84] *e.g.* his own private income, or payments from his natural parent: see *Snow* v. *Snow* (*supra*). The existence of such funds may be relevant to *quantum*, however.

[85] *B.* v. *B.* [1969] P. 37; *Bowlas* v. *Bowlas* (*supra*); *S.* v. *S.* (*supra*).

[86] *Caller* v. *Caller* [1968] P. 39.

[87] " The fact that . . . when everything was rose-coloured, the husband had said or intimated that he was going to marry her, and make the children members of the family seems to me to be beside the point. One has to see what the position was at the time of the marriage. The justices ought to have asked themselves: did this man, on the day that he married, marry this woman on the basis that he was then accepting the children as the children of the family? " (*per* Salmon L.J., *Bowlas* v. *Bowlas* (*supra*) at p. 462; *Snow* v. *Snow* (*supra*).

[88] *Snow* v. *Snow* (*supra*).

[89] *Ibid.*

[90] *Kirkwood* v. *Kirkwood* [1970] 2 All E.R. 161.

[91] *B.* v. *B.* (*supra*) where it was held that, by the time the husband had sufficient knowledge to accept his wife's children (see *infra*, p. 277), the family unit had been destroyed.

[92] *R.* v. *R.* [1968] P. 414; *Re L.* [1968] P. 119; *B.* v. *B.* (*supra*).

facts at the time of the purported acceptance. In *R.* v. *R.*,[93] for instance, the parties married in 1943. A child was born in 1956. It was brought up normally by the father as his child. In 1961, however, he discovered documents which led him to believe that he was not the father. He immediately repudiated wife and child and started divorce proceedings. Blood test evidence [94] was available, which established conclusively that he was not the father. It was held that he had not " accepted " the child:

> " The fact that for 5 years the petitioner maintained the child and treated her as his daughter would ordinarily be regarded as overwhelming evidence both of his consent to receive her and of his acceptance of her as one of the family. In this case, however, the petitioner acted in this manner throughout that period solely because he believed, and had every reason for believing, that the child was in fact his. It was not until 1961 that it became reasonably clear to him that she was not. It was then that he first had the opportunity with knowledge of the material facts either to consent to receive her as one of the family or to refuse to receive her. Without any hesitation he refused to receive her."

The result of this holding was that no orders for custody or maintenance could be made in respect of the eleven-year-old girl (and it was too late [95] to start affiliation proceedings against the natural father).

It should be stressed that the court cannot exercise *any* of its statutory powers unless the child is a child of the family: in *B.* v. *B.* [96] a deserted husband sought *access* to the children, of whom he was fond, and to whose maintenance he was prepared to contribute. It was held that the court had no jurisdiction to make such an order, since the children were not within the statutory definition. But the courts refused to carry the principle to extremes: in *Kirkwood* v. *Kirkwood* [97] the husband denied that he had accepted the wife's children, since he had believed them to be *legitimate* children of her former marriage, whereas in fact they were *illegitimate*. It was held that his misapprehension was not of such a fundamental character to negative acceptance. The difference from the earlier case is that there the husband had never, at the time when he was treating the child as a child of the family [98] any doubt that it was his own child. He therefore never directed his mind to the question whether he was prepared to accept another man's child or children into the family.[99] If the husband knows at the time of the alleged acceptance that the child is not his, and that he therefore has a *choice* whether to accept it or not, non-disclosure of material facts about the child is immaterial.

[93] *Supra.*
[94] See *infra*, p. 317.
[95] *Infra.*
[96] [1969] P. 37.
[97] [1970] 2 All E.R. 161.
[98] *Per* Bagnall J., *Snow* v. *Snow* [1972] Fam. 74, 89F. The significance of the learned judge's use of the formula " treated " as a child of the family will emerge below: p. 280.
[99] *Per* Ormrod J., *Kirkwood* v. *Kirkwood* [1970] 2 All E.R. at p. 164.

It remains to be said that in *Snow* v. *Snow* one member of the Court of Appeal [1] suggested that "accepted" had nothing to do with offer and acceptance, and could be equated with "treated as" or "taken in" as a child of the family. This, it is respectfully submitted, is good sense, but difficult to reconcile with the earlier authorities, which must be treated as good law until overruled.

Quantum of awards

Although the first object is to enable orders to be made in respect of a step-child, the second object is that justice should be done as between husband, wife and any other person concerned (such as the child's natural father). [2] The Act therefore provides [3] that—

> "In considering whether any, and if so what, [maintenance] provision should be included in a matrimonial order for payments by one of the parties in respect of a child who is not a child of that party, the court shall have regard to the extent, if any, to which that party had, on or after the acceptance of the child as one of the family, asumed responsibility for the child's maintenance, and to the liability of any person other than a party to the marriage to maintain the child."

The courts also consider any other relevant matter to enable a decision to be reached as to what is a fair provision. [4]

Extent of responsibility assumed

It is the *extent* of the obligation which is relevant, not the *length of time* for which it has endured: in *Roberts* v. *Roberts* [5] the husband had only assumed responsibility for the child's maintenance for four months and in *Snow* v. *Snow* [6] for not more than fourteen weeks. Since in each case he had assumed *full* responsibility during that period, he was fully liable. It has been said that quantum may be anything from 0 to 100 per cent. [7]

Liability of other persons

The "other person" will normally be the child's natural father (against whom an affiliation order might be obtained). [8] If payments are actually being made by a third party the court would take this into

---

[1] Davies L.J. at p. 114, a somewhat surprising dictum in view of the fact that in *Re L.* (*supra*) the same learned Lord Justice had assumed the correctness of *R.* v. *R.* in which the "contractual" test was adumbrated.

[2] *Snow* v. *Snow* (*supra*), *per* Sir J. Simon P. at p. 98.

[3] s. 2 (5).

[4] *Snow* v. *Snow* (*supra*).

[5] [1962] P. 212.

[6] *Supra.*

[7] *Per* Willmer L.J., *Bowlas* v. *Bowlas* [1965] P. 450, 458.

[8] *Infra*, p. 321. Or there may be an order in previous matrimonial proceedings: a child who has been held to be a child of the family in a divorce suit may, as a result of his parent's remarriage, become the child of another family: *Newman* v. *Newman* [1971] P. 93.

account on general principles in assessing the proper quantum of maintenance. The specific direction under this head will normally arise
where the natural parent might be put under a legal obligation to support
the child, although he is not currently liable under a judgment or order.

The court must have regard to the extent to which this liability
could in practice be enforced rather than its theoretical extent. In *Snow*
v. *Snow* [9] it was argued that, since the natural father of an illegitimate
child is liable to maintain him to the full, then if his identity is known
and traceable, and there is no bar to obtaining an affiliation order against
him, the husband step-father was exempt from liability. This argument
was dismissed as "insupportable." [10] It would produce absurd results
and mean that no order could be made in most cases where the natural
father was identified and alive, even if he were a tramp living on supplementary benefit, whereas the husband was a millionaire. If an order
has been obtained, the "liability" is prima facie the amount of the order.
If it has not, the liability is the amount that would be ordered in the
relevant proceedings.[11]

Discretion

Even if the husband has fully accepted the child, and there is no
third party under a liability the court retains a residual discretion to do
what is just in all the circumstances. In *Smith* v. *Smith* for instance, the
facts [12] were that:

> "The petitioner husband, who is a labourer, was married on
> December 23, 1957, to a wife who was a widow with two children.
> ... Under the influence, no doubt of matrimonial bliss, he treated
> them as children of the family. ... But though matrimonial bliss
> produced the birth of a child of the husband and wife on
> November 10, 1958, the bliss in fact only lasted for about 4 months,
> because at the end of that period the husband was ejected by the
> wife from her house, and within a month of the birth of his child
> the wife committed adultery, it appears, with another man. In those
> circumstances, the footing upon which the children were adopted or
> treated as members of the family must have suffered something of
> a blow."

In these circumstances no order at all was made: "it would have been
very unjust to saddle the husband with the maintenance of these two
children for whom he was in no way responsible."

---

[9] *Supra.*

[10] *Per* Edmund Davies L.J. In *Roberts* v. *Roberts* the Divisional Court held that when
it is proved that an illegitimate child formed part of its father's household within
12 months of its birth, that is prima facie evidence that he has paid money for the
child's maintenance. Paradoxically, therefore, if the mother has lived in the same
household as her child's father immediately after the birth she will probably be able
to bring affiliation proceedings against him, even long after the 12 months (now 3
years—see *infra*, p. 323) period, and thus reduce her husband's potential liability to
the child. If, however, she has never lived with the father, and successfully deceived
her husband for many years, it will be too late to get an affiliation order, and
(assuming *R.* v. *R.* to be correct) the husband will be under no liability.

[11] *Snow* v. *Snow* (*supra*).   [12] *Per* Danckwerts L.J.

Divorce Courts—Statutory Jurisdiction

Children of the family

The objections to the definition discussed above are:

(a) It may operate in a bizarre way, by preventing the court making orders for access, in relation to children who have formed part of the social unit created by the family. If applied to divorce proceedings it may prevent the court inquiring into whether satisfactory arrangements have been made for such a child,[13] notwithstanding that he has for many years been a dependent member of it.

(b) The child's welfare was at risk. As the Law Commission put it [14]:

> " It may be hard for a cuckolded husband to have to continue to bear a responsibility which he has assumed in ignorance of some of the relevant facts. But his ignorance is not the fault of the child but of the wife whom he took for better or worse, and the hardship to the child of being deprived of support is even greater."

Furthermore, the provision did not promote reconciliation: if a husband discovered that the child was not his, the safest course was to repudiate it immediately, to prevent his being fixed with full liability for maintenance on the basis of acceptance.[15]

A new definition of " child of the family " was therefore incorporated into the Matrimonial Proceedings and Property Act 1970.[16] For the purposes of proceedings under the Matrimonial Causes Act 1973 [17]:

> " child of the family," in relation to the parties to a marriage, means—
> (a) a child of both of those parties; and
> (b) any other child, not being a child who has been boarded-out with those parties by a local authority or voluntary organisation,[18] who has been treated by both of those parties as a child of their family; "

This provision was intended to change the law, in the proceedings to which it applies, to overcome the cases on " acceptance " discussed above.[19] It has successfully done so: in *W. (R. J.)* v. *W. (S. J.)* [20] the

---

13 Under s. 41, M.C.A. 1973, *supra*, p. 271.   14 Law Commission 25, para. 28.
15 See, *e.g. B.* v. *B.* (*supra*) but *cf. per* Ormrod J., *Holmes* v. *Holmes* [1966] 1 W.L.R. 187: " I hope that this valuable power that the court now has to protect the children who have in fact been accepted into the family will not lead people to rejecting the children lest they be saddled with the maintenance for them . . . the court should be very cautious when it is asked to hold that a child has been accepted as a child of the family without evidence of some explicit agreement between the spouses. Proof of acceptance, of course, may be given by evidence of conduct, but it must be clear and unequivocal. To hold otherwise is to encourage explicit rejection of such children and thus to promote a deal of unkindness to these unhappy children."
16 s. 27 (1), now s. 52 (1), M.C.A. 1973.
17 *I.e.* divorce, nullity, judicial separation (or wilful neglect if brought in the Superior Courts).
18 This means children taken into care by a local authority, and then boarded out by them with foster parents. The reason for excluding such children was that the authority was in *loco parentis* to the child: see Law Commission 25, para. 31.
19 *Cf. per* Davies L.J. in *Snow* v. *Snow* at p. 114, who regarded this provision as support for the view that " accepted " and " treated " were synonymous.
20 [1972] Fam. 152.

facts were very similar to those in *R.* v. *R.*[21] The husband had assumed that he was the father of the children. As soon as he discovered that he was not, he repudiated them. It was held (in contrast to the result in *R.'s* case) that they were children of the family, because they had been " treated " by both spouses as such, even though the husband had been under a misapprehension as to their parentage. Park J. (who had decided *R.* v. *R.*) rejected arguments that " treated " must mean " treated with knowledge of the material facts," and that where the wife deceived the husband about paternity she could not treat the children as members of the family (because she must have had a mental reservation that they were not members of the family). The test of " treatment " seems purely objective, and it is immaterial *for the purposes of deciding whether a child falls within the definition* that the wife has deceived the husband.

The fact that a child is held to fall within this definition does not mean that the spouse who is not his natural or adoptive parent will be held liable to maintain him in full, irrespective of the circumstances. The court is specifically directed,[21] in deciding whether, and if so how, to exercise its power to order financial provision :

> " to have regard (among the circumstances of the case)—
>> (a) to whether that party had assumed any responsibility for the child's maintenance and, if so, to the extent to which, and the basis upon which, that party assumed such responsibility and to the length of time for which that party discharged such responsibility;
>> (b) to whether in assuming and discharging such responsibility that party did so knowing that the child was not his or her own;
>> (c) to the liability of any other person to maintain the child."

These provisions are designed to enable the court to achieve substantial justice. Subsection (a) will cover the unusual case where there was no assumption of financial responsibility, or only the assumption of a *limited* responsibility (*e.g.* " I will be responsible for any needs over those covered by covenanted payments from the child's grandfather "). It will also enable the court to reduce maintenance in cases where the assumption of responsibility has only lasted for a short period. Subsection (b) recognises that, although the husband's ignorance of the truth no longer deprives the court of all its powers, it may well be highly relevant to quantify his liability. Subsection (c) largely follows the old law, but will extend (for instance) to allow the liability of the natural parents of a child of neither spouse to be considered.

The High Court: The Wardship Jurisdiction

This jurisdiction originated in the prerogative power of the Sovereign as *parens patriae*.[22] Traditionally, it was delegated to the Lord Chancel-

---

21 s. 25 (3), and see s. 27 (4) (wilful neglect).
22 Craffe, *op. cit.*, p. 68 *et seq.*, and p. 187 *et seq.*; Latey Report, para. 192 *et seq.*; Cross (1967) 83 L.Q.R. 200.

lor and other judges of the Court of Chancery and between 1875 and 1971 it was exercised by the judges of the Chancery Division of the High Court. The Administration of Justice Act 1970 transferred the jurisdiction to the Family Division,[23] which, however, still acts on the principles developed over the years in the Chancery Court.

The minors in respect of whom jurisdiction is exercised are called "Wards of Court." The original function of the court was to protect the property of a minor whose parents were dead or unavailable,[24] and was in practice only of concern to the wealthy:

> "The typical Ward of Court of the 18th and 19th Centuries was a wealthy orphan—the 'pretty young ward in Chancery' of the Lord Chancellor's song in 'Iolanthe.' The chief function of the Court was to supervise the administration of the ward's property by his or her guardian and, if she was a girl, to consider—and if thought fit to approve—proposals for her marriage and to see that her property was safeguarded by a suitable marriage settlement." [25]

The jurisdiction was invoked by bringing proceedings for the administration of a settlement under which the child was a beneficiary, although it became increasingly common to settle a small sum [26] *ad hoc* for the express purpose of starting wardship proceedings. In 1949, the necessity to resort to this expedient was abolished, and it was provided [27] that

> "(1) Subject to the provisions of this section no infant shall be made a ward of court except by virtue of an order to that effect made by the court.[28]
>
> (2) Where application is made for such an order in respect of an infant, the infant shall become a ward of court on the making of the application, but shall cease to be a ward of court at the expiration of such period as may be prescribed by rules of court unless within that period an order has been made in accordance with the application."

In 1950, Legal Aid became available and the number of applications increased substantially: in 1967 there were some 2,000 wards of court, and in a high proportion of the cases legal aid was involved.[29]

The main characteristics of the wardship jurisdiction are as follows:

(1) The court exercises an extensive and, if necessary, detailed [30]

---

[23] s. 1 (2).

[24] Latey Report, para. 193.

[25] Memorandum of the Judges of the Chancery Division to the Latey Commission, quoted at para. 200.

[26] Usually £50. See Report of the Denning Committee, Cmd. 7024, para. 32.

[27] Law Reform (Miscellaneous Provisions) Act 1949, s. 9. The object of this measure may have been partly to avoid children becoming wards of court without this being either intended or appreciated: *Re N.* [1967] Ch. 512.

[28] It has been held that the result is that the court can no longer exercise its inherent powers over a child unless he has been made a ward under this provision: *Re E. (An Infant)* [1956] Ch. 23 but *cf. Re N.* [1967] Ch. 512 and *L. v. L.* [1969] P. 25.

[29] Cross, *op. cit.*, p. 203.

[30] For an example, see the order noted in *Re R.(P.M.) (An Infant)* [1968] 1 All E.R. 691, which deals *inter alia* with the number of letters to be written to the ward and arrangements for collecting luggage.

control over the ward, whose custody vests in the court[31]: all important issues affecting the ward must be brought before the court[32] which will decide where it should live, where it should be educated, whether it should be allowed to marry, and so on. The court's jurisdiction is exhaustive, and it seeks to offer all the protection of a parent.[33]

(2) Any minor[34] may be made a ward. The jurisdiction is not subject to the restrictions in Divorce and Magistrates Courts proceedings, and there is no need for any matrimonial or other dispute to exist between his parents. "The only way in which a boy or girl over sixteen who has committed no criminal offence can be subjected to judicial control is by making him or her a ward of court."[35]

(3) Wardship proceedings can be started by any person having a sufficient interest[36]: a grandmother, for instance, could start proceedings if she considered that neither parent was suitable to exercise control.[37] She would have no *locus standi* in any matrimonial proceedings between them, nor could she invoke the *statutory* procedure under the Guardianship of Minors Acts 1971–73.

4. Even if another court or administrative agency has taken decisions under statutory powers about the child's welfare, the wardship jurisdiction is not for all purposes ousted or abrogated. The jurisdiction may be invoked as the residual protection for children.[38]

5. The procedure of the court ensures a thorough ventilation of the issues involved. In the words of Lord Cross of Chelsea[39]:

"Clearly a wardship case differs altogether from ordinary litigation. In an ordinary action the court has before it two parties, each of whom asserts that he has a legal right to a decision in his favour. The function of the judge is to act as umpire at the fight and to decide which side has won. In a wardship case the court is asked to take the child into its care and to decide how and with whom it is best for the child to be brought up. The role of the parties is simply to put before the judge for his consideration their suggestions with regard to the ward's upbringing."

The distinctive features of the procedure include:

The use of the Official Solicitor to represent the ward's interest

The Official Solicitor will be appointed *guardian ad litem* in cases

31 *Re W. (An Infant)* [1964] Ch. 202.
32 See *F. v. S. (Adoption: Ward)* [1973] 2 W.L.R. 178. For a striking illustration see *Bolton v. Bolton* [1891] 3 Ch. 270, where a man applied for (and obtained) leave to pay his addresses to the ward in terms which would comply with the court's directions and orders.
33 Latey Report, para. 193.
34 *i.e.* a person under 18: see Family Law Reform Act 1969, s. 1.
35 Cross, *op. cit.*, p. 204.
36 *Cf. Re Dunhill* (1967) 111 S.J. 113, where a night club owner made a 20-year-old girl a ward of court largely for publicity purposes. It is now necessary for the applicant to state his relationship to the minor and the proceedings may be dismissed if they are an abuse of the process of the court.   37 Cross, *op. cit.*, p. 204.
38 See *infra*, p. 305, for the limitations on this principle.   39 *Op. cit.*, at p. 207.

where the court feels that the ward should be separately represented [40]—
i.e. almost invariably when proceedings have been started because of a
disagreement between the ward on the one hand and the parents on the
other, and frequently where the dispute is between parents over the
upbringing of a young child. The object is to ensure that the ward's
interests and point of view may be represented by an objective outsider,
and to insulate the child so far as possible from the effects of any conflict
between the parents and to ensure that decisions are taken in the child's
interest.[41] The Official Solicitor plays a dual role: he is an officer
of the court and the ward's guardian, and he is a solicitor whose client is
the ward—not his parents.[42] In all cases he makes a full investigation
and reports to the court. He will see not only the people directly concerned, but others including specialists where useful [43]: indeed, if it is
desired to introduce psychiatric evidence the Official Solicitor will decide
(subject to the views of the court) whether an examination is desirable,[44]
and he will instruct the psychiatrist so as to ensure that he has
unbiased instructions, all relevant material, can see all parties, and
not be subject to the temptation to take the side of the party instructing
him.[45] In the (common) case where the proceedings have been started
by parents to break up what they consider to be an undesirable
association between their daughter and a man, the role of the Official
Solicitor has been vividly described by the Latey Commission [46]:

> " The Official Solicitor ordinarily sees the girl first and hears her
> side of the story. In the words of the . . . Judges it often comes as a
> surprise to these girls to find that the Official Solicitor is not there
> simply to ' rubber stamp ' their parents' views—but to consider
> dispassionately what is really best for them; and here, of course, lies
> the possibility of success. But obviously without some measure of
> co-operation—if only passive and grudging co-operation—from the
> ward herself the chances of success are small. . . .
>   The Official Solicitor then sees the parents, probes their evidence
> and finds out as much as he can of the family background, seeing
> others where useful. Finally he sees the young man concerned.
> He then makes a written report and submissions to the Judge."

The Official Solicitor's department discharges its duties with humanity
and expertise,[47] and often the full and sympathetic investigation of an
emotional problem itself has a therapeutic effect. The Official Solicitor
is not however bound, in making his report to the court, to accept the
views of the ward or any expert instructed by him, nor is the court bound
to accept his recommendations. But his report will ensure that the facts
are considered.

[40] There were 67 new references in 1971: Civil Judicial Statistics, Table 15.
[41] Latey Report, paras. 206–207.
[42] *Per* Goff J., *Re R. (P. M.)* [1968] 1 All E.R. 691, 692.   [43] Latey Report, para. 213.
[44] Although if both sides agree on the need for an examination and the identity of the
psychiatrist, the court will normally give effect to their wishes.
[45] *Per* Cross J., *Re S.* [1967] 1 All E.R. 202, 209; *Re R. (P. M.)* (*supra*); *B. (M.)* v.
B. (R.) [1968] 3 All E.R. 170.
[46] Paras. 209–210.   [47] Latey Report, para. 214.

Special rules of evidence

Wardship proceedings are not subject to the normal rules of evidence and procedure applicable to ordinary litigation where the judge is simply an arbiter between two parties, and need only consider what they choose to put before him. The judge may see the child and perhaps one or other or both parents in private. It is the practice [48] to admit hearsay evidence if that is the best available, and the judge may take into account the contents of a confidential report (*e.g.* by the Official Solicitor) without disclosing its contents to the parents, even though the ordinary rules of natural justice might require the disclosure to them of any adverse allegations against them. The judge will attach very great weight indeed to the principle that he should not base a conclusion adverse to a parent on information which that party has not seen and has had no opportunity of challenging or contesting, not only because of the conflict with the rules of natural justice, but also because this may engender a sense of grievance—itself adverse to the ward's welfare—in the parent. In many cases a solution to the conflict will be found in disclosing the contents of the confidential report to the parties' legal advisers on terms that they will not be disclosed to the parties personally. But if the judge is satisfied that disclosure will result in real harm to the ward, he is entitled to keep the contents secret.[49]

Privacy

Wardship proceedings are heard in Chambers, in private. There may be cases, however, where publicity is sought—*e.g.* to try to establish the whereabouts of children who have been removed by one party.[50] Committal orders for contempt are normaly heard in private, although details of any order made are given in open court.[51]

The existence of a wide range of ancillary powers

The following should be noted:

(i) The court has a wide power to enforce its orders by injunction, breach of which will be a contempt.[52] Orders are commonly made preventing the removal of a child from the jurisdiction,[53] or (perhaps

---

48 This practice may be open to review in the House of Lords: *Re K.* (*Infants*) [1965] A.C. 201; *Rossage* v. *Rossage* [1960] 1 All E.R. 600.

49 *Re K.* (*Infants*) (*supra*); see also *Re D.* (*Infants*) [1970] 1 All E.R. 1088; *Re P. A.* (*An Infant*) [1971] 3 All E.R. 522; Cross, *op. cit.*, pp. 208–209.

50 See *e.g. Re Wolfe* [1958] C.L.Y. 1619. But it is often difficult in practice to trace a ward, since the police usually are not prepared to assist. But the records of various government departments may be examined in an attempt to trace a ward or the person with whom the ward is said to be: *Practice Note* (*Disclosure of Addresses*) [1973] 1 W.L.R. 60.

51 R.S.C., O. 52, r. 6.

52 Punishable by fine (which is rarely imposed—see Latey Report, para. 204) or imprisonment.

53 There is a special Home Office procedure available to stop unauthorised removal: *Practice Note*, July 13, 1963 [1963] C.L.Y. 1804. The court seeks to discourage " kidnapping " cases, where a parent refused custody in one country brings the child here in the hope that the court will not allow him to be taken away. The court

less often today) prohibiting an intended marriage or association. In spite of the wording of section 9 of the Law Reform (Miscellaneous Provisions) Act 1949 [54] it is possible to obtain an interlocutory injunction at very short notice even before a summons has been issued.[55] It is not uncommon for applications to be made even on Sundays to judges at their homes to prevent a child being removed from the country.[56]

(ii) Under the Family Law Reform Act 1969 [57] the court has power to order either parent of a ward of court to pay [58] weekly or other periodical sums to the other parent or to any other person having control of the ward. The payment may be continued until the ward attains twenty-one, and a former ward between eighteen and twenty-one has an independent right to apply for an order.[59]

(iii) In a wardship case, the court retains custody (in the wide sense of this term) of the infant and only makes such orders in relation to that custody as amount to a delegation of certain parts of its duties.[60] It may, therefore, in the exercise of its inherent powers require a ward to reside at a particular place. The Family Law Reform Act 1969 [61] conferred two statutory powers similar to those exercised by the Divorce Court in matrimonial proceedings:

(a) Power to commit a ward to the care of a local authority if there are " exceptional circumstances making it impracticable or undesirable " for him to be or to continue to be under the care of either of his parents or of any other individual.

(b) Power, if there are " exceptional circumstances " to make a supervision order in favour of a local authority or welfare officer. The wardship procedure is therefore elaborate and careful. In recent years it has sometimes been suggested that it is too elaborate: the procedure involves much filing of affidavit evidence, and very considerable delays are often encountered.[62]

---

will order the child to be sent back, without detailed examination of the merits, provided there are no compelling reasons to the contrary: *Re H.* [1966] 1 All E.R. 886; *Re E. (D.)* [1967] Ch. 761; *Re G.* [1969] 2 All E.R. 1135; *cf. Re T. A. (Infants)* (1972) 116 S.J. 78; *Re S. M.* [1971] Ch. 621; *Re L.* (1973) *The Times,* November 9.
[54] *Supra,* p. 282.   [55] *Re N. (Infants)* [1967] Ch. 512.
[56] As in *Re N. (supra).* See *Rayden,* 11th ed., p. 953, and the authorities there referred to.
[57] s. 6. The Chancery Court had probably no inherent power to order a parent to maintain his child. All that it could do was to direct that the child's own property be properly applied for his maintenance. The practice therefore grew up of coupling with the wardship application an application under the Guardianship of Minors Act: see Latey Report, para. 250. This involved additional work and expense.
[58] But not to his *illegitimate* child: s. 6 (6).
[59] s. 6 (4).
[60] *Re W. (An Infant)* [1964] Ch. 202, *per* Ormrod J. at p. 210. In practice the court's intervention is often only sought in a narrow issue, and in such a case it will make no order as to custody (in the sense of physical care), care or maintenance, " for that remains in the hands of unimpeachable parents, and the court does not interfere in relation to such matters ": *per* Lord Evershed M.R.; *Re M. (An Infant)* [1961] Ch. 328, 345.   [61] s. 7.
[62] See, *e.g. J.* v. *C.* [1970] A.C. 668. Attempts have been made to reduce these delays: see *Practice Direction* of July 26, 1966 [1966] 3 All E.R. 84.

A child automatically ceases to be a ward on attaining his majority—
i.e. eighteen—and no order can be made in respect of a person who has
attained eighteen.[63] The Latey Committee rejected a suggestion that the
age be reduced to sixteen on the ground that between " sixteen and
eighteen many young people have not yet achieved stability or maturity;
the intervention of the court can do good much more often in that age
group " than in that between eighteen and twenty-one.[64]

The court may also at any time, either on application by a party
or of its own motion, order that a ward shall cease to be such.

Particular uses of the jurisdiction

Four examples of cases in which the wardship jurisdiction is
commonly invoked may be given:

(i) Where the court's superior procedure is needed. Thus, although
magistrates have an extensive jurisdiction over children, they have no
power to issue injunctions to prevent their order being defied. In an
appropriate case, therefore, the court will exercise its powers to supplement the magistrates' order.[65] The same principle may justify the
court exercising the jurisdiction for some limited purpose (*e.g.* the grant
of injunctions or orders for access) in supplementation of the statutory
powers of a local authority.[66]

(ii) Cases where there is a custody dispute between estranged parents.
In these cases, the children are often made wards because divorce proceedings have not yet been started (particularly if one parent threatens
to take the child abroad). The transfer of the wardship jurisdiction to the
Family Division means that there is no longer even a theoretical possibility
of conflicting orders being made in different divisions of the High Court
if divorce proceedings are subsequently taken.

(iii) Where foster-parents or potential adopters seek to retain the
custody of a child against his natural parents. If a parent withdraws
consent to adoption, the prospective adopter may make the child a ward
in the hope that the court (which, in contrast to the rule in adoption
cases,[67] is solely concerned with the child's welfare [68]) will allow him to
retain care and control. In *Re E.*,[69] for instance, the English mother (a
Roman Catholic) of an illegitimate child whose father was of mixed
Cuban and Chinese blood handed him over for adoption. Seven weeks
after the proposed adopters had taken the child to their home, the mother
wrote to them stating that she had changed her mind and wanted the
child to be brought up a Roman Catholic. The proposed adopters
retained the child, however, and applied unsuccessfully for an adoption

63 Family Law Reform Act 1969, s. 1.
64 Para. 238.
65 *Re Andrews (Infants)* [1958] Ch. 665; *Hall* v. *Hall* [1963] P. 378; *Re H. (G. J.) (An
Infant)* [1966] 1 All E.R. 952; *Re P.* [1967] 2 All E.R. 229.
66 *Re G. (Infants)* [1963] 3 All E.R. 370. See further *infra*, p. 306.
67 *Infra*, p. 354.
68 *Infra*, p. 289.
69 [1963] 3 All E.R. 874.

order. They then made the child a ward of court, and asked for care and control. The mother objected, asking that the child be moved to a Roman Catholic institution and then, if one could be found, to a Roman Catholic family for adoption. It was held that the interests of the child and the essential wishes of the mother could best be effectuated by continuing the wardship, giving care and control to the prospective adopters on their undertaking to bring up the child in the Roman Catholic faith. The House of Lords has [70] rejected the argument that such an order amounts to a *de facto* adoption. The two are entirely different in concept, nature and legal consequences: an adoption order is permanent, while the wardship can be varied at any time; an adoption order extinguishes parental ties, and replaces them with new ones; in adoption, the child is normally brought up without knowledge of his true parentage. This legal distinction is no doubt clear enough; but it may be difficult for the court to ensure that the distinction is preserved in practice. In *J.* v. *C.* [71] the courts refused to order a child who had been brought up by foster parents in England for most of the ten years of its life to be handed over to its natural parents, who were Spaniards resident in Spain. The court ordered that steps be taken to bring up the child in the knowledge and recognition of his parents, in the Roman Catholic faith, and with knowledge of their language. In spite of that, the evidence revealed that the child could speak only pidgin Spanish, and the controversy was sparked off by an application by the foster parents formally to change his religion. Unless there is someone able and willing to supervise the carrying out of such orders, it is difficult to be sure that they will be observed. Short of a supervision order, there is no available procedure.

If the child is in the care of a local authority, or the subject of a care order, the court may refuse in any case to interfere. This is dealt with below.[72]

(iv) Finally, there is the so-called " teenage wardship " where parents make their daughter a ward of court because they disapprove of her mode of life and she takes no notice of their protests.[73] In these cases it has been said,[74]

> " the ward is nearly always a girl or young woman . . . who is having, or is plainly about to have, sexual intercourse with some man of whom her parents disapprove. . . . The objections which the parents entertain to the man in question are, of course, very varied. Sometimes he is himself married. . . . Sometimes he has a criminal record of greater or less seriousness. Sometimes he has a record of seduction of young women. Sometimes he has no apparent means of support and appears to be battening on the ward. Sometimes again the chief objection is social class or colour. . . ."

70 *J.* v. *C.* [1970] A.C. 668.　　　　　　　　　　　　　　　71 *Supra.*
72 p. 305.
73 Cross, *op. cit.*, p. 203.
74 *Ibid.* pp. 209–210.

The number of cases in which the jurisdiction is invoked for this reason will no doubt have fallen since the age of majority was reduced to eighteen.[75] But the jurisdiction shows no signs of declining, as the following table [76] indicates:

Year	No. of Applications	No. of Children Involved	Orders Made Confirming Wardship	Dewarding Orders Made
1951	74	109	33	7
1956	86	121	49	47
1961	258	368	115	99
1966	444	609	159	190
1971	622	969	138	169

Principles on Which the Custodial Jurisdiction is Exercised

The Guardianship of Infants Act 1925, s. 1,[77] laid down the general principle that the first and paramount consideration in all proceedings where the custody or upbringing of a minor is in question is the welfare of the minor. This principle had been adopted by the Chancery Court as the proper test to be applied in exercising the wardship jurisdiction, and is now to be applied in all courts, *i.e.* the Family Division in its wardship and matrimonial jurisdiction, the courts exercising jurisdiction under the Guardianship of Minors Acts 1971–73, and magistrates under the Matrimonial Proceedings (Magistrates' Courts) Act 1960 or otherwise. The application of this principle will, however, inevitably produce different results at different periods of time [78]: decisions will reflect and adopt the changing views of reasonable parents as to the proper treatment and methods of bringing up children.[79]

The Act of 1925 in terms forbade the court from taking into consideration whether the claim of the father, or any common law right to custody was superior to that of the mother or vice versa. However, the " welfare principle " is not limited to disputes between parents, but is of universal application. There is no rule of law which entitles the rights and wishes of the natural parents to prevail over other considerations;

---

75 Although the number of cases in the 18–21 group seems to have been comparatively small—in the years 1962–65 never higher than one-sixth: Latey Report, para. 226.

76 Extracted from figures supplied by the Lord Chancellor's Office.

77 Now s. 1, Guardianship of Minors Act 1971.

78 For a striking illustration, see *Re Thain* [1926] Ch. 676, where a father who had no means of looking after his eight-month-old daughter on his wife's death, accepted an offer by the child's aunt and uncle to look after her. Six years later (having remarried, and being in a position to provide the child with a permanent and suitable home) he obtained an order that she be handed over to him. Although the correct principles of law were applied (see *J.* v. *C.*, *supra*) the decision on the facts would almost certainly be different. The trial judge's statement (" It is said that the little girl will be greatly distressed and upset at parting from Mr. and Mrs. Jones. I can quite understand it may be so, but, at her tender age, one knows from experience how mercifully transient are the effects of partings and other sorrows, and how soon the novelty of fresh surroundings and new associations effaces the recollection of former days and kind friends, and I cannot attach much weight to this aspect of the case ") would not now be adopted.

79 *J.* v. *C.* (*supra*), *per* Lord Upjohn at pp. 722–723.

there is no presumption that a child's welfare is best served by his living with his parents.[80]

Each case must depend on its own facts, and it is dangerous to place reliance on precedents.[81]

Meaning of welfare

The welfare of a child is not to be measured by money only nor by physical comfort only.[82] It " must be read in its largest possible sense, that is to say, as meaning that every circumstance must be taken into consideration, and the court must do what under the circumstances a wise parent acting for the true interests of the child would or ought to do. It is impossible to give a closer definition of the duty of the court in the exercise of this jurisdiction." [83]

First and paramount consideration

The law is not that the welfare of the child is the *sole* consideration. But the requirement to treat it as the first and paramount consideration means

> " more than that the child's welfare is to be treated as the top item in a list of items relevant to the matter in question. [The words] connote a process whereby, when all the relevant facts, relationships, claims and wishes of parents, risks, choices and other circumstances are taken into account and weighed, the course to be followed will be that which is most in the interests of the child's welfare as that term now has to be understood. That is the first consideration because it is of first importance and the paramount consideration because it rules upon or determines the course to be followed." [84]

Amongst the factors which the court takes into account are:

The wishes of the natural parents

In disputes between natural parents whose conduct is unimpeachable and an outsider (*e.g.* a foster-parent)

> " the natural parents have a strong claim to have their wishes considered: first and principally, no doubt, because normally it is part of the paramount consideration of the welfare of the infant that he should be with them but also because as the natural parents they have themselves a strong claim to have their wishes considered as normally the proper persons to have the upbringing of the child they have brought into the world." [85]

But this does not mean that the courts start by accepting the parents' views, and will only yield to clear proof that these will be harmful to the

---

[80] *J*. v. *C*. (*supra*), where the authorities are exhaustively reviewed.
[81] *M*. v. *M*. *and G*. (1962) 106 S.J. 877, per Willmer L.J.
[82] *Re McGrath* [1893] 1 Ch. 143, 148, *per* Lindley L.J.
[83] *Per* Kay L.J., *R*. v. *Gyngall* [1893] 2 Q.B. 232, 248.
[84] *Per* Lord MacDermott, *J*. v. *C*. (*supra*), at pp. 710–711.
[85] *Per* Lord Upjohn, *J*. v. *C*. (*supra*), at p. 724.

child.[86] The parental wishes are to be considered " only as one of the factors . . . as bearing on the child's welfare " [87]; they " must be assessed and weighed in conjunction with all other factors relevant to that issue " [88]; but they are " capable of ministering to the welfare of the child in a special way, and must therefore preponderate in many cases." [89] If, therefore, there is no clear advantage to the welfare of the child in one of several alternative courses of action, the wishes of the parents will no doubt be followed.

The conduct of the parents

The conduct of the parents in relation to the child is obviously relevant in determining what is in its best interests. Difficulty is caused when the dispute is between estranged parents, and the question arises as to how far misconduct and responsibility for the breakdown of the marriage (as distinct from conduct towards the child) is to be taken into account in deciding custody issues. It was for long a settled rule of the divorce court that a mother who had been guilty of adultery should be deprived of care and control.[90] This is no longer so,[91] but the conduct and wishes [92] of each parent must still be taken into account. In the comparatively recent case of *Re. L.*[93] the Court of Appeal employed somewhat strong language to make this point:

> " It is not the law, and it never has been, that no consideration shall be given to the spouse who has been deserted, whose home has been blasted, whose matrimonial felicity has been ended through no fault of his. If a wife chooses to leave her husband, for no ground which she chooses to put forward, but because she has a fancy or passion for another man, as this woman has, she must be prepared to take the consequences. She is a curious woman in

---

[86] If a parent abandons his child and allows it to be brought up at the expense of another, s. 3, Custody of Children Act 1891, provides that he can only regain custody if he proves he is a fit person to have it. But this provision has been restrictively interpreted.

[87] *Ibid., per* Lord Guest at p. 697.

[88] For this balancing process, see further *Re F.* [1969] 2 Ch. 238, *infra*, p. 293.

[89] *Ibid., per* Lord MacDermott at p. 715 (Lord Pearson concurring). The precise formulation of the extent to which the parents' wishes are to be taken into account is a matter of some difference: in *Re Adoption Application 41/61* [1963] Ch. 315, 329 Danckwerts L.J. pointed out that if the welfare of the child was to be the " first and paramount consideration " then " other considerations must be subordinate. The mere desire of a parent to have his child must be subordinate to the consideration of the welfare of the child, and can be effective only if it coincides with the welfare of the child. Consequently, it cannot be correct to talk of the pre-eminent position of parents or of their exclusive right to the custody of their children, when the future welfare of those children is being considered by the court." In *J.* v. *C.*, Lord Guest (at p. 697) regarded this as a " very clear and accurate " statement of the position, as did (apparently) Lord MacDermott (see pp. 713–714) (and thus also Lord Pearson). In this view, apart from material factors, the natural relationship of parent and child is relevant " not on the basis that the person concerned has a claim which has a right to be satisfied, but, if at all, and to the extent that, the conclusion can be drawn that the child will benefit from the recognition of this tie " (*per* Wilberforce J., *Re Adoption Application 41/61* (No. 2) [1964] Ch. 48, 53). Lord Upjohn on the other hand thought that these dicta of Danckwerts L.J. and Wilberforce J.: " hardly did justice to the position of natural parents " (see p. 724). This probably represents no more than a difference of emphasis, but see Eekelaar, 89 L.Q.R. at p. 217.

[90] See, *e.g. Clout* v. *Clout* (1861) 2 Sw. and Tr. 391.

that she seems to have no consciousness that she has duties as well as rights." [94]

This last sentence suggests that any conflict with the " welfare " test is more apparent than real.[95] The court refused care and control to an adulterous wife who left home taking her two daughters, aged four and six, with her, but the reason was not simply her adultery. Although perfectly satisfactory " as a day-to-day mother " she had nevertheless neglected her duty to the children to maintain for them a joint home with both their parents.[96] And " in so far as she herself by her conduct broke up that home, she is not a good mother." [97] Further, giving care and control to the innocent father on the facts of this case meant that there was still some possibility of a reconciliation.[98] At first sight it might seem unfortunate to use the effective guardianship of the children as an inducement to a couple to forget their differences; on the other hand since the welfare of the children would be so much better served by a reconciliation than by any other course the result is still within the basic " welfare " principle. Increasingly, now that both parents have equal rights at common law, the courts may simply make orders for care and control and access. If the parties cannot then agree on other matters, the court will decide.

The age and sex of the children

Statements will be found in the reports that as a general rule it is better (i) that very young children should be in the care of the mother,[99] and (ii) that older boys should be in the care of their father, and girls with their mother.[1] But these are not principles or rules [2]: they are simply judicial statements of general experience, whose application depends on the facts of every case.[3] Similar considerations apply to the alleged " principle " that brothers and sisters should not be separated.[4]

The wishes of the child

It is not uncommon for the judge in wardship cases to interview the ward privately.[5] In other cases, the child's views may emerge from reports and will be taken into account. There may be occasions when they count for very little, either because they are " merely reflections of

---

[91] *Willoughby* v. *Willoughby* [1951] P. 184.
[92] See, *e.g. Re O.* [1962] 2 All E.R. 10.
[93] [1962] 3 All E.R. 1.
[94] *Per* Harman L.J. at p. 4.
[95] *Cf. Re F.* [1969] 2 Ch. 238, discussed *infra*, p. 295, and *Laxton* v. *Laxton* [1966] 2 All E.R. 977.
[96] *Per* Russell L.J. at p. 5.
[97] *Per* Lord Denning M.R. at p. 3. See also *Re R.* (*M.*) [1966] 1 W.L.R. 1527.
[98] *Cf. Re F.* (*supra*).
[99] *Re S.* [1958] 1 W.L.R. 391; *Re F.* [1969] 2 Ch. 238.
[1] *W.* v. *W. and C.* [1968] 3 All E.R. 408.
[2] *Re B.* [1962] 1 All E.R. 872; *H.* v. *H. and C.* [1969] 1 All E.R. 262.
[3] *Re B.* (*supra*); *Re C.(A.)* [1970] 1 All E.R. 309.
[4] *Re P.* [1967] 2 All E.R. 229.
[5] *Re K.* [1963] Ch. 381, 406, 411.

the wishes of one of the parents which have been assiduously instilled into the ward " or because, although genuinely his own, they are plainly contrary to his long-term interests.[6]

Education and religion

The court will consider the educational advantages and disadvantages of a particularly proposal.[7] Religion may still be of importance,[8] but the court no longer allows contests as to the child's religious upbringing to predominate over considerations of its true welfare.[9]

Material advantages

It has already been said that welfare is not to be equated with material advantage.[10] But there may be cases where the inability to provide an adequate home environment is a determining factor.[11]

Medical factors

The danger of psychological harm arising from a change in custody is now widely recognised and forms part of the general knowledge and experience of judges.[12] In recent years it has become common for the evidence of a psychiatrist or educational psychologist to be tendered where there is a dispute about custody. If the infant is suffering from some physical, neurological or psychological malady or condition, then such evidence will be necessary and will weigh heavily with the court. But where it is a case of a happy and normal child (or even " the perfectly ordinary case of a broken home "),[13] and the evidence is simply general evidence of the dangers of taking a particular course in the proceedings, the courts (whilst emphatically denying that they " live in the past and have no time for psychiatrists and such new-fangled nonsense ")[14] will not hesitate to go against such evidence if the balance of probabilities indicates that the child's welfare will be thus better served.[15]

Balancing the considerations

The judge must take all relevant factors into account. The process has been vividly described by Megarry J.[16]:

---

[6] *Re S.* [1967] 1 All E.R. 202, 210; see also *D.* v. *D.* [1958] C.L.Y. 981, *Re T.* [1969] 1 W.L.R. 1608.   [7] See, *e.g. Re S. (supra).*
[8] See *Re M.* [1967] 3 All E.R. 1071.
[9] See *J.* v. *C. (supra)*, per Lord Upjohn at p. 717.   [10] *Supra*, p. 290.
[11] *Re F.* [1969] 2 Ch. 238; *Re Story* [1916] 2 I.R. 328, 345.
[12] *J.* v. *C. (supra)*, per Lord Upjohn at p. 726. Contrast the passage from *Re Thain* (n. 78) *supra*, and *cf.* the attitude of the House of Lords in *J.* v. *C.*, particularly *per* Lord MacDermott. Generally on this topic see N. Michaels, " The Dangers of a Change of Parentage in Custody and Adoption Cases," 83 L.Q.R. 547; " Alternatives to ' Parental Right ' in Child Custody Disputes involving Third Parties," 73 Yale L.J. 151.
[13] *Per* Cross J., *Re S. (supra)*, at p. 207.
[14] *Ibid.*, at p. 208.
[15] *J.* v. *C. (supra)*, per Lord Upjohn at p. 726; *Re C. (M. A.)* [1966] 1 All E.R. 838. As to the necessity to obtain an *independent* report, see *supra*, at p. 284.
[16] *Re F.* [1969] 2 Ch. 238, 241–242.

" I do not think that one can express this matter in any arithmetical or quantitative way, saying that the welfare of the infant must, in relation to the other matters, be given twice the weight, or five times the weight, or any other figure. A ' points system ' is, in my judgment, neither possible nor desirable. What the court has to deal with is the lives of human beings, and they cannot be regulated by formulae. In my judgment, I must take account of all relevant matters; but in considering their effect and weight I must regard the welfare of the infant as being first and paramount. If it is objected that this formulation does little to define or explain the process, I would reply that it is precisely a process such as this which calls for the quality of judgment which inheres in the Bench; and this is a quality which in its nature is not susceptible of detailed analysis."

Factors (such as the parties' conduct or wishes) must be weighed in the scales, but they will be considered primarily from the viewpoint of their effect on the child's welfare. The welfare consideration

" may so clearly point in one direction that it concludes the matter, even if every other consideration points in the opposite direction. On the other hand, it may be that the welfare of the infant would be equally served whichever parent has care and control; or the balance may fall on one side by only a small amount. *In those circumstances, the other considerations may be sufficiently strong to determine the matter.*" [17]

Thus if both parties can provide equally good facilities and stability for the child, the fact that one is morally blameless in relation to the break up of the marriage may tip the scales; but if the one party, however innocent he may be, cannot provide the necessary physical and emotional environment, nothing can derogate from the court's duty to provide the solution which is for the child's welfare. It must always be borne in mind that custody orders can be varied if circumstances change.

The application of the welfare principle is often one of great difficulty. But that it prevails over other considerations can be illustrated by two recent cases: in one [18] leave was given for a boy's mother and stepfather to take him to New Zealand as an emigrant even although this would affect his relationship with his father [19] and of course deprive the court of any further effective control over him. In the other,[20] custody of a sixteen-year-old boy had been given to the mother on divorce, as well as care and control. His father's application for *access* was refused, although the father was deeply devoted to the child, and his character as a parent was absolutely untarnished. The reason was simply that the " principle " that the court will only deprive a parent of access if he is not a fit and proper person to be brought into contact with the child

[17] At p. 241, italics supplied.
[18] *P. (L. M.)* v. *P. (G. E.)* [1970] 3 All E.R. 659; see also *Nash* v. *Nash* [1973] 2 All E.R. 704.
[19] Some arrangements were made in an attempt to preserve the relationship.
[20] *B.* v. *B.* [1971] 3 All E.R. 682.

at all [21]—perhaps because he has a criminal record, or is disposed to cruelty against children—is subordinate to the principle that the court will do what best serves the child's welfare.[22] Since the boy had formed a fixed determination not to see his father, an order for access could not do good, and might do harm. The court had to resolve the issue as it stood. It was not material, therefore, that the child might have been influenced by his mother against the father, or that the father had thus had a " raw deal."

INTERRELATION WITH WELFARE SERVICES

THE POLICY CONSIDERATIONS

The legal rules discussed earlier in this chapter are only a tiny part of the corpus of legislation designed to deal with the problems of " children in trouble." [23] Child welfare has in the twentieth century, been seen as a major problem of social welfare, and the resulting machinery is of great complexity. The following strands can be seen in the law:

(i) *Prevention of ill-treatment of children by criminal sanctions.* In 1889, the Prevention of Cruelty to, and Protection of Children Act was passed. Its principles have been much extended by later legislation,[24] and penalties can be imposed on those having the care of children or young persons for a wide range of misconduct—ranging from the general (failure to provide adequate food, clothing, medical aid or lodging, or failing to use the facilities of the Department of Health and Social Security to procure them [25]) to the specific (allowing a child to be in a room containing an unguarded heating appliance, resulting in serious injury to him,[26] causing the death of a child under the age of three by overlaying it in bed,[27] or being drunk in a public place while in charge of a child aged under seven).[28]

(ii) *Preventing the economic exploitation of children.* The Factory Act 1933 (which outlawed the employment of children under nine in textile mills) was the precursor of a large body of regulatory legislation. Again, this ranges from the general to the specific: the Children and

---

[21] Access is " no more than the basic right of any parent. . . . To say of a woman that she is a bad wife and mother may be an excellent reason for not giving her care and control, but . . . is not sufficient ground for depriving her of any kind of access ": *per* Willmer L.J., *S.* v. *S.* [1962] 1 W.L.R. 445.

[22] See also *M.* v. *M.* [1973] 2 All E.R. 81; see A. H. Manchester, (1973) 123 New L.J. 738.

[23] See *Bevan*, Chaps. 1–5, for fuller details. On the history, P. H. Pettit, in *Graveson and Crane*, Chap. 4.

[24] See now the Children and Young Persons Act 1933; Children and Young Persons (Amendment) Act 1952; Children and Young Persons Act 1963; Children and Young Persons Act 1969. See *Bevan*, Chaps. 6 and 7.

[25] Children and Young Persons Act 1933, s. 1 (2) (*a*).

[26] *Ibid.*, s. 11, as amended by ss. 8 and 9, Children and Young Persons Act 1969.

[27] *Ibid.*, s. 1 (2) (*b*), but only if the defendant was under the influence of drink when he went to bed.

[28] Licensing Act 1953, s. 2 (1).

Young Persons Act 1933 prohibits altogether the employment of children under the age of thirteen, whilst the Employment of Children Act 1973 enables more detailed regulations to be made.

(iii) *Education and health.* There is now a statutory duty [29] on parents to ensure that every child of compulsory school age receives " efficient full time education suitable to his age, ability and aptitude, either by regular attendance at school or otherwise." Failure to do so is punished by criminal sanctions.[30]

There are also numerous provisions designed to prevent children engaging in activities which are considered unhealthy—it is, for instance, an offence to sell to a person apparently under the age of sixteen years any tobacco or cigarette papers, whether for his own use or not.[31]

(iv) *Juvenile delinquency and social services.* The realisation that juvenile delinquency might be merely a symptom of social maladjustment and that (in any case) special measures were needed to deal with juvenile offenders led to the creation of a system of juvenile courts, applying a special code of law, and remedies. Although penal sanctions may have some part to play in protecting children, punishment of an adult will not necessarily improve the child's position. The problem began to be seen [32] as one, in the first instance, of providing help through the medium of the social services rather than compulsion through legal process (whilst still preserving that as a last resort). At the same time the existence of a clear dividing line between the punishment of delinquent behaviour (albeit that might be seen as therapeutic rather than retributive) and the treatment of misfortune began to be questioned. It has become

> " increasingly clear that social control of harmful behaviour by the young, and social measures to help and protect the young, are not distinct and separate processes. The aims of protecting society from juvenile delinquency, and of helping children in trouble to grow up into mature and law-abiding persons, are complementary and not contradictory." [33]

The implications of this view are by no means universally accepted,[34] but the law is now heavily influenced by it.[35] The main features of the legislation are as follows:

The Children Act 1948—taking into care

This Act imposed [36] on local authorities a duty to receive into their care any child in their area appearing to them to be under the age of seventeen, if it appears:

---

[29] Education Act 1944, s. 36.
[30] *Re Baker* [1962] Ch. 201.
[31] s. 7, Children and Young Persons Act 1933.
[32] See Report of the Committee on Children and Young Persons (Ingleby) Cmnd. 1191 (1960); The Child, the Family and the Young Offender, Cmnd. 2742 (1965); Children in Trouble, Cmnd. 3601 (1968).
[33] Cmnd. 3601, para. 7.
[34] See the Parliamentary debates on the Children and Young Persons Act 1969.
[35] See further O. M. Stone, 33 M.L.R. 649; J. Temkin, 36 M.L.R. 569.   [36] s. 1.

(a) that he has neither parent nor guardian or has been and remains abandoned by his parents or guardian or is lost; or

(b) that his parents or guardian are, for the time being or permanently, prevented by reason of mental or bodily disease or infirmity or other incapacity or any other circumstances from providing for his proper accommodation, maintenance and upbringing; and

(c) in either case, that the intervention of the local authority under this section is necessary in the interests of the welfare of the child.

In the year ended March 31, 1972 there were no fewer than 53,365 such cases.[37] Only a small proportion of these cases represent a long term social problem[38]: many children are taken into care during a short term emergency in a satisfactory home, and return when that emergency ends: in 1972 the largest single group (15,624) was received into care because of the short term illness of the parent or guardian. Other significant categories were:

Deserted by mother, father unable to care	4,984
Confinement of mother	4,413
Unsatisfactory home conditions	3,522
Child illegitimate and mother unable to provide	2,046
Long term illness of parent or guardian	1,095
Family homeless because of eviction	1,155
Family homeless through a cause other than eviction	1,833

In addition 9,559 children were taken into care following the making of a care order by a juvenile court under the Children and Young Persons Act 1969.[39]

There are two main ways in which the local authority may discharge its obligation[40] to provide accommodation and maintenance for a child in care,[41]

either boarding him out (i.e. placing him with foster parents who agree to provide a temporary home) or placing him in a residential institution (a "community home" or "voluntary home"). Some 41 per cent. of children in care in 1972 were boarded out, and it has usually been assumed[42] that the provision of a normal domestic environment in this way is the most satisfactory way of providing for the needs

---

[37] Children in Care, 1972, Cmnd. 5434.
[38] But there is a high correlation between the proportion of children in care and the existence of community social problems: 6·4 children per 1,000 of the estimated population under 18 are in care in England and Wales as a whole, but the figure for Tower Hamlets is 27·2 and for Kensington and Chelsea 25·2: ibid., Table II.
[39] Infra, p. 302.
[40] For the general duty of a local authority see s. 12, Children Act 1948, but cf. s. 27 (2) and (3), Children and Young Persons Act 1969.
[41] s. 49, Children and Young Persons Act 1969.
[42] But see Dinnage and Kellmer Pringle, Foster Home Care, Facts and Fallacies; Residential Child Care Facts and Fallacies.

of most children in care, and avoiding the dangers of institutionalisation.[43]
There are detailed provisions providing for the supervision of foster-
homes.   In particular, it should be noted that foster parents will be
required to give a statutory undertaking to return the child to the local
authority if called upon to do so.[44]   Difficulty is sometimes caused when
foster-parents are faced with a demand to return the child for whom
they have cared for many years [45]: proposals have been made which would
enable them to apply for guardianship (which would confer legal rights of
custody) and adoption, subject to safeguards,[46] but at present they have
no such rights or security, and must return the child.   The only
alternative is for the foster-parents to make the child a ward of court,
and ask for care and control.   This possibility is discussed below.[47]

If a child is taken into care, *in the absence of further procedures
outlined below*, the legal rights of its parent or guardian to custody are
unaffected.   On the contrary, it is expressly provided [48] that—

> " Nothing in this section shall authorise a local authority to keep
> a child in their care under this section if any parent or guardian
> desires to take over the care of the child, and the local authority
> shall, in all cases where it appears to them consistent with the welfare
> of the child so to do, endeavour to secure that the care of the child
> is taken over either—
>
> (a) by a parent or guardian of his, or
> (b) by a relative or friend of his, being where possible, a person
>   of the same religious persuasion as the child or who gives
>   an undertaking that the child will be brought up in that
>   religious persuasion."

It has been held [49] that this provision does not impose a mandatory
duty on the authority to *hand over* a child whose parent makes a demand
for his return.   It does, however, remove its right to *keep* the child in
care, and it would seem that the parent could obtain an order of *habeas
corpus* for the child to be handed over, unless: (i) The child were of an
age [50] when the court would not order a child to return to the custody
of a parent against its will.[51]   (ii) The authority (or some third party)
made the child a ward of court, when consideration of the child's welfare
would be the paramount consideration.[52]   (iii) The authority obtained

---

[43] Note, however, that the requirement imposed on a Local Authority by the Children
Act 1948 (ss. 11 and 13) to board out children unless it was impracticable or
undesirable to do so has been replaced by more flexible provisions: s. 49, *supra*.
[44] Boarding out of Children Regulations 1955, S.I. 1377 of 1955.
[45] See *Re A.B.* [1954] 2 Q.B. 385; *Re G. (Infants)* [1963] 1 W.L.R. 1169; *Re K. R. (An
Infant)* [1964] Ch. 455; *Re S. (An Infant)* [1965] 1 W.L.R. 483.
[46] Houghton Committee, para. 120 *et seq.*
[47] *Infra*, p. 305.
[48] s. 1 (3), Children Act 1948.
[49] *Krishnan* v. *Sutton London Borough Council* [1970] Ch. 181; *Re K. R. (supra)*.
[50] Traditionally 14 in the case of a boy and 16 in the case of a girl: *Re Agar-Ellis* (1883)
24 Ch.D. 317.
[51] As in *Krishnan* v. *Sutton L.B.C.*, *supra*, where the child was nearly 18.
[52] See the cases cited in n. 45, *supra*, and *infra*, p. 305. This was done in *J.* v. *C.*
(supra).

parental rights under the procedure laid down in section 2, Children Act 1948, discussed below.

In practice, the main reason why children do go out of care is that care is taken over by a parent, guardian, relative or friend.[53] If this cannot be done the Act provides [54]

> " Where a local authority have received a child into their care under this section, it shall, subject to the provisions of this Part of this Act, be their duty to keep the child in their care so long as the welfare of the child appears to them to require it and the child has not attained the age of eighteen."

In 1972 only 5,803 children went out of care because they attained eighteen.

Prevention measures

The 1948 Act makes adequate provision where the family unit has broken down, however temporarily. The Children and Young Persons Act 1963 introduced two measures designed to reduce the necessity to take children into care:

(i) A duty is laid [55] on local authorities " to make available such advice, guidance and assistance as may promote the welfare of children by diminishing the need to receive children into care . . . or to bring children before a juvenile court." Provision is also made [56] for co-operation with voluntary organisations for the provision of this advice, guidance or assistance.

The mischief aimed at by this provision was the fragmentation of services dealing with the problems of a single family, and the consequent difficulty facing the citizen in knowing where to go for advice and assistance. For instance, a family whose children were at risk might well find its problems being handled without much co-operation by the Local Authority Children's Department, the Housing Department and the Education Department, with, for good measure, other agencies like the Salvation Army, National Marriage Guidance Council and Citizens' Advice Bureau being involved.

The Act did not, however, provide an adequate solution to the problem, which has been tackled far more radically by the Local Authority Social Services Act 1970. This followed a full investigation by the Seebohm Committee on Local Authority and Allied Personal Services,[57] and requires the formation of a " social services committee "

---

[53] In 1972 38,863 children (out of a total of 50,486) went out of care for this reason, or because they had become self-supporting.

[54] s. 1 (2), Children Act 1948.

[55] s. 1 (1).

[56] s. 1 (2).

[57] Cmnd. 3703 (1968). For useful information on the provision of social services by local authorities see the inquiry carried out by Margaret Harrison and Alan Norton for the Committee on the Management of Local Government, *Local Government Administration in England and Wales*, particularly Vol. 5, 1967, Chap. 12, " Some Aspects of the Children's Service." This arouses doubts about the wisdom of delegating wide powers

to provide a more integrated service [58] and the appointment of " Directors of Social Services." [59]   It is too early to assess the effectiveness of these measures.

(ii) A more limited provision of the 1963 Act probably produced greater results: it was provided [60] that provision might be made for giving assistance " in kind or, in exceptional circumstances, in cash." Whereas in 1965 only £88,000 was expended, the figure had risen to £261,000 in 1968–69.[61]   Provision may be made in this way for the payment of arrears of rent and other debts, avoiding a threatened eviction. It has been rightly said that this power is " now one of the major levers used by social workers of the better local authorities to give help to keep families together, thus avoiding the misery, not to mention the public cost, of their disintegration." [62]   Since in 1971–72 it cost nearly £25 per week to keep a child in a local authority home,[63] this expenditure can also be justified on purely economic grounds.[64]

Assumption of parental rights

Taking a child into care, we have seen, does not affect the " rights " of his parents.   But there are two ways in which these rights may be suspended [65] and vested in the local authority:

(a) *Section 2 of the Children Act 1948*

This provides an *administrative* procedure whereby the local authority can acquire " all the rights and powers " [66] of a parent or guardian over a child which it has in its care under section 1 of the Act. It is made a criminal offence for the parent or any other person to take

to local authority committees (as distinct from trained local authority officials).   For instance, it would seem that there is often a feeling that the Children's Committee is a " ' Cinderella,' ranking low in the committee hierarchy . . ." (para. 21).   Not surprisingly, some officials had a low opinion of the abilities of committee members: " One children's officer had said that, apart from one member who was a trained social worker, committee members (who had an average age of over 65) tended to have a completely wrong outlook and no real comprehension of the sort of problems being handled.   Another said the committee had never been known to produce a new idea or intelligent criticism. . . .   One officer went so far as to say that, with the exception of one member of considerable calibre, the committee were, in the main, people whom they can't fit in anywhere else ' " (para. 9).

[58] s. 2 and Sched. 1.   But the welfare activities of education and housing committees are excluded.   For a criticism of this and other points see J. Harris, (1970) 33 M.L.R. 530.

[59] s. 6.

[60] s. 1 (1).

[61] Home Office Report on Work of the Children's Dept. 1967–69, para. 12.

[62] O. M. Stone (1970) 33 M.L.R. 652.

[63] Children in Care 1972, Cmnd. 5434, Table III.

[64] Although it costs far less to board a child out, the comparable figure being £4·66 per week: Table III, Cmnd. 5434.   It should also be noted that the parents of children under 16 in care can be made to contribute according to their means, to the cost of upkeep.   These contributions amounted to only £1,380,466 as against an expenditure of £74,130,769.

[65] For the consequences see *Re K.*; *Re M.* [1972] 3 All E.R. 769.

[66] s. 2 (1), s. 3 (1) and (2) Children Act 1948.   But the authority may not cause the child to be brought up in any religious creed other than that in which it would otherwise have been brought up (s. 3 (7)) and does not affect the parental obligation to maintain: s. 3 (6).

away such a child without lawful authority,[67] and the local authority will not be controlled by the court in a bona fide exercise of the powers thus conferred on it.[68]

To achieve these drastic consequences the local authority makes a resolution. It must "appear" to the authority that at least one of the following conditions [69] is satisfied:

    (a) The child's parents are dead, and it has no guardian; or

    (b) That "a parent or guardian" [70] has abandoned him; or

    (c) The whereabouts of "any [71] parent or guardian of his" have remained unknown [72] for not less than twelve months; or

    (d) That a parent of guardian suffers from some permanent disability rendering him incapable of caring for the child; or

    (e) That a parent or guardian suffers from a mental disorder (within the meaning of the Mental Health Act 1959 or the Mental Health (Scotland) Act 1960) which renders him unfit to have the care of the child; or

    (f) That a parent or guardian has so persistently failed without without reasonable cause to discharge the obligations of a parent or guardian as to be unfit to have the care of the child; or

    (g) That a parent or guardian is of "such habits or mode of life as to be unfit to have the care of the child."

Unless there is no parent or guardian, or the parent or guardian has consented in writing to the making of the resolution, the authority must [73] give notice to the parent or guardian. This must tell him of his right to object to the resolution and of the effect of any objection made by him.

The effect of an objection is to cause the resolution to lapse on the expiration of fourteen days from service [74] *unless* the authority not later than fourteen days from receipt of the objection makes a "complaint" to the juvenile court.[75] The resolution then remains in force until the court determines the complaint: It may do so either by making no order (in which case the resolution lapses, so that the child remains in care subject only to the provisions of section 1 of the Act) or by ordering that the resolution shall not lapse. It may only do this, however, if it is satisfied that the person objecting either—(i) had abandoned the child; or (ii) is unfit to have custody of the child by reason of (a) mental disorder, *or* (b) "his habits or mode of life," [76] *or* (c) "by reason of his

---

[67] s. 3 (8) added by Children and Young Persons Act 1963.

[68] *Re S. (An Infant)* [1965] 1 W.L.R. 483; *Re K. (an infant)* [1972] 3 All E.R. 769 (putative father's right to apply for access under Guardianship of Minors Act 1971, ss. 9 (1) and 14 (1), effectively ousted); see further p. 305, *infra*.

[69] Children Act 1948, s. 2 (1), as extended by s. 48, Children and Young Persons Act 1963.

[70] *I.e. semble* the condition need only be satisfied as to *one* parent, etc.

[71] This would apparently enable an authority to acquire parental rights even if the surviving parent were alive and of fixed abode.

[72] s. 10 of the Act imposes an obligation on the parent of a child in care under s. 1 to keep the authority informed of his address

[73] s. 2 (2).

[74] s. 2 (2).

[75] s. 2 (3).

[76] s. 2 (3).

persistent failure to discharge the obligations of a parent or guardian."
Thus, paradoxically, the court could not order the resolution to remain
in force on the grounds of permanent physical disability rendering the
parent or guardian incapable of caring for the child (unless perhaps
this so affects his " habits and mode of life " to make him " unfit ").[77]

Even if the resolution remains in force (whether because an objection
is made, or for some other reason) the juvenile court may at any time
terminate the resolution if satisfied either (a) that there was no ground
for the making of it, *or* (b) that this should be done in the interests of
the child.[78]   In this case the onus is on the parent or guardian to prove
his case, whereas in the objection hearing it is for the local authority
to prove its case.[79]

In the absence of any juvenile court determination, the resolution
will remain in force until the child attains eighteen,[80] unless the authority
determines it on the basis that rescission will be for his benefit.[81]

The fact that parental rights have been assumed by the local authority
does not, as a general rule,[82] prevent the authority allowing the child
" either for a fixed period or until it otherwise determines " to be under
the charge and control of a parent, guardian, relative or friend.[83]   This
power may be used in an attempt over a trial period to re-establish a
proper relationship with the natural parent.[84]

(b) *Care proceedings under the Children and Young Persons Act 1969*

Apart from this administrative procedure, a child may be committed
to the care of a local authority by court order.   The court's power to
make such an order in the exercise of its divorce [85] or other matrimonial
proceedings,[86] and in the exercise of its wardship jurisdiction,[87] has been
mentioned elsewhere.   The powers now under consideration stem from
the powers conferred on juvenile courts [88] to deal with children who
(although not guilty of a criminal offence) were beyond parental control,
or in need of care and protection.   The present law is contained in the
Children and Young Persons Act 1969 which represents a shift towards
the view that delinquency may be simply a symptom of the need for care.
Unfortunately, as a result of a policy of not bringing into force certain
crucial parts of the Act, the criminal sanctions are still retained for those
who commit offences, whilst powers which might have been justifiable
in cases of delinquency are applied to those who have committed no

[77] s. 48 (2), Children and Young Persons Act 1963.
[78] s. 4 (3), Children Act 1948.
[79] *Re L. (A. C.)* [1971] 3 All E.R. 743.
[80] s. 4 (1).
[81] s. 4 (2).
[82] But *cf.* s. 22 (4), Children and Young Persons Act 1969.
[83] s. 13 (2).
[84] *Cf. Re T. (A. J. J.)* [1970] Ch. 688.
[85] M.C.A. 1973, s. 43; *supra*, p. 264.
[86] Matrimonial Proceedings (Magistrates' Courts) Act 1960, s. 4 (1); *ante*, p. 260.
[87] *Ante*, p. 281.
[88] The history is traced in the Ingleby Committee's report (Cmnd. 1191), para. 52 *et seq.*

breach of the law. Thus in proceedings which are not criminal, so that " there is no lower age limit, and no finding of guilt, . . . the result may be what is regarded as the severest punishment for an offence, namely the sending of [a] child to a " community home.[89]

Under the Act the court has power to make orders if satisfied that any person aged under seventeen who has not been married is :

(a) in need of care and control which he is unlikely to receive unless the court makes an order, *and*

(b) that any one of the following conditions is fulfilled :

(i) His proper development is being avoidably prevented or neglected, his health is being avoidably impaired or neglected or he is being ill-treated.

(ii) It is probable that the condition set out in the preceding paragraph will be satisfied in his case, having regard to the fact that the court or another court has found that that condition is or was satisfied in the case of another child or young person who is or was a member of the household to which he belongs.[90]

(iii) He is exposed to moral danger.

(iv) He is beyond the control of his parent or guardian.

(v) He is of compulsory school age within the meaning of the Education Act 1944 and is not receiving efficient full-time education suitable to his age, ability and aptitude.

(vi) He is guilty of an offence, excluding homicide.[91]

If these conditions are satisfied, the court may make one of the following orders :

(i) An order requiring his parent or guardian to enter into a recognisance to take proper care of him and exercise proper control over him.

(ii) A supervision order.

(ii) A care order (other than an interim order).

(iv) A hospital order within the meaning of Part 5 of the Mental Health Act 1959.

(v) A guardianship order within the meaning of the Mental Health Act 1959.

In practice, supervision and care orders are those primarily relevant to " welfare " (as distinct from " offence "). A *supervision order* places the child under the supervision of a local authority [92] (or a probation officer, but only if the local authority requests this course, and an officer is already involved with the child's household [93]). The Act contains elaborate provisions as to the requirements which may be imposed in a supervision order (*e.g.* that the child reside in a particular place,[94] or

89 Ingleby Committee, para. 57.
90 See *Surrey C.C.* v. *S. and Ors.* [1973] 2 W.L.R. 649.
91 s. 1, Children and Young Persons Act 1969.
92 s. 11.
93 s. 13 (2).
94 s. 12 (1).

receive treatment [95]) but the essential idea is that it provides " compulsory ' care' without removing the child from his home surroundings " [96] except on a temporary basis.

A *care order* commits the child to the care of a local authority [97] which is then given the same [98] powers as his parent or guardian would have had. The authority is bound to " keep " the child in care " notwithstanding any claim by his parent or guardian," [99] and may restrict the child's liberty " to such extent as the authority consider appropriate." [1] This does not, of course, mean that the child must be kept in detention: the authority may board him out, keep him in a community or voluntary home, or make " such other arrangements as seem appropriate," and may allow him to be under the charge and control of a parent, guardian, relative or friend—exactly the same powers as are exercised in relation to other children in care.[2] However, the blurring of the distinction between the punitive and welfare functions, with the result that provision has to be made under the same code for the violent young criminal and the inadequate deprived child has meant that a glass has had to be put on the authority's general duty [3] to exercise its powers so as to promote the development of his character and abilities. It is now provided [4] that the authority may act contrary to this duty if it appears necessary for the purpose of protecting members of the public; furthermore the Secretary of State may, if he considers it necessary for the purpose of protecting members of the public, give directions to the local authority (*e.g.* that the child be kept in a particular community home) and the authority must comply with these directions, notwithstanding this general duty. These discretions might have been justifiable in the context of an Act whose principal object of permitting only " care " proceedings in respect of all those under the age of fourteen years and bringing as many young people as possible within such proceedings, " was to try to stop dealing with deprived, even if socially dangerous, young people as criminals." [5] But since this object has been rejected by the present government (by refusing to bring the parts of the 1969 Act restricting criminal—as distinct from care—proceedings into operation, save in the case of children under twelve) the unfortunate result is that the statute confers on authorities extensive powers only really justifiable in the context of major anti-social behaviour. It is therefore even more likely that the result of the Act (as has been said [6]) may be " to nudge those children

95 s. 12 (4).
96 *Eekelaar*, p. 169.
97 s. 20 (1).
98 Subject to the rule that his religion may not be changed: s. 24 (3).
99 s. 24 (1).
1 s. 24 (2).
2 s. 49.
3 s. 12 (1), Children Act 1948.
4 s. 27 (2).
5 O. M. Stone (1970) 33 M.L.R. 649, 658.
6 *Ibid.*

who have been neglected or ill-treated but show no anti-social tendencies into what largely amounts to a juvenile delinquents' court and sphere of treatment."

The Act provides a minor safeguard for the child whose destiny is so entirely committed to the discretion of a local authority: if a person over the age of five is in a residential establishment which he has not been permitted to leave during the preceding three months for ordinary educational attendance, or to go to work, the local authority must appoint an independent visitor for him if contact with his parents or guardian has broken down.[7] The person appointed must satisfy conditions to be laid down by the Secretary of State with a view to securing that he is independent of the local authority in question and unconnected with any community home. He will, however, be appointed by the local authority in whose care the child is. Such a visitor—presumably a magistrate, clergyman or other public-spirited individual—will have the right to apply to the court to discharge the order,[8] and is also under a duty to visit, advise and befriend the child. A care order, unless varied or discharged by the court, remains in force until the child is eighteen (or in some cases, nineteen).[9]

The right to bring proceedings under the Act is only available to local authorities, constables, or specially authorised persons (*e.g.* inspectors of the N.S.P.C.C.).[10] It is no longer possible for a parent to bring his own child before the court as being beyond his control. Extensive duties are laid on local authorities to investigate cases where proceedings may be appropriate,[11] and to prepare reports for the use of the court.[11a]

Substantial use was made of " fit person orders," the precursor of the care order: in the year ended March 31, 1970, 4,998 children came into care in this way, of whom 1,641 had been found guilty of a criminal offence.[12] As many as 23,336 out of the 71,210 children in care at that date were the subject of " fit person " orders. This indicates that taking into care under the Children Act 1948 procedure is often a comparatively short-term measure, in contrast to the fit person procedure. The other main difference is the element of compulsion in the " care order " procedure. Although once a child is in care under the Children Act the authority may (under the section 2 procedure) compulsorily acquire parental rights, a child cannot compulsorily be brought into care. Under the care order procedure he may be.

CONTROL BY THE COURT

The powers of the juvenile court under the 1948 and 1969 Acts have been mentioned. There are rights of appeal to the (essentially criminal) Crown

---

7 s. 24 (5).
8 s. 24 (5) (ii); s. 21 (2).
9 ss. 20, 21.   10 s. 1 (1).
11 s. 2.   11a s. 9 (1).
12 The comparable figure for 1971–72 is 9,559, but the statistics do not reveal how many of these were offenders.

Court. Sometimes, however, an attempt is made to invoke the prerogative powers of the wardship jurisdiction in order to question the exercise of the local authority's powers.[13]   The danger is that it may be used to appeal in cases where a full investigation has been made, and delay and expense caused.   The following principles emerge from the cases:

(i) The general rule [14] is that the prerogative right of the Queen, as *parens patriae* in relation to infants within the realm, is not for all purposes ousted or abrogated as the result of the exercise of the duties and powers by local authorities under the Children Act 1948, or other legislation.   The right to make a child a ward of court is not directly affected.

(ii) But, although the jurisdiction exists, it will not as a general rule be exercised, *if the authority has obtained parental rights* (whether under section 2 of the Children Act 1948,[15] or by reason of a care order [16]).   A judge will not in wardship proceedings substitute his own views as to the best course to be adopted in relation to the care and control of an infant for the views of the local authority, when an order has been made and remains in existence in the authority's favour.[17]

To this rule there are a number of exceptions—

(a) The court will interfere if the local authority is shown to be acting outside its statutory powers [18] or is not exercising them in good faith.   But if such an allegation is made the court should investigate the limited issue of whether prima facie grounds exist which would exceptionally justify intervention by the court, and not embark on a full hearing unless it is so satisfied.[19]

(b) The court will not deprive a child of the protection of the wardship jurisdiction if, for some reason, there is confusion about the validity or propriety of the local authority's assumption of rights.[20]

(c) The court will (*e.g.* by granting an injunction) exercise the juris-

---

[13] For a notorious example, see *Re T. (A. J. J.)* [1970] Ch. 688 where a local authority decided to return a child in its care under a fit person order to its mother for a trial period.   The foster parents made the child a ward: the trial judge heard full evidence on facts and merits, and agreed with the local authority that the trial return was justified in the interests of the child's welfare.   The hearing before Ungoed-Thomas J. involved solicitors, three counsel, and a judge for eleven days; in the Court of Appeal the four-day hearing involved three Lords Justices and no fewer than six counsel. The cost to the public cannot be less than £5,000 (the parties were legally aided), a sum which would pay the annual salaries of several child care officers.   Yet it is difficult to see how any of this expenditure contributed to the welfare of this (or any other) child.   See further D. Lasok (1970) 120 New L.J. 817; S. M. Cretney (1970) 33 M.L.R. 696.

[14] *Re M.* [1961] Ch. 328.

[15] *Ibid.*

[16] *Re T. (A. J. J.) (supra).*

[17] Per Russell L.J., *Re T. (A. J. J.) (supra),* at p. 690.

[18] *Re M. (supra).*

[19] *Re T. (A. J. J.) (supra).*

[20] *Re L. (A. C.)* [1971] 3 All E.R. 743.

diction to *assist* the authority, but not in a matter expressly provided for by statute.[21]

(iii) If, however, the child is only in care under section 1 of the Children Act the courts will more readily exercise the wardship jurisdiction. The reason has been said to be the transient nature of the authority's rights. In the words of Lord Denning [22]:

" . . . the statute gives to a natural parent the right to demand that the local authority give the child up to him or her if he or she desires to take over the care of the child. The imminence of such a demand is a very relevant consideration. Their care may be terminated at any moment. That puts the welfare of the child at peril. It may be taken away from a good home with foster-parents and removed to a very undesirable home with its natural parents whom it does not know in the least. In order to avoid this peril and secure the welfare of the child, the jurisdiction of the Court of Chancery [23] must be maintained. After all, the Court of Chancery exercises the power of the Crown as *parens patriae* and its jurisdiction is not to be taken away without express words: and there are none in the statute. The court would not, of course, interfere in any ordinary case with the care and control being exercised by the local authority. Nevertheless the fact has to be faced that emergencies may arise— and threats may be made—under which the natural parent may seek to take the child contrary to the best interests of the child. If there is any danger of this happening, the Court of Chancery should continue its wardship: and it should receive evidence for the purpose: and see where it is best for the child to be."

If, therefore, a local authority is faced with a demand from the natural parent for the return of a child in care under section 1 it may make the child a ward, and refuse to hand him over pending the court order. Similarly, foster-parents who wish, in defiance of their undertaking, and the local authority's wishes, to retain a child boarded out with them, may invoke the wardship jurisdiction and have the issue of the child's welfare examined by the High Court. Since they could not do this if the local authority had assumed parental rights, the paradoxical result is that where the legislature has carefully left parental rights unaffected they are most at risk to a possible claim in the High Court by foster-parents.

There are other instances where the court, on grounds of public policy, restricts the wardship jurisdiction:

(i) The court will not normally investigate the welfare of an individual child (as against questions of welfare of children generally) if a child

---

21 *Re Baker* [1962] Ch. 201 where a local authority sought to enforce school attendance by means of the wardship jurisdiction. It was held that the Education Act 1944 provided machinery for this purpose, and had put it outside the proper scope of the wardship jurisdiction to enforce it. *Sed quaere*: see D. E. C. Yale [1961] C.L.J. 137, 139.

22 *Re S. (An Infant)* [1965] 1 W.L.R. 483, 487. See also *Re G.* [1963] 1 W.L.R. 1169; *Re K. (R.)* [1964] Ch. 455, but *cf. Re A. B.* [1954] 2 Q.B. 385; *Re C. (A.)* [1966] 1 W.L.R. 415, 422; *Krishnan* v. *Sutton London Borough Council* [1970] Ch. 181.

23 Now the Family Division.

has been taken by one parent out of the jurisdiction of a foreign court in order to seek an advantage by having the case decided under the wardship jurisdiction in England: "kidnapping" of children by one spouse must be discouraged, and children brought here in those circumstances will normally be dewarded unless there is "some obvious danger or obstacle" in so doing.[24] This is so even although no foreign court has made an order affecting the child.[25]

(ii) If a magistrates' court is seised of a matter affecting a child, the High Court (although it has *power* to interfere) will normally only do so if relief is sought which the magistrates' court cannot give (*e.g.* an injunction to prevent a child being taken out of the jurisdiction)[26] or if there is some very special reason to do so.[27]

(iii) The general principle that the court will not exercise its jurisdiction to determine what is in a child's interests so as to interfere with legitimate decisions taken under a statutory power applies even if those decisions are not motivated by consideration of the child's welfare: the court will not, for instance, allow the wardship jurisdiction to be invoked so as to interfere with a decision of the immigration authorities refusing an infant Commonwealth citizen leave to stay in this country, nor would it interfere with a lawful posting overseas of a ward serving in the Armed Forces.[28]

---

[24] *Re H.* [1966] 1 All E.R. 886; *Re E.* [1967] Ch. 761; *Re G.* [1969] 2 All E.R. 1135. But *cf. Re A.* [1970] Ch. 665 (where there was no deceit involved in the children's removal, and they were in need of protection); *Re T. A. (Infants)* (1972) 116 S.J. 578; *Re L. (Minors)* (1973) *The Times*, November 9.
[25] *Re T.* [1968] Ch. 704.
[26] *T. v. T.* [1968] 3 All E.R. 321.
[27] *Re P.* [1967] 2 All E.R. 229; *Re K. (K. J. S.)* [1966] 3 All E.R. 154.
[28] *Re Mohamed Arif* [1968] 1 Ch. 643.

CHAPTER 8

LEGITIMACY AND ILLEGITIMACY

LEGITIMACY, for the lawyer,[1] is a legal concept whereby a couple's child is entitled to full recognition as a member of their family group, enjoying the legal rights which that status involves. The law determines who shall enjoy this status; it also defines the legal consequence of legitimacy or illegitimacy. It is important to bear in mind that the law does not directly govern the *social* consequences of illegitimacy, which depend on the circumstances of the case. The children of an unmarried couple who have a long-standing, stable relationship and home may suffer few social disadvantages. Their placement as members of a socially recognised group is quite clear. At the other extreme, the offspring of an unmarried mother's casual encounter with an unknown man may suffer from a realisation that it is the fruit of a relationship different from that which contemporary society regards as the norm. Legally there is little or no difference between the two cases; socially there may be a lot.[2]

Changing the legal *consequences* of illegitimacy will not necessarily affect the social consequences: the law might for instance make the right to succeed to a parent's property depend entirely on biological paternity,[3] but it cannot provide the fatherless child with a father, or change the attitude of society to such unconventional social groupings. The law may, however, operate indirectly to change attitudes to illegitimacy. The removal of legal distinctions may result in less attention being paid to the status. Giving the same legal rights to members of a " stable illicit " family group as those enjoyed by other families may, by removing one obvious distinction from other family groupings, give its members greater security. The law may also operate indirectly by making the fact of illegitimacy less obtrusive (*e.g.* by providing for a form of birth registration which does not involve public notice of illegitimate birth). But the law's power is limited. It is sometimes said [4] that it is not the child who is illegitimate but the parents. In strictness it is neither: it is the *legal relationship between* parent and child which is illegitimate. We consider, firstly, the circumstances in

---

1 For analyses of the sociological concept of legitimacy, see *Readings on the Family and Society* (ex. W. J. Goode), Chaps. 4–6; W. J. Goode, *The Family*, Chap. 3; C. C. Harris, *The Family*, pp. 44–48; for material on the causes of illegitimacy, see *Foote, Levy and Sander*, pp. 89–100; see also *Marsden*, pp. 86–92; *Eekelaar*, pp. 25–32.
2 On the " stigma " of illegitimacy, see *per* Sachs L.J., *S.* v. *McC. and M.* [1970] 1 All E.R. 1162, 1167.
3 See *e.g.* the Status of Children Act 1969 (New Zealand), s. 3: " For all the purposes of the law of New Zealand the relationship between every person and his father and mother shall be determined irrespective of whether the father and mother are or have been married to each other."
4 Baroness Summerskill. Hansard (H.L.) Vol. 280, col. 710.

which a child is treated as if he is legitimate; secondly, the consequences of legitimacy and illegitimacy. Finally, we shall consider defects in the law, and suggestions for its improvement.

LEGITIMACY AND LEGITIMATION

THE COMMON LAW

At common law, a child was legitimate if, and only if, he was *either* born, *or* conceived at a time when his parents were validly married to one another.[5] The typical case of legitimate birth involves both conception and birth during the parents' marriage. But the effect of the common law rules is that a child born after the marriage had been ended by the husband's death or by divorce [6] was legitimate,[7] as was a child born after the marriage has been solemnised, whenever he was conceived.

Any child born before his parents' marriage however was forever illegitimate. English law steadfastly refused to recognise the doctrine of legitimisation by subsequent marriage, which had been incorporated into the Canon Law from Roman Law, and thence into the laws of most civilised states.[8]

These rules were thought to serve the " main end and design of marriage " and to encourage matrimony

> " to which one main inducement is usually not only the desire of having *children*, but also the desire of procreating lawful *heirs*. . . . For if a child be begotten while the parents are single, and they will endeavour to make an early reparation for the offence, by marrying within a few months after, our law is so indulgent as not to bastardize the child, if it be born, though not begotten, in lawful wedlock: for this is an incident that can happen but once; since all future children will be begotten, as well as born, within the rules of honour and civil society." [9]

In 1253 the Bishops tried to persuade the Barons and Earls to adopt the Canon Law rule, but the assembled peers cried out with one voice: " Nolumus mutare leges Angliae." [10] It was almost 700 years before a change was made. The hardship of the common law was mitigated in two respects:

> (i) A child born to a married woman was presumed to be her husband's legitimate issue.[11] That presumption was virtually con-

---

5 *Blackstone*, Book I, Chap. 16, p. 454.

6 *Knowles* v. *Knowles* [1962] P. 161.

7 Assuming that he has been conceived whilst the marriage subsisted. If he had been conceived *before* the marriage, he would probably still be treated as legitimate. See Bromley, *Family Law*, 4th ed., p. 228.

8 See Fitzpatrick (1904) 6 J.Comp.Leg. 22; White (1920) 36 L.Q.R. 255.

9 Blackstone, *op. cit.*, pp. 455–456.

10 *Ibid.* For historical background, and an account of the bastard eigné and mulier puisné doctrine, see *Jackson*, pp. 42–53. Generally on the common law, see H. Nicolas, *Adulterine Bastardy* (1836).

11 " Pater est quem nuptiae demonstrant."

clusive, however unlikely it may have been that he was the true father.[12]

(ii) Although legitimation by subsequent marriage was not a doctrine of English law, if the child's father was domiciled in a country which accepted that doctrine both at the time of the child's birth and the subsequent marriage, English law would recognise the status so conferred.[13]

The common law has now been modified by statute in three respects:

(i) The doctrine of legitimation by subsequent marriage has been accepted into English law.

(ii) The issue of a voidable marriage which has been annulled remain legitimate, notwithstanding the fact that the decree [14] had a retroactive effect.[15]

(iii) In certain circumstances the issue of a *void* marriage is treated as legitimate.[16]

We deal with these in turn.

LEGITIMATION PER SUBSEQUENS MATRIMONIUM

The Legitimacy Act 1926 introduced into English law the principle that a child who has been born illegitimate is legitimated by the subsequent marriage of his parents [17]:

(i) The father must be domiciled in England [18] at the date of the marriage. It is not, however, necessary that he be domiciled here at the date of the child's birth.[19]

(ii) Under the 1926 Act, a child was only legitimated if neither parent was married to a third person when the child was born.[20] This refusal to legitimate the *filius adulterinus* was justified [21] on the grounds that it would result in a serious weakening in respect for marriage; a powerful deterrent to illicit relationships would be removed, with disastrous results for the status of marriage as at present understood.

The Legitimacy Act 1959 was ultimately passed, so that a child may now be legitimated notwithstanding the fact that one or both of his parents was not free to marry at the date of his birth. The practice of expediting the making absolute of a divorce decree so that the child

---

12 See *infra*, p. 315.
13 *Re Goodman's Trusts* (1881) 17 Ch.D. 266.
14 If made before August 1, 1971, when the Nullity of Marriage Act 1971 (now s. 16, M.C.A. 1973) came into force.
15 *Supra*, p. 65.
16 s. 2 (2) of the Legitimacy Act 1959.
17 s. 1 (1).
18 If the father was at that time domiciled in a foreign country by the law of which the child became legitimate by virtue of the subsequent marriage, that status is now recognised in English law: s. 8; *cf.* the common law rule, *supra*, p. 310. Further consideration of the topic is outside the scope of this work: see *Dicey and Morris*, Rule 64.
19 s. 1 (2).
20 *Ibid.*
21 Morton Commission, Cmd. 9678, paras. 1172–1183.

of one of the parties may be legitimate is no longer necessary, but is still used to enable the child to be *born* in wedlock as distinct from being subsequently legitimated.

(iii) The Acts only apply to legitimate a person who is alive at the date of the marriage[22] (or when the relevant Act came into force[23] if later). This may be important for purposes of succession.[24]

(iv) The Acts are not retrospective. If the parents of an illegitimate child had married before the relevant Act came into force, he was only legitimated with effect from that date. Thus if X were born in 1901, and his parents married in 1902, he would be legitimated on January 1, 1927. If, however, either of his parents had been married to a third party at the time of his birth, he would only have been legitimated on October 29, 1959.[25]

(v) It is a matter for proof that the child in question is the child of both parties to the subsequent marriage. This is dealt with below.[26] The mere fact of marriage is *some* but perhaps only very weak evidence that the husband accepts paternity of the child.[27]

(vi) It is only the subsequent *marriage*[28] of the parents which, in English municipal law,[29] can legitimate their child. There is no counter-part to the system which exists in many countries of legitimation by recognition.[30]

Effects of legitimation

It is provided[31] that a legitimated person shall have the same rights and be under the same obligations in respect of the maintenance and support of himself or anyone else as if he had been born legitimate, and legislation relating to claims for damages, compensation, allowances, etc. apply to him in the same way as to a legitimate child. But legitimation does not enable the legitimated person or his spouse or issue to take any interest in property, save in so far as legislation expressly confers such rights on him.[32] To a large extent, his position in this regard has now been equated to that of a legitimate child, but this topic is dealt with separately.[33]

---

[22] s. 1 (1), Legitimacy Act 1926; s. 1 (2), Legitimacy Act 1959.
[23] *Ibid.* The dates are respectively January 1, 1927, and October 29, 1959.
[24] *Infra*, p. 330.
[25] Provided that he survived until that time; *supra*, n. 22. But if either or both parents had died after marriage but before the relevant date, the child's legitimation would not be affected: *Re Lowe* [1929] 2 Ch. 210.
[26] See p. 315.
[27] *Gardner* v. *Gardner* (1877) 2 App.Cas. 723; *La Cloche* v. *La Cloche* (1872) L.R. 4 P.C. 325; *Battle* v. *Att.-Gen.* [1949] P. 358.
[28] *Sed quaere* whether a subsequent " marriage " which is void may legitimate: see *infra*, p. 313.
[29] Legitimation by (*e.g.*) recognition *may* be recognised in English law in certain circumstances: see *Dicey and Morris*, pp. 441–444.
[30] See Lasok, 10 I.C.L.Q. 123.
[31] Legitimacy Act 1926, s. 6.
[32] s. 1 (3).
[33] *Infra*, p. 330.

Nothing in the Acts affects the succession to any dignity or title of honour, or renders any person capable of succeeding to or transmitting a right to succeed to any such dignity or title.[34] Such rights depend on birth in lawful wedlock.[35]

Birth certificates

Provision is made for the re-registration of the birth of a legitimated person born in England and Wales.[36] A duty is placed on the parents to give the necessary information (i.e. proof of the marriage and of paternity [37]) to the Registrar-General so that re-registration may be effected.[38]

LEGITIMACY OF THE CHILDREN OF A VOIDABLE MARRIAGE

The parties to a voidable marriage which was annulled were treated as if they had never been married [39]; hence, any children of the marriage were bastardised by the decree. In 1937, certain exceptions were made to this rule when the decree was granted on the grounds of insanity, epilepsy, or venereal disease [40]; and finally in 1949 the principle was generalised to preserve the legitimacy of the children of all voidable marriages.[41] Decrees of nullity granted after July 31, 1971, no longer have retroactive effect [42] so that provision is no longer needed to preserve the legitimacy of the issue.

CHILDREN OF A VOID MARRIAGE

If the child of a voidable marriage was illegitimate, so a fortiori was the child of a void marriage. Logical though this might be, it could cause hardship: suppose that, unknown to both parties, the mother had been a few days short of her sixteenth birthday when the marriage ceremony took place, or that her husband, whom she reasonably believed to be dead, was then alive, or that the parties were unknowingly within the prohibited degrees, any children would be illegitimate. It is quite true that in the first two cases (i.e. non-age and bigamy [43]) the matter might, if both parties were still alive and willing at the time the defect was

---

34 s. 10 (1), Legitimacy Act 1926.
35 The Strathmore Peerage Claim (1821) 6 Bli.(N.S.) 489; Shedden v. Patrick (1854) 1 Macq. 535.
36 Births and Deaths Registration Act 1953, s. 14 (extended by the Legitimation (Re-registration of Birth) Act 1957).
37 See s. 14 (1), proviso, Births and Deaths Registration Act 1953.
38 Legitimacy Act 1926, s. 1 (4), Sched. The Registrar-General has power to call for information: ibid. s. 14 (2). There are penal sanctions for breach: Legitimacy Act 1926, Sched., para. 6, as amended.
39 Supra, p. 65.
40 s. 7 (2), Matrimonial Causes Act 1937.
41 s. 4 (1), Law Reform (Miscellaneous Provisions) Act 1949, now M.C.A. 1973, Sched. 1, para. 12. The old law had worked hardship since a child might have been born (e.g. if conceived by artificial insemination: R. E. L. v. E. L. [1949] P. 211) to a marriage which was voidable for incapacity or wilful refusal.
42 s. 16, M.C.A. 1973, supra, p. 68.
43 Assuming in this case that the marriage to the first husband had been terminated by death or divorce.

discovered, be rectified by a subsequent ceremony, but in the third case the possibility did not exist. In order to deal with this hardship the civil law adopted the doctrine of the " putative marriage " [44] under which the children of such a union are treated as if they were legitimate provided that the defect rendering the marriage void was not known to the parties. The Morton Commission [45] recommended that this principle be adopted in England, and the Legitimacy Act 1959 accordingly provided [46] :

> " . . . the child of a void marriage, whether born before or after the commencement of this Act, shall be treated as the legitimate issue of his parents if at the time of the act of intercourse resulting in the birth (or at the time of the celebration of the marriage if later) both or either of the parties reasonably believed that the marriage was valid."

The rule applies only if the child's father was domiciled in England at the time of the birth.[47]

It has been aptly said [48] that the effect of this provision, taken in conjunction with legitimation *per subsequens matrimonium*, is to make the status of legitimacy

> " no longer the product of a legal marriage, it is the product of a moral union. A child is legitimate if the parents were married (put things right, even if belatedly) or thought that they were married (perfect propriety again)."

But it should be noted that it is only necessary for *one* of the parties to believe in the validity of the marriage: for instance, the child of a union which, known to the father but unknown to the mother is bigamous, will have the benefit of the Act.

The Act gives rise to a number of points of difficulty:

(i) The burden of proof seems to lie on the person seeking to establish his legitimate status.[49] It may be difficult for him to show the state of his parents' minds at the date of his conception.

(ii) It must be shown that the belief was " reasonably " held. It may be that the reasonableness or otherwise of the belief must be assessed by an *objective* standard [50]; it may also be that a mistake of law cannot

---

[44] See E. J. Cohn (1948) 64 L.Q.R. 324; *Jackson*, pp. 50–53.

[45] Para. 1186. This seems paradoxical, in view of the Commission's refusal to accept legitimation of the adulterine bastard: if H (being married to X) had a child by W, it could not be legitimated by the subsequent marriage of H and W, even if W had been unaware of H's status at the material time. But if H had deceived her into a bigamous " marriage " the child was to be legitimate even though its parents had never been married.

[46] s. 2 (1). See generally O. Kahn-Freund (1960) 23 M.L.R. 56 and A. Samuels (1966) 29 M.L.R. 559.

[47] Or, if he died before the birth, was so domiciled immediately before his death: s. 2 (2).

[48] A. Samuels (1966) 29 M.L.R. 561.

[49] He will normally be the petitioner, and will thus have to show his entitlement to the relief: *Sheward* v. *Att.-Gen.* [1964] 1 W.L.R. 724.

[50] *Hawkins* v. *Att.-Gen.* [1966] 1 All E.R. 392.

be reasonable.[51] In so far as legitimacy under this Act involves a moral judgment on the behaviour of the parents, it is difficult to see why it should be necessary to show not only that the belief was honestly held, but that there were sound grounds for holding it. Obviously the further the belief diverges from the reasonable, the more difficult it will be to satisfy the court that it was honestly held, but if such proof is available it seems harsh to deny the child the status of legitimacy. If it is the case that a mistake of law can never be reasonable, the position is even more absurd: the child of a woman who is told by her solicitor (in error) that her divorce decree has been made absolute could rely on the Act, but if she had been advised (erroneously) that her foreign divorce would be recognised in this country, the child apparently could not.

(iii) The child must be the offspring of a " void marriage," rather than of " no marriage at all." " If a person is under the delusion of having gone through a ceremony he or she is not living in a ' void marriage.' " [52] But it not clear where lies the dividing line between these two concepts.[53] The Act defines [54] a void marriage as:

> " a marriage, not being voidable only, in respect of which the High Court has or had jurisdiction to grant a decree of nullity, or would have had such jurisdiction if the parties were domiciled in England."

This presumably simply means that one or both parties must have been able to make out one of the grounds of nullity set out in the Matrimonial Causes Act 1973.[55]

(iv) The Act applies to children whether born before or after the Act came into force, but rights under an intestacy occurring or a disposition made before that date are not affected.[56]

PROOF OF PATERNITY

THE PRESUMPTION OF LEGITIMACY

There will normally be no difficulty in establishing two of the three essential elements for a child's legitimacy, first, that a valid marriage exists, and secondly that the wife is the child's mother. But it may be difficult to prove that her husband is the father. In view of the serious social and legal consequences of illegitimacy, the law therefore adopted

---

51 This is apparently the rule in Scotland: see *Purves' Trustee* v. *Purves* (1895) 22 R. 513; *Philip's Trustees* v. *Beaton*, 1938 S.C. 733; Walton, *Husband and Wife* (3rd ed.) pp. 233–234; *cf. Hawkins* v. *Att.-Gen.* (*supra*).

52 Kahn-Freund, *op. cit.*, n. 46, at p. 58.

53 See *supra*, p. 68.

54 s. 2 (5).

55 *Supra*, p. 57.

56 s. 2 (4). Rather curiously, the Act seems to apply to govern the succession to titles of honour if the child is born after the commencement: s. 2 (3). It is expressly provided, however, that nothing in the Act affects the succession to the throne: s. 6 (4), so that the child of parents who should have obtained the sovereign's consent under the Royal Marriage Act 1772, but who through ignorance failed to do so, would not be eligible to succeed.

a *presumption* of legitimacy—*i.e.* the mother's husband is presumed to be the father of any child born during the marriage.[57] Furthermore it was not at common law sufficient to show a *probability* that the husband was not the father; it had to be shown *beyond reasonable doubt* that he *could not have been* so.[58] In the New Zealand case of *Ah Chuck* v. *Needham*[59] the wife bore a child who displayed markedly asiatic features. The husband and wife were both of unmixed European descent, and the mother had been associating on intimate terms with a Chinese. It was held that the presumption of legitimacy had not been displaced; if the husband could have had intercourse with his wife at the material times, then he was[60] to be held the father of the child, " even if she had committed adultery with one, two or twenty men."[61] This strong presumption was intended to protect the child's interest, but there must be many cases in which it failed to do so. As the Law Commission put it[62]—

> " Where a husband has denied being the father of his wife's child, but has been unable because of the strength of the presumption of legitimacy to prove that he is not, the emotional and financial effect on the child is not likely to be beneficial if the husband is nevertheless still firmly convinced that he is not its father. The trial judge may even have stated that he is satisfied as to the balance of probability that the husband is not the father; see *e.g. Watson* v. *Watson. . . .*"

In 1969,[63] therefore, the presumption of legitimacy was made rebuttable by proof *on the balance of probability*, thus perhaps showing that Parliament thought that public policy no longer required special protection to be given to the status of legitimacy.[64] The presumption remains; the onus of proof remains on a person seeking to bastardise a child born to a married woman. But it will be much less difficult to rebut the presumption[65]: " even weak evidence against legitimacy must prevail if there is not other evidence to counterbalance it."[66]

[57] *Banbury Peerage Case* (1811) 1 Sim. & St. 153.
[58] *Watson* v. *Watson* [1954] P. 48; *Cotton* v. *Cotton* [1954] P. 305.
[59] [1931] N.Z.L.R. 559.
[60] There were a number of exceptions to the generality of this rule: (i) the husband might prove that he was sterile or impotent at the relevant time: *Banbury Peerage Case* (*supra*); (ii) non-access might be proved—*i.e.* that the husband and wife did not have intercourse at any relevant time: *Aylesford Peerage Case* (1885) 11 App.Cas. 1.
[61] *Gordon* v. *Gordon* [1903] P. 141, 142, *per* Sir Francis Jeune P.
[62] Blood tests and the Proof of Paternity in Civil Proceedings (Law Commission No. 16), para. 14. See also *S.* v. *McC.* [1972] A.C. 24, 55, *per* Lord Morris: " It will be no benefit to a child to have a ' father ' from whom no recognition, no affection and no benevolence will come."
[63] Family Law Reform Act 1969, s. 26.
[64] *Per* Lord Reid, *S.* v. *McC.* [1972] A.C. 24, 43.
[65] Law Commission No. 16, para. 15, *S.* v. *McC.* [1972] A.C. 24; *T.* (*H.*) v. *T.* (*E.*) [1971] 1 W.L.R. 429.
[66] *Per* Lord Reid, *S.* v. *McC.* (*supra*), at p. 41.

BLOOD TESTS

The presumption of legitimacy was particularly important because of the difficulty of obtaining reliable evidence [67] about the facts of paternity. Blood test evidence may now supply this evidence, and make the necessity to rely on the presumption unusual.[68]

The scientific background.[69] It has been known since the beginning of this century that human blood exhibits certain characteristics which can be classified into groups. These characteristics are transmitted from one generation to another by recognised principles of genetics. A comparison of the characteristics of a child's blood with that of his mother and a man may show that the man *cannot* be the father. It cannot show (directly) that he *is* the father, but simply that he *could* be the father.

A test may, however, *indirectly* establish paternity: if, for instance, it is known that at the material times the mother has had intercourse only with H (her husband) and B,[70] and the blood test excludes H but not B as a possible father, it must follow that B is the father.

Tests may also provide evidence of paternity even if they do not exclude all possible fathers except one. They will show what blood group genes the child must have inherited from its father; it will then be possible to calculate the proportion of men in the population with the necessary combination of blood group genes. Hence, if the characteristics displayed by the child's blood are so uncommon [71]

" that if they were not derived from the husband they could only have been derived from one man in a thousand then the result of the test would go a long way towards proving (in the sense of making it more probable than not) that the husband was in fact the father because it would be very unlikely that the wife had happened to commit adultery with the one man in a thousand who could have supplied this uncommon characteristic. And if it appeared that only one man in a hundred or one man in ten could have been the father, if the husband was not, that might go some way towards making it possible that the husband was the father. Such an inference might not be lightly drawn, but it should not be ruled out." [72]

67 Even evidence of facial resemblance will be admitted, but little weight will normally be given to it: *C.* v. *C. and C.* [1972] 3 All E.R. 577.

68 Hence the brief account of it given in the text. See further *Cross on Evidence*, 3rd ed., p. 109. For striking examples of utility of blood test evidence, see *R.* v. *R.* [1968] P. 414; *B.* v. *Att.-Gen.* [1967] 1 W.L.R. 776.

69 The most accessible account is in App. B. to Law Commission 16. See also Taylor, *Medical Jurisprudence*, 12th ed., Vol. 2, pp. 46–50; and, on the legal background, Lanham (1966) 6 Medicine, Science and the Law 190; Bartholomew, " The Nature and Use of Blood Group Evidence " (1961) 24 M.L.R. 313.

70 See *e.g. Sinclair* v. *Rankin*, 1921 S.C. 933; *Robertson* v. *Hutchinson*, 1935 S.C. 708.

71 In an extreme case where uncommon blood characteristics are present, the incidence of possible fathers could be as low as one in fifty million: Law Commission 16, para. 5.

72 *S.* v. *McC.* (*supra*) *per* Lord Reid at p. 42. See also *T.* (*H.*) v. *T.* (*E.*) (*supra*), where the blood test evidence (a) did not exclude the husband's paternity, and (b) indicated that approximately 11 per cent. of western Europeans had blood groups compatible with the paternity of the child by the husband. It was held that this evidence went some way towards making it probable that the husband was the father.

The reliability of the tests is extremely high, provided that they are properly carried out.[73]

Use in legal proceedings. Although blood group evidence was used [74] to prove paternity, the court had no power to *order* an adult to take a blood test,[75] and there was considerable doubt as to the circumstances in which, once proceedings had been started, a child's blood should be tested if the result might be to bastardise him.[76] The Law Commission made a full investigation of the problem in 1968,[77] and its recommendations have been substantially implemented in the Family Law Reform Act 1969, which now [78] governs the matter. The court may now direct [79] blood tests to be taken in all civil proceedings. The power is discretionary: it seems probable that tests will usually be ordered if they are likely to establish the truth.[80]

BIRTH REGISTRATION

The law requires the registration of all births occurring in this country.[81] Regulations prescribe the details which have to be supplied.[82] These are then recorded. A birth certificate is simply a certified copy of the entry made in the register, and is evidence of the birth to which it relates.[83] Hence, the production of a birth certificate is often prescribed (*e.g.* by the Passport Authorities) to establish that a person was born in this country, or is of a certain age. If a child is illegitimate, this fact would probably emerge from a study of the entry in the register: either his father's name would not be given,[84] or it might differ from that of the mother. In order to avoid the embarrassment which is frequently caused,[85] provision was made in 1947 for a short form of birth certificate

---

73 Law Commission No. 16, App. B, paras. 5–6.
74 See *e.g. Liff* v. *Liff* [1948] W.N. 128, and Bartholomew, *op. cit.* n. 69, *supra.*
75 *W.* v. *W.* (No. 4) [1964] P. 67 (but *cf. S.* v. *McC.* [1972] A.C. 24, 46, *per* Lord MacDermott).
76 See *S.* v. *McC.* (*supra*) and the earlier cases there cited; M. Hayes, "The Use of Blood Tests in the Pursuit of Truth" (1971) 87 L.Q.R. 86; J. C. Hale [1971] C.L.J. 34; C. Tapper (1970) 33 M.L.R. 202.
77 Law Commission 16, see n. 73 (*supra*).
78 The relevant part (Part III) of the Act was brought into force on March 1, 1972, by the Family Law Reform Act 1969 (Commencement No. 2) Order 1971, S.I. 1971/1857. Much of the procedure under the Act is governed by rules: the Blood Tests (Evidence of Paternity) Regulations 1971, S.I. 1971/1861, lay down rules for the administration of tests etc., and there are separate procedural rules for different courts: see Supreme Court (Amendment No. 5) Rules 1971, S.I. 1971/1861, and Practice Direction (Blood Tests: Paternity) [1972] 1 W.L.R. 353, County Court (Amendment No. 3) Rules 1971, S.I. 1971/2127, and Magistrates' Courts (Blood Tests) Rules 1971, S.I. 1971/1991.
79 This does not mean "compel." If a person refuses to comply with a direction the court may draw inferences adverse to him, but cannot take any further action against him.
80 But *cf. R.* v. *R.* [1973] 1 W.L.R. 1115.
81 Births and Deaths Registration Act 1953, s. 1.
82 Registration of Births, Deaths and Marriage Regulations 1968, S.I. 1968/2049.
83 *Ibid.* s. 34 (6).
84 See *infra*, p. 319.
85 Vivid illustrations are given in the parliamentary debates on the Births and Deaths Registration Bill—see particularly the 2nd Reading Debates: Hansard (H.C.) Vol. 432, col. 2107; (H.L.) Vol. 145, col. 851.

to be issued.[86] This is an *extract* from the register, and must not contain any particulars relating to parentage or adoption.[87] The form currently in use gives simply the name, surname, sex, date and place of birth of the child.[88] It does not, therefore disclose that a child is illegitimate [89] or adopted.[90] It is still possible to obtain a full birth certificate (or copy entry in the Adopted Children Register). The short form costs less,[91] on the basis that this should make it more generally used. It is understood that the registration authorities normally issue the short form, unless the full form is specifically asked for. However, the fact that the full form may be demanded is a potential embarrassment to illegitimate children. It is sometimes suggested that it should not be available save in special circumstances—*e.g.* if it is necessary to prove the contents in legal proceedings. If the name of a man who is not married to the mother is entered as the father in the register, this is evidence of his paternity.[92] This is the nearest that English law approaches to allowing the father to make a formal recognition of the fact of his paternity.[93] In order to protect men, the Act provides [94] that in the case of an illegitimate child no entry shall be made about the father, save at the joint request of the mother and the person acknowledging himself to be the father.[95] It should also be noted that no entry can be made except with the consent of the mother: the father cannot insist, against her wishes, that his paternity be noted, even if they are living in a stable illicit union. There is no provision in English law (unlike some foreign systems) whereby a mother can be forced to disclose the identity of her child's father. It is sometimes asserted that " every child has a right to know who his father is," and that disclosure should be mandatory. But it would be impossible to introduce any such rule unless and until machinery were made available for giving binding judicial declarations of paternity: although there may now be proceedings which, incidentally,[96] involve

---

86 See s. 33, Births and Deaths Registration Act 1953.
87 s. 10 (2).
88 Birth Certificate (Shortened Form) Regulations 1968, S.I. 1968/2050.
89 But if the child is a foundling, this fact may be revealed by the certificate which will state that he was born " on or about . . ." and was " found at . . . on . . ." certain dates. 90 *Infra*, p. 364.
91 Registration of Births, Deaths and Marriages (Fees) Order 1972, S.I. No. 911 of 1972.
92 s. 34, Births and Deaths Registration Act 1953; *Jackson* v. *Jackson* [1964] P. 25; *Mayo* v. *Mayo* [1949] P. 172.
93 It is not, however, conclusive. 94 s. 10.
95 The Family Law Reform Act 1969, s. 27, enables the father's request and acknowledgement to be made by statutory declaration, rather than personal attendance, and provides for entries to be amended to give details of paternity if both parents request this: see the Registration of Births, Deaths and Marriages (Amendment) Regulations 1969, S.I. 1969/1811.
96 An exception exists under s. 45, Matrimonial Causes Act 1973; it is possible to petition for a declaration that the petitioner is legitimate or that he or his parents or grandparents are or were validly married. In such a case, paternity is directly in issue, and a declaration binds the persons given notice of the proceedings or made parties (including the Crown) and anyone claiming through them unless the decree was obtained by fraud or collusion. But there is no power to make a declaration of *illegitimacy*: *B.* v. *Att.-Gen.* (*B. Intervening*) [1966] 2 All E.R. 145n., and no analogous procedure in which the paternity of an illegitimate person is the direct issue before the court. See generally Law Commission P.W.P. No. 48.

a finding that someone other than the mother's husband is the child's father,[97] but these are not conclusive.

LEGAL CONSEQUENCES OF ILLEGITIMACY [98]

The common law looked on a bastard as *filius nullius* or *filius populi*.[99] The consequences of this premiss were worked out rigorously and to a logical conclusion.[1] The illegitimate child was a stranger in law not only to his father, but to his mother and all other relatives, and had no legal right to maintenance or other benefits deriving from the status of parent and child. When a judge [2] in 1841 asked rhetorically, " How does the mother of an illegitimate child differ from a stranger " it was subsequently said that he was not speaking ironically, but " rather stating bluntly the legal doctrine." [3] Legal intervention had been primarily concerned to protect the community against the financial consequences of bastards becoming a charge on the poor relief.[4] The poor law began the formal association between illegitimacy and criminality, relics of which still remain.[5]

In the twentieth century, legislation has gradually [6] assimilated the rights of an illegitimate child to those of a legitimate child in many respects.[7] Furthermore, legislation has indirectly improved the position of the illegitimate child, by enabling him to become legitimate.[8] But although the policy of the law is not to discriminate against illegitimate children,[9] there remain important differences between the legal rights of illegitimate and legitimate persons. We examine in turn: (i) Support obligations; (ii) Succession; and finally (iii) Custody and other issues.

MAINTENANCE AND THE ILLEGITIMATE CHILD

There are two special procedures whereby maintenance payments may be ordered for the benefit of an illegitimate child. First, the

---

[97] *E.g.* the question whether a child's father was the husband or an alleged adulterer used often to arise in divorce proceedings brought on the ground of adultery. Affiliation proceedings involve a finding that a man is the " putative father " of a child. See *infra*, p. 321.

[98] For valuable comparative material, see Sackville and Lanteri (1970) 44 A.L.J. 3.

[99] *Blackstone*, I, p. 459.   [1] *Per* Lord Herschell, *Barnado* v. *McHugh* [1891] A.C. 388.

[2] Maule J., *Re Lloyd* (1841) 3 Man. & G. 547.

[3] *Per* Lord Herschell, *Barnado* v. *McHugh* (*supra*), at p. 398.

[4] The preamble to 18 Eliz. 1, c. 3 (which empowered justices to order a mother or putative father to maintain the child or be imprisoned in default of payment) reads " concerning bastards begotten and born out of lawful matrimony (an offence against God's and men's laws) the said bastards being now left to be kept at the charges of the Parish where they be born, to the great burden of the same Parish and in defrauding of the relief of the impotent and aged . . . and to the evil example and encouragement of the lewd life. . . ."

[5] See *infra*, p. 324. For an analysis of the " relationship between " the law and social attitudes to illegitimacy, see Pinchbeck: Social Attitudes to Illegitimacy (1954) British Journal of Sociology, p. 315.

[6] The National Council for the Unmarried Mother and her Child (founded in 1918) has had a significant impact on this reforming legislation.

[7] Workmen's Compensation Act 1906 (dependants included illegitimate relatives); Fatal Accidents Acts 1846–1959; Family Allowance Act 1945; Legitimacy Act 1959 (Guardianship); Matrimonial Proceedings (Children) Act 1958.   [8] *Supra*, p. 311.

[9] See *per* Lord Denning M.R., dissenting: *Sydall* v. *Castings* [1966] 3 All E.R. 770, 773.

mother can seek an affiliation order against the father. Secondly, the law imposes a general obligation on both men and women to maintain their children, whether legitimate or illegitimate.[10] If that obligation is broken, so that benefits have to be paid by the Supplementary Benefits Commission, the sum involved may be recovered from the defaulting parent.

These two procedures are not, however, exhaustive of the ways in which a child who is born illegitimate may be the subject of legal proceedings to secure maintenance. First, the father of an illegitimate child may be prepared to enter into an agreement for its maintenance. Secondly, such a child may be legitimated or adopted, in which case any right to payment under an affiliation order will normally [11] cease, and other procedures become available for enforcing supporting obligations. Thirdly, if the mother marries a third party,[12] liability to support the child as a " child of the family " [13] may arise.

AFFILIATION ORDERS
The applicant

The Affiliation Proceedings Act 1957 provides [14] that " a single woman who is with child, or who has been delivered of an illegitimate child, may apply by complaint to a justice of the peace for a summons to be served on the man alleged by her to be the father of the child." But this apparently simple provision requires a considerable amount of explanation.

A " single woman " is not limited to women who are not married. It has been held to extend to a married woman who is (a) in fact separated from her husband, and (b) has lost the common law right to be maintained by him [15]—e.g. by having committed uncondoned adultery,[16] or by deserting him.[17] It seems [18] that the test of factual separation is the same as that applied in desertion: thus if husband and wife are living under the same roof, evidence will be required to rebut the prima facie inference that they are living together, but it is basically a question of fact whether they are doing so.[19]

The application of these principles is well illustrated by the case of *Jones* v. *Evans* [20] where the mother was the wife of a soldier serving [21]

10 Ministry of Social Security Act 1966, s. 22. In the case of a man the obligation only extends to those of which he has been adjudged the putative father by legal process.
11 But not if the child is adopted by the mother alone: s. 15 (2), Adoption Act 1958. If the child is legitimated, the order may remain in existence, but is unlikely to be enforced.
12 There may be rare cases in which marriage to the child's father does not legitimate the child. In that case, the " child of the family " provisions will also operate.
13 See *supra*, p. 274.   14 s. 1.
15 See generally pp. 217–219, *supra*.
16 *Jones* v. *Evans* [1944] 1 K.B. 582.
17 *Supra*, p. 217. *Mooney* v. *Mooney* [1953] 1 Q.B. 38.
18 *Whitton* v. *Garner* [1965] 1 All E.R. 70; *Giltrow* v. *Day* [1965] 1 All E.R. 73.
19 *Supra*, n. 16, and *Watson* v. *Tuckwell* (1947) 63 T.L.R. 634. The separation must not be merely colourable: *Jones* v. *Davies* [1901] 1 Q.B. 118.
20 [1944] K.B. 582.

abroad. The husband knew that she had committed adultery. He did not stop his allowance, and wrote her a letter saying " I have decided to forgive you to a certain extent, until I get the luck to get home." It was held that she was a " single woman ": she had (a) been separated from her husband for a considerable time, and (b) committed an uncondoned [22] matrimonial offence which deprived her of the right to maintenance and the right to live with her husband.

The reason for giving this extended meaning to the expression " single woman " was in the nineteenth century said to be that having " rendered herself unworthy of her husband's protection, she returns to the same state as if she were not married." [23]

A wife whose adultery has resulted in the birth of a child will cease to be a single woman if her husband condones that adultery. As a result he will in practice have to bear the whole burden of the child's upkeep. The rule may thus prejudice the prospect of reconciliation and remove a possible source of financial help without any compensating advantage.

Until 1959, the relevant time for determining whether the mother qualified as a " single woman " was the time of the application.[24] This would prevent a woman who married after the birth, but before the application, from obtaining an order. By the Legitimacy Act 1959 [25] it was provided as an alternative [26] that the mother may apply if she was a single woman at the date of the birth of the child whether or not she is a single woman at the time of the application. It seems probable on authority [27] that if she is not a single woman at either of these dates (but, for instance, only at the date of conception) she cannot apply.

There seems little point in these requirements: "... the question whether the woman ought to receive money for the support of her child must surely depend on her circumstances at the time when she seeks the order." [28] The assessment of these circumstances can properly be left to the discretion of the court. There seems little to justify depriving a family of support where the husband has married (knowing that his wife is pregnant by another) particularly when there would be a different result if he marries immediately after the child is born.

The application must be to a magistrate. There is an appeal to the Crown Court on law or fact, and from either the magistrates' court or Crown Court, on a point of law by way of case stated, to the Family Division of the High Court.[29] The court is normally to be that for the

---

[21] Compulsorily, cf. Marshall v. Malcolm (1917) 87 L.J.K.B. 491, distinguished in Jones v. Evans (supra).

[22] The letter written to the wife was not a sufficient reinstatement to amount to condonation: Keats v. Keats and Montezuma (1859) 1 Sw. & Tr. 334, see supra, p. 103.

[23] Per Littledale J., R. v. Flinton (1830) 1 B. & Ad. 227, 230.

[24] Jones v. Davies [1901] 1 K.B. 118; Gaines v. W. [1968] 1 Q.B. 782.

[25] s. 4.

[26] Gaines v. W. (supra).

[27] R. v. Pilkington (1853) 2 E. & B. 546.

[28] Gaines v. W. (supra).

[29] Administration of Justice Act 1970, s. 1 (2) and Sched. I.

area where the mother resides,[30] but it is now immaterial where the child was born.[31]

Time limits

The mother's complaint may be made before the child is born [32]: in this case it must be made on oath.[33] The hearing will not, however, take place until after the child's birth.[34] Hence although the court has power to order a putative father to pay the expenses incidental to the birth of the child,[35] there is no procedure for the mother to obtain the money at the time when it is most likely to be needed. The advantage of applying before the birth is that it may enable a hearing to take place very shortly after the birth,[36] and that any order for weekly payments may in this case be backdated to the date of birth.[37]

A complaint which is made after the birth must generally be made within three years from the child's birth.[38] However, there are three cases in which this time limit does not apply:

(a) A complaint may be brought at any subsequent time [39] if it is proved that the man alleged to be the father [40] of the child has within the three years next after the birth paid money for its maintenance.

If an illegitimate child formed part of the father's household, that is prima facie evidence that the father has paid money for its maintenance.[41] Hence the time bar will probably not operate where the child is the product of a stable illicit union.[42]

(b) If the man alleged to be the father ceased to reside in England within three years of the birth [43] proceedings may be brought within twelve months after his return.[44]

(c) If before the birth the mother was a party to a marriage which

---

30 s. 3 (1).

31 *R.* v. *Bow Road Justices (Domestic Proceedings Court),* ex p. *Adedigba* [1968] 2 Q.B. 572.

32 s. 1. Only 6 per cent. of the complainants in the Bedford College Survey did so: p. 177.

33 s. 3 (1) (*b*).

34 Magistrates' Courts Rules 1968, r. 31.

35 s. 4 (2) (*b*).

36 In recent years, there has been an increase in the delay between the issue of the complaint and the hearing: see the Bedford College Survey, Table 113.

37 s. 4 (3).

38 s. 2 (1) (*a*), as amended by the Affiliation Proceedings (Amendment) Act 1972.

39 s. 2 (1) (*b*), as amended. But it seems probable that an order cannot be made after the child has attained the age of 13; *cf.* s. 6, which empowers the court to " continue " orders after that age until the child is 16.

40 It suffices if payments have been made by someone acting as the father's agent: *G. (A.)* v. *G. (T.)* [1970] 2 Q.B. 643.

41 *Roberts* v. *Roberts* [1962] P. 212. In the Bedford College Survey 40 per cent. of complainants proved that money had been paid within 12 months after the child's birth, and about 20 per cent. of all complaints were brought more than a year after the birth: p. 177.

42 The Bedford College Survey found that around one-fifth of the couples in their sample had cohabited before the application. Nearly half of those cohabitations had lasted for more than three years: see pp. 185–186 and Table 128.

43 Or before the birth: *R.* v. *Evans* [1896] 1 Q.B. 228.

44 s. 2 (1) (*c*), as amended.

would have been valid but for the statutory provisions which invalidate marriage where either party is under sixteen [45] she may make a complaint at any time, provided that the other party had access to her within twelve months before the birth, notwithstanding that he may not within the three years next after the birth have paid money for the child's maintenance. This provision is unlikely to be of much practical importance since if either party reasonably believed the " marriage " to have been valid, the child must be treated as legitimate, with the result that maintenance for him will have to be sought under the code applicable in such cases.[46]

The hardship caused by these rigid time limits has been somewhat mitigated by the extension from one year to three years effected by the Affiliation Proceedings (Amendment) Act 1972. But it is questionable whether any limits are necessary. The availability of blood test evidence means that there is a 70 per cent. chance of conclusively excluding paternity if the defendant is not the father. Even if blood tests do not provide an exclusion result, any unreasonable delay is a factor the court could properly take into account in assessing the credibility of the complainant's evidence.

The hearing and procedure

After the complaint has been made, a summons will be served on the alleged father. Service is normally effected by the police. In spite of this and other outward trappings of the criminal law, the proceedings are technncally civil proceedings.[47] They are " domestic proceedings," [48] so that they take place in private, and press reporting is limited.

The court is no longer obliged to hear evidence from the mother. In many cases such evidence will be given, since the burden of proof is on the applicant. If it is, it must be " corroborated in some material particular by other evidence to the court's satisfaction." [49]

A common form of defence is to seek to show that the mother had intercourse with men other than the defendant at the material times. The possibility of a hostile cross-examination about her private life is a factor which deters many women from bringing proceedings.[50] In fact only about 13 per cent. of mothers of illegitimate children apply for orders. Although some mothers will be living in stable illicit unions, whilst others will have private maintenance arrangements, it seems clear that many " either cannot or will not complain to the court." [51] It has been suggested [52] that the reason is

---

[45] *Supra*, p. 16.
[46] *i.e.* under the Guardianship of Minors Act 1971, or in an application for relief ancillary to a decree of nullity. See *supra*, p. 185.
[47] *S.* v. *E.* [1967] 1 Q.B. 367.
[48] Legitimacy Act 1959, s. 5.   [49] s. 4 (2).
[50] It seems that in only about 25 per cent. of the applications actually made is the fact of paternity contested: Graham Hall Report, para. 185.
[51] Bedford College Survey, p. 187. For a consideration of the evidence normally given, see Josling, *Affiliation Law and Practice* (3rd ed.), pp. 60–67.   [52] *Ibid.*

" [f]rom their point of view they will receive the same assistance [*i.e.* from the Ministry of Social Security [53]] whether or not they establish a legal claim against the father. It is hard for a wife to resist the suggestion of the social security authorities that she seek a maintenance order against the husband who has deserted her but the mother of an illegitimate child is in a stronger position. If she has been promiscuous, she may be unable to establish a claim. On the other hand, if she dislikes the prospect of subjecting herself and her lover to unpleasant proceedings in a criminal atmosphere, she can easily decline to complain. It is also the more likely that she will act in this way if she hopes to establish a permanent relationship with the father of her child."

Orders that can be made

If the court finds the case proved, the defendant will be adjudged the putative father.[54] An order may then be made that he pay [55]:

(a) The expenses incidental to the birth of the child.[56] In assessing these expenses, the court must not take the mother's entitlement to maternity benefit into account.[57] It seems probable that the sums to be taken into account are payments actually made by the mother (*e.g.* for the child's initial clothing) rather than money which she may have lost (*e.g.* wages) by reason of the pregnancy.[58] The power to make such an order is entirely discretionary: in the Bedford College Survey one quarter of the defendants in 1961 were ordered to make such payment, but by the next year this figure had halved.[59] Since 77 per cent. of the complainants' babies had been delivered in National Health Service hospitals,[60] it seems unlikely that this power will often be exercised for large amounts.

(b) Funeral expenses, if the child has died before the making of the order.[61]

(c) A sum of money weekly, for the maintenance and education of the child.[62] There is now no financial limit on the amount which may be ordered.[63] Since one of the chief characteristics of men subject to affiliation orders is their low earning power,[64] it seems doubtful whether

53 See *infra*, p. 327.
54 This finding is now admissible in other proceedings, and will establish the putative father's paternity unless the contrary is proved in the subsequent proceedings: Civil Evidence Act 1968, s. 12.
55 s. 4 (1). It is only an order for such payments which is an " affiliation order ": *Oldfield* v. *N.A.B.* [1960] 1 Q.B. 685. This may be important where the Supplementary Benefits Commission wishes to obtain an order in its own right: see *infra*, p. 328.
56 s. 4 (2) (*b*).
57 National Insurance Act 1965, s. 25 (2).
58 See *Halkett* v. *McSkeane*, 1962 S.L.T. 59.
59 Bedford College Survey, p. 179.
60 *Ibid.*, Table 126.
61 s. 4 (2) (*c*). No order of any kind can be made if the child is stillborn: *R. de Brouquens* (1811) 14 East 277.
62 s. 4 (2) (*a*).
63 Maintenance Orders Act 1968, s. 1, Sched., implementing the recommendations of the Graham Hall Report.
64 Bedford College Survey, pp. 178–180. The maximum order of 50s. per week seems to have been only rarely made before 1968: *ibid.*

the change will have much practical effect. There is no power to order a lump sum or secured provision for the child, however wealthy the father.

It was said in successive editions of Stone's Justices' Manual (the *vade mecum* of magistrates' courts) that in exercising their discretion over quantum the court might take into account the relative ages and social position of the parties, the mother's character, and whether she was the seduced or the seducer. This statement (for which there was no judicial authority) has been omitted in recent editions, but it may be that some courts, in the absence of guidance, will take such factors into account. In general, however, it seems that economic factors are usually the only relevant circumstances.[65] There may be cases, however statistically insignificant, in which the putative father is wealthy whilst the mother comes from a relatively modest background: there is no guidance as to whether the court should be guided by the standard of living of the father or mother.[66] If the parties agree that the father pay a lump sum or periodical payments in consideration of the mother not applying for an affiliation order, it seems that this does not oust the jurisdiction of the court[67] (although the agreement does bind the father).

Costs may also be ordered.[68]

Duration of orders

Unless the order contains a direction that it shall continue until the child is sixteen, it ceases to be effective when he is thirteen.[69] It is believed that it is now common form so to direct. There is then power to extend the order if it appears to the court that he is or will be engaged in a course of education or training.[70] Such extensions may be for periods not exceeding two years at a time, but cannot extend beyond the age of twenty-one.[71] There are complex provisions as to the right to make applications and receive payments once the child is eighteen, or if the mother becomes incapacitated.[72]

If the child[73] or putative father[74] dies, the order is automatically discharged.

---

65 See n. 64 (*supra*) and the Graham Hall Report, *passim*.
66 Although no doubt it would be a factor in influencing the exercise of its discretion; see *Bromley*, p. 484.
67 *Follitt* v. *Koetzow* (1860) 2 E. & E. 730. Similarly, if an order has been made, the mother's releasing the father from liability under it in consideration of a lump sum or other payment is not binding: *Griffith* v. *Evans* (1882) 48 L.T. 417.
68 Magistrates' Courts Act 1952, s. 55 (1).
69 s. 6.
70 s. 7 (2).
71 s. 7 (3).
72 Family Law Reform Act 1969, s. 5 (2).
73 s. 6.
74 *Re Harrington* [1908] 2 Ch. 687.

Variation, etc. of orders

The court has a general power to revoke, revive or vary an order which it has made.[75] This power is little used: in the Bedford College Survey of orders live on January 1, 1966, only 13 per cent. had been varied (6 per cent. increased and 7 per cent. reduced). Seventy per cent. of those variations were for amounts less than £0·75.[76]

There is also provision for variation so that payments due under the order may be made to a person other than the mother, if she has died or for some other reason no longer has custody of the child.[77]

All the evidence suggests that affiliation orders are an inadequate way of securing the child's claim to maintenance.[78] It seems difficult to justify a special code for the illegitimate child. Admittedly there must be a procedure for judicially determining paternity, but once that is done there seems no reason why all applications for support should not be dealt with under the same code.

THE PUBLIC LAW OBLIGATION

The affiliation order procedure is historically rooted in the right of the Poor Law authorities to recover expenses incurred in providing for an illegitimate child.[79] Although the harsh penal attributes of the old law have been done away with, it remains the policy of the law to enforce the legal obligation to maintain [80] against the parents of an illegitimate child, if breach of that obligation involves the community in expense. The two agencies principally concerned are (a) the Supplementary Benefits Commission, which may have paid benefit to meet the requirements of an illegitimate child, and (b) local authorities, who may have taken an illegitimate child into care. The relevant procedures are considered separately.

The Supplementary Benefits Commission

A large proportion of mothers of illegitimate children resort to supplementary benefit: in 1965 there were some 36,000 such cases.[81] Such payments will normally include an allowance in respect of the child.[82] The Commission may seek to recover this cost in one of two ways:

(a) *Variation of existing order*

If the mother has herself obtained an order, the Commission may apply to have it varied to provide for payment to the Minister of Social

---

[75] Magistrates' Courts Act 1952, s. 53.
[76] Bedford College Survey, pp. 180–181, Table 118.
[77] s. 5. There are provisions whereby the justice may appoint a guardian if the mother has died, is of unsound mind, or in prison: s. 5 (4).
[78] See the relevant parts of the Bedford College Survey and Graham Hall Report.
[79] *Supra*, p. 320.
[80] s. 22, Ministry of Social Security Act 1966, *supra*, p. 321.
[81] Graham Hall Report, Table 17 (a), p. 92.
[82] As at October 1973 ranging from £2·05 per week for a child under five, to £3·70 for a child of 13 to 15.

Security, or to such other person as the court may direct.[83] This power may be exercised (on the assumption that benefit is paid for the child) even if the mother has died, and no person has been appointed to have the custody of the child.[84] If this procedure is adopted, the Commission may enforce the order direct against the father. It is a pre-condition that benefit should have been given in relation to the child, but once made the order will not expire simply because benefit ceases. In these circumstances, the mother may apply to have it varied again, to provide for payment to her.[85]

Furthermore, the mother may authorise the father to make payments to the Commission, rather than to the clerk of the court, who would normally receive them on her behalf.[86] If this is done, the Commission will give the mother a book of orders to enable her to obtain at a post office the total of benefit and affiliation payments to which she is entitled.[87]

(b) *Independent right to an order*

If no affiliation order [88] is in force, the Commission may itself apply for one within three years from the time when any payment by way of benefit in respect of the child has been made.[89] This right is wholly independent of that of the mother: the present code constitutes the supplementary benefit authorities the successors to the Poor Law guardians, who for long had a statutory independent right to apply for a summons against a man in respect of a child who had become chargeable to the parish.[90] This fact involves some curious consequences:

(i) An order can be made, even if the mother herself would have been debarred from obtaining one because she was out of time,[91] or was not a single woman,[92] or if the mother's own application has been dismissed by the court on its merits.[93]

(ii) Once the order has been obtained, its operation is not limited to the period during which benefit is paid.[94] The mother may apply to have it varied, so that payments shall thenceforth be made to her or to a person having custody of the child.[95]

Although there is some evidence that the authorities seek to persuade

---

83 s. 24 (6), Ministry of Social Security Act 1966.
84 *Ibid.*, s. 24 (7).
85 *Cf. Payne* v. *Critchley* [1962] 2 Q.B. 83, *per* Lord Parker.
86 s. 52 (1), Magistrates' Courts Act 1952, *supra*, p. 215.
87 See further *supra*, p. 227 for this procedure. In 1965 one-quarter of complainants had authorised payments to be made in this way: Bedford College Survey, p. 186.
88 *i.e.* an order containing provision for payment, as distinct from a mere finding of paternity: *Oldfield* v. *N.A.B.* [1960] 1 Q.B. 635.
89 s. 24 (2), Ministry of Social Security Act 1966.
90 *Clapham* v. *N.A.B.* [1961] 2 Q.B. 77, *per* Winn J.
91 *N.A.B.* v. *Mitchell* [1956] 1 Q.B. 53.
92 *N.A.B.* v. *Tugby* [1957] 1 Q.B. 506.
93 *Clapham* v. *N.A.B.* (*supra*), where evidence was available which destroyed the defendant's alibi.
94 *Payne* v. *Critchley* (*supra*).
95 *Ibid.*, s. 24 (6); Ministry of Social Security Act 1966.

mothers to take legal proceedings to enforce support obligations,[96] they seem largely unsuccessful in doing so. Of the 36,000 mothers of illegitimate children supported by the National Assistance Board, 9,000 had court orders, and a further 7,000 had private maintenance agreements.[97] This means that 20,000 were without either. The Commission's power to apply for a direct order seems very little used—it had been resorted to in only 2 per cent. of the cases in the Bedford College survey.[98]

Local authorities

Local authorities provide extensive social services for children in need [99]: these services include the provision of children's homes, and the making of arrangements to board children out with foster parents. In the twelve months up to March 31, 1972, 2,046 children came into care because they were illegitimate and the mother was unable to provide.[1] No doubt illegitimacy was also a contributory factor in cases grouped under other headings in the statistics.

It is a general principle that the parents of a child under sixteen years of age who is in care are liable to contribute to the cost of his maintenance, according to their means (although in practice the amounts involved are not large, averaging £0·35 per child in the financial year 1971–72 [2] compared with an average *expenditure* per child of £12·92 [3]). This right is normally enforced by obtaining a contribution order against the parent.[4] There is nothing to stop such an order being obtained against the mother of an illegitimate child [5] if she has the means to contribute. In practice, however, it is more important to be able to obtain contributions from the father, and local authorities are given powers to do so by means of the affiliation order process. As with the Supplementary Benefits Commission, there are two ways in which this can be done: either the authority may itself apply in respect of a child in care for an affiliation order if the mother has not done so,[6] or it may apply to vary an existing order so that the sums due thereunder are payable to the authority rather than the mother.[7] There are significant differences in detail [8] between the rights of a local authority and the Supplementary Benefits Commission, but the general principles are the same. It should,

---

[96] *Supra*, p. 226.
[97] See n. 81, *supra*.
[98] p. 186.
[99] *Supra*, p. 295.
[1] Children in Care 1972, Cmnd. 5434, Part I, Table I.
[2] *Ibid*. para. 12.
[3] *Ibid*., Table III.
[4] s. 87, Children and Young Persons Act 1933, as amended.
[5] *Ibid*., ss. 86–87, 24 (2); Children Act 1948, s. 4, imposes the liability on the " father and the mother " of a child. The interpretation section of that Act (s. 59 (1)) does not define these terms, but defines " Parent " to mean an illegitimate child's mother, to the exclusion of his father.
[6] Children Act 1948, s. 26, as amended.
[7] Children and Young Persons Act 1933, s. 88, as amended; s. 5 (2), Affiliation Proceedings Act 1957.
[8] See J. F. Josling, *Affiliation Law and Practice*, pp. 146–154.

however, be noted that if the child is in the care of a local authority no order can be extended to require further payments after he is sixteen, unless he is in fact residing with his mother.[9]

The Social Consequences of Affiliation Jurisdiction

There are many purely legal anomalies in the code governing affiliation law and practice which have been dealt with above. The major difficulties, however, seem to be social rather than legal: only a small proportion of mothers obtain orders, the defendants are poor (so that only small amounts are ordered) and payments are only made irregularly. About one third of all orders in the Bedford College Survey " live " on January 1, 1966, were in arrears, the majority fall into arrears before the order was two years old.[10]

The problem of the illegitimate child is simply one aspect of the problem of fatherless families generally, which is now under investigation.[11] It seems unlikely that reforms of the affiliation procedure as such would have much impact on this problem.[12]

MAINTENANCE AGREEMENTS

Many men prefer to avoid the embarrassment and possible publicity of affiliation proceedings by entering into an out-of-court agreement to maintain the child. It is significant that of the mothers receiving National Assistance in 1965, almost as many had voluntary arrangements as had court orders.[13] The more affluent the family the greater the incidence of voluntary arrangements is likely to be. Such agreements are actionable.[14] It has been held [15] that a mother's agreement not to take or enforce proceedings is ineffective to prevent her doing so.

SUCCESSION RIGHTS

The status of illegitimacy involved three major disadvantages in the field of succession rights. First, at common law an illegitimate child, as *filius nullius*,[16] had no right to participate on the intestacy of either of his parents, and likewise neither parent had any right to succeed on his intestacy. *A fortiori*, an illegitimate child had no right to take on the intestacy of a grandparent or brother or sister (whether illegitimate or not) and vice versa.

Secondly, although it was possible for a testator to make provision

9 Affiliation Proceedings Act 1957, s. 7 (4), (5) and (6).
10 Bedford College Survey, pp. 179 and 185.
11 By the Finer Committee on One Parent Families.
12 Generally, see Virginia Wimperis, *The Unmarried Mother and her Child* (1960), and cf. *Foote, Levy and Sander*, p. 66 *et seq.*; *Hambly and Turner*, p. 497.
13 7,000 as against 9,000.
14 *Jennings* v. *Brown* (1842) 9 M. & W. 496. It is not entirely clear what the consideration for the father's promise is: see *Ward* v. *Byham* [1956] 2 All E.R. 318, and Treitel, *Law of Contract*, 3rd ed., p. 80 (most such agreements are probably under seal).
15 *Follit* v. *Koetzow* (1868) 2 E. & E. 730.
16 *Supra*, p. 310.

by will for an illegitimate child, such a gift might be adversely affected by the application of one of three rules [17]:

(i) A *rule of construction*, under which words in a will or other disposition, denoting family relationships were construed as referring to legitimate relations, excluding those tracing the relationship through an illegitimate link.[18] Hence in *Sydall* v. *Castings*,[19] where a group life assurance scheme made provision for a class including " descendants " of a member, it was held that his illegitimate daughter could not benefit.

(ii) A *rule of public policy* whereby an illegitimate child conceived after the date of a settlement or the testator's death could not take, however clear it may have been that such children were intended to take.[20] Thus, if the male partner to a stable illicit union made a settlement of capital for the benefit of his children (expressly extending the meaning of that word so as to negative the rule of construction set out above) his after-born children could not take (although existing children could). This rule was justified on the basis that such gifts encouraged immorality.

(iii) A *rule of evidence* whereby a gift to the illegitimate children of a man (conceived after the date of the will) would fail (if they were described by reference to the fact, rather than the reputation, of paternity) because this would involve an inquiry which the court would not undertake.[21]

Thirdly, if (whether as a result of the operation of these rules in a testator's disposition, or his failure to make one) an illegitimate son or daughter were left without reasonable provision on the death of either parent, there was no legal remedy. The definition of " dependants " in the Inheritance (Family Provision) Act 1938 did not extend to illegitimate children.[22]

The Legitimacy Act 1926 [23] effected a minor reform by giving an illegitimate child and his mother certain (limited) reciprocal rights of succession on the other's intestacy.[24] In 1964, a Committee was set up (under the chairmanship of Russell L.J.) to consider whether any alterations were desirable in the law of succession in relation to illegitimate persons. The Committee recommended [25] major changes in the law, and these were effected by the Family Law Reform Act 1969. Although the Act goes a long way to remove the major succession disabilities attached to illegitimacy, it does not reduce the importance of the distinc-

---

17 For further details, see *Theobald on Wills* (13th ed.), Chap. 29.
18 *Hill* v. *Crook* (1873) L.R. 6 H.L. 265.
19 [1967] 1 Q.B. 302.
20 *Crook* v. *Hill* (1876) 3 Ch.D. 773; *Re Shaw* [1894] 2 Ch. 573; *cf. Re Hyde* [1932] 1 Ch. 95.
21 *Re Bolton* (1886) 31 Ch.D. 542; *Re de Bochet* [1901] 2 Ch. 441; *Re Shaw* [1894] 2 Ch. 573; *Re Homer* (1916) 86 L.J.Ch. 324.
22 *Re Makein* [1955] Ch. 194.
23 s. 9, applicable to deaths intestate after December 31, 1926.
24 See *Theobald on Wills* (13th ed.), para. 2051.
25 Cmnd. 3051 (1966).

tion between legitimate and illegitimate status. The Act does no more than to "create limited and carefully defined rights in favour of [illegitimate] persons, which fall far short of the rights which would arise if legitimate relationship and illegitimate relationship were given exactly the same legal status." [26] In practice, however, the changes will have a revolutionary effect, and much improve the rights of illegitimate persons.

We now consider the main changes effected by the Act to see how it affects the three disabilities referred to above; for detailed consideration, reference should be made to the standard works. [27]

Intestate Succession

The Act introduces two major changes [28]:

(i) It gives an illegitimate child [29] a right to share on the intestacy of both his father and his mother on the same basis as if he had been born legitimate. [30]

(ii) It gives both parents the same right to succeed on the illegitimate child's intestacy, as if he had been born legitimate. [31]

Two important points should be noted:

(a) The extent of the right conferred is very restricted. The Act does not permit participation by an illegitimate person in the estate of an ancestor more remote than a parent (*e.g.* a grandparent) or in the estate of collaterals. Nor does it allow any person except his surviving parent, surviving spouse or issue to succeed on the intestacy of an illegitimate person. Examples [32] may make the operation of the rules clearer:

(i) A has an illegitimate daughter, X, who predeceases him, leaving an infant illegitimate son, Y, whom A has taken into his house and treated as a member of his family. On A's death intestate, Y has no rights (although he would do if he had been X's *legitimate* child). Even if X had been A's *legitimate* child, her illegitimate son would have no right to succeed to the grandfather's estate. [33]

(ii) A and B had for many years lived as man and wife. They have two children, C and D, one of whom (C) is an invalid. After the death of A and B, C is supported by his brother, D, and by A's parents (*i.e.* C's grandparents). C dies intestate without having married or had children. Neither D nor either grandparent is

---

[26] E. C. Ryder, "Property Law Aspects of the Family Law Reform Act 1969" [1971] C.L.P. 157, 161.

[27] See *Theobald, op. cit.* Chap. 29; E. C. Ryder, *op. cit. supra*, n. 26. See also A. Samuels: "Succession and the Family Law Reform Act 1969" (1970) 34 Conv.(N.S.) 247; J. H. C. Morris: "The Family Law Reform Act 1969, sections 14 and 15" (1970) 19 I.C.L.Q. 326.

[28] The Act applies only to intestacy occurring after it came into force on January 18, 1970.

[29] Or if he is dead his (legitimate) issue.

[30] s. 14 (1). For these rights, see *supra*, p. 166.

[31] s. 14 (2).

[32] Many of these are based on the author's annotations to the Act in *Current Law Statutes Annotated*.

[33] Family Law Reform Act 1969, s. 14 (1) (3).

entitled to any part of his property. It will thus devolve on the Crown as *bona vacantia*.[34]

(b) The Act draws no distinction between the case where a genuine familial relationship has existed between an illegitimate child and his natural parents, and others. In each case, the fact of paternity is a matter for proof. If it can be established, there is a right of succession, irrespective of previous recognition or acknowledgment of paternity. Thus:

(i) I dies leaving surviving a legitimate son, A, an illegitimate daughter, B, whom he has accepted into his family, and an illegitimate son, C, of whose existence he was unaware, A, B and C are equally entitled on his intestacy.

(ii) I, a youthful, illegitimate, but immensely wealthy pop-star dies intestate after a motor accident. His father (who had never contributed to his maintenance despite all the pleas of the mother) is entitled to share in his estate equally with the mother.

Dispositions in Favour of Illegitimate Children

The rule of construction

The Act provides that:

" In any disposition made after the coming into force of this section—

(*a*) any reference (whether express or implied) to the child or children of any person shall, unless the contrary intention appears, be construed as, or as including, a reference to any illegitimate child of that person; and

(*b*) any reference (whether express or implied) to a person or persons related in some other manner to any person shall, unless the contrary intention appears, be construed as, or as including, a reference to anyone who would be so related if he, or some other person through whom the relationship is deduced, had been born legitimate."

The object of this section is simply to reverse the old principle of construction referred to above whereby gifts by will or settlement to children or other relations are prima facie to be construed as referring only to legitimate persons (or to those who trace their relationship exclusively through legitimate links). A gift by will to " the children of A " will now prima facie benefit A's illegitimate as well as legitimate children. The following points should be noted:

(a) The new rule only applies to " dispositions."[35] It does not, therefore, affect the rule of construction in relation to statutes or other legal documents. Examples can be found in the Act itself: section 14 (1) provides that where either parent of an illegitimate child dies intestate,

---

[34] Although the moral claims of dependants and others for whom the intestate might reasonably have been expected to provide may be recognised by means of an *ex gratia* payment: Administration of Estates Act 1925, s. 46 (1) (vi); Intestates' Estates Act 1952, s. 4, Sched. 1.

[35] Defined in s. 15 (8).

that child " or, if he is dead, his issue " shall be entitled to take as if he had been born legitimate. The word " issue " means " legitimate issue " with the consequences set out above.[36]

(b) The new rule does not apply to dispositions made before January 1, 1970. For these purposes a will is made on the date when it is signed (not the date of the testator's death).

(c) In sharp contrast to the intestacy provisions, the new rule applies to the whole range of relationships, and not simply to those of parent and child. A gift " to the grandchildren of X " will include (i) the legitimate child of an illegitimate child of X; (ii) the illegitimate child of a legitimate child of X; and (iii) probably, the illegitimate child of an illegitimate child of X.[37]

(d) The new rule only applies " unless a contrary intention appears." [38] Such contrary intention may be express (*e.g.* the use of the expression " lawfully begotten " children) or implied from all the relevant circumstances.[39]

A number of technical problems arise as a result of the abolition of the old rule of construction.[40] The Russell Committee opposed the change for more general reasons. They considered [41] that any

> " change in the present prima facie rule of construction would . . . lead to more problems than it would solve. A father would be faced with the alternative of either benefiting against his wishes bastards who might be born to his daughter, or of extending to her by the terms of his will the gratuitous insult of expressly excluding the possible outcome of her possible immorality."

The problems caused by the new rule are of two kinds. First, should a lawyer taking instructions for a will specifically draw his client's instruction to the new rule in case he wishes to negative its effect (perhaps at the cost of embarrassment) or should he as a matter of common form exclude the operation of the new rule? [42] Second, administrative difficulties might be caused since it will normally be impossible for Personal Representatives to be *certain* that a male testator has no illegitimate issue. (The testator may himself be unaware of their existence.) The former type of difficulty is a human one to which no easy solution can be offered. The latter is a legal one, which the Act largely solves by administrative provisions protecting personal representatives against liability if they distribute in ignorance of an illegitimate relationship.

[36] p. 332.
[37] See E. C. Ryder, at p. 164, *et seq.*
[38] s. 15 (1).
[39] See, for some possible difficulties, Ryder, *op. cit.*, pp. 166–167.
[40] See E. C. Ryder, *op. cit.*, p. 164.
[41] Para. 57.
[42] See R. T. Oerton (1970) 120 New L.J. 290; *cf.* A. Samuels, *op. cit.*, n. 27, *supra*, p. 249 *et seq.*; E. C. Ryder, *op. cit.*, p. 161.

The Rule of public policy

This Rule is expressly abolished by the Act, which provides [43]:

> " There is hereby abolished, as respects dispositions made after
> the coming into force of this section, any rule of law that a dis-
> position in favour of illegitimate children not in being when the
> disposition takes effect is void as contrary to public policy."

Thus a settlement for the benefit of X for life, and then to X's children
will prima facie include X's illegitimate children whenever born.

The Rule of evidence

This Rule is not expressly abolished, but it is presumably abolished
inferentially.   Section 15 (1) of the Act assumes the very thing that the
old rule forbade—namely that the court should investigate the *fact*
(rather than the mere reputation) of paternity.

Rights under the Inheritance (*Family Provision*) *Act 1938*
and Related Legislation

This legislation [44] confers a power on the court to order reasonable
provision for certain categories of dependants in cases where the court
considers that in all the circumstances it should have been but has not
been made.   Under the Family Law Reform Act [45] illegitimacy will no
longer be a bar to an application by a son or daughter of the deceased.
No special criteria are laid down by which the court is to determine
what is reasonable: will it make any (and if so what) difference if the
deceased has ignored or accepted the blood link?   There is no reported
case in which the point has arisen.

CUSTODY AND MISCELLANEOUS ISSUES

It is now a general principle that courts in deciding questions affecting
the custody or upbringing of a minor must regard his welfare as the
first and paramount consideration.[46]   It is tempting, therefore, to say that
his status as legitimate or illegitimate cannot be relevant.   This is an
over-simplification.   First, not all questions affecting the custody and
upbringing of children come before a court, so that we must examine
what rights either parent may have independently of legal proceedings.
Secondly, even in legal proceedings, the court may pay special regard to
the wishes of a parent entitled to custody; it is therefore important to
know how far the status of illegitimacy affects this matter.   Thirdly, there
are procedural distinctions which to some extent depend on the child's
status.

[43] s. 15 (7).
[44] *Supra*, p. 177.
[45] s. 18, implementing the recommendations of the Russell Committee (paras. 29, 36–46).
[46] Guardianship of Minors Act 1971, s. 1, *supra*, p. 289.

The natural right to custody

In the late nineteenth century it was established by the House of Lords that the mother of an illegitimate child had the legal right to its custody.[47] This was based on two grounds:

(a) even if, at common law, the child was *filius nullius*, so that no person had any legal rights over him, the Poor Law (which imposed a duty on the mother to maintain the child) gave her a correlative right to custody.[48]

(b) the mother had a natural right to have her views taken into account: "the desire of the mother of an illegitimate child as to its custody is primarily to be considered." [49]

The mother therefore has all the legal rights to her child's custody, unless and until those rights are displaced by court order or other competent act.[50] This is so even if the child is the product of a stable illicit union: the father has no rights in the absence of legal proceedings. This is not affected by the Guardianship Act 1973, which expressly provides that the powers conferring equal rights on a child's mother and father [51] shall not be taken as applying in relation to a minor who is illegitimate.[52]

Rights in custody proceedings

Once legal procedings have been brought, the court is bound by the general rule that the child's welfare is the first and paramount consideration.[53] This is a question of fact. Thus, *other things being equal*, the mother's views will be respected on such matters as religious and secular education:

> "an illegitimate child's mother's wishes are of great significance, and must not merely not be disregarded; they must be very seriously regarded by the court. The court will certainly not substitute its views [about religious upbringing] for hers, but they must be considered with all other matters bearing on the welfare of the child (both long term and immediate). The court is not bound to give effect to them when satisfied that the child's welfare requires otherwise, and in giving effect to them the court has power to do so in such a manner as it may consider to be best in the child's interest." [54]

The natural father of an illegitimate child is not in this special legal

---

[47] *Barnardo* v. *McHugh* [1891] A.C. 388.

[48] *Per* Lord Halsbury L.C. and Lord Herschell [1891] A.C. at pp. 395, 398. Since a man who has been adjudged the putative father is now also bound to support the child (s. 42 (2), National Assistance Act 1948), if this reasoning is correct he should be equally entitled to custody.

[49] *Per* Lord Herschell, *ibid.*; *R.* v. *Nash* (1883) 10 Q.B.D. 454.

[50] *E.g.* a resolution of a local authority assuming parental rights over the child: s. 2, Children Act 1948, *supra*, p. 300.

[51] *Supra*, p. 251.

[52] s. 1 (7).

[53] Guardianship of Minors Act 1971, s. 1.

[54] *Per* Wilberforce J., *Re E.* [1963] 3 All E.R. 874, 879.

position [55]: although there is now a procedure [56] by which the natural father may claim custody this procedural change did not give him any additional rights, either against the mother or third parties. His position is not the same as that of the father of a legitimate child [57] and remains as laid down by courts exercising the wardship jurisdiction.[58] Although there have been occasions on which the court may seem to have given special recognition to the blood tie between the natural father and his child [59] the true view seems to be that the

> " tie (if such is shown to exist) between the child and his natural father (or any other relative) may properly be regarded in this connexion, not on the basis that the person concerned has a claim which he has a right to have satisfied, but, if at all, and to the extent that, the conclusion can be drawn that the child will benefit from the recognition of this tie." [60]

Procedural matters

It is possible for any person (including the natural father) to invoke the custodial jurisdiction of the court by making the child a ward of court.[61] This necessarily involves formality and expense.

The availability of other procedures may be affected by the child's illegitimate status:

(i) Custody of a child may be claimed, by anyone entitled thereto, in the High Court by bringing Habeas Corpus proceedings. The natural father will not, however, be entitled to custody unless he has obtained that right by previous legal proceedings [62] or appointment.[63]

(ii) The father of an illegitimate child has since 1959 had the right

---

55 For an example where the court preferred proposals made by the natural father to those made by the mother, see *Re A.* [1955] 2 All E.R. 202. But *cf. Re C.(A).* [1970] 1 All E.R. 309, 311, *per* Harman L.J.: The father " has no rights such as the right to forbid an adoption, as the mother of an illegitimate child has, but nevertheless he is a person who is not to be ignored, and his wishes, when he is a person who in many respects is a perfectly respectable member of society, can be given some weight. They will not be given much weight against the mother; but here there is no mother. . . ."
56 Legitimacy Act 1959.
57 *Re Adoption Application 41/61* [1963] Ch. 315; *Re Adoption Application 41/61 (No. 2)* [1964] Ch. 48; *Re O.* [1965] Ch. 23; *Re C.(A.)* [1970] 1 All E.R. 309; see also *Re M.* [1955] 2 Q.B. 479.
58 *Re Adoption Application 41/61 (No. 2)* [1964] Ch. 48; *Re C.(A.)* [1970] 1 All E.R. 309, 311, *per* Harman L.J. In *Re C. (M. A.)* [1966] 1 W.L.R. 646, counsel reserved the right to argue, in the House of Lords, that the Act had changed the substantive law, and given the natural father the same rights as a lawful father.
59 See *e.g. Re C.(M. A.)* [1966] 1 W.L.R. 646, a case which received undeserved publicity on the (erroneous) assumption that it accorded some special weight to the " blood tie "; *cf. Re G.* [1956] 1 W.L.R. 911, where the Court of Appeal expressed the view that any presumption that it was in the child's interests to know *both* his parents proceeded on the premise that the parents are legitimate, lawful parents.
60 *Per* Wilberforce J., *Re Adoption Application 41/61 (No. 2) (supra)* at p. 53; *cf. Re O. (supra)* at p. 28, *per* Lord Denning M.R.: " The natural father is not in the same position as a legitimate father. He is a person who is entitled to special consideration [*sic*] by the tie of blood, but not to any greater or other right. His fatherhood is a ground to which regard should be paid in seeing what is best in the interests of the child; but it is not an overriding consideration."
61 *Supra,* p. 281.
62 *E.g.* Wardship or Guardianship proceedings or an order by the divorce court.
63 *E.g.* by will.

to apply to the court (High Court, County Court or Magistrates' Court) for custody of or access to the child.[64]   There is, however, no power to make orders for maintenance under the 1959 Act [65]: the mother is left to her rights under the Affiliation Proceedings Act.[66]   *If* a custody order is made in favour of the father, he has a right by deed or will to appoint any other person to be the guardian after his death.[67]   This appointment will only be effective if he is entitled to custody immediately before his death.[68]

(iii) There is a special power under the Affiliation Proceedings Act [69] by which, if the mother dies, becomes of unsound mind, or is sent to prison while an affiliation order is in force, the justices may appoint some other person to have custody of the child and receive payments due under the order.

(iv) A person who is not the father or mother of an illegitimate child has no right to apply for custody or access under the Guardianship of Minors Act.   This may occasionally cause problems where such a child has been accepted into the family unit created by the marriage of one parent to a third party.   The step-parent could apply for custody under the Matrimonial Proceedings (Magistrates' Courts) Act 1960 if one of the grounds for a complaint therein provided [70] could be established, or application could be made to the divorce court [71] if matrimonial proceedings are pending there.   But apart from this the only way in which the step-parent can get an order is by invoking the wardship jurisdiction. This is unlikely often to be of practical importance, but it demonstrates the unnecessary procedural complications which arise.   Given that any interested person may invoke the jurisdiction of the courts through the wardship procedure, there seems no justification for not allowing access to the courts in other (less formal) procedures.

CONSENT TO MARRIAGE

One final curious anomaly may be mentioned: if an illegitimate minor under the age of eighteen wishes to marry he must obtain parental consent.   The Marriage Act 1949 [72] specifies that the consent required is that of the mother unless (a) she is dead, in which case the guardian appointed by the mother must consent, or (b) she has been deprived by order of the court of the infant's custody, in which case the consent of the person to whom custody has been committed by order of the court must be obtained.   The testamentary guardian appointed by the father

[64] ss. 14, 9, Guardianship of Minors Act 1971.
[65] s. 14 (2).
[66] *Supra*, p. 321.
[67] s. 14 (3).   The appointee will act jointly with the mother: s. 4 (3), see further *supra*, p. 251.
[68] *Ibid.*
[69] s. 5 (4).
[70] *Supra*, p. 211.
[71] *Supra*, p. 266.
[72] Sched. II, see *supra*, p. 52.

has no rights, nor has he himself unless (a) he has obtained a custody order, and (b) the mother has been deprived of the right to custody. The exclusion of the testamentary guardian is no doubt an oversight; the exclusion of the father himself is indicative of the reluctance to accord him paternal rights.

CHAPTER 9

ADOPTION

ADOPTION, in English family law, has a restricted meaning [1] : it is the process whereby a court extinguishes the parental links between a child and his natural parents, and creates analogous links between him and the adopters.[2] It is impossible to adopt a child without a court order: a mere agreement whereby a parent seeks to transfer his rights and duties to someone else is ineffective for this purpose [3]; similarly *de facto* assumption of parental rights over a child is ineffective to vest parental rights and duties in those who have put themselves *in loco parentis* to the child.[4]

Adoption in England is entirely the creature of statute.[5] No provision for it was made until 1926. English law thus differs sharply from Civil law systems which, inheriting the Roman concepts of *adoptio* and *adrogatio*, recognise legal transfers from one family group to another. Again, in England adoption is normally associated with a desire to nurture a young child as if he were the natural child of the adopters. Although adoption has important effects on succession and other legal rights,[6] these rights are usually incidental to the factual relationship of dependence between parent and child,[7] and adoption is not used primarily to govern succession rights. In Civil law systems (which, unlike English law, often permit the adoption of one adult by others) [8] adoption is sometimes used to confer succession rights on the adopted person.[9] The English freedom of testation [10] made that unnecessary in English law.

---

[1] *Cf.* Shorter O.E.D. " to take voluntarily into any relationship . . . especially that of a son."

[2] s. 13 (1), Adoption Act 1958.

[3] *Humphreys* v. *Polak* [1901] 2 K.B. 385; *Brooks* v. *Blount* [1923] 1 K.B. 257; s. 1 (2), Guardianship Act 1973.

[4] As to the effect of such placements on parental rights and duties, see Chap. 7.

[5] Now Adoption Acts 1958 to 1964. The Adoption Act 1968 deals with adoptions involving a foreign element and implements the 1965 Hague Convention (Cmnd. 2613); it is outside the scope of this book: for details see McClean and Patchett, 19 I.C.L.Q. 1.

[6] See Adoption Act 1958, s. 16, *infra*, p. 362.

[7] See *Re A.* [1963] 1 All E.R. 531 where an adoption order was refused since it was sought solely to give the adopted person (who was aged 20) British nationality; *cf. Re R.* [1966] 3 All E.R. 613 where an adoption order was made in respect of a 20-year-old national of a totalitarian state, who wanted not only to acquire British nationality, but also to become a member of the applicant's family.

[8] Only a person under 18 can now be adopted under English law: see Adoption Act 1958, ss. 1 and 57, as amended by Family Law Reform Act 1969, Sched. 1, Part 1.

[9] *E.g.* the attempt of Mr. Somerset Maugham (then aged 88) to adopt under French law his male secretary, Mr. Alan Searle (then aged 57). The object was to defeat the claim of Lady John Hope (his only daughter) to a *legitima portio* on his death: See *Dicey & Morris*, p. 466.

[10] *Supra*, p. 165.

340

HISTORICAL BACKGROUND

Adoption in the sense of " the complete severance of the legal relationship between parents and child and the establishment of a new one between the child and his adoptive parent " [11] is now universally accepted and widely practised.[12] But it has evolved into something very different from what was originally envisaged, both in concept and acceptability.[13] *De facto* adoptions had probably been common in the industrial slums for many years, when charitably disposed neighbours would bring up an orphan (who would otherwise go to an institution) as their own child.[14] But attention tended to be concentrated on a very different phenomenon: in Victorian times, pregnant unmarried women would arrange for their child to be delivered in a private lying-in house, the owner of which would receive a lump sum of money [15] in exchange for arranging the baby's " adoption." The child was removed to "the worst class of baby-farming house " [16] the owners of which received either a small lump sum or an inadequate weekly allowance. There the children were " so culpably neglected, so ill-treated, and so badly nurtured " (*e.g.* on a diet consisting of a mixture of laudanum, lime, cornflour, water, milk and washing powder) " that with rare exceptions they all of them die in a very short time."

The worst features of baby-farming were stamped out by legislation, but the commercial exploitation of those who had an unwanted child, or those who wanted to bring up a child as their own troubled the legislature for many years to come. The practice of *de facto* adoption grew considerably in the first part of the twentieth century, perhaps for the following reasons [17]:

(i) The 1914-18 war led to an increase [18] in the number of orphans who were available for adoption. In addition, it may have led to an increase in the number of those who were unable or unwilling to look after their own children.

(ii) Increased knowledge of child psychology led to a preference in informed circles for a child to be brought up as a member of a family in normal home surroundings rather than in an institution.

[11] Houghton Report, para. 14.
[12] There were 23,399 adoption orders in the United Kingdom in 1971 and 641,406 orders have been made since 1927. Houghton Report, Appendix B.
[13] Report of the Departmental Committee on the Adoption of Children (" Hurst Report ") (1954) Cmd. 9248, para. 9.
[14] Major C. R. Attlee in the debate on the Adoption Act 1926: Hansard (H.C.) Vol. 917, col. 931.
[15] The sum seems to have varied from as little as £5 to £50 or even on occasion £100.
[16] This and the following quotations are from the Report of the Select Committee on the Protection of Infant Life B.P.P., 1871, vii, 607, which is not recommended to the squeamish.
[17] See the Report of the Committee on Child Adoption (1921) Cmd. 1254 B.P.P. 1921, ix, 161 (" The Hopkinson Report ") particularly para. 62; and the Report of the Child Adoption Committee, First Report (1925) Cmd. 2401, B.P.P. 1924–25, ix, 337 (" the Tomlin Report "), particularly at para. 6 *et seq.*
[18] There is no statistical evidence available: see the Tomlin Report, para. 4, expressing the view that the phenomenon was transient.

(iii) There was an increasing tendency to value child life and "to desire association with and the companionship of children on the part of those who have no children of their own or desire another child." [19]

(iv) Societies formed to encourage adoption gave publicity to the matter.[20]

Demand for reform of the law came from two main sources:

(a) Those who were concerned to provide security for the adopters. Since the law forbade a parent to bargain away his parental rights and duties, he might (at any time) seek to reclaim his child from the adopters; conversely, a mother who had placed her child with adopters might at any time be forced to take him back.[21] In 1921 it was said [22] to be "no uncommon thing, when a child has reached an age at which it can work and earn wages, for parents who have habitually rejected it and left it to be brought up by a relative or even a stranger, to claim it back simply in order to take its earnings."

(b) Those who were concerned with the evils of child trafficking.

Under the law as it then stood children could be handed from one person to another with or without payment or sent out of the country without any record being kept; intermediaries could accept children for adoption and dispose of them as and when they chose; and "homes" and institutions for the reception of children existed which were not subject to any system of inspection or control.[23] A particularly obtrusive feature was the use of newspaper advertisements, often inserted by professional agents who would charge both the natural parent and the adopters large fees. The following are specimens,[24] (all inserted by the same person):

"I's a lovely baby boy. I'm lonely and sad without mummy or daddy to make me glad; will anyone adopt me?"
"Adoption — beautiful blue-eyed boy wishes to be adopted where he would give love in return for parents and home."
"Good refined home required for Army officer's twin boy and girl, fortnight old."

Pressure led to the appointment of the Hopkinson Committee in 1921,

---

[19] The Hopkinson Report, loc. cit.
[20] According to the Tomlin Report, their activities gave adoption a "prominence which is somewhat artificial and may not be in all respects wholesome." Loc. cit.
[21] Hurst Report, para. 12.
[22] Hopkinson Report, para. 13. The Tomlin Report (whose general approach to adoption was unenthusiastic) suggested that such apprehensions had "but a slight basis in fact," since the courts had long recognised that any application by the natural parents to recover the custody of his child would be determined by reference to the child's welfare and by that consideration alone: para. 9. This is correct as a statement of principle: see J. v. C. [1970] A.C. 668, supra, p. 289 but its application in practice was far less certain, Re Thain [1926] Ch. 676.
[23] Hopkinson Report, para. 61.
[24] Taken from para. 30 of the Report of the Departmental Committee on Adoption Societies and Agencies (1937) Cmd. 5499, BPP 1936–37, ix, 1 ("the Horsburgh Report").

which reported that legal provision for the adoption of children should clearly be made, and that the question had become urgent.[25] Adoption was the next best thing to a stable home with natural parents; satisfaction of the natural desire of the childless to have the care and bringing up of a child was a proper object of the law, and was often in itself the best guarantee of the adopted child's welfare.[26] The Committee recognised that legal adoption would never be more than " one link in the chain " [27] and proposed measures to prevent abuses of long term child care arrangements.[28]

This report prompted attempts to introduce legislation,[29] but in view of the differences of opinion which the debates revealed, the Government appointed a second committee, under the chairmanship of Tomlin J. This Committee's report was sceptical about the validity of the arguments for legal adoption, but nevertheless concluded that a case had been made out for giving some legal recognition to the link between the adopter and the adopted child, and some procedure for the transfer of parental rights and duties. The Committee drafted a Bill,[30] which was the basis of the Adoption Act 1926. This laid the basis for the modern law, but many changes of principle have been effected by later legislation which has accepted the principle that so far as possible an adopted child should be treated as the legitimate child of the adopters for all purposes.

We shall consider: (i) the main characteristics of the existing law; (ii) criticisms of the existing law and proposals for its reform.

ADOPTION UNDER THE ADOPTION ACTS 1958-64
WHO MAY ADOPT AND BE ADOPTED

The first striking feature of English law is that it lays down detailed rules which "attempt to embody in precise legal rules two general judgments of what constitutes unsuitability to adopt." [31]

(a) There are age restrictions designed to ensure that the adopters are sufficiently mature to undertake the responsibilities of adoptive parenthood [32]:
> (i) if the applicants are a married couple, the normal rule is that one of them must be at least twenty-five and the other twenty-one.[33] If either of the spouses is the child's parent

---

25 Para. 9.
26 Para. 14.
27 Para. 59.
28 It also made other valuable recommendations, some of which have still got to be implemented—e.g. that all statutes dealing with children be consolidated and put into a form convenient for reference.
29 2nd Report, Cmd. 2469, BPP, 1924–25, ix, 349.
30 Ibid.
31 Houghton Committee Working Paper (1970) para. 60.
32 Ibid.
33 Adoption Act 1958, s. 2 (2) (b).

there is no age requirement [34]; if either of them is a
" relative " [35] of the child an adoption order can be made
provided both are twenty-one.[36]

(ii) If the application is by an individual, the rules are that he
must be twenty-five unless he is the child's parent (in which
case there is no age restriction), or a relative who has
attained twenty-one.[37]

(b) An adoption order can be made in favour of an individual
or a married couple.[38] There is no power to make a joint adoption
order except to a couple who are married: this means, for instance,
that an elderly brother and sister cannot jointly adopt their young
nephew; it also means that a couple who are not legally married
cannot adopt a child even if he is the natural child of one of
them, and is being brought up in a common household. An
individual married person can adopt a child only with the consent
of his spouse.[39] It is provided that the court may dispense with
the consent of the spouse of an applicant for an adoption order
if it is satisfied that the person whose consent is to be dispensed
with cannot be found or is incapable of giving his consent or that
the spouses have separated and are living apart and that the
separation is likely to be permanent.[40]

(c) There is no rule preventing a single woman from adopting a
male child (whether or not she is related to him). But an adoption
order is not to be made in respect of a female child in favour of
a sole applicant who is male, unless the court is satisfied that there
are special circumstances which justify as an exceptional measure
the making of an adoption order.[41] The fact that the applicant was
the natural father of the child has been held insufficient.[42]

(d) The person to be adopted must never have been married
and must be under eighteen.[43]

(e) The Act contains special rules defining the jurisdiction of
the courts where either the adopters or the child are not both
resident and domiciled in this country. Consideration of these
rules is outside the scope of this book.[44]

---

[34] *Ibid.* s. 2 (2) (*a*). As to the reasons why adoption might be indicated in such a case,
see *infra*, p. 360.
[35] Defined in s. 57 (1) to mean a grandparent, brother, sister, uncle or aunt (of the full
or half blood), and (if the child is illegitimate) any persons who would be relatives
if he were legitimate.
[36] Adoption Act 1958, s. 2 (2) (*b*).
[37] *Ibid.*, s. 2 (1).
[38] s. 1 (1) (2).
[39] s. 4 (1) (*a*).
[40] s. 5 (4).
[41] s. 2 (3).
[42] *Re R. M.* (1941) 193 L.T.Jour. 7 (C.A.); *cf. Re H., Petitioner*, 1960 S.L.T.(Sh.Ct.) 3,
where an order was made when the applicant's wife had died after the child had
been taken into their care, but before a joint application could be made.
[43] Adoption Act 1958, s. 1 (1); s. 57 (1), as amended by the Family Law Reform Act 1969.
[44] See n. 5, *supra*.

It should be stressed that these rules are simply pre-conditions. The court has a discretion whether or not to make an adoption order, it *cannot* do so if any of the pre-conditions is not complied with; it *may* not do so even if they are.[45] In order to discharge its statutory duty of deciding whether adoption will be for the child's welfare [46] the court will require a great deal more information about the adopters than the conditions set out above might indicate: the *guardian ad litem* [47] is specifically required to report on a wide range of topics—for instance, he is required to draw the attention of the court to the difference in age between the applicant and the infant if it is less than the normal difference in age between parents and their children,[48] and to the reason why a married applicant's spouse does not join in the application.[49] If the child has been placed with the prospective adopters by an adoption agency (as distinct from a direct placement—*e.g.* with a relative—or a placement arranged by an individual mediator, such as a doctor or solicitor),[50] far more searching inquiries will normally be made in an attempt to assess the suitability of the proposed adoption.[51]

LEGAL PRE-REQUISITES TO ADOPTION
Probationary Period

In order to allow a period for the child to settle in the home and for the applicants to adapt to their new role as parents,[52] the Act lays down [53] that an adoption order shall not be made in respect of any infant unless he has been continuously in the care and possession of the applicants for at least three months immediately preceding the date of the order, not counting any time before the date which appears to the court to be the date on which the infant attained the age of six weeks.

There have been difficulties in interpreting what meaning to give the expression " continuously in the care and possession of the applicant ": in one case [54] the prospective adopters allowed the child to go to its natural mother (who subsequently resisted the making of an adoption order) for two consecutive nights and one further night during the three-month period. Roxburgh J. held that this voluntary

---

45 1958 Act, s. 1 (1); *Re A.* [1963] 1 All E.R. 531.
46 1958 Act, s. 7 (1) (*b*), *infra*, p. 359.
47 See *infra*, p. 346.
48 Adoption (High Court) Rules 1959, Sched. 2, para. 12.
49 *Ibid*. para. 1 (*h*).
50 See *infra*, p. 366.
51 See " A Guide to Adoption Practice " (a handbook prepared in 1970 by a joint committee appointed by the Advisory Councils on Child Care of England and Wales, and Scotland), Chap. III.
52 In 1966, out of 9,614 adoptions arranged by adoption societies in England and Wales, some 1·1 per cent. of the children placed were returned to the societies, usually at the request of the adopters: " Some Casework Implications in the Study of Children Reclaimed or Returned before Final Adoption " by M. Kornitzer and J. Rowe (1968).
53 1958 Act, s. 3 (1).
54 *Re C. S. C.* [1960] 1 All E.R. 711.

surrender of the child interrupted the necessary period, so that the condition precedent to the making of an order had not been satisfied. Yet the words of the section are not to be construed literally, otherwise an adoption order could rarely be made in the case of minors who no longer need continuous care [55] or babies whose prospective adopters employ a nurse for periods when they are away.[56] The basic test is: where is the infant's home and has there been a parental relationship with the applicants during the period? Have the applicants throughout the period exercised quasi-parental control over the child even if there has been no continuous physical propinquity? [57]

Notification to the Local Authority

Unless the applicant (or one of two joint applicants) is a parent of the child, no adoption order is to be made in respect of a child who at the hearing of the application is below the upper limit of the compulsory school age unless the applicant has, at least three months before the date of the order, given notice in writing of his intention to adopt the child to the local authority within whose area he was then resident.[58] The effect of giving such notice is that the child becomes a " protected child," [59] and the local authority is required to secure that he be visited from time to time by officers of the local authority, who must satisfy themselves as to the well-being of the children and give such advice as to their care and maintenance as may appear to be needed.[60] The Act contains various powers permitting local authority officers to inspect premises where protected children are kept,[61] to prohibit the placement of a child if it would be detrimental to the child to be kept by the applicant in the premises concerned,[62] or to apply to the court [63] for his removal to " a place of safety " if circumstances justify this course.

Appointment of a Guardian Ad Litem

The court must appoint a *guardian ad litem* of the infant whose duties are to safeguard the interests of the infant before the court.[64] In cases

---

[55] *Re A.* [1963] 1 All E.R. 531 (" Infant " aged 20, artificiality of test commented on).
[56] *Re B.* [1964] Ch. 1.
[57] *Re A.*; *Re B.* (*supra*).
[58] 1958 Act, s. 3 (2).
[59] s. 37 (1) (*b*). In most cases the child will be a " protected child " in any case, since the expression also includes any child below the upper limit of the compulsory school age when arrangements have been made by a person other than his parent or guardian for placing him in the care and possession of a person who is not a parent, guardian or relative of his but who proposes to adopt him: s. 37 (1) (*a*) as amended by s. 52 (4) (*a*), Children and Young Persons Act 1969. A child taken directly from the mother without third party intervention would, however, be within s. 37 (1) (*b*) but not s. 37 (1) (*a*).
[60] s. 38.
[61] s. 39.
[62] s. 41. There is a right of appeal against such a prohibition: s. 42.
[63] *i.e.* a juvenile court. But a single justice of the peace may make such an order if there is imminent danger to the health or well-being of the child: s. 43 (1).
[64] s. 9 (8).

brought in the High Court,[65] the guardian will normally be the Official Solicitor; in the county court and juvenile court the local authority's children's officer, who will delegate the function to a child care officer, is usually concerned.[66] Rules of court prescribe the extensive duties of a guardian [67]: he has a primary duty to verify all the statements contained in the adoption application, to ascertain that all the requisite consents [68] have been freely given and to discover whether everyone who has the right [69] has also the opportunity to be heard.[70] His report is confidential,[71] the parties have no right to be informed of its contents, but where a report contains allegations against a party directly affecting his rights, efforts are to be made to apprise him of what is said against him, so that he can seek to meet the allegation.[72]

Consent of Parents and Guardians

An adoption order is not to be made except with the consent of every person who is a parent or guardian of the child,[73] although there is a limited discretion to dispense with consents in certain cases.[74]

The putative father of an illegitimate child is not, for this purpose, a parent [75]: his consent to the adoption is thus not required. In certain circumstances, however, he has *a right to be heard* by the court:

(i) if he is liable by virtue of an order or agreement to contribute to the maintenance of the child, the rules of court stipulate [76] that he must be notified of the application, and may attend the hearing.[77]

(ii) Even if he is not so liable, the *guardian ad litem* has a duty to inform the court if he learns of any person claiming to be the father who wishes to be heard by the court on the question of whether the adoption order should be made or not.[78] The extent

---

[65] For the jurisdiction of the various courts, see *infra*, p. 359.
[66] If the local authority is itself the placing agency (see *infra*, p. 365), a probation officer or neighbouring children's officer may be appointed: see Adoption (County Court) Rules 1959, r. 8 (2) and " A Guide to Adoption Practice," para. X, 2.
[67] See *e.g.* the Adoption (High Court) Rules 1971, Sched. 2.
[68] *Infra.*
[69] *Infra.*
[70] " A Guide to Adoption Practice," para. X, 4.
[71] *Re J. S.* [1959] 3 All E.R. 856.
[72] *Re G.* [1963] 2 Q.B. 73, *per* Donovan L.J.; *Re M.* [1973] Q.B. 108. The court may adopt the practice of allowing disclosure to the affected party's counsel: *cf. Re K.* [1965] A.C. 201.
[73] s. 4 (1) (*a*).
[74] Dealt with fully below: see p. 351.
[75] *Re M.* [1955] 2 Q.B. 479; *Re Adoption Application 41/61* [1962] 2 All E.R. 833; affirmed [1963] Ch. 315.
[76] See *e.g.* Adoption (High Court) Rules 1971, r. 17 (*c*).
[77] Until the 1958 Act, a putative father's consent was required if he had contributed to the child's maintenance. The provision was removed (following the recommendation of the Hurst Committee) because (i) the requirement led to anomalies, and (ii) on occasion, to a mother refusing to seek an affiliation order.
[78] Adoption (High Court) Rules 1971, Sched. 2, para. 9.

to which different guardians and courts conceive it their duty to seek out the putative father varies.[79]

(iii) The father of an illegitimate child has the right to apply for *custody*.[80] If he does so, procedural complications may arise: the applications may be in different courts,[81] and even if (as is the proper procedure [82]) arrangements are made for the adoption application and custody suit to be heard at the same time and in the same court, appeals may lie to different courts.[83] Furthermore, there may be difficulty in avoiding the disclosure of the prospective adopters' identity to the natural parents [84] if both applications are heard at the same time in the same court.

The test to be applied in determining the custody proceedings is [85]: what is for the welfare of the child? The court may, therefore, dismiss the father's application for custody because it thinks the child's welfare will be better served by making an adoption order,[86] even in circumstances where it could not be said that a parent whose consent was required to the proposed adoption was being unreasonable in withholding it.[87] The court may thus in effect reject a putative father's objections to the making of an adoption order when it would not be able to dispense with the consent of a lawful parent. The effect of giving the putative father a right to apply for custody is thus in no way to equate his right to object to adoption with that of a lawful

---

[79] In *Re Adoption Application 41/61 (No. 2)* [1964] Ch. 48, Wilberforce J. stated that there is no duty on a guardian to seek out the putative father or (in the absence of special circumstances) to make any inquiries as to the existence, whereabouts or attitude of a putative father. But practice differs: *cf.* Houghton Working Paper, para. 181: " Some [courts] insist on every effort being made to seek him out;" and the Report of the Standing Conference of Societies Registered for Adoption on Difficulties arising from the Adoption Act 1958.

[80] s. 14, Guardianship of Minors Act 1971, replacing s. 3, Legitimacy Act 1959. This enables him to apply (in the county court or Magistrates' Court as well as the High Court) under the statutory provisions; he has always been able to apply to have the child made a ward of court: *Re A.* [1955] 2 All E.R. 202; *Re Adoption Application 41/61* [1963] Ch. 315.

[81] As in *Re Adoption Application 41/61* [1963] Ch. 315.

[82] *Ibid.; Re O.* [1965] Ch. 23.

[83] As in *Re E. (P.)* [1969] 1 All E.R. 323, where competing custody and adoption applications were heard in the county court; an appeal lay in the custody application initially to the High Court (Guardianship of Minors Act 1971, s. 16 (2)), whereas the appeal in the adoption application was direct to the Court of Appeal. There is no reason why a putative father should not simply put his case in the adoption proceedings: *Re Adoption Application 41/61 (No. 2)* [1964] Ch. 48.

[84] See *infra*, p. 350. But these are not necessarily insoluble: *Re Adoption Application 41/61 (No. 2)* [1964] Ch. 48; *Re O.* [1965] Ch. 23, *per* Lord Denning M.R.—the correct course is to hear the applications separately, but not to give judgment on either until the conclusion of both hearings.

[85] s. 1, Guardianship of Minors Act 1971; *supra*, p. 289.

[86] As in *Re Adoption Application 41/61 (No. 2)* [1964] Ch. 48.

[87] See *infra*, p. 353. There have been cases where the court has refused to make an adoption order (because the parent's consent is not available, and cannot be dispensed with) but have yet made a guardianship order in favour of the prospective adopters (thus allowing them to retain custody of the child): see *e.g. Re E.* [1963] 3 All E.R. 874. As to the distinction between custody and adoption in such cases, see *J.* v. *C.* [1970] A.C. 668 and *supra*, p. 288.

father.[88] His fatherhood is only one factor in assessing the best interests of the child.[89]

What is for the welfare of the child depends on the particular facts of any case: the effect of an adoption order will be to extinguish any tie that may exist between the child and his natural parent, and the court must therefore consider the blood tie between the child and his natural father " not on the basis that the person concerned has a claim which he has a right to have satisfied, but, if at all, and to the extent that, the conclusion can be drawn that the child will benefit from the recognition of this tie." [90] There may be cases where, on the facts, the continued recognition of this tie may be sufficiently beneficial to the child to outweigh the advantages of adoption [91] but in many cases the fact that an adoption order will remove the stigma of illegitimacy [92] and give the child security [93] will outweigh the advantages to be gained from recognition of a father (even one devoted to the child) [94] at least if the father is not himself able to provide a satisfactory domestic environment for the child.[95]

A *guardian* is a person who has been so appointed by deed or will, or by a court, under the provisions of the Guardianship of Minors Act 1971.[96] Even if the court grants the custody of an illegitimate child to his natural father, under the statutory provisions [97] he does not become a " guardian " within the meaning of the Adoption Act, and his consent to adoption is not required.[98]

How consent is given

The consent which is required is a consent to the making of an order by the court. It is, therefore, only effective if it exists at the date of the hearing and order.[99] The simplest method of giving such consent is to attend the hearing, and give the consent in the face of the court. But to expect the mother to do this—apart from prejudicing the confidentiality of the proceedings—could cause emotional and

---

[88] *Re Adoption Application 41/61 (supra)* not following *Re B.* (July 27, 1961) (unreported); *Re O. (supra) per* Lord Denning M.R.; *cf. per* Harman L.J. The correctness of this view is open to question in the House of Lords: *Re C. (M.A.)* [1966] 1 All E.R. at 849.

[89] *Per* Lord Denning M.R., *Re O. (supra).*

[90] *Re Adoption Application 41/61 (No. 2) (supra), per* Wilberforce J. at p. 53.

[91] See *e.g. Re C. (M.A.)* [1966] 1 All E.R. 838 where the recognition accorded to the blood-tie, and the supposed " instinctual " bond between father and child were the decisive factors: see at p. 847B, and *cf.* the powerful dissenting judgment of Willmer L.J., particularly at p. 855I.

[92] *Re E. (P.) (supra), Re F. (T.)* [1970] 1 W.L.R. 192.

[93] *Re Adoption Application 41/61 (No. 2) supra* at p. 57.

[94] As in *Re E. (P.).*

[95] *Cf. Re E. (P.)* and *Re C. (M.A.) (supra).*

[96] *Supra,* p. 251.

[97] *Supra.*

[98] *Re Adoption Application 41/61 (No. 2) (supra).*

[99] *Re Hollyman* [1945] 1 All E.R. 290; *Re K.* [1953] 1 Q.B. 117; *Re F.* [1957] 1 All E.R. 819; *Re W.* [1972] Q.B. 589 (reversed, but not so as to affect the point [1971] A.C. 682).

practical problems.[1] It is therefore provided [2] that where a child's parent or guardian does not attend at the hearing then, subject to conditions, a document signed by the person consenting is admissible as evidence of consent. The conditions are:

(i) if the consent is that of the mother, the infant must be at least six weeks old on the date of the execution of the document,[3] and

(ii) the document must (if the mother is the signatory) be attested by a justice of the peace, county court officer or justice's clerk.[4] If the consent is that of any other person it is not *necessary* that it be attested in this way; if it is, however, it is admissible without further proof of the signature of the person by whom it is executed.[5]

(iii) The consent must be to a specific adoption: the identity of the applicant may be disguised by the use of a serial number, but it is not possible to consent to adoption generally.[6]

Signature of such a form of consent is in no way final: the form of consent states in terms [7] that the signatory understands the documents may be used as evidence of his consent " unless I inform the court that I no longer consent "; furthermore, the guardian *ad litem* is expressly charged to ascertain that every consent to the making of an order is freely given and with full understanding of the nature and effect of an adoptive order.[8] The fact that a mother has signed such a form has been said to be wholly irrelevant [9] in determining whether her consent is being unreasonably withheld. There are certain exceptions to the principle that signing a form of consent is immaterial if it is subsequently withdrawn:

(i) once consent in the statutory form has been given the parent or guardian can only remove the child from the care and possession of the applicant with leave of the court, and in considering whether to grant or refuse such leave the court shall have regard to the welfare of the infant.[10] Until that time, a parent has a right to require the child to be handed over to him.[11] This gives

---

[1] Hence the Hurst Committee refused to recommend a return to the requirement that the mother should attend to attest her consent.

[2] 1958 Act, s. 6 (1).

[3] s. 6 (2).

[4] s. 6 (3). Special rules apply if it is executed outside England and Wales.

[5] s. 6 (1).

[6] *Ibid.*, and s. 4 (2). The consent may, however, impose a condition about religious upbringing: s. 4 (2).

[7] Adoption (High Court) Rules 1971, r. 9, Form 3, para. 3.

[8] *Ibid.* Sched. 2, para. 7.

[9] *Re K.*, and see the other cases in n. 99 *supra.* If a parent has *vacillated* in deciding whether to consent or not that may be evidence of unreasonableness in withholding consent; but the fact that consent has at one time been manifested in the statutory form is immaterial.

[10] s. 34.

[11] Although a person having the child in his possession could frustrate this right by making the child a ward of court: see *supra*, p. 281.

an important tactical advantage to the adopters; the longer a child stays in the custody of the prospective adopters the less likely it is that the court will order him to be handed back to the parent.[12]

(ii) If a person gives his consent [13] to the making of an adoption order without knowing the identity of the applicant (*i.e.* under the serial number procedure referred to above) a subsequent withdrawal of consent on the ground only that he does not know the identity of the applicant shall be deemed unreasonable [14] (with the consequence that the court may dispense with it [15]). In practice this is unimportant: it would be an unimaginative parent or guardian who could not put forward some other reason to justify his change of heart.

Dispensing with consent of the parent or guardian

Although the scheme of the Act is that parental consent is an essential ingredient,[16] nevertheless, the court has a dispensing power in cases where the difficulty or impossibility of getting the requisite consents would make it harsh or unjust to refuse an order, or where it is unjust to allow a person to veto an adoption.[17] In some cases this is a matter of procedural convenience (*e.g.* if the parent is insane), but in others a wide and ill-defined discretion is given (*e.g.* if consent is unreasonably withheld). The exercise of this discretion is one of the most controversial features of the modern law. In statistical terms it is not very significant: in 1966, for instance, of 9,614 children placed for adoption by adoption societies 2·1 per cent. (205 children) were reclaimed by the natural mother before the court hearing. In only thirty-four cases was an application made to the court to dispense with consent, and in twelve cases the court did dispense with consent.[18] But these figures give a misleading impression of the significance of the court's powers: it has already been seen that the parent's consent can be withdrawn at any time up to the making of the order, and that the law can be said to encourage vacillation in this regard. All prospective adopters will be aware of the possibility of a withdrawal since cases in which an application is made to dispense with consent receive a great deal of publicity. This factor must be responsible for considerable tension on the part of applicants for an adoption order. The possibility

---

12 But *cf. Re C. (M. A.) (supra).*
13 *Semble* whether in the prescribed form or informally.
14 1958 Act, s. 5 (3).
15 *Infra*, p. 353.
16 *Per* Karminski L.J. *Re F. (R.)* [1970] Q.B. 385.
17 *Per* Buckley J., *Re R.* [1966] 3 All E.R. 613. It is doubtful whether the statement that the injustice must arise from a " defect of character " can stand with the House of Lords decision in *Re W. (infra).*
18 Report of Standing Conference of Societies Registered for Adoption to the Home Office on Difficulties arising from the Adoption Act 1958; *cf.* the (lower) figure in the sample taken by the Home Office Research Unit: A Survey of Adoption in Great Britain (Home Office Research Studies 10) (1971), pp. 66–67.

that even if consent is withdrawn, the court may dispense with it, may place the adopters in a cruel dilemma, particularly if the natural parent has vacillated in the past: should they hand the child back, or fight the case?   The Act provides (s. 5):

> " (1) The court may dispense with any consent required by paragraph (a) of subsection (1) of section four of this Act if it is satisfied that the person whose consent is to be dispensed with—
> (a) has abandoned, neglected or persistently ill-treated the infant; or (b) cannot be found or is incapable of giving his consent or is withholding his consent unreasonably.
> " (2) If the court is satisfied that any person whose consent is required by the said paragraph (a) has persistently failed without reasonable cause to discharge the obligations of a parent or guardian of the infant, the court may dispense with his consent whether or not it is satisfied of the matters mentioned in subsection (1) of this section."

These provisions derive from earlier legislation, and lack any logical pattern. The grounds are separate and independent.[19]

(a) *Parent abandoned, neglected or persistently ill-treated the infant* [20]

The substance of this provision dates back to the original 1926 Adoption Act,[21] following the recommendation of the Hopkinson Committee.[22] It has been restrictively interpreted: in *Watson* v. *Nikolaisen* [23] the mother of an illegitimate child handed him over to prospective adopters, signing a form of consent which she believed and intended would destroy her parental rights. She made no payments for its upkeep; but on the contrary drew, and kept for herself, children's allowance. Two years later she withdrew her consent. The Divisional Court held that she had not, within the meaning of this section, " abandoned " the child, for that word had to be construed in its context of neglect or persistent ill-treatment. Hence it meant such conduct as would expose a parent to the sanctions of the criminal law.[24] The mother had not left the child to its fate, but simply given it over to people who desired to adopt it, and in whom she had confidence. On this construction, there can be few acts (short of leaving a child on a doorstep [25] or otherwise abandoning him) which will satisfy the condi-

---

[19] *Per* Lord Donovan, *Re W*. (*An Infant*) [1971] A.C. 682, 724.

[20] Adoption Act 1958, s. 5 (1) (a).

[21] s. 2 (3) provided that consent could be dispensed with if the parent had " abandoned or deserted " the child. These words seem to have been derived from s. 1 of the Custody of Children Act 1891, and have been held to involve leaving the child to its fate: *Mitchell* v. *Wright*, 7 F. (C. of S.) 568. The present wording dates from s. 3 (1) (a), Adoption Act 1949.

[22] p. 33.

[23] [1955] 2 Q.B. 286.

[24] Under s. 27, Offences against the Person Act 1861 or s. 1, Children and Young Persons Act 1933.

[25] *R.* v. *White* (1871) L.R. 1 C.C.R. 311 ; *cf. R.* v. *Whibley* [1938] 3 All E.R. 777 (leaving five children in a moment of passion in a magistrates' court not sufficient).

tions.[26] A similarly restricted meaning has been put on the word
"neglected." [27] There is no authority on the words "persistently
ill-treated" but it seems likely that they would also be interpreted in
the same way, involving criminal neglect or ill-treatment. This ground
is only made out if the *infant* has been ill-treated. Thus, the court could
not dispense *under this head* with the consent of a father who had killed
the mother, and been convicted of manslaughter on the grounds of
diminished responsibility.[28]

(b) *Parent cannot be found or is incapable of giving his consent* [29]

This provision (which seems to be invoked more often than any
other) [30] will normally apply to cases where the whereabouts of the
person whose consent is required are unknown and cannot be discovered, or where he lacks the mental capacity to give consent.[31] A
person "can be found" if his address is known [32]; normally notice
must be served on each person whose consent is required,[33] and if
this is not done the court may give leave to appeal against an adoption
order out of time if in all the circumstances it is right to do so.[34] If,
however, the circumstances are such that, although a person's physical
whereabouts are known, there are no practical means of communicating
with him, he "cannot be found for the purposes of this section." In
Re R.,[35] where the parents lived in a totalitarian country and any
attempt to communicate with them would involve embarrassment and
danger, it was held that they "could not be found," for this reason. It
was also held that they were incapable of consenting since even if they
were able to be asked, it was unlikely that they would be allowed freely
to give their consent. This decision probably carries the law to its
extreme limit, but in practical terms it may not be important.

(c) *Parent is withholding his consent unreasonably* [36]

Under the 1926 Act there was power to dispense with the consent
of a person if he was "a person whose consent ought, in the opinion

---

26 See also *Re R.* [1966] 3 All E.R. 613, 616: infant refugee from totalitarian country
   had not been abandoned by his parents, even though they were prepared to let him
   go without expectation of exercising any further control over him.
27 *Re W. (Spinster) (An Infant)* (1962), unreported: see *Re P.* [1962] 3 All E.R. 789, 793.
28 *Re F. (T.) (An Infant)* [1970] 1 W.L.R. 192.
29 s. 5 (1) (b), reproducing s. 2 (3) of Adoption of Children Act 1926.
30 Adoption Survey Table 4 (13).
31 *Re R.* [1966] 3 All E.R. 613, 616, *per* Buckley J. Note, however, that infancy does
   not *per se* prevent a person having the capacity to consent: *Re K.* [1953] 1 Q.B. 117.
32 *Re B.* [1958] 1 Q.B. 12.
33 *Re F. (R.) (An Infant)* [1970] 1 Q.B. 385, where the applicants had written to the
   mother at her last known address, advertised, and made inquiries through the Post
   Office. It appeared that they did not inquire of her father although they knew his
   address. The mother first learnt of the order two months after it was made, and her
   appeal was allowed out of time, the case being remitted to the county court. See also
   Re B. (supra).
34 *Ibid.*
35 [1966] 3 All E.R. 613.
36 s. 5 (1) (b). See generally Blom-Cooper (1957) 20 M.L.R. 473.

of the court and in all the circumstances to be dispensed with." [37]
That provision gave the court the widest possible discretion,[38] but
there is no evidence that it was often used. In the 1949 Act (a private
member's measure) the present formula was substituted.[39] The object
according to the Hurst Committee [40] was to focus the attention of the
courts on the welfare of the child when considering whether consent
should be dispensed with. But the courts took a different view. It was
held in a series of cases that (although it was a pre-requisite to the
making of an order that the court should be satisfied that the order
if made would be for the child's welfare [41]) the mere fact that the
order if made would conduce to the child's welfare does not make
the withholding of consent unreasonable.[42] A parent could perfectly
well say: " good as it might be for my child to be adopted and looked
after by someone else, I am not prepared that my child should be
removed entirely out of my life and no longer be a member of my
family and that I should be as if I had never had the child at all." [43]
There was a fundamental difference between custody proceedings (in
which the child's welfare was the paramount consideration [44]) and
adoption proceedings: a parent may have forfeited his rights to have
the care and custody of a child, but it is quite another thing to say
that he must therefore consent to the child being adopted so that it
becomes a member of the family of the adopting parents and the
natural parents lose all parental rights.[45] This may mean that the courts
will commit the care and custody of a child to applicants whose request
for an adoption order has failed because of a refusal or withdrawal
of consent.[46] There may seem little difference to a parent who is told
that his child is to remain in the custody of third parties between that
and adoption, but adoption and custody are entirely different in concept,
nature and legal consequences [47]: an adoption order is permanent
and irrevocable, while a custody order can be varied at any time; under
an adoption order the family ties with the natural parents are severed
forever, in most [48] cases the adopted child remaining ignorant of his
true parentage, while under a custody order the natural parents might
well have access and remain parents for all purposes, the child normally
being brought up in recognition of that parentage.[49] In custody cases

---

[37] s. 2 (3).
[38] *H.* v. *H.* [1947] K.B. 463, *per* Lord Goddard.
[39] s. 3 (1) (*c*).
[40] (1954) Cmd. 9248, para. 117.
[41] Adoption Act 1958, s. 7 (1) (*b*).
[42] *Re K.* [1953] 1 Q.B. 117; *Re F.* [1957] 1 All E.R. 819.
[43] *Hitchcock* v. *W. B.* [1952] 2 Q.B. 561 *per* Lord Goddard. See also *Re F. (An Infant)* [1957] 1 All E.R. 819.
[44] See *supra*, p. 289.
[45] *Watson* v. *Nikolaisen* [1955] 2 Q.B. 286, 296.
[46] As in *Re E.* [1964] 1 W.L.R. 51. See also *Re W.* [1965] 1 W.L.R. 1259.
[47] *J.* v. *C.* [1970] A.C. 668; see *per* Lord MacDermott at p. 714, and *supra*, p. 288.
[48] But not invariably: *Re B. (M. F.)* [1972] 1 W.L.R. 102.
[49] *J.* v. *C.* (*supra*).

" what is in question is the custody, care, or control of the child, or perhaps the administration of his property, and that is why his interest is the first and paramount consideration. But in adoption cases, what is in issue is the parent-child relationship itself, and in that relationship the parent as well as the child has legitimate rights " [50] In one line of cases it was held that these parental rights would only be forfeited if the parent's refusal to consent could be said to show a callous or self-indulgent indifference to the welfare of the child in the broad, long-term sense of that word.[51] If, therefore, a mother in refusing consent to an adoption displayed indifference to specific medical evidence demonstrating a prognosis of long term harm to the particular child concerned in the proceedings (as distinct from general psychological theory [52]) she would be said to be unreasonable in withholding consent; the provisions requiring parental consent to adoption were for the protection of the parent and a decision to overrule a parent's refusal had penal aspects.[53] Hence, the test was not the child's welfare, but the attitude of the natural parent to his welfare.[54] Other views had, however, received judicial support,[55] and the conflict was finally resolved by the House of Lords.[56] The following propositions seem now to be the law:

(i) It is not necessary, in order to dispense with consent, that the refusal be culpable or self-indulgent or that a failure or possible failure of parental duty is made out. " Unreasonableness is one thing. Culpability is another. It may be that all or most culpable conduct is unreasonable. But the converse is not necessarily true." [57] The unambiguous words of the Act must be given their normal meaning.

(ii) The welfare of the child is not the sole, or primary consideration in adoption cases. The distinction between adoption and custody cases must be insisted on.[58] The legal relationship of parent and child is not to be sundered lightly and without good reason.[59]

(iii) But it does not follow that considerations of the welfare of the child are to be *ignored* in determining whether a refusal of consent is unreasonable [60]:

[50] *Re W. (An Infant)* [1971] A.C. 682 at 693, *per* Lord Hailsham of Marylebone L.C.
[51] *Re C.(L.) (An Infant)* [1965] 2 Q.B. 449.
[52] *Re W. (An Infant)* [1970] 2 Q.B. 589 (C.A.). As to medical evidence in adoption cases see Hopkins, *Medicine, Science and the Law*, Vol. 9, p. 31.
[53] See *Re C.(L.) (An Infant) (supra)* and *Hitchcock* v. *W. B. (supra)*.
[54] See, for an excellent summary of this point of view, *per Sachs* L.J. [1970] 2 Q.B. 589.
[55] *Re L.* (1962) 106 S.J. 611 ; *Re C.* [1965] 2 Q.B. 449 ; *Re B.* [1970] 3 All E.R. 1008.
[56] *Re W. (An Infant)* [1971] A.C. 682.
[57] *Per* Lord Hailsham of St. Marylebone L.C. at p. 695.
[58] *Ibid.*, at p. 693 ; see also *Re P. A.* [1971] 1 W.L.R. 1530.
[59] *Per* Lord MacDermott at p. 708.
[60] See *per* Lord Sorn in *A. B.* and *C. B.* v. *X's Curator*, 1963 S.C. at pp. 137, 138 approved in *Re W. (supra)*.

" . . . the fact that a reasonable parent does pay regard to the welfare of his child must enter into the question of reasonableness as a relevant factor. It is relevant in all cases if and to the extent that a reasonable parent would take it into account. It is decisive in those cases where a reasonable parent must so regard it." [61]

(iv) The test is an objective one in the light of the facts of each individual case. A mother's "anguish of mind is quite understandable; but still it may be unreasonable for her to withhold consent. We must look and see whether it is reasonable or unreasonable according to what a reasonable woman would do in all the circumstances of the case." [62]

(v) In deciding whether the refusal is unreasonable all the circumstances which would weigh with a reasonable parent are to be considered, including the child's prospects and outlook if adopted as compared with those if unadopted. Material and financial prospects are relevant as are "education, general surroundings, happiness, stability of home and the like." [63] Nevertheless, prima facie it remains reasonable for a parent to refuse his consent to adoption.[64] The court must not simply substitute its own view for that of the parent:

" Two reasonable parents can perfectly reasonably come to opposite conclusions on the same set of facts without forfeiting their title to be regarded as reasonable. The question in any given case is whether a parental veto comes within the band of possible reasonable decisions and not whether it is right or mistaken. Not every reasonable exercise of judgment is right, and not every mistaken exercise of judgment is unreasonable. There is a band of decisions within which no court should seek to replace the individual's judgment with his own." [65]

In effect, therefore, a decision will only be held to be unreasonable if no reasonable parent could have taken it.

The facts of *Re W.* were summarised (by Lord Donovan [66]) as follows:

" A young girl (the natural mother) left home at the age of seventeen and went to live with a man by whom she had two illegitimate daughters. He left her and she then formed a liaison with another man by whom she had the present child—also illegitimate. Both fathers have deserted her. Before this third child was born she decided to have it adopted and after its birth she signed the required form of consent. Having settled down in better accommodation provided by the local council she withdrew this consent

[61] *Per* Lord Hailsham, *Re W. (supra)*, at p. 699.
[62] *Per* Lord Denning M.R., *Re L.* (1962) 106 S.J. 611, a statement regarded as " authoritative " by Lord Hailsham in *Re W. (supra)* (at p. 698) and as putting the natural construction " in a nutshell " by Lord MacDermott (*ibid.* at p. 711). See also *per* Lord Hodson at p. 719, Lord Guest at p. 723, and Lord Donovan at p. 725.
[63] *Per* Davies L.J., *Re B.* [1971] 1 Q.B. 437, 443 a statement which (*per* Lord Hodson in *Re W., supra*) " I cannot improve on. . . ."
[64] See particularly *per* Lord Hailsham at p. 700, and *per* Lord MacDermottt at p. 708.
[65] *Per* Lord Hailsham at p. 700; followed in *O'Connor* v. *A. and B.* [1971] 2 All E.R. 1230, H.L.(Sc.) (see *per* Lord Simon at pp. 1237–1238).
[66] At p. 727.

about a month later and decided that she would keep the child. She is keeping her other two illegitimate children, and looks after them well with the help of her own mother and sisters and a female cousin of twenty-seven who lives with her. She does not work but lives on social security payments. There is no male influence in the home, beyond an uncle of the mother, aged about thirty-four, who visits the home about once a week. She hopes to get married later.

The appellants were described by the guardian ad litem as an extremely pleasant happily married couple with whom the infant has made good progress. They have two other children, one adopted, one natural. The adoptive father works in the printing trade and earns £25 a week. He and his wife can give the infant greater stability and security. As compared with this, there must be, as the judge clearly thought, ' an enormous question mark ' in relation to the respondent, and quite plainly, and quite legitimately, he could not put out of his mind the possibility of another association leading to another unwanted child. He assessed this as a grave risk."

On these facts, the mother's consent was dispensed with.

The application of the law to the facts of any particular case is essentially a matter for the court of first instance: if correct passages from the authorities are recited, and no manifest error of law or other misdirection occurs in the judgment, an appellate court will be reluctant to interfere.[67] The decision in Re W. is legally somewhat limited and much of the old case law remains relevant. In particular, the operative time for assessing reasonableness or otherwise is the time of the hearing.[68] In many cases, the mother will have withdrawn a consent previously given: this is not necessarily to be held against her,[69] but in weighing up all the circumstances the court will give considerable weight to the known dangers of a change of environment for a young child.[70] It would appear (after some doubt) that the impact of the refusal on the prospective adopters may also be taken into account,[71] although little weight could be given to this factor by itself.

Although the legal significance of the case may be comparatively small, it may have repercussions on the willingness of courts to dispense with consent. In O'Connor v. A. and B. [72] an appeal from Scotland decided some three months later, the House of Lords refused to interfere with a decision dispensing with the consent of both natural parents of a child, where marriage to each other had legitimated him, and who could provide the child with an adequate home (although not so good as the prospective adopters). It is difficult to believe that this decision

[67] See O'Connor v. A. and B. (supra) (particularly per Lord Wilberforce).
[68] Re L.; Re W. (supra); Re S. [1973] 3 All E.R. 88 (time of appellate hearing).
[69] Re W. (supra), particularly per Lord MacDermott, p. 708.
[70] Re C. (L.) (An Infant) [1965] 2 Q.B. 449; Re W. (supra); O'Connor v. A. and B. See N. Michaels, " The Dangers of a Change of Parentage in Custody and Adoption Cases " (1967) 83 L.Q.R. 547.
[71] O'Connor v. A. and B. (supra) per Lord Simon at p. 1237 and per Lord Reid at p. 1232; see also Re P. A. (An Infant) [1971] 3 All E.R. 522.
[72] Supra.

(thought to be the first of its kind) would have been taken in the years before *Re W*.

In one case, the statute gives a clear rule about withholding consent. If [73]

> " a person who has given his consent to the making of an adoption order without knowing the identity of the applicant therefor subsequently withdraws his consent on the ground only that he does not know the identity of the applicant, his consent shall be deemed for the purposes of this section to be unreasonably withheld." [74]

(d) *Failure to discharge parental obligations*
The Act provides [75] that if—

> the court is satisfied that any person whose consent is required by the said paragraph (a) has persistently failed without reasonable cause to discharge the obligations of a parent or guardian of the infant, the court may dispense with his consent whether or not it is satisfied of the matters mentioned in subsection (1) of this section.

This was a new provision introduced in 1958, partly to take account of the narrow interpretation given by the courts to the " unreasonable withholding " provisions.[76] The obligations referred to have been held [77] to include both the natural and moral duty of a parent to show affection, care and interest towards his child, and the legal duty of a parent to maintain his child. In one case,[78] a father of Spanish nationality and residence was held to have shown such neglect where he had wanted legal custody of his daughter (born in England after his separation from the wife) but had taken no active steps to assert his claim, or support her, even though the child had been placed for adoption some days after birth. It seems paradoxical that a parent could be held so to have neglected his child, and yet not to be unreasonable in withholding his consent to adoption. The answer may be that unreasonableness is judged at the time of the hearing: if he then wants the child, is fit to have him, and is able and willing to support him, he could not be held unreasonable in withholding consent [79]; yet if he had *in the past* neglected the child consent could be dispensed with under this subsection. The court can only act if two conditions are fulfilled: (i) there must be *persistent* failure. This probably connotes a *permanent* abrogation [79a]; and (ii) the failure must be " without reasonable cause." In one case [80] it was held that an unmarried mother's wish to conceal the birth from her parents was a sufficiently reasonable cause.

[73] Under the procedure of serial numbers, explained *supra* at p. 350.
[74] s. 5 (3).
[75] s. 5 (2).
[76] See Hurst Committee Report, para. 120: the Committee intended this to be *substituted* for the " unreasonable withholding " ground discussed above.
[77] *Re P. (Infants)* [1962] 1 W.L.R. 1296.
[78] *Re B. (S.) (An Infant)* [1968] 1 Ch. 204.
[79] *Re W. (supra)*.
[79a] *Re D.* [1973] Fam. 209.
[80] *Re M. (An Infant)* (1965) 109 S.J. 574; see A. Samuels (1965) 109 S.J. 799.

Dispensing with consent of the adopter's spouse

The court has power to dispense with the consent of the applicant's spouse in certain circumstances.[81] This has already been dealt with.[82]

THE COURT AND ITS FUNCTIONS

The High Court (Family Division), the County Court, and Magistrates' Courts (juvenile court) have jurisdiction to make adoption orders. The county court is now the most widely used forum, hearing some 60 per cent. of applications; juvenile courts hear some 34 per cent. of applications. Fewer than fifty cases are heard in the High Court each year. The county court has increased in popularity over the years [83] particularly for third party adoptions.[84] The reasons have been said to be that county court judges are prepared to exercise a greater discretion than magistrates, that they accept affidavit evidence, and that there is a greater confidentiality about proceedings.[85] The diversity of choice is not, perhaps, a serious matter but it is regrettable that appeals are dealt with differently, those from the High Court and county court going to the Court of Appeal while those from magistrates go to a Divisional Court.[86]

The court's functions are laid down by the Act,[87] and by detailed rules made thereunder. The court must be satisfied—

> " (a) that every person whose consent is necessary under this Act, and whose consent is not dispensed with, has consented to and understands the nature and effect of the adoption order for which application is made, and in particular in the case of any parent understands that the effect of the adoption order will be permanently to deprive him or her of his or her parental rights;
>
> (b) that the order if made will be for the welfare of the infant; and
>
> (c) that the applicant has not received or agreed to receive, and that no person has made or given or agreed to make or give to the applicant, any payment or other reward in consideration of the adoption except such as the court may sanction.
>
> (2) In determining whether an adoption order if made will be for the welfare of the infant, the court shall have regard (among other things) to the health of the applicant, as evidenced, in such cases as may be prescribed, by the certificate of a fully registered medical practitioner, and shall give due consideration to the wishes of the infant, having regard to his age and understanding."

The provisions as to consent have already been explained: the discharge of the duty of explaining the effect of an order is often in

---

[81] s. 5 (4).
[82] See *supra*, p. 344.
[83] See Adoption Survey, Table 1 (3).
[84] *Ibid*. Table 2 (2).
[85] See Report of the Standing Conference of Societies Registered for Adoption to the Home Office on difficulties arising from the Adoption Act 1958.
[86] See Adoption of Children (H.M.S.O.) (1970), para. 189.
[87] s. 7.

practice placed on the guardian *ad litem*.[88] That relating to payments is designed to prevent trafficking in children and is considered below.[89] The rules make elaborate provision for medical examination.[90]

The requirement that the court must be satisfied that the order will be for the welfare of the child gives rise to more complex problems, on which some general principles have been laid down, in addition to the matters specifically referred to in the Act (*i.e.* the health of the applicants and the wishes of the child):—

(i) It is a benefit to a child to have the stigma of illegitimacy removed. This has been said to be a solid advantage, which should not be thrown away simply to preserve the rights of access which the natural father of an illegitimate child may have.[91] It is for this reason that adoptions by the mother (alone) of her own illegitimate child [92] have to be justified: adoption used to confer certain advantages relating to succession rights,[93] but this is no longer the case.[94] The courts tend to use emotive language in describing the stigma of illegitimacy,[95] but with the removal of the proprietary disadvantages of the status and a change in attitude it may be questioned how far the issue of a certificate showing that the child is adopted [96] rather than a birth certificate (which may, but need not,[97] reveal illegitimacy) is by itself a significant advantage.

(ii) In the majority of cases, the principal benefit to the child will be that of being brought up against the background of a normal family life, by parents who will have the legal security of knowing that the child cannot be reclaimed by the natural parents or anyone else.[98] If the adoption is not intended to confer the benefits of a real parent/child relationship the applicant will normally be refused.[99]

---

[88] In *Re G. (T. J.) (An Infant)* [1963] 2 Q.B. 73, it was held that a guardian's report sufficed to indicate the views of the infant, but in county court and juvenile court cases the rules now prescribe that a child who is capable of understanding shall attend the court, in the absence of special circumstances: Adoption (County Court) Rules 1959, rr. 11, 13. Adoption (Juvenile Court) Rules 1959, rr. 11 (2), 14.

[89] *Infra*, p. 366.   [90] *e.g.* Adoption (High Court) Rules 1971, r. 11.

[91] See *Re E. (P.) (An Infant)* [1969] 1 All E.R. 323 (which is to be referred to on the rights of a putative father); *Re C., P. and P. v. C.* (1969) 113 S.J. 721.

[92] There were only 22 applications by one parent alone out of 3,400 in a survey made in 1966: Adoption Survey Table 2 (8).   [93] *Re D.* [1959] 1 Q.B. 229.

[94] As a result of the improved succession rights conferred on illegitimate children by the Family Law Reform Act 1969, see *supra*, p. 330.

[95] See *e.g. Re E. (P.) (An Infant) (supra)* [" It does not seem to matter to the father that the child will remain a bastard. The effect of the Adoption Act 1958, is to to remove that stigma, so far as it can be removed, and to give children in that unfortunate position a fresh start in life without the slur attaching to their origin." *Per* Harman L.J. at p. 324] *cf.* the divergence of views in the Court of Appeal in *S.* v. *McC.* (orse S.) and M. (D. S. intervening) [1970] 1 W.L.R. 672.

[96] See *infra*, p. 364.   [97] See *supra*, p. 318.

[98] *Re B. (M. F.)* [1972] 1 W.L.R. 102.

[99] *Re A. (An Infant)* [1963] 1 All E.R. 53: the object was to confer on a 20-year-old Frenchman British nationality and the right to stay in this country with freedom from exchange control regulations which affected his interests under certain settlements; *cf. Re R. (Adoption)* [1966] 3 All E.R. 613, where an adoption order was made in respect of a 20-year-old refugee from a totalitarian country. The fact that the adoption would confer British nationality was not a bar (although security checks would be a pre-condition) and the child in that case would receive the social and psychological benefits of truly belonging to a family as a member of it, with the attendant legal status and rights.

In the typical case of adoption by strangers, care is taken to ensure that there should be no contact between the child and his natural parents. This is the view taken by adoption agencies and by the courts.[1] But the rule is not inflexible, and there may be exceptional circumstances where continued contact may be justified.[2] However, in a significant proportion of cases,[3] adoptions are by relatives other than the natural parent (*e.g.* grandparents, uncles and aunts). In some of these cases the natural parents will have died, but in others (*e.g.* the adoption of a daughter's illegitimate child) serious risks arise because the child and its natural parent " must inevitably remain in association to a greater or less degree, and it is impossible to exclude the risk of grave psychological strain and emotional disturbance. . . . The ostensible relationship of sisters between those who are, in fact, mother and child is unnatural, and its creation might sow the seeds of grievous unhappiness. . . ." [4] In such cases, adoption orders should only be made with great caution and in special circumstances.[5] It has been suggested [6] that such adoptions should no longer be permitted save in such exceptional circumstances, a matter referred to further below.[7]

In the exercise of the jurisdiction, individual courts differ a great deal in their approach to the procedure.[8] In the juvenile court and county court the personal attendance of the applicants is necessary, but much of the evidence may be given on affidavit. If the adoption is contested, however, it is vital that the court should see all parties, as well as considering the reports before it.[9] Dissatisfaction has been expressed about the way in which hearings are conducted in some courts.[10]

The court has power to impose conditions in the making of an adoption order (*e.g.* as to religious upbringing), and may require the adopter to make for the child provision by bond or otherwise.[11] Any such conditions should be clearly drafted; in the event of non-compliance the child can be made a ward of court, enabling the court to enforce the conditions.[12]

Interim Orders

The Act [13] provides that—

> . . . the court may, upon any application for an adoption order,

---

[1] *Re B.* (*M. F.*) (*supra*); *Re J.* [1973] Fam. 106. See also Houghton Report, para. 296.
[2] *Ibid.*
[3] 5 per cent. in a survey of applications in 1966: Adoption Survey, Table 2 (6).
[4] *Per* Vaisey J., *Re D. X.* (*An Infant*) [1949] Ch. 320.
[5] *Re D. X.* (*An Infant*) (*supra*); *Re G.* (*D. M.*) (*An Infant*) [1962] 1 W.L.R. 730; *Re B.* (*M. F.*) (*supra*); see also the materials in *Hambly and Turner*, pp. 633–639.
[6] In the Houghton Committee Report, Chap. 5.
[7] See *infra*, p. 369.
[8] For a brief description see the Houghton Report, paras. 266–270.
[9] *Re F.* (*R.*) (*An Infant*) [1970] 1 Q.B. 385.
[10] See Houghton Committee Working Paper, paras. 195, 216; Report of Standing Conference of Societies Registered for Adoption on Difficulties arising from the Adoption Act 1958.
[11] s. 7 (3).
[12] *Re J.* [1973] Fam. 106; *cf. Re G.* (*T. J.*) (*An Infant*) [1963] 2 Q.B. 73.
[13] s. 8 (1).

postpone the determination of the application and make an interim order giving the custody of the infant to the applicant for a period not exceeding two years by way of a probationary period upon such terms as regards provision for the maintenance and education and supervision of the welfare of the infant and otherwise as the court may think fit.

This power is infrequently exercised. In 1969, 32 orders were made by juvenile courts.[14] Apparently, many of the interim orders are in respect of applications by a natural parent and a step-parent, or by grand-parents, and are used where the court is uneasy about the placement and wants to ensure a longer period of supervision. But it is only rarely that a full adoption order is not made in the end. There is a difference of opinion about the desirability of this practice.[15] Although the same consents are needed as for a final adoption order (the court having the same power to dispense)[16] the full legal consequences of adoption only arise in the making of the final order.[17] An interim order is wholly different from a so-called "Provisional Adoption Order," the object of which is to enable a foreign domiciliary to take a child out of Great Britain so as to adopt him under the laws of his own country.[18]

Revocation of Orders

The making of an adoption order is normally a final and irrevocable step. To this there are two exceptions:

(i) An appeal may be made,[19] within statutory time limits, against the grant or refusal of an adoption order. In exceptional circumstances, an appeal may be allowed outside this time limit, but it would have to be very exceptional if some years had gone by.[20]

(ii) If an illegitimate person has been adopted by his mother or father alone, the order may be revoked if the subsequent marriage of his parents has legitimated him.[21] It is thought that this will be advan-tageous to the child.

Effects of an Adoption Order

The general effect of an adoption order is to destroy the legal bond between both natural parents and the child, and to put him in the

---

[14] No figures are available for other courts. The contents of this paragraph are based on para. 309 of the Houghton Committee Report.

[15] Houghton Committee Working Paper, para. 238, Report, paras. 309–311.

[16] s. 8 (2).

[17] s. 8 (5).

[18] s. 53. Consideration of such orders is outside the scope of this book.

[19] If the court has refused to make an order, the Act provides (s. 35) that the child must be handed back to the placing agency (adoption society or local authority) within 7 days. There is no jurisdiction to order a stay pending appeal: *Re C. S. C.* [1960] 1 All E.R. 711. However, it may be possible to achieve the same result by making the child a ward of court. If the child has not been placed by an agency, there is no such obligation, and the natural parent must take proceedings to recover the child if it is not voluntarily handed over.

[20] *Re F. (R.) (An Infant)* [1970] 1 Q.B. 385.   [21] s. 26.

position of a legitimate child of his adopting parents. The Act provides[22]:

"(1) Upon an adoption order being made, all rights, duties, obligations and liabilities of the parents or guardians of the infant in relation to the future custody, maintenance and education of the infant, including all rights to appoint a guardian and (in England) to consent or give notice of dissent to marriage, shall be extinguished, and all such rights, duties, obligations and liabilities shall vest in and be exercisable by and enforceable against the adopter as if the infant were a child born to the adopter in lawful wedlock; and in respect of the matters aforesaid (and, in Scotland, in respect of the liability of a child to maintain his parents) the infant shall stand to the adopter exclusively in the position of a child born to the adopter in lawful wedlock.

(2) In any case where two spouses are the adopters, the spouses shall in respect of the matters aforesaid, and for the purpose of the jurisdiction of any court to make orders as to the custody and maintenance of and right of access to children, stand to each other and to the infant in the same relation as they would have stood if they had been the lawful father and mother of the infant and the infant shall stand to them in the same relation as to a lawful father and mother."

However, this general principle only relates to the matters specified in the Act. All existing orders relating to custody or maintenance will therefore cease automatically,[23] as will care orders and resolutions under section 2 of the Children Act 1948.[24] There is an exception to this general principle if an illegitimate child is adopted by his mother alone, she being a single woman[25] at the time of the order[26]: she will continue to be entitled to payments under an affiliation order or agreement. Otherwise such orders and agreements cease to have effect, and no affiliation order can be made in the future. It should be noted, that succession rights are not in all respects equated to those of a legitimate child.[27]

Secondly, although the Act provides[28] that for the purpose of marriage an adopter and the adopted person shall be deemed to be within the prohibited degrees (even though the child may subsequently have been adopted by a third party) it makes no other provision to bring an adopted child within the prohibited degrees to members of his adoptive family. Hence he may marry his adoptive parents' daughter; equally, if he were (however innocently)[29] to go through a ceremony of marriage with the daughter of his natural parents, that marriage would be void.[30]

---

[22] s. 13.   [23] *Crossley* v. *Crossley* [1953] P. 97.
[24] s. 15 (3), (4), as amended by Children and Young Persons Act 1969, ss. 5 and 6.
[25] See *supra*, p. 321.
[26] s. 15 (1).
[27] The adopted child has only limited rights under settlements made before the adoption: s. 16 (2).   [28] s. 13 (3).
[29] Some protection against this risk may exist in that, under the present practice, the adopters will know the surname of the natural parents: see *infra*, p. 365.
[30] *Supra*, p. 14.

REGISTRATION OF ADOPTIONS—ANONYMITY

The Registrar-General maintains an Adopted Children's Register,[31] and entries are made in it whenever an adoption order is made by an English court.[32] Certified copies of entries in the Register in effect replace the child's birth certificate: it gives his names (normally with the surname of the adopting parents [33]) and is sufficient evidence of the date and place of his birth.[34] The Registrar-General may issue a short form of birth certificate in respect of an adopted child.[35] This will contain no reference to his parentage, or to the fact that he has been adopted. For most purposes, therefore, outsiders will not discover that he is an adopted child. The Register is open to public search, in the same manner as the Register of Births.[36]

The Registrar-General is required to keep " such other registers and books, and make such entries therein, as may be necessary to record and make traceable " the connection between entry in the Adopted Children's Register and the child's original registration of birth.[37] It follows that it is possible to trace the original name and true parentage (so far as that is recorded on the birth certificate) of a child who has been adopted. However, these materials are not open to the public, and no information about them will be given save by court order.[38] It is understood that applications for such orders are few, and that the number of orders actually granted is very small indeed.[39] English law thus effectively prevents an adopted child finding out the true facts about his parentage. The Houghton Committee recommended that a child should, on reaching the age of eighteen be entitled as of right to see his original birth certificate. If further information from court records were sought, this would be within the court's discretion. This was based on research into the similar practice now existing in Scotland. This worked satisfactorily and many adopted persons have a psychological need to know as much as possible about their origins, which can occasionally only be satisfied by knowledge of the names of their parents, and perhaps by seeking them out.[40]

At this stage, the law seems primarily concerned to protect the natural parents who have placed the child for adoption in the belief that it would not subsequently be possible for them to be traced.[41] At the earlier stage of the placing and court hearing, the law is more con- cerned to protect the adopters from any subsequent approach by the

---

[31] s. 20.   [32] s. 21.
[33] s. 21 (2).
[34] s. 20 (2) ; s. 21 (2).
[35] *Supra*, p. 318.
[36] s. 20 (3).
[37] s. 20 (4). The original birth register entry is simply marked " adopted ": s. 21 (4).
[38] s. 20 (5).
[39] Houghton Committee Working Paper, para. 235.
[40] The research in Scotland suggests that such attempts are not often successful: Houghton Report, para. 301.
[41] Houghton Committee Working Paper, para. 232.

natural parents.[42] Their identity can be disguised by means of a serial number,[43] and attempts are made to ensure that the identity is not revealed to anyone not already aware of it.[44] But there is no provision to preserve the anonymity of the natural parents, whose name will or may appear on the consent form, the child's birth certificate and on the application form, with the result that the adopters will know of them. It has been suggested [45] that (in spite of the procedural difficulties) a serial number procedure should be available to protect the natural parents' anonymity.

ADOPTION PRACTICE—THE SOCIAL BACKGROUND [46]

" The crucial decision in the whole process of adoption is the decision regarding the actual placement of the child." The considerations which should be taken into account are matters for the social worker, rather than the lawyer. The majority of adoptions are arranged through adoption agencies. Traditionally, these have been voluntary societies, often with a religious inspiration. The Adoption Act 1958 provided [47] that all local authorities should have power to make and participate in adoption, but only some 96 out of 172 authorities in England and Wales have taken advantage of these powers.[48] To give some idea of the scope of the work, in 1971 voluntary societies placed a total of 5,640 children; in the same year local authorities placed some 4,130.[49]

Control is exercised over voluntary societies (which must be charities) [50] by the requirement [51] that they be registered with the local authority where their administrative centre is situated. Although registering authorities have a number of specific powers to refuse registration,[52] and certain powers to make investigations [53] it has been said that the " present requirements for registration are inadequate and

---

[42] Secrecy about the child's whereabouts originated in the practice of adoption societies, before legalised adoption was made possible in 1926, to avoid (as far as possible) a mother making a claim to recover the child which might be legally difficult to resist. The Tomlin Committee considered (para. 28) that secrecy was unnecessary and objectionable once adoption was given legal force.

[43] See e.g. Adoption (County Court) Rules 1959, r. 15.

[44] This may cause difficulties: Re O. (An Infant) [1965] Ch. 23, per Harman L.J. In Scotland, an attempt is made to avoid these difficulties by appointing a reporter to interview all the parties: see O'Connor v. A. and B. [1971] 2 All E.R. 1230.

[45] Houghton Committee Report, paras. 297–298.

[46] " A Survey of Adoption in Great Britain " (Home Office Research Papers, 10) (1971) is the major source of statistical information. See also " A Guide to Adoption Practice " by the Advisory Councils on Child Care [H.M.S.O. 1970] a useful source of information on this topic; See also M. Kornitzer, " Adoption " (1959).

[47] s. 28 (2).

[48] Houghton Report, para. 33.

[49] Ibid., App. B, Table 4. The proportion placed by Local Authorities has increased sharply in recent years.

[50] s. 30 (3).

[51] s. 29 (1). Provisions for registration were first introduced by the Adoption of Children (Regulation) Act 1939, after the Departmental Committee on Adoption Societies and Agencies (The Horsburgh Committee, Cmd. 5499, 1937) had looked into expressions of disquiet about the evils associated with unlicensed, unregulated and unsupervised adoption.

[52] s. 30.

[53] s. 33.

indeed registration has been variously treated by local authorities as a mere formality or as a serious exercise." [54] Consideration of these matters is outside the scope of this book, but the principal defect is that a comprehensive adoption service is not necessarily available to all persons throughout the country: some voluntary societies impose religious or other tests on applicants, whilst not all local authorities provide a service.[55] The Houghton Committee recommended the provision of a nation-wide comprehensive [56] service (which would still make use of the voluntary societies).[57]

It is *not* illegal for a private individual [58] to make arrangements for adoption. The Act forbids the making of payments in consideration of the making of adoption arrangements,[59] and contains provisions designed to prevent the worst abuses of baby-farming.[60] But there is nothing to stop private individuals arranging adoptions provided they do so without payment, and some 4 per cent. of adoptions in 1966 were of this kind.[61] There are two major criticisms of this practice: first, the agent will often lack any understanding of the complex issues involved; second, he may be primarily concerned, not with the welfare of the child but with the needs of the natural parents or adopters.[62] The Hurst Committee [63] particularly criticised the " deplorable cases in which a doctor acts as third party for the benefit of a patient whose neurotic condition he seeks to remedy or whose marriage he hopes to stabilise by this means. An example (which, it was stressed, was not typical) was quoted of a letter from such a doctor to a social worker:

> "Mrs. X tells me that her husband threatens to leave her unless another baby is forthcoming, and adoption is the only way. I feel myself that, although the home is not ideal, a baby might go a long way to settle down the whole family and without itself suffering in the process."

On the other hand it has been said that third parties arranging adoptions are usually well-intentioned people consciously offering a service,[64] and that there may be certain advantages to the parties in a privately-arranged adoption—for instance, speed, personal control of

[54] Houghton Committee Working Paper, para. 37.
[55] Houghton Committee Report, para. 32.
[56] But not a single national service: Report, para. 40.
[57] *Ibid*. Recommendations 2 and 3.
[58] As distinct from a " body of persons "—see s. 29 (1).
[59] s. 50 (1) (*d*). Agencies may charge expenses reasonably incurred: s. 50 (3). Some Adoption Societies seek donations from adopters: Houghton Report, para. 64.
[60] Parts IV and V. The effect of the Children Act 1958, as amended by ss. 51–59 of the Children and Young Persons Act 1969, is to give local authorities wide powers over *de facto* adoptions.
[61] Adoption Survey, p. 48.
[62] Houghton Committee Working Paper, para. 66. Some prospective adopters claim to have paid inflated fees for infertility investigations on the understanding that a child would be found for them to adopt, and some mothers have claimed that nursing home facilities have been provided on the understanding that the child would be placed for adoption: Houghton Report, para. 87.
[63] Cmd. 9248 (1954) para. 43.
[64] A Guide to Adoption Practice, para. VIII, 15, and see Houghton Report, para. 85.

the situation and self-reliance, a feeling of privacy, and greater apparent certainty.[65] But in most cases an independent adoption deprives the parties of adequate safeguards and expertise at the crucial moment of placement. It has therefore been suggested that such placings should no longer be permitted, and that only an adoption agency should be permitted to place a child for adoption with non-relatives.[66]

CRITICISMS AND PROPOSALS FOR REFORM

The present law of adoption has been criticised on the following main grounds [67]:

(i) The welfare of the child is not paramount, or even as important as the rights of its natural parent. In particular, there is concern about a number of children who have been reclaimed by the natural parent, perhaps after several years in a foster home.

(ii) The timing and arrangements for the giving of the natural parent's consent impose a considerable strain on her, cause anxiety to the prospective adopters, and in some cases, disturbance to the child.

(iii) There is ambiguity about the position of the natural father of an illegitimate child, and a divergence of practice in the extent to which the court insists on his being sought out.[68] In any case the procedural arrangements whereby he may not directly intervene in the adoption proceedings, but may do so indirectly by applying for custody, are unsatisfactory.[69]

(iv) There is a variety of practice about the extent to which the husband of a married woman placing a child for adoption must be sought out. Unless evidence to the contrary can be given, he will be deemed [70] a lawful parent whose consent is required. Some courts (it has been said [71]) accept an affidavit or personal statement by the mother as evidence of non-access, but others insist on the husband being contacted in any case, even though the couple may have been separated for years. In other cases, subsisting marriages may be jeopardised by revealing to a husband his wife's infidelity.

(v) There is confusion about the supervision of children placed for adoption and unnecessary duplication of effort.[72] The position and status of the *guardian ad litem* is also thought to be unsatisfactory.

[65] *Ibid.*, para. VIII, 2.
[66] Houghton Committee Report, paras. 84–90.
[67] Adapted from Houghton Committee Working Paper, para. 3, and the Report of the S.C.S.R.A. (*supra*).
[68] See Adoption Practice, App. B, paras. 5–6.
[69] *Supra*, p. 348.
[70] As to this presumption, see *supra*, p. 315.
[71] Adoption Practice, *loc. cit.*, para. 7.
[72] See particularly the S.C.S.R.A. Report on this point.

(vi) Adoption resources vary from area to area, and many voluntary societies have inadequate resources.

(vii) There is concern about direct and third party placements, and particularly about the position where grandparents adopt, and legal relationships are created which conflict with natural relationships.[73]

In 1969 a Departmental Committee [73a] was set up to consider the law, policy and procedure on the adoption of children, and what changes are desirable. A Working Paper giving the Committee's provisional proposals was published in 1970, and a Final Report appeared in 1972. The recommendations [73b] include:

1. The creation of a comprehensive adoption service, integrated into local authorities' child care and family casework provisions.[74]

2. Since decisions on the suitability of prospective adopters were primarily matters for the professional judgment of agencies and the courts, the attempts in the existing law to lay down conditions of eligibility [75] should be abandoned. The basic legal conditions of eligibility should be limited to the domicile, residence, and marital status of the adopters, and their relationship (if any) to the child.[76]

3. Although adoption should still require the consent of the child's parent, (a) statute should provide that in interpreting what is " reasonable " and " unreasonable " the court should have regard to all the circumstances, first consideration being given to the effect of the decision on the long-term welfare of the child [77] and serious ill-treatment of the child should also be a ground upon which consent may be dispensed with if the court is satisfied that rehabilitation of the child in the family is unlikely.[78] (b) A new procedure should be permitted to discourage the temptations to vacillation inherent [79] in the present law. Adoptions arranged by agencies could be in two stages: (i) A relinquishment stage, in which the parent would relinquish her rights over the child, with a view to his adoption. At this stage, the rights and interests of any other relevant person or body (e.g. the natural father of an illegitimate child) should be considered, before the court vested parental rights in the agency, who would retain them until the adoption was finally made. This relinquishment would be irrevocable.[80] (ii) The Adoption agency would in due course be able to consent to an adoption order. In the meantime it would have parental rights over the child.

---

[73] Adoption Practice, loc. cit., para. 8.   [73a] The Houghton Committee.
[73b] See C. Davies (1973) 36 M.L.R. 245; A. Samuels, ibid. p. 278.
[74] Recommendations 2 and 3.
[75] Supra, p. 343.
[76] Recommendation 11.
[77] Recommendation 51. This would probably codify the existing law, in the light of Re W. (supra).
[78] Recommendation 52.
[79] Supra, p. 350; see Recommendations 37 to 44.
[80] If no adoption order were made within 12 months the mother could apply for restoration of her rights.

4. The Committee favoured an extended use of long-term *guardianship*, as a means of giving legal recognition and security to relatives, and foster parents who had cared for a child for some time.[81] It was felt that this would overcome some of the tensions in the existing system, caused by the fact that adoption often seems the only way in which such legal assurance can be given.

5. Guardianship would usually be the appropriate relief for relatives looking after a child. It would then be possible to avoid (as a general rule) adoptions by relatives, which are often undesirable not only because of the ambiguity of relationship already referred to,[82] but because (particularly in the case of an adoption by a natural parent and a step-parent) they might cause the severence of existing family links.[83] The Committee recommended that (a) an adoption order should only be made in favour of a natural parent alone in exceptional circumstances; and, (b) that if other relatives (including a step-parent applying jointly with his spouse) sought adoption, the court should first consider whether guardianship would not be more appropriate, the first consideration being given to the long-term welfare of the child.[84]

6. In cases where the putative father of an illegitimate child was actively concerned about it, his involvement should be encouraged. He should, in such a case, be a respondent to any relinquishment application, and his rights determined in it. If, however, the father shows no interest, or cannot be found, his rights would expire after a time limit fixed so that the child's status could be finally determined without long delay.[85]

Similarly, if there is satisfactory evidence that the mother's husband is not the father of the child, and he has not been involved with his upbringing, it should not be necessary to approach him.[86]

The Government has declined to give any undertaking as to when legislation will be introduced, but consultations are taking place.[87]

---

[81] Recommendation 21, and Chap. 5.
[82] *Supra*, p. 361.
[83] Working Paper, paras. 86–95; Report, para. 107.
[84] Report, Recommendations 18, 20. Adoptions by parent and step-parent are common under the existing law, amounting to some 29 per cent. of all adoptions in 1966: see Adoption Survey, Table 2 (6).
[85] Recommendations 47–48.
[86] Recommendation 50 *supra*, p. 348.
[87] See the House of Commons Debate on November 9, 1973. A private member's Bill to give effect to some recommendations (the Children Bill 1973) received a first reading on November 22, 1973.

INDEX

371